# The Media

**Pearson Education**

We work with leading authors to develop the
strongest educational materials in media studies,
bringing cutting-edge thinking and best learning
practice to a global market.

Under a range of well-known imprints, including
Longman, we craft high quality print and electronic
publications which help readers to understand and
apply their content, whether studying or at work.

To find out more about the complete range of our
publishing, please visit us on the World Wide Web at:
www.pearsoneduc.com

# The Media: An Introduction

Second edition

Edited by
## Adam Briggs & Paul Cobley

Longman

An imprint of **Pearson Education**

Harlow, England · London · New York · Reading, Massachusetts · San Francisco · Toronto · Don Mills, Ontario · Sydney
Tokyo · Singapore · Hong Kong · Seoul · Taipei · Cape Town · Madrid · Mexico City · Amsterdam · Munich · Paris · Milan

**Pearson Education Limited**
Edinburgh Gate
Harlow
Essex CM20 2JE

*and Associated Companies throughout the world*

*Visit us on the World Wide Web at:*
www.pearsoneduc.com

First published 1998
**Second edition published 2002**

ISBN 0 582 42346 5

**British Library Cataloguing-in-Publication Data**
A catalogue record for this book is available from the British Library

**Library of Congress Cataloging-in-Publication Data**

The media : an introduction / edited by A. Briggs & P. Cobley. – 2nd ed.
    p. cm.
  Includes bibliographical references and index.
  ISBN 0-582-42346-5
  1. Mass media.  I. Briggs, Adam.  II. Cobley, Paul, 1963–

P90.M364  2002
302.23–dc21                                        2001036933

10  9  8  7  6  5  4  3  2  1
06  05  04  03  02

Typeset in 10/12pt New Baskerville by 35
Printed in Great Britain by Henry Ling Ltd., at the Dorset Press, Dorchester, Dorset

# Contents

*List of contributors*                                                        ix
*Acknowledgements*                                                           xvi

**1  What you need to know before you start to use
     this book**                                                              1
Adam Briggs and Paul Cobley

**Part I   What are the Media?**                                              9
Introduction to 'What are the Media?'                                        11
Adam Briggs and Paul Cobley

**2  Comics**                                                                14
Roger Sabin, 'Eurocomics: "9th art" or misfit lit?'

**3  Book publishing**                                                       23
David Saunders, 'The book publishing industry'

**4  Advertising**                                                           39
Iain MacRury, 'Advertising and the new media environment'

**5  News agencies**                                                         57
Oliver Boyd-Barrett and Terhri Rantanen, 'Global and
national news agencies: opportunities and threats in the age
of the Internet'

**6  Public relations and journalism**                                       70
David Miller, 'Promotion and power'

**7  Newspapers**                                                            89
James Curran, 'The sociology of the press'

**8  Magazines**                                                            104
Brian Braithwaite, 'Magazines: the bulging bookstalls'

9   **Radio**                                                          121
    Andrew Crisell, 'Radio: public service, commercialism and
    the paradox of choice'

10  **Television**                                                     135
    Richard Paterson, 'A framework for analysing contemporary
    television'

11  **Cinema**                                                         148
    Anne Jäckel, 'Cinema in Europe'

12  **Pop music**                                                      164
    Roy Shuker, 'Marketing and mediating popular music
    in Europe'

13  **Technology**                                                     180
    Brian McNair, 'New technologies and the media'

**Part II   'Outside' the Media**                                      193
    Introduction to '"Outside" the Media'                              195
    Adam Briggs and Paul Cobley

14  **Economics**                                                      198
    Patrick Barwise and David Gordon, 'The economics of
    the media'

15  **Policy**                                                         217
    Sylvia Harvey, 'Making media policy'

16  **Models of media institutions**                                   231
    Ralph Negrine, 'Media institutions in Europe'

17  **Audience research**                                              245
    Ray Kent, 'Administrative research of audiences'

18  **'Effects'**                                                      259
    Guy Cumberbatch, 'Media effects: continuing controversies'

19  **'Impacts and influences'**                                       272
    Jenny Kitzinger, 'Media influence revisited: an introduction
    to the "new effects research"'

20  **Active audiences**                                               282
    Joke Hermes, 'The active audience'

21  **Approaches**                                                     294
    John Corner, 'Why study media form?'

**Part III  In the Media**                                             305
    Introduction to 'In the Media'                                     307
    Adam Briggs and Paul Cobley

22 **Sexuality**                                                    313
   Andy Medhurst, 'Tracing desires: sexuality in media texts'

23 **Gender**                                                       326
   Irene Costera Meijer and Liesbet van Zoonen, 'From Britney
   Spears to Erasmus: women, men and representation'

24 **Social class**                                                 340
   Joanne Lacey, 'Identifying characteristics of class in
   media texts'

25 **Race and ethnicity**                                           357
   Sarita Malik, 'Race and ethnicity the construction of Black
   and Asian ethnicities in British film and television'

26 **Youth**                                                        369
   Bill Osgerby, '"The good, the bad and the ugly": post-war
   media representations of youth'

27 **Disability**                                                   383
   Jessica Evans, 'Making up disabled people: charity, visibility
   and the body'

28 **Nationality**                                                  401
   Andrew Higson, 'National identity and the media'

29 **Sport**                                                        415
   Neil Blain and Raymond Boyle, 'Sport as real life:
   media sport and culture'

30 **News production**                                              427
   Jerry Palmer, 'News values'

31 **Parliamentary politics**                                       444
   Ivor Gaber, 'The media and politics'

32 **News photography**                                             464
   Patricia Holland, '"The direct appeal to the eye"?
   Photography and the press'

33 **Pornography and censorship**                                   477
   Linda Ruth Williams, 'Sex and censoriousness:
   pornography and censorship in Britain'

*Index*                                                             497

# Contributors

**Patrick Barwise**

Patrick Barwise is Professor of Management and Marketing and Chairman of the Future Media Research Programme at London Business School. His publications include *Television and its Audience* (with Andrew Ehrenberg, Sage, 1988), *Predictions: Media* (with Kathy Hammond, Phoenix, 1998), and *Advertising in a Recession* (NTC Publications, 1999). He is also managing editor of *Business Strategy Review* and a regular contributor to *FT Creative Business*.

**Neil Blain**

Neil Blain is Professor of Media and Culture at the University of Paisley. Recent work includes *Sport in Media Culture: New Perspectives* (edited with Alina Bernstein, Frank Cass, 2002) and *Media, Monarchy and Power* (written with Hugh O'Donnell, Intellect, 2002).

**Oliver Boyd-Barrett**

Oliver Boyd-Barrett is Professor, Department of Communication, at California State Polytechnic University, Pomona. His primary area of research is international communication and news agencies. Among recent works he is author of *The Media Communications Book* (with Chris Newbold and Hilde van Bulcke, Arnold, 2001), and *The Globalization of News* (with Terhi Rantanen, Sage, 1998). He authored UNESCO's *Final Report of the Workshop on News Agencies in the Era of the Internet*. Dr Boyd-Barrett was previously development director for the MA in Mass Communication at the University of Leicester, and has innovated distance learning courses in mass communications at the Open University (United Kingdom). He has consulted for NATO, the Government of Dubai, UNESCO, the Royal Commission on the Press, and the Parliamentary Committee on Science and Technology.

**Raymond Boyle**

Raymond Boyle is a Senior Lecturer in Film and Media Studies and a member of the Stirling Media Research Institute at Stirling University. He is co-author (with Richard Haynes) of *Power Play: Sport, the Media and Popular Culture* (Longman, 2000) and sits on the editorial board of the journal *Media, Culture and Society*.

**Brian Braithwaite**

Brian Braithwaite is a retired magazine publisher (Board Director of National Magazine Company for 23 years). He has worked on many titles and he launched *Harpers & Queen, Cosmopolitan* and *Country Living*. He has co-authored two books on the business of women's magazines and seven books on magazine nostalgia. He is the author of *Women's Magazines: the First 300 Years* (Peter Owen, 1995). He is a regular broadcaster on the subject of consumer magazines.

**Adam Briggs**

Adam Briggs is Principal Lecturer in Cultural and Historical Studies at the London College of Fashion. He has published articles on subcultures, marketing and fashion. He is currently researching the relationship between production and consumption in fashion.

**Paul Cobley**

Paul Cobley is Reader in Communications at London Guildhall University. He is the author of *Narrative, The American Thriller* (Routledge, 2001) and *Introducing Semiotics* (with Litza Jansz, Icon Books, 1999). He is also the editor of *The Communication Theory Reader* and *The Routledge Companion to Semiotics and Linguistics*.

**John Corner**

John Corner is Professor in the School of Politics and Communication Studies at the University of Liverpool. His recent books include *Studying the Media: Problems of Theory and Method* (Edinburgh University Press, 1999), and *Critical Ideas in Television Studies* (Clarendon Press, 1999). He is currently working on studies of the history of television current-affairs documentary and of media-political relations. He an editor of the journal *Media, Culture and Society*.

**Andrew Crisell**

Andrew Crisell is Professor of Broadcasting Studies at Sunderland University and the author of *Understanding Radio* (Routledge, 1994) and *An Introductory History of British Broadcasting* (Routledge, 1997). He is presently completing a second edition of the latter and editing a collection of essays entitled *More than a Music Box: Radio in a Multi Media World*.

**Guy Cumberbatch**

Guy Cumberbatch is a Chartered Psychologist and currently Director of The Communications Research Group in Birmingham, specialising in media research. His particular interests have been in content analysis – particularly minority group representation on television – and more generally in media audiences.

**James Curran**

James Curran is Professor of Communications at Goldsmiths College, University of London. He is the author or editor of thirteen books about the mass media including *Power Without Responsibility* (with Jean Seaton, fifth edition, Routledge, 1997), *Media, Ritual and Identity* (edited with Tamar Liebes, Routledge, 1998) and *De-Westernizing Media Studies* (edited with Myung-Jin Park, Routledge, 2000).

**Jessica Evans**

Jessica Evans is Senior Lecturer in Cultural and Media Studies at The Open University. She is the editor of *The Camerawork Essays* (Rivers Oram Press, 1997) and co-editor of *Visual Culture: The Reader* (Sage, 1999) and *Identity: A Reader* (Sage, 2000), and has written widely on visual culture and photography.

**Ivor Gaber**

Ivor Gaber is Professor of Broadcast Journalism (Emeritus) at Goldsmiths College, University of London and the author (with Steve Barnett) of *The Westminster Tales; the 21st century crisis in political journalism* (Continuum, 2001). He is also a freelance journalist and an independent radio and television producer.

**David Gordon**

David Gordon is the Secretary of the Royal Academy of Arts. He was formerly Chief Executive of ITN, and for 12 years Chief Executive of The Economist Group, where he had been a journalist. He is the author with Fred Hirsch of *Newspaper Money* (Hutchinson, 1975).

**Sylvia Harvey**

Sylvia Harvey is Professor of Broadcasting Policy at Sheffield Hallam University and Principal Associate Director of the AHRB Centre for British Film and Television Studies. Her current research is in the area of broadcasting policy and regulation and she is the author of *May '68 and Film Culture* and co-editor of *The Regions, the Nations and the BBC* (BFI, 1993) and *Television Times: A Reader* (Arnold, 1996). She has written about Channel 4 Television, British independent cinema and documentary film and television.

**Joke Hermes**

Joke Hermes is Lecturer in Television Studies at the University of Amsterdam. She is editor of the *European Journal of Cultural Studies*. Her book *Reading Women's Magazines* was published by Polity Press (1995).

**Andrew Higson**

Andrew Higson is Professor of Film Studies at the University of East Anglia. His is the author of *Waving The Flag: Constructing a National Cinema in Britain* (Clarendon Press, 1997); the editor of *Young and Innocent? The Cinema in Britain, 1896–1930* (University of Exeter Press, 2002); and co-editor of *British Cinema, Past and Present* (with Justine Ashby, Routledge, 2000) and *Film Europe and Film America* (with Richard Maltby, University of Exeter Press, 1999).

**Patricia Holland**

Patricia Holland has contributed to many publications on aspects of television, photography and popular media. With Jo Spence she co-edited *Family Snaps* (Virago Press, 1991) and is currently working on an updated version of her book *What is a Child?* She is the author of *The Television Handbook* (Routledge, 2000).

**Anne Jäckel**

Anne Jäckel is Visiting Research Fellow at the University of the West of England. She has contributed many chapters and articles to books and academic journals (including *Media Culture and Society, French Cultural Studies* and *The Canadian Journal of Communication*) on film policy, European cinema (East and West) and cinematographic co-productions. She is the author of the forthcoming BFI book on the *European Film Industries*.

**Ray Kent**

Ray Kent is Senior Lecturer in the Department of Marketing at the University of Stirling. He is editor of *Measuring Media Audiences* (Routledge, 1994) and the author of *Marketing Research: Measurement, Method and Application* (ITP, 1999) and *Data Construction and Data Analysis for Survey Research* (Palgrave, 2001).

**Jenny Kitzinger**

Jenny Kitzinger is Director of the Centre for Media and Communications Research at Brunel University (West London, UK). She is co-author of *The Mass Media and Power in Modern Britain* (Oxford University Press, 1997) and *The Circuit of Mass Communication* (Sage, 1998) and co-editor of *Developing Focus Group Research: Politics, Theory and Practice* (Sage, 1998).

**Joanne Lacey**

Joanne Lacey is Lecturer in Design History in the School of Historical and Critical Studies, University of Brighton. She has published in the areas of popular culture, class and gender. She is currently writing a book on gender and popular film audiences and co-editing (with Andy Medhurst) *The Representation Reader* for Sage Publications.

**Iain MacRury**

Iain MacRury is Senior Lecturer in Media and Advertising at the University of East London. He is co-author of *The Dynamics of Advertising* (Harwood, 2000) and co-editor of *Buy This Book: Studies in Advertising and Consumption* (Routledge, 1997). He is a director of The U.E.L. Centre for Consumer and Advertising Studies and has worked as a brand consultant on a number of commercial research projects.

**Brian McNair**

Brian McNair is Reader in Film and Media Studies at the University of Stirling, and a member of the Stirling Media Research Institute. He is the author of many books on the media, including *The Sociology of Journalism* (Arnold, 1998), *Journalism and Democracy* (Routledge, 2000), and *Striptease Culture* (Routledge, 2002).

**Sarita Malik**

Sarita Malik has researched and written extensively on race, media and ethnicity. She is currently Head of Asian Arts at Watermans Art Centre in London and is author of *Representing Black Britain: Black and Asian Images on Television* (Sage, 2002).

**Andy Medhurst**

Andy Medhurst teaches Media and Cultural Studies at the University of Sussex. His recent publications include *A National Joke: Popular Comedy and English Cultural Identities* (Routledge, 2002), *Lesbian and Gay Studies: A Critical Introduction* (co-edited with Sally Munt, Continuum, 1997), and is currently co-editing (with Joanne Lacey) *The Representation Reader* for Sage Publications.

**Irene Costera Meijer**

Irene Costera Meijer is a Senior Associate Professor at the Department of Communication, University of Amsterdam, The Netherlands. Her most recent books are *Reality Soap* (2000) and *Talk/Show* (2001). She specializes in questions of citizenship in relation to journalism, advertising and popular culture.

**David Miller**

David Miller is a member of the Stirling Media Research Institute. He is co-author of *Open Scotland: Journalists, Lobbyists and Spin Doctors* (Polygon, 2001) and co-author of *Market Killing: What Capitalism Does and What Social Scientists Can Do About It* (Longman, 2001).

**Ralph Negrine**

Ralph Negrine is Director of the Centre for Mass Communication Research and Dean of the faculty of the Social Sciences at the University of Leicester. He is the author of *The Communication of Politics* (Sage, 1996); *Television and the Press since 1945* (Manchester University Press, 1999) and *Parliaments and the Media* (Pinter, 1999).

**Bill Osgerby**

Bill Osgerby is a Senior Lecturer in Cultural Studies at the University of North London. His main publications include *Youth in Britain Since 1945* (Blackwell, 1998) and *Playboys in Paradise: Masculinity, Youth and Leisure-Style in Modern America* (Berg/New York University Press, 2001). He is also co-editor of *Action TV: Tough-Guys, Smooth Operators and Foxy Chicks* (Routledge, 2001).

**Jerry Palmer**

Jerry Palmer is Professor of Communications at London Guildhall University, where he teaches communications strategy and the ethics of communication. He is the author of four books and numerous academic articles on popular culture and popular narrative as well as a recent book on news journalism, *Spinning into Control; News Values and Source Strategies* (Continuum, 2000).

**Richard Paterson**

Richard Paterson is Head of Knowledge at the British Film Institute where he leads the BFI's digitisation programme. He is also Honorary Professor of Media Management at the University of Stirling. His publications include *Working in Television* (OUP, forthcoming).

**Tehri Rantanen**

Terhi Rantanen is Director of the MSc Global Media and Communications Programme at the London School of Economics and Political Science. Her books include *The Globalisation of News* (Sage, 1998), edited with Oliver Boyd-Barrett, and *The Global and the National: Media and Communications in Post-Communist Russia* (Rowman & Littlefield, 2002).

**Roger Sabin**

Roger Sabin is a Lecturer in Cultural Studies at Central St. Martin's College of Art and Design, London, and a freelance journalist. His books include *Adult Comics: An Introduction* (Routledge, 1993) and *Comics, Comix and Graphic Novels* (Phaidon, 2001).

**David Saunders**

David Saunders is Professor and former Dean of Arts at Griffith University, Australia. His books include *Authorship and Copyright* (Routledge, 1992) and *Anti-lawyers: Religion and the Critics of Law and State* (Routledge, 1997). He is co-editor (with Ian Hunter) of *Natural Law and Civil Sovereignty: Moral Right and State Authority in Early Modern Political Thought* (2002).

**Roy Shuker**

Roy Shuker is an Associate Professor in the School of English and Media Studies at Massey University, Palmerston North, New Zealand. He is the author of *Understanding Popular Music* (second edition, Routledge, 2001) and *Key Concepts in Popular Music* (Routledge, 1998).

**Linda Ruth Williams**

Linda Ruth Williams is a Senior Lecturer in Film Studies at the University of Southampton. She is the author of *D. H. Lawrence* (Northcote House/The British Council, 1997), *Critical Desire: Psychoanalysis and the Literary Subject* (Edward Arnold, 1995) *and Sex in the Head: Visions of Femininity and Film in D. H. Lawrence* (Harvester Wheatsheaf, 1993) and is working on a further three books on film and cinema.

**Liesbet van Zoonen**

Liesbet van Zoonen is Professor of Gender and Multimedia at the University of Maastricht in the Netherlands. She is also affiliated with the Amsterdam School of Communications Research. Apart from her writings on gender and media, she is known for her work on the articulations of politics and popular culture. She has published in numerous academic journals, and is the author and editor of *Feminist Media Studies* (Sage, 1994), *The Media in Question* (Sage, 1998) and *Women, Politics and Communication* (Hampton Press, 2000).

# Acknowledgements

The editors would like to give a big thanks to Sarah Caro who originally commissioned this book and whose energy, commitment and cheerfulness were indispensable to getting the first edition published. We would also like to acknowledge the good humour and diligence of Matthew Smith in bringing about the new edition that is now in your hands.

Clearly, this book could not go ahead without the cooperation of the contributors to this volume, a distinguished body of experts who have generously provided samples of their own leading work in the field of media studies. We owe a debt to their professionalism and accomplishment.

Finally, we must acknowledge those who suffered the perspiration (as opposed to the inspiration) required to produce this book: Philippa and Alison.

# Chapter 1

# What you need to know before you start to use this book

ADAM BRIGGS AND PAUL COBLEY

As editors, we expect that this book will be invaluable to students of media, communications and cultural studies in learning what the media actually are. What the media 'are', however, is never static: media are constantly changing. Hence the second edition of this book, each of whose chapters has been thoroughly updated from the last edition and accompanied by three chapters on additional topics.

This introduction therefore seeks to do two things. First, it aims to help you use this book as an effective study tool. This introduction gives information on how this book is structured and how it can be most fruitfully read.

Second, it aims to focus attention on the difficulty of arriving at an understanding of what this thing 'the media' is. What is often forgotten is that the term 'media' is the plural of 'medium'. What is often referred to as 'the media' (implying singular) is actually a diverse collection of industries and practices, each with their own methods of communication, specific business interests, constraints, and audiences.

The enormity and complexity of the public arena known as 'the media' has meant that the study of media has entailed constant reiteration of questions of definition. Is 'the media' a collection of industries? Is it a collection of practices? Is it a collection of representations? Is it a collection of the products of economic and statutary regulations? Is it a collection of audiences' understandings? Is it a means of delivering audiences to advertisers or is it a public service?

The answer to all these questions is 'yes'.

Of course, the media are *also* in a state of perpetual flux. As consumers of media we know very well that the media's content changes from day to day. Also media outlets are continually being bought, sold and created. Regulations change; so do technologies and audiences.

Undoubtedly, when we are in the thick of media study, these facts are crucial. Before this study can begin, however, we need some means of grasping the broader picture. Our first task is to acquire an initial overview of the general scope of media.

One way of achieving this is to consider the media in terms of a communications process. What all media entail is a process that involves senders, messages and receivers as well as a specific social context in which they operate.

## Senders

'Senders' of media messages can usefully be understood as institutions. These institutions

- are economic entities which have to maintain a sufficient cash flow to continue/expand their activities
- work within legal and governmental frameworks of regulation
- are peopled by professionals implementing specialized practices
- facilitate the transmission of certain messages embodying certain worldviews (and not others).

## Messages

Media 'messages'

- differ from medium to medium
- are not simple reflections of the world
- are thoroughly constructed entities
- emanate from 'senders' operating within the parameters noted above
- are often aimed at target audiences
- are often rich and open to interpretation
- are subject to political, cultural and legal constraints

## Receivers

The 'receivers' of media messages

- are commodities sold to advertising agencies
- have demographic characteristics
- are not passive consumers or 'cultural dupes'
- make meaning of messages according to pre-existing values, attitudes and experiences
- sometimes apprehend depictions of themselves in messages and assess the nature of these depictions, sometimes fail to apprehend depictions of themselves and sometimes notice their absence from messages

## Specific social context

The 'specific social context' of the media discussed in this book is **Europe**. Europe has

- its own models of media operation and regulation
- diverse national traditions, languages and audiences
- diverse traditions of representation
- an ambiguous relationship to American media

The book is divided into three sections, each of which, in different ways, is concerned with European media.

Part I, '**What are the Media?**', as the section title suggests, describes the media as a series of *separate* and *distinct* industries and practices rather than as a monolithic entity.

Part II, ' **"Outside" the Media**', deals with those issues which directly impinge (from without) on the different media: audiences and beliefs about 'effects', broadcast policy and differing traditions of organizing, studying and funding media. These issues may seem like a 'backdrop' to media but they are more than this; in fact, they *determine* the kinds of media that we get. The discussion of such determinants also serves to demonstrate that there is some accuracy in the common sense understanding of a monolithic 'media' in that it draws attention to the way in which separate media are increasingly being linked by common owners and technologies.

Part III, '**In the Media**', examines some of the things that actually appear (and *do not* appear) in the media. This section deals with the manner in which different media represent different facets of the 'real' world.

This book is not designed to be read sequentially, all at once, like a novel. Use this volume as a sourcebook: each article is self-contained and can be consulted

- as an introduction to the particular medium in question ('**What are the Media?**'),
- as an introduction to relevant external influences upon the media we consume (' **"Outside" the Media**'),
- as an introduction to the kind of representations and agendas which occur across the media ('**In the Media**').

However, you should *not* simply use this book to gain a little information on one specific topic which has an appeal to you. You will learn more from reading about other topics covered in this volume, over and above those in which you are especially interested. Such a reading strategy will enable you to

- compare, contrast and thereby recognize the distinctiveness of a given topic
- identify consistencies across topics.

As well as providing introductions, each chapter will enable you to pursue further study by offering subjects for discussion (in the form of questions) and by suggesting further reading. In many cases you will find references to published works in the main body of the chapter. This can serve two purposes: for the author of the chapter the reference supplies details of the evidence being used; for the reader, it supplies a source for further study in whatever facet of the area is under discussion. You will also find at the end of each chapter a set of further readings which are annotated with comments in order to give you a sense of the topics and approaches of these readings.

## Are we already experts?

There can be no doubt that the study of media is rapidly expanding. One reason is that in the early twenty-first century the media are increasingly a central part of our lives, our cultures and global economies. Another reason, not unconnected to this, is that the study of media is very exciting.

What makes the study of contemporary media special is that the ubiquity of media, and the human engagement that it allows, means that we are all already, in a sense, experts. This book seeks to go beyond the knowledge that accrues as a consequence of our daily media consumption into a realm much different from our *experience* of radio, film, books, TV, newspapers, magazines, etc. The consuming of various media products is a different activity to the *understanding* of what those products consist of and how they have come about. The *study* of media, like the media themselves, is not a singular practice but is made up of a range of different approaches.

## The study of the media and media studies

The study of contemporary media – as opposed to the study of media throughout human history (oral cultures, cave painting, theatre, illuminated manuscripts, town criers, and so on) – emerged alongside the contemporary mass media, and pre-dates the establishment of the discipline known as 'Media Studies'. Various disciplines cast their gaze over the developing media in a way similar to the current moment where media are still the object of study in a range of disciplines such as sociology, politics, economics, psychology, cultural studies, anthropology, electronics, communications, cybernetics, geography and history, to name but a few.

Leaving technical considerations aside, two broad strands of media study can be identified in the early decades of the twentieth century. The first was made up of American sociologists and psychologists who sought to *measure* the content and the 'effects' of mass media. The crux of their research involved a use of 'scientific' method to establish the power of the mass media in individuals' lives. The second evolved in Europe and can be closely identified with the Frankfurt School of Social Research in Germany (Adorno and Horkheimer 1973; originally 1944) and the work of literary critics such as F. R. Leavis in Britain (Leavis 1930; Leavis and Thompson 1933) who, in spite of their different academic and political perspectives, claimed to recognize the detrimental effect of the media on their audiences. Leavis and the Frankfurt School feared what they believed to be a 'mass culture' which, in a crude outline of their view, was vulgar and homogenized, created a community of uncritical and passive consumers (apart from elites such as themselves, of course), excluded engagement with 'higher things', and rendered the 'masses' acquiescent to the owners/controllers of the mass media (which sometimes included the state). For Leavis, these features of 'mass culture' – a newly developed phenomenon characteristic of what is now known as 'modernity' – threatened the values which he believed to underpin a 'great tradition' in Britain; for the Frankfurt School they acted as a narcotic distracting from mass social organization against the ruling order (see Swingewood 1977).

As can be seen from a cursory glance at these broad strands, much theorizing about the media has been concerned less with the internal workings of the media themselves than with identifying data to inform speculations about their social and political consequences. On the other hand, particularly in the American tradition (but elsewhere as well), much research into media has been carried out for commercial purposes rather than strictly academic ones. Paul Lazarsfeld, one of the founding fathers of this tradition, described such work as 'administrative' (as opposed to 'critical') research (Lazarsfeld 1941). Frequently, data which might be incorporated into media study was (and remains) less concerned with 'understanding' audiences, for example, than with conceptualizing audiences as tradeable commodities and transforming audiences' media consumption into statistical entities which could serve as the basis for financial transactions between media executives and advertisers.

Like all areas of knowledge, then, the study of media is bound up with interests, biases, influences, arguments, motives and instrumental applications.

## Pluralism and perspectives

Clearly, all serious writing and investigative work takes place within its own perspective. Work funded by media industries, for example, will have its own agenda and uses; work carried out from a political standpoint will also have its own characteristic slant; work using different theoretical tools will produce different data; work focusing on different aspects of a subject will, again, produce different forms of understanding (an emphasis on media institutions will produce accounts of media differing from those which emphasize audiences or output). Different perpectives act to frame information and lead to different varieties of knowledge.

Not only is it necessary, therefore, to identify perspectives, it is also useful to be able to identify

- that which is absent from any account of a subject
- the way in which one perspective challenges, or is in conversation with, the premises of another perspective.

Taking this as a cue, then, we should offer some comments on the partiality of the volume presently in your hands.

What this book does not contain is a 'toolkit' or systematic introduction to approaches for the study of media. Such a toolkit would consist of expositions of 'narrative', 'genre', 'realism', 'semiology/semiotics', 'psychoanalytic theories', 'identity', 'deconstruction', 'discourse analysis', 'feminisms', 'post-colonialism', 'queer theory' and accounts of their usage as concepts in the understanding of media representations; plus expositions of 'hegemony', 'public sphere', 'political economy', 'globalization/localization', 'post-industrialism', 'post-modernism', 'culture', 'community' and accounts of their usage as concepts in the understanding of media institutions (these lists are by no means exhaustive; see Barker 2000; Boyd-Barrett and Newbold 1995; Branston and Stafford 1999; Mosco 1996; Storey 1997).

There are, however, numerous perspectives which you will find in this book although they will not necessarily appear in isolation with strict definitions attached. As a reader, you will need to be active in identifying the perspective which informs each discussion. You may even find that not only does this volume as a whole contain many different perspectives but individual articles fruitfully utilize arguments from different traditions and viewpoints. In this respect, this book can be described as 'pluralist', containing multiple perspectives without giving overt privilege to one and recognizing the equal validity of seemingly contradictory ideas.

Moving on from *this* collection of media studies, we now examine 'media studies' as a distinct discipline. 'Media studies' emerged in the 1970s, evolving from sociology, 'mass culture' theory and the study of 'mass communications'. While often attempting to be 'pluralist' and open, in general media studies tended to incorporate the agendas which were already embedded in its ancestors. Nevertheless, it might be argued that, at present, a different tension bifurcates the field. Media studies has found that its scholastic aspirations have been continually called into question by students, the media industries, selected academics and educational policy-makers, all of whom have argued the need for a more practical/vocational emphasis within the field. Put simply, such arguments have criticized an exclusive devotion to hostile analyses of the media and demanded a practical education in the skills necessary for working in the media industries.

It is worth considering the way in which this distinction between 'vocational' and a more 'critical' approach to media may be a false dichotomy on a number of levels. Exclusive hostility towards the media implies a position of distance from both the media industries and the consumers or – as the 'mass culture' theorists would have it – 'dupes' of the media. Unsurprisingly, this attitude encourages elitism and a withdrawal from anything other than a purely intellectual engagement with media. However, a singular emphasis on the supposed 'vocational' aspects of media – 'learning on the job', using a camera or sound equipment, for example, without prior planning, thought or cultural knowledge – can only ever equip students with a competence to deal with some technical, plugs 'n' sockets aspects of the media.

In short, an effective and credible vocational emphasis in the study of media cannot exist without a 'critical' component. It is important to realize that 'critical' here does not necessarily entail an endless catalogue of media sins against humanity; instead, it points to the acquisition of a thoroughgoing insight into the media, their uses, their significance in contemporary life and their modes of operating. Potential future media employees will, of course, benefit from a knowledge and understanding of media institutions as economic and professional entities; they will also gain much from a prior knowledge of the diversity of media audiences and what brings audience members together as possible constituencies; they will also be well placed if they are equipped with an understanding of the social realities of audiences and how this impacts on media consumption (Who likes football? What makes who change channel, switch off, cancel a subscription, switch newspaper, fail to buy a CD, etc.? What kind of things do people want to hear, see, read, subscribe to, etc.?).

Even for those who do not aspire to be a future media employee the study of media is central to any understanding of the culture in which we live and yields its own competencies and transferable skills. In the same way that students of English literature are not necessarily motivated by the desire to be a novelist, poet or play-wright – in fact, very few English graduates *do* go on to publish novels, poems or plays – students of media do not have to be motivated by pre-established career plans.

Whatever your motivation, nobody could deny that the study of media offers access to a cultural literacy befitting the contemporary world.

## Questions

1   Compare media studies to any other discipline studied in higher education. How does it differ from other disciplines and how is it similar?

2   List all the things that the creator of any media representation may need to know before embarking upon the creative process. Leave your list for a while and then reread it, adding components where necessary. Will the list need to be substantially changed for different kinds of representation (e.g. news as opposed to 'fiction')?

3   Using knowledge gained from this book and elsewhere try to construct a list of possible
   (a)   media 'senders'
   (b)   media 'messages'
   (c)   media 'receivers'
   (d)   media 'contexts'
Do not worry if your lists become very long.

## References

Adorno, T. W. and Horkheimer, M. (1973) *Dialectic of Enlightenment*, London: Allen Lane (originally 1944).

Barker, C. (2000) *Cultural Studies: Theory and Practice*, London: Sage.

Boyd-Barrett, O. and Newbold, C. (1995) *Approaches to Media*, London: Arnold.

Branston, G. and Stafford, R. (1999) *The Media Student's Book*, 2nd edn, London: Routledge.

Lazarsfeld, P. F. (1941) 'Remarks on critical and administrative communication', *Research Studies in Philosophy and Social Science* IX: 2–16.

Leavis, F. R. (1930) *Mass Civilization and Minority Culture*, London: Heffer.

Leavis, F. R. and Thompson, D. (1933) *Culture and Environment*, London: Chatto and Windus.

Mosco, V. (1996) *The Political Economy of Communication*, London: Sage.

Storey, J. (1997) *An Introduction to Cultural Theory and Popular Culture*, 2nd edn, Harlow: Prentice Hall.

Swingewood, A. (1977) *The Myth of Mass Culture*, London: Macmillan.

**Part I**

---

# What are the Media?

# Introduction to 'What are the Media?'

ADAM BRIGGS AND PAUL COBLEY

As we have been at pains to stress, the media are diverse. Part I addresses this diversity in detail by providing definitions and descriptions of various important media.

It may seem strange to start off with a chapter on comics. Often we think of the media as dominated by the high-profile products of electronic communication. Yet, as Roger Sabin demonstrates in Chapter 2, much of our media consumption is specialized, private and motivated by specific enthusiasms and prejudices. Our choice not to consume certain media forms – for example, tabloid newspapers, comics – may be informed by prejudices about form and cultural value. However, a medium such as the comic – which has been a victim of such value judgements – is as much a part of 'the media' as newspapers or cinema are.

David Saunders similarly deals with 'a neglected topic' in Chapter 3. The publishing industry in Europe is huge but has singularly failed to become a repeated focus of media studies in the way that, say, television has. This is curious because it has many different points of interest for media students. One such issue is that of intellectual property: who owns the copyright of the 'content' of media texts? Another is the relation of print publishing to the new electronic media: why has the book failed to die out? Yet another is the diversification of formats within this medium: the book has proved to be very flexible.

One *traditional* area of media study is advertising. More often than not, however, there has been an emphasis on the texts of advertising – the advertisements – at the expense of an attention to their production. Iain MacRury's Chapter 4 rectifies this and examines both the history of, and current changes in, the advertising industry. He does this by considering communications technology and the organization and the use of media, alongside broader cultural transformations.

Unlike advertising, which is popularly recognized as being in the business of selling products/services and changing behaviour, news is often thought to consist of 'information'. Granted, it is widely believed that news is often presented by newspapers, radio and television within certain *perspectives* (party political or otherwise); but this still presupposes that there is some 'objective' entity out there called 'news'. Even before it is collected, news is subject to sifting, selection, evaluation, structuring and classification (see Palmer, Chapter 30 in this volume). One of the first links in the chain of collecting news, as Oliver Boyd-Barrett and Terhi Rantanen discuss in Chapter 5, is the news agency. But, news is not just a matter of collection. As David Miller shows in Chapter 6 on journalism and promotional strategies, news is often *delivered* with an in-built perspective and thoroughly managed by interested parties. In this sense it is often difficult to judge what is news and what is public relations 'spin'.

In addressing the press, therefore, James Curran in Chapter 7 shows that it is difficult to utilize only one simple perspective. He explores the current state of British newspapers by comparing and synthesizing two very different approaches to understanding this medium. The first he characterizes in general as 'liberal' and presenting, for many, an 'optimistic' view about the workings of the press. The second he characterizes as 'radical' – this approach, he suggests, offers a far more critical and 'pessimistic' understanding. Neither approach, he states, can offer an adequate account of the role of the press in society.

Much different from those media involved in conveying news, are those which are (usually erroneously) considered as exclusively 'entertainments' media: magazines, radio, cinema, television, pop music. There is clearly a problem with the notion of 'entertainment' as a distinct entity which imputes a singular character to certain media. For instance, supposedly non-entertainments media such as newspapers are themselves often responsible for entertainment: features, lifestyle coverage, reviews, etc. Moreover, that which has traditionally been understood as news has been increasingly *packaged* as entertainment. Conversely, for many, television is the main source of *news and current affairs* (McNair 1999) which also constitutes large parts of much of radio and many magazines. Although it must be conceded that the pop music industry and cinema *are* devoted to entertainment, pop groups and film stars are an increasingly frequent staple of news output.

Magazines, as Brian Braithwaite demonstrates in Chapter 8, are currently the subject of rapid expansion. Two main reasons for this concern niche markets and technological advances. Technology has enabled more cost efficiency in producing media which reach more accurately the readers who are also target markets for advertisers (see also McNair, Chapter 13 in this volume). This avoids what is known as 'wastage' – i.e. buying advertising space in publications which reach a broad set of readers, many of whom may not belong to the desired target market.

The development of the 'invisible medium', radio, has had a similar trajectory in its recent profusion of services. Radio appears to have been used as a kind of policy testbase for the process of 'deregulation'. As Andrew Crisell shows in Chapter 9, many different markets for radio have existed for some time; but, has diversity truly been delivered by the move from a small number of radio stations to a larger number of stations catering for what are often niche markets? The limits of radio's ability to satisfy the diverse musical tastes of the British public are clearly demonstrated by the health of the many pirate radio stations.

In the case of the television industry, Richard Paterson adopts the concept of the value/supply chain in Chapter 10 to analyse the recent dispersal of the medium's functions. Rather than conceiving television as a group of companies which control every stage of the supply of television services to audiences, he shows that it is now more accurate to consider the television industry as comprising a number of contributors to a 'supply chain'. *Radio*, given current uncertainties about the introduction of digital audio broadcasting, continues to operate, despite considerable recent expansion, within the limits of spectrum scarcity. Television in Europe, on the other hand, is now in the midst of a new multi-channel digital revolution.

The indigenous cinema in Europe, by virtue of its eclipse by Hollywood, has received a woeful lack of attention. As Anne Jäckel illustrates in Chapter 11, this may be because of the European cinema's size (relatively small) and its profitability (again relatively small). Much focus on film has taken the film text – narrative, photography, genre – as its primary interest. Jäckel, on the other hand, discusses the way in which film texts come to be produced in the European context. A similar lack of attention to the industry has characterized previous studies of pop music which have usually been concerned with the subcultural influences on the production and consumption of music. Roy Shuker shows in Chapter 12 that there is actually an elaborate network of practices responsible for the production and marketing of pop music. Between the producers and consumers there lies a number of important mediating factors: radio, clubs, concert tours and festivals, videos, the music press and the charts. Furthermore, pop music is embodied in different technologies – from live performance to CDs to MP3 – each of which entails a different relationship between producers and consumers. Pop music is not just spontaneous expression; it is a highly complex multi-million-dollar (or yen) global business.

'What are the Media?' concludes with a topic that impinges on all media and is rapidly producing new ones. In one sense, as Brian McNair discusses in Chapter 13, the new technology produces new kinds of media and new audiences. An example of this is the new media texts and the immediate feedback which the Internet makes possible. But the new technologies also provide different (and sometimes quicker) ways of producing the 'old' media such as newspapers or pornography. Moreover, there are new digital technologies which have and will continue to have a radical influence on the distribution of media.

This has thrown up new issues of media policy and regulation which are addressed in Part II.

# Reference

McNair, B. (1999) *News and Journalism in the UK: A Textbook*, 3rd edn, London: Routledge.

## Chapter 2

# Comics

EUROCOMICS: '9$^{TH}$ ART' OR MISFIT LIT?

**ROGER SABIN**

This chapter seeks to explore the role of comic books in Europe. The focus is on European 'album' culture and its history. By examining the ways in which the economics of comics production have influenced their reception, we can begin to understand why they have attained such a high level of cultural respectability (in France, they are known as 'the ninth art'). A secondary theme of the chapter is to ask why in the UK comics have never been accepted as an artform in the same way.

This chapter is about comic books. Why, you may ask, should such a subject be relevant to a book about media studies? The answer is simple, but commonly not expected: that comics constitute 'a medium' just like film, television, novels, virtual reality, and any other medium you care to mention, and are therefore equally worthy of consideration within the parameters of media studies. They have their own properties, and generate their own 'kick': they are not 'movies on paper', and nor are they some half-way house between 'literature' and 'art'. Rather, they involve a co-mingling of words and pictures that can be breathtaking in its sophistication (as well as sometimes groan-inducing in its banality), and which rivals any other medium for depth of expression. (On the mechanics of how comics work, see McCloud 1994; Witek forthcoming.) In other words, comics matter.

In Europe, comics matter more than in most parts of the world, and in keeping with the focus of the rest of this book, our attention will be turned to here. There are, of course, notable comics traditions elsewhere (most of the histories available focus on the USA); but in Europe, the form has become culturally respectable in a way that is unmatched anywhere in the world, with the possible exception of Japan. To be more specific than this, we can say that although there are as many comics traditions in Europe as there are countries, it is fair to talk of a unified comics market. This is because comics in Europe share properties that are distinct from any other region in the world: these include not just cultural status, but also kinds of format, and, above all, underlying economics. One European country, however, does not fit into this template: namely, Britain. In comics, as in politics and so much else, Britain remains separate. A secondary theme of this chapter, therefore, is what makes British comics so different, and why the country has never become part of the 'European Comics Community'.

The most immediate way to obtain a sense of the place of comics in European life is to make a few basic observations. First and foremost, European comics culture is essentially an 'album' culture. This is to say that comics are produced as hardback books, usually of about 48 pages in length, containing a single self-contained story, with high-quality production values and full colour throughout. The artwork is often superb, and they have an aesthetic value that until recently was virtually unknown in Britain and the USA. This is duly reflected in the price (between roughly £7 and £20), and the fact that they are sold not from newsagents, but from bookshops. These comics are not intended to be read and thrown away after one sitting, but to be kept on bookshelves and returned to.

There are some exceptions to this rule. There exist, for example, monthly comics magazines that consist of anthologies of serialized stories. However, they are, again, usually of a much higher quality than their British and American counterparts, and the publishers' aim is typically to 'pre-publish' stories so that they can then be collected into album form at a later date. This system has a long history in Europe, and originally had the advantage of 'testing the waters' in the sense that if a story did not prove popular in the magazine, it would not make it into hardback. Today, however, stories are almost always guaranteed to be released as albums, and the magazines play a less significant role. Moreover, the trend since the mid-1980s has been for first publication to be in album form, thus circumventing the magazines altogether.

In terms of content, we can also observe that the subject matter covered by the comics includes 'something for everybody'. A quick scan of the shelves in a typical Parisian bookshop, for example, reveals an extensive range, from 'funny animal' stories for young children to hard porn for adults. In between, the storytelling styles can encompass the dumbest-of-dumb pulp fiction to hyper-literate meditations on philosophy and art. The point is better made by considering a random handful of hit albums dating from the 1980s to 2001:

- *The Town That Didn't Exist* (in translation through Titan Books). Written by acclaimed French novelist Pierre Christin (also a Professor of Journalism at Bordeaux University), with artwork by Enki Bilal (born in former Yugoslavia), the story revolves around the impossibility of building a utopia. In an (unspecified) age of industrial decline, a mysterious wheelchair-bound woman inherits a fortune and proceeds to spend it on constructing a city where no one need work ever again. A downbeat, often very weird, allegory for the contradictions of Marxist theory.
- *The Towers of Bois Maury: Babette* (in translation through Titan). Written and illustrated by Belgian 'Hermann' (Hermann Huppen), this historical drama, set in the early medieval period, concerns the rape of peasant girl by a noble, and the murderous events this sets in train. Plenty of action – swordfights, jousting and hideous torture – all rendered in exquisite photo-referenced linework, and held together by a meticulously researched script. What it lacks in wit, it makes up for in pace and atmosphere.
- *Pixy* (in translation through Fantagraphics). Written and drawn by Dane Max Andersson, the frankly indescribable story involves a procession of bizarre characters and inventions, including buildings that eat people, and gun-toting

foetuses. There is a satirical theme underpinning the strangeness, but this is basically an ultra-violent surrealist nightmare: alternately compelling and repulsive.

- *Little Ego* (in translation through Catalan). Written and illustrated by Italian Vittorio Giardino, a slice of soft porn about a beautiful brunette ingenue (Ego) who can't help losing her clothes. The storytelling and artistic style is a nod to the classic American newspaper strip 'Little Nemo', about a little boy's dreams, and Ego's deeply politically incorrect erotic fantasies are always set in the world of the surreal (the publisher's blurb asks, disingenuously: 'Who could object to Ego's frolics – with men, women, the occasional reptile or household implement – when it's all just a dream?').
- *Lea* (in translation through Fantagraphics). French writer Serge Le Tendre and artist Christian Rossi collaborated on this gripping thriller, which owes as much to Hitchcock and Truffaut as any comics tradition. An innocent man is branded a child-killer, and descends into mental breakdown. At once an effective psychodrama and a meditation on scapegoating: filmic, fast-moving, and terrifying.
- *Blueberry: Chihuahua Pearl* (in translation through Epic Comics). Written by novelist Jean-Michel Charlier and illustrated by fellow countryman Jean Giraud, one of the most acclaimed artists in the industry, this gritty Western has the feel of a Sergio Leone movie. Long coats, cigar-chewing, and stubble are *de rigeur* for both goodies and baddies, as US cavalryman Lieutenant Blueberry investigates misdeeds across the Tex–Mex border. A pretty basic shoot-em-up, redeemed by evocative artwork.
- *The Incal: Volume 1* (in translation through Titan). Written by Chilean filmmaker Alexandro Jodorowsky and illustrated by 'Moebius' (a pen-name for Jean Giraud, as above), this first part of a science fiction 'cosmic epic' features the adventures of private detective John Difool on a faraway planet. New Age and Tarot card references add colour to this Philip K. Dick-influenced story, packed with violence, grotesque monsters, and vast spaceships. Narratively drivesome in places, but a feast for the eyes.
- *Comix 2000* (L'Association). Intended as a 2000-page anthology for the year 2000, this huge volume was edited by French 'independent' publishers L'Association, and had two guiding principles: that the strips be about the twentieth century, and that they contain no words (in order to appeal to the widest possible audience). Contributors hailed from around the world, and subject matter ranged from basic gag humour to more serious concerns (e.g. AIDS and politics in South Africa). The quality, perhaps inevitably, was mixed.

You might notice that this selection of titles is essentially aimed at a teenage and adult audience. This is a fair reflection of the bulk of European comics publishing in recent years, at least in terms of numbers (for reasons we shall explore in a moment). However, it is important to add that the really big hitters in regard to sales rely on more traditional formulas, and are orientated towards a juvenile and family readership. In particular, two characters dominate: Tintin and Astérix. Both have been around for decades (Tintin since the 1930s, Astérix since the 1950s), and such is their fame, both in the UK and the USA, that we need not detail their history here (on Tintin, see Thompson 1991; Peeters 1992; on Astérix, see Kessler 1995). Suffice to say that between them, the be-quiffed boy-reporter and the diminutive ancient Gaul have sold more comics than any other characters put together (sales of Tintin albums alone are estimated to be in the hundreds of millions). Today, although the creator of Tintin (Georges 'Hergé' Remi) and the writer of Astérix (René Goscinny) are dead, the back-catalogues for both characters continue to sell extraordinarily well, and they are also stars of stage, screen, television, computer game, and – in the case of Astérix – theme park. At the time of writing, the big publishing event in France is the imminent publication of the new Astérix book, the name of which is being kept secret, yet which will appear in a (worldwide) print run of six million.

Other big sellers after Tintin and Astérix also tend to be marketed towards a juvenile/family audience, and are worth mentioning in passing. For example, translations of Disney comics do very well throughout Europe (famously, Eurodisney is in bitter competition for punters with the Astérix park), while other successful European-originated titles include The Smurfs (from the Netherlands), about cute blue elves; Lucky Luke (from France), about a gormless cowboy; and Blake and Mortimer (from Belgium), about a pair of time-travelling English detectives. Most of these comics have also developed huge adult followings on top of their intended young readership.

Continuing our survey, we can tell one more thing simply by looking at the titles available in the shops: that some countries are more important than others in terms of who publishes what. It soon becomes clear, for example, that France is the centre of the Eurocomics world. More titles are published here than anywhere else, while there is a long tradition of cartoonists from all over Europe being published by French houses. Companies like Dargaud (who publish Astérix), Flammarion (who publish Tintin), Glénat, and L'Association are prolific and powerful. Similarly, the Benelux countries have strong industries (it is a point of pride among Belgians that statistically more comics are sold per head here than in any other part of Europe). It is difficult to say which countries come next in ranking order. The north of Europe, including Scandinavia and Germany, is served by the giant corporation Carlsen, based in Germany, which often publishes translations of titles originated elsewhere in Europe. Meanwhile, Italy and Spain are certainly big comics consumers, and have thriving indigenous titles.

Moving away from the specific comics in the shops, we can also observe that in Europe, due to such a wide-ranging industry, there has developed a culture surrounding the form that is unique. For example, people commonly learn to read using comics, and continue to buy them throughout their lives. There is no 'cut-off' point as there has been traditionally in Britain and the USA. Thus, many comics characters become household names, and their exploits permeate everyday parlance. Perhaps the most visible expression of this love of comics are the comics festivals, which take place every year in most European nations. These tend to be large-scale events, not just for committed fans, but for all members of the family. The biggest, in Angoulême in south-western France, takes over the whole of the town for a period of several days, with exhibitions, talks, film shows, stalls, and, of course, artists' signing sessions (if you're lucky you get a sketch too). Angoulême markets itself very much as 'pour la famille', and regularly attracts over 100,000 visitors: in other words, roughly 100 times as many as the comparable (fan-orientated) event in Britain, and 20 times that in America. Other no less lively festivals are held in Lucca (Italy), Brussels (Belgium), Grenoble (France), and Frankfurt (Germany).

That's probably as far as we can go in analysing the European scene just by looking. To dig a little deeper, we need to explore two areas that are not immediately obvious: the comics' history and their underlying economics. Both themes are very closely linked, of course, and both are essential elements of any media studies investigation. Let us begin with the extraordinary level of intellectual respect that comics command in Europe, something that has influenced their history quite considerably. It is true to say that they are written about and deconstructed in the same way as any other artform. To give the most prominent example of a scholar with an interest: whenever the Italian Umberto Eco (author of *The Name of the Rose*) holds forth about contemporary culture, in books, TV and radio documentaries and newpaper columns, he invariably includes comics. (Eco's best-known book (in translation) to deal with comics is *The Role of the Reader* (1981), which includes a classic essay on Superman.) He's not the only one: academics all over Europe have made comics an integral part of degree courses. There are serious critical magazines about the subject, and specialist archives and study centres (such as those in Angoulême and Brussels).

This embracing of comics by Europe's 'intellectual class' (as it is still often referred to there) itself has a history. The trend dates back to the 1960s (although before this it is possible to find erudite discussions of titles like Tintin), and in particular to the French 'rediscovery' of early American comic strips. Comics study groups started to emerge, which focused primarily on strips like 'Little Nemo', 'Krazy Kat', 'Flash Gordon', and 'Dick Tracy'. A similar process had started in the late 1950s, when French intellectuals started to take American movies seriously – at the time, a very unusual concept. Now comics were being given the same treatment, and it was not long before critical and theoretical magazines were founded, and exhibitions organized. Undoubtedly an important moment in the growth of the movement was an exhibition of (largely American) comics at no less prestigious a venue than the Louvre in 1968 (the catalogue for the exhibition was published as a book: Couperie *et al.* 1968).

The cooption of comics into serious cultural debate continued into the 1970s. European intellectuals increasingly concentrated on European rather than American comics, and the new decade saw the form being referred to as 'the ninth art' (film and television had been added to the list a few years earlier). More than this, and partly as a result, the whole notion of what constituted 'culture' *per se* was being reconfigured. Old notions dating fom the Victorian era that culture essentially meant 'high culture' – for instance, fine art, classical music, opera, and literature drawn from a 'respected' canon of authors (Shakespeare, Goethe, etc.) – were being challenged as (mainly) French intellectuals progressively elevated 'low culture' (movies, television, jazz and rock music, and, of course, comics) to the status of bona fide artforms. It was an exciting period in intellectual history, and perhaps had its ultimate flowering in the works of French philosopher Roland Barthes, who argued that culture should include everything, and that the distinctions between 'high' and 'low' were outdated (see in particular Barthes, 1977). Barthes, too, discussed comics.

A corollary of this shifting of cultural priorities was that there developed close links between European comics and other artforms – especially with movies. It is possible to argue that the same kind of thing happened in Britain and America: but in these countries, comics, because of their low cultural status, were primarily seen as 'raw materials' to be stolen from at will by moviemakers. In Europe, a far more respectful tradition took shape whereby comics creators and film-makers collaborated and shared ideas. The career of the great Italian movie director Federico Fellini is very instructive in this respect. He was a founder member of an important comics study group in the early 1960s (The 'Centre d'Etudes des Literatures d'Expression Graphique', or CELEG for short), and frequently paid homage to comics in his films. Later in his career, he would collaborate with comics artists to produce comics albums, notably *Trip to Tulum* (1989), drawn by Milo Manara, which was based on a once-discarded film script. Other European film-makers closely associated with, and influenced by, comics include the Frenchmen Alain Resnais and Jean-Luc Godard. Equally, comics creators often worked in the movies: Enki Bilal, for instance, directed his own film, a science-fiction yarn entitled *Bunker Palace Hotel* (1990).

A similar process was evident with regard to novelistic fiction. Writers of comics would also pen novels, while novelists would try their hand at comics. For example, in our list of hit comics albums above, two of the writers happen also to be internationally recognized novelists: Pierre Christin and Jean-Michel Charlier. There are many more such examples, notably Jerome Charyn, a Europhile American author, whose collaborations with French artist Francois Boucq (*The Magician's Wife, Billy Budd: KGB*) have produced some of the best comics thrillers in recent years.

Because of this relative parity among the artforms, comics creators command a level of respect in Europe that is comparable to film directors or novelists – again, a concept that would be totally alien to the comics scene in Britain or America. Sometimes, it is even true that star creators assume the status of 'auteurs' (a French word denoting a creative artist who has a controlling influence over their work). Such is the case with the above-mentioned Jean ('Moebius') Giraud, and to a lesser extent with Enki Bilal and Milo Manara. In the case of these creators, comics can be marketed on the basis of their names, just in the same way as novels are sold as 'the new William Gibson' or films as 'the new Francis Coppola'.

These factors have greatly influenced, and have been influenced by, the economics of comics production in Europe. Because of the cultural respect that comics command, creators have never been exploited in the same way that they have in Britain and the USA. Rather, comics have traditionally been a natural place for upcoming creative talents to ply their trade – as natural as working in movies, novels, advertising, illustration and so on. The crucial issue has always been rates of pay: for, whereas in the USA and the UK creators have traditionally been paid a flat fee calculated by the page, in Europe, creators receive royalties as well: in other words, they earn a split of any profits their work may make.

The development of the album system was a major step forward in this respect. It was the Tintin albums that established the form, in the 1930s. What was unusual about them was that they were published by a Catholic publisher, Casterman (who were bought by Flammarion in 2000), whose code of practice evidently entailed a 'moral obligation' to pay creators a decent royalty. Thus, not only did Tintin's creators receive a royalty when strips appeared first in magazine form, but also a second royalty when they were collected together as albums. This system has endured through the decades since throughout the European comics industry, and has ensured not only a reasonable living for creators but also a higher standard of work. For it stands to reason that if creators are paid well, then they take more pride in what they are doing: this in turn means that it is easier to take comics seriously as an artform.

Most creators also retain copyright over their creations, which means that they rather than the publishers determine what happens to them. For example, if a creator decides to stop producing stories starring a particular character, then there is no way a publisher can step in and hire another creator to continue the strip without the originator's permission (which would additionally require financial remuneration). More than this, control of copyright means that it is the creator who benefits from any film or TV adaptations – always very important in the world of comics, as we have seen.

Other historical factors have also combined to bolster the economics of the comics industry. For example, there has been a more successful history of unionization and collective bargaining among comics creators in parts of Europe than in the USA and the UK. This has meant that when disputes arise, they are settled in a manner which at least takes the views of creators into account (very rare in the latter countries). Also, the intervention of governments in some European countries has meant certain advantages for the industry. For instance, after the Second World War, the French government introduced a law which limited the importation of comics from abroad: the French industry was thus protected against foreign competition, and allowed to develop at its own pace. More recently, governments in some countries have actually subsidized the comics industry. The most famous example of this was the construction of a sizeable museum and study centre in France (Centre nationale de la bande dessinée et l'image, or CNBDI), part-funded by the government to the tune of millions of francs. Once again, the fact that comics have cultural kudos was a major factor in the government's decision: the centre was opened by the then Minister for Culture, Jack Lang.

So we can see that economics and cultural acceptance have combined in Europe to create a unique comics culture. But the question remains, what about Britain? Of course, Britain is a part of Europe in many respects; but in terms of comics, there is different sensibility at work. Certainly, the British industry has produced its own classic titles in the past – *The Beano, The Eagle, 2000AD* and *Viz* to name just a few. But it can be argued that these have been successful despite the production system rather than because of it. For in Britain, comics have traditionally been culturally despised as either lowest-common-denominator trash, or as literature for children, or both. Underlying this prejudice, as we have seen, there has existed an iniquitous economic situation that has meant that comics have usually been the last place anybody would want to work.

Thus, the comics tradition in Britain has been dominated by titles aimed at an 8-to-12 age-range, produced on cheap, poor-quality, paper, and designed to be binned after one read. As for the contents, despite some notable exceptions, the norm has been mediocre storylines, produced to string the reader along for week after week, and unexceptional artwork. In other words, the work-for-hire, fee-per-page, system that has prevailed in Britain has ensured that comics remain the preserve of hacks, and thus have never acquired any kind of cultural respectability. Many of the beneficial aspects of comics production that we have discussed with regard to European comics, and which are largely taken for granted there – the collecting of stories into albums, the way in which royalties are split among creators, how they retain copyright, and so on – have (historically) barely made an impact on the British scene. Arguably this is one reason why the British industry has shrunk from its heyday in the 1960s to its present level, consisting of merely a handful of publishers of weekly and monthly product (notably Rebellion, publishers of *2000AD*; IFG Ltd, publishers of *Viz*; and DC Thomson, publishers of *The Beano*), plus a few book publishers who put out a limited range of 'graphic novels' – more about which in a moment.

Yet recently, things have been changing. With the growth since the late 1970s of a network of specialist shops orientated towards hard-core comics fans (usually, it should be said, fans of American superhero titles), there has developed a more European approach to the economics of comics production. Today, many publishers offer creators royalty splits, plus control over copyright – concessions that were very rare only a decade ago. Part of this evolution has been due to the particular economics of the specialist shop system (see Sabin 1992: Chapter 5), but partly it has been due to the influence of the European industry itself. For example, people involved in the British scene have become more aware of working conditions in Europe since the mid-1970s, when fan shops began to import European albums aimed at an adult and teenage audience. This was followed by a spate of translations of top albums by small British and US publishers, and the emergence of a British fan following for Eurocomics (albeit a very limited one). This gradual rise in awareness prompted some publishers to question previous employment practices, and some creators to press for change.

The rise of the 'graphic novel' in Britain and America in the 1980s was part of this process. Graphic novels are basically lengthy comics in book form – in other words, an indigenous version of the European album. Although other factors were involved in their origination, the European paradigm was certainly influential: anglophone creators had long sought the opportunity to experiment with longer stories and more sophisticated artwork in tune with their European counterparts. So, too, the European idea of selling comics from bookshops was exploited more fully: graphic novel shelves were erected, and efforts were made to ensure that they were reviewed in the literary pages of the newspapers. In this way, a readership was solicited which might not otherwise have come across comics – the kind of readership that publishers in Europe had been serving for decades. Progress, as ever, is slow.

Thus, the question of whether Britain can ever join the European Comics Community is not entirely closed. Graphic novels and European albums are pretty much the same in terms of format, quality, and price, and this does mean that the comics are more easily sellable across the markets. Yet, when it comes to content, it is still true that Britain has a lot of catching up to do before publishers can offer the same range of subject matter as exists in Europe. Things are improving, and there have been a few British hits across the Channel, just as there have been a few Euro-hits in the UK. But any realistic appraisal of the situation would have to conclude that in 2001, British readers still prefer British and American comics, while European readers prefer European comics. In the end, each finds the other 'a bit too foreign'.

## Questions

1   Is it possible to talk of a 'European Comics Community'?

2   Why is the British comics industry distinct from the rest of Europe?

3   How far have economic factors influenced the history of Eurocomics?

## References

Barthes, R. (1977) *Mythologies*, Harmondsworth: Penguin.

Couperie, P. *et al.* (1968) *The History of the Comic Strip*, trans. E. B. Hennessy, New York: Crown.

Eco, U. (1981) *The Role of the Reader*, London: Hutchinson.

Kessler, P. (1995) *Astérix Complete Guide*, London: Hodder.

McCloud, S. (1994) *Understanding Comics*, London: HarperCollins.

Peeters, B. (1992) *Tintin and the World of Hergé*, Boston, MA: Little, Brown.

Sabin, R. (1992) *Adult Comics: An Introduction*, London, Routledge.

Thompson, H. (1991) *Hergé and his Creation*, London: Hodder & Stoughton.

Witek, J. (forthcoming) *The Comics Page*, Jackson: University of Mississippi Press.

## Further reading

Unfortunately, there is not very much in English about European comics. The most detailed and up-to-date information is available in fanzines, and readers are encouraged to track down the regular column 'Eurocomics for Beginners' by Bart Beaty in the American zine *The Comics Journal* (Fantagraphics). The more academic *International Journal of Comic Art* (John A. Lent) has frequent, useful articles. The Internet is also a good source, though sites tend to come and go without much warning. One reliable example is: *European Comics on the Web* (http://lcg-www.uia.ac.be/~arikt/comics/welcome9.html) which has links to a variety of specialist sites. Comics encyclopedias can be useful, e.g. M. Horn *The World Encyclopaedia of Comics* (New York: Chelsea House, updated edition, 1998), while some of the essays in A. Magnussen and H. Christiensen (eds) *Comics Culture* (Copenhagen: Museum Tusculaneum Press, 2000) give a theoretical perspective. The following volumes also cover European territory, but are out of print, and therefore only available from libraries: R. Reitberger and W. Fuchs *Comics: Anatomy of a Mass Medium* (London: Studio Vista, 1972); H. Kurtzman, *From Aargh! to Zap!* (New York: Prentice Hall, 1991); A. and L. Clark *Comics: An Illustrated History* (London: Greenwood, 1991). My own books *Adult Comics: An Introduction* (London: Routledge, 1992) and *Comics, Comix and Graphic Novels* (London: Phaidon, 1996) both contain short chapters on the subject.

# Chapter 3

# Book publishing

THE BOOK PUBLISHING INDUSTRY

**DAVID SAUNDERS**

Book publishing was the first cultural industry. This chapter presents basic book trade factors – categorization of books and readerships, book pricing, legal conditions of trade – and considers today's tumultuous publishing scene of deregulated markets, massive mergers and digital agendas.

## Background

Whether it will be remembered as a confidence trick pulled by the information technology industry, or as a demonstration of an enduring capacity for popular panic in the most 'advanced' countries, or even whether it will be remembered at all, the Y2K 'event' carried an important cultural lesson: not everything changes overnight. This lesson is relevant when we are considering a commercial enterprise and a cultural institution with a 500-year history: the European printed book industry. This industry has contributed to building and destroying religious, moral and political values. Its product, the book, along with sermons, has been at the heart of wars and genocides, yet it has also entertained millions of people, once they acquired interest and competence in reading for pleasure. The range of uses persists today: the book is a vehicle for the commercial writer of the best-selling work of popular fiction bought by all, but also for the publicly funded academic writer of hyper-intellectual critiques of late capitalism prescribed in university curricula.

Yet despite its history (or because of it), book publishing is also said now to face an uncertain future (Nunberg 1996). The factors are several. Some are commercial. Through the 1980s and 1990s, as in other spheres of industrial production and commercial distribution, national and cross-national mergers and acquisitions broke the book trade's traditional patterns of ownership. Equally antique patterns of work and relations of labour were disrupted, supposedly to gain competitive advantage in local, national and international markets. Other new factors are political and legal. Within its delegated powers, the European Union trading bloc presented once nationally based publishing industries with novel political, legal and administrative obligations and opportunities. On the international level, a major battle-line has emerged over the future handling of international copyright material between the European Geneva-based World Intellectual Property Organization (WIPO) and the

US-based World Trade Organization (WTO) which, in 1995, established the WTO Agreement on Trade-Related Aspects of Intellectual Property (TRIPS).

Then, as the mention of Y2K suggested, there is the new communications technology. The first technological revolution in publishing is converging with the second in the confluence of printing and computing. In the multimedia environment, publishers consider turning from printed books to off-line optical publishing such as CD-ROMs and to on-line services such as are now routinely available via telephone to the legal and medical professions, conveniently passing on to consumers the choice and cost of producing the hard copy. Finally, there are the cultural factors. With the mental attention of the young endlessly diverted to playstation screens, discursive literacy levels are falling . . . or so it is asserted by those who think yesterday was better than today. In their pessimistic account, civilization as we have known it is in danger because the young are no longer habituated to the discipline and cultural regimen of readers of print.

Whatever the case, given such a catalogue of factors, talk of uncertain futures in the book industry is no surprise. After all, it is more than thirty years since the cultural 'prophet' Marshall McLuhan foretold that the book would disappear as the epoch shifted from linear print to non-linear electronic communication. Yet he was wrong. Unlike movable type, print publishing itself is far from having been moved into the museum. The computer may have changed publishers' printing methods but their product, the book, has not disappeared from daily life. A hundred years ago English publishers, as major players on the international publishing stage, produced 6000 titles annually. At the start of this twenty-first century, each year some million titles will be published worldwide. European publishers now produce some 300,000 book titles annually in 300 million copies, to say nothing of newspapers and the proliferating magazine sector. Indeed, unlike in film, television and recorded music, in book publishing Europe is not in deficit to the USA, outproducing the Americans by a ratio of three titles to one.

As for distribution and retailing, even in the USA in 1980–90 bookselling came second only to fast food as the fastest-growing retail sector. It is a sign of life, not death, that book promotions are stronger than ever, from international trade shows such as the Frankfurt Buchmesse and the London International Book Fair to national events such as la Fureur de lire in France and Belgium, the Bologna children's book show and Now Read On in the UK. And this is to say nothing of the solid achievement and future promise of e-commerce where new channels of book purchasing are concerned. Amazon.com was an unknown name five years ago.

The printed book might be an analogue product with half a millennium of history, but the publishing process is anything but pre-technological. Over-excitement about new technology, however, might explain the relative neglect of book publishing in today's curriculum. For all its history and present scale, publishing has not been taken up as a subject of study to the same extent as journalism, media and communications (although there are courses at Loughborough, Napier, Oxford Brookes, Robert Gordon, Stirling and Thames Valley Universities; also, as the web sites listed at the end of this chapter suggest, there is now a substantial range of source materials available on-line to students). Communications and media scholars have produced innumerable works about 'text'; however, studies of the 'book' are by comparison relatively few. Talk of text allows meanings to be endlessly deepened and invites theory; talk of the book concerns an industrial, commercial and intellectual product and requires descriptive work.

To grasp something of European book publishing in its commercial, legal, technological and cultural circumstances, this chapter will therefore be descriptive rather than critical or socially transformative. Our discussion of book publishing will not be an occasion for critique or a platform for counter-politics. Nor is it clear that we would understand the book trade any better by referring readers to some higher theory or deeper structure. Instead, we assume readers have a fair idea of the division of labour between publishers, printers and booksellers, and some sense of what is involved in the publishing process itself – identifying markets, investing capital, commissioning authors, obtaining readers' reports, editing, design and graphics, legal arrangements, manufacturing, promotion and publicity, sales to distributors and booksellers, stockholding, payments and accounting.

## What is a book?

First things first: some basic definitions. These turn out to be less self-evident than might be expected. What is a book? To count how many books are published, it has first to be decided what should count as a book rather than, say, a leaflet. Is there a minimum number of words, sentences or pages? Is a printed musical score a book? Is a substantial government document a book? Who is to decide? In 1964 UNESCO defined a 'book' as 'a non-periodical printed publication of at least 49 pages excluding covers'. Likewise, to assess how many publishers there are, a decision is needed on what to count as a publisher. The Fédération des éditeurs européens (FEE) set the limit at firms that published at least five titles per year and achieved a turnover of at least 100,000 ECU (£80,000).

All such boundaries are arbitrary and could be different. Their adoption as standards is a cultural and administrative achievement, as is the invention of categories such as 'average print run' – the total number of titles published divided by the total number of copies printed. In 1994 in France, for instance, according to the Syndicat national de l'édition, the average print run across the 41,560 titles rose by 5.8% to 9069 (it had been 9180 in 1992 but dropped to 8753 in 1993). For paperbacks (*livres de poche*) there were fewer titles but larger printings, the average print run being 12,727 across 9674 titles, a rise of 4.6% (it had been 13,409 in 1992 and 12,170 in 1993). In this instance, the 1994 average print run figures suggest modest confidence in a small increase of demand. But in France as elsewhere, publishing remains a risk business. It is still the case that 20% of titles generate 80% of revenue. Unfortunately for publishers, that 20% cannot be identified with absolute certainty in advance, even with the best available market research and promotion. The ratio of copies of books that remain unsold (and are returned to publishers) to copies sold can be very high.

## Categories of books

European publishing is segmented by language differences and cultural variations. For all the talk of media globalization, and despite the reality of transnational media corporations such as the German-based Verlagsgruppe Bertelsmann or the US-based News Corp, print publishers still do most of their business in their national home market, particularly for newspapers and magazines, but also for books. This is especially significant for publishers in languages other than English. Each national territory in Europe has a developed print publishing industry, hence the calls for cultural protection of specific language-area publishing to preserve a local heritage. National industries have also differentiated their products according to multiple sub-sectors and local circumstances, developing different kinds of book for different kinds of reader.

With these cultural and economic processes of differentiation and specialization operating at the national (or sub-national) level, the definition and, especially, the adoption of a unified global set of book categories by subject marks a fascinating challenge for commercial and administrative practice. It is not simply a matter of mega-categories such as 'trade' and 'academic', or 'consumer' and 'professional' (these are categories of publisher as well as of publications). In the UK, the Publishers' Association *Book Trade Year Book* employs the following basic categories to classify titles published in paperback and in hardcover: fiction, non-fiction, children's books, school texts, STM (scientific, technical, medical), academic/professional. To an extent, as is predictable, the categories used by the French Syndicat national de l'édition correspond to those of the UK Publishers' Association, but not entirely. The French organization also includes *sciences humaines*, *histoire et géographie*, *littérature générale*, *encyclopédies et dictionnaires*, and *livres d'art*. The point is not that the one classification is truer than the other. The value of this system, like that of any system of categories, depends on how appropriate the system is to its circumstances and how well it meets its purpose.

At the global level, the UNESCO *Statistical Yearbook* uses twenty-three subject categories, these being derived from the Universal Decimal Classification. However, as we might expect, the *European Specialist Publishers Directory* deploys a yet larger range of categories of books. No less, in fact, than the following fifty-five: agriculture and farming; animals; antiques and collecting; archaeology and anthropology; architecture and design; atlases and maps; aviation and transport; bibliographies and library science; biography and autobiography; building and construction; business and industry; careers and vocational training; children's; computing and computer software; crafts and hobbies; directories and yearbooks; DIY (Do it yourself); earth sciences; educational and textbooks; ethnology; fashion and costume; film; financial; fine and limited editions; fine art and art history; food and drink; gardening; gay and lesbian; genealogy and local history; health and beauty; history; humour; languages and linguistics; law; life sciences; literature and criticism; marketing and advertising; military and war; music; new age, magic and the occult; periodicals, magazines and newsletters; photography; physical sciences; poetry; politics and current affairs; printing and publishing; psychology and sociology; reference; religion and philosophy; science fiction and fantasy; sports and games; STM; theatre and drama; travel and travel guides; women's studies.

Each of these categories marks off a particular 'demographic' or consumer group, defined by its interests but also by its willingness to pay for books published in its preferred category or categories. But there is more. The trade may further subdivide the categories, depending on how publishers 'segment' their target market. For instance, children's books – and it is hard to imagine arguing for a future in which children will be bookless, at least while Harry Potter has a say – are further segmented according to age-group norms: 0–5, 6–8, 9–12, and teenage. We can take these developments as signs of movement away from an undifferentiated mass market and towards a highly segmented market (although the mass-marketing of best-selling authors and titles will remain a staple of major publishers' income, if not always profit given the scale of advances and the costs of publicity). The trend towards special interest publications, in respect of books as in respect of magazines (see Braithwaite, Chapter 8 in this volume), generates categorizations that are finer but whose future shelf-life is impossible to predict.

A novel circumstance, generated by forces entirely external to the book trade, may bring a certain category of book into massive favour, especially when an element of coercion is involved (which may not be a bad thing!). For instance, when governments legislate to introduce a National Curriculum, the category of 'school textbooks' can grow in importance. This was the case in the UK following the 1988 Education Reform Act. However, after three years' growth in school texts associated with the new National Curriculum, the Publishers' Association *Year Book* for 1995 records a decline of 4.8%. In France in 1993, school texts could record an 11% increase while sales of children's books were declining by 5.3%.

## Prices

Publishing is a wonderfully impure activity. It combines but does not synthesize commerce and culture, business profit and civilizing mission. At least in respect of commerce and profit, its worth might appear calculable. Yet though we can say that British publishers achieved a turnover of some £3 billion per year in the 1990s, thanks to something of a natural monopoly in selling to a worldwide market of Anglophone readers, the question remains: what is a fair price for a book?

How should the price of a book be determined? This can be a grittier question than we might expect, given that the fortune of each title is different and unpredictable. Should price be decided by material weight or length? By conceptual genre, such that philosophy should be priced above (or below) agriculture? Should anticipated sales decide the price? Should a reprint be priced at the same level as a new title? Given that most new titles achieve their maximum sale within one year from publication and rarely remain in print for longer, should the price of a book unsold after a year be adjusted upwards in step with inflation, remain the same, or be reduced to encourage a sale? Even the Goldilocks principle fails us here.

Whatever the answer, unlike public broadcasting product, the book has always been and remains an object and commodity of commerce. On the other hand, it has been and remains also a subject of culture and a bearer of values, whether institutional or personal, not least with regard to the issue of national sovereignty and identity. To be completely and exclusively committed to the cultural view would be to believe that books should be protected from the price factor and the market. This high-minded view – that the book has its special status as a bearer of culture and thus possesses singularity as a public good – for a long time constituted the UK publishers' defence of a practice that had lasted across forty years into the 1990s: price fixing or, more cosmetically, retail price maintenance. Under the consensual name of the Net Book Agreement (NBA), retail price maintenance came into force in 1957, in the days before governments became possessed by the religion of the market and faith in deregulation of commerce. The NBA codified an existing practice whereby the Publishers' Association enforced a minimum price for books by making admission to the register of booksellers dependent on a bookseller agreeing to adopt the price fixed for those titles that the publishers deemed 'net books'. Only marginal flexibility was allowed, such as temporary price cutting during an annual National Book Sale and the 1994 provision that allowed a publisher to remove a title from the list of net price books six months after publication. The stated purpose of the NBA was to maintain an orderly market in books.

In 1962 the NBA was challenged in the Restrictive Practices Court. High-mindedly, the publishers argued the special nature of the book as something more than just another commodity. As such, the book deserved public support in the form of legal recognition of publishers' entitlement to fix a minimum price. Without the NBA, they claimed, book prices would rise, the number of titles would fall, and fewer bookshops would hold widely based stocks. In fact, whenever we hear someone say 'It's not the money, it's the principle', we should always suspect that it's the money! Commentators remained ambivalent on the economic argument, seeing the NBA as 'rigidifying' the book market by preventing open competition but conceding that a 'cultural' case might be made (Curwen 1986: 213). In the event, the Court found in favour of the publishers and the NBA was not curtailed.

However, in 1995 the NBA collapsed under commercial pressure from the major UK retail bookselling chains such as Dillons and Waterstones which had come to hold one third of the book market. Control of the levers of distribution, not those of production, was now what mattered. As a result, it is the major booksellers that now call the tune on the prices charged to the public, marketing books just like any other commodity. A regulated market has given way to a deregulated environment in which booksellers pursue the US mode of retail exposure: direct selling, price promotions on certain titles or imprints, and telemarketing. Indeed, in the USA, given continental scale and the uncontrollable variety of local jurisdictions and trading practices, price fixing British-style never took hold. A further factor – e-commerce – has subsequently impacted on bookselling. Amazon.com may in part be an epiphenomenon of stock-market fantasy and business credulity, given that it will not make an actual profit in our lifetimes. But a visit to the Amazon web site, or to that of Barnes & Noble, the older US bookselling chain now owned by Bertelsmann, will underscore the powerful marketing modes of an e-commerce in books that is international in reach.

Elsewhere in Europe the picture is less clear, although the web site of the FNAC bookselling chain, based in France but operating also in Belgium and Spain, shows that others can deregulate too. Price-maintenance remains in the Netherlands and Germany – historically speaking, price maintenance was established in Germany in the late nineteenth century and taken up by British publishers early in the twentieth. It has been dropped in Italy, although the Italian scene might be better described as unregulated, rather than deregulated. The European Commission and the European Court have ruled against net book pricing as a restraint of trade when applied across national boundaries. The Federation of European Publishers, however, has held to the 'absolutely imperative maintenance of the fixed book price'. This is the view of Joost Kist (1992: 201) on a pricing policy to protect publishing in the Dutch-language area, a regional policy for which he seeks legal buttressing in the form of a general regulation. Publishing thus stakes a claim to protection, the polar opposite of free trade in the Single Market. Against this regionalist logic must be set transnational publishing initiatives such as co-production, whereby contributors from different nations collaborate on a book too costly for any one national company but viable if published in multiple language versions.

The French case history on price fixing is interesting, given the statutory buttress provided by the Law of 10 August 1981. Driven by Jack Lang, Minister of Culture in the Socialist government, this legislation responded to the 1979 abolition of the *prix conseillé* or recommended price, as a consequence of which publishers had cut slow-selling titles from their lists, large booksellers had lowered prices but small booksellers had raised them, and books had generally risen in price. The 1981 law required the fixed price to appear on the book, and limited discounting to no more than 5% of that price for two years from publication. This provision was contested by FNAC, the French chain offering purchasers a general 20% discount on books.

The once-sacred relation of author and publisher is also price-dependent. Authors' royalties are calculated as a percentage – typically between 2% and 10% – of the published price on copies sold, although this is very variable by contractual agreement, as when massive advance payments go to best-selling authors. The typical royalty rate seems minuscule when set against the fact that publishers may pass the retailer as much as 50% of the published price. Around 15% is allocated to manufacturing costs, the publisher's own costs and profit being met from the balance that remains.

## Subsidies and taxes

By comparison with those media sectors such as broadcasting that have operated in public service mode, directly subsidized by government as a welfare provision, the European book publishing industries have always depended for their profit, and survival, on a paying public of readers. The rule of the game has been commercial. Even in France, in the late 1980s direct state aid made up less than 2% of total publishing revenues. Other fiscal and administrative measures played a role, such as the 0.02% tax on book sales and the 3% tax levied on the sale price of reprographic equipment. This revenue passes to the Centre National Littéraire, an agency that 'enables the state to intervene in the life of books and authors', is 'administered with the participation of authors and professionals of the book' and 'has as its purpose to encourage writing, publishing, circulation and reading of high-quality works' (Vessilier-Ressi 1993: 82).

Other fiscal arrangements impact on the publishing industry, such as postal rates for printed materials. The major taxation issue on which European publishers have campaigned is that of Value Added Tax (VAT). As things now stand, for cultural goods that aid the free flow of ideas and information, states may introduce rates below the standard 15% VAT but not less than 5%. The publishers' organizations, however, call for a zero rate for books, magazines and newspapers. In the UK, where VAT was introduced in 1973, the zero rate for books has been maintained.

## Laws

Different facets of book publishing are regulated by different areas of law: property by copyright, publishing markets by trade practices law and competition law, published content by laws against defamation. These different areas of law each have their particular purposes and history.

Copyright has been an element of the English book trade from 150 years before the 1710 Statute of Queen Anne, an Act 'for the Encouragement of Learning, by vesting of the copies of printed books in authors or purchasers of such copies during the times therein mentioned'. Since Tudor times, English monarchs had issued royal patents to protect printing monopolies on certain categories of books that were important to the government of the state, such as prayer books or the books of statutes. The famous Stationers' Company, whose members owned the 'rights in copies', had received its Charter of Incorporation from Queen Mary in 1557. Today the legal conditions bearing on book publishing are different but no less important to the trade. For instance, the European Commission issues directives on the duration of copyright and the photocopying of protected works, while EC committees of inquiry wrestle with the issues of copyright protection in a digitalized environment such as the protection to be accorded to electronic databases.

However, movement towards uniform copyright legislation in Europe faces divergent legal traditions. In the common law systems of England and the USA, copyright was, and is, an exclusive economic right created by the legislator. The statute authorizes the copyright holder to exclude other persons from making copies of the work and to take legal action against them if they do. A different conception, more coloured by natural law thinking, emerged in the civil law systems of France and Germany in the nineteenth century: that of author's right (*droit d'auteur* or *Urheberrecht*). Here the rationale was to protect the personality of the individual creator. We can distinguish between copyright as a property right attaching to the work and authors' right as a personality right attaching to the individual author of the work. The author's right system expands the sphere of personal rights in order to protect the non-economic 'moral right' (*droit moral*) of individual authors. The moral right has two principal components: the right of attribution (the author can require users of the work to identify its authorship) and the right of integrity (the author can exercise control over uses of the work, in particular to prevent unauthorized alterations that interfere with the work's 'integrity'). The right of integrity embodies a natural law notion of the individual's ideal inviolability, our intellectual creations being seen as an inviolable (and inalienable) part of our very person.

The conceptual distinctions between copyright and author's right have their importance, but at a practical level they are often blurred. The 1988 UK Copyright, Designs and Patents Act thus provides a qualified protection for moral rights. The overarching international law on copyright, the 1886 Berne Convention for the Protection of Literary and Artistic Property, requires all signatory states to extend to authors of other member states protection of creators' moral rights. In late 1996, the Diplomatic Conference of the WIPO adopted two treaties, the WIPO Copyright Treaty and the WIPO Performances and Phonograms Treaty (WPPT). These treaties, now in the process of awaiting signature and domestic legislation by member states of the Berne Convention, did not deal with book publishing issues directly, but they show the lawyers and legislators grappling with the challenges of the 'digital agenda'.

As with taxation regimes, so too with legal arrangements. The European Commission aims for cross-national standardization in place of historically divergent national policies. In 1993, for instance, the Commission 'harmonized' the post-mortem term (or period of copyright protection after the author's death). To have terms that vary from nation to nation, it was said, impedes fair competition by creating the anomaly whereby a work is protected in one national territory but not across the border in another. As a directive to member states, the Commission adopted a norm of seventy years post-mortem protection, thereby raising copyright protection to the highest (German) standard. This change created problems for the book reprint industry that had operated on the basis of a life plus fifty-year copyright. Empirically speaking, it is not in fact clear that this progressive extension of after-death protection makes the best sense when, for almost all books published, the maximum return to authors from sales comes in the first year following publication. What the extension of copyright clearly does, however, is to lock up works for a still longer time before they enter the 'public domain'.

The advent of the Single Market and the free movement of goods within Europe has raised another issue: territorial copyright and parallel importation, that is, the exclusive right to publish a given title in a given national territory. For British publishers, the Single Market both offers an opportunity and poses a threat. The opportunity is that of obtaining exclusive English-language rights to publish a work in the whole of Europe. The threat is that European booksellers will import editions of English-language titles legally (and more cheaply) published in the USA and then re-export them to English booksellers, undercutting prices for English publishers. Before we sympathize with them, the British publishers' traditional practice has been to remorselessly control their own exclusive rights to distribute in the English-speaking territories of the Commonwealth such as Australia, thus restricting the market to themselves by excluding the lower-cost American editions as 'piracies', regardless of the interests of Australian book-buyers.

Like other protectionist devices, this one is ambivalent. Territorial copyright is defended by its advocates on commercial and cultural grounds as protection for indigenous industries but attacked by advocates of free trade and lower prices to consumers. Copyright and competition law clash over parallel importation (although the Amazon.com factor may resolve the issue by transferring whatever profitability there may be to the Americans!). You will appreciate, perhaps, why we cannot easily say to what extent the European book trade is an unjustly protected industry, or to what extent cultural protection via territorial copyright unfairly denies the interests of the book-buying public.

## Bureaucracy

Law alone, unsupported by governmental and industry bureaucracy, does not do everything, indeed it does not do too much. In Europe today much of the legal-cultural action is driven and administered through two of the European Commission's twenty-six Directorates-General, DG XIII and DG XV. The former has responsibility for telecommunications, information markets and exploitation of research, and thus has carriage of policy-making for the Information Society. DG XV has responsibility for the internal European market and financial services. Here too, it seems, there is a tension. The January 1996 *Newsletter* of the European Magazine Publishers' Federation records 'one of the great tussles of our age being conducted between DG XIII, widely seen to be on the side of "the producers" of new media, and DG XV, taking the side of "the creators".' It remains to be seen who is on the side of the readers who buy the books.

Despite the European Commission's 1988 Green Paper on *Authors' Rights and the Technological Challenge* and the 1993 White Paper on *Growth, Competitiveness and Employment*, publishers have for the most part criticized the Commission for giving too little attention to the print media. Certainly the 1988 Green Paper neglects the industry of the printed word. While noting the *Community Plan on Books and Reading* approved by the European Council of Ministers in 1989, Ruipérez (1992: 224) can thus conclude that 'in practice few resolutions of lasting importance have been passed', that is, resolutions dealing with book pricing, taxation and international trade. However, this relative neglect of print publishing is in keeping with an important fact which has already been mentioned and which consistently distinguishes publishing from other media institutions: the book trade is much less the object of governmental regulation than the telecommunications industries. It is important to be alert to these sectoral variations. After all, deregulation has less bite in a sector that was already so much less regulated than others in respect both of subsidy and of content.

Perhaps to compensate for the lack of public controls, the publishing industry has its own bureaucratic agencies. These include the Federation of European Publishers, the European Magazine Publishers Federation, and the European Booksellers Federation. The common aim of these organizations is to promote the publishing industry. Bureaucracy, fortunately, is not a feature of the state sector alone.

# Publishers

The 1980s saw economic recession. The 1990s, especially in the Anglo-Saxon countries, pursued deregulation of markets, reduction of governmental provision and minimization of public spending as the key to unlock endless future prosperity and lower taxes. In such circumstances, extraordinary corporate acquisitions and unprecedented mergers occurred, and continue to occur. From all this the publishing industry has been anything but immune. Indeed, change in the book industry has been further intensified by the advent of digital technology as a new means for creating, storing and distributing information.

From the 1980s, traditional commercial relations in the UK book trade were transformed by significant concentrations of ownership. Formerly independent family-based publishing houses became component parts of larger publishing groups. These larger combinations were in turn incorporated – with varying degrees of autonomy – into sprawling industrial conglomerates with transnational interests beyond publishing and, sometimes, beyond communications. In the UK, for instance, in 1987 the US publisher Random House acquired the British group of Chatto & Windus, Virago, Bodley Head and Jonathan Cape, together with Century Hutchinson two years later. More recently, in 1998 Random House was itself acquired by the world's largest book publisher, the German Bertelsmann AG. On a smaller but still massive scale, International Thomson embraced Routledge (now independent again) and Nelson. Pearson incorporated Addison Wesley Longman, Penguin, Viking, Michael Joseph and Hamish Hamilton; Pearson also came to own the *Financial Times* in the UK, Les Echos in France and the Recoletos group in Spain. Reed International (now Reed-Elsevier) includes Butterworths, the leading publisher of law texts.

The jury is still out on the results of such concentrations of capital, some of which were driven as much by short-term stock market hope as by long-term strategic publishing advantage. But this is not a call to romanticize independence. Having remained independent does not guarantee that Cambridge University Press and Oxford University Press will publish only sweet-scented 'progressive' works (whatever that might mean). Nor in fact do things move only in the one direction towards greater and greater concentration. The historic publishing house of Routledge regained independent status when purchased by Cinven, a major venture capital company, from the previous owner, the Thomson group. Routledge is now largely a self-managing publisher of books and journals under the umbrella of the Taylor and Francis Group. For the present, then, the only verdict is that there is as yet no verdict.

Changes continue among the major publishers, often driven by cross-national strategies. Most recently, in 2000, the UK Macmillan Press (not Pan Macmillan, which is the general books not the reference and academic publishing arm of the company) amalgamated with the US-based St Martin's Press, creating a single unit to publish out of the UK and the USA. This new bi-national entity will operate under the Palgrave imprint. Such a development is typical. Others have been on an even grander scale. Thus the German publishing and media corporation, Bertelsmann AG, has made deep inroads into the US publishing scene. This followed the trend to concentration of ownership in Germany where some 5% of the 2000 recognized publishers hold 65% of the market, by far the largest turnover being that of the Bertelsmann group. Primarily concerned with print publishing, the group also has interests in music and media production, having entered the European and American English-language print market with its purchase of the British Corgi and American publishers Doubleday, Bantam Books and Dell. Already by 1994, Bertelsmann had become the fifth largest US consumer magazine publisher with its purchase of the New York Times Company's women's magazines, followed by the 1998 acquisition of Random House. As noted above, Random House had previously acquired the British group of Chatto, Virago, Bodley Head and Jonathan Cape, together with Century Hutchinson. Add in the 1997 acquisition of the trade division of Reed Books and it becomes evident why Bertelsmann AG is the world's largest book publisher.

No less striking an international creation is Reed-Elsevier, formed by the 1993 merger of the British Reed Group and the historic Dutch publisher, Elsevier (the founder of the house, Louis Elzevir, published his first book in Leyden in 1583!). Elsevier is now world leader in scientific journals and the second largest newspaper publisher in the Netherlands. This giant publishing corporation has since purchased Mead Data Central, an American company specializing in electronic distribution. With this purchase, Reed-Elsevier has become the major European-owned on-line publisher.

In France too, national concentration has been a feature of the recent history of book publishing and distribution. Some 60% of the market is held by just two major publishing corporations, Hachette and the Groupe de la Cité, the former much the larger and more diverse in its interests, the latter much more focused on publishing. To concentrate its book publishing capacities, the Groupe de la Cité acquired Bordas, Larousse, Laffont and, through Havas, France-Loisirs, the principal French book club. By contrast, Hachette has major interests not only in publishing but also in distribution and retail sales, as well as in film and television. Hachette's Book Distribution Centre can handle half of France's published materials while its Nouvelles Messageries monopolizes deliveries to news stands and magazine kiosks. Alongside this duopoly are famous medium-scale publishers such as Albin-Michel, Flammarion, Gallimard and Le Seuil. Such companies have a reputation for quality which, perhaps fortunately, perhaps not, makes them targets for takeover. One such target – unsuccessful as it turned out – was Gallimard in 1990.

## Book futures

'Old economy' book publishing must now compete with 'new economy' virtual reality for market capitalization. Printed books compete with off-line CDs and on-line Internet service providers for our disposable income. The prudent view is that both, older and newer technologies, will survive and interact. CD-ROM is an established sector of the publishing market. This is no longer news. From 1994 to 1995 the Frankfurt Book Fair – whose 1992 slogan was already 'Frankfurt goes electronic' – saw a doubling of the number of exhibitors in the electronic publishing section and a 50% rise in visitors. The major German publishing interests have long been active in the new field: Bertelsmann, Suhrkamp and Burda, with a catalogue of 17,000 CD titles and an average edition of 4000, sell around 5 million copies annually. The German publishers and booksellers' association – the Börsenverein des Deutschen Buchhandels – estimates that an ever-increasing percentage of German publishing will be in electronic mode.

To date, the impact of CDs and on-line delivery on the book trade is variable. The market for reference works, for instance, is more affected by electronic alternatives to print than the market for novels, notwithstanding one-off gestures such as Stephen King's Internet serial publication of his most recent novel (King can trade off a reputation built on his traditional book sales and, interesting though his experiment is, on-line 'print on demand' has yet to prove its general commercial viability). This differential impact is clear from the success of CD and on-line versions of reference works such as the *Oxford English Dictionary* or the great encyclopedias. More specialist materials, such as the vast collection of historical law reports under the title of the *English Reports*, remain in electronic form a purchase affordable only by well-endowed law libraries. In the emerging circumstances, policies on pricing, marketing and retailing are being rethought in relation to the new media. Legal issues are being settled: for instance, the complex issue of recognizing the multiple intellectual property rights involved in multimedia products. It is, however, no surprise if there is still uncertainty as to precise conditions of access and use by third parties, given the novel ease of (illicit) copying that comes with digital technologies. As with licensing of on-line uses of copyright materials, these problems of development and distribution are being resolved as issues are tested in the courts and workable systems of remuneration and regulation are legislated. The time is long past when Internet meant anarchy.

Meanwhile, the traditional 'hard copy' printed book, carried in the hand or pocket and read on the bus or in bed, is anything but dead. Paperbacks, be they 'livres de poche', 'Taschenbuchen' or 'tascabili', have now become a key part of the European book scene (although the Venetian printer Aldus Manutius invented the 'pocket book' format in 1501). Among recent 'phenomena' of this domain of publishing, in Italy in 1992 Marcello Baraghini of *Stampa Alternativa* (Alternative Press) launched his *libro a millelire*, the 1000-lira 'book costing less than a cup of coffee'. The launch title – well out of copyright to avoid any payment to authors – was the *Lettera sulla felicità* (Letter on Happiness) of Epicurus. This is not the place to explore the historical conflict between Epicurean self-interest and utility, on the one hand, and Stoic–Christian pretensions to universal moral values, on the other. What is clear is that the new format provoked a category of books now known as *supereconomici* from other Italian publishers, both smaller competitors such as Newton Compton as well as older established majors such as Rizzoli and Mondadori. In the UK Penguin followed suit, responding to the Wordsworth Editions' Classics (at £1), and in 1995 announced the Penguin 60s (60 titles at 60 pence each to mark the company's 60th anniversary). This series was then augmented by Penguin 60s Classics. Also in the UK, Orion's Phoenix 60s also imitated the Italian initiative, including Epicurus's *Guide to Happiness* among the list of titles. In France the *livres d'un soir*, books you can read in a night, made their appearance.

It is not clear that the micro-format has a significant future, even if definite savings accrue to the publisher whose authors have been dead well beyond the European Commission's new 70-year post-mortem copyright term. However, the factors of fresh format, low price and new channels of mass distribution – Baraghini operated less through bookshops than through direct mail lists and news-stands – showed how the printed book, after half a millennium, need not be facing impending demise. A gesture such as Baraghini's also has a concrete lesson for those studying today's media: entry costs and capitalization for print publishing are far lower than for telecommunications, as is the level of government regulation. In fact the book publishing industry and the new media – networked or CD-based – reveal a similar structure where, alongside a few very large firms, many small to medium enterprises specialize in niche marketing to particular audiences. There may be more to learn about the future of communications from studying the book trade than from deconstructing the ostensible meanings of mass audience television programmes.

## Acknowledgements

My thanks to Jeanette Gilfedder for her invaluable help with this chapter.

## Questions

1 Which features of the book publishing industry justify making it a more significant focus for contemporary media studies?

2 Develop arguments for and against the proposition that books are different from other media products and therefore deserve specific measures of protection.

3 Using concrete examples, map the changing relations between production and distribution in the UK book trade from the 1980s.

4 Will books as we know them become extinct in the foreseeable future?

## References

Curwen, P. (1986) *The World Book Industry*, London: Euromonitor Publications.

Kist, J. (1992) 'The Netherlands in the European Community: a cultural area of modest proportions with a few large publishing companies with international interests', in F. Kobrak and B. Luey (eds) *The Structure of International Publishing in the 1990s*, New Brunswick, NJ, and London: Transaction Publishers.

Nunberg, G. (ed.) (1996) *The Future of the Book*, Berkeley, CA: University of California Press.

Ruipérez, G. S. (1992) 'The publishing industry and the Single European Market', in F. Kobrak and B. Luey (eds) *The Structure of International Publishing in the 1990s*, New Brunswick, NJ, and London: Transaction Publishers.

Vessilier-Ressi, M. (1993) *The Author's Trade. How Do Authors Make a Living?* New York: Center for Law and the Arts, Columbia University School of Law.

# Further reading

## *Article and books*

Altbach, P. G. and Hoshino, E. S. (eds) (1995) *International Book Publishing. An Encyclopedia*, New York and London: Garland Publishing, Inc. Offers a valuable compendium of facts and policies relating to many aspects of book publishing in all the major publishing nations.

Birkets, S. (1994) *The Gutenberg Elegies: the Fate of Reading in an Electronic Age*, Boston, MA: Faber & Faber. Offers speculation as to the impact of digital technology on literate culture.

Clark, G. (1994) *Inside Book Publishing*, London: Blueprint. Offers a 'coalface' view of the operations of the British book trade.

Curwen, P. (1986) *The World Book Industry*, London: Euromonitor Publications. Represents an earlier but still interesting international survey of the state of the book trade.

Feather, J. (1988) *A History of British Publishing*, London: Routledge. Provides the fundamental historical background to today's book publishing scene by the foremost historian of the British trade.

Feather, J. (1993) 'Book publishing in Britain: an overview', *Media, Culture and Society* 15(2): 167–81. Provides a short but helpful scan of themes for studying the local British scene in book publishing by the foremost British historian of the book trade.

Johns, A. (1998) *The Nature of the Book: Print and Knowledge in the Making*, Chicago, IL: University of Chicago Press. A rather massive but rewarding exercise in the historical study of print as material culture.

Kobrak, F. and Luey, B. (eds) (1992) *The Structure of International Publishing in the 1990s*, New Brunswick, NJ, and London: Transaction Publishers. Another collection of studies that throw light on the evolving global character of book publishing.

Lanham, R. A. (1993) *The Electronic Word: Democracy, Technology and the Arts*, Chicago, IL: University of Chicago Press. Represents one of the best explorations of the impact of digital technology on literate culture, by a great historian of rhetoric.

Owen, P. (1993) *Publishing Now*, London: Peter Owen. Offers a readable view of the publishing scene by an established British commentator.

Saunders, D. (1992) *Authorship and Copyright*, London: Routledge. Offers a historical comparison of copyright regimes in Britain, France, Germany and the USA, and treats publishing as a legal reality.

Unseld, S. (1980) *The Author and his Publisher*, Chicago, IL: University of Chicago Press. Represents what is now almost a nostalgic account of the once-sacred bond between authors and publishers.

## *Journals*

The following journals, here grouped under a number of headings according to their field of interest, provide access to current information and debates on book publishing:

(a) Trade journals that deal with commercial, policy and other business matters:
*European Bookseller*
*ISBN Review*
*European Bookseller*
*Publishers' Weekly*
*Publishing News*

(b)  Academic journals that deal with publishing and authorship as themes of historical and archival scholarly work:
  *Book History*
  *Book Research Quarterly*
  *Publishing History*

(c)  Academic journals that locate book publishing within the media studies perspective:
  *Convergence: a Journal of Research into New Media*
  *Journalism History*
  *Media History Monographs* (on-line)

## *Directories and yearbooks*

The following trade publications provide essential statistics and other reference information on and for the book trade
*The Book Trade Year Book*, London: The Publishers' Association.
*Multilingual Directory of Publishing, Printing and Bookselling*, London: Cassell and the Publishers' Association.
*UNESCO Statistical Yearbooks.*

## Web sites

The following web sites, here grouped according to their organizational character, offer a variety of information updates, reportage and discussion of issues relevant to a study of book publishing:

(a)  Media corporations
  www.bertelsmann.com/themes/book/book.cfm
  www.vivendi.com

(b)  Book publishers
  www.penguin.co.uk
  www.cup.org

(c)  Booksellers
  amazon.com
  www.fnac.com

(d)  Reference libraries
  lc.web.loc.gov/loc/cfbook

(e)  Scholarly organizations and groups
  indiana.edu/~sharp
  english.cam.ac.uk/hobo
  uni-mainz.de/FB/Geschichte/buwi/buchwissenscaft.html

Chapter 4

# Advertising

ADVERTISING AND THE NEW MEDIA ENVIRONMENT

**IAIN MacRURY**

Advertising is a global economic and cultural industry. At the beginning of the new millennium annual world expenditure approaches $300 billion. Advertising has been central to the formation of the contemporary media landscape, which depends heavily upon advertising revenue. In turn advertising is dependent on the media to provide audiences. Accelerating changes in communications technology and in the organization and the use of media, alongside broader cultural transformations, have forced advertising institutions to face up to a challenging new marketing environment.

## Advertising: growing global

Advertising is the distinguishing cultural form present in all modern industrial market economies. Emerging in the USA and Europe after the Industrial Revolution, modern advertising rapidly developed in the twentieth century to become today's global industry. In financial terms alone advertising is a significant economic activity. Global advertising expenditure in 1989 was estimated at US$167 billion. It grew to US$276 billion[1] in 1998, the bulk (over 40%) of which was spent in North America. European spending increased by almost 40% in the same period (to US$83 billion in 1998). Europe accounts for about 30% of global expenditure on advertising.

Advertising's global presence is extending. Expenditure doubled in more than 20 national markets between 1989 and 1998. Advertising activity has recently been increasing most rapidly in former Eastern bloc countries, following the fall of the Berlin wall and in China as a consequence of market liberalization. In this period expenditure fell in only three countries (*World Advertising Trends 2000*: 4).

At a national level advertising is a key sector of economic activity. In 1998 advertising expenditure in the five highest spending national markets was at a level of between 0.67% (in France) and 1.32% of GDP (in the USA) (*World Advertising Trends 2000*: 16).[2] Twelve advertisers spent above £50 million in the UK alone in 1999[3] with the largest, Procter & Gamble, spending more than three times that amount (*Advertising Statistics Year Book* 2000: 227).

These levels of expenditure can be made more comprehensible by looking at the estimated advertising outlay per person in some of the largest national markets. In the UK, for instance, the per capita expenditure on advertising has increased by over

*Table 4.1* Per capita advertising expenditure in five largest markets 1989 and 1998 (US$)

|      | UK    | USA   | Germany | France | Japan |
|------|-------|-------|---------|--------|-------|
| 1998 | 293.4 | 415.9 | 241.8   | 166.0  | 237.4 |
| 1989 | 191.1 | 291.6 | 175.4   | 129.7  | 234.9 |

*Source*: *World Advertising Trends 2000*, World Advertising Research Centre

50% in the past decade – to US$293pcpa (about £180pcpa). As Table 4.1 indicates, quite significant disparities are evident between national marketplaces – France and the USA, for example.

Primarily these national and international expenditure statistics are of interest because they indicate some important themes and developments in advertising. First, the increase in global advertising expenditure is clear evidence for, and a direct consequence of, ongoing market globalization. Second, the continuing year-on-year increase in advertising expenditure within mature industrial economies, such as the UK and the USA, is evidence of the growing pressure to produce and circulate commercial imagery in the media.[4] Advertising and marketing, always important considerations for businesses, have become increasingly central components in the thinking and activity of corporations selling goods and providing services. Third, while the growing expenditure figures imply a prosperous and effective advertising industry able to gain healthy revenues for its expertise, they also point to the increased cost of advertising in effective media spaces. This results in part from the difficulty advertisers face in captivating contemporary audiences.

Lastly, for people living in contemporary societies, these expenditure figures, and the level of media and advertising activity they represent,[5] go a little way to explaining something of the character of contemporary experience. The assertion that we are bound to a 'promotional culture' (Wernick 1993) seems increasingly accurate, as lives play out against a media landscape of competing images and signs.

## The emergence of modern advertising

### *Advertising and market relationships*

Modern advertising has a relatively short history. The conditions and commercial tensions, which led to its emergence, directly shaped the contemporary advertising industry. While 'advertising' activity of various kinds has been identified in earlier societies,[6] advertisements in the specific form we recognize, and the commercial institutions that produce them, have developed only since the early decades of the nineteenth century. The key driver which provided the conditions for the emergence of modern advertising was the change in the rate and volume of manufacture and supply of goods born of the Industrial Revolution. The key condition for advertising's development was the extension of the media infrastructure. More broadly speaking, cultural changes were important. Some argue that cultural changes were partly a consequence of early advertising – as consumers were 'constructed' (Ewen 1976). On the other hand, there is strong evidence that the rise of 'the consumer', in the USA and in Europe, was attached to a deep-rooted long-range dissolution and transformation of traditional value systems and practices, predating the Industrial Revolution. These changes underpinned the disposition towards consumption necessary for mass production to succeed (Campbell 1987; Mukerji 1983; Schudson 1984; McCracken 1990).

Advertising, considered as a communications process, is 'a relationship' which takes place 'between a producer (or distributor) who advertises, an agency that creates the ad, and an audience to whom the ad is directed' (Schudson 1984: 168–9). In the nineteenth and twentieth centuries, as low-cost and high-volume industrial productivity developed, the links in this new chain of commercial relations began to grow, connect and solidify (Table 4.2).

An eighteenth-century household[7] was organized to produce a majority of its inhabitants' needs (clothes, food, etc.). A localized rural economy, scarcity allowing, provided the rest. By contrast, a typical early twenty-first-century suburban household and its surrounds (directly) produce almost none. This juxtaposition illustrates, at a basic level, the transformation out of which advertising institutions arose. The redistribution of production to non-local mechanized industries[8] and the increase of colonial imports led to an increase in the volume (and novelty) of goods available to the market. These factors and the need to manage and ensure demand for what had

*Table 4.2* Ingredients in the emergence of the modern advertising industry

| Production | Media | Consumption |
| --- | --- | --- |
| Supply | | Demand |
| • Sufficient levels of production achieved by industrial manufacturing | • A crucial prerequisite is the existence of national media and networks of local media channels, journals, periodicals and local newspapers | • Sufficient levels of accessible potential consumers brought about by increasing levels of (urban) population – and improved literacy |
| • Extended networks of distribution – including a national transport system and retail outlets – transforming local 'customers' to distant 'consumers' | | • Culturally based legitimacy and motivation for goods consumption – a propensity to consume |

• Media will grow, extending the means of mass communication as technology develops additional media
• Advertising emerges alongside these developments and contributes to their acceleration. However, it is difficult to pinpoint simple relationships of cause and effect between production and consumption

been made or imported were central to the emergence of advertising. Advertising has a role when relationships to the 'system of provision' (Fine 1995: 145) become less direct. The important features of these new relationships were first, the *distance* separating the producer from the consumer, and second, the subsequent mutual *anonymity* of the producer and the consumer.

As new relations between producers and consumers became more prevalent, a commercial intermediary became a necessary function, as producers sought, in the words of nineteenth-century economist Walter Bagehot, 'to find without effort, without delay, and without uncertainty, others who want[ed]' what they produced (Bagehot 1870 cited in Caplin 1959). Various entrepreneurial institutions and commercial roles grew out of the attempt to manage and develop the emergent networks of commerce by mediating between producers and consumers. While retail was a necessary and powerful provider of such an 'interface', producers quickly became aware of the advantages of asserting their own relationship with consumers. Numerous 'advertising agents' appeared on producers' doorsteps offering to provide access to the means of communication, necessary to enable producers to communicate with consumers directly. Producers remained dependent upon the retail sector for distribution, but the advertising of product and price information promised a vital degree of control, in particular of retail 'mark-up'.

The growing means of mass communications (which in the nineteenth century meant the newspapers[9]) were crucial to enable this second producer–consumer interface to emerge. Space in the media became a commercial resource – a commodity to be traded. The first function of the embryonic 'advertising' agencies was the buying and selling of this space. Sometimes allied to the newspapers and sometimes independent, 'space brokers' or 'space farmers' (Nevett 1983) were able to offer a service to media owners and to potential advertisers; providing and selling space, and easing payment and collection of advertisers' debts (the latter function developed into account management). Agents received commission from the media owners in the process, which was a percentage of the media cost paid by the advertiser to the media owner.

The value advertising promised to businesses lay in the commercial advantage gained by increasing demand for their goods and maintaining control of prices. A necessary correlate of this was the emergence of branding. Branding, as it remains, was the most convenient way of distinguishing the commodities sold by one manufacturer from those of competitors. It is in this period that well-known national and international brands were born; e.g. Kodak, Guinness, Heinz and Coca-Cola.[10] It was quickly recognized that branding had the potential not only to functionally distinguish products but also to assert qualitative distinctions in the form of brand images and values. Advertising became integral to the development of branding as it assumed a form suitable not just as the vehicle for the communication of product information, but also as the carrier of brand symbolism – transforming the commodity into a specific and meaningful 'good'. The potential mistrust of faceless and placeless commodities could now be overcome by the trustworthy symbolism of a familiar brand name. Advertising served to counteract two problems faced by industrial manufacture: a logistical difficulty born of distance and a social difficulty born of anonymity of products for consumers.

The range of product sectors using advertising today in the UK is far larger than in the earlier decades of the twentieth century. In a number of sectors organizations have sought to overcome difficulties faced as the relationship between production and consumption has shifted in some way. Advertising has often been presented as part of the solution to communications problems attendant upon restructuring. For the adverting industry the use of their expertise by providers of such an ever-broadening array of products and services has contributed inestimably to both its financial success and its social significance. There are two main categories of 'new' advertisers.

First are the former nationalized industries: most relevant here are rail, electricity, gas, water, and telecoms. When these were privatized in the 1980s users stopped being 'owners' and became 'customers'. A new relationship was instituted between providers and consumers. Advertising in these sectors emerged in the 1980s to help manage consumers' new relationship to market provision. Nationally owned commodities became 'brands' and used advertising in their communications strategies.

The second group is professional institutions, such as banking, medical,[11] educational, accounting, and legal services. These types of organization began to advertise following the loosening of legal restraints on their promotional activities. A further and more significant factor, however, has been the deep-rooted changes in the structure of their relationships with the public, e.g. from formal, often rather hierarchical, professional relationships to 'service' relationships, and from face-to-face communications to call centres (and the Internet).

Once changed – or 'marketized' – these service industries turned to advertising. Advertising serves not just to boost demand but as an alternative way of achieving consumers' trust in the absence of the formal relationships which were characteristic of earlier times. Providers of all types of public services, from politicians and government departments to universities and charities, are now routinely communicating in forms developed by the advertising industry in the early decades of the twentieth century. The post-war era saw the authority structures, which formally underpinned communication in the public sphere, continually challenged by the demands for modes of openness, entertainment and accessibility for which advertising provides powerful models. Advertising becomes one of the modes of information most congenial to that particular spirit of 'democracy' created in the post-modern marketplace. There is much understandable ambivalence about the role of advertising in these areas.

## Advertising institutions

The advertising images we see around us are the product of institutions the model for which was fully formed before the Second World War. In the final three decades of the nineteenth century advertising agencies, such as A. J. Ayer and J. Walter Thompson in the USA and Mather and Crowther[12] in the UK had fully established themselves. Gradually key principles were instituted. First, advertising agencies became formally independent of the media owners from whom they gained commission (at

15% of media cost). Second, agencies would carry accounts from only one producer in a product sector to avoid conflicts of interest.

Agencies began to offer clients a range of services supplementary to basic space dealing. Making the ads was the logical step on from arranging the media space. Creative services developed quickly as the twentieth century began. It was easier to sell space to a client by promising to fill it too. A copywriting department was of particular importance as ads relied heavily on detailed written text to provide persuasive appeal (Pollay 1984). As the century unfolded and advertising became a more visual and figurative mode of communication, artistic input (across the media) took on greater prominence under the guidance of a creative director.

As advertising agents sought to persuade the business community of the power and respectability of advertising,[13] they began to undertake research; primarily into demographics ('nose counting') but also into attitudes to consumer products. Media owners ratifying and detailing circulation information of considerable commercial significance echoed this strategy. Bodies constituted between media and advertising agencies now jointly audit circulation and audience information. The Audit Bureau of Circulation was set up in 1931 in the UK (other media have other bodies, e.g. BARB for TV and JICNAR for newspapers).

The presentation of 'the science of advertising' (the title of a 1923 text by advertisement agent Claude Hopkin) and the espousal of professional advertising 'principles' were part of the agencies' attempts to justify (and increase) advertisers' expenditure. Primarily a genuine exploration of the market – checking effectiveness and exploring consumer demand – research departments also serve as guarantor of credibility and accountability, easing advertisers' anxiety about the imprecision and risky nature of advertising communications (Lury and Warde in Nava *et al.* 1997).

Research has a key role in guiding creative strategy. The stereotype depicts relations between research and 'creativity' as tense. This is mostly a result of the perception that the two share different agendas and different definitions of advertising effectiveness. It is likely that the roles promote different temperaments. Nevertheless the interplay of these two ways of approaching the consumer (which, generously, could be thought of as 'art' and 'science') serves to regulate the excesses of both partners.

Advertising and marketing research of various kinds are crucial and ongoing projects for communications in a market economy, contributing, as they do, to the profitability of businesses and the work of moderating the relationships between production, the marketplace, and consumers. That said, the validity of much advertising research is often held in doubt – not least by advertising professionals, who are disappointed with its regular inability to deliver new, useful and effective knowledge. This recognition of the impotence of much research does not, however, allay fears among critics of the industry that market and advertising research provides the basis for media and advertising practices which *institute* the creation and construction of 'needs' and audience divisions which research pretends merely to *discover.* As markets extend globally, research will be central to the project of market definition. There is doubt that transnational research can do this with genuine sensitivity to cultural differences and with sufficient accuracy to allow advertisers to navigate effectively (*Admap* April 1999: 19).

## Advertising and marketing

Advertisements are just one part of the much larger productive enterprise of the promotional industries. It is important to try to distinguish advertisements from the array of other promotional activities, which have become central to social, economic and cultural life. Advertising represents one form (or genre) of communication which takes its place alongside a vast and intricate array of commercially produced signs and stories. These include the work of public relations, package design, corporate sponsorship, and retail display and innumerable other small acts of face-to-face promotion. The advertisement is one communication option among many available to the corporation or other body wishing to project promotional messages into public arenas. It is an ingredient in what is known as 'the marketing mix', one which not all corporations are obliged to include.

Marketers' shorthand has traditionally distinguished advertisements from other kinds of marketing activity in a division made between 'above-the-line' and 'below-the-line' approaches to promotion.[14] 'Above the line' refers to those communications placed in media space bought, through an advertising agency, from a media owner. 'Below the line' refers to promotional activity that does not depend upon the purchase of media space and might include brochures, direct mail shots or point-of-sale materials.

One of the key features of the changing marketing environment is the blurring of the boundaries marking this distinction, which is becoming increasingly redundant in the face of the new media environment. The continual attempts to customize promotional packages to a more tightly defined audience segment has led some advertisers to buy out of the expertise associated with large-scale advertising campaigns and into the targeted procedures of direct mailshots, or the localized immediacy of ambient ads. Price cutting and promotional deals with large retail outlets have been an alternative marketing strategy. In other strategic restructurings of the marketing mix, programme sponsorship has been selected as an alternative to paying for a range of ill-defined national TV slots.

The shrinkage of advertising's role in the promotional mix can be overstated. Promotional expenditure through the main media is still on the increase. But pressures contributing to the de-centring of main media advertisements in corporations' promotional policies are mounting. This trend is evident in Figure 4.1 (below) in the proportionate contraction of TV and press spending and the parallel year-on-year growth in direct mail. The impact of imminent changes in the media environment are likely to hasten this process – as marketers establish ways of using the Internet, digital television and mobile telephone technology in coherent and effective promotions.

## Advertising and the media: crisis and continuity

### *Advertising revenue: dependence and interdependence*

From its origins and by its nature advertising is intimately bound to other media. Primarily it is economic interdependence that dictates the terms of their relationship.

But it is also worth observing that media and advertising companies often share personnel and technical and creative expertise in complex, formal and informal networks of association. Increasingly too, media content, ideas, images and celebrities 'inspire' advertising – and vice versa.

Advertising revenue usually has great significance for the life of a publisher or broadcaster. In commercial media, advertisers' expenditure partially or entirely under-writes the production and publication or broadcast of media 'content'. In return the media owner displays the advertisements. Advertising revenue supports media, either directly, or more usually indirectly, through a holding company or network of commissioning channels.[15]

Advertising revenue provides a commercial rationale for the existence of the other channels of media communication, such as television, newspapers and magazines, but it does so without, however, being the singular *reason* for the form, existence and proliferation of other media.[16] These perform a range of social and cultural roles extending well beyond the basically commercial intentions of advertisers and media owners.

Nevertheless complex relationships between advertising and the other media are an important and long-running concern.[17] Tensions about the relation between 'art' and commerce (often a feature of agency–client disagreement) are redoubled in commentaries on inter-industry relations. A common observation is that media outlets overly dependent on advertising revenues are liable to 'dumb down' media content – for instance, by reducing the quality of current affairs and news output – in pursuit of higher circulation, or larger audiences, who are regarded as wanting films, soaps and sitcoms.

There are further concerns, not always legitimate, about the likelihood of censorship and political bias in a media implicitly beholden to the ideology of the market and the, sometimes unconscious, prejudices, interests and values, either of an economic elite – or the imputed populism of 'the majority' – or both at once.

General arguments about 'falling standards' are simplistic – competition for audiences might just as easily drive standards 'up'. It seems more than plausible, however, that dependence on advertising revenue can restrict editors, producers or commissioners facing the pressure to deliver up specific audience sectors. Despite considerable professional and ethical resolve – which are real, but intangible, safeguards against the instrumentality of commercial decision making – it seems likely that the search for ad revenue can encourage the media to play safe. Broadcasters will privilege the production of formulaic content about derivative themes using 'proven' formats. Newspapers will increase the prevalence of 'consumer lifestyle journalism'. Such policies make it easier for media buyers to join the dots linking programming, features and ad slots, but their contribution to informative and creative media work is questionable.

In the face of the evidence of much contemporary media content it is as hard to deny the legitimacy of such anxieties. It is also, however, difficult to defend some of the often elitist and puritanical assumptions, and the political orthodoxies, of both left and right, which are their usual correlates.

Working in the media has increasingly come to include criteria of success measured in terms of good levels of space sales, the delivery of a well-defined audience and, ultimately, provision of an income stream to a holding company. However, media content is, to an extent, insulated against these pressures. Advertising revenue cannot dictate content. The realities of commercial dependence are at a remove, delegated to a rational system of media sales.

Typically a media group (e.g. EMAP, IPC or News International) will bundle together its sales operations offering space in a range of its titles or channel schedules, each of which promises access to differently constituted audience segments. Media titles advertise themselves to decision makers in the media buying departments of the advertising agencies (often through the trade press e.g. *Advertising Age* in the USA and *Campaign* in the UK). The 'product information' in their ads typically includes information on circulation and the demographic characteristics of the audience or target readership.

The significance of media in the mind of the advertiser is equally great. Selection of slots in the media is almost invariably delegated to the expertise of an advertising agency's media planner, or increasingly even further, to specialist media buyers, who also offer the benefits of expenditure savings from bulk purchasing, allowing space purchasers to band together and assert market power.

A crucial part of the organization of an advertising campaign lies in the strategic use of what is traditionally known as the 'media mix' which offers an array of options and decisions about how and in what mode a message is communicated. The traditional strengths of the main media are outlined in Table 4.3 along with some problems advertisers (increasingly) encounter.

*Table 4.3* The 'media mix'

| Major medium | Is good because . . . | But consumers . . . |
| --- | --- | --- |
| TV<br>Typically 30-second<br>commercial breaks | Large national audiences offer reach and this medium offers high creative scope. Can provide regional audiences too. Digital promises smaller but better segmented audiences | Channel hop, watch videos, find ads stupid or boring, and are increasingly harder to identify and group. Digital TV has begun to fragment the audience, making national reach impossible |
| RADIO<br>Short 10–30-<br>second slots | Ads can be related to the locality and daily routines (breakfast, drive to work etc.), and are relatively cheap | Have now many choices and don't tend to recall the rather low-impact ads. Non-commercial radio remains popular |
| PRESS<br>Newspapers,<br>magazines | Offers frequent publications, and identifiable audiences | Flick past dull formats and have an immense array of choices – and sections within newspapers |
| OUTDOOR<br>Posters, transport | Excellent and witty high-impact ads and improves with traffic congestion | Are typically hard to identify and target and don't pay much attention |
| CINEMA<br>30–60-second slots | Captive audience, usually well segmented (by age and gender for example), sees well-crafted ads in good conditions | Are relatively few in number and tend to be limited to the young |

While the fundamental advertising task remains to present the best ad to the right audience in the right way, the management of the media mix is becoming an increasingly complex part of the advertising process. In the 1970s and 1980s it was well acknowledged that the idea of a mass audience was a fiction and that different groupings or 'segments' were the correct object of 'targeting'.

Then, the problems of reaching an audience were most usually conceived in terms of 'clutter'. Because consumers were subjected to thousands of advertising addresses per day the key priority was to get noticed. Then as now, advertising agencies habitually contested this worry by an appeal to the psychological idea that we 'filter' out non-'salient' messages. The way to get 'below the radar' ad agencies suggest is via the excellence (and expense) of a strong focused creative execution: using humour, parody, celebrities or other distinguishing stylistic devices resonant for the relevant audience. The creative boom discerned in post-1970s advertising is attributed to the success of agencies such as Bartle Bogle Hegarty in persuading their clients of the validity of such arguments (Mort 1996: 106).

## Fragmentation and segmentation

Ad clutter has hardly abated (for advertisers or for everybody else) but concerns about how to use the media environment are now expressed in terms of *media* (and therefore *audience*) 'fragmentation'. Audiences are not switched off, they're switched over. A related set of problems (explored and managed by market researchers) focuses on social fragmentation. The advertiser is faced with the difficulties of catering to an ever more diverse set of lifestyle segments, social groupings and taste patterns. While these subcultures are an opportunity to forge ahead into ever new markets, they impair the effectiveness of producers' communications strategies when they hope to profit from the economies of scale afforded by selling to audiences seen as largely coherent cultural groupings. Once there was profit in seeking out common cultural denominators, now the denominations have become higher, and harder to scale. Advertisers addressing contemporary audiences want to use the media to hit a number of diffuse and moving targets – and even their best shots bounce off. Saturation offers one strategy. Smart targeting is an increasingly attractive alternative.

As the number of media choices increases the audience for any one channel or publication is likely to diminish – although there is no evidence that this will take place proportionately. The threat of such 'splintering' puts the traditional techniques and strategies of national brand advertising in jeopardy. The greatest anticipated problem lies with digital TV. In the UK the 1998 launch of ONdigital and Sky's digital service considerably augments the range of additional channels provided by terrestrial and satellite TV services (Table 4.4). It also brings closer the viability of online retailing and service provision, not via PCs but through the convergence of television with Internet technology.

Digital and satellite delivery of media (including radio), combined with the strength of global corporations and global media ownership brings the prospect of global

*Table 4.4* The multiplication of traditional media choices in the UK

|  | **1982** | **1999** |
|---|---|---|
| Commercial TV stations | 1 | 100+ |
| Commercial radio stations | 28 | 200+ |
| Consumer magazines | 1300 | 2600+ |
| Business magazines | 2000 | 5400+ |
| National daily and Sunday papers | 21 | 21 |

*Source*: From Tilley (1999) in *Excellence in Advertising* by L. Butterfield. Reprinted by permission of Butterworth-Heinemann

market for media space more realistic. This intensification of globalization (the emergence of a global commodities market in advertising space) is a cause for concern. Expansion is likely despite the recalcitrance of audiences facing the necessary blandness of trans-cultural commercial communication (*Admap* June 2000: 17) and the inevitable problems of cross-border regulation.

Advertising is a business which has become expert in assuaging clients' anxiety about the value of commercial communications and the capacity of ads to solve business problems. The threat of ongoing audience *fragmentation* – 'how do I speak to all my potential consumers at once?' – implicit in media multiplication (Table 4.4) is fended off by the opportunity advertising has to take advantage of more precise *segmentation*. The assumption is that the *splintering* of media provision will result in the further *specification* of media audiences. A closer fit can then be negotiated between message and audience. Using the 'creativity' of the advertisements themselves, and the detail of media placement strategy, advertisers can speak to audience segments more effectively. Segmented audiences, charted by computer-generated clusters of data showing demographic, psychographic and a range of other classificatory lifestyle indicators (for example, TGI and ACORN) inform the selection of media slots. The promise is that in the new media environment audiences will see ads they like for products they are likely to want. Advertising agents (and media owners) will hope to persuade their clients that the loss of media 'reach' is more than made up for by the erosion of consumer anonymity, allowing a new intimacy born of improved marketing intelligence.

Since the practice of segmenting audiences is (and always has been) the fundamental task of almost all research in media, advertising and marketing, it is unlikely that this particular challenge of the new media environment will be beyond the ingenuity of the industry and its rhetoric. Nevertheless certain changes in media planning strategy will arise. It is anticipated that 'The business of media will shift from the focus on negotiation and buying power that characterised the 1980s and 1990s towards creative and imaginative planning' (*Admap* January 1999: 19). The name for this is 'integrated marketing communications'. This is, on the one hand, the continuation of what media planners have always done: get the mix right (Surmanek 1995: x). On the other hand, it is the death knell of advertising as a mode of commercial information distinctive for its 'below-the-line' marketing 'stalemates'

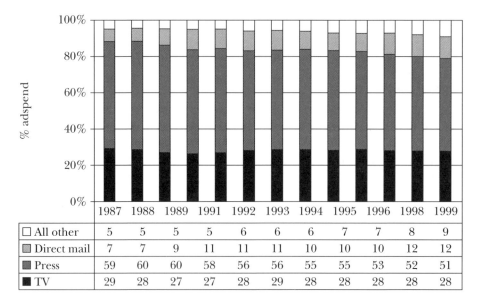

| | 1987 | 1988 | 1989 | 1991 | 1992 | 1993 | 1994 | 1995 | 1996 | 1998 | 1999 |
|---|---|---|---|---|---|---|---|---|---|---|---|
| ☐ All other | 5 | 5 | 5 | 5 | 6 | 6 | 6 | 7 | 7 | 8 | 9 |
| ▨ Direct mail | 7 | 7 | 9 | 11 | 11 | 11 | 10 | 10 | 10 | 12 | 12 |
| ▨ Press | 59 | 60 | 60 | 58 | 56 | 56 | 55 | 55 | 53 | 52 | 51 |
| ■ TV | 29 | 28 | 27 | 27 | 28 | 29 | 28 | 28 | 28 | 28 | 28 |

**Figure 4.1** Distribution of total advertising expenditure across main media in the UK

(Wilmshurst and Mackay 1999: 127), direct mail, ambient media,[18] PR, sponsorship and the diverse informational, promotional and retail uses of the Internet. These last are currently in their infancy.

While a crisis in advertising and the media is (once again) on the horizon, the balance of media expenditure remains fairly stable in the UK (Figure 4.1). Press continues its gradual decline – which the Internet will speed as it comes to dominate key sections of classified advertising,[19] notably recruitment. The gradual rise of the two marginal media categories, 'All other' and 'Direct mail', is indicative of a growing desire to initiate 'one-to-one' relationships with consumers. This is seen by some as an alternative to the wider net cast by main media advertisements. It is more realistic to see it as a powerful but supplementary way of relating to audiences.

## The mediation of consumption

After McDonald's the two largest spending brands advertised in 1999 in the UK were Sainsbury's product range and ONdigital's television service. More than half of the top 16 advertising brands were large national retailers. Three of these were supermarkets. These figures, ostensibly good news for the industry in terms of a healthy level of expenditure by big clients, at the same time point to a crisis in an area which is traditionally advertising's staple – big brand commodity advertising.

Since the emergence of mass production and mass consumption there has been a co-dependent rivalry between advertisers and retail distribution. This rivalry is the necessary consequence of their shared ambition to profitably manage the relationship between consumption and manufacture. Today supermarkets are successfully outselling big-name brands with their own ranges and thus reducing the premium prices established by brand name products. There is a threat that goods will be 'commoditized' as the distinctive and profitable value of a brand name exerts increasingly less power over the consumer – who will happily select generic alternatives on the basis of price. This risk is increased due to the potential of the Internet to provide quick and detailed comparative information. Brand owners' struggles with retailers to inhabit and manage the consumer interface was one which, through advertising and branding, was settled in favour of the powerful large brand-owning corporations such as Procter & Gamble, Cadbury's, Lever Brothers etc. In the UK, 'a nation of shopkeepers' became a nation of consumers. At the turn of this century this settlement is unravelling due to the increasing market power of the major retailers and the rapid developments of new means of communication that have the potential to bind the promotional and informational function of advertising, with the final act of consumption – purchase.

While the difficulties of media planning are high on the agenda, due to anxieties about the Internet, perhaps most pressingly the convergence of Internet and TV technology through digital television, these fears underlie a more fundamental one which goes to the heart and the origins of modern advertising. This is that the relationship between consumer and producers which advertising was uniquely equipped to manage in form and in function is being radically transformed. This is not to say that there will no longer be widespread dissemination of promotional material by the media. But it is to register that modern advertising and the institutions, which produce it will have to continue to adapt, as they are, to the market conditions respecting agendas, heavily inflected by the interests and wishes of consumers, advertisers, retailers and the new media.

## Concluding comments

From an industry perspective advertising will approach the challenges of the new media and marketing environment on two fronts. The threat posed by the ever-increasing fragmentation of the media audience will be confronted by ever more variegated use of the media. The trend for finding increasingly opportunistic spaces for advertising will continue. Fragmentation will be addressed by the use of ever more complex computer-generated marketing data alongside novel qualitative research techniques. The attenuation of the division between main media advertising and the other aspects of the media and marketing mix will promise a tighter fit between what consumers see and hear about the marketplace and what they want from it. This is summed up in the notion of integrated marketing communications (IMC) (*Admap* September 2000). Whether advertising (and the market) can deliver on such a promise is, as ever, in doubt.

In so far as main media national advertising has been the 'flagship' mode of consumer communications in the past, the future will see it remain prominent but partially de-centred, making space for other modes of consumer interface under the rubric of CRM – consumer relationship marketing. Organizations will turn their attention more carefully to the Internet, loyalty cards and other points of contact and information exchange as they attempt to satisfy more needs (real and imagined) more completely and more profitably than their competitors.

From the perspective of consumers it is likely that advertising and marketing will continue to offer opportunities to make practical decisions about the usefulness and value of goods – a function of advertising ignored by cultural critics but a fundamental part of communication in many product sectors and central to the functioning of the marketplace. There is much anxiety about the capacity of advertising to manipulate the consumer. This concern remains high on the agenda in critical commentaries on advertising's social influence (see Williams 1960: 170–95 and Goldman 1992 for detailed accounts on this position). This position has often been contested by theoretical and evidence-based work claiming that consumers are largely 'resistant' to advertising – both as a cultural force (changing our minds and values) and a commercial force (making us buy for no good reason). To point to advertising as an artistic and cultural 'benefit' is to overstate the case. Nevertheless academic studies and practitioners of advertising need to keep in mind the resilience of contemporary audiences and the uses, psychological and social, to which they can put goods – as represented to the market in advertisements.

Advertising and other promotional imagery are the cultural consequence of transitions in societies, global and local. Ongoing changes in the relations between producers and consumers lie at the root of the emergence and transformation of the advertising form. Much is pathological about the patterns and relations that constitute contemporary capitalism. Much, too, is progressive. Advertising, directly, but more often indirectly, reflects, and *reflects on*, contemporary social and personal experience. It can be the occasion of our dismay at contemporary life but, like other, more respectable, cultural forms, it tells us also about its pleasures and pains, our creativity and our alienation.

## Questions

1   What threats and what opportunities confront advertisers in the new media environment? Think of ways in which changes impact on the industry and on consumers.

2   Explore reasons why institutions such as universities, hospitals, government agencies and political parties increasingly use advertising in their communications strategies. Why might we be ambivalent about the use of advertising in such institutions?

3   If advertising is ultimately a relationship between producers and consumers, who 'wears the trousers?' Discuss with particular reference to gender politics.

# Notes

1　Global and international statistics have been taken from *World Advertising Trends 2000* and the *Advertising Statistics Year Book*. Figures are adjusted to allow for inflation. The figures provided are estimates based on the best evidence available. Particular caution is advised in regard to international and historical comparisons. Figures are exclusive of production costs which can run to £1 million for a 30-second spot.

2　In the UK expenditure on media space alone (and excluding marketing and research) was measured at 1.24% GDP in 1999 (*Advertising Statistics Yearbook* (2000)). As a comparison public managed expenditure on primary and secondary education was 4.5% GDP or about £600 per capita (HM Treasury: Office for National Statistics).

3　These immense sums can be put in perspective when compared with other costs in the world of corporate competition. In 2000 investment bankers Morgan Stanley Dean Witter paid 100 staff Christmas bonuses of £1 million each – an expenditure *double* the above-the-line advertising expenditure of McDonald's in the UK.

4　The figures cited are exclusive of non-media commercial communications such as retail display and direct promotional work.

5　The figures cited are exclusive of the far larger marketing expenditure which underwrites much of the commercial imagery and marketing activity in contemporary societies.

6　For instance, in Elizabethan London and even ancient Athens (Nevett 1982). Eighteenth-century man of letters Samuel Johnson was famous among advertisers for remarking, in 1758, on what has come to be known as advertising 'clutter', that,

> Advertisements are now so numerous that they are very negligently perused and it is therefore become necessary to gain attention by magnificence of promises and by eloquence sometimes sublime and sometimes pathetick (Johnson, cited in Caplin 1959: 17).

7　This production depended on agriculture, other modes of subsistence living and, for the wealthy, the domestic labour of household staff.

8　A key change in provision is that agriculture has developed from a local concern to become a national and global industry in the period of the nineteenth and twentieth centuries.

9　Which had expanded circulation in the nineteenth century due to urbanization, improving literacy and deregulation of the press. As other media developed, with governmental restrictions on the commercial use of their airtime advertising agencies dealt in their space too. Commercial television, which began in 1955, has consistently been the second-largest advertising medium.

10　The 1875 Trade Marks Registration Act gave legal protection in the UK to manufacturers who wanted to use a sign to identify their products – against imitation. Similar US legislation was passed through Congress in 1870 and 1905.

11　In the UK the education and health services remain largely under public ownership – though much reorganization and mimicry of private sector management techniques has increased their participation in promotional culture.

12　The forerunner of Ogilvy and Mather, now based in London's Canary Wharf which is, like J. W. Thompson, among the largest, now global, advertising agencies.

13　Advertising had strong associations with the patent medicine trade which was prevalent from the seventeenth to the nineteenth centuries. Cure-all potions were hawked, doing severe damage to the credibility of all other kinds of commercial speech promising improvements by the purchase and use of new products.

14　This distinction is an artefact of accounting procedures in marketing departments of advertisers – with media expenditure records being placed 'above the line' on the accounts page and 'below the line' below it.

15   Typically revenue for magazines or newspapers will be composed of cover price revenues and revenue from the sale of advertising space. For instance, *The Daily Mail* gets over half (approx. 60%) of its revenue from advertisers.

16   As numerous other chapters in this book attest.

17   This argument was summed up by mid-century mass society theorists using the following mottos: 'he who pays the piper calls the tune' and in the observation that media owners were unlikely to 'bite the hand that feeds them'.

18   Ambient media is the heading given to a growing range of novel media options such as bus tickets, airport trolleys and petrol pumps.

19   There is no indication that Internet advertising will be immense though the general contribution of the Internet to the spectrum of marketing and retail activity, in a range of sectors, can only increase.


## References

*Admap* (January 1999) 'Re-thinking media'.

*Admap* (April 1999) 'Studying the entrails: The future of market research'.

*Admap* (June 2000) 'Cross-cultural communications'.

*Admap* (September 2000) 'Frontier becomes homeland'.

*Admap* (December 2000) 'Managing customers or relating to them'.

Berman, M. (1983) *All That is Solid Melts into Air*, London: Verso.

Campbell, C. (1987) *The Romantic Ethic and the Spirit of Modern Consumerism*, Blackwell, Oxford.

Caplin, R. S. (1959) *Advertising: a General Introduction*, London: IPA.

Ewen, S. (1976) *Captains of Consciousness: Advertising and the Social Roots of Consumer Culture*, McGraw-Hill, New York.

Fine, B. (1995) 'From political economy to consumption', in D. Miller (ed.), *Acknowledging Consumption*, Routledge: London.

Goldman, R. (1992) *Reading AAS Socially*, London: Routledge.

McCracken, G. (1990) *Consumer Culture and Consumption: New Approaches to the Symbolic Character of Symbolic Goods*, Indiana University Press.

Mort, F. (1996) *Cultures of Consumption: Masculinities and Social Space in Twentieth Century Britain*, Routledge: London.

Mukerji, C. (1983) *From Graven Images: Patterns of Modern Materialism*, New York: Columbia University Press.

Nevett, T. (1982) *Advertising in Britain: A History*, Norfolk: History of Advertising Trust.

NTC (2000) *Advertising Statistics Yearbook*, Henley-on-Thames: NTC.

Packard, V. (1957) *The Hidden Persuaders*, Harmondsworth: Pelican.

Pollay, R. (1984) 'Twentieth century magazine advertising: determination of informativeness'. *Written Communication*, 1(1): 56–77.

Surmanek, J. (1995) *Media Planning: A Practical Guide*, Chicago, IL: NTC.

Tilley, A. (1999) 'The strategic importance of media' in L. Butterfield (ed.), *Excellence in Advertising*, Oxford: Butterworth-Heinemann.

Schudson, M. (1984) *Advertising: The Uneasy Persuasion*, London: Routledge.

Wernick, A. (1993) *Promotional Culture: Advertising, Ideology and Symbolic Expression*, London: Sage.

Williams, R. (1960) 'Advertising: the magic system' in *Problems in Materialism and Culture*, London: Verso.

Wilmshurst, J. and MacKay, A. (1999) *The Fundamentals of Advertising*, Oxford: Butterworth-Heinemann.

*World Advertising Trends 2000*, World Advertising Research Centre.

## Further reading

Butterfield, L. (1999) *Excellence in Advertising*, Oxford: Butterworth-Heinemann. A highly practical account of a variety of issues and practices in the advertising industry. Convincing insights into the way advertising agencies operate and a useful complement to generalized depictions of the industry presented in cultural and political analyses.

Hamilton, C. (2000) *Absolut: Biography of a Bottle*, New York: Texere. Entertaining account of the rise and rise of the Absolut Vodka brand. Insight into the precedence marketing development takes over product – 'making something out of nothing'. Branding history in a novel format and insightful accounts into promotional culture and global branding.

Mayhew, L. (1997) *The New Public: Professional Communication and the Means of Social Influence*, Cambridge: Cambridge University Press. A useful account of the extension of communications techniques originating in advertising and marketing into politics and other social discourses. Offers bleak conclusions about the state of social communication.

Nava, M., Blake, A., MacRury, I. and Richards, B. (eds) (1997) *Buy This Book: Studies in Advertising and Consumption*, London: Routledge. Useful collection of essays. See in particular Nava on academic theorists' 'incrimination' of advertising, Lury and Warde on the 'real' functions of market research, Schroeder on corporate advertising, O'Donohoe on ethnographic approaches to ad reception, Falk on Benneton, Nixon on the masculinities of advertising executives, Jobling on history of condom advertising and MacRury on advertising 'readership'.

Richards, B., MacRury, I. and Botterill, J. (2000) *The Dynamics of Advertising*, Harwood Academic Press. Useful overview of academic approaches to advertising, detailed exploration of changes in advertising content in three product sectors tracing some interesting changes in advertising appeals. Proposes a psychodynamic models of advertising reception and an assessment of its psychosocial role.

Schudson, M. (1984) *Advertising: The Uneasy Persuasion*, London: Routledge. Comprehensive assessment of the cultural and commercial role of the advertising industry. Detailed, balanced and well argued. Good, US-based historical perspectives.

## *Key articles*

Nava, M. (1992) 'Discriminating or duped' in *Changing Cultures*, London: Sage.

Williams, R. (1960) 'Advertising: the magic system', reprinted in *Problems in Materialism and Culture*, London: Verso.

Winship, J. (2000) 'Advertising, controversy and disputing feminism in the 1990s', *International Journal of Cultural Studies* 3(1): 27–55.

## *Other learning resources*

www.warc.com World Advertising Research Center: WARC provides access to over 13,000 articles and case studies in virtually all areas of advertising, marketing and media activity worldwide.

www.hatads.org.uk Excellent resource. Particularly strong on UK advertising marketing materials. Saves marketing materials wholesale for historical, scholarly and industry research.

scriptorium.lib.duke.edu/hartman Web site of superbly run historical US advertising archive at Duke University. Rich range of materials and on-line ad access.

Chapter 5

# News agencies

GLOBAL AND NATIONAL NEWS AGENCIES: OPPORTUNITIES AND
THREATS IN THE AGE OF THE INTERNET

## OLIVER BOYD-BARRETT AND TERHI RANTANEN

This chapter introduces the institution of the news agency, with particular reference
to the developing challenge of the Internet to news agencies' operations, and to the
contribution of news agencies to the processes of globalization. The major international news agencies and some of the national news agencies of developed countries
may be among the first traditional media systems to generate profitable business
models for the Internet. One impact of the Internet is a further blurring of the line
between traditional 'wholesaler' and 'retailer' roles of news agencies and their media
clients, respectively. The chapter notes that both international and national news
agencies have contributed significantly to, and are affected by, globalization. For
many national news agencies globalization is a factor that negatively impacts upon
an already precarious economic situation. Media-owned agencies find themselves
constrained by their owners in how far they can respond proactively to market opportunities. Many state-owned agencies experience a mixture of reduced subsidy and
continued political intervention. Current trends invite the question of whether there
is a future for national news agencies.

## What are news agencies and why are they important?

News agencies were classically defined as *'wholesale' media*, gathering news for the purpose of distributing it to other – *'retail'* – *media*, mainly newspapers and broadcasters,
who packaged news agency news for their own distinctive readers and audiences.
Until recently, news agencies did not have a direct access to an audience consisting
of individuals; their services were mediated through their subscribers. This classic
definition of news agencies still holds true in good measure, but now needs to be
extended and recontextualized. In addition to their traditional 'wholesale' role, news
agencies have become increasingly important as 'retail' sources of information not
only for media but also for *individual citizens*. This has been in evidence for some time
in the provision of financial news services for financial institutions, brokers, exchange
agencies etc., but is every day more in evidence in the provision of general news
through the Internet. However, even on the Internet, clients typically access news
agency news through secondary, or 'retail' agents consisting of general interest (e.g.
Yahoo!) and corporate web sites, the web sites of newspaper and television stations,

or through Internet portals such as Netscape. The 'wholesale' role of news agencies is therefore still important, but today it is easier for the individual news consumer to access large quantities of news agency news whose text has not been subject to rewriting by a 'retailer' who controls the channel through which the news has been disseminated.

The result is that increasingly the news agencies are thinking of their markets in terms not of media clients but of large numbers of individual news consumers. Associated Press established The Wire, an on-line news service accessible through the sites of AP member media, in 1996, and began offering on-line access to its Photo Archive in 1997. Reuters' chief executive, Peter Job, said in the company's half-year report (July 2000) that 'our strategy to make Reuters fully Internet ready is gaining great momentum'. Also, 'We see the Internet as a fast and deep current running through all our activities . . . Whereas we have historically dealt with customers in the hundreds of thousands, we will now be able to serve tens or even hundreds of millions of people'. In the company's 1999 annual report Job had referred to Reuters' 'strategy to accelerate its use of Internet technologies, open new retail markets, and migrate its core business to an Internet-based model'. Hoover's Online report for Reuters in August 2000 noted that the company had recently announced that it would invest $800 million over four years for the conversion of its core business to an Internet model.

In August 2000, the three biggest participants in the foreign-exchange market – Deutsche Bank, Chase Manhattan and Citigroup – teamed up with Reuters to offer a range of foreign exchange services over the Internet. Reuters and Electronic Broking Systems (EBS), owned by a consortium of banks, already ran two rival interbank electronic foreign exchanges, but these had few non-bank customers. Given the scale of news agency operations, and the extent to which Internet delivery could bring savings to business customers that have been accustomed to paying handsomely for specialized financial news and transaction services, it began to seem by the autumn of 2000 that the news agencies, and in particular Reuters, would be among the first media organizations to realize the profit potential of the Internet. This was at a time when the Internet ventures of many 'retail' media were judged a failure (see *The Economist*, 'The failure of new media', 17 August 2000). Almost none of the World Wide Web's roughly 32,000 news sites – mainly subsisting on advertising revenue – were earning a profit. Even the *Wall Street Journal*'s Internet site with 461,000 paying subscribers had lost money in all but one month of its five years in operation. Total Web advertising revenues had risen to $4.6 billion in 1999, but competition for that revenue had increased even more sharply (Piller 2000).

Another development that blurs the 'wholesale' and 'retail' division is evidence that some news agencies buy into 'retail' media. An example is Reuters' 20% ownership, at the time of writing, of Independent Television News (ITN), the flagship of television news for commercial terrestrial television in the UK. Yet a further change is that some traditional news 'retailers' have begun to act more like news 'wholesalers'. This has long been the case with syndicated news services such as those of the New York Times News Service, for example, but recent years have seen the emergence of worldwide news organizations such as CNN that have extensive news-gathering facilities of their own, and whose news is often used by other retail news organizations.

Despite all these changes in communications technology and media markets, most news agencies still perform their traditional role as wholesalers of news for media. However, as the authors of this chapter have remarked (see, for example, Boyd-Barrett and Rantanen 2000), the times for news agencies are rapidly changing. What will happen to them in the future is not certain, but through news agencies it is possible to link with many of the key issues that concern scholars of media and society.

## Origins of global news system

News agencies can be said to have been among the first highly visible manifestations of 'globalization' in the nineteenth century, a process of the interlinking of different national economies through the activities of transnational economic and financial trade. However, the agencies (especially at national level) have also been important symbols of national identity as well as contributing to the development of the nation-state by rationalizing the national organization of news collection and dissemination.

In postulating five stages of globalization, Robertson (1992) argues that a second phase began in Europe in 1750–1870. While he places international communication only in his third, 'take-off' phase (1875–1925), news agencies had already started their global operations earlier. If we define globalization, as Waters (1995) does, as a social process in which the constraints of geography on social and cultural arrangements recede and in which people become increasingly aware that they are receding, it is of considerable significance that news agencies operated as the first electronic media playing a major role in the process of transmitting news instantaneously from different parts of the world and thus overcoming the constraints of geography. Equally, however, we cannot overlook the relationship between geographic centres of power, and the major hubs of worldwide news gathering and dissemination, which is to say that globalization is not a neutral nor an egalitarian process.

The French agency Havas (predecessor to AFP), founded in 1832, is considered by many scholars to be the world's first news agency. It started by translating items from domestic and foreign newspapers. In the beginning it was a private firm owned by a former banker, Charles Havas. The Associated Press was founded in New York as a press cooperative in 1848. A second major agency in Europe, the German Wolff, was founded in 1849. Its owner, newspaper proprietor Bernhard Wolff, first delivered economic news to his own newspaper *National-Zeitung* and extended it to other newspapers and enterprises. Contemporaneous with Wolff, Julius Reuter (originally Isaac Beer Josaphat) founded a news agency in Paris. Both Reuter and Wolff had once worked for Havas in Paris. The new Reuters agency soon had to move, first to Aachen and then to London, where it started operations in 1851. Establishment of these agencies was subsequently followed by a national agency in almost every European country. By the end of the century most European countries had their own news agencies, and the trend has continued worldwide in the ensuing 150 years.

By its very nature, news transmission has always been international, crossing the boundaries of nation-states. Before the first news agencies were founded, newspapers received their foreign news mainly by quoting foreign newspapers or, if they could afford it, used reports from their own correspondents. When the news agencies started operations, foreign news-gathering then became primarily their responsibility. That is why, even in the early years of the first news agencies, foreign news transmission played a major role. The three pre-eminent European agencies – Havas in France, Wolff in Germany and Reuters in Britain – transmitted foreign news in the first years of their operation, while other agencies continued to operate mainly within a national framework. Reuters was the only agency that began its operations as an international agency. A separate agency (the Press Association) was established in 1868 to provide domestic news to national newspapers in the UK and Ireland. These major agencies specialized in political and financial news, above all else, and their clients were mainly news media, financial institutions and governments. Political and financial affairs have always had a strong international component, and transnational links of this kind had grown much stronger, more intense, and more numerous in the wake of industrialization.

Simultaneously, news was commercialized and monopolized. The news agencies established exchange arrangements between themselves in order to further reduce costs and rationalize operations as well as in the interests of controlling competition and protecting markets. The first extant and verifiable agreement among the three big agencies was signed in 1859. These arrangements were revised periodically and constituted the foundation of a powerful news cartel that lasted for more than seventy years. Although the cartel itself was dismembered in the 1930s, its long period of operation established an institutional hierarchy or global news system which bequeathed very significant advantages to some of its leading members, notably, Reuters, Havas and its successor – Agence France-Presse – and finally to Associated Press, originally a junior member of the cartel.

Through the cartel agreements, the global agencies allocated themselves control over given territories on an exclusive or shared basis. For example, according to the 1909 agreement, Reuters controlled outside its home territory Canada, India, most of the Far East, Australia, New Zealand, and its dominions in Africa, while it shared certain other territories with Havas. Each global agency was to negotiate appropriate agreements with a national agency in its domain. The national agencies obtained through these agreements exclusive rights to the news from the global agencies. News from the cartel agencies would be funnelled through to the national agency by the particular global agency with which a national agency had to deal. Inevitably, this caused great concern on the part of some national agencies and their respective governments about the ways in which news of the world was represented by the global agency, and about how the global agency represented news of their country to the rest of the world through the cartel. In signing these agreements, national agencies relinquished their right to transmit news abroad, either directly or through any other agency. They could send this news only through the global agency with which they had concluded the agreement. In addition, the national agencies paid commission to the global agencies, not vice versa.

There were several attempts to break the cartel by national agencies, but it was only the partnerships established with other national agencies by the two rival US agencies, the United Press (founded by W. Scripps in 1907, and later to become United Press

International or UPI) and the Associated Press (AP), that finally crushed the system. The German Wolff had already lost its position as a global agency after the German defeat in the First World War, and its former territories were taken over by Reuters and Havas. The United Press, which had operated outside the cartel, had already started to serve South America, previously Havas territory, and the AP followed it. The AP managed to extract a major concession from the cartel in 1918, when it concluded a separate agreement with Havas that gave the AP a free hand in South America.

Both US agencies were interested in the Asian market as well. While the United Press operated outside the cartel and successfully competed with it, the AP became increasingly anxious to operate freely without the restrictions set by the cartel (AP became a formal member of the cartel in 1927). United Press was free to start operations in Asia, therefore, but the AP faced the problem that the Far East belonged to Reuters, which was much stronger there than Havas had been in South America. The cartel finally collapsed in 1934 with the US agencies playing the decisive role. If the Second World War had not broken out when it did, the US agencies would have become completely global by the late 1930s. The USA became the only country to have two global agencies in the world's news market (indeed, for several decades there were three, including Hearst's International News Service). The other two Western agencies that now dominate the global print news market are the French Agence France-Presse (AFP, founded in 1944 as a direct successor of Havas) and Reuters.

## The 'global' news agencies

News agency identity has a variety of geographical markers. Most celebrated of the genre are the major global print news agencies, including AFP, AP and Reuters. While these do operate globally, gathering news independently from most countries of the world, and selling it to clients in most countries, each of these also has a long-established national identity (though Reuters rather less than the other two), and two of the 'Big Three' have a strong European identity. Of the big three news agencies, one, Reuters, has become spectacularly wealthy, as a result of a 1970s redirection of core business towards computerized information and transaction services for financial markets. The other two major agencies, AP and AFP, control substantial worldwide human resource and communications assets; but they do not typically generate substantial revenues in excess of operating expenditures, nor have they been constituted for that purpose. Both these agencies derive the largest share of their revenues from their domestic markets.

Once a private limited liability company owned by the national and provincial daily newspaper press of the UK and Ireland, Reuters is today a commercial company quoted on the London stock exchange. In 1999, it earned total revenues of $5049 million ($1011 million profit before taxation), and had net assets of $13,827 million. It is listed as one of the leading UK companies, and is one of the world's largest media enterprises. It employed 17,067 people in June 2000. These included 1957 journalists, located in 185 bureaus in 98 countries. Services were distributed in 153 countries and 275 markets were reported in real time. Over 80% of Reuters revenue is denominated in non-sterling currencies. Most of its revenue (53%) is earned from Europe, the Middle East and Africa (mainly Western Europe); 31% from the Americas (mainly the USA), and 16% from the Asia/Pacific region. In June 2000, Reuters had 521,000 users worldwide and subscribers in 52,400 locations. Information contributors numbered 5021.

The company focuses on three business areas. Reuters Financial is described as the 'core business' and is grouped around the financial markets business area. This comprises two divisions. One of these is Reuters Information (accounting for 53% of total revenue), which is responsible for the development and sale of information products for professionals in financial institutions and their clients. The other is Reuters Trading Solutions (accounting for 25% of total revenue) that comprises: Applications and Enterprise Solutions, which operates (a) a software infrastructure business providing sophisticated software for the enterprise-wide distribution of real-time information and order flow data within customer organizations; (b) pre- and post-trade risk management applications; and (c) the Transactions group, comprising Money/Foreign Exchange and Securities Transactions. In addition, Reuters has established Instinet (accounting for 17% of revenue), which it describes as the world's largest electronic agency brokerage firm. Instinet is a member of 18 equities exchanges in North America, Europe and Asia.

Another division, Reuterspace, groups together: Reuters Media (both traditional and Internet media sales), Reuters Enterprise (providing information to the business-to-business e-commerce market), an investment arm called The Greenhouse Fund, and a number of partnerships including a fifth ownership of ITN and a joint venture with Dow Jones – Factiva – which combines the businesses of Reuters Business Briefing and Dow Jones Interactive (Factiva still showed a loss in the first half of 2000). Reuters Media includes Reuters Television News, which serves 350 subscribers and their networks and affiliates in over 90 countries. The importance of the media market to overall revenue stood at less than 6% in the mid-1990s. But by 1999, the traditional media market had been subsumed as one component of a larger division, Reuters Ventures (renamed that year Reuterspace). The total Reuterspace division contributed only 5% of total revenue in 1999 (rising to 6% in the first half of 2000), and made a loss. Half-year results for the year 2000 also showed Reuterspace divisional revenue making a loss. Within Reuterspace, however, Reuters Media revenue had increased 5% to approximately $113 million. Traditional media revenue declined 9% but Internet-based new media revenue rose 250% to $21 million (Reuters provides news and information on-line to over 900 web sites with over 140 million page views per month). Television revenues had declined as selected existing services were cut back and effort refocused towards on-line delivery of video.

Reuters' major competitors in the financial news markets include Bloomberg L.P. (20% owned by Merrill Lynch), Bridge Information Systems, and Dow Jones, all of which also combine financial with general news (aided by partnerships with each other or with general news agencies such as AFP, AP, or CNBC). In August 2000, Bloomberg's web site claimed a total of over 140,000 users in 100 countries, accessing services in five languages: English, French, Spanish, German and Japanese. In 2000, the company earned $2.8 billion in total revenues, just over half those of Reuters' $5.3 billion. It distributed by web, television and radio. The company employed 5150 people in sales offices, data centre and bureaus around the world of which the ten largest were situated in New York, Frankfurt, Hong Kong, London, Princeton, San Francisco, Sao Paulo, Singapore, Sydney and Tokyo. Bridge Information Systems, described by Hoovers Online in August 2000 as 'struggling' and acquired by Reuters in 2001, had 300,000 financial clients, employed 5001 people and achieved sales of $1470 million. Dow Jones and Co, employer of 8175 people, also publisher of the *Wall Street Journal* and its corresponding subscriber web site WSJ.com (375,000 subscribers in 1999), and virtually tied to *US Today*, earned $2.2 billion in 2000, two fifths that of Reuters. Total electronic publishing venture revenues were $400 million, accounting for approximately a fifth of total company revenues. Dow Jones Newswires had 318,000 subscribers earning revenues of $209 million; and subscribers for Factiva's combination of Dow Jones Interactive and Reuters Business Briefing were 1,000,000. In 1999, Dow Jones sold its share of Telerate; no mention is made in the Dow Jones annual report for 1999 of its older partnership with AP (AP-Dow Jones had delivered economic, business and financial news to subscribers outside the USA).

Associated Press is a not-for-profit cooperative news agency owned by 1550 daily newspapers of the USA (98% of the total). Altogether, according to the AP web site in August 2000, its news services (a daily total of 20 million words) were distributed to 5000 radio and television and 1700 newspapers (including daily, weekly, non-English and college newspapers) in the USA, of whom 1550 were members. Sales in 1998 were $574 million, less than a tenth of Reuters' total revenues, but well in excess of Reuters' 2000 revenue for its new Reuterspace division ($235 million), and the companies are possibly comparable in terms of their respective non-domestic media activities. The agency predicted revenues of $600 million for the year 2000. AP's financial health has improved with the decline of competition from United Press International, its long-time but struggling rival. Of all AP's broadcast clients, 55 take AP's All News Radio, a 24-hour news radio network, 750 take AP Network News. Overseas, AP services 8500 newspaper, radio and television subscribers in 112 countries overseas. It claims 3500 employees working in 240 bureaus around the world, of which 145 are located in the USA and 95 are located in a total of 78 other countries. A total of 330 international broadcasters receive APTN television news services: these include among other things a broad selection of specialized television news services, broadcast services, customized coverage for the Middle East, a productions division, weekly and daily entertainment news, and an extensive video archive library. It also has a strong digital phone network offering 1000 photos a day worldwide, and a 24-hour continuously updated on-line news service (The Wire) which is available to subscribing newspaper or broadcast members to incorporate into their own web sites (there were 450 such subscribers in 2000). This includes international and national, but not state news. From 1999 this includes AP Money Wire, a site for financial market data and personal financial coverage, including stock tables, mutual fund prices and Hoover's Online profiles for all companies. It also has a digital advertising delivery service AdSEND. From 1999, AP offers news organizations daily video news and audio news packages via RealNetworks' Real Broadcast Network and its distributed multi-tier Internet broadcast architecture indicating that AP, like Reuters, is shifting its core business on-line. Altogether the agency distributes 20 million words a day in five languages, including English, German, Dutch, French and Spanish. In recent years, AP has faced criticism from some of its members, especially larger newspapers who complain about the agency's increasing sales of AP news to web sites. But AP has a commitment to members to keep annual assessment increases below the rate of inflation. Revenue from web sites has helped AP to add 50 editorial positions in the last few years. Some members are also concerned about the way in which links between their web sites and that of AP's may tend to draw readers away from the members' web sites into other AP linkages (Rose 2000).

AFP is a public entity constituted according to French law, with headquarters in Paris and controlled by a governing council on which is represented the French newspaper press, the agency's journalists, and its major state clients. State clients still account for approximately half of the agency's revenue, and the bulk of this derives from French media and other clients. The AFP web site in August 2000 claimed that the agency had bureaus in 165 countries, and employed a full-time staff of 2000 of whom 950–1200 were journalists and 150–200 were news photographers (the numbers vary between AFP's French-language and English-language web sites) augmented by a network of 2000 freelancers or stringers. Revenue in 1998 was $228 million, although the profit–turnover ratio was zero. AFP also offers photo and television. The agency distributes 2 million words, 250 photos and 80 graphics each day in six languages (French, English, Spanish, German, Arabic, and Portuguese) and claims to serve a total of 10,000 media clients either directly or through national agencies. It liaises with Financial Times Information and other financial news sources in the provision of financial news services, including a partnership with Bloomberg for the international dissemination of television financial news by cable for Canal television satellite and cable networks.

These brief company reviews reveal a number of distinctive features. One is the phenomenal growth of the financial information and transaction market, and the pre-eminent role within it of Reuters. Apart from Reuters, the main players are US companies. With the decline of UPI (once considered a member of the 'Big Four'), which in 2000 was sold to the News World Communications, owners of the *The Washington Times*, the number of major players in the traditional general news agency business has declined. This decline has been offset to some extent by the availability of 'retail' media services worldwide, such as those of the BBC, CNN, and other newspapers and broadcasters that command independent worldwide news-gathering networks, although the strongest of these are principally American or British. Furthermore, the scope for Associated Press and Agence France Presse to develop alternative entrepreneurial markets is limited by the terms of their establishment and by cooperative ownership structures that oblige them to mould new business activity to the interests and requirements of their members.

The television news agency world has been reduced to two major players, Reuters Television News and APTV (which absorbed what had been the third largest player, WTN, in 1998), and there are signs in 2000 of some retrenchment by Reuters Television News while the company plays out its multi-media and Internet strategies. Thus another outstanding feature is the gathering importance of the Internet for the largest news agencies. These are the most able to benefit from the advantages that the Internet affords them in terms of cost reduction, speed of news-gathering and dissemination, and access to 'wholesale' news services for mass markets. Some of the outstanding characteristics of the news agency field, however, are long-standing ones, most notably perhaps, the dominance of this industry by organizations headquartered in New York, London and Paris, and their close affiliations with and their principal dependence on the markets of North America and Western Europe.

The global news agencies represent the archetype of 'syndication' and in this way they raise questions about whether the apparent diversity of 'retail' media is much less than it seems if those same diverse media are in fact drawing from the same sources of supply. The argument applies not only to the number of supply sources but also to their representativeness. Concern extends to content. The agencies reflect the usual 'Western' news values (e.g. priority to elite nations, elite sources, recency, negativity – see Palmer, Chapter 30 in this volume), values which today probably influence the news selection practices of most mainstream media in most parts of the world; they are primarily in business to provide news of major 'national' stories of economic, political and military affairs, and sport – the stories thought most likely to interest international audiences – as well as news of international relations and conflict; they are interested in events more than processes.

## National news agencies

The global news agencies are sometimes regarded as the most significant players of a global news system made up of global, national and city news media. Global news agencies monitor local media, they often develop stories that have been first identified in local media, and they customize local news for distribution to and consumption in global markets. Their local clients include national news agencies with which they often maintain close ties. National news agencies are popular: most nation-states have them, and new nation-states are generally quick to establish them. They may be seen as component parts of the iconography of nationhood (Boyd-Barrett 2000a: 299–321). National news agencies are often the largest domestic news-gathering organizations, connecting central and peripheral media in a network with the national agency at its centre, collecting news from the different provinces, compiling a service of national and regional news for national dissemination. Some national agencies were originally established directly by or with the aid of the global agencies, and many were junior partners in a global network of news exchange in which the global agencies were dominant.

The global agencies typically supply their international news services to national agencies. Directly, or indirectly through national agencies, national media take international news from the global agencies (which are often the sole first-hand news sources for such news), and their news priorities are influenced by the global agencies. Local media usually have access to other sources of international news, including the international press and broadcasters (much of it North American and

European, including publications such as *Time, Newsweek*, the *Asian Wall Street Journal*, and the *International Herald Tribune*, or broadcasters such as the BBC or CNNI). These international 'retail' media are not necessarily first-hand sources, since their international coverage will have been influenced by and to a varying extent drawn from the global news agencies, even while they are also adding valuable and sometimes more in-depth coverage of leading news events and issues.

At the beginning of the twenty-first century, many national news agencies appeared vulnerable in the face of a range of external and internal problems; the nature of the problems varied between different kinds of news agency. A year 2000 review (Boyd-Barrett 2000b; Boyd-Barrett and Rantanen 2000) of European news agencies argued that the industry as a whole could be described as in a state of crisis. European national news agencies showed a modest annual average turnover in 1998 of only $16.5 million, although these figures did not in all cases take account of 'daughter' companies charged with more entrepreneurial activity. Profit–turnover ratios were low, with an average of only 1%. Before-tax profits averaged only 0.15 million Euro. There were a few strong national agencies, including the Press Association of the United Kingdom, and dpa of Germany. AFP, dpa, EFE (Spain) and ANSA (Italy) also engaged in significant international news gathering and dissemination, but of these all but dpa showed zero profit–turnover ratios.

Most national news agencies in Europe demonstrate some features of 'cooperative' structure, in as much as they depend on the cooperation of different and possibly competing media that share a common interest in securing a cheap and reliable source of news, or, sometimes, on the cooperation of private media, public media and state agencies. Cooperative agencies often experience tensions between the interests of their owners in saving money as against the interests of their managers in improving/conserving service, between owner preference for exclusivity of membership (to shut out competitors) against management preference for universality of service to maximize revenue, between owners' minimalist goal of covering their costs as against managers' entrepreneurial ambitions to explore new markets and new services even where these conflict with private business interests of their owners, between the owners' vision of a closed 'business-to-business' operation as against managers' interest in a more open 'business to customer' ethos.

More fortunate managers have been able to persuade their owners to give national agencies some freedom to explore entrepreneurial activities in return for rate reductions on the mainstream news services. Less fortunate managers encounter reluctance among owner–clients to maintain desired levels of investment and rates of subscription. Rate restrictions imposed by owners were a common cause of dispute between owners and agency managers. These sources of tension may be most in evidence in the case of those cooperative agencies that depend very heavily for their income on media markets and therefore have the furthest to move in order to diversify into new services and markets. Some of the older, cooperative agencies are among those most heavily wedded to traditional media markets: in Europe, agencies depend on media markets for an average 64% of turnover, rising to a high as 88% in the case of the Swedish news agency, whose cooperative structure fell apart in 1999.

Globalization presents a somewhat different source of threat to the role of the traditional news agency. Media members of a national news agency cooperative increasingly find themselves subsumed within larger international corporations that have little sensitivity or respect for local news markets, needs or customs, and have a strong interest in cost reduction and profit maximization. The result may be pressure to reduce staff and to lower rates, or even to develop separate agencies whose sole mission is to serve the news needs of their owner corporation. This may be particularly dangerous in markets that are characterized by a high degree of concentration. In these cases, a small number of corporations control both the media and the national news agency which serves them: if one of these corporations withdraws from the cooperative then it seriously undermines the agency's claim to be 'national', and its ability to sustain a viable concern. Many national agencies in Europe have experienced competition that emerges from within their memberships, although to date most such efforts have been repulsed or contained by incumbent national agencies. Such competition may sometimes take the form of regional challenges to centrally dictated news agendas.

National news agencies that have or have had strong ties to their respective national governments, among them the agencies of Central and Eastern Europe, face a somewhat different range of problems. Just as dependence on government for subsidy or for custom is itself a problem for agencies that are dependent on such funding, equally so, and for different reasons, are reductions in government subsidy or custom, a worldwide trend in the wake of processes of deregulation and political transition. These same processes simultaneously open the doors to competition from the global agencies that establish national or financial news services for local markets. The post-cold war states of Central and Eastern Europe have had to develop new models for the relationship of state and news agency, and a variety of solutions have emerged, of which some offer substantial protections from undue political interest, but mostly have made their national agencies prisoners of the state.

Globalization, deregulation, privatization, and commercialization are all processes that have changed the nature of the relationship between state, agency and media clients, in particular driving news agencies to provide for more fragmented broadcast, satellite, cable and Internet news markets, more concentrated print media markets and overall more 'infotainment-ization' of news. There is greater and greater pressure on news agencies to 'diversify'. The range of identified diversification strategies include Internet portals; the sale of advertising space and the distribution of advertising to client media; specialized country, county, issue, industry, sports, and classified advertising services; consultant services; media management services (information, market assessment, feasibility, negotiating deals); public relations wires; direct print-to-customer pagination; screen-ready services; teletext services; specialist statistical or data services (e.g. financial, sports); financial services (share prices, performance graphs, unit trust company information and graphics, investment analysis graphics), weather services (national, regional and international weather graphics, symbol charts, text forecasts and reports, comparative data, detailed analysis, world temperature tables, satellite pictures), television listings, special features.

## Issues

This chapter addresses a number of key issues. A principal issue of concern is diversity of supply. Are there enough sources of international and national news supply? Do the international and national agencies represent a sufficiently comprehensive (including geographical, ethnic, political) diversity of voices, topics, issues and interests? A second issue has to do with revenue generation. Can these agencies survive economically while maintaining a commitment to their core mission as news-gatherers and suppliers? How far do pressures to diversify their economic base in order to generate additional revenue, or in other ways to adjust to the new conditions of deregulated and globalized markets, conflict with their core mission? Third, we should ask how far are traditional structures of ownership and control – including the different examples available of cooperative and state ownership – suited to the new world order in which the agencies find themselves, to the pressures on them to diversify economically and to demonstrate credibility by maintaining independence of political and corporate interests? A fourth issue has to do with new technology and in particular the impact of the Internet. What are the likely implications for cost reduction, news-gathering practices, service delivery, revenue structure (for example, does the Internet indicate greater dependence of agencies on advertising as opposed to subscription), and market competition?

But perhaps the biggest question of all is whether there is still a role for national news agencies, and if so, how that role should best be performed in a global economy. It may be self-evident that there is a role for a national news agency in developing countries where the few media that exist are likely to be concentrated in urban areas, and where there is strong need for a vehicle that can be harnessed to developmental campaigns, for example, of agriculture or education, and where the national agency can provide a national news service that is also a contribution to the government's own internal channels of information. But in media-saturated, developed countries, the clarity of role may be less obvious, and this may indicate a need for a fundamental reclarification of purpose and potential about the very nature of the news agency business at national level.

## Questions

1   What is the distinction between 'wholesale' and 'retail' media? Why has this been important in the past? Is it still important?

2   What are the contributions of news agencies to the gathering, distribution and social construction of news?

3   In what ways might the operations of news agencies be said to facilitate or to impede plurality of news sources for print and broadcast media?

4   How do news agencies contribute to globalization?

# References

Boyd-Barrett, O. (1980) *The International News Agencies*, London: Constable.

Boyd-Barrett, O. (2000a) 'Constructing the global, constructing the local: news agencies represent the world', in M. Abbas and P. K. Anandam (eds) *The Global Dynamics of News*, Stamford: Ablex.

Boyd-Barrett, O. (2000b) 'National and international news agencies: issues of crisis and realignment', *Gazette. The International Journal for Communication Studies* 62/1: 5–18, February.

Boyd-Barrett, O. and Palmer, M. (1981) *Le Traffic des Nouvelles*, Paris: Alain Moreau.

Boyd-Barrett, O. and Rantanen, T. (1998) *The Globalization of News*, London: Sage.

Boyd-Barrett, O. and Rantanen, T. (2000) 'European national news agencies: the end of an era or a new beginning?' *Journalism* 1(1): 86–105.

Boyd-Barrett, O. and Thussu, D. K. (1992) *Contra-Flow in Global News*, London: Sage.

Cohen, A. A., Levy, M. R., Roeh, I. and Gurevitch, M. (1996) *Global Newsrooms, Local Audiences*, London: John Libbey.

Fenby, J. (1986) *The International News Services*, New York: Shocken Books.

Ingmar, G. (1973) *Monopol på nyheter: Ekonomiska och politiska aspekter på svenska och internationella nyhetsbyråers verksamhet 1870–1914*, Uppsala: Esselte Studim.

Johnston, C. B. (1995) *Winning the Global TV News Game*, Boston, MA: Focal Press.

Piller, C. (2000) 'Web news sites fail to click', *Los Angeles Times* 18 August, 1.

Rantanen, T. (1990) *Foreign News in Imperial Russia: The Relationship between Russian and International News Agencies, 1856–1914*, Helsinki: Suomalainen Tiedeakatemia.

Rantanen, T. (1994) *Howard Interviews Stalin: How the AP, UP and TASS Smashed the International News Cartel*, Roy W. Howard Monographs, no. 13, Bloomington, IN: Indiana University Press.

Rantanen, T. and Vartanova, E. (1995) 'News agencies in post-Communist Russia: from state monopoly to state dominance', *European Journal of Communication* 10(2): 207–20.

Read, D. (1998) *The Power of News*, 2nd edn, Oxford: Oxford University Press.

Robertson, R. (1992) *Globalization, Social Theory and Global Culture*, London: Sage.

Rose, M. (2000) 'Big newspapers say AP's moves boost web rivals', *Wall Street Journal* 31 August, B1.

Tunstall, J. and Palmer, M. (1991) *Media Moguls*, London: Routledge.

Waters, M. (1995) *Globalization*, London: Routledge.

Wilke, J. (1991a) *Die Nachrichten-Macher*, Cologne: Bohlau Verlag.

Wilke, J. (1991b) *Telegraphenburos und Nachrichtenagenturen in Deutschland*, Munich: KG Saur.

# Further reading

Boyd-Barrett, O. and Rantanen, T. (eds) (1998) *The Globalization of News*, London: Sage. This reader offers a broad-ranging review of the major Western-based print, television and financial news agencies, and of national news agencies in many different parts of the world. There is an emphasis on the role of news agencies in periods of political and social transformation.

Read, D. (1999) *The Power of News. The History of Reuters*, Oxford: Oxford University Press. Probably the best history of a single news agency.

Chapter 6

# Public relations and journalism

PROMOTION AND POWER

DAVID MILLER

This chapter examines the rise of promotional culture and public relations and debates how to understand their increased importance in the contemporary world. It
notes the key importance of the state and business in disseminating and suppressing
information as well as the countervailing tactics which are used by pressure groups
and other activists. The chapter examines the relative success of various tactics and
groups in managing the news and in exercising political and economic power. It
points to future developments in ownership and control of the media and promotional industries and argues that this will tend to narrow the space for free debate. As
coporate power both increases and is increasingly subject to challenge, the question
of curbing 'promotional culture' is raised.

## Introduction

Contemporary society has become more promotional. Public relations (PR) and promotional strategies are now central concerns of government, business, trades unions,
popular movements and even the smallest single-issue protest group. The rise of
'promotional culture' (Wernick 1991) parallels, and is intimately intertwined with,
the expansion of the role of the media in societal decision making and development.
In Britain and many other countries, the sheer amount of media space which needs
to be filled has markedly expanded since the end of the 1970s. The need to plan
promotional strategies has brought with it the rise of promotional professionals in
advertising, marketing and especially public relations. As Robert Jackall has remarked:
'Few areas of our social lives are untouched by the visual images, narratives, jingles,
rhetorics, slogans, and interpretations continuously produced by these experts with
symbols' (Jackall 1994: 7). So how should we understand the relationship between
promotion, the media and power in society?

## News and media strategies

In liberal pluralist theory the media provide a public space in which information is
shared and the public informed. By this means the free media function as a watchdog

on the actions of government. Free competition for media space and political power ensures that a variety of voices are heard in the media (Gans 1980; Blumler and Gurevitch 1995; Sigal 1986). In contrast, much Marxist theory sees the media as an agency of class control in which official messages are reproduced by journalists, the masses are indoctrinated and the stability of capitalism assured (see Curran 1991; Curran and Seaton 1995, Chapter 16).

It has been widely noted, however, that the identification of these two positions as self-contained opposites can rather overstate the difference between them (Curran *et al.* 1982). While some differences between the approaches remain, until recently both have been highly 'media-centric'(Schlesinger 1990: 64) in their analyses and explanations of promotional strategies. They have tended to assess the activities of sources by either examining media content or interviewing journalists and have therefore failed to examine 'source–media relations from the perspectives of the sources themselves' (Schlesinger 1990: 61; Ericson *et al.* 1989: 24).

The use of media-centric methods of research has affected the kinds of analysis of source power available. In one variant of Marxist theorizing about the media, often referred to as 'structuralist', it is argued that the opinions of the powerful receive a 'structured preference' in the media and become 'primary definers' of media coverage (Hall *et al.* 1978). This approach has tended to overemphasize the power of official sources and to underestimate the extent to which pressure groups and others can manage the news (Miller 1993). Crucially it also assumes that managing the news is tantamount to exercising power in society.

By contrast, pluralist approaches tend to underemphasize the crucial importance of official sources of information and overplay the fluidity of competition. An approach which moves beyond 'media-centrism' and directly examines the promotional strategies of government, business and interest or pressure groups has been advocated and a number of studies are now in existence (e.g. Anderson 1991, 1997; Cook 1989; Davies 2000a,b; Deacon and Golding 1994; Ericson *et al.* 1989; Manning 1998; Miller 1994; Miller *et al.* 1998; Schlesinger and Tumber 1994; Schlesinger *et al.* 2001; Tilson 1993). The following sections of this chapter review some of the important issues in understanding promotional strategies and their relationships with the media and power in society. First we briefly examine the rise of public relations and promotional culture.

## The rise of 'promotional culture'

The rise of public relations as a specific profession occurred around the turn of the twentieth century in the USA and slightly later in Britain. The development of propaganda and public relations suggests that public opinion became more important in this period. But why did public opinion suddenly become so important that it needed to be managed? According to Bernays (in 1923) twentieth century-capitalism brought with it:

> an increased readiness of the public, due to the spread of literacy and democratic forms of government, to feel that it is entitled to its voice in the conduct of large aggregations, political, capitalist or labour (cited in McNair 1995: 112).

Thus universal suffrage and other democratic reforms were a key factor in increasing the influence which could be exerted by the populace on decision making. In other words, the rise of public relations as a specialism was a *response* to the modest democratic reforms of this period. These followed increased social unrest and the rise of organized labour (L'Etang 1998).

At the same time new communication technologies were being developed and it became possible to reach a new mass market. Some writers suggest that it was advancing communications technology which pushed the powerful into propaganda techniques. However, it should be remembered that one of the key reasons for the development of the new communications technologies were the use to which they could be put in wartime propaganda.

PR posts have tended to be established at moments of crisis for the powerful, whether at war, under attack from colonial possessions or organized labour. For example, the Foreign Office and the armed forces first appointed press officers during the First World War and in 1919 Prime Minister Lloyd George's aide set up a covert propaganda agency to incite hostility against trades unionism, funded by employers (Middlemass 1979). Business PR became important after the end of the Second World War. An organization called Aims of Industry was founded by business leaders in 1942/43 and it soon saw action assisting the medical profession in resisting the introduction of the National Health Service and campaigning against the nationalization of the sugar and iron and steel industries (Kisch 1964). In the US it has been argued that the conservatism of the 1950s was 'politically constructed' in part by the 'intellectual reconquest' or the USA by big business (Fones-Wolf 1994: 285). Since 1945 we have witnessed a mushrooming of information posts in British government (Tulloch 1993), both in civil ministries (Crofts 1989) and in colonial counter-insurgency (Carruthers 1995), leading latterly to the rise of the 'public relations state' (Deacon and Golding 1994: 4) and in the political parties the emergence of the 'spin doctor' (Jones 1995, 1997, 1999). Corporate PR has also expanded and adapted to new challenges, such as the threat to business interests of the environmental movement or of business competition. According to some accounts the PR activities of, for example, McDonald's (Vidal 1997), British Airways (Gregory 1996), and consultancies like Burson Marstellar (Hager and Burton 1999) have often strayed over the line of good faith and even legality (Beder 1997; Rampton and Stauber 2001; Stauber and Rampton 1995).

The Conservatives' release of the free market from 1979 had an explosive impact on PR. Between 1979 and 1998 the PR consultancy industry in the UK increased elevenfold in real terms (Miller and Dinan 2000). PR consultancies expanded on the back of the mass privatizations of publicly owned assets and the increased international mobility of capital fostered by conservative regimes in the UK, the USA, Japan and elsewhere.

In the political world too PR and marketing techniques have become much more important. The obsession with controlling image and perception evident in the Labour Party under Blair led to the jettisoning of Labour's distinctive policy platform (Heffernan and Marqusee 1992), to be replaced by spin and presentation. The accounts of this period which have appeared make it clear that a small group of modernizers around Blair (especially pollster Philip Gould and spin doctor Peter Mandelson) conspired to reshape the party in a new market-friendly guise (Gould 1998; Macintyre 2000; Routledge 1999). In government after 1997, Labour's biggest change to the civil service was the mass cull of almost all heads of information in Whitehall (Franklin 1999; Oborne 1999). It has been widely alleged that centralized and politicized information control by the Prime Minister's press secretary Alastair Campbell, surpasses that experienced under the Thatcher administration (Jones 1999; Oborne 1999).

With the growth of PR has come myriad specialisms such as media relations, public affairs, issues management and lobbying (Moloney 1996). The activities of lobbyists have themselves become a major public issue following the exposure by the media of the cash-for-questions controversy when some MPs were revealed to be secretly working for undeclared lobbying interests (Greer 1997; Leigh and Vulliamy 1997). Soon after the election of the New Labour government in 1997 the tight networks of power around New Labour were exposed when Labour-friendly lobbyists offered direct ministerial access to an undercover journalist posing as a businessman. In a similar sting in 1999 lobbyists targeting the new Scottish Parliament were also exposed as offering access to ministers for cash (Schlesinger *et al.* 2001). The covert and media-shy activities of lobbyists have unquestionably become more important in policy making (Hollingsworth 1991; Silverstein 1998), but calls to regulate British lobbyists have so far gone unheeded in the UK. In Scotland, however, the Edinburgh Parliament has, in 2001, moved decisively towards regulation (see http://staff.stir.ac.uk/davidmiller/lobbying.html).

It was only in the 1970s that organizations such as trades unions started to appoint PR officials and prioritize media relations (Jones 1986). As the media have become increasingly important or as other avenues for influence or change are closed off, so pressure groups and other campaigners have been forced to try to attract the attention of the media in order to pursue their aims. Since the 1970s there has been a change in the character of protest. Mass marches and demonstrations have become less popular and are increasingly seen as ineffective (Engel 1996; Porter 1995). Instead radical or countercultural movements increasingly understand the value of smaller and more focused actions which are more likely to have televisual appeal (Grant 1995; Vidal and Bellos 1996). This can be seen particularly in the campaigns against Genetically Modified (GM) food, where campaigners have damaged crops wearing protective clothing and with TV cameras in tow.

The focus of much lobbying and public relations activity has also shifted from the centres of power in the nation-state to transnational bodies. In Europe, Brussels has become a much more important target for both pressure groups (Greenwood 1997; Mazey and Richardson 1993) and the PR industry (Anderson and Eliassen 1995; Miller and Schlesinger 2000). The global level has also become markedly more important. Corporations are increasingly able to move capital globally to seek higher and quicker profits. Consequently institutions of global governance such as the World Bank, International Monetary Fund and World Trade Organization have become more important in regulating the 'free trade'. But in the wake of the globalization of capital has come the globalization of protest. The protests in Seattle against the WTO and in Prague against the IMF in 2000 signalled the public emergence of a heterogeneous assemblage of different interests from the developed and developing world united by their opposition to the free market and the dominance of predominantly US multinationals. Anti-capitalist protests have occurred across the world as the global reach of corporations has made clear the interconnectedness of local protests.

One key aspect of the protests is a specific opposition to the marketing, PR and advertising strategies of multinationals. This is expressed by pressure groups such as the Canadian adbusters group (http://adbusters.org) and chronicled in Naomi Klein's anti-branding polemic *No Logo* (Klein 2000).

## Promotional resources

The contemporary experience is that government, business and pressure groups actively compete for media space and definitional advantage. However, in the competition for access there are very marked resource inequalities between organizations. One obvious way in which this is the case is in financial and personnel budgets. Government promotion is carried out by the Government Information and Communication Service, which employs around 1200 Information Officers, plus support staff and has a budget running into hundreds of millions of pounds. The top 150 PR consultancies earned £440 million in fee income in 1995 (Miller and Dinan 2000: 11). It is only government, corporations and the bigger interest groups who can afford long-term support from PR consultancies. In other words, the central institutions of the state and big business enjoy structured advantages in the competition. By resources, however, we also mean the extent to which an organization is institutionally secure. For example, the central institutions of the state are plainly among the most institutionalized, whereas government-created statutory bodies are less institutionally secure. Outside the ambit of the state are major pressure groups such as Greenpeace or professional associations such as the British Medical Association. These are long-term bodies, which may not always be fully secure. The least institutionalized organizations are those with little formal organization, arising out of specific campaigns or circumstances, whether as a result of attempts to block new motorways or bypasses or to stop the closure of a local school. A third type of resource is cultural. Respectability, authoritativeness and legitimacy are all key elements here. These are largely decided by and dependent on the perceptions of others and can decisively influence the credibility of an organization. Cultural capital resides even in the smallest feature of personal presentation such as the accent of the speaker and how they dress. On the basis of the unequal distribution of resources we can identify some groups as 'resource-poor' (Goldenberg 1975) or resource-rich. However, the resources available to the institutions of the state also exist in the context of broader structures of power and authority. Both the state and business have markedly more power to police disclosure and enclosure than others.

## Policing enclosure and disclosure

The state is a key site for the policing of information. It controls a huge bureaucratic machinery for the production of research, official statistics and public information. The backbone of the machinery of media management in Britain is the system of mass unattributable briefings, known as the lobby system by which journalists receive the latest 'off-the-record' comment and political spin on the stories of the day. These appear in news reporting with the source of the information disguised in phrases such as 'the government believes' or 'sources close to the Prime Minister suggest'. The advantage for the government is that since the information is not attributed it is, as one minister put it, 'no skin off anyone's nose if it turns out to be wrong' (Cockerell *et al.* 1984: 33; see also Cockerell 1988; Franklin 1994; Harris 1990; Ingham 1991).

The production of government information can itself be influenced by party-political or class interests and there have been a number of controversies in Britain about the accuracy of official statistics (Levitas and Guy 1996). Furthermore, the accuracy of government information in general has been increasingly questioned. From the massaging of the figures for unemployment to disinformation in times of war state personnel regularly involve themselves in misinformation.

Successive Cabinet Secretaries have provoked opprobrium for their slippery definitions of the concept of truth. Sir Robert Armstrong famously acknowledged in an Australian court that he had been 'economical with the truth' in the British government's attempt to suppress the book *Spycatcher*. In the Scott inquiry into the Arms to Iraq affair, his successor Sir Robin Butler maintained that Parliament had not been misled even though it had only been given partial information. 'Half the picture can be true' he stated (see Norton-Taylor 1995: 91).

However, such evasions can be complemented by wholesale falsehoods when governments face conflict. In Northern Ireland, before the IRA ceasefires, both the police and the Army engaged in disinformation. In the case of the 1988 Gibraltar shootings, quite false information was given to the media (about a non-existent bomb, and a gun battle which did not happen) to suggest that the killing of three unarmed members of an IRA Active Service Unit was legitimate (Miller 1991; Bolton 1996). During the Gulf War in 1991, Western governments built up a picture of Saddam Hussein as a Hitler figure, threatening western civilization (Philo and McLaughlin 1995). Atrocity stories similar to those of the First World War involving Iraqi troops looting incubators and leaving the babies occupying them to die were circulated by PR company Hill and Knowlton for the Kuwaiti government. These stories were false, but had their effect in influencing sceptics in the US Congress to vote for war (Kellner 1992; MacArthur 1993: 37–77). Furthermore, the war was presented as a hi-tech operation in which the Western forces were able to attack targets with 'surgical precision' using 'smart' weapons. However, such weaponry accounted for only 7% of weapons used in the Gulf and 40% of those apparently missed their targets (Kellner 1992: 163). The key result was that, in this 'clean' war, an estimated 30,000–40,000 Iraqis (around 20–25% of them civilians) died (MacArthur 1993: 255–57) and as the BBC's John Simpson concluded after the war 'we didn't see much of that' (cited in Philo and McLaughlin 1995: 155).

The state also defines the laws which govern the disclosure of official information (the Official Secrets Act among others) and the suppression of other categories of information (Leigh 1980). For example, there are powers in the Prevention of Terrorism Act, the Emergency Provisions Act, the Police and Criminal Evidence Act and the Criminal Justice Act to seize journalistic materials. Furthermore the use of such legislation has increased markedly since the 1970s (Miller 1994, Chapter 1).

Of course, the existence of such laws is not a strict limitation on the ability to communicate. In fact the disclosure of official information by state personnel is sanctioned so as to allow selective communication (Downing 1986). As Margaret Thatcher's former Press Secretary Bernard Ingham acknowledges:

> I must tell you that I . . . have never regarded the Official Secrets Act as a constraint on my operations. Indeed, I regard myself as licensed to break the law as and when I judge necessary; and I suppose it is necessary to break it every other minute of every working day. (Ingham 1991: 348)

However, the concept of public service and the limited public accountability of government does mean that they have a greater openness than large corporations whose activities are not required to be publicly scrutinized (Gandy 1992; Stauber and Rampton 1995; Rowell 1996, Chapter 4). PR and lobbying companies too operate secretively since as PR practitioners acknowledge the best PR leaves no trace.

## Promotional strategies: lobbying versus media relations

Resources determine the strategies which organizations are able to employ. But resource-rich organizations do not always devote the main part of their efforts to managing the media. It may be that low-profile and discreet lobbying in Whitehall, Brussels or at the WTO is seen as a more effective way of pursuing interests. Indeed it has been suggested that the groups most able to implement this type of 'insider' strategy (Grant 1995) are by definition resource-rich since they have superior contacts and are perceived as more respectable, credible and authoritative or representative.

Furthermore, given that British society is characterized by marked inequalities of wealth, power and status, the defenders of the current order are only likely to need to engage in media management in so far as change is threatened or desired. This is one explanation of the observation that business tends not to be as visible as its critics in the media (Tumber 1993).

Both of these factors influence the strategies of resource-poor groups. An absence of contacts with government and the aim of political or cultural change can condemn resource-poor groups to strategies and tactics which resource-rich organizations would rarely even consider. Moreover, resource-poor groups may not wish to become entangled in consultative procedures with government for ideological or strategic reasons (Grant 1995).

The tactic of outing allegedly gay bishops or MPs is an example of such a strategy as is the use of demonstrations, anti-road protests and even that of armed struggle.

More prosperous groups tend to concentrate on more orthodox media relations. Nevertheless, resource-poor groups are sometimes able to gain coverage in the media and can on occasion influence public debate. This is particularly the case with issue-based campaigning groups which appear to gain a higher profile than those which simply attempt to raise resources or their own profile (Deacon 1996). For example, Peter Tatchell of the lesbian and gay activist group Outrage has commented:

> We produce very good quality press releases that back up what we say with hard facts and statistics. It makes it much easier for people to take us seriously (cited in Miller and Williams 1993: 132).

The imaginative and highly controversial tactics of Outrage allowed them to capture the media spotlight for lesbian and gay issues at an unprecedented level in the 1990s. It is this kind of skill and innovation in campaigning strategy which can help the resource-poor group even in marginalized parts of the developing world. For example, the Zapatista peasants of Chiapas Province in Mexico made highly entertaining use of new technology in their fight with the Mexican government (http://www.ezln.org). Spokesperson 'Sub commandante Marcos' fires off statements to the media by email:

> It's Marcos's communications skills that have helped to make his modern
> revolution . . . A reporter who interviewed him in July 1994 asked: 'So where did you
> pick up the American accent?' 'While I was working as a waiter in San Francisco,
> until they sacked me for being gay', he joked to the *Houston Chronicle.* The Mexican
> government seized on the gaffe. 'Marcos admits to being homosexual', the front
> pages of the government newspapers taunted. In response Marcos issued one of his
> characteristically quirky communiqués from his tropical forest. Marcos is gay in San
> Francisco, a Palestinian in Israel, a Jew in Germany . . . a pacifist in Bosnia, a housewife
> alone on a Saturday night in any neighbourhood of any city in Mexico, a reporter
> writing filler stories for the back pages, a single woman on the metro at 10PM and,
> of course, a Zapatista in the mountains of South-east Mexico. So Marcos is a human
> being, any human being, in this world, resisting and saying 'Enough!' (*The Guardian,*
> 20 February 1995)

But however sophisticated their public relations skills, small alternative groups are unlikely to be able to gain sustained positive media coverage in the face of strong competition from resource-rich organizations.

## Problems of coherence and division

Conversely, resource-rich organizations are not always able to plan and execute coherent and unified promotional strategies. All organizations, whatever their resources, are likely to contain a variety of competing agendas, political perspectives and professional rivalries. In government departments, for example, there is a history of rivalry between promotional professionals and administrative civil servants (Miller 1993). Furthermore, the involvement of a variety of official bodies in a particular issue can lead to, or be symptomatic of, serious disputes over strategy and tactics. The rivalry between different government agencies in Northern Ireland such as the police, the Army the various intelligence bodies and the Northern Ireland Office are well known and in 1974 the divisions were so serious that a strike by Protestant workers succeeded in bringing down a power-sharing assembly in the face of the government's inability to speak with one voice (Miller 1993). In recent years the food scares over salmonella (in 1988/89) and BSE (Mad Cow Disease in 1990 and 1996) have revealed significant divisions between the Department of Health with its brief for public health and the Ministry of Agriculture with its concern for the farming industry which have resulted in the two ministries issuing contradictory advice to the public and even attacking each other in off-the-record briefings to the media (Miller and Reilly 1995).

When powerful and resource-rich organizations suffer serious internal problems, are caught in indefensible positions, are attacked by seeming allies or try to maintain a low media profile, resource-poor groups are often able to step into the media spotlight to provide answers to the apparent crisis or fill the news vacuum. Thus in relation to salmonella, radical pressure groups such as the London Food Commission or, in relation to BSE, alternative 'experts' such as Professor Richard Lacey or Stephen Dealler were able to some extent to take the PR initiative (Miller and Reilly 1995). But we should remember that for all their efforts the government was able to stonewall proper investigation of BSE for a decade (Miller 1999; http://www.bse.org.uk).

Too much publicity can be dangerous for radical organizations. Success in gaining media coverage may lead to internal dissent as spokespersons become media-friendly. The suspicion within the organization that the newly visible spokesperson might become infatuated with their own celebrity and have 'sold out' is never far from the surface (see Anderson 1993; Gitlin 1980; Miller *et al.* 1998). Furthermore, divisions over strategy and tactics are common, especially of radical or countercultural movements or groups. Divisions within environmental and animal rights groups have increasingly appeared as some become more mainstream. The divisions between organizations campaigning for rights for people with disabilities are absolutely typical. Here the old style of incremental campaigning now competes with the more radical direct action approach of organizations such as the Disabled People's Direct Action Network (DAN), which eschews the gradualist approach and agitates for civil rights rather than 'charity' and sympathy. One campaign slogan, fusing radical politics with newsworthy punchiness, reads 'piss on pity'. For the old-style campaigners such tactics are more likely to alienate policy makers. According to one: 'if you go up to an MP with that on I don't think he or she's likely to warm to you – if they're not already interested' (Parker 1995: 6). For the radicals such an approach smacks of tried and failed reformism. Such differences of emphasis on strategy, tactics and goals are of course partly genuine political differences, but can also indicate strategies of 'product differentiation' and a means of generating extra pressure on decision makers.

Of course, there are occasions on which it is seen as better to cooperate on particular issues. Resource-poor groups can enter tactical or long-term alliances with their resource-rich competitors or even with their apparent enemies. But more commonly pressure groups will join other statutory and non-statutory bodies to create a common strategy, perhaps at the European or global levels (Mazey and Richardson 1993; Miller and Schlesinger 2000).

## Media factors

The media operate within a complex set of pressures of ownership, editorial control and economic interest. Journalists do have some measure of autonomy in their daily work routines. But this varies greatly between radio, television and the press, between different channels or newspapers and even between different formats, be they news, current affairs or discussion programmes in the broadcast media or news, features, columns and editorials in the press. These variations are in part a result of variations in news values, but they also reflect the promotional networks which form around varying journalistic beats. At the pinnacle of the news values of broadcasting, the broadsheet press and some elements of the tabloid press is hard news. This typically revolves around the news beats of central government which are covered by political correspondents or lobby journalists. Down a notch in terms of news value are more peripheral government departments such as Defence, Education, Agriculture or Health, which typically have their own corps of specialist journalists. As a result of this form of organization the bulk of political news originates with the central bureaucracies of Whitehall and the political party's news management apparatus. However, the specialist correspondents are also engaged in attempting to cover the major policy debates or new developments in their field. Furthermore, they may have a special page devoted to their output in broadsheet newspapers such as the health, science or education pages. Such factors do mean that specialists can be more interested in the intricacies of policy debates or in the activities of resource-poor groups than their non-specialist colleagues on the news desk. As a result resource-poor groups who target specialist journalists can often build up a valuable relationship with them and will tend to gain more access to the inside specialist pages than to other sections of the paper. The relationship also has advantages for the specialist journalist in that pressure groups can be used as a research resource. On the other hand, specialists do tend to gravitate towards official sources in their area and may be less likely to view pressure group stunts as newsworthy than their news desk.

Deacon and Golding (1994) suggest that journalists tend to see news sources as either *advocates* of a point of view or constituency who can be used to give a 'balancing' comment, or as *arbiters*, as 'expert witnesses' who can judge the significance or import of events. Both rich and poor groups can move between these designations though achieving arbiter status is harder than advocate status. Groups at the poorer end of the resource spectrum may only be designated arbiters by specialists. When an issue leaves the specialist pages to move higher up the news agenda to the front pages, most likely when official pronouncements or action are involved, an organization may have to contend with reverting to advocate status. Such differences are also inflected by varying news values across the media. For example, 'cuddly charities', the ones which deal with animals, children or health, are more heavily featured in tabloid and television coverage (Deacon 1996). But the media are increasingly subordinate to commercial imperatives. In the press investigative journalism has declined, to be replaced by lifestyle and consumer writing. On television 'reality TV' has squeezed out programmes which periodically make powerful interests uncomfortable or provide the public with useful information (Barnett and Seymour 1999; Cohen 2000; Stone 1999). In TV news the obsession with 'liveness' is substituted for explaining the world (Snow 2000).

## The impact and success of promotional strategies

The success and impact of promotional strategies are hard to measure, first, because they have myriad aims which are not always clearly conceptualized. Second, they work at different levels. That is, some groups target local opinion, while others simply want to raise funds. Clearly, to misquote Mao, a revolution is not a jumble sale.

The self-denying status of propaganda, the behind-the-scenes nature of lobbying and the endemic secrecy surrounding the policy process in Britain are further reasons why evaluations of success or impact are difficult. Finally, we should beware of judging success in terms simply of the amount or quality of media coverage, since media coverage does not necessarily or straightforwardly translate into influence (cf. Cracknell 1993).

Governments, business and interest groups try to manage the media because of a widespread recognition that media reporting can impose limits on organizational action and provide opportunities for influencing public opinion, and the distribution of power and resources in society (Walsh-Childers 1994: 827; Linsky 1986). However, one of the key limitations of much media and cultural studies is the reluctance to examine the outcomes of successful (or unsuccessful) media management (Philo and Miller 2000: 70–71). The influence of media reporting on public opinion and, most importantly, government and corporate decision making require to be directly investigated.

Media strategies can also help to sell government policies such as the privatization of the public utilities in the 1980s (Miller and Dinan 2000; Philo 1995). Conversely, even flagship policies of strong governments such as the Poll Tax can fail despite concerted marketing campaigns (Deacon and Golding 1994). In the longer term the strategies of social movements and associated struggles can lead to marked changes in the status and power of social constituencies such as women, Black people and lesbians and gay men. The emergence of issues like racism, violence against women, child sexual abuse, homophobia and even the environment were preceded by long and, on many occasions, apparently unsuccessful campaigns to raise awareness and change society (cf. Tiffen 1989: 197–8).

## Changing trends?

In contemporary Britain as in many other advanced societies we are witnessing an ever-increasing spiral of expertise and sophistication in promotional strategies. One indication is the use by pressure groups such as Greenpeace of Video News Releases which are supplied to news rooms complete with commentary and newsworthy footage. In an increasingly competitive and deregulated international media market strongly influenced by commercial pressure, the ability of business and government sources to supply 'information subsidies' is likely to become more not less important.

In addition, public relations and journalism industries are increasingly converging. One symptom of this is the practice of journalists giving training in public relations technique to politicians or business people, such as the media training venture set up by HTV in 1995. In March 1996 BBC journalists were warned about the potential conflict of interest in giving media training to people they are subsequently required to interview, although media training activities were not outlawed (Methven 1996).

Furthermore, Independent Television News (ITN) owns a half share of Corporate Television Network (CTN). CTN makes video news releases for corporate clients, some of which had been shown on ITN bulletins (Brooks 1995). This highlights the potential for increased conflict of interest as media companies grow larger and diversify into other parts of the industry. The fact that PR multinational Burson Marstellar owns the other half of the agency also indicates that there is a potential for conflict of interest, a potential which some have alleged has had an impact. CTN made a corporate video for Shell on its role in Ogoniland in Nigeria which according to one observer was 'total porkies . . . Its claims on environmental damage are incredible' (Monbiot 1998). Separately, an ITN journalist had interviewed Ogoni leader Ken Saro Wiwa. This was Saro Wiwa's last interview before his arrest by Nigerian authorities, but ITN refused to broadcast it because 'Shell might sue us'. The journalist involved later raised the question of whether the relationship between Shell and CTN was 'the reason for ITN's refusal to run the Ogoni story?' (Whitehead 1998). In another example two journalists in Florida were 'bullied, censored, and then fired' for their investigation of the adverse effects of a cattle growth hormone produced by Monsanto. Coincidentally, or not, their employer Fox TV is owned by Rupert Murdoch who also owns Actmedia, a promotions company which counts Monsanto among its clients (Cohen 1999b: 138). Such, trends will tend to place limits on journalistic integrity as increasingly multinational media conglomerates move into both promoting and reporting news.

## And finally . . .

This brings us back to debates about the effects of 'promotional culture' on the democratic process. On the one hand, it can be argued that there has been an increasing sophistication in news management on the part of the powerful, especially in government and business. On the other, that some countervailing pressure has been exerted and that particular social constituencies have to some extent advanced their position in our culture. This seems to speak of an increasing sophistication of promotional strategies on the part of the powerless too. Yet, before we embrace the comforting pluralist notion of relatively open competition for power and resources we should examine the extent of inequality, the relative prominence of official sources in the media and the results of promotional strategies on the distribution of rewards and resources in society. While winners and losers vary and the type and extent of inequality in contemporary society does change, it is clear that Western countries remain radically inegalitarian societies. Indeed in some cases, (such as Britain) whatever the victories of the resource-poor in the media, inequalities of wealth and power have actually become dramatically wider since the beginning of the 1980s (Philo and Miller 2000). In other words wealth can be systematically moved from poor to rich even as the media are awash with stories about 'fat cats' in big business.

Contemporary corporate and governmental public relations activities are terminally lacking in good faith, they debase the political language and stride forward hand in hand with an increasingly commercialized media – ever ready to take handouts from PR operatives. The campaign against corporate promotion is gathering pace. From Seattle and Prague to critiques of New Labour 'spin', there is resistance to the misinformation and distortion which are central to the PR business. There are possibilities for pressure groups and the powerless to intervene in this process. It is also possible to plan and execute promotional strategies on behalf of the powerless which do not compromise either radical politics or a respect for truth. The key question for the future is whether the systematic distortions of promotional culture can be curbed in the interests of democratic deliberation and decision making.

## Questions

1  Are multinational corporations able to manipulate the media to safeguard their interests?

2  Are pressure groups condemned to rely on publicity stunts to promote their aims?

3  Does spin work? Is it successful in (a) managing the media; (b) influencing public opinion; (c) legitimizing government policies?

4  Using an example selected from contemporary news coverage, analyse the promotional strategy of one or more of the following: a government department, a corporate organization, a pressure group and attempt to assess the relative success or failure of the strategy.

## References

Andersen, S. and Eliassen, K. (1995) 'EU Lobbying: the new research agenda', *European Journal of Political Research* 27: 427–41.

Anderson, A. (1991) 'Source strategies and the communication of environmental affairs', *Media, Culture and Society* 13(4): 459–76.

Anderson, A. (1993) 'Source–media relations: the production of the environmental agenda', in A. Hansen (ed.) *The Mass Media and Environmental Issues*, Leicester: Leicester University Press.

Anderson, A. (1997) *Media, Culture and Environment*, London: UCL Press.

Barnett, S. and Seymour, E. (1999) *'A Shrinking Iceberg Travelling South . . .' Changing Trends in British Television: A case study of drama and current affairs*, London: Campaign for Quality Television .

Beder, S. (1997) *Global Spin: The Corporate Assault on Environmentalism*, Totnes, Devon: Green Books.

Blumler, J. and Gurevitch, M. (1995) *The Crisis of Public Communication*, London: Routledge.

Bolton, R. (1996) 'Death on the Rock' in B. Rolston and D. Miller (eds) *War and Words: The Northern Ireland Media Reader*, Belfast: Beyond the Pale.

Brooks, R. (1995) 'ITN "has fingers in both pies" on video news', *Observer* 10 September: 4.

Carruthers, S. (1995) *Winning Hearts and Minds: British Governments, the Media and Colonial Counter-Insurgency 1944–1960*, Leicester University Press.

Cockerell, M., Hennessy, P. and Walker, D. (1984) *Sources Close to the Prime Minister*, London: Macmillan.

Cockerell, M. (1988) *Live from Number 10*, London: Faber.

Cohen, N. (1999a) 'The death of news' in Cohen, N. *Cruel Britannia: Reports on the Sinister and the Preposterous*, London: Verso, pp. 123–34.

Cohen, N. (1999b) 'Modified news' in Cohen, N. *Cruel Britannia: Reports on the Sinister and the Preposterous*, London: Verso, pp. 137–40.

Cohen, N. (2000) *Cruel Britannia: Reports on the Sinister and the Preposterous*, London: Verso.

Cook, T. (1989) *Making Laws and Making News*, Washington, DC: Brookings Institution.

Cracknell, J. (1993) 'Issue arenas, pressure groups and environmental agenda', in A. Hansen (ed.) *The Mass Media and Environmental Issues*, Leicester: Leicester University Press.

Crofts, W. (1989) *Coercion or Persuasion: Propaganda in Britain after 1945*, London: Routledge.

Curran, J. (1991) 'Rethinking the media as a public sphere', in P. Dahlgren and C. Sparks (eds) *Communication and Citizenship*, London: Routledge.

Curran, J. and Seaton, J. (1995) *Power without Responsibility*, 4th edn, London: Routledge.

Curran, J., Gurevitch, M. and Woollacott, J. (1982) 'The study of the media: theoretical approaches', in Gurevitch, M., Bennett, T., Curran, J. and Woollacott, J. (eds) *Culture, Society and the Media*, London: Methuen.

Davies, A. (2000a) 'Public-relations campaigning and news production, the case of the "new unionism" in Britain', in Curran, J. (ed.) *Media Organisations and Society*, London: Arnold.

Davies, A. (2000b) 'Public relations, news production and changing patterns of source access in the British national media', *Media, Culture and Society*, 22: 39–59.

Deacon, D. (1996) 'The voluntary sector in a changing communication environment: a case study of non-official news sources', *European Journal of Communication* 11(2): 173–99.

Deacon, D. and Golding, P. (1994) *Taxation and Representation*, London: John Libbey.

Downing, J. (1986) 'Government secrecy and the media in the United States and Britain', in Peter Golding *et al.* (eds) *Communicating Politics: Mass Communications and the Political Process*, Leicester: Leicester University Press

Engel, M. (1996) 'Protest locale that can't square the circle', *The Guardian*, 25 March: 2.

Ericson, R. *et al.* (1989) *Negotiating Control: a study of news sources*, Buckingham: Open University Press.

Fones-Wolf, E. (1994) *Selling Free Enterprise, The Business Assault on Labor and Liberalism, 1945–60*, Urbana IL: University of Illinois Press.

Franklin, B. (1994) *Packaging Politics*, London: Edward Arnold.

Franklin, B. (1999) *Tough on Soundbites, Tough on the Causes of Soundbites*, London: Catalyst Trust. http://www.catalyst-trust.co.uk/pub3.html

Gandy, O. (1992) 'Public relations and public policy: the structuration of dominance in the information age' in E. Toth and R. Heath (eds) *Rhetorical and Critical Approaches to Public Relations*, Hillsdale, NJ: Lawrence Erlbaum.

Gans, H. (1980) *Deciding What's News*, London: Constable.

Gitlin, T. (1980) *The Whole World is Watching*, University of California Press.

Goldenberg, E. (1975) *Making the Papers: The Access of Resource-Poor Groups to the Metropolitan Press*, Lexington, MA: D. C. Heath.

Gould, P. (1998) *The Unfinished Revolution, How the Modernisers Saved the Labour Party*, London: Abacus.

Grant, L. (1995) 'Just say no', *Guardian Weekend*, 3 June: 12–22.

Grant, W. (1995) *Pressure Groups, Politics and Democracy in Britain*, 2nd edn, Hemel Hempstead: Harvester Wheatsheaf.

Greenwood, J. (1997) *Representing Interests in the European Union*, Basingstoke: Macmillan.

Greer, I. (1997) *One Man's World, The untold story of the cash-for-questions affair*, London: Andre Deutsch.

Gregory, M. (1996) *Dirty Tricks: British Airways' secret war against Virgin Atlantic*, revised edn, London: Warner Books.

Hager, N. and Burton, B. (1999) *Secrets and Lies, The Anatomy of an Anti-environmental PR Campaign*, Nelson, NZ: Craig Potton Publishing.

Hall, S., Critcher, C., Jefferson, T., Clarke, J. and Roberts, B. (1978) *Policing the Crisis: Mugging, the State and Law and Order*, London: Macmillan.

Harris, R. (1990) *Good and Faithful Servant*, London: Faber.

Heffernan, R. and Marqusee, M. (1992) *Defeat from the Jaws of Victory, Inside Kinnock's Labour Party*, London: Verso.

Hollingsworth, M. (1991) *MPs for Hire, The secret world of political lobbying*, London: Bloomsbury.

Ingham, B. (1991) *Kill the Messenger*, London: HarperCollins.

Jackall, R. (ed.) (1994) *Propaganda*, London: Macmillan.

Jones, N. (1986) *Strikes and the Media*, Oxford: Blackwell.

Jones, N. (1995) *Soundbites and Spin Doctors*, London: Cassell.

Jones, N. (1997) *Campaign 1997, How the General Election Was Won and Lost*, London: Indigo.

Jones, N. (1999) *Sultans of Spin, the media and the new Labour government*, London: Victor Gollancz.

Kellner, D. (1992) *The Persian Gulf TV War*, Boulder, CO: Westview Press.

Kisch, R. (1964) *The Private Life of Public Relations*, London: MacGibbon and Kee.

Klein, N. (2000) *No Logo*, London: Flamingo.

Leigh, D. (1980) *The Frontiers of Secrecy*, London: Junction Books.

Leigh, D. and Vulliamy, E. (1997) *Sleaze: the corruption of parliament*, London: Fourth Estate.

L'Etang, J. (1998) 'State propaganda and bureaucratic intelligence, the creation of public relations in 20th century Britain', *Public Relations Review* 24(4): 413–41.

Levitas, R. and Guy, W. (eds) (1996) *Interpreting Official Statistics*, London: Routledge.

Linsky, M. (1986) *Impact: How the Press Affects Federal Policymaking*, New York, W. W. Norton.

MacArthur, J. (1993) *Second Front: Censorship and Propaganda in the Gulf War*, Berkeley: University of California Press.

Macintyre, D. (2000) *Mandelson and the Making of New Labour*, London: HarperCollins.

McNair, B. (1995) *Political Communication: an introduction*, London: Routledge.

Manning, P. (1998) *Spinning for Labour, Trade unions and the new media environment*, Aldershot: Ashgate.

Mazey, S. and Richardson, J. (1993) 'Pressure groups and the EC', *Politics Review*, 3(1): 20–24.

Methven, N. (1996) 'BBC restates ban on outside work by freelances', *UK Press Gazette*, 22 March.

Middlemass, K. (1979) *Politics in Industrial Society, The experience of the British system since 1911*, London: Andre Deutsch.

Miller, D. (1991) 'The media on the Rock: the media and the Gibraltar killings', in B. Rolston (ed.) *The Media and Northern Ireland: Covering the Troubles*, Basingstoke: Macmillan.

Miller, D. (1993) 'Official sources and primary definition: the case of Northern Ireland', *Media, Culture and Society*, 15(3): July, 385–406.

Miller, D. (1994) *Don't Mention the War: Northern Ireland, Propaganda and the Media*, London: Pluto.

Miller, D. (1999) 'Risk, science and policy, BSE, definitional struggles, information management and the media', *Social Science and Medicine*, special edition on 'Science speaks to policy' 49: 1239–55.

Miller, D. and Dinan, W. (2000) 'The rise of the PR industry in Britain 1979–98', *European Journal of Communication* 15(1): 5–35.

Miller, D. and Reilly, J. (1995) 'Making an issue of food safety: the media, pressure groups and the public sphere' in D. Maurer and J. Sobal (eds) *Eating Agendas: Food, Eating and Nutrition as Social Problems*, New York: Aldine De Gruyter, pp. 305–36.

Miller, D. and Schlesinger, P. (2000) 'The changing shape of public relations in the European Union', in R. L. Heath and G. M. Vasquez (eds) *The Handbook of Public Relations*, London/Thousand Oaks CA/New Delhi: Sage Publications, pp. 675–83.

Miller, D. and Williams, K. (1993) 'Negotiating HIV/AIDS information: agendas, media strategies and the news', in Eldridge, J. (ed.) *Getting the Message*, London: Routledge.

Miller, D., Kitzinger, J., Williams, K. and Beharrell, P. (1998) *The Circuit of Mass Communication, Media Strategies, Representation and Audience Reception in the AIDS Crisis*. London: Sage.

Moloney, K. (1996) *Lobbyists for Hire*, Aldershot: Dartmouth.

Monbiot, G. (1998) 'Dressed for the job', *Journalist* July/August: 20–21.

Norton-Taylor, R. (1995) *Truth is a Difficult Concept: Inside the Scott Inquiry*, London: Guardian Books.

Oborne, P. (1999) *Alastair Campbell, New Labour and the Rise of the Media Class*, London: Aurum.

Parker, I. (1995) 'Spitting on charity', *Independent on Sunday Review* 9 April: 4–6.

Philo, G. (1995) 'Television, politics and the rise of the new right', in G. Philo (ed.) *The Glasgow Media Group Reader Vol. II*, London: Routledge.

Philo, G. and McLaughlin, G. (1995) 'The British media and the Gulf War' in Philo, G. (ed.) *The Glasgow Media Group Reader Vol. II*, London: Routledge.

Philo, G. and Miller, D. (2000) *Market Killing, What the free market does and what social scientists can do about it*, London: Longman.

Porter, H. (1995) 'Crowd control', *Guardian* 12 October: 2–3.

Rampton, S. and Stauber, J. (2001) *Trust Us, We're Experts: How Industry Manipulates Science and Gambles with Your Future*, New York: Jeremy P. Tarcher.

Routledge, P. (1999) *Mandy, The Unauthorised Biography of Peter Mandelson*, London: Pocket Books.

Rowell, A. (1996) *Green Backlash: Global Subversion of the Environment Movement*, London: Routledge.

Scammell, M. (1995) *Designer Politics: How Elections are Won*, Basingstoke: Macmillan.

Schlesinger, P. (1990) 'Rethinking the sociology of journalism: source strategies and the limits of media-centrism', in M. Ferguson (ed.) *Public Communication: The New Imperatives*, London: Sage.

Schlesinger, P. and Tumber, H. (1994) *Reporting Crime*, Oxford: Clarendon Press.

Schlesinger, P., Miller, D. and Dinan, W. (2001) *Open Scotland? Journalists, Spin Doctors and Lobbyists*, Edinburgh: Polygon.

Sigal, L. (1986) 'Who? Sources make the news', in R. K. Manoff and M. Schudson (eds) *Reading the News*, New York: Pantheon.

Silverstein, K. (1998) *Washington on $10 Million a Day, How lobbyists Plunder the Nation*, Monroe, ME: Common Courage Press.

Snow, J. (2000) 'Journalism, the techno revolution, and the art of disinformation', *The Hetherington Lecture*, 1 November, Stirling Media Research Institute, Stirling University. http://www-fms.stir.ac.uk/Hetherington/2000/index.html

Stauber, J. and Rampton, S. (1995) *Toxic Sludge is Good for You: Lies, Damn Lies and the Public Relations Industry*, Monroe, ME: Common Courage.

Stone, J. (1999) *Losing Perspective: Global Affairs on British Terrestrial Television 1989–1999*, London: Third World and Environment Broadcasting Project. http://www.ibt.org.uk/4tv%20Research/Losing%20Perpective/losing.html

Tiffen, R. (1989) *News and Power*, Sydney: Allen and Unwin.

Tilson, D. (1993) 'The shaping of "eco-nuclear" publicity: the use of visitors centres in public relations', *Media, Culture and Society* 15(3): 419–36.

Tulloch, J. (1993) 'Policing the public sphere: the British machinery of news management', *Media, Culture and Society* 15(3): 363–84.

Tumber, H. (1993) '"Selling scandal": Business and the media', *Media, Culture and Society* 15(3): 345–62.

Vidal, J. (1997) *McLibel: Burger Culture on Trial*, Basingstoke: Macmillan.

Vidal, J. and Bellos, A. (1996) 'Protest lobbies unite to guard rights', *Guardian*, 27 August: 5.

Walsh-Childers, K. (1994) '"A death in the family" – A case study of newspaper influence on health policy development', *Journalism Quarterly* 71(4): 820–29.

Wernick, A. (1991) *Promotional Culture*, London: Sage.

Whitehead, B. (1998) 'Why did ITN kill my story?' *Journalist*, October/November: 14–15.

## Further reading

### *On the PR industry and corporate PR*

Hager, N. and Burton, B. (1999) *Secrets and Lies, The Anatomy of an Anti-environmental PR Campaign*, Nelson, NZ: Craig Potton Publishing. Based on hundreds of pages of leaked documents on the activities of PR giant Burson Marstellar in environmental destruction in New Zealand.

Miller, D. and Dinan, W. (2000) 'The rise of the PR Industry in Britain 1979–98', *European Journal of Communication*, 15(1): 5–35. Gives an account of the rise of the PR industry in Britain and its links with Conservative policies and business interests.

Rampton, S. and Stauber, J. (2001) *Trust Us, We're Experts! How industry manipulates science and gambles with your future*, Madison, WI: Tarcher/Putnam.

Stauber, J. and Rampton, S. (1995) *Toxic Sludge is Good for You: Lies, Damn Lies and the Public Relations Industry*, Monroe, ME: Common Courage.

Both these books, by the editors of *PR Watch*, are critical accounts of the PR industry and its manipulation of the news and policy making.

## On PR history

Carey, A. (1995) *Taking the Risk out of Democracy*, edited by Andrew Lohrey, Sydney: University of New South Wales Press: (1997) Urbana, IL: University of Illinois Press. A critical examination of the beginnings of PR in the USA, UK and Australia.

Ewen, S. (1996) *PR! A social history of spin*, New York: Basic Books. The historical relationship between big business and PR in the USA.

Fones-Wolf, E. (1994) *Selling Free Enterprise, The Business Assault on Labor and Liberalism, 1945–60*, Urbana, IL: University of Illinois Press. How big business attacked democratic and redistributionist government policy in the 1950s USA.

L'Etang, J. (1998) 'State propaganda and bureaucratic intelligence, the creation of public relations in 20th century Britain', *Public Relations Review* 24(4): 413–41. Tells the mostly unknown history of the British PR industry.

## On lobbying

Hollingsworth, M. (1991) *MPs for Hire, The secret world of political lobbying*, London: Bloomsbury. Reveals the attempts of the lobbying industry to influence MPs in the Westminster parliament.

Leigh, D. and Vulliamy, E. (1997) *Sleaze: the corruption of parliament*, London: Fourth Estate. How the *Guardian* broke the cash-for-questions lobbying scandal.

Miller, D. and Schlesinger, P. (2000) 'The changing shape of public relations in the European Union', in R. L. Heath and G. M. Vasquez (eds) *The Handbook of Public Relations*, London/Thousand Oaks CA/New Delhi: Sage Publications, pp. 675–83. An account of the growing importance of lobbying in Brussels for decision making in member states.

## On government information and spin

Franklin, B. (1999) *Tough on Soundbites, Tough on the Causes of Soundbites*, London: Catalyst Trust. http://www.catalyst-trust.co.uk/pub3.html. A critical account of New Labour's news management.

Gould, P. (1998) *The Unfinished Revolution, How the Modernisers Saved the Labour Party*, London: Abacus. The 'official' account by a key New Labour adviser of the benefits of spin and focus groups.

Jones, N. (1999) *Sultans of Spin, the Media and the New Labour Government*, London: Victor Gollancz. A first-hand account of New Labour news management.

Macintyre, D. (2000) *Mandelson and the Making of New Labour*, London: HarperCollins.

Oborne, P. (1999) *Alastair Campbell, New Labour and the Rise of the Media Class* London: Aurum.

Routledge, P. (1999) *Mandy, The Unauthorised Biography of Peter Mandelson*, London: Pocket Books.

The above three books are journalistic accounts of two of the key architects of New Labour's spin and news management techniques.

Schlesinger, P., Miller, D. and Dinan, W. (2001) *Open Scotland? Journalists, Spin Doctors and Lobbyists*, Edinburgh: Polygon. An inside account of the impact of devolution in Scotland on journalism, government news management and lobbyists.

Tulloch, J. (1993) 'Policing the public sphere: the British machinery of news management', *Media, Culture and Society* 15(3): 363–84. A good review of the development of government public relations in Britain.

### On pressure groups and the new anti-corporate activism

Cracknell, J. (1993) 'Issue arenas, pressure groups and environmental agenda', in A. Hansen (ed.) *The Mass Media and Environmental Issues*, Leicester: Leicester University Press. Thoughtful account of the importance of promotion in environmental campaigning.

Klein, N. (2000) *No Logo*, London: Flamingo. The key polemic against the practice and effects of corporate branding and promotion.

### On the release of the free market and the shortcomings of media and cultural studies especially in relation to 'outcomes'

Philo, G. and Miller, D. (2000) *Market Killing, What the free market does and what social scientists can do about it*, London: Longman.

## Web sites

Adbusters adbusters.org The site for the subversion of corporate advertising.

Center for Media and Democracy www.prwatch.org Publishers of *PR Watch* which provides public interest reporting on the PR industry.

Institute of Public Relations www.ipr.press.net/ The organization for PR people in the UK.

Media Channel, Media activist site www.mediachannel.org A clearing house of alternative media information.

O'Dwyer's Public Relations reporting site www.odwyerpr.com US reporting on the PR industry.

Public Relations Consultants Association www.martex.co.uk/prca The umbrella group representing British PR consultancies.

*PR Week*, trade weekly www.prweek.com/

# Chapter 7

# Newspapers

THE SOCIOLOGY OF THE PRESS

**JAMES CURRAN**

The sociology of the press offers two contrasting views. One is of the press as a 'bottom-up' agency shaped by consumer demand, the professional concerns of journalists, pluralistic competition between news sources, and the shared values of society. The other is of the press as a 'top-down' agency of control, shaped by big business ownership, advertising power, powerful institutional news sources, state pressure and elite cultural dominance. A case study of the British press suggests that these opposing views can be usefully synthesized. The British press, it is argued, is linked to the power structure of contemporary Britain without being wholly intregrated into it.

According to liberal orthodoxy, the capitalist press is an autonomous institution which empowers the people. This upbeat view is at the very heart of conventional liberal press history (e.g. Emery 1972; Alexander 1981). Thus, in Britain, the press supposedly evolved from being an agency of the state to becoming the adjunct of political parties, before its final liberation through commercialization (Koss 1981/1984). This resulted, it is argued, in the press being controlled by market-led pragmatists who follow public demand. The dominating influence over the press in this final 'free' phase is said to be the sovereign consumer (Koss 1984).

This celebratory historical tradition is implicitly qualified by liberal ethnographic studies of news organizations. These tend to play down the influence of consumers, and stress instead the central role of media professionals who are sometimes uninformed about their audiences but have strong views about what they need. The best known of these ethnographies, a study of American news media by Herbert Gans (1980), advances the key argument that the division of labour within media organizations leads to a dispersal of control. For example, the separation of advertising and editorial departments results in story selection and advertisement placements taking place separately, and only coming together at the last moment, in a way that limits the power of advertisers. Similarly, the power of owners, Gans claims, is limited by the delegation and subdivision of authority within news organizations. While big business corporations are 'nominal managers', 'news organizations and journalists are the actual ones' (Gans 1980: 229).

Gans's second key argument is that 'delegation of power also takes place because the news organization consists of professionals who insist on individual autonomy' (Gans 1980: 101). In his account, pressures on journalists to follow a line or suppress information are rare, and are strongly resisted. They conflict with the professional values of journalists who derive their self-respect from their professionalism, and who receive strong support from their peers in doing so. This professional orientation includes a strong commitment to detachment and objectivity, and a belief in the importance of ensuring that the public is adquately informed.

Gans's conclusions find support in Tunstall's pioneering study of British specialist correspondents (Tunstall 1970) and Hetherington's later study of British news organizations (Hetherington 1985). However, all three studies contain 'small print' statements qualifying their general conclusions. Reporters, it is acknowledged, often have less personal decision-making power than they think because they are part of a production process. They do not control whether their copy is published, nor how it is subbed. They also tend to feel free because they are inclined to internalize the norms of their employing organization, or regard its routine requirements as legitimate. Research since Gans's landmark work also suggests that American news media have become more subject to consumer/market influence, and less the bastions of professional independence (Hallin 2000; McManus 1994). Tunstall's latest study (1996) also indicates that editors in the British national press have become more assertive, while increasing casualization in the industry has weakened professional autonomy.

If liberal history celebrates the consumer, and liberal ethnography salutes more guardedly the media professional, there is a third liberal tradition that focuses on the news source. According to this third tradition, it is the suppliers of news, not its purveyors or consumers, who are the real figures of power. Allegedly, only an excessive 'media-centrism', an undue preoccupation with internal organizational processes, has masked the extent to which control lies outside news media (Schlesinger 1990). Liberal versions of this argument, such as that advanced by Hansen (1991), emphasize open competition between news sources, reflecting the variety of different groups vying for media attention and influence (see Miller, Chapter 6 in this volume).

A fourth strand of liberal interpretation sees the media as reflecting the cultural values of a socially harmonious society. The news judgements employed by journalists, and the premises and assumptions on which their reports are grounded, are said to be framed by the common culture of society. Good examples of this general approach are provided by two studies of the Swedish press which demonstrate that newspaper editorials and advertising came to express more egalitarian values (Nowak 1984; Block 1981). This is attributed to a shift in the core values of Swedish society, also registered in a movement towards a more egalitarian distribution of incomes.

Clearly, these different arguments can be woven together into a coherent liberal synthesis (of which the most skilled is a version advanced by Schudson 2000). News media can be seen as being shaped by consumer demand, the professional concerns of media workers, pluralistic source networks, and the collective values of society. While there is no consensus within the liberal tradition about the relative weight that should be accorded to these different influences, there is broad agreement about one thing: 'free' media serve the public.

There is also beginning to develop a distinctive postmodernist version of this approach. Essentially, it rehearses traditional liberal themes but in a context of society characterized by rapid change, fluid identities, and increasing pluralism. An eloquent example of postmodernism is the work of Angela McRobbie (1994, 1996) on womens' magazines. In contrast to traditional radical feminists who have been inclined to view the womens' press as vehicles of patriarchal culture, McRobbie argues that the womens' magazine press is changing, and that some successful magazines now offer relatively liberated definitions of what it is to be a contemporary woman. This is, she suggests, a direct consequence of the way in which these magazines operate. They conduct market research into what their readers want; they respond to circulation shifts in a competitive market overflowing with titles; they recruit young journalists, some exposed to feminism through media studies courses, many of whom have developed a strong rapport with their readers; and as organizations they are subject to 'complex and contested social processes'. It is because these publications are exposed to a multiplicity of influences that they are responsive to the flux and change around them, and in particular to changing gender values.

## Radical challenge

Such accounts are shrugged off by radical critics as naive. According to this alternative viewpoint, both liberal and postmodernist approaches overstate the power of human agency because they fail to grasp the way in which personal choices are structured by standard formats, organizational norms and the play of power. What is meant by this rather intimidating line of argument?

One standard radical theme is that media enterprises have grown from relatively small, independent organizations, their characteristic form in the nineteenth century, into units within large business corporations that are strongly oriented towards maximizing profits rather than promoting good journalism. These corporations have also extensive holdings in industry and finance (Tunstall and Machin 1999; Herman and McChesney 1997), and consequently a vested interest in the tax, interest rate, labour relations, industrial and contractor policies of the government. This influences both their orientation towards government and the politics of the media under their control (Herman and Chomsky 1988; Waisbord 2000). Furthermore, a corporate culture and web of interlocking directorships have evolved in a form that has encouraged the development of a shared outlook between commercial media and other business leaders (Murdock 1982a,b). Rather than functioning as an independent fourth estate, media businesses are thus increasingly commercial mercenaries. As Douglas Kellner (1990: 172–3) writes, 'it is because of the control of media institutions by multinational capital (big business) that the media have been biased towards conservatism, thus furthering what they see as their own economic interests. . . .'

Media owners, and those they delegate power to, shape the ethos of media organizations. They determine overall policy, set budgets, make senior appointments and establish a reward structure that encourages staff conformity. Dissident staff tend not to be given good assignments, and are liable to be shunted sideways or simply sacked. However, controls usually operate unobtrusively through initial staff selection, and through self-censorship, rather than through overt coercion (Parenti 1993; Chomsky 1989; Herman 1999).

The power of owners is supplemented by that of advertisers and the capitalist state. Advertisers provide the main source of revenue of most newspapers and free-to-air TV channels. They sometimes use this economic power, it is argued, to promote their ideological commitments, as well as to silence radical critics (Baker 1994; Bagdikian 1992). The state also features in some radical accounts, particularly of broadcasting organizations, as a source of direct and indirect censorship exercised through control over appointments, funding and broadcast regulation (Miliband 1973).

The general thrust of this analysis is to see the media as being subject to multiple controls exercised by a dominant class or group in a deliberate and intentional way. However, there is another strand of radical argument that owes more to neo-Keynsianism than to Marxism. This argues that the media are subject to constraints rather than controls, and that these arise out of impersonal processes that are largely unsought (Golding and Murdock 2000; Gustafsson 1993; Curran 1986). Yet, their effect is to skew profoundly the way in which the media relate to the wider public.

First, high market entry costs exclude resource-poor groups from starting and owning their own mass media. This limits competition, and encourages the marginalization of their interests and viewpoints. Second, there is a recurring tendency for media concentration to develop, leading to reduced choice and less consumer control. Third, advertising is distributed disproportionately in favour of media reaching affluent audiences, which encourages media producers to privilege their concerns. Finally, the economic benefits of size create a magnetic pull, it is argued, towards the terrain of maximum sales and, consequently, the ideological middle ground.

This approach is paralleled by radical social organizational studies. These argue that the media are bureaucracies guided by procedures directed towards serving their welfare rather than that of the public (Curran 2000; Kaniss 1997; Sigal 1987; Tuchman 1978). For example, news media organize news-gathering around a network of powerful institutions and groups because these seem to be at the centre of things, and employ public relations executives who make the work of journalists easier. News stories are written within formats which are designed to make it easy for journalists with limited time to write fast, in relation to topics that they need know nothing about, in ways that give limited offence. The result is twofold: news organizations typically rely on a narrow range of elite sources, and they use self-effacing formulae (such as quoting opposed statements, the truth of which is not evaluated) that result in delegating considerable editorial control to these sources. The implications of this argument can be wrenched, as we have seen, into a pluralist groove by stressing source competition. However, the way this argument is usually presented in traditional radical research is to maintain that the media reflect the elite consensus (Hall 1986; Fishman 1982).

A further way in which informal control is exercised over the media is through the dominant discourses of society patterned over time by the superior symbolic and material resources available to powerful groups. An eloquent illustration of this argument is provided by Graham Murdock (1984) in a study of news reporting of urban disturbances in the early 1980s. He shows how reporting drew upon a conservative 'common sense' view of the sources of civic disorder, partly prompted by news informants but also cued by a readily available repertoire of imagery and explanation. This derived from recent reporting of muggers, football hooligans and Irish terrorism but also drew upon time-worn themes from the past developed around alien agitators, black hordes and 'King Mob'. News media absorbed and reproduced right-wing interpetations that were carried, like pollen, in the air that journalists breathed.

These different radical descriptions of the media have been synthesized in a number of accounts. The most influential of these is that offered by Herman and Chomsky (1988) who see the media as being controlled through a combination of private ownership, advertising power, elite sources, state pressure and cultural dominance. These are likened to 'filters' that siphon out radical meanings, leaving only a residue of largely conservative interpetation. Some debate takes place within the media but, generally, only within defined limits consonant with the interests of established privilege.

## Context and confrontation

We are thus presented with diametrically opposed accounts of the media. In the traditional liberal approach, the media are bottom-up channels of popular power; in the traditional radical one, they are strictly top-down agencies of control.

One explanation for this disagreement is that different conclusions arise from different circumstances. There are significant national differences in the way in which the media are organized, and in the societal influences to which they are exposed. The significance of national difference has tended to be obscured by the tendency of the English-language literature to advance universalistic conclusions on the basis of a small sample of unrepresentative but homogeneous countries (Curran and Park 2000).

This said, divergencies of interpretation also arise from different perspectives. Opposed traditions portray the media system in the *same country* in different ways (contrast, say, Seymour-Ure's 1996 account of the British media with that of Eldridge, Kitzinger and Williams 1997). There are also incompatible accounts of the media in the same type of society. For example, Chomsky's (1989) portayal of the media as propaganda agencies sustaining 'thought control' in liberal democracies is fundamentally at odds with Parsonian sociologist, Jefferey Alexander's idealization of the media as institutions that enable liberal democracy to commune with itself and express shared beliefs (Alexander 1981).

One response to this irreconcilable core of conflicting interpretation at the heart of media sociology is to take sides, and sign up with one camp or the other. Another is to draw selectively upon opposed traditions in constructing a new synthesis that is properly contextualized. The case study that follows suggests that this latter approach has much to recommend it. The British press, as we shall see, is subject to both top-down and bottom-up 'countervailing' influences. Elements of both liberal and radical interpretation can be combined in a way that seems to illuminate the influences that shape British newspapers.

## British newspapers: economic regulation

In contrast to most other countries, Britain has a dominant national newspaper press which accounts for about two thirds of total daily circulation. In 2000, the national press comprises ten daily and nine Sunday titles operating in a highly competitive market. This is in marked contrast to the local press which consists largely of local monopoly daily papers, and local weekly (paid and freesheet) papers which are generally part of a regionally dominant newspaper chain.

The national press is more right-wing than the public. Only in one general election in the twentieth century – in 1997 – has national newspaper support for the Labour Party exceeded Labour's electoral support in the country, and this was due to an opportunist, tacit alliance formed in early 1997 between the media mogul, Rupert Murdoch, and the New Labour leader, Tony Blair. In every other general election during the twentieth century, editorial opinion was to the right of electoral opinion. Thus, in the previous three general elections (1983, 1987, 1992), the Conservative vote never rose above 42%. Yet the Conservative press accounted for between 64% and 78% of national newspaper circulation (Seymour-Ure 1996: 218–19). In other words, press support exceeded by at least half the Conservative Party's share of the vote.

One reason why the press is so right-wing is the 'closed shop' nature of publishing. It costs over £20 million to establish a new national daily newspaper. This high cost excludes most social groups from being represented in the press through ownership of a newspaper.

A further, subsidiary reason is the sclerotic nature of the newspaper market. Over half the national paper titles in Britain were launched over 80 years ago. All the remainder were started, or acquired, by an established publishing group. No new independent publisher has launched a national paper still in existence, and retained control, since the First World War. All successful new entrants are tycoons or corporations who have *bought* their way into the national press by acquiring a new title or titles.

This pattern of market exclusion and recruitment has resulted in the national press (with the exception of the trust-owned Guardian group) being controlled by the corporate business sector. Some groups like News Corporation and the Telegraph Group are part of global media empires: others like the Mail Group (Associated Newspapers) are centred in Britain. All of them have business interests outside the press industry. The main publishers of the national press thus have a shared interest in government policies favourable to large-scale, corporate enterprise.

However, what differentiates the press from many other large commercial organizations is that most newspaper groups are still dominated by a single shareholder. These dominant shareholders are currently more interventionist than their predecessors in the 1960s, and have tended to flex their power by promoting right-wing positions in their newspapers. Typical of this more interventionist generation of publishers is Rupert Murdoch. 'Murdoch, the paper spread out before him', recalls a former *Sunday Times* editor, 'would jab his fingers at some article or contribution and snarl, "What do you want to print rubbish like that for?" or pointing to the by-line of a correspondent, assert that "That man's a Commie"' (Giles 1986: cf. Evans 1983). His successor at the *Sunday Times*, Andrew Neil, selected by Murdoch partly because he had strongly right-wing views, describes how his proprietor dominated his thoughts even when he was absent:

> Rupert has an uncanny knack of being there even when he is not. When I did not hear from him and I knew his attention was elsewhere, he was still uppermost in my mind . . . Rupert expects his papers to stand broadly for what he believes: a combination of right-wing Republicanism from America mixed with undiluted Thatcherism from Britain . . .' (Neil 1996: 165).

The second main way in which economics influences the national press is more indirect. Advertisers pay more to reach high- than low-income readers. This skews the structure of the national press. Five out of ten national daily papers are prestige papers aimed at the top end of the market. They cater for, and articulate, the interests of Britain's political class. They also help to sustain elite domination of British politics since they are now the only national newspapers that provide detailed coverage of public affairs. There have been other newspapers offering full accounts of public affairs, written from a different class perspective and some with far larger circulations, but they all closed because they reached less affluent readers and failed to attract adequate advertising. Thus, what keeps alive a prestige press, and amplifies elite perspectives, and denies an equivalent voice to others, is an unequal advertising subsidy rooted in disparities of income and wealth in society (Curran and Seaton 1997).

## Political regulation

The American scholar, Michael Schudson (2000), complains that political economists tend to focus on the economic to the exclusion of the political. The implication is that restrictive political controls tend to be understated.

Certainly, the British press is subject to more restrictive laws than those in the USA. In particular, limitations on free speech arising from national security and defamation law in Britain are more curtailing than their equivalents across the Atlantic (Barendt and Hitchens 2000; Robertson and Nicol 1992). The Human Rights Act (1998) offers qualified protection for freedom of expression, and this will shortly be supported through a new Freedom of Information law offering a conditional right of access to public information. However, these affirmative measures stop short of the protections provided, for example, by the US or German constitutions.

There are various other ways in which state regulation or policy impinge on the press. Since 1965, the press has been subject to special anti-monopoly rules designed to restrict the growth of press concentration. Broadcasting regulation has also limited the expansion of the press into terrestial television and radio. In addition, the press receives a very large subsidy in the form of zero VAT rating on newspaper sales. The Press Complaints Commission, the heir to the Press Council, with a remit to investigate public complaints against the press, also exists only because of external political pressure.

In principle, therefore, there are a number of regulatory levers that could be manipulated by public officials in order to secure a favourable press. But in practice, this has not happened. The Press Complaints Commission has no legal powers, and its strictures can be – and are – ignored (O'Malley and Soley 2000). Anti-monopoly controls limiting the growth of press concentration have been consistently ineffectual over a 35-year period, while limits on cross-media ownership were substantially eased by the 1996 Broadcasting Act. No government has threatened to withdraw the press's VAT concession. Indeed rather than the press being intimidated by government, it would be truer to argue that successive governments have been intimidated by the press. In reality, the press largely defines the regulatory environment in which it operates (Tunstall 1996).

## Press and politics

Yet although the press is 'deregulated', it has been at times intensely loyal to the government. During the run-up to the 1987 election, for example, the 'free' press consisted mainly of passionately pro-government newspapers. During the same period the broadcasting system, which is linked to the state and subject to extensive regulation, offered much more space to critical and anti-government perspectives.

What this seeming paradox highlights is the limitations of conventional liberal analysis. This portrays the press as an independent institution for ever locked into an adversarial relationship with government which it oversees on behalf of the people. Only the extension of state powers over the press, according to this view, can 'chill' the press's zeal in critically scrutinizing the actions of government. What this conventional analysis overlooks is that the press is not fully independent as a consequence of being privately owned. The press can be loyal to the government of the day because those who own and control it are government supporters. What it also fails to grasp is that it is possible for a media organization like the BBC to be an institution of the state, yet owe its allegiance to the public.

The key to explaining the politics of the press during the 1980s was the Thatcherite mobilization of a social coalition, coordinated by the Conservative Party, that included large-scale business. Under Thatcher's leadership, the Conservative government promised economic regeneration on the basis of low taxes, a slimmed-down state, anti-union legislation and privatization, and for a time seemed to be delivering on its prospectus. Much of the national press were the government's principal cheerleaders.

Yet, this relationship was more fragile than it appeared at the time. It was not rooted in party funding of the press, as in the early twentieth century. Nor was it part of a stable relationship between senior politicians and publishers, both integrated into Westminster politics, at a time of strong, stable party loyalties, as in the 1950s. Powerful publishers like Murdoch and Black (owning between them six normally Conservative national papers) were global business tycoons with right-wing views but with no special attachment to the Conservative Party as an institution. During 1994–5 much of the Conservative press attacked the Conservative Prime Minister, John Major, with a vehemence usually reserved for the left. Disenchantment with Major's leadership provided the context for the tactical partnership between Murdoch and

Blair, mentioned earlier. Blair, a market-friendly politician, seemed certain to win the next election (1997). He also signalled in 1996 that he would be sensitive to Murdoch's business interests when his team attacked as excessive the Conservative government's anti-monopoly restrictions on big publishers, contained in its Broadcasting Act. Indeed, Tony Blair as Prime Minister even phoned his counterpart in Italy in an attempt to facilitate Murdoch's expansion into the Italian media market. His friendliness was reciprocated: some of Murdoch's papers supported Blair in 1997 and afterwards, though on terms that made clear their continuing commitment to right-wing policies.

## Some countervailing influences

Yet the press is not simply the product of those who own and control it. Nor is it a mere mouthpiece of the economic interests of the corporate sector. The press is also influenced by countervailing influences both inside and outside newspaper organizations.

The power of owners is constrained by the professional culture of journalists. This professional culture has a craft element based on pride in a technical job well done, which is essentially conformist. But it has also a normative element rooted in beliefs about how journalists should serve society. It is this public interest component, transcending newspaper organizations, which provides a potential counterbalance to press control.

Thus, journalists at the *Sunday Times* put up a determined rearguard action during the early 1980s against what they saw as a management-inspired, right-wing shift in the paper's news agenda. Their colleagues at the *Observer* went even further, and were considerably more successful, in resisting changes during the same period also inspired by a new owner, Tiny Rowland. Thus, Rowland backed down in 1984 after ordering his editor, Donald Trelford, to suppress a report of atrocities in Zimbabwe, which jeopardized the parent company's extensive business activities in that country. The reason for Rowland's humiliating reversal was that he was opposed not only by his editor but also by the paper's entire journalistic staff in a row that became embarrassingly public.

Professional norms are not confined to journalists but also penetrate deep into the culture of newspaper management, a significant number of whom are former news reporters. It also transcends political differences. One key reason (among several) why the Conservative press turned on the Conservative government after 1992 was because it became associated with political 'sleaze'. Politicians' sale of influence in return for money, symbolized by the asking of Commons questions for cash payments, was exposed and attacked as much by newspapers on the right as on the left. It violated journalists' own professional norms, and what they thought should be the norms of democracy.

The professional culture of journalists has also contributed to the evolution of news conventions and formats. These are currently in a process of transition. Traditional distinctions between fact and opinion are weakening with the gradual blurring of news and features; so-called 'straight' reports are giving way to more transparently angled ones; professional standards of accuracy are seemingly in decline. But it is still the case that contending opinion is routinely quoted in news reports of contentious issues in the national press. This convention significantly limits the partisanship of national newspapers.

One of its consequences is that the press routinely responds to shifts in the balance of power in society because this leads to changes in the composition and status of 'accredited' news sources. The relationship between societal change and source change is imperfect because the press is skewed towards elite sources (an issue discussed further by Miller in Chapter 6 in this volume). But the very fact that the news convention of 'balance' exists at all means that the press responds, however inadequately, to changes in the political environment. Thus, Stuart Hall and his colleagues (1978) show how in the early 1970s the press responded to a closed loop of news sources – the police, judiciary and politicians – who fostered a moral panic about muggers, and promoted a repressive law and order agenda. Yet Schlesinger and Tumber (1994) show how law and order had become almost two decades later a highly contested terrain in which effective pressure groups, with significant political and other allies, gained access to the press (especially broadsheets) and opened up a fusillade of criticism concerned with prison reform, police violence and miscarriages of justice. The contrast seemingly reflected the intensification of pressure group and campaigning activity. Similarly, Deacon and Golding (1994) offer a classic exposition of how popular, political, local state and specialist professional opposition profoundly influenced press representations of the poll tax, including coverage in papers supporting the Thatcher government which introduced the new tax.

If professional and source influences are potentially a countervailing force limiting economic control of the British press, so too is the culture of society. The political culture of Britain is ambivalent. It contains profoundly conservative elements symbolized by the retention of the House of Lords. But it also contains residual radical elements, which penetrate all sections of society. These generate an opposed stream of images and explanations to those that are dominant. When tabloid newspapers in the 1990s called highly paid senior executives (like Cedric Brown) 'fat cats', they were giving voice to this radical element in British culture. Similarly, when even some right-wing newspapers responded in 2000 to train crashes and delays by questioning the efficacy of rail privatization, they were keying into tenacious social democratic attitudes that lie beneath the surface of 'market hegemony'.

The nature of British political culture changes over time. This influences the press in a variety of ways, not least by influencing how journalists approach a story. Different conventions are employed in reporting and commenting on the news. There are some topics and times (e.g. Remembrance Day) when journalists feel that they have an obligation to celebrate and affirm the shared values of society. There are other topics which are the subject of legitimized controversy (e.g. the government's autumn Budget) where journalists tend to adopt a more formally neutral approach by quoting or paraphrasing opposed views. And, lastly, there are times when journalists assume the role of social critic in condemning anti-social groups or behaviour (such as paedophilia) on the assumption that they are speaking for society. Which register – celebratory, neutral or condemnatory – is adopted by journalists depends in part on the prevailing climate of opinion.

This is borne out by changing conventions in reporting the Royal Family. In the late 1970s and early 1980s, immediately following the Jubilee celebrations and the marriage between Prince Charles and Lady Diana, the Royal Family were reported in a largely celebratory way: they were projected as symbols of national unity and family values. But in response to their own domestic upheavals, the accelerated erosion of social deference, and the revival of republicanism, the Royal Family came to be reported in the 1990s in a more critical way. They were featured irreverently as figures in a long-running soap opera. The monarchy even moved almost from the category of consensus to that of controversy, reflected in the publication of some news reports in which the comments of royalists were balanced by those of critics. Indeed, one member of the Royal Family – 'Fergie', Duchess of York – acquired for a time the status of 'moral deviant', and came to be denigrated in a journalistic voice usually reserved for social outcasts. In other words, the way in which the Royal Family were reported changed because underlying attitudes towards the 'Royals' had shifted.

A key dynamo in this process of connecting the press to social change is consumer power. Admittedly, this power is weakened by the oligopolistic structure of the national press. Just five, relatively centralized groups controlled in 2000 94% of national newspaper circulation so that the large number of national newspaper titles exaggerates the real range of choice available (Audit Bureau of Circulation 2000). Consumer influence is also limited, in political terms, by the increasing dominance of entertainment content in the tabloid press with the result that a growing number of people select newspapers without reference to their political allegiance. But even so, the freedom of press controllers to preach right-wing politics is constrained by the freedom of readers, with different views and perhaps more importantly different social experiences, to buy only those papers that they find pleasurable. This sets up a field of tension between the ideological commitments of press controllers and the different perspectives of large numbers of readers.

This conflict has been negotiated in different ways. Historically, one way has been for political coverage to shrink in relative terms in favour of content that is more interesting to the generality of readers, such as human interest stories, entertainment features and sport. This led to a cumulative contraction in the proportion of space devoted to public affairs in the popular press during 1936–76 (Curran, Douglas and Whannel 1980). This trend appears to have continued since then, although the evidence is contradictory (McLachlan and Golding 2000; Rooney 2000).

Another way has been for the market to overule the publisher. An example of this was when the *Star* secured an exclusive story about Princess Diana making nuisance calls to her former friend, Oliver Hoare, which was spiked on the instructions of the paper's proprietor, Lord Stevens, on the grounds that the story would damage the Royal Family. The *News of the World* then obtained the story, forcing the *Sunday Express* (also controlled by Lord Stevens) to run it as a 'spoiler'. Audience demand for soap opera stories about the Royal Family overpowered the protective conservatism of a traditionalist proprietor.

At other times, however, publishers have imposed their views in opposition to those of many of their readers. This is borne out by the wide gap, cited earlier, between editorial and electoral opinion. At still other times, the conflicting demands of propaganda and profit are left unresolved resulting in tensions, contradictions or a 'lack of fit' between different elements of the same paper. For example, most right-wing tabloids published leaders during the mid-1980s extolling the need for the regeneration of Britain through the cultivation of a free enterprise culture. But this injunction was not carried over into the entertainment pages. There were very few articles glamourizing business leaders and holding them up as models for admiration and emulation (in the way that model workers were celebrated in the Soviet press in support of an opposed value system). Press controllers, operating in a market environment, instinctively knew that this form of capitalist evangelism would have invited derision and boredom – and falling circulations.

Finally, market pressures give rise to different sorts of newspapers catering for different sorts of readers. These pressures are imperfect due to the distortions exerted by advertising, market entry barriers, oligopoly and the advantages of size. But they are still a pervasive form of influence. Perhaps their most important consequence has been to sustain two national newspaper groups (out of seven) that publish centre-left newspapers. One of these, the Trinity Mirror group, has senior executives who are strongly anti-socialist. But its national papers are broadly committed to the causes of social democracy, because this is thought to be commercially advantageous.

In short, a number of influences propel the British national press towards the orbit of established privilege. But national newspapers are also exposed to countervailing pressures, pulling in a contrary direction. This gives rise to an ambiguous press system which is linked to the power structure of contemporary Britain, without being wholly integrated into it.

## Questions

1  What are the main strengths and weaknesses of the radical and liberal approaches to understanding the media?

2  In what ways – if at all – can they be usefully combined in a single analysis?

3  Take a newspaper, and see if you can infer from its content some of the influences – cultural values, professional norms, its ownership, sources, market pressure, etc. – that shape it.

## References

Alexander, J. (1981) 'The mass media in systemic, historical and comparative perspective', in E. Katz and T. Szescho (eds) *Mass Media and Social Change*, Beverly Hills, CA: Sage.

Audit Bureau of Circulation (2000) Certified average issue circulation, January–June.

Bagdikian, B. (1992) *Media Monopoly*, 4th edn, Boston, MA: Beacon.

Baker, C. E. (1994) *Advertising and a Democratic Press*, Princeton, NJ: Princeton University Press.

Barendt, E. and Hitchens, L. (2000) *Media Law*, Harlow: Longman.

Block, E. (1981) 'Freedom and equality; indicators of political change in Sweden, 1945–1975', in K. Rosengren (ed.) *Advances in Content Analysis*, London: Sage.

Chomsky, N. (1989) *Necessary Illusions*, Boston, MA: South End Press.

Curran, J. (1986) 'The impact of advertising on the British mass media', in R. Collins, J. Curran, N. Garnham, P. Schlesinger and C. Sparks (eds) *Media, Culture and Society*, London: Sage.

Curran, J. (2000) 'Literary editors, social networks and cultural tradition', in J. Curran (ed.) *Media Organisations in Society*, London: Arnold.

Curran, J., Douglas, A. and Whannel, G. (1980) 'The political economy of the human-interest story', in A. Smith (ed.) *Newspapers and Democracy*, Cambridge, MA: MIT Press.

Curran, J. and Park, M.-Y. (eds) (2000) *De-Westernizing Media Studies*, London: Routledge.

Curran, J. and Seaton, J. (1997) *Power Without Responsibility: The Press and Broadcasting in Britain*, 5th edn, London: Routledge.

Deacon, D. and Golding, P. (1994) *Taxation and Representation*, London: Libbey.

Eldridge, J., Kitzinger, J. and Williams, K. (1997) *The Mass Media and Power in Modern Britain*, Oxford: Oxford University Press.

Emery, E. (1972) *The Press in America*, 3rd edn, Englewood Cliffs, NJ: Prentice-Hall.

Evans, H. (1983) *Good Times, Bad Times*, London: Weidenfeld and Nicholson.

Fishman, M. (1982) 'News and non-events: making the visible invisible', in J. Ettema and D. C. Whitney (eds) *Individuals in Mass Media Organizations*, Beverly Hills, CA: Sage.

Gans, H. (1980) *Deciding What's News*, London: Constable.

Giles, F. (1986) *Sundry Times*, London: Murray.

Golding, P. and Murdock, G. (2000) 'Culture, communications, and political economy', in J. Curran and M. Gurevitch (eds) *Mass Media and Society*, 3rd edn, London: Arnold.

Gustafsson, K. (1993) 'Government policies to reduce newspaper entry barriers', *Journal of Media Economics* 6(1).

Hall, S. (1986) 'Media power and class power' in J. Curran, J. Ecclestone, G. Oakley and R. Richardson (eds) *Bending Reality*, London: Pluto.

Hall, S., Critcher, C., Jefferson, T., Clarke, J. and Roberts, B. (1978) *Policing the Crisis*, London: Macmillan.

Hallin, D. (2000) 'Commercialism and professionalism in the American news media', in J. Curran and M. Gurevitch (eds) *Mass Media and Society*, 3rd edn, London: Arnold.

Hansen, A. (1991) 'The media and social construction of the environment', *Media, Culture and Society* 13(4).

Herman, E. (1999) *The Myth of the Liberal Media*, New York: Lang.

Herman, E. and Chomsky, N. (1988) *Manufacturing Consent*, New York: Pantheon.

Herman, E. and McChesney, R. (1997) *The Global Media*, London: Cassell.

Hetherington, A. (1985) *News, Newspapers and Television*, London: Macmillan.

Kaniss, P. (1997) *Making Local News*, Chicago: University of Chicago Press.

Kellner, D. (1990) *Television and the Crisis of Democracy*, Boulder, CO: Westview.

Koss, S. (1981/1984) *The Rise and Fall of the Political Press in Britain*, 2 vols, London: Hamish Hamilton.

MacLachlan, S. and Golding, P. (2000) 'Tabloidization in the British press: a quantitative investigation into changes in British newspapers, 1952–1997', in C. Sparks and J. Tulloch (eds) *Tabloid Tales*, Lanham, MD: Rowman and Littlefield.

McManus, J. (1994) *Market-Driven Journalism*, Thousand Oaks, CA: Sage.

McRobbie, A. (1994) *Postmodernism and Popular Culture*, London: Routledge.

McRobbie, A. (1996) '*More!* New sexualities in girls' and women's magazines', in J. Curran, D. Morley and V. Walkerdine (eds) *Cultural Studies and Communications*, London: Arnold.

Miliband, R. (1973) *The State in Capitalist Society*, London: Quartet.

Murdock, G. (1982a) 'Class, power and the press: problems of conceptualisation and evidence', in H. Christian (ed.) *The Sociology of Journalism and the Press*, Keele: University of Keele Press (Sociological Review Monograph 29).

Murdock, G. (1982b) 'Large corporations and the control of the communications industry', in M. Gurevitch, T. Bennett, J. Curran and J. Woollacott (eds) *Culture, Society and the Media*, London: Methuen.

Murdock, G. (1984) 'Reporting the riots: images and impact', in J. Benyon (ed.) *Scarman and After*, Oxford: Pergamon.

Neil, A. (1996) *Full Disclosure*, London: Macmillan.

Nowak, K. (1984) 'Cultural Indicators in Swedish Advertising 1950–1975' in G. Melischek, K. Rosengren and J. Stappers (eds) *Cultural Indicators: An International Symposium*, Vienna: Verlag der Osterriechischen Akademie der Wissenschaften.

O'Malley, T. and Soley, C. (2000) *Regulating the Press*, London: Pluto.

Parenti, M. (1993) *Inventing Reality*, 2nd edn, New York: St. Martin's Press.

Robertson, G. and Nicol, A. (1992) *Media Law*, 3rd edn, Harmondsworth: Penguin.

Rooney, D. (2000) 'Thirty years of competition in the British tabloid press: the *Mirror* and the *Sun* 1968–1998', in C. Sparks and J. Tulloch (eds) *Tabloid Tales*, Lanham, MD: Rowman and Littlefield.

Schlesinger, P. (1990) 'Rethinking the sociology of journalism: source strategies and the limits of media-centrism', in M. Ferguson (ed.) *Public Communication*, London: Sage.

Schlesinger, P. and Tumber, H. (1994) *Reporting Crime*, Oxford: Clarendon.

Schudson, M. (2000) 'The sociology of news production revisited (again)' in J. Curran, J. and M. Gurevitch (eds) *Mass Media and Society*, 3rd edn, London: Arnold.

Seymour-Ure, C. (1996) *The British Press and Broadcasting since 1945*, 2nd edn, Oxford: Blackwell.

Sigal, L. (1987) 'Sources make the news' in R. Manoff and M. Schudson (eds) *Reading the News*, New York: Pantheon.

Tuchman, G. (1978) *Making News*, New York: Free Press.

Tunstall, J. (1970) *Journalists at Work*, London: Constable.

Tunstall, J. (1996) *Newspaper Power*, Oxford: Clarendon.

Tunstall, J. and Machin, D. (1999) *The Anglo-American Connection*, Oxford: Oxford University Press.

Waisbord, S. (2000) 'Media in South America: between the rock of the state and the hard place of the market', in J. Curran and S. Waisbord (eds) *De-Westernizing Media Studies*, London: Routledge.

# Further reading

Allan, S. (1999) *News Culture*, Buckingham: Open University Press. A useful review that combines a cultural studies and sociological approach.

Berkowitz, D. (1997) (ed.) *Social Meanings of News*, Thousand Oaks, CA; Sage. A good anthology of essays putting news in a wider context, with an American bias.

Curran, J. and Seaton, J. (1997) *Power Without Responsibility*, 5th edn, London: Routledge. A widely used book about the British press and broadcasting, now in its fifth edition.

Curran, J. and Park, M.-Y. (eds) *De-Westernizing Media Studies*, London: Routledge. A collection of essays from around the world which emphasizes the importance of national differences in shaping media systems in opposition to globalization and universalistic theories.

Franklin, B. (1997) *Newszak and News Media*, London: Arnold. A well written, UK-oriented critique, with concrete examples.

Herman, E. (1999) *The Myth of Liberal Media*, New York: Lang. An eloquent presentation of the radical perspective (with an American emphasis).

Herman, E. and McChesney, R. (1997) *The Global Media*, London: Cassell. A key radical book that marshals extensive evidence from around the world about the growing dominance of media mega-corporations.

McNair, B. (1999) *News and Journalism in the UK*, 3rd edn, London: Routledge. A clear, useful and informative textbook, from a sociological perspective.

Seymour-Ure, C. (1996) *The British Press and Broadcasting Since 1945*, Oxford: Blackwell. A clear, useful and informative textbook, from a political science perspective.

Schudson, M. (2000) 'The sociology of news production revisited (again)', in J. Curran and M. Gurevitch (eds) *Mass Media and Society*, London: Arnold. A clever liberal synthesis of media sociology.

Sparks, C. and Tulloch, J. (2000) (eds) *Tabloid Tales*, Lanham, MD: Rowman and Littlefield. A recent, useful contribution to the tabloidization of the press debate.

Stephenson, H. and Bromley, M. (1998) *Sex, Lies and Democracy*, Harlow: Longman. A useful collection of essays, mainly from a practitioner's perspective.

Tumber, H. (1999) (ed.) *News*, Oxford: Oxford University Press. A useful collection of essays, with a stress on the sociology of news organizations.

Tunstall, J. (1996) *Newspaper Power*, Oxford: Clarendon. A good, well-researched book on the British press.

## Chapter 8

# Magazines

MAGAZINES: THE BULGING BOOKSTALLS

**BRIAN BRAITHWAITE**

The magazine industry is flourishing, for both the consumer and 'business-to-business' titles. A significant contributor over the past decade has been the explosion of new titles in the contract sector – customer magazines sold or distributed free to consumers and businesses. Another area which has surprized the publishing pundits has been the recent reappearance and meteoric growth of men's magazines – a moribund sector back in the 1970s. And there has been a considerable shift in the revenue pattern of bookstall consumer magazines: no longer is advertisement revenue dominant. Now only 36% of total revenue is generated from advertising. But business publications still take 82% of their revenue from this source. (Consumer magazine cover prices tend to stay ahead of inflation, with small but constant increases, while advertising is a supremely competitive market which tends to overlook the traditional concept of rate cards while enjoying a huge range of media buying choice.) Subscriptions have become a vital strategy to consumer publishers. Once a minor factor in the publishers' treasury, postal subscriptions now deliver nearly 14% of total sales. And supermarkets, only comparatively recently interested in magazines as a commodity, have latterly enthusiastically seized on all the more popular titles and take 30% of market share. Seismic changes continue to rock this once comparatively staid medium. A look at the bookstalls is evidence of the robust, competitive jungle in which the industry operates.

## The medium

The final years of the twentieth century witnessed the thrusting and ever-expanding activity of electronic media – terrestrial, satellite and cable television, the explosion of new radio stations, the domestic revolution of video recorders and the resurgence of the cinema, attributed to the expansion of multi-screen complexes as well as 'block-buster' films. But against this exciting explosion of feverish growth the magazine industry across Europe is not only alive and kicking but ever innovative and expansive with new products. In the UK there are over 2700 consumer magazines and 5000 specialized, professional and 'business-to-business' journals. In the rest of Europe there are over 9000 consumer magazines and about 30,000 professional trade titles. An estimated total of world magazine publishing produces the impressive figure of 87,500 titles. (Figures from FIPP/Carat.)

(In general, magazines are defined as 'consumer' providing readers with leisure-time information and entertainment, or 'business and professional', providing information relevant to readers' working lives. There are also 'specialist' titles, aimed at readers with particular interests such as cars, boats, hobbies, and so on.)

This is an industry which is intensely competitive within itself, constantly evolving and (the secret of its success?) able to split itself into myriad niches to attract and retain audience segments that will appeal to advertisers. This is the factor that makes magazines so singularly unique among the media. Not for magazines the broad sweep of the general audience with the attendant dissipation (or 'wastage') of advertisers' money. (The US magazine business received the message in the 1950s when it endeavoured to compete with television, with the resultant crash of the dinosaurs *Life*, *Look* and the *Saturday Evening Post*.) Magazines have niche markets of women, men, motorists, slimmers, parents, gardeners, teenagers, retired people, 'telly addicts', computer freaks, train spotters, farmers, golfers, holidaymakers, photographers and other specialized reading groups. The range of women's magazines, for instance, is so wide and diverse that advertisers can select their potential audience by age, social class, hobby or leisure interest. Industry research has always shown intense and discrete loyalty of readers to their magazines – a 'one-to-one' dialogue between editor and reader that is symptomatic of the strength of the medium. Publishers, of course, are never slow to exploit this selling ingredient.

And we are still looking at a growth industry. In the decade 1987–1997 the number of consumer titles in the UK rose by 31% and business/professional by 44%. The yearly rate of magazine launches in this decade rose from 300 in 1987 to almost 700 in 1997.

## The players

### The UK

The magazine industry in the UK has experienced considerable ownership changes since the 1950s, particularly in the consumer sector. The formation of the International Publishing Corporation (IPC) in 1968 mopped up, through various takeovers, the distinguished prewar companies of Fleetway, Newnes, Odhams and Hulton Press. So under one roof (in the high-rise offices on London's South Bank, originally dubbed by the trade the Ministry of Magazines) came a complex near-monopoly of women's weekly and monthly titles and specialized magazines. Previous 'eyeball to eyeball' rivals such as *Woman* and *Woman's Own*, *Amateur Gardening* and *Popular Gardening*, *Ideal Home* and *Homes and Gardens*, were suddenly working cheek by jowl and subsequently were to be marketed together. But there were other contenders in the women's market. Two American-owned companies have operated in the UK since 1910 and 1916 respectively: the National Magazine Company and Condé Nast, both specializing in British versions of their successful USA titles including *Vogue*, *Good Housekeeping*, *House and Garden*, *Cosmopolitan*, *Country Living*, *Brides* and *Harpers & Queen*.

### The German 'invasion'

The 1980s saw the emergence of two significant magazine publishing companies. From Germany came Gruhner & Jahr (G & J of the UK) with its new monthly *Prima*, already successful in mainland Europe. The magazine, after a successful launch, is still the highest selling women's monthly in the UK. After *Prima* G & J launched the weekly *Best*. G & J was followed into the UK by H. Bauer, publishing the weekly *Bella*. Bauer also publishes the weeklies *Take a Break* (the UK's biggest selling weekly for women) *That's Life*, and *TV Quick*. The UK-based publishing company which has made important strides since the 1970s has been EMAP (East Midland Allied Press). Originally a local newspaper company, based in Peterborough, EMAP expanded into specialized newsprint titles in the fishing and motorcycle areas. It moved in the 1980s into teenage titles (*Just 17* and *More*) and made an important move later in the decade by acquisition, notably buying the Murdoch magazines when that giant media company decided to concentrate on newspapers and television. EMAP owns a portfolio of important women's magazines, including *Elle, New Woman* and *Red*. It also boasts the mega-success of the men's title *FHM* which outsells all women's and men's monthly titles. EMAP also has a considerable portfolio of specialized titles. Note that in 2001 G & J was bought by the National Magazine Company, the British end of the American Hearst Corporation.

### The publishing giants

The BBC, the publisher of *Radio Times* since 1923, has emerged in recent years as a leading contender in consumer titles, allied to their television and radio programmes. BBC *Gardeners' World, Good Food, Homes & Antiques* and *Wildlife* are successful titles with sales helpfully exploited on the relevant programmes.

A seismic change in ownership took place in 1998 when Reed–Elsevier, the merger of Reed and the Dutch Elsevier in 1994, sold all the IPC magazines as a going concern to its management, a big financial deal which helped to sharpen the Corporation's competitive edge. In 2001 the entire IPC Group was sold to AOL Time Warner.

Although there are still many other publishers, often with single publications, the consumer publishing business is dominated by these giants. The Continental influence is also evident, apart from the Germans, with *Hello!* from Spain and *Marie Claire* from France. The Dutch company VNU publish a string of puzzle magazines as well as many computer titles. D. C. Thomson in Scotland still publish *People's Friend* (began 1869) as well as their famous children's comics, *The Beano* and *The Dandy*.

The pages of *British Rate & Data* (BRAD) illustrate the massive scope of all magazine titles in the UK – not only in the number of titles but also in the width of ownership. There are similar publications for all other European countries.

### Europe

Magazines are big business right across Europe. France, for instance, has 1444 consumer titles (1317 business/professional), Finland 281 (2012), Germany 1950 (4300), Italy 975 (9175) Switzerland 123 (1724) and the Netherlands 1330 (4520). (Figures from FIPP/Carat.) Giant players include Germany's Bertelsmann, Axel Springer, Burda and H. Bauer, Italy's Mondadori, France's Bayard Presse and Fillipacchi and Hachette, the Netherlands' VNU and Sweden's Bonnier Group, to name just a few. Many publishing companies also own newspaper and/or television interests.

Some titles have successfully crossed national frontiers including *Vogue, Cosmopolitan, Essentials, Hello!, Reader's Digest, House and Garden, Prima, Marie Claire, Elle, GQ* and *Esquire*. This cross-fertilization of suitable titles is a trend that is likely to develop right across the world. Usually, but not always, the editorial is entirely indigenous – only the titles and the editorial ethos are the same.

## Cost structures

The medium has witnessed monumental changes in the past decades. This was a medium dominated by photogravure and litho-printing for the big circulation magazines and by letterpress printing (hot metal) for the thousands of titles with circulations under 100,000 copies. The advent of new technology with computer typesetting and desktop computers, giving editorial staff the ability to interpret their words and designs, has created a publishing revolution that is not only creative but also financial. Design work stations enable the designer to create layouts, including colour originals, tinted lettering and panels as well as incorporating text. Pages of text and mono originals can be made-up on screen and output via a laser printer, with the cost of software being within the resources of even small publishers. Although colour scanning is still in the domain of the professional repro house, the whole effect of the giant strides in printing technology in the pre-press area has meant significant savings in the editorial and advertising departments.

### *The publisher as a juggler*

The magazine publisher has three revenue streams: cover price, advertising and 'brand extensions' – the latter the newer area of creating profit from extraneous activities such as editorial offers, books, exhibitions, franchising etc. Advertising revenue is the main boost to the publisher's treasury but is obviously dependant on so many external forces: competition, the economy, circulation fall etc.). In 1989 consumer magazines enjoyed a revenue of £449 million from display advertising which deteriorated to £374 million in 1996 (at current prices – figures from Advertising Association 1997). Cover price revenue is obviously more in the immediate control of the magazine publisher and, in fact, cover prices have steadily risen over the decade. The split between the two main sources of revenue for consumer magazines was 38% advertising and 62% circulation. For business/professional the figures are 82% and 18%. (PPA/ Advertising Association 1997.)

Magazine publishers have two economic weapons at their disposal to endeavour to counteract rising costs or falling revenue. They can increase cover prices and/or increase the advertising rates. These options can offer an esoteric balancing act. Cover price rises tend (but it is not a cast-iron rule) to depress circulations, even if sometimes only temporarily. In the case of falling circulations (if not readership) the advertiser will resist rate-card increases. It is a delicate balance to preserve and one that constantly occupies the minds of publishers.

Publishers' rate cards are notoriously unscientific. A newly launched magazine, for instance, will assess the competition and base the page rates on a comparable, if competitive, rate structure. Advertising rates have increased significantly over the years – generally above the rate of inflation – and in the cutting edge of media competition, coinciding with the explosive development of media-buying shops and media specialists, the rate card has become at best elastic and at worst obsolescent (in extreme cases, obsolete). The advertiser buys not only on circulation but also on readership, and the six-monthly National Readership Survey (NRS) figures are keenly picked over for falls and rises and other more subtle nuances. So publishers who allow the cover price rise to outstrip reader demand, and who see readers leaving for a competitor because of price (quality is another matter), could easily see their circulation counteracted by a fall in the advertising revenue.

### Quality of readership is the key

But advertisers also buy on 'quality' of circulation: breakdowns of sex, age and class. The NRS is keenly reflective of the quality of the reader so a powerful magazine like *Vogue*, with its wealthy and aspirational readership, has an influence for the advertiser far beyond the mathematics of its circulation or even readership figures. But publishers who are able to charge their customers a premium on their pages have to continue to justify that premium or join the slippery slopes of falling revenues.

The whole history of the magazine business is attended by continual deaths of titles as they run out of editorial steam or fail to deliver the right audience at the right price to their advertisers. Competitors, already existing or those waiting in the wings, are eager to take advantage of a magazine 'on the skids', sometimes as a result of editorial obsolescence but sometimes because a publisher has failed to balance the important cost factors which will keep the magazine economically attractive to both readers and advertisers.

It is relevant to note that across Europe the big weekly is still popular and a successful formula. Germany's *Stern* and *Neue Revue*, Spain's *Ola!* and France's *Paris Match* are examples of the genre still up and running. Perhaps the UK could in theory resurrect a popular title like *Picture Post* but in practice the dominance of the dozen 'free' newspaper colour magazines and the enormous popularity of television in the UK (backed by the 80% ownership of video recorders) must be a deterrent to would-be big circulation magazine enterprises.

### Distribution

Distribution is the basic engine of the magazine industry – the function of getting the magazine into the hands of the reader at the right time at the right place. Good distribution builds circulations with the minimum of wastage at a reasonable price to the publisher. This simple-sounding operation is, however, beset with difficulties, problems, politics, recriminations and sometimes (but not often) chaos.

There was a time when distribution was a basic function of the publisher who delivered the copies to the wholesaler who, in turn, delivered them to the retailer. Sometimes the copies were 'firm sale' (at a subsequent loss to retailers if they were left with unsold copies at the end of the magazine's on-sale period) or more recently 'sale or return' (SOR), which tends to encourage retailers to be bolder in their ordering but opens up the possibility of waste in the system. But this is simplifying what has become a highly complex set of possibilities for the magazine publisher.

## Changing times

The whole distribution chain has been subject to a great deal of change, basically engendered by the newspaper industry which has cut the number of wholesalers throughout the UK in order to reduce costs and make the business more efficient. Many small private and family businesses have gone to the wall as the bigger wholesalers have been appointed on exclusive geographical contracts. The 'big three' wholesalers in the UK are still WH Smith, John Menzies and Surridge Dawson. John Menzies sold all their retail shops in 1998 to WH Smith and now concentrate on wholesaling.

The third force in the distribution chain has emerged since the early 1970s. This is the distributor – the link between the publisher and the wholesaler – and ultimately the retailer. The distributor is appointed by the publisher on a brokerage basis to handle the circulation sales – responsible for the contact with the wholesalers and the bigger retailers. Many of the biggest publishers tend to own and run their own distribution companies, which also take on third-party contracts for other publishers. For instance, Britain's leading distributor is COMAG, jointly owned by Condé Nast and the National Magazine Company. Not only does COMAG distribute all the titles published by both companies but it also holds contracts to circulate a large number of other magazines for outside companies. Even without these client publishers COMAG finds itself, when distributing the house titles, selling into the trade such hugely competitive titles as *Vogue, Harpers & Queen* and *Tatler*. The dominant financial partner in COMAG is the National Magazine Company but it means that Condé Nast (a confrontational company in selling advertising against the National Magazine titles) enjoys revenue from every copy of such successful magazines as *Cosmopolitan* and *Good Housekeeping*.

The whole concept of third-party contracts has become popular in the business in the UK. IPC, in addition to distributing its own eighty or so titles, actively encourages outside business. The BBC and EMAP own a joint distribution company called Frontline to handle house titles (including *Radio Times*) and third-party magazines.

So the publishing director of a magazine has quite a few people to hold responsible when explaining a downturn in circulation, but could, of course, personally take the full credit for an upturn! The director can blame the distributor, the wholesaler or the retailer, and will probably also have an in-house circulation department to liaise with the distributor.

Distribution is a difficult game, particularly when the going gets tough. A fall in circulation can be attributed to many areas – poor editorial, a weak front cover, lively competition, inadequate publicity, lack of advertising funding, late delivery from the printers, and so on. A look at the bookstalls on railway stations, or the so-called 'news runs' in the local WH Smith, is immediate evidence of the problem: a bewildering mass of magazines all calling for attention. And the shelf life is all too ephemeral, particularly for the weeklies.

So let us examine the three methods of distribution open to the publisher.

### The news trade

The news trade is broadly divided into the CTN multiples (CTN is the trade abbreviation for Confectioner, Tobacco, Newsagent, the three prongs of existence for the retail shop) such as WH Smith, Martins and Forbuoys, with many smaller provincial chains, and the 'corner shop', which still survives in the UK. With each type of store there is a diversity of product: books and stationery in the multiples and anything from drinks to groceries, or even film processing, in the corner shops. Each outlet will have costed the priority to selling magazines as against, say, dog food in the corner shop or books in the multiples. Distributors can play a useful role in advising the retailer on display and setting up better news-runs to be able to carry more titles, preferably 'full face' to the potential customer.

The news trade in the UK still boasts over 30,000 shops nationally, despite falling numbers over the years. Many shops are opening as 'convenience stores' (such as '7/11') which stay open long hours and sell magazines as part of their general mix of products. But the conventional news trade, which often offers home delivery, is still the important backbone of the magazine distribution process. Across Europe there is a dominance of kerbside kiosks, selling newspapers, tobacco and magazines, rather than the newsagent shops. Other vital sales points are at railway stations and airports.

Despite the ever-increasing encroachment of the supermarkets on magazine sales, the independent newsagents in the UK, typified by the Asian-run corner shop, still represents 45% of sales with an annual revenue estimated at £750 million. Magazines offer a profit margin of 25% and cover prices are never diffident of steady increases. This is a higher return than those offered by confectionery, tobacco and most newspapers. Space is a problem for the smaller newsagent but, even so, the average number of titles carried by the independents is 472. The multiples, headed by WH Smith, are responsible for about 24% of the retail market.

### Supermarkets

The ever-expanding supermarkets are now an important factor in selling more magazines. At first in the UK supermarkets were confined to the sale of just two titles, *Family Circle* and *Living*. These two magazines, which were not on sale through the news trade, were owned by the late Canadian newspaper tycoon Roy Thomson, who negotiated with supermarkets for the exclusive availability of his two titles. Not only were they the only magazines in the supermarkets but also, equally importantly, they were situated at the check-outs: the supreme position for last-minute impulse purchases. The success of the magazines was phenomenal, with *Family Circle* gaining an unheard-of circulation of 1 million copies at the height of its success. Distributors and wholesalers were not involved – Thomson's circulation staff looked after the supply and distribution of the magazines. (Not popular with the news trade!) The ubiquitous IPC purchased the titles from Thomson in the late 1980s and by doing so opened the floodgates for other magazines, both at the check-outs and in news runs in the stores. Tesco was quick to see the advantages of magazine sales (quite effective against many grocery products) but Sainsbury's was slower off the mark. Both groups of stores, and many other supermarkets throughout the UK and mainland Europe, are now fully converted to the big profits to be made from selling magazines, particularly those of interest to women. Sainsbury's now publishes its own title *Sainsbury's, the Magazine,* which is exclusive to the stores and has become a best-seller.

The supermarkets are supplied by the wholesalers, although there are fears in the trade that the big stores are now so powerful that they could move into a position of negotiating directly with the publishers. This could be to the fundamental detriment of both the publishers and, of course, the wholesalers. A trade criticism of supermarkets, convenience stores and garage forecourts has been that they 'cherry pick' the best titles, in other words they select only the biggest and fastest selling magazines and are not interested in handing a wide range of titles outside the top 200. The corner newsagent feels umbrage at this, being expected to handle many more titles which are not such attractive fast movers.

Back in 1995 the supermarket share of the magazine market was 19%. Wissenden Marketing in their report *Magazine Retailing towards 2000* forecast a significant increase of this market share to about 27% at the start of the millennium. Even this forecast figure may be conservative as the superstores expand both their branches and their news-runs.

## Subscriptions

Subscriptions in the UK are a newer phenomenon. At one time the concept of receiving a copy of a consumer magazine by post was simply not considered practicable or viable. The reader had to be charged the cost of the magazine plus hefty postage. Before the days of polythene wrappers, which deliver the product flat and pristine, a magazine would arrive in the letter box rolled up with a tear strip that often damaged the edges of the magazine. (Professional journals, not available through the news trade were, of course, totally reliant on postal subscription.) So the potential reader of, say, *Good Housekeeping* or *Vogue* would find it easier and less expensive simply to call in to the local WH Smith and buy a copy, which would probably have been in the shop some days before the postal copy.

But the business has changed and moved on. The British Post Office came up with sensible and viable postal rates for printed matter and the polythene wraps were a revolution. Publishers began to advertise their subscription services persistently, either by direct mail or through the magazines themselves. In order to make subscriptions attractive to the reader they have to offer inducements: straight price cuts or tempting presents or extras. British customers have taken to postal subscriptions in a big way

– there are national titles with as much as 30% of their circulations obtained this way. It is expensive to maintain subscription departments with their attendant computer systems and mailing devices but the publishers obtain the full cover price with no discounts to the trade. (The normal trade discount is about 45%, with 25% to the retailer while the distributor takes about 10% brokerage: figures vary.) All in all, a subscription nets about the same to the publisher as a trade copy when the various costs are weighed up.

Subscriptions also have one advantage. A subscription copy is a sold copy, with no returns. So publishers can set their print orders with more confidence when they know that a particular percentage of the print run is spoken for.

The news trade – retailer, wholesaler and distributor – are unenthusiastic about the growing move to subscriptions. Retailers feel aggrieved because every postal copy is, in theory but not necessarily in fact, a lost sale to the shops. Retailers' indignation grows more intense when they realize that many of the magazines on their shelves are carrying subscription advertisements or pull-out leaflets offering the magazine to the potential subscriber at less than the cover price in the shops. Much dialogue has taken place between publishers and the trade but subscription selling is so effective in increasing circulations that protestations of unfair practice fall on deaf publishing ears.

The trade estimates subscription sales for consumer magazines to be 11% of average issue sales but the volume rose by 23% in the 1993–6 period compared to a 6% increase in the average issue volume of retail sales. Forecasts suggest subscriptions could reach 14% by 2000. Obviously titles like *Reader's Digest, Which?* and *Saga* are all or mostly subscription sales but many leading national titles are also heavily into subscription selling, often at cut rates or with tempting preumium offers.

### The system works!

The distribution of magazines is a sort of internecine war but the whole system does work and millions of copies of magazines are sold over the counters of retail shops, the railway station units and the CTNs, or bought in the supermarkets or received in the post.

Do not be left with the impression that the distribution of the hundreds of consumer titles is a mess. The distributors and the wholesalers have spent millions of pounds since the mid-1980s in setting up complex computer systems to analyse the sales patterns of each title – where they would be most likely to sell and in what quantity. Their systems will allocate the number of copies a retailer should receive and the possibilities of reordering when supplies are sold out. Magazine fulfilment has become almost an art – an inexact science full of imperfections maybe, but rationalization and technology are constantly striving to make the complicated business work better.

Out of the melée of corner shops, multiples, supermarkets and subscriptions consumer spending on magazines rose by 74% over the last decade, reaching £1.5 billion in 1998. Total magazine circulation is now over 1.4 billion copies annually and rising. The figures are considerably aided by the explosion of men's magazines, the 'playstation' titles and the constant battle of the celebrity weeklies.

## *Europe*

The divide between subscriptions and retail sales differs widely across Europe. In Finland, for instance, 91% of magazine sales are by subscription with 60% in Sweden and the Netherlands. In France 70% of sales are retail and 56% in Germany. Italy sells 81% through the shops, Norway 65% and Ireland 90%. Greece eschews the subscription route entirely with all copies sold through retail. And in the UK, despite the immense strides made by the publishers, still 89% of titles are sold through the trade.

## Lifestyle

'Lifestyle' is a buzzword much bandied about in the world of magazine publishing. Although the word may have sprung into more general usage in the 1960s and the 1970s, the concept is as old as magazines themselves. The very nature of magazine editorial is to associate itself with lifestyle, or the mode of living of the sort of reader it seeks to attract.

Women's magazines have always been positive in this approach to the cultural subdivisions of their audience. The first woman's magazine, *The Ladies Mercury*, was published in 1693. It was publicized as aiming to answer all 'the most nice and curious questions concerning love, marriage, behaviour, dress and humour of the female sex, whether virgins, wives or widows', so we may assume that the editor was seeking to attract a positive lifestyle; not only women, but also women with a positive attitude to their lives. Down through the ages women's magazines have classified their potential readerships into such broad categories as domestic, the working woman, the sportswoman, the socialite, the fashion conscious, the political, the flighty, the serious or the light-hearted. The very nature of magazine publishing is to exploit those cultural differences.

If you had the time or the inclination to spend a couple of hours at the news runs of WH Smith or any other magazine store, you could peruse the acres of glossy pages to ascertain that although many titles seem to be not unidentical (every successful new title speedily acquires a like-minded competitor), all those editors of all those magazines are out to find a particular lifestyle to make the magazine a 'must' purchase every week or every month. One lifestyle may well be repelled by another – the magazine for ferret fanciers will not necessarily appeal to the readers of *Majesty* or *Vogue*.

## *The general magazine – RIP*

The day of the general magazine is long dead, when *Picture Post* and *Illustrated* were the big-selling photo-story titles, with *John Bull* and *Everybody's* supplying general interest, light-hearted cartoons and fiction. The norm circulation for these titles was about 1 million, an easily acquired figure in those days before television. In the USA, the big picture magazines reached mega-millions – eventually to die because the television audience found moving pictures more enthralling than still ones and the magazines were unable to compete against the television ratings. Cheaper and cheaper subscriptions, in order to emulate the television millions, helped the magazines along the road to ruin. The same pattern occurred in the UK thus necessitating the search for the lifestyle of readerships to deliver to advertisers segments of the sort of people they specifically wanted to reach. They could purchase the mere bulk of millions of consumers either in the newspapers or else on TV. In publishing jargon, magazines were offering the rifle sharp-shooting approach against the mass readership blunderbuss.

Another factor came into the lives of magazine publishers. Electronic media have one outstanding virtue: they move very fast. A major piece of news flashes around the country and the world minutes after the event, whether by radio, television, teletext or on the Internet. The newspapers can pick up the story next day and shade in the picture, fleshing it out with comment and analysis. So we no longer rely on our newspaper to give us the hot news – we have heard it or seen it hours before. The tabloid newspapers became only too aware of this failing and increasingly have turned to 'features' to keep their readers' attention. These features are frequently of particular interest to their women readers: fashion, beauty, diets, and so on. A study of the pages of the *Daily Mail, Express, Mirror* and other tabloids (and to some extent the broadsheets) compared to the same papers in the mid-1970s will emphasize this. It cannot therefore be a coincidence that during this period the circulations of the big women's weeklies (*Woman, Woman's Own*, etc.) have considerably declined. In the 1950s the circulation of *Woman* was 3 million copies a week and *Woman's Own* 2.5 million. In the mid-1990s those circulations were down to about 800,000 each; much of their natural editorial ground has been occupied by the popular press. Many magazines over the same period with lower circulations and weaker editorial personalities have sunk without trace.

## *Magazines are a lifestyle*

A magazine has to be certain that it is projecting a positive lifestyle. By necessity this lifestyle will not attract vast quantities of readers – the days of the 3 million weekly have gone for ever. The woman's weekly is not yet dead, however; there are currently thirteen in this crowded market. The top seller is the German *Take a Break*, topping the market at 1.5 million. But if this appears a bit contradictory it should be noted that a new ingredient is part of this weekly mix. Puzzles and competitions, led by *Take a Break*, occupy many pages with attractive prizes for many of the competitions, while others are just coffee-break time-fillers.

The monthly magazines pursue the lifestyle image with particular vigour. They are very clearly divided into the living styles and aspirations of their traders – the extensive range of home interest titles from *House and Garden* to *House Beautiful*, or fashion (*Vogue*), or society (*Tatler, Harpers*), or slimming, beauty, parenthood, teenagers, brides, crafts and the young women's titles such as *Cosmopolitan, Company, New Woman* and others which have taken an increasing and almost obsessional interest in sex since the mid-1980s.

## Enter the men's magazines

Men are not to be left out of the equation. The male sex has always, if rather sporadically, been a lifestyle target for the magazine publisher. The first men's magazine, *The Gentleman's Magazine*, was published as early as 1731, and actually coined the description 'magazine'. There were several examples of male magazines in Victorian days and the genre was particularly lively in the 1930s to the late 1950s, when the accent was on pocket magazines with a strong humour content. By the early 1960s they had all ceased publishing, more the victims of the publishing mergers of the period rather than the lack of audience.

The re-emergence of magazines which deliberately emphasized 'lifestyle' came with the launches in the 1980s of *Arena* and *The Face*. Their coverage of fashion, films, music and travel was bisexual but with a slight bias towards men. The male magazine sluice gates really opened with the appearance of *GQ* from Condé Nast, a British version of the old-established American title. This was swiftly followed by National Magazine's *Esquire, FHM, Men's Health, XL, Loaded* and *Maxim*. Publishers are always swift to leap on a bandwagon and the sudden surge of men's magazines is as much publishing rivalry as a hungry demand from the male sex for their own magazine capacity.

The men's magazine market has been the success of the 1990s. From a slow beginning of 'style' titles the explosion began with the launch of *Loaded* from IPC – all lads, bosoms and lager – swiftly followed and emulated by *FHM* (regenerated by EMAP) and *Maxim*. *FHM* has broken all circulation records, topping all the other bookstall monthlies, male and female. The six leading titles sell over two million copies and the genre has createn niche titles of the niche. The myth that men don't read magazines, except for sports or hobby titles, is destroyed for ever.

So is the general magazine a lost dinosaur? Such a question seems to be confounded by the phenomenal success of *Reader's Digest*, the monthly title which is the epitome of general interest and sells one million copies a month. The magazine sells a paltry number on the bookstalls – the secret of its success is its cunning and brilliant employment of direct mail techniques, including its occasional sweepstakes. (The jest that it is impossible to get off the subscription list once on it, because of the direct debit system and the publisher's persistence, bears the hallmark of some truth.) Otherwise it is difficult for an objective commentator to assess the widespread reader appeal of comparatively banal editorial to such an historically high audience. The magazine must be the exception that proves the rule.

## General or specialized?

Other magazines with a more general appeal are harder to find. The *Spectator*, originally published in 1828, is doing better than ever with a circulation of 50,000 copies weekly. Although the kernel of the editorial content is political, the magazine carries many features on books, the arts and general comment. It does considerably better than the *New Statesman*, which has declined from its former glory of a 100,000 sale to one-fifth of that figure. *The Economist* is an impressive international success but the content is entirely financial and business comment. *Time* and *Newsweek* (the leading

US news magazines) both have British and European editions but have never achieved the prestige or circulations they would like. Their editorial slant is perhaps too transatlantic.

Europe still publishes its big general magazines in several countries (*Paris Match, Stern*, etc.) but it might be worth noting that television advertising does not have such full rein as it does in the UK or the USA.

Mention has to be made of the television listing magazines, which received a shock when British television programme copyright was 'decontrolled' in the mid-1980s. This meant that all newspapers could carry programme details, which were no longer the exclusive publishing property of either the BBC's *Radio Times* or ITV's *TV Times*. Two more weeklies quickly appeared – *TV Quick* from the German Bauer and *What's On TV* from IPC (who also own *TV Times*). Together they sell over 5 million copies every week, an interesting circulation considering the free and extensive publication of programme details in all the newspapers. But the television magazines run plenty of features about personalities and 'behind the scenes' so one might accept that, in some way, they are lifestyle papers – if you consider television addicts a market segment and watching television a lifestyle.

## Customer magazine growth

Customer magazines, titles which are produced under contract for companies and either distributed free or sold to the customers, have seen a rise in industry turnover of almost 300% since 1990. The editorial and production standards of these titles are high, with Redwood Publishing, John Brown and Premier being three of the largest specialist publishers working for clients. The distribution of the customer magazine has tended to change over recent years with an increasing number of titles distributed at newstands and retail outlets with high cover prices. But the majority of magazines are still mailed or distributed through client outlets. The annual turnover of this sub-industry reached £250 million in 1999 and is fast-growing.

Retail stores, financial institutions, estate agents, airlines, car manufacturers, cable and satellite companies, senior citizen organizations and credit card companies are typical successful and prolific users of customer magazines. The Automobile Association mails nearly four million members and Sky TV sends out to 3.5 million customers every month. *Saga Magazine,* for senior citizen members, goes out to over 800,000 on their mailing list. Marks & Spencer, one of the pioneer users, distributes a million copies – free to card holders and £1 cover price to others. Sainsbury's has an exclusive magazine only on sale in their stores – a glossy product selling over 400,000 copies at the competitive price of £1.

The customer magazine has been one of the most successful sectors of the magazine industry in the 1990s and is destined to considerably expand in the future.

# The future

The future of the magazine industry is bright. The state of the art shows a higher degree of professionalism than ever before, in editorial, business and technology. The rationalization in publishing companies, and the methods of distribution, together with the high standards of the magazines themselves, point the way to an industry which knows where it is going and which has the ability to compete with the 'mega-bucks' poured into the newspaper and electronic media.

Magazines have strategic benefits. We have seen their unique quality of the classification of audiences for the assistance of advertisers and the advantage of their long life when compared to the ephemeral flash of the television or radio commercial or the necessarily limited on-sale period of the daily or Sunday newspaper. Magazines have staying power, quality of presentation, honed editorial talents and the ability to talk to their vertical audiences with authority, energy and a unique one-to-one quality.

The magazine industry is so diverse and so brilliant at finding audiences for the hundreds of categories of literate readers, from the glittering array of the women's market, to sports and hobbies, professional titles, the explosion of computer magazines and the thousands of business-to-business titles covering every trade activity. Perhaps it is the *Hello!* society gossip or the sexual exploits of the *Cosmopolitan* editorial which make the headlines but bear in mind the importance of the trade and professional journals which are required, essential reading in their respective fields. Magazines like *New Scientist, Farmers' Weekly, The Economist, The Lancet, The Builder, Nursing Mirror, The Grocer* and *Caterer and Hotelkeeper*, to take some random examples, uphold the traditions of their own spheres of influence and are paradigms of the unique power and prestige of the magazine business. Right across Europe publishers are providing highly respected professional journals to their industries.

## *Plenty more to come*

There will be plenty of new titles over the years, occasionally replacing more obsolescent ones and sometimes brilliant new ideas to catch the moods of new audiences or new mores. The fact is that people love magazines. The Internet may represent the flashier future but magazines will continue reaching out to their specialized audiences who still enjoy the power of words and pictures. Magazines enjoy a universal marketplace: in 1995 there were 54,000 sales outlets in the UK and the trade expected these to grow by at least another thousand during 1996. The efficacy of magazines as a contact advertisement medium is confirmed by the quality and quantity of response rates obtained by offers and coupons. Magazines have been most creative in exploiting this response factor with imaginative advertising promotional pages, 'widgets', perfume sachets, stick-on reply cards and other aids to easy response.

Sales of magazines will continue to grow, as will the number and variety of titles, despite the millions of 'free' colour magazines given away by the weekend newspapers, often with high editorial quality. But newspapers with their characteristically generalized readerships cannot take the place of magazines with their targeted audiences any more than the electronic media will destroy the printed word.

## Appendix: some 'snapshot' figures

### Numbers of titles

| | |
|---|---|
| Sports | 340 |
| Computer | 48 |
| Motoring | 146 |
| Medical | 580 |
| Social science | 261 |
| Business management | 399 |
| Women's interest | 139 |
| Home interest | 85 |
| County town & local | 187 |
| Travel & tourism | 173 |
| Hobbies | 105 |

(*Source*: BRAD 1998)

### Sources of revenue

| | |
|---|---|
| Consumer magazines: | |
| advertising revenue | 38% |
| circulation revenue | 62% |
| Business and professional: | |
| advertising revenue | 82% |
| circulation revenue | 18% |

### Circulation growth

Since 1991 UK magazine circulation has grown by 23%
Biggest circulation weekly: *What's On TV* 1.7 million
Biggest circulation monthly: *Reader's Digest* 1.3 million
Value of consumer magazine sales in UK: £1.5 billion plus
Consumer magazine publishing receives *c* £900 million net cover price revenue per year.

### Estimated net advertising revenues in UK (1998)

| | |
|---|---|
| All magazines | £1932 million |
| Consumer | £714 million |
| Business/professional | £1218 million |

### Readership

84% of women in UK read a consumer magazine
80% of adults in UK read a consumer magazine
95% of decision makers read relevant business magazine.

## European magazines' share of total advertising revenue (over all other media): 1997

| | |
|---|---|
| Austria | 22.5% |
| Belgium | 22.5% |
| Denmark | 11% |
| France | 28% |
| Germany | 25.2% |
| Greece | 25.2% |
| Ireland | 4.9% |
| Italy | 18.4% |
| Netherlands | 24.8% |
| Norway | 10% |
| Portugal | 10% |
| Spain | 15.3% |
| Sweden | 12.6% |
| Switzerland | 16% |
| UK | 17% |

## Questions

1  You want to launch a new magazine. You can consider consumer, specialized or 'customer'. Will you take the subscription option, newsstand sales or another distribution route? How will you balance the equation between income from cover price and advertisement revenue?

2  Magazines are becoming increasingly international, even in the polyglot European market. How will national publishers cross the European borders in the future, taking into consideration the developments of the past few years?

3  Will magazines survive in the future world of more and more electronic media, including digital TV and The Net? If so, how and why? Can magazine publishers themselves exploit the new technology?

## References

Braithwaite, B. and Barrell, J. (1988) *Business of Women's Magazines*, London: Kogan Page.

*British Rate & Data* (BRAD) (1998) 33–39 Bowling Green Lane, London EC1R 0DA.

Federation of International Publishers, *World Magazine Trends*, London: FIP.

Periodical Publishers Association (PPA), *Magazine Handbook*, London: PPA.

## Further reading

Braithwaite, B. (1996) *Women's Magazines: The First 300 Years*. London: Peter Owen.

Periodical Publishers' Association (1996) *A Career in Magazines*, London: PPA.

Periodical Publisher' Association (1996) *Magazine Magic. A brief summary of the research-based case for consumer magazine advertising*. London: PPA.

Periodical Publisher' Association (1996) *The Power of Business Magazines* (brochure). London: PPA.

Periodical Publishers' Association (1997) *The Magazine Handbook*, London: PPA.

Wharton, J. (1992) *Managing Magazine Publishing*, London; Periodicals Training Council.

*Note*: The address of the PPA, FIPP and PTC is Queen's House, Kingsway, London WC2 6JR. Tel 020 7404 4166; Fax 020 7404 4167; E-mail info1@ppa.co.uk; website www.ppa.co.uk

# Chapter 9

# Radio

RADIO: PUBLIC SERVICE, COMMERCIALISM AND
THE PARADOX OF CHOICE

**ANDREW CRISELL**

Radio is expanding at national, regional and local levels and exploiting the new platforms of cable, satellite, digital technology and the Internet. Yet the range of its content has narrowed. For historical reasons radio has changed from a mixed-programme to a streamed, background medium, and only BBC Radio 4 continues to celebrate its imaginative and intellectual strengths. By resigning 'choice' (an often timid, conservative faculty) to a diet of mixed-programming, its listeners are uniquely enriched.

## Radio at the millennium: sound in health?

On the face of it, radio in Britain is thriving as never before. The publicly funded BBC, which tradition places at the heart of the broadcasting system, has four FM networks, one AM network, and 38 regional and local stations – all of them commanding respectable audiences. The latter are normally calculated in terms of 'weekly reach', the number of people who listen to a particular station for at least five minutes in an average week. At the end of the first quarter of the year 2000 Radio 1's weekly reach was 11.3 million listeners, Radio 2's 10.5 million, Radio 3's 2.1 million, Radio 4's 9 million, and Radio 5 Live's 6.1 million – while the total weekly reach of the regional and local stations was 10.6 million, second only to Radio 1's (source: RAJAR). Since 1995 the Corporation has also offered a digital radio service, a technology which in quality of signal and number of channels offers the same vast opportunities for sound as for vision (Williams 1995: 61).

But thanks to the Broadcasting Act of 1990 the most remarkable expansion of radio has been in the 'independent' or commercial sector. ('Independent' was a sly term devised for commercial television at its inception in the 1950s: the aim was to disguise its money-making intentions and at the same time to imply that its rival was feebly dependent on government largesse!) Whereas in 1984 the public could tune to a mere 48 independent stations, there were 248 by 2000, outnumbering the BBC's by more than six to one.

The expansion of independent radio during the 1990s was significant not just in numerical terms but for the levels of its provision: for the first time in the seventy-year history of British broadcasting listeners could tune in to legal, home-based, *national* commercial stations. Classic FM launched in 1992, Virgin 1215 in 1993, and Talk Radio UK (now broadcasting as TalkSPORT) in 1995. Also for the first time, *regional* commercial stations could be heard, as well as vastly more stations at *local* level. Early in 1995 commercial radio's total audience at last matched that of the BBC, and since November 1999 the commercial sector has also boasted a digital national multiplex service, Digital One. By March 2000 the Radio Authority had awarded 13 local digital multiplexes (source: Radio Authority).

This expansion of the independent sector has brought with it a long-awaited boom in radio advertising (Horsman 1996: 17) and, mercifully, some rise in the production standards of radio commercials. Advertising revenue rose from £141 million in 1992 to £481 million in 2000 (source: Radio Advertising Bureau). Though advertisers tend naturally to exaggerate, their recent promotional slogan for the medium itself seemed no more than the strict truth: 'Commercial radio. It's time has come'. Between 1993 and 1996 the annual increase of revenue was 23%, and radio became an attractive prospect for companies which already had substantial holdings in other media and were keen to expand into new sectors. It was made even more attractive by the Broadcasting Act of 1996, which relaxed most of the remaining rules on cross-media ownership.

Even this is not the full story of radio's recent growth. For some years the Radio Authority has licensed cable and satellite services (by 2000 there were 15 of the former and 19 of the latter), and it has also issued a large number of restricted service licences (RSLs), which allow particular establishments or locations or events to make low-powered broadcasts, usually for a limited period. The main beneficiaries of the RSLs have probably been hospitals and educational establishments.

But without doubt the most important of the recent developments is Internet radio, whose nature and possibilities have been summed up thus:

> [It] enables the output of even the smallest, most localized station to achieve literally worldwide reach – and at relatively little cost. It breaks down the territorial boundaries that have historically restricted a station to a particular catchment area, thus disrupting regulatory controls on scope of operation and content; and it adds value to the station as an advertising vehicle (Barnard 2000: 253).

It is now a commonplace irony that stations which have been issued with RSLs by the Radio Authority can quite legally use the Internet to reach listeners on the far side of the globe and to continue broadcasting long after their RSLs have expired. Though often widely scattered, the audiences for Internet stations are not necessarily large but they gain the potential for interactivity: they can download music and other material, join on-line chat groups, order merchandise.

Yet it must be a matter of some uncertainty whether, in coexisting with computer images, Internet radio *is* radio in the strict sense. Do the images merely complement the radio output or – as may be more likely since sight is our dominant faculty – does the radio output become an adjunct to the images, the mere soundtrack of a broader 'multi-media' experience? Of course, unless we are unsighted or listening with our eyes shut, even traditional radio is a constant accompaniment to the things we are looking at, such as dishes in the sink or traffic on the road ahead. But the crucial point is that its output has *no need of* these images: it is quite unrelated to what we can see – in its own terms, self-sufficient. And this is why, notwithstanding those scholars who discount its significance (Shingler and Weiringa 1998: 1; Crook 1999: 62), blindness is the crucial, indeed determining, feature of the radio medium.

Listeners to Internet radio may, of course, ignore any associated images on their screens or listen to it while accessing other, unrelated material from their computers. But even if we are still happy to regard it as the genuine article there are two reasons why Internet radio might reasonably be omitted from the present study. First, it is for the time being much less portable and flexible than radio which is heard through conventional receivers (although mobile phones linked to the Internet are likely to change this in the very near future). Second, in Britain at least, Internet radio is still listened to by only a fraction of those who tune into the traditional BBC and commercial stations.

For these reasons I shall focus on the familiar BBC/commercial duopoly, which as we have already noted has been marked since the early 1990s by an absolute increase in the number of stations, and for the first time by competition between the sectors at all three geographical levels. But has the numerical increase brought with it a commensurate increase in choice? The answer would appear to be no. Commercial radio has enriched output in one or two areas, notably pop and rock music, but not in many others such as documentary, features, drama, comedy and light entertainment, where the BBC's near-monopoly has been left largely unchallenged.

The apostles of consumer sovereignty, such as Professor Sir Alan Peacock, would be unfazed by this. In 1985 Professor Peacock was appointed by the government to chair a committee to consider new ways of financing the BBC. Though the committee recommended the short-term retention of the Corporation's licence fee it proposed the adoption of subscription funding when more TV and radio channels became available, thus introducing a closer connection between supply and demand (McDonnell 1991: 95–103).

The essence of Peacock's view was that types of programming should stand or fall entirely on the strength of consumer demand for them. However, it could be claimed that demand and choice are a more complex and elusive matter than free market economists might assume – a claim which Peacock half acknowledged when he conceded that consumers are sometimes willing to pay as taxpayers and voters for what they are not prepared to buy as consumers (McDonnell 1991: 99). What we choose and what we esteem are not always the same thing: choice is often made on the basis of ignorance and timidity, of pleasure rather than benefit. We might greatly enjoy or gain from what we would not freely have chosen to listen to, and few would agree with the proposition that the best programme is defined by what is preferred by the greatest number.

However if we look back at the history of broadcasting we can see how a purely quantitative approach to audience choice has led not only to a lack of it with respect to certain *types* of programme but to an overall reduction in the *number* of those programmes. As we noted earlier, only BBC radio continues to broadcast features, plays and comedy, but whereas these could once be found on each of the three networks it operated, they are now largely confined to one: Radio 4.

## Early radio and the 'brute force' of monopoly

Although they have been explored in detail elsewhere (Crisell 1994), we will begin with a brief description of the characteristics of radio. It is an entirely non-visual or 'blind' medium in the sense that it lacks not only the pictures of television or cinema but the visible symbols of print. This means that its messages lack the 'stability' of literary and to some extent television texts since they exist in time rather than space. However one important and invincible advantage of radio is that it is a 'secondary' medium: its messages can easily be absorbed while the person who is receiving them is engaged in some other activity such as driving, cooking or even dozing.

Before the mid-1960s there was a little regional but almost no local radio in Britain: sound broadcasting was mostly conducted on a network or national scale and was the virtual monopoly of the non-commercial British Broadcasting Corporation. However the BBC had originally been a quasi-commercial organization, the British Broadcasting Company, which was itself a consortium of wireless manufacturers such as Marconi, British Thomson Houston, General Electric and Metropolitan Vickers.

With the beginnings of 'wireless' (the older name for radio) in the early 1920s, many of these manufacturers had individually sought broadcasting permits from the Post Office, at that time the government body overseeing public communications, and several were licensed on a temporary and local basis. They wished to broadcast in order to stimulate the sale of their wireless receivers, but the Post Office, fearing the kind of aerial melée which was developing in the USA, where scores of stations were trying to drown one another out of scarce spectrum space, invited the manufacturers to form a single consortium to which it would grant a *de facto* though not a *de jure* monopoly.

The British Broadcasting Company therefore went to air in 1922, but without any government prescription as to what its programmes should consist of. Within the laws of the land, they might be as trivial or populist as the need to sell wireless sets dictated. Nevertheless, the company's first general manager, John Reith, took a rather more elevated and moralistic view of broadcasting's capabilities. He believed that so scarce and precious a form of communication should offer the best of everything to everyone who cared to receive it and quickly evolved a philosophy of what came to be known as 'public service broadcasting'. It had four main tenets (Briggs 1961: 235–8):

1 The British Broadcasting Company, which was largely funded by a licence fee levied on the listeners, did not exist solely to make money. Unlike its constituent companies it did not depend on the profit motive.
2 It aimed to serve everyone in the community who wished to listen.
3 It maintained unified control as a monopoly which would resist sectional pressures, whether commercial or political.
4 It pursued high programming standards, setting out to provide the best of everything.

These tenets, which on 1 January 1927 resulted in the BBC becoming a public corporation, a status it has maintained ever since, were embodied in the principle of *mixed programming*. At first the BBC operated a single network, but soon added a second (known respectively as the National Programme and the Regional Programme); and in 1945–6 it established three: the highbrow Third Programme, the middlebrow Home Service, and the populist Light Programme. But each of these networks contained a variety of output – news, drama, sport, talks, light and classical music, religion, features, light entertainment, specialized programmes for women, children, farmers and so on – in which, during the early years at least, routine scheduling was largely avoided.

The aim of mixed programming was not simply to provide 'something for everyone' but, at whatever level, 'everything for someone': that is, to cater for the particular interests that the individual already had, but also to introduce her to areas of experience she had not previously encountered – to enlarge knowledge and foster new enthusiasms. Though radio was a scarce medium, there was certainly room for more than one broadcaster on the spectrum. But Reith insisted on what he called the brute force of monopoly. If the BBC were allowed a rival, each would be under pressure to maximize its audience by abandoning minority and quality programming and offering merely that which was preferred by the greatest number: or, put the other way round, if the listener were allowed a choice she would be likely to avoid the challenge of new experiences inherent in mixed programming and opt for the less demanding fare that a competitor of the BBC would almost certainly provide. Indeed despite Reith's demands that the monopoly be defended, the BBC was embarrassed before the Second World War by competition from two commercial stations, Radios Normandie and Luxembourg, which were able to circumvent Post Office restrictions by transmitting into Britain from the European mainland.

## Telly versus tranny

The public service notion of mixed programming made good sense as long as radio remained the primary broadcasting medium. But when television overtook it during the 1950s, its audience did not merely decline – it plummeted. By 1959 the average number of the BBC's evening listeners had fallen by five and a half million in ten years (Paulu 1961: 155). If television was both far more popular than radio and had the advantage of vision along with sound, it was a much more appropriate medium for mixed programming. It is true that from 1955 BBC television was exposed to competition from ITV, but since the latter had its own very different source of income the competition was not cut-throat; and in any case ITV was also in some measure bound by the Reithian principles of public service. The question, then, was what role would be left to radio. Would it even disappear altogether?

Fortunately a new technology was at hand which would guarantee the medium's survival yet also help to confirm its secondary role – ensure that it would seldom be the primary object of attention it had often been in the days before television. This new technology was a tiny semiconductor device called a transistor. Previously radio receivers were objects whose size, weight and attachment to aerials and the mains electricity supply made them difficult to move about. They contained valves (known as 'tubes' in America) which looked rather like light bulbs, and when the set was switched on these took time to heat up before anything could be heard. Valves were also fragile and expensive to replace.

The transistor, which was developed in 1947 at Bell Laboratories in the USA, performed all the functions of the valve without any of its disadvantages. It was much smaller, lighter and stronger. It consumed less power, produced less heat, cost less money – and the result was a new generation of radio receivers which could be economically powered by small batteries. They were cheap, light, small, reliable and very easily carried about. The first transistor radio to appear in Britain was made by Pye in 1956 and called 'Pam', and transistor sets soon became so popular that for many years 'tranny' was the main name by which a radio set was known, especially among young people.

The major consequence of the transistor was that it changed the way in which the sound medium was used. In the old days of the immovable mains receiver, wireless was often treated as a background or secondary medium, but also, during leisure periods and in the absence of television, not infrequently used as a focus. In the evenings or at weekends people might choose to do nothing but sit and listen to the radio, or at any rate to do only those things which could accompany the primary business of listening, instead of listening as a merely incidental accompaniment to the primary business of work.

In its leisure role as the main focus of attention radio was, as we have seen, rapidly superseded by television, and the transistor meant that radio was used in an almost entirely secondary way. But it could be so used in many more places and situations than ever before – not just in the kitchen, sitting room or workplace but in the garage, the garden, the countryside, at the beach or in the car. One kind of output which was well suited to secondary listening was, of course, music, and for the inter-mittent attentiveness of so many modern listeners the short and simple tunes of pop music were positively ideal. How convenient, then, that the arrival of rock music should coincide with that of the transistor! For the craze for Elvis Presley and Bill Haley also developed in 1956. By the early 1960s radio's largely musical destiny was becoming steadily clearer (Crisell 1997: 133–8).

Nevertheless the BBC was in a difficult position. Despite its rapidly dwindling radio audience, its *raison d'être* as a public service broadcaster was to provide a range of programming, not just popular music; and in any event the number of records it could play was restricted by Phonographic Performance Limited, the organization which acted on behalf of the record companies and in league with the Musicians' Union. Radio Luxembourg, on the other hand, was bound neither by PPL nor by public service dogma and was much more in touch than the BBC was with contem-porary developments in popular music (Briggs 1979: 759).

Yet Luxembourg was also limited. Its programmes in English were broadcast only during the evenings and its signal in many parts of the country was weak. Those of us who are of a certain age will have vivid memories of being huddled under the bedclothes with a 'tranny', and – we hoped – out of earshot of our parents as we struggled to retune the fading sounds of the Everly Brothers, Jerry Lee Lewis, Little Richard and Buddy Holly.

As is well known, it was the arrival of the offshore pirate stations in 1964 which most clearly signposted the future of radio. Their growth and impact has already been much chronicled (for example, Harris 1970; Baron 1975; Chapman 1992). Here it must suffice to say that as typified by the two most successful, Radio Caroline and Radio London, they were professional and highly commercial operations, and most were not only dedicated to pop music but based their playlists on the current Top 40. Presented at last with a choice between two clearly audible kinds of sound broadcasting, millions of listeners rallied to the Jolly Roger, putting the conservative programming policy of the BBC under ever severer strain.

The Labour government of Harold Wilson swept the pirates off the air with the Marine Broadcasting (Offences) Act of 1967, but only on the understanding that the BBC would satisfy the huge demand they had created, or at least identified. Its response was to launch a streamed pop music network, Radio 1, on one of the Light Programme's old frequencies. The other three networks were renamed Radios 2, 3 and 4, but for a further two and a half years continued to offer mixed programming. Hence public service broadcasting was there if you wanted it, and not if you didn't: but since, as we have seen, this kind of choice was inimical to public service in its original Reithian form, there was a sense in which it had disappeared altogether.

## One, two, three – format!

In April 1970 Radios 2 and 3 also moved into streamed, specialized programming, the former offering mostly middle-of-the-road, the latter mostly classical, music. BBC local radio, which had begun in Leicester in 1967, was already confined mainly to sequences of information and light music, so Radio 4 remained the only repository of mixed programming – news and current affairs, talks and discussions, drama, documentaries and features, special interest programmes, comedy shows, quiz games – though it broadcast very little music. Thus although programme variety was lost at highbrow and populist levels it persisted on Radio 4: but if the networks were taken as a whole, there was clearly much less of it than before.

The streaming or specialization of output became known during the 1970s as 'format radio'. As has already been hinted, the ideal material for formats is music, but certain kinds of speech content, notably rolling news or current affairs, also suit the routinized, background use to which radio is often put. In essence 'rolling news' consists of a sequence of segments, some updated and some simply repeated – headlines, weather forecasts, traffic and travel information, stock market bulletins, interviews, correspondents' reports – these catering for the intermittent listener in the way that pop songs do.

In fact the trend towards formats has been all but unstoppable. When independent local radio (ILR) began in 1973, its regulator, the Independent Broadcasting Authority, was expected by the government to impose public service requirements on the stations in the form of some programming variety. Such variety was, however, completely at odds with commercial radio's need to target consumers, and in order to stay afloat most of the stations soon moved to (mainly pop and Top 40) formats, with the reluctant consent of the Authority. BBC Radio 5 tried to buck the trend in 1990 by launching as a mixed programme channel, but it failed to win a coherent audience and was obliged to relaunch four years later as a news and sport format.

Within the huge majority of stations that are now formatted, a further large majority are devoted to mainstream pop, whether chart (Radio 1 and most ILR stations); adult rock (Virgin Radio and the Irish-based Atlantic 252); or golden oldies (the 'Gold' stations on AM, most of them ILR operations). Some stations offer specialist or ethnic music (Classic FM, Jazz FM, Asian Sound Radio, Choice FM), and yet others offer speech formats, such as News Direct and TalkSPORT.

Although in the provision of pop music there is a greater diversity than before (yet not, perhaps, quite the diversity that is implied by the proliferation of names: indie, reggae, ragga, house, trance, garage, hip-hop, jazz-funk, punk, nu-metal, rap-metal, etc.), it is hard to see how formats have increased or even matched the overall range of output which was once provided by three BBC networks; and even if they have, they are individually uniform and predictable in what they provide. This is, of course, their whole point: it is always open to the individual to introduce her own element of relief or variety by tuning to another channel. But what is largely lost is, as we shall see, the exposure to new radio experiences *by chance*.

## The polarities of modern radio

We might plot the position of the various radio stations along two axes. The first axis is *national*, or network, and *local* (regional is a third category, though one which makes little difference to the discussion that follows); and the second axis is *format* and *mixed programme*.

In Britain, home-based commercial radio began at local level: there was no national station until 1992. Why? Part of the reason was to parallel the already regional nature of commercial television, which had itself been something of a reaction to what was seen in the 1950s as the excessively centralized, metropolitan nature of the BBC. But the main reason was to exploit the modern technology of VHF/FM, which would allow a large number of stations on to the spectrum and give advertisers the opportunity to target local as well as national markets. There was also the hope that the system would yield locally originated programming and even afford broadcasting access to local listeners.

Virtually all the stations do carry local elements: news, sport, phone-ins, advertising; but as the preponderance of pop music formats implies, the pull of cosmopolitan culture is almost irresistible. Whether in Cornwall or Durham, ILR is, like McDonald's hamburgers, a reassuringly uniform experience, its music originating in neither and mediated by mostly 'accentless' presenters whose pleasantries and platitudes seldom assume a knowledge of the locality or its culture.

This relative absence of local flavour has largely been matched by a lack of local ownership. Colin Seymour-Ure points out (1996: 84) that there was at first a fair spread of local investors in ILR, including the press, but that as the stations became quoted on the Stock Exchange their ownership dispersed and with it their local character. Later, as market competition and economies of scale began to take effect, ownership became concentrated among a few large groups: Crown Communications and Capital Radio during the 1980s and later Capital, the East Midlands Allied Press (EMAP) and Great Western Radio (GWR). It has been tersely observed that independent local radio is now

> anything but: GWR's portfolio of stations embraces localities as different as Bournemouth and Coventry, Norwich and Gloucester, while EMAP and Capital each have a brand of stations (Magic and Gold respectively) that do not even identify their locality in their name (Barnard 2000: 61).

Broadcasting technology itself conspires with concentration of ownership to work against localism and individuality in programme origination, for the output of a local station which is part of a group can in theory originate from another station in the group which may be on the far side of the country. It is common practice, especially for transmission at the dead of night, for the principal station of an ILR group to feed its computerized output to all the other stations, where the lack of localness may be disguised by the insertion of local commercials and sometimes also by an '0800' number which listeners can use to telephone their 'local' presenter situated fifty or more miles away. We might describe this as networking by stealth or as a kind of syndication, the process by which whole programme packages are centrally produced and pre-recorded and then delivered to a spread of local stations. Syndication has long been a feature of local broadcasting in the USA (Fornatale and Mills 1980: 143–5; Tunstall 1986: 153).

It seems fair to say that BBC local radio, with its news and chat programmes, phone-ins and reports on neighbourhood issues, has focused to a much greater extent on the communities it serves than ILR has. Nevertheless it has been dogged by difficulties. In an organization which has always been highly centralized on London and whose great achievements have been on a national or even international scale, it seems all but a contradiction in terms.

Not surprisingly, local radio has never been able to claim a high priority within the BBC. It has been poorly funded, and to minimize costs many of its stations form regional networks during off-peak listening periods. Though the aggregate audience of BBC local radio looks large, it is also true to say that the listening figures for some of its stations are fairly modest. Moreover, there is a common impression both outside and inside the Corporation that it became involved in local radio not through any ideological commitment but in order to exploit VHF/FM technology and pre-empt the influence of ILR, and that it maintains its involvement only because local radio feeds the networks with news stories, programme ideas and promising young journalists and production staff. The problems of BBC local radio have hardly changed since they were acutely summarized many years ago (Lewis and Booth 1989: 95).

If from the standpoint of the listener 'national' has largely overshadowed 'local', whether institutionally, as in the case of the BBC, or in the sense that the content of ILR is largely indistinguishable from that of the networks, we might also say that 'format' has almost totally extinguished 'mixed programming'. Except on one network . . .

## What is this Radio 4?

The only network which offers anything like the old Reithian programme diet is Radio 4, and even here there is a virtual absence of music. There is also some output, notably *Today* in the early morning, which does not so much resemble programmes in the traditional sense as the kinds of rolling sequence that we expect from stations broadcasting an all-news format.

Nevertheless Radio 4 swims against the current of modern radio in a highly distinctive and significant way, and it is worrying that the BBC's own management seemed not to recognize this when it decided during the 1990s to combine radio and television within a single administration.

The network is distinctive first of all because in the variety and nature of its output it presupposes a *listener*, not someone for whom radio is merely a noise in the background. Certainly there are aspects of both its form and content which acknowledge the likely secondariness of its consumption (traffic information for motorists is only one obvious example); but it is one of the few surviving stations which would not dissatisfy anyone who chose to treat its output as primary.

Certain of its programme genres paradoxically demonstrate radio's strengths by pushing against its limitations. Drama, which is normally a spectacle, something to be watched, thrives here by stretching the listener's imagination. Comedy, another genre which normally depends on the visual, must on radio literally live by its wits – survive on its more cerebral ability to create laughter through words alone. What Radio 4 does above all is to reclaim for its audiences, situated as they are at the end of several centuries of a predominantly 'literate' culture, something of the archaic value and pleasure of listening to 'talk' or speech.

Because we inhabit a culture of writing and print many of us feel that there is something trivial and self-indulgent about talk. In much broadcasting it is often apologetically referred to as 'chat'. But the value of orality is something quite distinct from, if equivalent to, that of literacy (Ong 1982: 31–77): it is language which is *dynamic* – inflected by the human voice and personality and often under pressure from thought or emotion rather than lying disembodied on the page. This dynamism is an important element in any kind of spoken language – interviews, discussion, argument, persuasion, explanation, anecdotes, jokes, sustained narratives – whether it is language which has never been anything other than speech or language which originated as writing.

Radio 4's *From Our Own Correspondent*, a collection of reports by its foreign news staff, is a type of programme which might seem to be better suited to the print medium, but few who hear it would agree. It is a classic instance of the peculiar power of the spoken word. Its reports, perhaps of a certain situation in Africa or Eastern Europe, typically comprise a vivid physical description – the sights, sounds and smells of the situation – together with certain more abstract observations of a social or political nature. Yet because the reports are spoken, everything seems to be transfigured by the correspondent's own consciousness and personality in a way which is much less obvious in the 'objective' medium of print. As well as accent and voice tone, we are acutely aware of the correspondent's choice of language, intellectual cast of mind, and the peculiar impression which the situation has made upon him or her.

Of course, television also offers the benefits and pleasures of 'talk', providing its own correspondents' reports, discussion programmes and much else besides, but not in an equivalent way. Radio talk is often 'secondary' in the sense that the listener hears it while doing something else, but paramount on its own terms because the medium is blind: with the possible exception of some accompanying noises which must in any case be verbally identified, words are all there is. Unlike television's, they are not drowned in an often superfluous visuality.

It is precisely this abstract quality of radio – its focus on language to the exclusion of almost all else – which makes it potentially a much more *intellectual* medium than television. Since it is mostly renowned for the banal chatter of its myriad music presenters, this may seem an astonishing claim to make. Yet it is supported by a look at the schedule for one random yet typical day on Radio 4: 29 June 2000. Among other offerings were an edition of *From Our Own Correspondent*; an examination of Singapore's new economic strategy in *In Business*, of cot deaths in *Leading Edge*, and of why musicians are reworking J. S. Bach in *Front Row*, and a discussion of legal issues in *Law in Action*, consumer issues in *You and Yours*, and of whether sex is an evolutionary necessity in *The Material World*. The primary point here is not that radio can be interesting, although the casual listener could hardly fail to be stimulated by some of this content, but that it is capable of being highly conceptual.

Yet Radio 4 is distinctive and significant not just because so many of its individual programmes are substantial enough to be listened to and not merely heard, but because of the overall *range* or variety of its programmes. It seems fair to say that no independent radio station could deliver such range because the lifeblood of commercialism is format: by typifying content you can typify the listener and deliver her to the advertiser. As Fornatale and Mills argue (1980: 61), differing formats are devised not to provide diversity for its own sake, nor in response to any government regulator's requirement, nor – in essence – to satisfy listeners' demands. They exist simply in order 'to deliver to advertisers a measured and defined group of consumers, known as a segment', and it is not surprising that the history of radio formats is closely linked to the history of market research.

In complete contrast, Radio 4 is built round the essentially Reithian principle of serendipity, the faculty of discovering pleasing or valuable things by chance. In a curious way the listener who chooses Radio 4 *resigns* the principle of choice in order to gain a less predictable, more varied and ultimately richer experience. From this it is apparent that although public service broadcasting is so often discussed in terms of television, it has a special relevance to radio. Though TV formats are on the increase, mixed programming remains more widespread on television than on radio; but from a modern public service point of view it makes rather less sense, since viewers are much more attentive and active in the use of their medium and can obtain as much variety as they feel they need by switching channels.

However, few take the trouble to switch channels on the radio because listening is generally secondary to some other activity. They are thus more likely to be exposed to fresh things by chance and to persevere with them – which makes mixed programming on the sound medium an especially valuable asset.

We will recall from its origins that what is of real importance about the mixed programming of Radio 4 is not its variety *per se* but the social and psychological values that underlie it. In fact the social context of radio is worth special study, not simply at the demographic level – which socio-economic groups listen to what stations? – but at the philosophical level. What do the different stations posit about human psychology and about what used to be called, in more generalizing times, human nature?

The commercial strategy of format, by ostensibly elevating individual autonomy and the principle of consumer choice, actually seems to take a reductive, deterministic view of human behaviour. It assumes that the individual is significant or definable only in terms of one particular interest or preoccupation, and that free choice is usually timid and conservative. Choice resists plenitude, settles for what is easy and familiar, declines to acknowledge the value of new experience or the possibility that benefit may sometimes be different from pleasure. Consequently, given a certain type of content, you can confidently predict that so many thousands or millions will listen to it.

Mixed programming, on the other hand, requires the listener's passive, old-fashioned submission to a selection of material which is made by others who presumably 'know better', the acceptance of a hierarchy of expertise and values which neatly complements the patrician approach of the early BBC. But its ultimate consequence is intellectual enlargement, the exposure to a much wider range of knowledge and experience, and thus the basis for autonomy of another kind. Mixed programming exalts the individual because it assumes that in the potentially infinite nature of their interests, listeners transcend the simple categories of market research: they are human beings even more than they are 'types of consumer'.

Radio may now be the Cinderella medium. Despite the proliferation of networks and stations there seems to have been an overall shrinkage of its content. Yet it still affords much food for thought, its inherent characteristics placing it at the heart of the public service debate.

## Questions

1   Most television commercials make great use of the varied visual resources of the medium. Select a radio commercial which in your opinion effectively compensates for, or even exploits, sound broadcasting's lack of vision, explaining how you think it does so.

2   Listen over a period of time to the output of Classic FM and then attempt some detailed analysis of it. In its presentation and promotion of classical music how far does the station resemble, how far differ from, a conventional pop music station, and what can you infer about the identity of its target audience?

3   Listen to a studio discussion programme on the radio and then watch a similar programme on the television. What difference did the visual dimension make? In enabling you to distinguish the speakers more clearly do you feel that it enhanced or detracted from your concentration on, and understanding of, the issues that were being discussed?

# References

Baron, M. (1975) *Independent Radio*, Lavenham: Dalton.

Barnard, S. (2000) *Studying Radio*, London: Edward Arnold.

Briggs, A. (1961) *The History of Broadcasting in the United Kingdom, Volume 1: The Birth of Broadcasting*, London: Oxford University Press.

Briggs, A. (1979) *The History of Broadcasting in the United Kingdom, Volume 4: Sound and Vision*, Oxford: Oxford University Press.

Chapman, R. (1992) *Selling the Sixties: The Pirates and Pop Music Radio*, London: Routledge.

Crisell, A. (1994) *Understanding Radio*, 2nd edn, London: Routledge.

Crisell, A. (1997) *An Introductory History of British Broadcasting*, London: Routledge.

Crook, T. (1999) *Radio Drama: Theory and Practice*, London: Routledge.

Fornatale, P. and Mills, J. (1980) *Radio in the Television Age*, Woodstock, NY: The Overlook Press.

Harris, P. (1970) *When Pirates Ruled the Waves*, 4th edn, London and Aberdeen: Impulse Books.

Horsman, M. (1996) 'On radio advertising's boom', *The Independent Section Two* 16 April: 17.

Lewis, P. M. and Booth, J. (1989) *The Invisible Medium: Public, Commercial and Community Radio*, London: Macmillan.

McDonnell, J. (1991) *Public Service Broadcasting: A Reader*, London: Routledge.

Ong, W. (1982) *Orality and Literacy*, London: Methuen.

Paulu, B. (1961) *British Broadcasting in Transition*, Minneapolis: University of Minnesota Press.

Radio Advertising Bureau web site: www.rab.co.uk

Radio Authority web site: www.radioauthority.org.uk

RAJAR (Radio Joint Audience Research) web site: www.rajar.co.uk

Seymour-Ure, C. (1996) *The British Press and Broadcasting Since 1945*, 2nd edn, Oxford: Basil Blackwell.

Shingler, M. and Weiringa, C. (1998) *On Air: Methods and Meanings of Radio*, London: Edward Arnold.

Tunstall, J. (1986) *Communications Deregulation*, Oxford: Basil Blackwell.

Williams, R. (1995) 'BBC switches on CD-quality radio', *The Independent* 28 September: 6.

# Further reading

Barnard, S. (1989) *On the Radio: Music Radio in Britain*, Milton Keynes: Open University Press. An extended study, with substantial historical backgrounding, of the ways in which British radio stations exploit popular music.

Barnett, S. and Morrison, D. (1989) *The Listener Speaks: The Radio Audience and the Future of Radio*, London: HMSO Books. A profile of the characteristic uses to which its listeners put radio. Also suggests that there are six different strands of public service broadcasting which have a particular significance for the medium.

Briggs, A. (1995) *The History of Broadcasting in the United Kingdom, Volume 5: Competition 1955–1974*, Oxford: Oxford University Press. This final volume of what, despite the title, is almost exclusively a history of the BBC gives a useful account of the launch of Radio 1 and of the reorganization of BBC network radio in 1970.

BBC (1969) *Broadcasting in the Seventies*, London: British Broadcasting Corporation. Explains the BBC's proposals to convert its old mixed programme networks, Radios 2, 3 and 4 (formerly the Light Programme, Third Programme and Home Service), into networks which were for the most part streamed and specialized.

Donovan, P. (1992) *The Radio Companion*, London: Grafton. An alphabetical guide to radio from its inception to the beginning of the 1990s. Contains entries on many of the historical matters referred to in this chapter.

Franklin, B. (1997) *Newszak and News Media*, London: Edward Arnold. A lively if pessimistic account of the way in which the newly deregulated media landscape has forced the news to become more populist. Includes a brief history of radio's broad transition from public service to market-driven medium.

Montgomery, M. (1986) 'DJ talk', *Media, Culture and Society* (8): 421–40. An illuminating analysis of how the presenter's monologue on music radio differs from other forms of radio talk.

Moss, P. and Higgins, C. (1984) 'Radio voices', *Media, Culture and Society* (4): 353–75. Explains that talk on the radio differs from other forms of talk because of the demands placed on it by the special character of the medium.

O'Sullivan, T., Dutton, B. and Rayner, P. (1994) *Studying the Media*, London: Edward Arnold. A helpful survey which shows how radio fits into the contemporary media landscape.

Peacock, A. *et al.* (1986) *Report of the Committee on Financing the BBC*, Cmnd 9824. Advocates a system of broadcasting which gives sovereignty to the choices of the consumer. Yet also acknowledges that certain forms of output cannot be provided by the market but are sometimes willingly supported by the consumer in her/his alternative guise of taxpayer and voter.

Reith, J. (1924) *Broadcast Over Britain*, London: Hodder and Stoughton. Reith's first attempt to articulate his philosophy of 'public service' broadcasting. Insists that while seeking to provide something of high quality for everyone, such broadcasting must not be constrained by the vagaries of consumer choice.

Scannell, P. (ed.) (1991) *Broadcast Talk*, London: Sage Publications. A collection of essays which analyse the character and purposes of talk in radio and television and suggest its overall importance.

Scannell, P. and Cardiff, D. (1982) 'Serving the nation: public service broadcasting before the War' in B. Waites, T. Bennett and G. Martin (eds) *Popular Culture: Past and Present*, London: Croom Helm. A fascinating account of how the 'public service' ideal was realized in the early BBC, but also of its gradual attenuation in the form of increased programme streaming during the 1930s and early 1940s.

# Chapter 10

# Television

A FRAMEWORK FOR ANALYSING CONTEMPORARY TELEVISION

## RICHARD PATERSON

Television is in transition throughout the world. The structures and organizational patterns of the days of spectrum scarcity, when television channels were only allocated a small part of the radio spectrum for broadcasting analogue signals, are fast becoming a distant memory. Digital television is now operational, the age of e-commerce is evolving very rapidly and the days of dominance of public service broadcasters in Europe are over. What analytical framework can we bring to bear on these changes in the TV industry which can explain its operations in the past, the present and the future?

In recent years the television industry has been marked by constant revolution. Until the late 1980s, in the UK and Europe, there had been a relatively settled regulatory and organizational structure based on a perceived scarcity of spectrum. The advent of first satellite transmission and later digital transmission increased the number of channels which could be delivered to viewers at an economic cost and led to a rapid proliferation of services. Market rules began to have a major effect on the television industry for the first time as competition between broadcasters intensified. In the UK, after an initial period of high risk investment, BSkyB emerged as the financially strongest TV company by the late 1990s only to come under pressure from competitors as digital television emerged across three platforms: digital satellite, digital terrestrial and digital cable. BSkyB's position, based on its dominance of the satellite market through providing the leading film and sports channels, with an increasing number of long-term exclusive deals with many of the leading sports and a virtual monopoly on licensing deals with the Hollywood studios, was put under pressure as market relationships evolved and it was forced to invest heavily to maintain its competitive position. Little original programming was produced in the early years of satellite operation with the exception of news and sports programming, as the satellite channels relied heavily on imports of fiction and entertainment programmes from the USA. The cable industry, after a slow beginning, also began actively to build its market share as a means of distribution and a greater concentration of ownership emerged. The launch of digital terrestrial television created another means of multi-channel distribution. The wider market for film and television evolved rapidly as telecommunications advances (such as streamed video on the Internet or through phone lines) enabled moving-image content to be distributed in new ways to consumers.

The terrestrial broadcasting companies in both the public and private sectors have had to respond to these developments. In the late 1990s there was continuing concentration in the commercial television sector in the UK with a series of takeovers of ITV franchises by the larger companies so that by summer 2000 there were two dominant companies (Carlton and Granada), as the franchise rules of only a few years were overturned by government keen to enable UK companies to achieve global economic success.

All television companies have been forced continually to evaluate the range of businesses in which they operate. The ITV companies' important competitive advantage has always been based on their dominant position in advertising sales. Their licences require them to use their privileged position to commission and produce high-quality and high-cost programmes which both mirror British society in its regional diversity and are attractive to viewers. Channel 4 has built an audience with a young and affluent demographic profile much desired by advertisers and found itself with a large revenue flow allowing it to plan new digital ventures and secure important US programming and sports rights. Strategy reviews have become endemic inside the BBC, as it has positioned itself for the competitive market. It retains the proceeds of the licence fee and continues to operate under a Royal Charter which empowers and obliges it to produce a diverse range of programming, but has been criticized by its competitors for unfair competition in providing a 24-hour news service and for its online activities. The BBC's 'new media' initiatives have been adroitly constructed to enable maximum impact in deploying its services through new outlets.

The far reaching changes in British television in the late 1990s led to repeated calls for changes to the regulatory structure. In 2000 the Government proposed the creation of a single regulator for the broadcasting and telecommunications industries (OFCOM) to provide a uniformity of approach across economic and content issues in the age of convergence.

This chapter provides a model for understanding contemporary television in Europe and the UK, and then briefly describes the changing structures, programming and audience response. What has been lacking heretofore in much media studies is an analytical framework which identifies the 'business' (or more accurately the 'businesses') of television. The basic analytical tool which I propose to introduce here is the 'value chain'. A common enough concept in any study of industry, it has great power in explaining significant relationships within the audio-visual industry. In particular, it enables an examination of the changing nature of television, and of the income streams for software, in the emerging digital domain.

## Value chain – an overview

The value chain model analyses the media industries as a series of interrelated but discrete activities, like most other industries. This value chain can be broken down in many ways but for the sake of this argument it can be understood as follows:

Contributors and rights holders → Content creation/programme making →
→ Broadcasting/Distribution → Gateway → Audience

Key terms of the value chain model may be defined as follows:

- **Gateway:** Advances in technology have resulted in a direct relationship
  between the broadcaster and the consumer using subscriber management
  and conditional access systems which enables only those who have paid a
  subscription to view the transmitted television signal. This is called a gateway.
- **Distribution:** In television the act of distribution has normally been called
  transmission and in the UK was dependent on scarce radio spectrum until
  satellite technologies allowed new services to be provided direct to the home
  or via a cable network.
- **Vertical integration:** Companies which have activities in different parts of the
  value chain are vertically integrated. So, for example, the BBC or Granada
  Media have both production activities and run television channels – they are
  vertically integrated companies.
- **Contributors and rights holders:** The key to any television programme is the
  ideas and those who realize them through their creative endeavour. With
  'ideas' come rights – intellectual property rights – which are protected by
  copyright and related laws to protect the interests of rights holders.
- **Content creation/programme making:** The makers of a programme – a
  production company – will take ideas and invest to create a programme.
  The source of the investment will vary – usually in the UK programmes are
  commissioned by one of the channels for their own schedule and they will
  retain the right to distribute the resulting production. With escalating costs
  there has been an increasing reliance on partnership funding through presales
  particularly of drama and high-cost documentaries, while format sales have
  increased in importance.
- **Regulation:** The need for a regulatory framework was initially based on the
  perception of television's political importance at a time when only a limited
  spectrum was available. Latterly the concern has become more oriented to
  business matters (which arguably could be as well monitored through
  competition law) with an increasing pressure to deregulate in content matters.

Until recent changes affected the place of the integrated 'broadcaster' in the value
chain there had been a relatively settled situation and spectrum space was allocated
because of its deemed 'scarcity'. In Britain, which introduced commercial television
in 1955, there was a division of the sources of income between the BBC and ITV –
respectively the licence fee and advertising revenue. For commercial broadcasters,
which were invariably vertically integrated organizations, profit margins were adequate,
indeed substantial. Individual companies were able to sustain their businesses and in
particular, the larger television companies like Granada Media produced, broadcast
and distributed their programmes within the regulated and protected broadcasting
economy. For ITV companies, the emphasis on the local flavour of their services was
paramount (and a licence requirement). However, these monopolies, or cartels, came
under increasing economic pressure from the mid-1980s onwards from various quarters.

In the UK this had started with the legislation setting up Channel 4 in 1981. Its remit included a requirement that the channel should give access to new voices and, in particular, that programmes should mostly be sourced from independent producers. When the Peacock Committee (ostensibly set up to report on the future financing of the BBC) suggested in 1987 a minimum 40% quota of independent productions on ITV and the BBC, the place of the independent producers in the UK television industry, or at least those that could survive the difficulties of uncertain commissions and low capitalization, was confirmed.

The independent sector grew rapidly in the 1980s until it was estimated there were more than 1000 independent production companies in existence by the early 1990s, most very small operations run by people who would find work as freelancers in between occasional commissions. Channel 4 continued to be the main source of commissions for smaller independents after 1990 with both the BBC and ITV (effectively forced to take 25% of independent productions by the 1990 Broadcasting Act), as well as Sky and other satellite channels, commissioning from relatively few, and usually larger, independent production companies. These larger companies have become better capitalized and some have ceased being 'independent' following the acquisition of equity stakes by broadcasters.

It was the introduction of a number of new means of broadcast distribution – satellite and cable – which disrupted the so-called cosy duopoly of BBC and ITV and then the value chain in British television. The new subscription gateway, requiring the provision of decoders, subscriber management and billing, underpinned the increasing financial strength of BSkyB as satellite penetration and later cable build increased. The value to be extracted and the distribution of power and profit across the chain have continued to change radically as control of the gateway to individuals and their ability to pay for TV programmes has become a new high-profit business. Furthermore, these changes are expected to become of increasing importance as they provide access to invaluable market information about consumer tastes as well as the pay-per-view market for premium programming.

The growth of a digital market – in its initial stages of development hugely subsidized – has provided a further range of competition with ITV Digital offering digital terrestrial television in competition with digital satellite and digital cable. Cable's natural advantage in delivering broadband services with interactivity has not been exploited in the UK due in part to fragmentation of ownership at a critical juncture in the developing competitive framework, but with the growing importance of e-commerce and its ability to deliver fast Internet access, this may change.

With the emergence of a highly competitive market in broadcasting, companies have constantly assessed their business strategies in the light of uncertainty over the future value of infrastructure, of distribution channels and of the content. Some believe ownership of content remains the fundamental to income generation so that the exploitation of rights in libraries of programming and new programming is seen as the key to profitability. However, the re-emergence of vertically integrated companies confirms the strength of a business strategy in which a company produces content as well as distributes it to viewers. Various large mergers in the international market including those of ABC and Disney, AOL and Time Warner, and Vivendi and Universal are based on this strategy. The competition authorities have taken alarm at the possibility that larger and more powerful conglomerates might gain a stranglehold on the market, with additional sensitivity because of the 'propaganda' fears associated with media ownership. In Europe, in both national parliaments and in the European Commission this has led to proposals for new regulations. However, in these times of rapid change, views have moved towards accepting further conglomeration as the ability for companies to compete in global markets has become seen as a central factor to economic success.

Such situations of increased market power of media companies have emerged before, particularly in the USA, and have led to action by competition authorities: the forced divestment of cinema theatres by Paramount in the late 1940s resulted from earlier fears of market domination; the introduction in the 1970s of the finance and syndication rule to prevent the networks dominating programme production. In Europe, however, there has never, until recently, been the potential for such market influence beyond national borders across the European audio-visual market, in part because of the previous dominance of a public service orientation in most European broadcasters (see Negrine, Chapter 16 in this volume). In the UK the constant lament that British companies seem to lack sufficient size to compete in global markets has led to an encouragement of mergers. In Europe the Granada Media Group is emerging as a potential global player alongside RTL (in which Pearson have a major share and which controls Britain's Channel 5) and Endemol (owned by Telefonica, the Spanish telecommunications group). Many of these groups are looking to exploit content through services over the Internet as well as through television.

The value chain is being pressured and altered because of new and different expectations of audience behaviour, with increasing competition for people's leisure time, and new relationships are being forged between companies in content and production, distribution and consumption.

## Key analytical issues

### *What is the business?*

At its simplest the television business is about making programmes and giving audiences the opportunity to view. However, as the supply chain model shows, this conceals a range of discrete businesses which have come under scutiny in an age of convergence. The uncertainties in organizations within the television industry about their future positioning in the market has led to a variety of strategies and to a range of changing alliances. These strategies are based on assumptions about the future economic drivers of markets and the need to align company strategy to maximize profitability. The competitive drivers in the industry are now constantly being reassessed with particular interest in the challenge of Internet delivery and its relationship to traditional broadcasting activity.

The control of rights in material is now generally recognized as of immense value within the audio-visual sector. In this regard, it is important to recognize that programme production requires conditions which sustain creativity and innovation in order to create cultural and commercial value, which in turn depends on the skills of the workforce to create images and representations that audiences want to watch.

It is the control of the gateway to services which provides the means to address audiences and access to their buying power. Programme production does not, in itself, add significant economic value but it remains critical in providing the material which will attract eyeballs (either paying ones or ones the advertisers themselves are wanting to speak to).

The development of an individualized gateway to members of the audience has induced businesses to begin to invest in new services. The involvement in television of telecommunication companies, each of which has enormous potential economic power but little knowledge of the value-added markets, of which the media is clearly one, has become highly significant. The change in relationships between companies is understood as convergence between formerly separate industries because of technological and organizational change, but in fact it is a convergence where the main interest of companies is where value will be added (and high profits can be made) in the future. Convergence has both economic and cultural consequences. Mergers have created companies with interests spanning areas such as telecommunications, on-line services, production, television channels and music. The regulatory authorities in Europe and the USA have intervened to prevent market dominance particularly when there is a likelihood of undue influence in particular sectors of the market.

One of the most significant political and cultural consequence of the new market realities will be their effect and lasting influence on public sector broadcasters as they engage with ever greater competitive forces. The picture remains complex and its outcome uncertain but the new age of multi-channel television will almost certainly have a fundamental long-term effect on programming and channel scheduling. Generalist channels like BBC 1 and ITV may survive for some time but their ability to attract large numbers of viewers and to afford to commission first-run high-cost drama might reduce over time as premium services emerge for which subscribers are willing to pay extra. Sport is sometimes seen as the precursor of many other genres in its biddability to the richest provider. There are no certainties in the competitive marketplace. There is a mix of evidence about audience behaviour. While there is evidence of an inertia of most viewers' habits, younger viewers are less hidebound by tradition and are more likely to use a range of niche channels to satisfy their needs. Higher-quality programming *may* be the long-term outcome as channels begin to compete for viewers, but equally there might be a reduction in programme quality as smaller audiences fail to support bigger-budget productions. It seems certain, however, that as the number of channels increases with the huge additional capacity provided by digital broadcasting we can expect to see ever more niche channels targeted at specialist audience groups.

If commercial companies have been concerned about future profitability the BBC has been concerned with its legitimacy and its future role in the new broadcasting environment. The BBC has a central place in British television but recognized both a political threat and new commercial imperatives in the early 1990s following the introduction of a 25% independent production quota. An internal market was introduced and a major restructuring ensued in 1996 into five Divisions (Broadcast, Production, News, Resources and Worldwide). The BBC redefined its core operations into the key parts of the broadcasting value chain. The new Director-General modified this structure in 2000 and began to rebuild the programme-making capabilities. Partnerships with the private sector have been used to develop the exploitation of BBC resources inside and outside the UK.

## Old models in Europe – public service and private

European television was distinctive in its public service orientation until the 1980s. Even in the UK, which had pioneered commercial television in the 1950s, this was undertaken within a definitive public service mode which obliged the ITV companies to provide a range of high-quality programmes in return for their monopoly in the sale of television advertising.

The economic model was based on a vertical integration which allowed programme making to develop within the broadcasting organization. That a TV service was many businesses (production, facilities, broadcasting and transmission) was masked by the priority given to the cultural or public service mission of television in Europe and the lack of competition and consequent protection of the different parts of the business. Despite the political support for public service broadcasting its role in the digital age is likely to remain in question for some time.

When a vital independent production sector re-emerged in Britain in the 1980s it created first uncertainty and then led to the gradual erosion of the duopoly's control. The certainties for the commercial ITV companies were swept away. A system based on monopsony and cartelization, in 'competition' with the BBC, had been justified culturally into the mid-1980s but in fact had become extremely inefficient.

> **Cartel:** A cartel is formed when a group of companies combine to exclude competition and maintain an agreed level of price of a good.
>
> **Monopsony:** A monopsony exists when there is one buyer and many sellers – a condition which pertained in UK commercial television until the early 1980s.

The justification for limited channel availability was technological and based on the limited radio spectrum available. Rationing broadcasting licences was necessary because of the need to plan frequency use and achieve near-universal service across the country (the fundamental access principle of public service broadcasting). But the elite position of television had led to an increasing range of interests – both commercial and cultural – calling for change. The recommendations of the Annan Committee on the Future of Broadcasting (1977) for an Open Broadcasting Authority led to the decisions in 1981 by the Conservative government to create Channel 4 with a remit to encourage a range of different voices on television. This model cleverly blended enough certainty for the ITV companies (who funded the channel's inception but sold and retained advertising revenue until 1992) with an opening for a new and vibrant 'independent' production sector.

New possibilities for additional channels were opened up in Britain from the late 1980s first by satellite technology then by the huge increase in channel capacity offered by digital transmission. The other mode of delivery, cable, had had varying success across Europe in the 1960s and 1970s but despite several attempts in the UK to increase uptake of cable (particularly in the mid-1980s) it took direct-to-home satellite broadcasts by BSkyB finally to break the BBC/ITV duopoly. Cable companies achieved a more significant market impact when allowed to sell voice telephony as well as entertainment services and thus broke the BT monopoly in the local loop with a competitive pricing strategy. The large investments by the American telecommunications and cable companies led to Britain acting as a laboratory for the cable–telephony interface.

### *New model*

Changes across the value chain in the television industry, alongside altered expectations of the role of small and medium-sized enterprises in the market, has had a profound effect on all sectors. Another way of thinking about the value chain is as a supply chain – with an upstream (where programmes are produced) and a downstream (where they are transmitted and viewed).

If we conceive of the television industry as a supply chain then the major companies, which previously operated as vertically integrated organizations, usually within national markets, have had to identify where the most efficient deployment of their capital can be achieved in an increasingly global industrial sector. Programme exports are no longer seen as an optional addition – merely confirming the high quality of UK television – but as a very important part of the financial envelope in television. No longer is there an assured situation of super-profits for the ITV companies based on an effective monopoly on advertising sales, nor a sufficiency of income for the public service broadcaster to undertake every activity. At one point in the 1980s the BBC was seen to want to be a part of every innovation in the industry. Only financial realism and competition changed this attitude, although through its investment in online services the BBC stole a competitive march on the commercial companies, who then complained about unfair competition.

All organizations have to address the problem of identifying their core business and which parts of their operational needs could be as well or better supplied by others. This raises the key question of where value is added, and the future income streams of the business. It is difficult to determine the answers when the industry is in flux. However, what is clear is that content will always be primary (to attract customers or the advertisers attracted by the customers), and that owning intellectual property rights on programming will ensure a continuing future income. Television once was seen as a single business. Now it is seen as a series of related activities. Furthermore, new businesses are emerging including the 'navigation' and tracking of customer or viewer preferences – effectively gathering intelligence from services offered in order to supply yet other services.

In the new European television system commerce doesn't just meet culture, it is feared that it might overwhelm it. At a political level in some European countries, television is still seen as above all else related to culture and citizenship – albeit aware of the American pre-eminence in the audio-visual industries. This has led to a series of measures from the European Commission seeking to protect the diversity of European culture and create a strong European audio-visual industry, but in the emerging global communications sector these political views may be swamped by the competitive needs of European firms to operate globally. Regulation may be the only means, however, to ensure that companies maintain production which reflects the 'national' and 'regional' cultures of the countries where they are based.

## Political concerns

In Europe (and in the USA) there has been a consistent concern to maintain a diversity of voices and opinions on the airwaves. In the new commercial era in European television the need to control cross-media ownership replaced previous concerns about press dominance, but this concern has in turn been overtaken by the focus on e-commerce. Regulation of ownership of media in different sectors (press, television, radio) and an insistence about transparency of shareholdings will continue but is likely to be superseded by rules which adapt to changes in modes of distribution. Competition policies of governments need to be sensitive to changing conditions to create a fair environment for public and private sector providers alike.

A second political concern in Europe has been the US dominance in the balance of trade in audio-visual products. This is seen as both a threat economically and in terms of loss of identity – the idea that television and film produced in a country will reflect and mirror society and sustain its self-image. The French government has historically been particularly keen to restrict American influence (or increase European influence) by imposing quotas on airtime for American product. Trade in audio-visual services will remain an important agenda item in the deliberations of the World Trade Organization for the foreseeable future.

One major fear of European governments, bred on insecurity and with memories of war and deprivation, is the loss of the social glue which public television represented. Social democracy and the welfare system are integral to European political life and their standing reinforced by media which convey and reassure through these messages of identity and unity within a diverse set of cultures.

Other political concerns have focused on areas of moral regulation. The influence of television is seen as potentially harmful and in an era when social cohesion is undermined television has often been labelled as the scapegoat. In Britain this has resulted in agreed practices like the 9.00 p.m. 'watershed' and Family Viewing policy (since the early 1960s), the drawing up of editorial guidelines within broadcasting organizations, and since the late 1980s the creation of the Broadcasting Standards Commission to offer guidance on questions of taste and decency. These issues have acquired a wider provenance in the age of the Internet with governments unsure how to act to protect groups perceived to be at risk.

## New market considerations

In the new audio-visual market 'content is king' and ownership of intellectual property is seen as crucial to future prosperity by many companies on both sides of the Atlantic. The supply chain is seen to require a constant input of new programming (content) as well as enabling the further exploitation of existing programming by rights' owners. For those with large libraries of material (whether produced and owned, or acquired) the key to profitability is to sell into secondary markets while continuing to produce or acquire new material.

New rules have begun to be applied in the new audio-visual marketplace under the influence of competition law and the public sector is facing increasing difficulties now that its protected position has disappeared. Where previously there was a guaranteed role for public broadcasters in all European countries this position has changed at a rapid rate. No longer possessing the largest guaranteed income (even when bidding together with public broadcasters from other countries) the public broadcasters are slowly losing their pre-eminent position within the national cultures. The global impetus in communications industries are benefiting large conglomerates able to take a controlling position, while the European public sector broadcasters, when they have tried to achieve the same end (through, for example, their pan-European sports channel, Eurosport) were found guilty of unfair competition. Indeed sport is an area where the new satellite broadcasters with large revenues available from subscription channels have been able to outbid the public broadcasters for rights to many events.

In analysing these changes the centrality of distribution – which for television means the control of broadcasting and commissioning – as the controlling function in the audio-visual industry becomes clear. It gives access to viewers and control of rights from commissions paid for by the profits generated. Rationalization is happening in television across all sectors with change in each part having some effect elsewhere in the industry. Global and local markets are being redefined with the market forcing these changes rather than any political settlement.

## Production consequences – skills and structures

There seems to be wide political agreement that the creative and information industries are of ever greater importance in the modern economies. One of the key factors for commercial prosperity in television is the availability of a skilled workforce, deployed effectively in a well-functioning industry able to harness and sell on its creativity.

A new functional map of the skills required in the television industry is emerging following the changes in the technical infrastructure associated with digitization. The changes are part evolution, part innovation, and require responses by firms acting in the market. Industries in the audio-visual sector need a well-functioning supply chain, supported at each stage by a sufficiently skilled workforce. In the UK television industry the previous certainties of employment in the BBC or one of the ITV companies was replaced in the 1990s by an increasing casualization of employment (estimated to be over 50% of the workforce) with potentially disastrous consequences for creative endeavour in the longer term.

## Outputs

Television output evolves gradually. The standard television genres are well known – fiction (single plays and TV movies, series and serials – crime, medicine, melodrama), factual (documentaries, current affairs), news, entertainment (including situation comedy), sport, features. Public service broadcasting on generalist channels has been characterized by the balance of tastes it has catered for – an attempt to please all the audience some of the time across the whole output: to inform, to educate and to entertain. TV fiction has been seen as both a mirror and window to the society it represents in all its diversity. The news is seen to play a key role in offering impartial information to citizens and to secure the functioning of the democratic processes.

There is continuity and innovation across the genres in programme output by TV channels in Europe and an appropriate mix, cleverly scheduled, can lead to ratings success. Recently, however, increased competition has come from niche channels (whether film, sport, children, documentary etc.) and this trend seems likely to continue. It is a truism that in most countries the locally produced fiction tends to attract the largest audiences but why US programmes should achieve great success in Europe when few European programmes are successful outside their country of origin is difficult to explain. If the US studios can offer universal narratives attractive to most of Europe then, it is often argued, European producers should be able to identify a winning solution to achieve the same end.

### The audience

All endeavours to alter television output are dependent on consumer uptake. Without an audience public service broadcasters lose their legitimacy, commercial television cannot sell advertising airtime and subscription channels go out of business. Most academic work and industry research on audiences in the UK has been ill suited to achieving an understanding of what uses audiences make of television. The notion of television as the glue for the nation's democratic future is untestable. The industry's use of the currency of the ratings, demographically interpreted, to conduct its business – whether the BBC in debates about its future or the commercial channels in negotiations with the advertisers – conceals much about the ways television is used in different types of household.

Recent academic research has shown the complexities of an individual's use of television. The industry now faces an uncertain future with little knowledge of how or why its audiences have engaged with its products in the past. The one certainty that seems to shape many current investment decisions is that while the future of the industry is uncertain it will be highly profitable for those players able to secure high-quality programming and ensure the continuing attention of their audiences. The range of choice on the digital platforms alongside the emergenece of competing leisure activities are altering TV's previously central place in the household,

## Conclusion

Television in the future will be different from the past and the changes in the regulatory structure (whether allowing the market to operate unfettered or within a 'lighter touch' set of rules), and in technology, in the form of opportunities to view, will have an impact on the programmes made, and how and where they are consumed. Whether it will be better or worse only time will tell, it will probably be different but we could never predict how much. That the different sectors which constitute the television industry remain ultimately dependent on the willingness of the viewer to watch remains unaltered. However, using the value chain as an analytical tool allows a clarity of approach for researcher, student, investor and policy maker, as these fundamental changes unwind in response to market developments.

## Questions

1 Review how the different television channels in the UK – BBC, Channel 4, ITV, Channel 5 and the cable and satellite channels – gain their supply of programmes. Comment on the different proportions of US and independently produced programming on each channel.

2 How do niche channels fit into the overall business of television? What sort of information about audiences and programmes would a business need to know before making an investment in a new channel? What is an appropriate framework for regulating the ownership of television channels in Britain in order to ensure a diversity of views on the airwaves?

3 If the three UK television channels in the 1970s were the glue for the democratic order what function do the numerous available channels play in the new century?

## References

BFI (1999) *Television Industry Tracking Study, Third Report (May 1999)*, London: BFI.

Bonner, P. (with Aston, L.) (1998) *Independent Television in Britain Vol. 5: ITV and IBA, 1981–92 The Old Relationship Changes*, Basingstoke: Macmillan.

Buonanno, M. (ed.) (1999) *Shifting Landscapes: Television Fiction in Europe*, Luton: University of Luton Press.

Council of the European Communities (1997) *Treaty on European Union 10.11.97 (incorporating changes made by Treaty of Amsterdam)*, Brussels: CEC.

DCMS (1998) *Creative Industries: Mapping Document 1998*, London: DCMS.

Gauntlett, D. and Hill, A. (1999) *TV Living: Television, Culture and Everyday Life*, London: Routledge.

Goodwin, P. (1998) *Television under the Tories: Broadcasting Policy 1979–1997*, London: BFI.

Home Office (1977) *Report of the Committee on the Future of Broadcasting (The Annan Report)*, Cmnd. 6753, London: HMSO.

Hood, S. (ed.) (1994) *Behind the Screen*, London: Lawrence and Wishart.

Mulgan, G. and Paterson, R. (eds) (1993) *Reinventing the Organisation*, BBC Charter Review No. 4, London: BFI.

Porter, M. (1985) *Competitive Advantage*, New York: Free Press.

Smith, A. (with Paterson, R.) (ed.) (1998) *Television: An International History*, 2nd edn, Oxford: Oxford University Press.

Stevenson, W. (ed.) (1993) *All Our Futures: The Changing Role and Purpose of the BBC,* London: BFI.

Tunstall, J. (ed.) (2000) *Media Occupations and Professions,* Oxford: Oxford University Press.

Venturelli, S. (1998) *Liberalizing the European Media: Politics, Regulation and the Public Sphere,* Oxford: Oxford University Press.

## Further reading

Gauntlett, D. and Hill, A. (1999) *TV Living: Television, Culture and Everyday Life,* London: Routledge. This book, based on a longitudinal study of the audience for television in Britain, offers important insights into the how television is used in households.

Goodwin, P. (1998) *Television under the Tories: Broadcasting Policy 1979–1997,* London: BFI. An analysis of the key developments of broadcasting policy which have wrought such significant changes in how television in Britain is organized.

# Chapter 11

# Cinema

CINEMA IN EUROPE

ANNE JÄCKEL

National cinemas are experiencing profound changes. In Europe, transnational part-nerships have been encouraged in the hope of producing films that cross cultural and national borders. In the 1990s, European and pan-European institutions' support mechanisms have contributed to bring about 'cross-cultural synergies' and to pro-mote cultural diversity but they have done little to improve the circulation of films between EU member states. The trend is now to focus on 'potentially commercial' films. Powerful private players are also emerging. European cinema is widely recog-nized as diverse and innovative as well as culturally and aesthetically different from (industrially based) 'Hollywood'. European films have traditionally been small-budget pictures, 'auteur films' and/or popular films which address a national audience. To what extent will new trends affect the future of cinema in Europe?

## Cinema an art but also an industry

European cinema has been defined and promoted in terms of 'art cinema' (the French call it 'the seventh art'). It is in Europe that cinema was first elevated to an art form and a strong tradition of film culture has developed and flourished through specific art movements whether international (avant-garde, surrealism) or national (Soviet cinema, German expressionism, the British documentary movement, Italian neo-realism, the French and Czech new waves), gaining critical recognition from film journals, theoreticians and intellectuals. Europe has a long-standing tradition of 'Auteur Cinema'. In film theory, 'la politique des auteurs' (an expression first used by the French film magazine *Les Cahiers du Cinéma* in the 1950s) is based on the proposition that the film director, like a literary author or any other artist, is the prime author of a film. In the 1970s, the theory became a critical method for evaluating films. According to this theory, a film became identified with its director, an 'auteur' with his or her own thematic concerns and a recognizable style. The theory has led to numerous debates over the years.

As Ginette Vincendeau noted:

> The subjective vision of individual *auteurs* has been part of national identity formation, providing a guarantee of authenticity and belonging and a personal 'refraction' of dominant national concerns . . . Some are synonymous with their whole country

(Bergman, Oliveira), some have acted as its 'humanitarian conscience' (Wajda), or raised its international profile, either in a repudiation of previous generations (the French New Wave film-makers) or after a period of oblivion (the New German *auteurs*); others have played the 'enfant terrible' or 'artiste maudit' (Polanski, Akerman, Godard) or militated in favour of a particular group (Brückner for women directors) or the whole of Europe (Beineix, Bertolucci and Tavernier during the [1993] GATT negotiations). Directors like Kieslowski and Wenders have almost ceased to be Polish or German, and become 'European': recently Wenders declared that working in the USA made him realise that it was 'a much nicer profession to be a European film-maker' . . . (Vincendeau 1995: xiv).

This tradition may have served Europeans well at crucial moments in film history (transition from silent to sound, competition from television), and cinema may well have been 'the art form of the twentieth century' but, in the last decades, lacking government support, several national industries have been struggling to survive. From the mid-1980s onwards, the share of national films in their domestic market also fell considerably while American films increased their share of the European market. (The strengths of 'Hollywood' lie as much in the current box-office performance of a few well-promoted blockbusters as in its libraries and worldwide delivery systems. That American cinema has always been able to adapt and to redefine itself also explains its dominant position.) Despite attempts made at European levels to improve the situation, European films are more often seen at film festivals and relegated to the 'art-house ghettos' than shown in mainstream cinemas, even in their country of origin.

The campaign for 'cultural exception' led by the French in 1993 revealed that US film exports to Europe generated US annual revenues of over $3.7 billion (£2.5 billion) while Europeans had to content themselves with less than 2% of the US market. No one doubted the supremacy of US popular culture in the audio-visual sphere (American films command between 80% and 85% of the world's film market) but to non-Americans, the US position in the long battle over the right of European countries to support their own film and television productions seemed greedy and 'imperialistic'. In the name of free trade, liberal USA called 'protectionism' what the French considered keeping a stake in their own culture and encouraging local creativity and talent. In December 1993, Europe obtained the (temporary) exclusion of audio-visual works from the General Agreement on Tariffs and Trade but, within Europe, the GATT negotiations exposed the uneven playing field in which film industries continue to operate. Benefiting from a whole array of subsidies and tax incentives, France was the only European country which could claim both a prolific film industry and a strong film culture.

Yet self-indulgence on the part of European directors, the reluctance of European actors and actresses to 'play the star game', along with the protective schemes that many governments continued to operate to support their domestic film industries have also been blamed for the poor commercial performance of European films throughout the 1990s.

Today, Europeans are repositioning themselves in order to compete in the global audio-visual environment. With the construction of multiplexes and the proliferation of distribution outlets (IMAX, satellite and cable television channels, video, CD-ROM) the cinema experience is also changing. At the beginning of the new millennium, the challenges facing Europeans are enormous.

## Funding

Film financing in Europe continue to depend on the various schemes operated by governments to support their national film industries. Subsidies take essentially two forms. One is an automatic aid in the form of a tax on cinema tickets which goes to a support fund to help producers raise finance for their next film; the other is a selective aid whereby projects are assessed by committees which give 'soft loans' for development and production (known as 'advance on receipts'). Some territories also have cultural and regional funds (France, Germany, Scotland) and tax incentives exist in many countries.

However, it is not local subsidies but television which is now one of the most important sources of financing in the larger European territories – France, Germany, Spain and Italy. In France, the five terrestrial television broadcasters have to invest 3% of their turnover in film production while the pay-TV channel, Canal Plus, invests around 20%. In Germany, government subsidies usually go to films which already have television backing. In the UK, broadcasters are under no obligation to invest in film production, but Channel 4 has a long tradition of commissioning films and the BBC recently started to follow suit. In the last few years, film and television have been discovered by the capital markets and private investors who wish to embark on ambitious programmes of expansion and internationalization (not to mention take advantage of local tax incentives) now invest heavily in film.

It has been argued that the network of conglomerates and powerful financial institutions willing to invest in films, along with local subsidies and television funding, has led to the creation of 'a three-tier European industry':

All the territories have producers who make low-budget films, supposedly 'art-house' films. A second tier of producers, mainly in the larger territories, also make medium-budget archetypal European films with international reputation such as *Toto le héros*, *High Heels*, *Europa Europa*, and *Mediterraneo*. The third tier of producers, best represented in France, provides the European blockbusters – *Cyrano de Bergerac*, *Atlantis* and *Les Amants du Pont Neuf* (Sheperd and McCartney 1992: 17).

While the failure of Besson's and Carax's films at the box-office illustrates the famous maxim of Hollywood novelist and screenwriter William Goldman, 'in the film business, nobody knows anything', least of all what a 'potential' blockbuster is, the concept of 'a three-tier industry' is particularly appropriate to describe and assess the state of the European film industry.

## Investments

In Europe, only France, Germany, Ireland and the UK – the latter with much help from American producers – appear to be able to raise finance for large-scale productions, although average film budgets are low (around $5 million in 1998) (*Screen Digest* October 1999: 261; see also Table 11.1) in comparison with the average cost of an 'American Major's picture' ($76 million – $51 million of which are production costs) (*Le film français* 1 March 2000: 36).

*Table 11.1* European film production investment 1989–1999 (million US dollars)

|  | **1989** | **1996** | **1997** | **1998** | **1999** |
|---|---|---|---|---|---|
| Austria |  | 18.73 | 16.12 | 14.55 | 15.38 |
| Belgium | 15.38 | 35.70 | 16.51 | 16.53 | 38.05 |
| Denmark | 20.79 | 39.65 | 52.20 | 33.60 | 33.56 |
| Finland |  | 9.58 | 11.55 | 12.30 | 21.36 |
| France | 492.14 | 642.52 | 792.34 | 838.07 | 732.58 |
| Germany | 126.63 | 309.59 | 298.19 | 279.26 | 380.45 |
| Greece |  | 5.94 | 4.08 | 3.94 |  |
| Ireland | 7.55 | 83.97 | 102.17 | 110.60 | 98.92 |
| Italy | 249.40 | 243.96 | 198.38 | 180.89 | 171.10 |
| Luxembourg |  | 3.45 | 3.01 | 1.93 | 1.44 |
| Netherlands | 10.18 | 29.41 | 27.31 | 26.73 | 41.89 |
| Portugal | 5.65 | 4.20 | 4.36 | 3.33 | 3.22 |
| Spain | 59.45 | 157.88 | 156.96 | 133.69 | 168.46 |
| Sweden |  | 40.25 | 56.90 | 31.46 | 34.70 |
| UK | 134.33 | 842.78 | 764.76 | 617.53 | 817.85 |
| EU | 1,121.51 | 2,467.61 | 2,504.85 | 2,304.41 | 2,558.96 |

*Source*: *Screen Digest*, June 2000: 186.

Many European large-scale films are now shot in the English language. Following the commercial success of the English-language films of Luc Besson after 1994 (*Leon*, *The Fifth Element* and *Joan of Arc*), French legislation has been altered to allow English-language films made by French film directors and with French technical and/or artistic input to be considered as 'French films' (with a reduced subsidy entitlement). 'French' conglomerates (Gaumont, UGC, Vivendi) have now developed close links with American partners to make 'global pictures' in English. German-based film funds are also financing English-language films (*Mission Impossible 2*, Neil Jordan's *The End of the Affair*). Small countries have developed strategies to attract the bigger players. In Ireland, the combination of financial incentives and the re-establishment of the Irish Film Board have helped raise the country's output from a mere three films in 1990 to 25 in 1998. However, the European country which has become the most attractive to film producers is the UK. The introduction of Lottery funds for film in the mid-1990s along with British technical expertise and artistic talent – and the possibility of making films in English – have all played a part in this. In 1996, Besson shot *The Fifth Element* (£50 million budget) in Britain but, in the late 1990s, it is largely American money which has filled British studios with the bigger productions (*Star Wars: The Phantom Menace, Saving Private Ryan* and *Mission Impossible 2*). While British studios have welcomed this influx of US productions, industry observers have remained cautious: 'if there is one thing we have learned from the British film history,' wrote Terry Ilott (BFI 1996: 26), 'it is that Americans cannot be relied upon to be consistent investors: the level of their activity rises and falls according to a host of factors, notably the exchange rate'. Indeed, total investments in US/UK films fell from £350.6 in 1996 to £261.2 million in 1999. Still, with the setting up of a new Film Council in May 2000, the UK has high hopes of becoming 'the Hollywood of Europe'.

## Large-scale European productions and their reception in Europe

In the decade cinema reached its first centenary, European producers with global ambitions have had little difficulty in raising finance and Europe developed a thriving industry in works rooted in a 'genuine' national culture by rediscovering its literary heritage and reconstructing an imaginary colonial past. The Merchant–Ivory films, Régis Warnier's *Indochine*, Bille August's *The House of Spirits*, Claude Berri's *Germinal*, Jean-Paul Rappeneau's *The Horseman on the Roof* are only a few in a long list of large-scale productions drawing on Europe's history and high culture and made to appeal to audiences worldwide.

However, several film critics, particularly in France, have suggested that these super-productions may be doing more harm than good to a European film culture which is still defined in terms of 'Auteur Cinema'. Large-budget historical film events such as *1492, Conquest of Paradise* had bad press in the early 1990s. (*1492*, the Colombus epic with Gérard Depardieu heading a mutinational cast, was labelled 'Europudding'.)

Heritage film's high production values include expensive sets and the use of stars and 'some European stars (Emma Thompson, Gérard Depardieu) are increasingly associated with the genre' (Vincendeau 1998: 446). The genre may have given some European actors 'an international profile' but star status rarely goes hand in hand with critical acclaim. Critics have not been kinder to the big-budget films of the new *enfants terribles* of French cinema, Besson (*The Big Blue, Leon, The Fifth Element*), Beineix (*IP5*), Carax (*Les Amants du Pont Neuf*) or Jeunet and Caro (*The City of the Lost Children*). In Europe, critical acclaim rarely concurs with box-office performance. Also, audiences are far less homogeneous than in the USA. Audience surveys show that Besson's films cater almost exclusively for young audiences' tastes while historical epics and melodramas are more popular with older and female audiences (*CNC Info* 1993).

Overall, the public reception of these film-events made in Europe has been mixed, ranging from overwhelming enthusiasm (*Delicatessen, Nikita, Indochine*) to mild approval (*The Horseman on the Roof, Ridicule*) and indifference (*IP5*) but there is some evidence that large-budget productions – particularly those shot in English and/or with American stars (*The Fifth Element, The Avengers*) – are easier to sell to agents and distributors and therefore more capable of reaching global audiences.

The second tier of films produced in Europe consists of medium- to low-budget pictures, usually financed by producers from more than one country and with the support of European programmes.

## European co-productions

Co-productions are nothing new in Europe. Many countries have a long and successful tradition of co-operation. (Not only did *Pelle the Conqueror* win the Cannes Palme d'Or (1988) but also Nordic consensus declared Bille August's film Best Swedish film in Sweden and Best Danish film in Denmark!)

In Europe, co-productions represent an activity without which small countries would not have a film industry (see Table 11.2). With a minute home market (6 million

Table 11.2 Film production figures 1989–1999 (of which co-productions)

| | 1989 | 1990 | 1991 | 1992 | 1993 | 1994 | 1995 | 1996 | 1997 | 1998 | 1999 |
|---|---|---|---|---|---|---|---|---|---|---|---|
| Austria | 10 — | 14 (5) | 11 (0) | 14 (0) | 26 — | 24 — | 19 (2) | 15 (2) | 15 (3) | 22 (5) | 20 (5) |
| Belgium | | 12 (9) | 3 (3) | 13 (8) | 10 (4) | 15 (6) | 10 (8) | 12 (6) | 8 (5) | 7 (6) | 14 (5) |
| Denmark | 18 (2) | 13 (1) | 11 (6) | 15 (5) | 14 (3) | 17 (3) | 17 (4) | 21 (8) | 23 (7) | 18 (12) | 16 (6) |
| Finland | 10 — | 13 (3) | 12 (6) | 10 (8) | 13 (2) | 11 (4) | 8 (4) | 11 (2) | 10 (1) | 8 (1) | 16 (1) |
| France* | 136 (70) | 146 (65) | 156 (83) | 155 (83) | 152 (85) | 115 (54) | 141 (78) | 134 (60) | 163 (77) | 183 (81) | 181 (66) |
| Germany | 68 (15) | 48 (10) | 72 (19) | 63 (10) | 67 (17) | 60 (11) | 63 (26) | 64 (22) | 61 (14) | 50 (11) | 74 (30) |
| Greece | 8 | 13 | 15 | 15 (3) | 16 (3) | 12 | 19 (17) | 17 (10) | 16 (10) | 15 | 16 |
| Ireland | 3 | 3 | 1 | 4 | 17 (2) | 17 | 22 | 18 (12) | 22 (6) | 25 | 23 |
| Italy | 117 | 119 (21) | 129 (18) | 127 (13) | 106 (20) | 95 (24) | 75 (15) | 99 (22) | 87 (16) | 92 (13) | 108 (16) |
| Luxembourg | 3 | 1 | 2 (1) | 4 (2) | 2 (2) | 0 | 0 | 5 (5) | 5 (5) | 3 (3) | 2 (2) |
| Netherlands | 13 | 13 | 14 | 13 (0) | 16 | 16 (4) | 18 (8) | 18 (6) | 15 (6) | 18 (5) | 14 (8) |
| Portugal | 7 | 9 (7) | 9 (3) | 8 (7) | 16 (8) | 13 (9) | 12 (11) | 8 (6) | 13 (4) | 10 | 10 |
| Spain | 47 (8) | 47 (10) | 64 (18) | 52 (14) | 56 (15) | 44 (8) | 59 (22) | 91 (25) | 80 (25) | 65 (18) | 97 |
| Sweden | 26 | 25 (5) | 27 (17) | 20 (11) | 29 (8) | 23 (8) | 23 (13) | 18 (15) | 29 (4) | 20 (7) | 23 (10) |
| UK** | 30 | 60 (8) | 59 (22) | 47 (13) | 67 (29) | 84 (32) | 78 (36) | 128 (52) | 116 (51) | 88 (45) | 103* |

Source: Figures compiled from Screen Digest, June 1997; June 2000; European Audio-visual Observatory (OBS), 1999.
Notes: *CNC Info May 2000; **BFI Yearbook 1999: 18; 2000: 26.
From 1991, figures for reunited Germany.

and 6.4 million respectively), a Greek or Portuguese film industry almost seems a contradiction in terms. In a country like Belgium which is divided into two cultural parts, the likelihood of an indigenous film-making a profit in its country of origin is small.

It is not only for Greek, Portuguese, Belgian or Danish film-makers that co-production has become a way of life. With production and post-production costs rising throughout Europe, all countries have felt the need to spread the financial burden of film production and, by the mid-1990s, the search for more co-production partners had become a necessity.

Multilateral arrangements have been encouraged by both the European Community Programmes, MEDIA and the Council of Europe Fund, EURIMAGES.

## European and pan-European initiatives

MEDIA (Measures to Encourage the Development of the Audio-visual Industry) was instigated in 1987 to provide aid and encourage initiatives designed to fulfil the needs of the entire audio-visual sector. EURIMAGES was set up in 1988 by the Council of Europe to create a pan-European fund supporting (fiction and documentary) film co-productions and their distribution.

### *MEDIA*

From a pilot scheme of ten projects in 1988 (ranging from script-writing to a European Film Academy), MEDIA grew into fully fledged Community programmes under the names of MEDIA 92 and MEDIA 1995. (In 1990, the Council of Ministers granted MEDIA a budget of Ecu200 million (£140 million) to be spread over five years. For a summary of the various projects supported by MEDIA, see Hill *et al.* 1994: 29–31. They included initiatives for research and development, finance, training, production, distribution and the encouragement of minority languages.) The aim was to create 'cross-border synergies' by establishing networks of cooperation among professionals.

Considering that MEDIA is a fairly modest programme – in financial terms – suffering from various ailments such as under-funding, lack of mechanisms for the recoupment of loans and the occasional duplication of resources, its achievements have been significant. Whether one looks at the several hundreds of projects and networks it has helped set up, at the number of producers and distributors it has encouraged or the range of ventures it has supported (fiction, animation and documentary films, dubbing and subtitling, etc.), the results are extremely valuable. Yet the development of those cross-border synergies has not brought about the arrival of a European audio-visual structure strong enough to face the future. In a larger European Union, MEDIA has been allowed to continue but the nineteen initiatives of MEDIA 95 have been trimmed down, and, given a modest budget of Ecu310 million (over five years), MEDIA II has, from 1996 onwards, concentrated its efforts on three action lines: training, development and distribution.

## EURIMAGES

Initially, the Council of Europe Fund supported only low- and medium-budget films (fiction and documentary). From its beginning, EURIMAGES has granted its support to 'works which uphold the values that are part and parcel of the European identity'. While there has been no attempt to define such an identity beyond general references to diversity and common cultural heritage, many of the EURIMAGES-supported films speak for themselves, inclined as they are to tackle contemporary issues (e.g. of belonging, or not belonging) and explore cross-cultural exchanges. They include Xavier Koller's *Journey of Hope*, Lars von Trier's *Europa* (1989), Jaco van Dormael's *Toto le héros* (1991), Gianni Amelio's *Il ladro di Bambini/ The Stolen Children* (1990), Fernando Trueba's *Belle Epoque* (1991), Kieslowski's *Blue* (1992) and Nikita Mikhalkov's *Urga* (aid for distribution).

The early success of EURIMAGES can be measured by the increasing number of applications to the Fund. It has been estimated that of all films made in Europe in 1994, over a quarter of them had applied to EURIMAGES (*Eurimages News* 1994). However, the number of applications dropped in the mid-1990s and an audit (Bipe Conseil) revealed that producers had complained about the Fund's rigidity and adherence to bureaucracy. The report also criticized the principle of tri-partite co-productions, pre-empting the decision by EURIMAGES management Board to open up the Fund to bi-partite films in 1998. By then, around half of Europe's co-productions were receiving EURIMAGES support (*Screen Digest* 1998: 127). (EURIMAGES membership has grown from the original twelve founding member states to twenty-five – a third of which from the former Eastern bloc; the UK briefly joined in 1993 and withdrew in 1995.)

The growth of co-productions involving European partners (from 144 in 1990 to 198 in 1993) has largely been responsible for the upward path taken by European production in the early 1990s. In 1994, production figures fell below 500 films for the first time since the 1940s but the adoption of new measures to encourage private or/and public investment in film production in certain territories since then, has contributed to a reversal of the trend. By the end of the decade, production had increased again ( just over 700 films in 1999) (see Table 11.2).

This has led to fears of overproduction. Noting that it has become easier than it had ever been to produce a film in the UK, industry analyst Nick Thomas noted for instance:

> Whether there is a sufficiently deep talent to justify more than 100 feature film projects each year is debatable, to say the least. Though the quantity of films produced is higher than for 40 years, there is little evidence of a comparable rise in the overall quality (Thomas 1999: 26).

The growth in production has not been matched with a greater cross-border appeal of European films. Bearing this in mind, the EURIMAGES Board had already decided, in 1993, to pay special attention to 'high-quality co-productions capable of pleasing large audiences' and put more emphasis on the Fund's recoupment of its interest-free loans. Since 1 January 2000, EURIMAGES awards assistance under two schemes: one for projects with 'circulation potential', the other for films 'of artistic value' (*Eurimages News* 2000). MEDIA has also pledged to support 'more commercially ori-entated projects'.

At the European Union level, it has been suggested that national subsidies should be available to all European producers, something which is possible in law but extremely difficult in practice (*Screen Digest* October 1999: 262). In the meantime, EURIMAGES plays the role of life-saver to many film-makers in central and eastern Europe.

## Unreleased European films

In France, only films which have a statutory theatrical release are allowed to qualify for cinema funding. Without such regulations, other European films often fail to secure a theatrical distribution deal even in their domestic country. In 1994, only 60% of the feature films made in Germany and Italy were screened at a cinema; the others went straight to television or video. In the UK, as many as 43.1% of films produced in 1997 remained unreleased with no plans to release them during 1999 and fewer British films receive a wide release (opening on 30 or more screens around the country) (BFI 2000: 24).

## Film distribution and exhibition

Britain was the first European country to welcome the multiplex revolution. The major cinema operators have been actively involved in the construction of multiplexes. Offering better and cheaper facilities, multiplexes have been responsible for the steady rise in cinema admissions from the late 1980s onwards. Today, multiplex sites continue to be developed even though, in some territories, admissions have begun to fall slightly. To date, the growth in sites and screens has not led to the creation of mini-circuits catering for specific niches with one recent exception: Bollywood films are becoming so popular with audiences in some parts of Britain that multiplexes have now started screening them. However, overall, the greater chances for 'independent films' to find exhibition space alongside mainstream films have not materialized. Mainstream movies (largely American) aimed at 15–24 year-olds continue to account for a major share of Europe's national markets (see Tables 11.3 and 11.4).

Few films find success without a significant promotion budget. At a time when the theatrical life of a film is made shorter by the development of ancillary markets, a film is expected to make more and more admissions in a small number of weeks and its promotion budget has become a sign of its commercial potential. Massive advertising and promotional support (including an ever-increasing number of copies) ensure that a small number of (mainly American) blockbusters are successful at the box office. In the European territories as in most major cinema markets around the world, the top 20 films now account for well over half of box office revenues. In 1998, *Titanic* made history taking over 10% of total box office revenues in four of the five major European markets. If France remains one of the few countries in Europe where domestic films regularly manage to get into the top 10 (the UK has recently joined France with films like *The Full Monty, Bean, Lock, Stock and Two Smoking Barrels*),

*Table 11.3* Market share of domestic films (%, including co-productions)

| | 1989 | 1990 | 1991 | 1992 | 1993 | 1994 | 1995 | 1996 | 1997 | 1998 | 1999 |
|---|---|---|---|---|---|---|---|---|---|---|---|
| Belgium | 0.4 | 1.4 | 2.2 | 5.0 | 1.6 | 1.1 | 0.3 | 0.1 | 0.9 | | |
| Denmark | 15.0 | 14.7 | 10.8 | 15.3 | 15.9 | 21.5 | 8.3 | 17.2 | 19.0 | | |
| Finland | 7.4 | 13.9 | 13 | 10.9 | 6.3 | 4.0 | 11.2 | 3.5 | 5.6 | | |
| France* | 34.3 | 37.5 | 30.6 | 35.0 | 35.1 | 28.3 | 35.2 | 37.5 | 34.5 | 27.6 | 32.3 |
| Germany | 16.7 | 9.7 | 13.6 | 9.5 | 7.2 | 10.1 | 6.3 | 15.3 | 17.3 | 8.1 | 14.0 |
| Greece | 9.0 | 8.0 | 7.0 | 2.0 | | | | | 4.0 | | |
| Ireland | 4.0 | 5.0 | 2.0 | | | | | | | | |
| Italy | 21.7 | 21.0 | 26.8 | 24.4 | 17.3 | 23.7 | 21.1 | 24.9 | 32.9 | 24.7 | |
| Luxembourg | 2.0 | 2.0 | 2.0 | 0.0 | 0.8 | 0.1 | 0.0 | | 1.7 | | |
| Netherlands | 4.6 | 3.0 | 2.3 | 13.0 | 4.1 | 0.6 | 7.6 | 5.4 | 3.4 | | |
| Portugal | 1.2 | 2.2 | 2.1 | 2.0 | 1.0 | | | | 2.0 | | |
| Spain | 7.4 | 10.4 | 10.9 | 9.3 | 8.8 | 7.1 | 12.2 | 9.3 | 13.1 | 11.9 | 13.9 |
| Sweden | 20.4 | 10.4 | 25.6 | 17.0 | 20.3 | 19.9 | 20.1 | 18.0 | 17.8 | | |
| UK | 10.0 | 7.0 | 6.8 | 2.5 | 8.8 | 12.3 | 10.2 | 12.8 | 28.1 | 14.2 | 17.8 |

*Source*: European Audiovisual Observatory (OBS), 1999.
*Note*: *CNC Info* 2000.

*Table 11.4* Market share of US films (%)

| | 1989 | 1990 | 1991 | 1992 | 1993 | 1994 | 1995 | 1996 | 1997 | 1998 | 1999 |
|---|---|---|---|---|---|---|---|---|---|---|---|
| Belgium | 68.4 | 79.1 | 78.6 | 69.3 | 75.8 | 72.4 | 69.7 | 73.7 | 71.9 | | 78.3 |
| Denmark | 63.7 | 77.0 | 83.3 | 77.7 | 74.1 | 66.5 | 81.1 | 67.1 | 66.0 | | 45.3 |
| Finland | 70.0 | 80.0 | 80.0 | 63.0 | 63.0 | 66.0 | 76.5 | 75.2 | 73.1 | | |
| France* | 55.5 | 55.9 | 58.0 | 58.2 | 57.1 | 60.9 | 53.9 | 54.3 | 52.2 | 63.2 | 53.9 |
| Germany | 65.7 | 83.9 | 80.2 | 82.8 | 87.8 | 81.6 | 87.1 | 75.1 | 70.5 | 85.4 | 76.5 |
| Greece | 86.0 | 87.0 | 88.0 | 92.0 | | | | | | | |
| Ireland | 85.0 | 87.0 | 91.5 | | | | | | | | |
| Italy | 63.1 | 70.0 | 58.6 | 59.4 | 70.0 | 61.1 | 59.7 | 55.5 | 46.7 | 63.8 | 62.1 |
| Luxembourg | 87.0 | 80.0 | 85.0 | 78.0 | 80.0 | 84.0 | 82.4 | 68.4 | | | |
| Netherlands | 75.6 | 85.8 | 92.5 | 78.8 | 89.3 | 89.9 | 82.0 | 89.7 | 84.5 | | 78.2 |
| Portugal | 67.4 | 63.5 | 67.8 | 68.4 | 97.0 | 95.0 | 66.5 | | | | |
| Spain | 71.4 | 72.5 | 68.7 | 77.1 | 75.7 | 72.3 | 71.9 | 78.2 | 68.2 | 78.5 | 64.2 |
| Sweden | 69.3 | 82.3 | 70.5 | 65.5 | 73.6 | 67.5 | 68.5 | 65.9 | 67.5 | 66.7 | 43.0 |
| UK | 86.2 | 88.0 | 89.0 | 92.5 | 94.2 | 85.6 | 85.2 | 81.7 | 69.3 | 83.7 | 80.5 |

*Source*: European Audiovisual Observatory (OBS), 1999.
*Note*: *CNC Info* 2000.

it is becoming increasingly reliant in financial terms on these top 10 films. In 1998 and 1999, the top 10 films took around 40% of the domestic market, in France but also in the UK, Denmark, Norway, Sweden, Poland and the Czech Republic (*Screen Digest* January 2000: 29).

It has been estimated that just over one-third of all films directly cover the cost of their cinema release; between 10% and 15% make a profit and about 24% recoup the cost of prints and advertising. The ways a film can recoup its costs have greatly increased with the proliferation of distribution outlets via the growth of video retail, cable, satellite, pay-TV, pay-per-view and CD-ROM but the commercial value of a film is still determined by the number of cinema tickets sold.

Limited medium-growth potential of the US market has led the large conglomerates to seek to strengthen their positions in European theatrical markets in order to maximize revenues and be ideally placed to exploit the latest technological advances in distribution. This has led to mergers between European and US distributors (Gaumont with Buena Vista and UGC with Fox in France). The companies which have taken the lead in establishing pan-European operations that work across traditional boundaries include Canal Plus, Mediaset, CLT-Ufa and Kinowelt. It remains to be seen whether they can sustain growth and support the expansion of Europe's film industries. Up to now, concentration in the distribution field has done little to improve the situation of European films but there are signs that, even in a world obsessed with economic performance, things are changing.

## Popular cinema

Large-budget films are not necessarily profitable. In the 1990s, the worldwide commercial performance of two British films (*Four Weddings and a Funeral* and *The Full Monty*) was hailed as a watershed. Yet the most successful 'British films' of the decade probably owe their success as much to corporate marketing strategies as to the films' creative teams. *Four Weddings and a Funeral* was launched by Polygram, shortly after the giant international record conglomerate had taken over Working Title – the small independent British company which had developed the project. (Hoping to become 'the only European-based studio', Polygram put all its weight behind the film.) Recalling the many tests, previews and the huge promotion efforts of the (then Dutch-owned) conglomerate, Duncan Kenworthy (1995), the producer of *Four Weddings and a Funeral*, declared: 'They were terrific . . . Polygram needed a hit – they were hurting for a hit – and we were happy to supply it.' Although widely considered 'British', *The Full Monty* was backed by an American studio after being turned down by Channel 4 and the Arts Council of England. Made on a $3.5 million budget, the film took $69 million in the UK and $205 million worldwide in 1997. Fox Searchlight spent over ten times the film's budget on its international marketing.

In the wake of the commercial – and critical – success of a small number of British comedies, Europeans are now spending a lot of money and effort in making more ambitious comedies (*Astérix and Obélix, Life is beautiful*) in the hope of breaking into the international market. Yet so far, Roberto Benigni's Oscar-winning film *Life is beautiful* (1999) remains the exception. Foreign-language comedies have not travelled well even if, on their domestic market, they remain the most popular genre. In 1993, *Les Visiteurs*, sold more tickets (13 million) in France than *Jurassic Park*, the 'world's uncontested top earner of the year', but elsewhere in Europe, the French hit was not a unique success story. In the Netherlands, drawing an audience of 1.2 million, Dick Maas' comedy, *Flodder does Manahattan* (*Flodder in Manhattan*) drove *Basic Instinct* into second place at the Dutch box office in 1992. The following year, *Der Bewegte Mann*

(*The Most Desired Man*) registered over 6 million admissions in Germany, Roberto Benigni's *Il Mostro* took $21.2 million at the Italian box-office and in Spain, the top two domestic releases were also comedies.

By relying on local audiences' knowledge of the national history and socio-political system as well as viewers' familiarity with comedians, language and other specific cultural icons, locally made comedies are often inaccessible to audiences coming from a different cultural background (Dyer and Vincendeau 1992: 3). However, the inexportability of local comedies should not be exaggerated. Both *Les Visiteurs* and *Astérix and Obélix* were considerable hits in the French-speaking regions of Belgium and Switzerland and also did well in other territories (Spain but also in Eastern Europe, with a little help from Unifrance, the French film export body). If the German hit *Schtonk*, a comedy based on the forged Hitler's diaries scandal, was a flop on the international scene in 1992, two years later, *Der Bewegte Mann* was an enormous success in Austria, Switzerland and Finland; its dubbed version also performed well in Spain. Spanish theatrical quotas for European productions then may well have been responsible for the greater popularity of those films in Spain compared to the rest of Europe but cultural affinities between regions (i.e. Nordic versus Latin) no doubt also play a part in the shared fortunes of many European titles.

## Films exploring European issues

In the mid-1980s, Vincent Porter asked:

> Can we look forward to a film culture which offers something more imaginative, which brings together the experiences and feelings that men and women of the different European cultures have in common and which plays down, or better still resolves, the nationalistic differences that can divide them? (Porter 1985: 6).

Many of the films supported by MEDIA and/or EURIMAGES correspond perfectly to Porter's longing for images of cultural collaboration, dealing as they do with love and friendship between people of different cultures (*Urga, Prague, Orlando, Before the Rain, The Extraordinary Adventures of Private Chonkin, Someone Else's America*); immigration (*Journey of Hope, Lamerica, Asphalt Tango*) or the search for a new identity in an indifferent or hostile modern environment (Theo Angelopoulos' *Ulysses' Gaze*, Kiewslowski's *White*, Tony Gatlif's *Gadjo Dilo*).

Interestingly, among the film-makers engaged in works that manage to reconcile the somewhat contradictory aims of the Council of Europe 'to work for European unity by protecting and strengthening pluralist democracy and human rights as well as seeking solutions to the problems facing European society', there are many directors from Central and Eastern Europe (Nikita Mikhalkov, Milcho Manchevski, Jiri Menzel, Goran Paskaljevic, Nae Caranfil). All of them have had the support of the French Centre National de la Cinématographie (CNC). Far from bearing the stigma attached to French/European cinema (narcissist and elitist), their films offer a cinematic expression which is essentially concerned with social and moral questions (Jäckel 1997).

During the last decade, those (medium- and low-budget) European co-productions commenting on socio-political issues in contemporary Europe have won critical acclaim and prizes at film festivals but have not fared well with audiences.

However, several low-budget films directed by a new generation of film-makers, often sharing the same thematic concerns as the co-productions of the Russian, Czech, Macedonian, Romanian or Polish directors, have not only been covered with awards, but they have also achieved critical and public success and been sold outside their national territory (Issac Julien's *Young Soul Rebels*, Cyril Collard's *Savage Nights*, Mathieu Kassovitz's *La haine/Hate*, Luc and Jean-Pierre Dardenne's *La Promesse* and *Rosetta*). *La Haine*, a black-and-white film about a day in the life of three young men in a deprived suburb outside Paris, even secured a distribution deal in the USA. The late 1990s have been marked by a rash of innovative films made by women film-makers. There are signs that young directors from eastern Europe have not only assimilated the ethical and aesthetic lessons of their elders but can also produce humane and funny movies capable of pleasing international audiences (Jan Sverak's *Kolya* and Radu Mihaileanu's *Train de Vie*).

## A changing marketplace

The rapidly changing audio-visual environment requires a new look at the market-place. At a time when films rely on ancillary outlets to recoup their cost and revenues from export overtake those from domestic takings, film commissions all over Europe are adopting an agenda for the future which includes making films for the global market and establishing a better distribution and marketing system. The European funds are not the only initiatives to have committed to support projects with 'commercial potential'. The UK's new Film Council has pledged to 'use public money to make better, more popular and more profitable films in real partnership with the private sector' (Parker 2000: 1). In France the automatic aid now takes into account export revenues and the Spanish subsidy system is to include box-office results in its allocation of grants.

However, the idea of 'making movies that make commercial sense' has been taken to tasks by European cinéphiles. Many argue that the *auteur* tradition, with its preference for works of personal expression, social commentary and aesthetic exploration, remains both an easily identifiable and valuable cultural practice and a well-established market niche. Besides, as the film critic Alexander Walker pointed out in his defence of a strong national British cinema, it is unlikely that anyone ever set out deliberately to make a film for small audiences . . . Mike Leigh, Kenneth Loach, Peter Greenaway, all hope their 'elitist Art-house' productions reach as wide an audiences as possible. (quoted in *London Evening Standard* 18 March 1994)

Paradoxically, it is outside their native country that the reputations of Loach and Greenaway have blossomed (France, Italy and Spain for the former, Germany, the Netherlands and France for the latter). Resnais, Rivette and Rohmer, the most 'elitist' masters of the old French New Wave, had little difficulty in exporting their 'unquestionably Art films' in the last decade. Thomas Elsaesser (1992) explained the success of *La Belle Noiseuse* by the fact that audiences saw in it 'a qualified but nonetheless comforting reaffirmation of the values not only of Art, but also of European Art Cinema'. 'Auteur' films are outside fashion and, with a little help from the boom in cultural and media studies of the last ten years, still cross borders. So do several low-budget films directed by young talented film-makers. For Thomas Vinterberg's film *Festen* only 1% admissions came from Denmark, its home country. In 1997, the $0.3 million budget film of young French director Cédric Klapisch, *When the cat is away*, took $7.6 million at the box-office worldwide. Like audiences and audiences' tastes, the strategies employed by professionals (distributors, sales agents, producers but also actors and directors) in their attempts to 'make film travel' vary greatly.

As far as European film industries are concerned, even though national productions are still predominantly made at home, there is some evidence that, on the one hand, producers and facilities/post-producers are linking as a part of a vertical integration policy, and, on the other, small companies working in the same field are coming together in order to attract lucrative US projects and the larger European projects (*Screen Digest* October 1999: 263). However, the power of capital must not be underestimated. In the global environment, relations of power are also changing. The production, distribution and marketing of films is an important part of that environment. The accelerating flows of people, technologies and images combine with the search for wider markets to imply growing homogeneity in film production (e.g. the number of remakes and/or sequels of a few successful small- and large-budget films). Technology needs to be 'demystified': it can be 'utilized to contest the forces of social amnesia, rather than reproducing the industry's incessant bottom-line drive towards newer, bigger, shinier tech'. (Kipnis 1998: 603)

Specialization on economic grounds is no guarantee of cultural diversity, difference or creativity. Film production and distribution may be conditioned by economic strategies but the rich variety of industries, individuals and films that constitutes European cinema also depends on the existence of regulation and film policies.

Even though everybody now accepts that to survive in the multimedia explosion a strong European film industry needs a preponderance of commercially viable products, few in Europe today would question the fact that support to established 'difficult' directors and incentives to encourage first-time film-makers are a cultural necessity. It also needs to apply corrective mechanisms to monopolies that have emerged (or may emerge) and to adopt some sort of system whereby success can be used to help local talent. It is not only a necessary condition for Europe as a whole but also for the various regions/peoples of Europe if they want to retain their specific identity as well as to renew it.

## Questions

1  To what extent can it be said that the economics of the European film industry determines the cinematic content of European films? Do modes of production, distribution and exhibition affect the characteristics of films?

2   Why might the survival of national film industries in Europe be important?

3   Can films be defined in terms of their origins (financial, technical and artistic input)?

## References

British Film Institute (1996) *BFI Film and Television Handbook 1996*, London: BFI.

British Film Institute (2000) *BFI Film and Television Handbook 2000*, London: BFI.

*CNC Info* (1993) 245 (January).

*CNC Info* (2000) 276 (May).

Dyer, R. and Vincendeau, G. (eds) (1992) *Popular European Cinema*, London: Routledge.

Elsaesser, T. (1992) 'Rivette and the end of cinema', *Sight and Sound* 1(12): 12.

*Eurimages News* (1994) 7 (September): 1.

Hill, J., McLoone, M. and Hainsworth, P. (eds) (1994) *Border Crossing: Film in Ireland, Britain and Europe*, London: British Film Institute.

Jäckel, A. (1997) 'Cultural cooperation in Europe', *Media, Culture and Society* 1(19): 111–20.

Kipnis, L. (1998) 'Film and changing technologies', in J. Hill and P. Church Gibson (eds) *The Oxford Guide to Film Studies*, New York: Oxford University Press, pp. 595–604.

Parker, A. (2000) 'Foreword', in *Towards a sustainable UK film industry*, London: Film Council.

Porter, V. (1985) 'European co-productions: aesthetic and cultural implications', *Journal of Area Studies* 12: 6.

Sheperd, L. and McCartney, N. (1992) 'Europe by numbers', *Impact* 4 (May): 17.

Thomas, N. (1999) 'UK film, television and video: overview', *BFI Film and Television Handbook*, London: BFI, pp. 16–52.

Vincendeau, G. (ed.) (1995) *Encyclopedia of European Cinema*, London: British Film Institute.

Vincendeau, G. (1998) 'Issues in European cinema', in J. Hill and P. Church Gibson (eds) *The Oxford Guide to Film Studies*, New York: Oxford University Press, pp. 440–48.

## Further reading

British Screen Advisory Council (1992) *The Challenge of Language in European Film*, London: BSAC/Media Business School Seminar.

*Cahiers du Cinéma* (1992) 'Il était une fois l'Europe', special issue. Collection of essays and interviews with film professionals on European cinema (in French).

Dale, M. (1997) *The Movie Game: The Film Business in Britain, Europe and America*, London: Cassell. Written from an economic perspective and packed with facts, figures and case studies, the book outlines the strategies of the various players in the film industry (Majors, Independents, foreign sales agents, etc.) and suggests that European film quotas and subsidies have had devastating effects on European cinema.

*Statistical Yearbook: Cinema, Television, Video and New Media in Europe* (1999) Strasbourg: European Audiovisual Observatory (OBS).

Everett, W. (ed.) (1996) *European Identity in Cinema*, Exeter: Intellect. Investigation into concepts of identity, whether personal, national and/or European in contemporary European cinema.

Finney, A. (1996) *The State of European Cinema: A new dose of reality*, London: Cassell. Critical review of the state of the European industry, Europe's subsidy funds, co-production trends and distribution systems as well as ten case studies (including *Trainspotting* and *Breaking the Waves*).

Hancock, D. (1996) *Mirrors of our Own*, Strasbourg: Eurimages. Collection of case studies on European organizations (Canal plus, Channel Four, Polygram) and small nations/regions (Catalonia, Iceland, Ireland and Wales) with a strong emphasis on cultural specificity and internationalization.

Hill, J., McLoone, M. and Hainsworth, P. (eds) (1994) *Border Crossing: Film in Ireland, Britain and Europe*, London: British Film Institute. A group of British scholars explore key questions on European cinema such as: What is the cultural value of cooperation? What relationship does film have to Irish, British and European cultural identities? Is there a European cinema?

Nowell-Smith, G. and Ricci, S. (eds) (1998) *Hollywood and Europe*, London: British Film Institute. An international group of scholars consider the long and complex history of competition and cooperation between Europe and America.

Petrie, D. (ed.) (1992) *Screening Europe*, London: British Film Institute. Collection of essays on image and identity in contemporary European cinema.

Sojcher, F. (ed.) (1996) *Cinéma européen et identités culturelles*, Brussels: Revue Universitaire de Bruxelles. Collection of essays on the various economic, cultural and legal issues facing European cinema (in French).

Sorlin, P. (1992) *European Cinemas, European Societies, 1939–1990*, London: Routledge. Looking at the way various nations have expressed their cultural individuality through film, Pierre Sorlin detects a common evolution towards federalism.

Vincendeau, G. (ed.) (1995) *Encyclopedia of European Cinema*, London: British Film Institute. Essential work of reference which offers comprehensive coverage of European cinema throughout the twentieth century.

## Web sites

www.bfi.org.uk (British Film Institute)

www.obs.coe.int (European audiovisual observatory)

www.cnc.fr (France's French film centre)

www.culture.coe.fr/eurimages

www.mediasalles.it

# Chapter 12

# Pop music

MARKETING AND MEDIATING POPULAR MUSIC IN EUROPE

**ROY SHUKER**

This chapter examines aspects of the production, marketing and consumption of popular music in Europe, particularly in the UK. Included are the structure of the international music industry; the various mediators of the music, operating between production and consumption; and three ongoing trends: the changing audience for popular music, the impact of new technology, including the Internet and MP3; and the increased importance of income generated from the sale of rights.

## Introduction

In 2000, the Recording Industry Association of America observed that, as the world's universal form of communication, music touches every person of the globe to the tune of US$40 billion annually. The Rolling Stones pulled in US$64.7 million in ticket sales for their 34 North American shows on their 1999 'No Security' tour, making the evergreen band the year's top-grossing concert attraction. In the UK, Shania Twain's 'Come On Over' was the biggest selling album of 1999, with almost one and a half million unit sales, boosted by her appearances in a high-profile Revlon cosmetics advertisement campaign and her *Top of the Pops* Special broadcast by the BBC in December. In May 2000 HMV opened a new Oxford Street (London) megastore using the latest in music retail trechnology, including catalogue database points, scan-activated listening posts, and a DVD cinema. In Germany, the IFPI (International Federation of the Phonographic Industry) shut down more than 100 illegal MP3 Internet music sites in 1999, and as problems with copying persisted, the IFPI declared 'war on European Napster clones' (*Music Week* 6 May 2000).

Such events and statistics indicate the international commercial and cultural significance of popular music. Defined here as commercially produced music for a mass market, and including the variety of genres variously subsumed by terms such as rock, pop, and electronic dance music, popular music is ubiquitous. We are exposed to it through 'muzak' in shopping malls; on the streets and in the parks with 'ghetto blasters' and the Walkman; on film soundtracks; on music video through MTV Europe and television shows like *Top of the Pops*; on radio in the home and workplace; 'live' in a variety of settings, from the stadium concert to pub gigs; in clubs; and in the music press.

In cultural terms, the significance of this consumption is clearly of enormous importance in people's daily lives, and for some consumers is central to the construction of their social identities. While there are problems with obtaining reliable figures, in economic terms the products of the music industry outweigh those of any other cultural industry, with income including the sales of recorded music, copyright revenue, tour profits, sales of the music press, musical instruments and sound systems.

This chapter examines some aspects of the production, marketing, and consumption of popular music in Europe, particularly the UK. My central concern is with the relationship between the power of the music industry to shape and even construct audience tastes, and the autonomy of market choice exercised by those who consume the music (see Negus 1999; Shuker 2001, Chapter 2). I consider the nature of the music industry, especially the relationship between the Majors and Independent record companies; the various mediators of the music, operating between production and consumption – live performance (the club scene; concerts; festivals), radio, music video, and the music press; and the role of the charts. The chapter ends with a brief look at three on-going trends: the changing nature of the audience for popular music, especially the decline of the traditional youth market; the promise and threats of new technology, including the Internet and MP3; and the increased importance to the music industry of income generated from the sale of rights.

The emphasis is on the political economy of popular music: the industry and its relationship to its audience. The brushstrokes are broad, and readers must look elswhere for detailed consideration of how the music industry operates on an everyday basis (Negus 1993, 1999; Hull 2000). I have also not had space to consider several important aspects: the important role of government, both local and central, in promoting and regulating popular music (see Bennett *et al.* 1994; Cohen 1991; Shuker 2001, Chapter 4); the nature of youth's creative engagement with popular music, through subcultures and practices such as home taping (Hebdige 1979; Willis *et al.* 1990) and the importance of local 'scenes' (see Johnson 1996; Bennett 2000) I have chosen to say little about musical trends and individual performers; the relative visibility of these can change rapidly, and can best be followed though readers' own eyes and ears.

## The music industry

The music industry is big business, an international multi-billion-dollar enterprise. While reliable data are difficult to obtain, various sources indicate the economic significance of the products of the music industry. At the global level, after a decline in the early-1980s, world sales reached a retail value of $US 21–22 billion in 1989, boosted by the increasing popularity of CDs (IFPI 1990). During the 1990s, worldwide music industry sales have continued to increase steadily, but at a slower pace (for up-to-data data, see www.riaa.com). Aside from the sales of recorded music in its various formats, there is also the considerable revenue to be gained from associated activities and products.

Historically, the music industry has been centred in the USA, with the UK making a significant artistic contribution to an Anglo-American popular music hegemony. This Anglo-American dominance waned during the 1990s, with the reassertion of the European market and the emergence of Japanese media conglomerates as major players in the music industry. Nonetheless, the Anglo-American market remained of major importance, not least for its frequent commercial legitimation of emergent trends. In terms of record sales, the European Community had overtaken the USA by 1990, when the retail value of discs and tapes sold in the twelve member states of the EC was $8.4 billion, equivalent to 35% of the global total and one-quarter higher than the 1989 total. US sales represented 31% (Laing 1992: 128). This picture remains relatively unchanged in 2000, with the US recording industry and the European Community each accounting for approximately one-third of the world's market (RIAA).

Recording companies are the most important part of the music industry. They fall into two main groups: the 'major' international companies and lower tiers of 'independents' although in terms of structure and operating practices, the distinction between these is frequently blurred (see Negus 1999). The 'indies' in many cases are dependent on the majors for distribution and also act as 'farm teams', finding and developing new talent for them. Record companies are hierarchically organized business structures, with clearly demarcated roles. In a larger enterprise these would include management, producers, marketing and public relations, publicity, promotion, business affairs, finance and legal, manufacture and distribution, administrative and secretarial (see Negus 1992: 38f.; Hull 2000). In the case of the record industry, while creating and promoting new product is usually expensive, actually reproducing it is not. Once the master copy is pressed, further copies are relatively cheap and economies of scale come into operation. A master recording may well cost hundreds of thousands of dollars to make, but its capacity to be reproduced and played is then virtually limitless. It needs to also be noted that the advent of cheap reproductive technologies has made piracy difficult, if not impossible, to control.

The international recording industry is now dominated by five 'majors'. Each company is part of a larger communications or electronics conglomerate, each has branches internationally, and each embraces a number of labels. For example, Sony Music is part of Sony Corporation, the Japanese electronics manufacturing company. In addition to its extensive consumer electronics division, Sony also owns or has significant interests in film production and distribution (through Columbia Pictures and Tri-Star Pictures), home video production and distribution, and television production. Sony Music includes Sony Music Publishing, and the labels Columbia, Epic, and Epic Associated Labels; Sony also owns half the Columbia House record club, Sony Distribution, and CD and tape production facilities in the USA. Sony expanded its music interests substantially through its acquisition of CBS Records for US$2 billion in 1988 from CBS. Sony's music group revenues amounted to around US$4.6 billion in 1997, some 56% of Sony's entertainment business revenues of US$8.2 billion, and about 10% of Sony's total revenues for that year (Hull 2000: 81; Hull provides useful sketches of each of the big five; see also Burnett 1996).

The trend towards concentration of the culture industries as a whole is increasingly obvious, with global communication now dominated by twelve major corporations.

This situation reflects the battle for global dominance of media markets, with companies attempting to control both hardware and software markets, and distribute their efforts across a range of media products – a process labelled 'synergy' – which enables maximization of product tie-ins and marketing campaigns and, consequently, profits (Herman and McChesney 1997; Schiller 1999).

The music industry has been part of this process of consolidation, heading towards a system of oligopoly (where a few sellers occupy the market). In 1998 two of the majors, Universal Music Group and Polygram, merged, with the resultant record company, Universal Music Group, becoming the largest record company in the world, with an estimated market share of 23% (Hull 2000: 79). However, this was soon surpassed with the January 2000 merger of Time Warner and EMI creating the world's biggest music company, worth around US$20 billion, and with a powerful foothold on the Internet through a planned merger between Time Warner and America Online. This will enable the new Warner EMI Music group to have access to millions of web, cable and magazine subscribers at a time when the Internet is transforming the music industry. (As I write this, in October 2000, the merger has been stalled by opposition from European regulatory agencies, concerned at the monopolistic situation it would produce.)

Estimates of the degree of market control exercised by the majors, and the relative share of the market enjoyed by each, are difficult to determine. Various authorities place the majors' market share of the global production, manufacture and distribution of recorded popular music at between 80% and 90% (Burnett 1996). In Europe, the dominance of the multinationals is clear, but varies in particular national contexts. IFPI figures for 1990 placed it around 90% in most European countries, ranging from Austria 94%, to Portugal 89%, France 83% and the Netherlands 75% (Laing 1992: 129). Since the late 1980s, several of the majors had embarked on 'a concerted effort to absorb locally owned record companies' (Laing 1992) For example, EMI absorbed Chrysalis in the UK (in 1991), Medley in Denmark (1991), Minos Matsas in Greece (1991), and Hispavox in Spain (1988). The major companies also take major shareholdings in independent labels with promising artists, an investment which can pay off: Oasis's label Creation is 49% owned by Sony. More recently, the share of national (as opposed to international) repertoire has increased slightly in several European countries (Rutten 1995); for example, in Germany, with the domestic impact of performers such as Sasha, whose debut album 'Dedicated To . . .' (WEA Germany) sold more than 400,000 copies in his home country, and also reached the top twenty in Austria, Switzerland, and the Netherlands (*Billboard* 19 June 1999: 51). (National repertoire is the recorded music performed by musicians living in the specific country. As this example shows, the local branches of the major recording companies will produce national repertoire if profitable.)

The crucial issue is does such concentration affect the range of opportunities available to musicians and others involved in the production of popular music, and the nature and range of products available to the consumers of popular music? Initial analyses of the relationship between concentration, innovation, and diversity in popular music suggested a negative relationship between concentration and diversity in the recording industry, relating this to a cyclical pattern of market cycles (Peterson and Berger 1975; Rothenbuhler and Dimmick 1982). The basis for this analysis was the proportion of top-selling chart records sold by the majors. During periods of greatest market concentration, there were fewer top-selling records. Conversely, during periods of greater market competition, with noticeable competition from the independents, there were a greater number of top-selling records in the charts.

This view was challenged by Burnett (1996) and Lopes (1992), who both argued that a very high level of concentration was accompanied by a high level of diversity. In a sophisticated analyses of the Dutch music industry, Christianen (1995) 'found a cyclical movement where, at present, we seem to witness an increase in competition together with an increase in diversity and innovation'. These analysts argue that innovation and diversity in popular music in a period of high market concentration depends on the system of development and production used by major record companies. Major record companies develop an open system of development and production, based on 'a multidivisional corporate form linked with a large number of independent producers' (Lopes 1992: 70). Negus (1992) points out the importance of the number of decision makers within a firm, as a variable in explaining the diversity and innovation generated by a major record company. Examining this situation, necessitates paying more attention to the gatekeeping process, the filtering processes at work before a particular piece of music reaches the charts.

An important aspect of the role of the majors in national popular music markets is the question of the possible conflict between the local and the global, in relation to national musical vitality. The basic concern is that the transnationals will promote their international artists at the expense of local artists, and international preferences and genres at the expense of more 'authentic' local popular music, and only developing local talents and genres with global sales potential. At a more general level, it is noteworthy that English is the dominant language of popular music, arguably a form of linguistic imperialism.

Do the policies and activities of the multinationals inhibit the development of indigenous music in the European popular music market? The response is complex, and varies from country to country (for examples, see Burnett 1996, on Sweden; Larkey 1993, on Austria; Rutten 1995, on the Netherlands).

## Marketing and mediating the music

There are a number of important media forms, institutions, and practices which serve to articulate the industy and the consumers of popular music, i.e. which stand between yet connect the two: the club scene; concerts and concert tours; music festivals; popular music on or in film; the music press; and, most important of all, radio and music video. All these forms mediate the music, creating a diegetic link between performer, text, and consumer. Their significance in determining meaning in popular music lies in the interrelationship of ritual, pleasure, and economics in the music. In various ways, each form operates to create audiences, to fuel individual fantasy and pleasure, and to create musical icons and cultural myths.

## The club scene

Clubs (and some pubs) are the main venues for live music on a regular and continuing basis. They serve as training grounds for aspiring performers operating at the local level, and provide a 'bread and butter' living for more established artists, often through being part of an organized circuit of venues. The equation of live performance with musical authenticity and 'paying your dues' as a performer remains a widely held ideology among fans, musicians, and record company executives, despite the challenge made to it by electronic dance music with its different sites of production and creative processes (see Reynolds 1998). Clubs have historically assumed mythic importance for breaking new acts, as with The Who at the Marquee in London in the early 1960s. They can also establish and popularize trends, as in English punk at London's 100 Club and the Roxy in the late 1970s (Savage 1992), and with techno and DJ culture in the mid-1990s (Thornton 1995).

A community network of clubs or pub venues can create a 'local' sound or scene, such as Liverpool 'Merseybeat' associated with the Beatles, Gerry and the Pacemakers, and the Searchers in the early 1960s; Algerian rai in Paris over the past twenty years; and the Manchester sound (the Happy Mondays, James, and the Stone Roses) of the early 1990s. While the cohesion of their 'common' musical signatures is frequently exaggerated, such localized developments provide marketing possibilities by providing a 'brand name' with which consumers can identify.

Despite the importance of music video as a marketing tool, club venues remain important for establishing new trends and their associated performers, such as the various forms of techno. A number of observers have documented the resurgence of the club and disco scene through the 1990s, particularly in the UK, with the popularization of electronic dance music (see *MUZIK* magazine; Reynolds 1998; Thornton 1995; Gilbert and Pearson 1999). The cult of the DJ (disc jockey) is a central part of the current club scene, a star figure whose skill is to judge the mood on the dance floor, both reflecting and leading it, all the while blending tracks into a seamless whole.

## On the road again: tours and concerts

One-off performances (gigs) and concert tours, expose performers and their music to potential fans and purchasers, building an image and a following. Through the 1980s and into the 1990s, live perfomances remained important to maintain audience interest in a successful act and a key factor in breaking a new one. Concerts are complex cultural phenomena, involving a mix of music and economics, ritual and pleasure, for both performers and their audience. (For a detailed discussion, see Weinstein 1991, Chapter 6.) Concert tours are about promotion as much as performance; artists appear on radio and TV shows, make personal appearances at record stores, and generally do anything that will help promote sales. In 1996, BBC Radio relaunched its Music Live festival as a three-week travelling roadshow of concerts and events around the UK, broadcasting live events, including Blur's only UK concert for that year (*Music Week* 18 March 1996).

## *From the Isle of Wight to WOMAD: rock festivals*

Festivals play a central role in popular music mythology. A number of festivals at the end of the 1960s helped to create the notion of a youth-oriented rock culture while confirming its commercial potential: Monterey, Woodstock, and the Isle of Wight. The 1980s saw the reassertion of the music festival, with the success – both financially and as ideological touchstones – of the politically motivated 'conscience concerts': the concert for Bangladesh, Live Aid, and the Amnesty International concerts. In recent years, the Glastonbury and WOMAD (World Music and Dance) concerts have become an established feature of the UK popular music scene, while major European festivals include Roskilde, in Denmark; Torhout-Werchter in Belgium; and Paleo in Switzerland.

As do concerts, festivals work at both the economic and ideological levels. They reinforce popular music personas, creating icons/myths. At the same time, the performers are made 'accessible' to those attending the concert, and, increasingly via satellite television, to a world-wide audience. This audience is created as commodity. The event itself, if it attracts the projected audience, is a major commercial enterprise, with on-site sales of food and souvenirs, the income from the associated TV broadcasts via satellite to a global audience/market, and the subsequent 'live' recordings.

## *Radio*

Until the advent of MTV in the mid-1980s, radio was indisputably the most important medium for determining the form and content of popular music. The organization of radio broadcasting and its music-formatting practices have been crucial in shaping the nature of what constitutes the main 'public face' of popular music. As listeners, we can all conjure up vivid memories of the sheer physical and emotional impact of first hearing a song which, associated with a particular period, event or person in our everyday lives, became part of our personal rock history. These songs were usually first heard on the radio, and radio airplay continues to play a crucial role in determining and reflecting chart success.

Radio stations are distinguishable by the type of music they play, the style of their disk jockeys, and their mix of news, contests, commercials and other programme features. The music is central to this mix, with station and programme directors responsible for ensuring a prescribed and identifiable sound or format. This is based on what the management of the station believes will generate the largest audience – and ratings – and consequent advertising revenue. Quarterly rating figures are crucial in the competition for audiences and advertising revenue: witness the bidding wars for new licences issued by the Radio Authority in the UK (see Frith 1996). Historically, radio formats were fairly straightforward, and included 'Top Forty', 'soul', and 'easy listening'. Recent formats are more complex, and include 'adult-oriented rock', 'golden oldies', and 'contemporary hits radio'.

High-rotation radio airplay clearly remains vital in exposing artists and styles, and building a following for them. Radio exposure is also necessary to underpin activities like touring, helping to promote concerts and the accompanying sales of records. The very ubiquity of radio is a factor here; it can be listened to in a variety of situations, and with widely varying levels of engagement, from the Walkman to background accompaniment to activities such as study, domestic chores, and reading.

Radio can play an important role in sustaining 'local' music. In the Netherlands, for example, in the mid-1990s Radio Noordzee Nationaal played 90% Dutch national music and gained a market share of some 10% of the national radio market (Rutten 1995). This supports the use of Dutch language for vocals by local rock and pop bands.

## Music video

The term 'music video' has several distinct yet overlapping meanings: MTV and similar cable/satellite music channels; individual programmes within general broadcast television channel schedules; and the long-form music video cassette, available for hire or purchase. Taken together, these exert enormous influence in the marketing of popular music (Goodwin 1992; Banks 1996). The common component of the three formats is individual music video clips, which follow the conventions of the traditional single. They are usually approximately three minutes long, and function, in the industry's own terms, as 'promotional devices', encouraging record sales and chart action.

The role of television popular music programmes is illustrated by the UK show *Top of the Pops*, which enjoyed a revival and increased audiences in the mid-1990s, with 8.4 million viewers by 1995. 'In the past twelve months, the programme has been transformed from an insipid showcase for mainstream single releases and unwatchable dance bands to a varied and bold show featuring album tracks, more live perfomances, new acts and celebrity presenters' (*The Times* 22 February 1995: 23: 'Top of the Pops back on track').

Launched in 1987, MTV Europe now broadcasts to 60 million plus households across the Continent. The language is largely English, but the veejays come from all parts of Europe and the channel aims to create programming that reflects tastes, styles and issues distinctly 'European', collapsing national distinctions in the process (Sturmer 1993; Banks 1996).

## The music press

The music press plays a major part in the process of selling music as an economic commodity, while at the same time investing it with cultural significance. Popular music and culture magazines don't simply deal with music, through both their features and advertising they are also purveyors of style. At the same time, these magazines continue to fulfil their more traditional function of contributing to the construction of audiences as consumers. The majority of popular music magazines, however, focus on performers and their music, and the relationship of consumers (fans) to these.

These magazines fall into a number of fairly clearly identifiable categories, based on their differing musical aesthetics or emphases, their socio-cultural functions, and their target audiences. To take the UK as an example: music retail chain's free magazines promote performers and genres as 'product' (e.g. *HMV Choice*); 'Teen glossies' emphasize vicarious identification with performers whose music and image is aimed at this youth market (e.g *Smash Hits*); *Melody Maker* and *New Musical Express* (the 'inkies') have historically emphasized a tradition of critical rock journalism, with their reviewers acting as the gatekeepers for that tradition; and the 'style bibles' (*The Face*) emphasize popular music as part of visual pop culture, especially fashion. Several relatively newer magazines offer a combination of the 'inkies' focus on an extensive and critical coverage of the music scene and related popular culture, packaged in a glossier product with obvious debts to the style bibles (*MOJO, Select, Hip-Hop Connection*). Musicians' magazines (*Guitar Player*) inform their readers about new music technologies and techniques.

The European music press is differentiated in a similar fashion. It includes *Les Inrockuptables*, France, with a bias towards contemporary 'alternative' acts; *Puls Furore*, a Norwegian weekly, mainly covering rock, but also techno, roots, and jazz; and *Popcorn*, a Bulgarian magazine aimed at younger readers, covering mostly rock and pop artists and styles.

This is a volatile and highly competitive market: *RAW*, the 'Britpop fortnightly' launched in 1995 to fill the gap between *Smash Hits* and the monthly *Select*, ceased publication after five months, despite selling around 40,000 copies per issue. It is also influential on consumption: an ICP survey of the readers of 27 music magazines showed that 57% of those who read music magazines buy an album every month and a further 30% do so every two to three months (*Music Week* 18 March 1996)

Music press reviews form an important adjunct to the record company's marketing of their products, providing the record companies (and artists) with critical feedback on their releases. In the process, they also become promotional devices, providing supportive quotes for advertising and forming part of press kits sent to radio stations and other press outlets. Both the press and critics also play an important ideological function, distancing consumers from the fact that they are essentially purchasing an economic commodity, by stressing the product's cultural significance. This is reinforced by the important point that the music press and critics are not, at least directly, vertically integrated into the music industry (i.e. not owned by the record companies). A sense of distance is thereby maintained, while at the same time the need of the industry to constantly sell new images, styles and product is met.

Popular music is mediated through its performance in clubs, concerts and festivals, via radio airplay and music video, and in the coverage of the music press. These forms merge consumer ritual and pleasure with economics, in the process imbuing a commercial product with ideological significance. The various media reinforce each other, in a cross-fertilization process; e.g. BBC Radio's first Music Live festival, in Birmingham over five days in May 1995, attracted more than 40,000 people and broadcast sixty hours of live music to a radio audience of around 11 million (*Music Week* 18 March 1996: 'BBC takes to the road'). It all coalesces around the charts.

## The charts

The record charts play a major role: 'to the fan of popular music, the charts are not merely quantifications of commodities but rather a major reference point around which their music displays itself in distinction and in relation to other forms' (Parker 1991: 205). The charts both reflect and shape popular music, especially through their influence on radio playlists, and controversies abound over perceived attempts to manipulate them.

# Trends and issues

We turn finally to three major trends evident in the marketing and consumption of popular music.

## *The changing audience for popular music*

As Goodwin (in Frith and Goodwin 1990: 259) observed at the end of the 1980s: 'older' music had become contemporary for audiences of *all* ages. Through the mid-1990s 'nostalgia rock' was to the fore in popular music, with the release of 'new' Beatles material ('Live at the BBC', etc); the launch of *MOJO* magazine, placing rock's past firmly at its core and with 35% of its readers aged 35-plus; and successful tours by the Rolling Stones, Pink Floyd and the Eagles, among other ageing stars. This continued high level of interest in popular music's past was evident among both greying consumers and younger people, with the latter being constructed by the popular and academic media, and the advertising industry, as 'Generation X': a very media self-conscious group of youth, primarily associated with 'grunge' as a style.

This repackaging/marketing of our collective memories is hardly new, of course, but the scale is different, and it raises questions about the vitality of popular music in the 1990s. As an age cohort, seen usually as around 13 to 24 years of age, youth have historically been popular music's major consumers, and young people remain a major consumer group with considerable discretionary income for the leisure industries to tap. The straightforward association of popular music with youth, however, now needs qualifying. The absolute numbers of young people entering the labour market in the UK and Europe for the first time declined during the 1980s, and continued to fall until the end of the century. The market for popular music has extended to those who grew up with the music in the 1950s and 1960s, and who have continued to follow it. During 1999, in North America consumers aged 35 and over accounted for almost 40% of album purchases, with pop and country dominating their selections (RIAA; the European situation appears similar, but 'hard data' is lacking). Ageing along with their favoured surviving performers of the 1960s, these older consumers largely account for the present predominance of 'golden oldies' radio formats and occupy an increasing market share of record sales, especially 'back catalogue' releases.

## *Copyright and new sound technologies*

Copyright is central to the music industry. The basic principle of copyright law is the exclusive right to copy and publish one's own work; the copyright owner has the right to duplicate or authorize the duplication of their property, and to distribute it. The full legal nature of copyright is beyond our scope here, its significance lies in its cultural importance. The role of new technologies of sound recording and reproduction have been associated with issues of intellectual property rights, copyright and the control of sounds. For the music industry, the 'bogey-man' of the new millennium is posed by threats to copyright.

In addition to deriving income from unit sales of records, record companies, performers, songwriters and music publishers derive income from the sale of rights.

Ownership of rights are determined by copyright in the master tape, the original tape embodying the recorded performance from which subsequent records are manufactured. The global music industry is now less concerned with the production and management of commodities, and more with the management of rights. As Frith (1993) observes, the advent of new technologies of sound recording and reproduction have coincided with the globalization of culture, and the desire of media/ entertainment conglomerates to maximize their revenues from 'rights' as well as maintaining income from the actual sale of records. What counts as 'music' is changing from a fixed, authored 'thing' which existed as property, to something more difficult to identify (see *Music Copyright Matters*, the quarterly journal of the music publishers association).

The Rome Convention and the Berne Covention are the major international agreements on copyright (see Frith 1993). The IFPI, the International Federation of the Phonographic Industries, globally regulates the application and enforcement of copyright, supported by various local and regional agencies (in the UK, the British Phonographic Industry). According to the IFPI, the UK music industry leads the developed world in the battle against piracy, which was slashed by 40% in the UK during the mid-1990s, after several high-profile raids and prosecutions. However, attempts to ensure international uniformity in coyright laws have met with only partial success; even within the European Community conventions and practices vary considerably. Attitudes towards copyright diverge depending whose interests are involved. There is hostility towards copyright among many music consumers and even some musicians, due to its regulatory use by international corporations to protect their interests. On the other hand, the companies themselves are actively seeking to harmonize arrangements and curb piracy, while the record industry associations (especially the IFPI), which are almost exclusively concerned with copyright issues, largely support the industry. Ultimately, it is market control that is at stake. As case studies of the legal and moral arguments in the cases associated with records by the JAMS, M/A/R/R/S, De La Soul, and others show, there are extremely complex issues involved. These centre around questions of what is actually copyrightable in music. Who has the right to control the use of a song, a record, or a sound? And what is the nature of the public domain?

Through the 1980s and 1990s new recording technologies continued to open up creative possibilities and underpinned the emergence of new genres, notably techno, dance, and rap and hip hop. Beadle (1993) addresses the profound changes being wrought by samplers, MIDI, and other new technological phenomena, which he credits with giving new life to a moribund music industry in the 1980s. Sampling can be viewed as part of rock's historic tendency to constantly 'eat itself', while also exemplifying its postmodern tendencies: 'The willful acts of disintegration necessary in sampling are, like cubism, designed to find a way ahead by taking the whole business to pieces, reducing it to its constituent components. It's also an attempt to look to a past tradition and to try and move forward by placing that tradition in a new context' (Beadle 1993: 24).

Digital sampling allows sounds to be recorded, manipulated, and subsequently played back from a keyboard or other musical device (see Theberge 1997). Introduced in the late 1970s and subsequently widely used, digital sampling illustrates the debates surrounding musical technologies. Its use is seen variously as restricting the employment of session musicians, and as enabling the production of new sounds, e.g. the use of previously recorded music in the creation of rhythm tracks for use in rap and dance remixes.

## Popular music on the Internet

The Internet has added a major new dimension to the marketing and reception of popular music, while creating new problems for the enforcement of copyright. It includes on-line music shops; web sites for record companies and performers; on-line music journals; on-line concerts and interviews; and bulletin boards. In sum, they represent new ways of interlinking the audience/consumers of popular music, the performers, and the music industry (Hayward 1995; Gurley and Pfefferle 1996). Most discussions of the significance of such electronic commerce emphasize the business/economic aspects: the benefits to firms and consumers; the barriers and difficulties associated with doing business via the Internet; the demographics of Net users; and the opportunities for companies on the Net. But there are also significant cultural issues associated with popular music on the Internet.

MP3 is a technology encoding recorded sound so that it takes up much less storage space than it would otherwise. MP3 files are small enough to make it practical to transfer high-quality music files over the Internet and store them on a computer hard drive, making CD quality tracks downloadable in minutes (see Mann 2000). MP3 has become very popular as a way to distribute and access music, and it has become the most sought-after word on search engines. There has been intense debate over the economic and cultural implications of this new technology. For consumers, MP3 enables access to a huge variety of music, most of it free, and they can selectively compile their own collections of songs by combining various tracks without having to purchase whole albums. For artists, MP3 means they can distribute their music to a world-wide audience without the mediation of the established music industry, but this opportunity also raises concerns about potential loss of income. For the major record companies, MP3 challenges their control over distribution and, since the format has no built-in way to prevent users from obtaining and distributing music illegally, can represent considerable lost royalties. The majors have joined to create the Secure Digital Music Initiative (SDMI; see www.sdmi.org), in an attempt to reassert control over music distribution. During 2000, there have been lengthy legal battles in the USA over the use of MP3 and Napster, the web site that enables people to access one another's hard drives for free music.

The Internet may create greater consumer sovereignty and choice by bypassing the traditional intermediaries operating in the music industry (primarily the record companies). Any new medium or technological form changes the way in which we experience music, and this has implications for how we relate to and consume music. In the case of the Internet, the question is, what happens to traditional notions of the 'distance' between consumer and product, and its technological mediation? Finally, the nature of intellectual property rights, and the regulation of these, has been brought into even sharper focus with the Internet's electronic retrieval possibilities, and the recent debate over the use of MP3 (see Mann 2000).

## Questions

1 Consider the implications, both economic and social, of the ageing of the market for popular music.

2 If possible, check out some music sites on the Internet (see end of chapter). What cultural and economic changes do they indicate for the future of popular music?

3 Investigate the music industry of one European country. Do the policies and activities of the multinationals inhibit the development of indigenous music in that popular music market?

4 Undertake a content analysis of one music magazine.

5 What is MP3, and what are the arguments (and associated 'players') surrounding its use?

## References

Banks, J. (1996) *Monopoly Television. MTV's Quest to Control the Music*, Boulder, CO: Westview Press.

Barnet, R. and Cavanagh, J. (1994) *Global Dreams. Imperial Corporations and the New World Order*, New York: Simon & Schuster.

Beadle, J. (1993) *Will Pop Eat Itself? Pop Music in the Soundbite Era*, London: Faber & Faber.

Bennett, A. (2000) *Popular Music and Youth Culture. Music, Identity and Place*, London: Macmillan Press Ltd.

Bennett, T. *et al.* (1993) *Rock 'n' Roll Politics, Policies, Institutions*, London: Routledge.

Bennett, T., Frith, S., Grossberg, L., Shepherd, J. and Turner, G. (1994) *Rock and Popular Music: Politics, Policies, Institutions*, London: Routledge.

Burnett, R. (1996) *The Global Jukebox. The International Music Industry*, London: Routledge.

Christianen, M. (1995) 'Cycles of symbolic production? A new model to explain concentration, diversity and innovation in the music industry', *Popular Music*, 14:1, 55–93.

Cohen, S. (1991) *Rock Culture in Liverpool. Popular Music in the Making*, Oxford: Clarendon Press.

Eisenberg, E. (1988) *The Recording Angel: Music, Records and Culture From Aristotle to Zappa*, London: Pan Books.

Finnegan, R. (1989) *The Hidden Musicians. Music-Making in an English Town*, Cambridge: Cambridge University Press.

Frith, S. (ed.) (1993) *Music and Copyright*, Edinburgh: Edinburgh University Press.

Frith, S. (1996) *Performing Rites: On the Value of Popular Music*, Cambridge, MA: Harvard University Press.

Frith, S. and Goodwin, A. (eds) (1990) *On Record Rock, Pop, and the Written Word*, New York: Pantheon Books.

Gilbert, J. and Pearson, E. (1999) *Discographies. Dance Music, Culture and the Politics of Sound*, London and New York: Routledge.

Goodwin, A. (1992) *Dancing in the Distraction Factory. Music Television and Popular Culture*, Oxford, Minneapolis: University of Minnesota Press.

Gurley, T. and Pfefferle, W. (1996) *Plug In. The Guide to Music on the Net*, Englewood Cliffs, NJ: Prentice Hall.

Hayward, P. (1995) 'Enterprise on the new frontier. Music, industry and the internet', *Convergence* 1:2, 29–44.

Hebdige, D. (1979) *Subculture: The Meaning of Style*, London: Methuen.

Herman, E. and McChesmey, R. (1997) *The Global Media: The New Missionaries of Global Capitalism*, London: Cassell.

Hull, G. P. (2000) 'The structure of the recorded music industry', in Greco, A. N. (ed.) *The Media and Entertainment Industries. Readings in Mass Communications*, Boston: Allyn and Bacon, pp. 76–98.

International Federation of the Phonographic Industries (1990) Hung, M. and Morencos, F. G. (compilers and editors) *World Record Sales 1969–1990: A Statistical History of the Recording Industry*, London: IFPJ.

Johnson, P. (1996) *Straight Outa Bristol. Massive Attack, Portishead, Tricky and the Roots of Hip Hop*, London: Sceptre (Hodder & Stoughton).

Jones, A. and Kantonen, J. (1999) *Saturday Night Forever. The Story of Disco*, Edinburgh and London: Mainstream Publishing.

Laing, D. (1992) ' "Sadeness", scorpions and single markets: national and transnational trends in European popular music', *Popular Music* 11: 2, 127–40.

Laing, D. (1995) 'The economic importance of music in the European Union', Research Report.

Larkey, E. (1993) *Pungent Sounds. Constructing Identity with Popular Music in Austria*, New York: Peter Lang Publishing.

Lopes, P. (1992) 'Aspects of production and consumption in the music industry, 1967–1990', *American Sociological Review* 57: 1, 46–71.

Mann, B. (2000) *I Want My MP3! How to Download, Rip, & Play Digital Music*, New York: McGraw-Hill.

Mitchell, T. (1996) *Popular Music and Local Identity*, London and New York: Leicester University Press.

Negus, K. (1992) *Producing Pop. Culture and Conflict in the Popular Music Industry*, London: Edward Arnold.

Negus, K. (1999) *Music Genres and Corporate Cultures*, London and New York: Routledge.

Parker, M. (1991) 'Reading the charts – making sense with the hit parade', *Popular Music* 10: 2, 205–17.

Peterson, R. and Berger, D. (1975) 'Cycles in symbolic production: the case of popular music', *American Sociological Review* 40: 158–73.

Reynolds, S. (1998) *Generation Ecstasy: Into the World of Techno and Rave Culture*, Boston, MA: Little, Brown & Company.

Robinson, D., Buck, E., Cuthbert, M. *et al.* (1991) *Music at the Margins. Popular Music and Global Diversity*, Newbury Park, CA: Sage.

Rothenbuhler, E. and Dimmick, J. (1982) 'Popular music: concentration and diversity in the industry, 1974–1980', *Journal of Communication* 32: 143–9.

Rutten, P. (1995) 'Global sounds and local brews. Musical developments and music industry in Europe', Research Report.

Savage, J. (1992) *England's Dreaming: Sex Pistols and Punk Rock*, London: Faber & Faber.

Schiller, D. (1999) *Digital capitalism: Networking the Global Market System*, Cambridge, MA: MIT Press.

Shepherd, J. (1991) *Music as Social Text*, Cambridge: Polity Press.

Shuker, R. (1998) *Key Concepts in Popular Music*, London and New York: Routledge.

Shuker, R. (2001) *Understanding Popular Music*, revised edition, London and New York: Routledge.

Sturmer, C. (1993) 'MTV's EUROPE. An imaginary continent?' in *Channels of Resistance. Global Television and Local Empowerment*, London: BFI Publishing, pp. 50–66.

Theberge, P. (1997) *Any Sound You Can Imagine: Making Music/Consuming Technology*, Hanover, NH: Wesleyan University Press.

Thornton, S. (1995) *Club Cultures. Music, Media and Subcultural Capital*, London: Polity Press.

Wallis, R. and Malm, K. (1992) *Media Policy and Music Activity*, London and New York: Routledge.

Weinstein, D. (1991) *Heavy Metal: A Cultural Sociology*, New York: Lexington.

Willis, P. *et al.* (1990) *Common Culture. Symbolic Work at Play in the Everyday Cultures of the Young*, Milton Keynes: Open University Press.

The daily operation of the music industry is best followed by trade publications, particularly *Music Week* (UK) and *Billboard* (USA). The British Phonographic Industry publishes an Annual Yearbook, which includes very comprehensive statistics.

Trends and performers can be followed through the music press, and on music video channels and programmes such as *Top of the Pops*.

## Further reading

Bennett, A. (2000) *Popular Music and Youth Culture. Music, Identity and Place*, London: Macmillan Press Ltd. Uses a series of ethnographic studies (UK; Germany) to examine the significance of place and associated youth cultures in shaping popular music consumption.

Frith, S. (1996) *Performing Rites: On the Value of Popular Music*, Cambridge, MA: Harvard University Press. Deals with how music is created and evaluated, in a sophisticated (but accessible) and wide-ranging discussion.

Hull, G.P. (2000) 'The structure of the recorded music industry', in A. N. Greco (ed.) *The Media and Entertainment Industries. Readings in Mass Communications*, Boston: Allyn and Bacon, pp. 76–98. An excellent succinct overview of the music industry; includes extensive statistical information.

Negus, K. (1999) *Music Genres and Corporate Cultures*, London and New York: Routledge. Explores the workings of the music industry as an example of corporate culture, and the strategies for managing and marketing styles and artists.

Shuker, R. (1998) *Key Concepts in Popular Music*, London and New York: Routledge. A 'beginner's guide', with particular attention to genres.

## Web sites

Internet popular music industry sites include:

The British Phonographic Industry www.bpi.co.uk/

Recording Industry Association of America www.riaa.com

*Music Week* www.dotmusic.com

Music Publishers Association www.mpaonline.org.uk

International Federation of the Phonographic Industries (IFPI) www.ifpi.org.uk/home

On popular music more generally, see:

Internet Music Resource Guide: www.teleport.com/~celinec/mus_gnrl.htm

which gives access to numerous other music sites.

# Chapter 13

# Technology

NEW TECHNOLOGIES AND THE MEDIA

**BRIAN McNAIR**

This chapter examines the impact of new information and communication technologies (NICTs) on the established print and broadcast media. Issues covered include the hanging media production process, and the impact of digitalization and the Internet on the future of regulation and censorship. The chapter seeks to avoid both the dystopian and utopian perpectives on the social impact of new technologies, and to present a realistic appraisal of the positive and negative consequences of their introduction.

One of the greatest challenges to the media in recent years – and one that will intensify further in the twenty-first century – is the potential impact of new information and communication technologies (NICTs) on the form and content of media output, the processes through which media messages are produced and consumed, and on the role of the media in society. Such challenges are not new, of course, and the history of the mass media is a history of technological development with profound social consequences and implications at every stage. But there are strong grounds for believing that contemporary media are undergoing particularly dramatic technologically driven change, heralding a qualitatively new phase in the cultures of advanced capitalism. This will be an era characterized by media interactivity, accessibility and diversity, with new freedoms for the audience (or the 'consumer', as we may prefer to call him or her). It will also be the era of universally available 'cyberporn', information overload, and the decline or disappearance of some traditional media.

This chapter examines these developments and attempts to assess their implications, positive and negative, for the media culture of the twenty-first century. It considers both print and broadcast media, and media which are neither print nor broadcast, such as the proliferating Internet services. The discussion will focus on news and journalistic media, around which public debate on the impact of NICTs is the most lively, but issues relating to entertainment and recreational media, such as the emergence of 'cyberporn' on the Internet, will also be included.

'Cyberporn' is one issue which has prompted some academics, politicians and other interested parties to be pessimistic about the impact of new media technologies on the quality of cultural life. Others have expressed optimism about the potentially democratizing, decentralizing effects of NICTs as they spread. This chapter will aim to make some contribution to that debate, while providing the reader with a fair summary of the issues and the evidence cited by those who participate in it.

## New technologies and the media industry: changing structures and practices

Before examining those debates, we must acknowledge the huge and continuing impact which the introduction of NICTs has had on structures of ownership and control, patterns of employment, and processes of production within the media industry. For four decades or so following the Second World War, media organizations enjoyed relative stability, and their employees relative security. British newspapers, for example, in the early 1980s still used printing methods first introduced in the nineteenth century. Journalists and technical staff were secure in their positions within the production process, enjoying high wages and status (members of the Fleet Street print unions were 'labour aristocrats' in the classic sense). Newspapers were not particularly profitable institutions, often being used by rich men as what Robert Maxwell once called 'megaphones' for the wielding of political influence. Then, in January 1986, Rupert Murdoch imposed new technology and associated working practices on a shocked staff, leading to mass sackings, resignations, and picketline violence of exceptional ferocity and bitterness.

When the Wapping dispute was over (won by Murdoch with the political support of the Thatcher government) the way was clear for a technologically driven 'revolution' in the British newspaper industry. The print unions were all but banished from the production process, and journalists forced to learn new computer-based methods such as direct-inputting. Both groups saw their wages driven down and their working conditions drastically altered. Newspaper profits increased sharply, allowing Rupert Murdoch to fund his Sky operation (McNair 1999) and unleashing the highly competitive pricing, promotional giveaways and design innovation that have characterized the British press environment since 1986.

These same pressures were at work in other countries (often initiated by the same companies and individuals, notably Murdoch, who were establishing themselves as truly global media barons) although not always as rapidly and ruthlessly an in the UK. In the USA, for example, Murdoch's News Corporation met with more effective resistance from the unions than was the case in the UK.

As James Curran predicted (Curran and Seaton 1997), the introduction of new technologies to the print media did not fundamentally change the long-established structures of ownership and control, which remained predominantly the preserve of a small number of proprietors. New technologies produced huge cost savings, certainly, but these were reinvested in the launching of competitive strategies such as the introduction of Saturday supplements and multiple sections by newspapers, or the price cutting which has been a key feature of the British newspaper market since 1993 or so. As a consequence, and with the obvious exception of Robert Maxwell's empire, those who dominated the press before the introduction of new printing technologies in the 1980s still do so now. Their employees, on the other hand, are rather less well-paid and secure, expected to do more, and more varied work for less money than in the days of 'hot metal'.

NICTs have had this impact on many other spheres of work – changing the nature of tasks, undermining professionalism, encouraging casualization and short-term contracts – but media workers have experienced the effects more severely than most.

For the newspaper and periodical industry the drive for change has been made more urgent by the development of electronic 'on-line' data services, distributed on the Internet (see below). In the early years of the information revolution, these took the form of highly specialized services providing, for example, up-to-date information about share prices to computer users in the finance industries, or abstracts of printed articles for researchers in academia. By their nature they were of little or no interest to the wider population, and quality journalism was not their priority. Now, however, the Internet is awash with electronic publications and news services of increasing journalistic quality which, in the view of some observers, threaten the long-term viability of print as a media form. Cultural futurologists have long speculated about the decline of print, but the debate has taken on a distinctly more apocalyptic tone as the Internet expands and penetrates into mainstream consumer markets across the globe.

Reports of the death of print are probably exaggerated since, as the American analyst Jon Katz (1995) has put it, 'newspapers are silent, highly portable, require neither power source nor arcane commands and don't crash or get infected. They can be stored for days at no cost and consumed over time in small, digestible quantities'. Newspapers and magazines (and printed books, also perceived to be at risk in the new era of electronic publishing) will always enjoy the unique selling point of their user-friendliness. Computer terminals are not suitable for a quiet read on the bus or in the pub. Reading from the printed page is a different and, in many respects, superior experience to that of scrolling through text on a computer screen. But the advent of electronic publishing on a commercial scale can nevertheless be expected to have some impact on the readerships and revenues of the traditional print media, and prudence dictates a response.

Most UK newspapers now publish on-line versions, eager to be seen as part of the information revolution rather than standing outside of it. New computer-aided design, layout and printing techniques are being used to make the look and content of print media attractive, and more contemporaneous in a world where the immediacy of information is highly valued. In these and other ways – most of which require radical change in working practices and conditions – newspapers and periodicals will strive to protect their market share in the twenty-first century.

## NICTs and broadcasting

In broadcasting, the changes have been somewhat slower and (by comparison with the Wapping experience) more sympathetically managed, but no less profound in their consequences for those who work in the industry. Digitalization and 'bi-media' (in which material is produced for transmission on both radio and television) has forced broadcasting professionals to become more flexible and adaptive in a context of ever-increasing competition from NICT-based media such as on-line data services (see above). As with workers in the print media, deskilling, casualization and permanent job insecurity are the consequences. Regardless of how we assess the impact of NICTs on media content (see below) they have made the lives of media workers more difficult and complex. In early June 1996 the BBC's director-general John Birt announced a further major restructuring of the corporation's management and production apparatus designed, as he put it, to prepare the BBC for the coming digital era of multi-channel broadcasting. The restructuring would include further merging of the BBC's television and radio news production in the name of 'bi-media' – a process that began in the early 1990s (McNair 1999) – leading, some critics argued, to a downgrading of the status of radio in the BBC's overall scheme of things (Tusa 1996).

Unpopular with employees though these and subsequent changes understandably are, they are viewed by BBC management as a necessary response to a changing media environment which could otherwise threaten the corporation – in its present form – with extinction. Digitalized television and radio services, disseminated through cable and satellite to audiences at home and abroad, promise hundreds of channels available to the average household in the near future. Since the mid-1980s there has already been a proliferation of channels in the UK, but within a framework recognizable as 'broadcasting'. The future will be one of 'narrowcasting', as increasingly specialized services are targeted, with the help of digital technologies, on ever more distinctive niche markets. These will, in the main, be pay-per-view subscription services, allowing 24-hour news junkies to have their daily fix of journalism, and sports fans to watch their activity round the clock. Consumers will use these services to make purchasing decisions, and to handle financial transactions. Electronic media will become like print in their form and function – distinctive packages of information and entertainment bought, as newspapers and periodicals are currently bought, by audiences willing to pay the premium.

The first British pay-per-view sporting event – the Frank Bruno versus Mike Tyson heavyweight boxing match – was transmitted by Skysport in early 1996, and few doubted that this was but a taste of things to come in the digitalized, multi-channel era ahead.

The BBC (and other broadcasting organizations) are compelled to enter this developing market, even while striving to maintain a public service broadcasting operation of sufficient quality and popularity to maintain the case for the licence fee. In John Birt's view his proposals for change were intended to allow the reconciliation of the two goals, supporting a 'free at the point of delivery' public service comprising the existing BBC TV and radio channels, with an expanding commercial element targeted on consumers who are willing to pay extra. Although it has survived the bitter anti-public service campaigns of the Thatcher years (not least due to the management's skilful negotiation of those troubled waters) the BBC cannot stand still while the digital revolution proceeds all around. On the contrary, as its managers see it, the BBC should use its immense stocks of resources, experience and reputation to become a leading player in the twenty-first-century media business. This, more than anything, will permit it to maintain its public service role in the domestic British market. At the Edinburgh television festival in August 2000 Birt's successor as Director General, Greg Dyke, presented his vision for the BBC in the digitalized environment which included expansion to seven 'branded' channels, targeting niche audiences. He also announced the end of the flagship *9 O'Clock News*, and a new *10 O'Clock* programme to replace it. In these and other ways (the development of BBC OnLine, for example), the post-Birtian BBC was continuing the process of reform and adaptation to the impact of NICTs which Birt had begun. By 2000, not only did the BBC have the Internet, cable and satellite to deal with, but also TIVO – a new kind of set-top box which would allow viewers to precisely tailor their own viewing, independent of the broadcasters' scheduling strategies.

Adaptation was required in the global market as much as in the domestic. NICTs have allowed national organizations like the BBC to become *global* broadcasters, transmitting their programmes to countries around the world. Both BBC and ITN supply news and current affairs material to the Russian market, for example, while the BBC World Service provides a vast range of radio (and increasingly television) services in a multitude of languages. In the twenty-first century the potentially huge global market for quality journalism and entertainment will be dominated by a small number of transglobal corporations, such as Ted Turner's Cable Network News and News Corporation. The BBC, of all British companies, is the best placed to compete in this market, having not only the experience and infrastructure developed for international operations, but also a reputation for quality unequalled by any other organization. With some justification the BBC is perceived around the world as the best provider of information, education and entertainment programming, a reputation persuasively reinforced by Mikhail Gorbachev when under house arrest in the attempted coup of 1991. At the most life-threatening moment of crisis, he testified later, he turned to the World Service for a reliable account of what was happening back in Moscow.

Having established its reputation in an earlier, less competitive time, the BBC aims to consolidate and strengthen its position in the expanding television market created by the introduction of NICTs, often in cooperation with commercial companies like Pearson, with whom it is cooperating in the establishment of new satellite channels.

Opponents of this approach are numerous, however. Dennis Potter's valedictory *Cold Lazarus* might be read (among other things) as an allegory of what happens when the values of public service and civic responsibility (represented by Frances De La Tour and her team of scientists exploring the brain of Daniel Feeld) are 'sold out' to those of commerce – in particular, to the global media industry. The playwright, as a leading practitioner of quality public service broadcasting in his lifetime, was clearly warning us off the superficial attractions of virtual reality and cultural globalization.

Similar views are held, if in less aesthetically refined form, by many concerned observers. As the BBC and others go digital, argue the pessimists, the needs of commerce will come to outweigh those of public service; quality (however we may define it) will be diluted; and electronic media will become a cultural desert filled with home shopping and cheap entertainment.

On the other hand, as is argued by the proponents of change, and especially by representatives of the organizations like Sky which are in the vanguard, the end result will be *more* television, *more* radio, *more* choice. In the past, for example, the British football fan had *Match of the Day* once a week, showing edited highlights of one or two games. Now, even before the digital revolution has taken hold, there are three dedicated sports channels on Sky, showing more football than anyone could have time to watch, and a host of other minority sports previously excluded from television. The service is not free, but if British sports fans are willing to pay the price, why the concern? Especially when, as a result of the competition from Sky, the traditional terrestrial broadcasters are forced to be more responsive to audience demands in their own sports programming, and the sporting bodies themselves are sharing in the new revenues?

Similar arguments can be made in other spheres of programming. Not everyone, for example, wants access to 24-hour news, but for those who do, Sky provides it. The BBC has used savings from the introduction of NICTs and 'bi-media' to set up Radio 5 Live and *BBC News 24.*

The key issue here is not whether digitalization and the other technology-driven processes associated with it are good or bad – they are unstoppable and irreversible – but the extent to which *existing* TV and radio services, on established BBC and commercial channels, can be protected, allowing a core of socially responsible, public service broadcasting to coexist with the new, market-driven products.

## NICTs and content

If the current phase in the development of NICTs is forcing major changes in the structure and practice of the media industries, it is also shaping the content of what they produce. This process has been most apparent in the sphere of television news and journalism, where it has also generated the most controversy (because of the perceived importance of this particular category of media output).

NICTs have (as was noted above) greatly increased the quantity of news and current affairs available to television audiences, by creating more transmission outlets. Cable and satellite technologies began the process, and Cable Network News (CNN) led the way in the 1980s, before being joined by other organizations. The digital revolution will accelerate it, and there will soon be more than enough news on the air for the most dedicated journalism junkie. But NICTs have also fundamentally altered the process by which news is gathered and made ready for audiences.

The development of technology has greatly improved the efficiency and immediacy of TV news. Until the 1960s TV news was filmed on 35 mm stock, meaning a two- or three-day delay in transmission. Telecommunications satellites increased the immediacy of news in the late 1960s, as did the coming of electronic news-gathering in the 1970s. More recently, portable VCRs (video cassette recorders) and edit suites, combined with satellite transmission of video and telephone reports, have gradually cut out the need for the processing of material, and enhanced the role of journalists in the field. For one observer, this is a 'fundamental development with lasting significance for the way in which events are reported on the television screens of the world' (McGregor 1994). We now live in the era of 'real-time news', where events are reported to us, in the comfort of our living-rooms, as they happen. Cruise missiles make their way through the streets of downtown Baghdad; rioters in Los Angeles loot shops and beat up truck drivers; a politician is assassinated – we are intimate witnesses to these events in a way that was never possible before the advent of electronic news-gathering.

From one perspective these are positive developments. More news, and more immediate news, is generally viewed as a good thing, strengthening the democratic rights of populations. Brent McGregor cites as an example the case of the 1992 pro-democracy riots in Bangkok, Thailand. Thanks to the speed of news-gathering and transmission, video-taped news footage of the events was circulating among particip-ants within twenty minutes of their taking place, thus spreading awareness about the unfolding crisis. During the 1991 coup in Moscow (in which NICTs such as e-mail and fax also played an important anti-coup role) Russian TV audiences were able to see with their own eyes (mediated by the journalists) that opposition to the plotters was widespread, including among the military. Resistance was strengthened, and the coup failed. In these cases and others, the immediacy of news was a positive influence on the development of the events being reported.

Some observers have, however, cautioned against the trend towards evermore immediate and 'live' news coverage of events, particularly in the international arena. For leading British television journalist Nik Gowing (1994), the development of real-time news has major and unwelcome implications for governmental crisis man-agement, especially in the sphere of foreign affairs. Because of the immediacy and all-pervasive nature of media coverage, politicians can no longer respond to conflicts and crises with what he characterizes as the desirable restraints of *control, confidentiality* and *coolness.* Instead, they must deal with a situation in which mass publics are gain-ing access to information as quickly as the politicians and their advisers themselves. Moreover, that information is undigested and raw – frightening, emotionally charged images of destruction and atrocities which may obscure the underlying complexities of an event or conflict and generate ill-informed, if well-intentioned and under-standable shifts in the public's mood. In a conflict situation where real-time news is present, in short, politicians *lack* control and confidentiality. Rather than maintaining coolness, they are under pressure to act in the heat of the moment. Real-time news may force a policy response geared to public opinion rather than the needs of the situation. As Gowing puts it, 'governments frequently go out of their way to appear to modify policy when little or nothing of substance has changed' (1994: 11). Politicians increasingly 'fear that emotive pictures provided by real-time TV coverage forces them into an impulsive policy response when the reality on the ground is different [from that portrayed in the news]'.

Of course, the impact of real-time news in this sense will be moderated by other factors. In Rwanda and Burundi, real-time images of massacre and genocide did not influence western policy. In Somalia (images of a dead US serviceman being dragged through the streets), Srebrenica (concentration camps) and Kurdish Iraq (refugees), they did. In this sense, TV coverage may be 'a powerful influence in problem recogni-tion, which in turn helps to *shape* the foreign policy agenda. But television does not necessarily *dictate* foreign policy responses' (Gowing 1994: 18).

The American journalist and writer James Fallows argues that the immediacy of news, combined with its relentless focus on drama, violence, and negativity, generates citizen apathy and a 'huge collective demoralisation for the people masochistic enough to watch [it]' (1996: 200). Contemporary news depicts a world out of control, a conclusion which applies as much to domestic as to international events. In the context of real-time coverage of the LA riots, or O.J. Simpson's failed attempts to flee after becoming a suspect in the murder of his wife, Fallows' observations are a useful qualifier to the general enthusiasm with which developments in news-gathering technology are greeted, not least by professional journalists:

> There is increasing evidence that [the news media's] cynical handling of issues and their contextless presentation of violent events make society's problems harder to solve than they would otherwise be (Fallows 1996: 202).

The term 'compassion-fatigue' has been used in the context of this discussion, with reference to the perception that television audiences are growing tired of hearing about (and watching) the tragedies of less fortunate societies unfold on their screens. Since the news coverage which accompanied the 1984 Ethiopian famine, it is argued, one crisis after another has generated a similar pattern of journalistic response. Armed with the latest in electronic news-gathering technologies, journalists are dropped into a crisis zone (Tien an Mien square, former Yugoslavia, Rwanda), from where they produce horrific images of human brutality and suffering for as long as editorial offices back home dictate that the event is a 'story'. After a certain period of time, determined by such factors as the presence of oil or some other strategic reason for western interest in the situation, newsworthiness declines and the journalists move on to another 'hot spot' where, again, horrific, decontextualized violence and cruelty is served up as news. Compassion fatigue signifies the gradual loss of interest (and compassion) on the part of audiences, as they grow tired of the feelings of guilt and powerlessness that often accompany exposure to such scenes. Just as some sociologists argue that watching fictional violence on television desensitizes the viewer to real-life violence, so too, it is argued, we become blasé and complacent about the never-ending succession of human tragedies presented to us as news.

While NICTs have made such news possible for the first time in human history, it is the pressure of competition which has encouraged its growth. Since CNN pioneered the concept of live 24-hour news in the 1980s, other broadcast news organizations have felt themselves obliged to participate. In the Gulf War, for example, news organizations accepted the restrictive demands made upon them by the military (such as the requirement that journalists work in 'pools', with military minders making sure that access to controversial or contentious material was denied) not least because they could not (or so they believed) afford to be left out. In the TV ratings battle which was a by-product of the conflict, every news organization wanted access to the war zone, and the images which it generated. For this, they were prepared to have their coverage sanitized and managed in such a way as to censor out images that might have presented their audiences with a messier, less technologically clean war (MacArthur 1992).

Commercial competition dictates that where one leading news organization goes – be it Burundi, Bosnia or Kosovo – others must follow, all with the objective of supplying what they genuinely perceive to be informative real-time news. Consequently, only audience dissatisfaction as measured in ratings, or direct efforts to manage and control coverage by political and military authorities, can be expected to moderate the tendency.

## NICTs and democracy: the Internet

Of all the developments in NICTs currently impacting on the production and consumption of media, the most significant is probably that of the Internet – the growing global network of linked computers – also known as the information superhighway – through which information can be passed at an unprecedented rate.

The Internet links millions of individual users and networks by satellite and cable, offering access to the WorldWideWeb – mainly used by commercial organizations – and Usenet, a network for private individuals organized into thousands of 'newsgroups'. These facilities can be used for advertising and promotion (including that of university departments, many of which now have a Web page profiling their activities); for on-line publishing of the type discussed earlier in the discussion of print media; and for communication between individuals by e-mail. The latter may be used for the circulation of data by researchers (for example, I subscribe to Moscow-based services supplying up-to-date information about the Russian media) or for two-way communication between geographically disparate users with a common interest. As the Internet develops and the infrastructure becomes more sophisticated it has become routine for 'virtual conversations' to take place in 'cyberspace', involving many individuals sending and receiving messages almost as quickly as if they were in the same room.

The power of the Internet was first demonstrated during the San Francisco earthquake of January 1994, when it was used to send out the first information about the disaster, beating CNN and other news organizations to the 'scoop'.

But the significance of the Internet for media culture goes beyond that of another leap in the speed of information dissemination. It constitutes an entirely new medium, harnessing the vast information-handling potential of modern computers, now easily accessible to the mass consumer market as well as the traditional scientific and industrial users, and the distributive power of cable and satellite delivery systems. For the first time, Marshall McLuhan's concept of the global village takes on real shape, as people in California 'talk' to people in the UK, Japan, Russia and Australia. The Internet presents a further, and to date the most radical dissolution of the barriers of time and space which have constrained human communication since we left the savannas and learnt to use language.

Speculation about what the Internet will do for and to human society abounds. From one perspective – which we might describe as utopian – the Internet does indeed herald the emergence of a true global village, a benign virtual community accessible to anyone with a computer terminal and a knowledge of how to use it. This perspective stresses the accessibility and interactivity of the new medium – the fact that it allows ordinary people to communicate across continents at the pressing of a 'Return' key, at relatively low cost (by comparison with telephone and fax), on all manner of topics and specialisms. The Internet is not owned by any state or multinational company, and no state or company can control its use. The Internet's relative freedom from the commercial and political constraints which have accompanied all previous communicative media, combined with its accessibility and interactivity, make it a uniquely democratizing technological innovation: a medium which evades censorship, regulation, and commercialization like no other.

An opposing, 'dystopian' view sees the Internet as the latest in a long line of dehumanizing technological developments, producing a population of 'computer-nerds' who, if they are not watching TV or fiddling with their playstations, are addictively 'surfing the Net'. The Internet, it is argued, encourages not communication but isolation, in which one talks not to real people, but disembodied screens.

Concerns about the implications of the Internet are often based on a fear of its anarchic, uncontrollable character – precisely the qualities welcomed by its most enthusiastic advocates. The Internet, it is argued, provides an uncensorable platform for the dissemination of all kinds of antisocial messages. Many US newsgroups are devoted to the rantings of extreme right-wing, pro-gun 'militias', for example. 'Cyberporn' is also cited in this connection, particularly in relation to children and young people. *Time* magazine in July 1995 devoted the bulk of an issue, and its cover, to the problem of cyberporn (Elmer-Dewitt 1995). The cover depicted a young boy, face reflecting the green light of a computer terminal, his eyes wide open with amazement. The article inside warned (and also pointed would-be users in the right direction) that the Usenet and WorldWideWeb networks were being used to distribute pornography all over the world, including – as the cover illustration made clear – to children and young adults. The material being distributed, moreover, was of the most extreme kind. An American academic's analysis of the cyberporn phenomenon concluded that 'computers and modems are profoundly redefining the pornographic landscape by saturating the market with an endless variety of what only a decade ago mainstream America defined as "perverse" or "deviant"' (Rimm 1995).

Cyberporn nicely illustrates the threat posed by the Internet, as seen by some. To a greater extent than is true with traditional forms of disseminating pornography (and this applies to all forms of morally or legally sanctioned information) the Internet permits a private mode of consumption (no need for guilty browsing among the top shelves); it is user-friendly, allowing a high degree of selection and choice for anyone familiar with the system; and it is free of censorship, respecting no 'community standards' (the usual test of obscenity) or national boundaries. Traditional means of regulating and restricting pornography are useless on the Net (McNair 1996). And as children and young people are known to be among the most frequent and adept users of the Internet, cyberporn thus emerges as a serious threat to new generations.

This dystopian view, which views the Internet as the harbinger of not only techno-logical slobbery and information overload, but also moral chaos and anarchy, without the control of legislators, acknowledges the inherent difficulty in imposing traditional constraints on the medium. As the *Time* article puts it, 'the key issue is whether the Internet is a print medium, which enjoys strong protection against government interference, or a broadcast medium, which may be subject to all sorts of government control' (Elmer-Dewitt 1995). In fact, the Internet is neither print nor broadcasting, but a qualitatively new medium, to which conventional means of exerting control are extremely difficult, if not impossible, to apply. It remains to be seen if the global community (and it would have to be a genuinely global effort) can agree on standards of taste and decency for the Internet which are both enforceable and acceptable to the growing population of users.

For this writer, neither the optimistic nor pessimistic views described above represent a realistic appraisal of the Internet's significance for media culture. Certainly, as the utopian perspective asserts, the Internet permits a qualitatively new level of communication between human beings, and hitherto unimagined access to all kinds of information. But the resulting 'global village' can be no more benign than the individuals who use it, and the materials sent down its superhighways and byways. The Internet, like all previous developments in communication technology, is destined to reflect the best and the worst that humanity has to offer. It will continue to evade state censorship and arbitrary moral regulation – undeniably a good thing – but it will certainly be subject to a creeping commercialization, as its economic potential becomes clear. This process has already begun, and will accelerate in the twenty-first century.

But if the optimists are perhaps a little too optimistic, so the dystopian perspective may be viewed as a familiar blend of moral panic, social conservatism and cultural elitism. Children and young people will not become drooling slaves to the computer terminals in their bedrooms. Some children will find and watch cyberporn on the Net, as earlier generations watched 'video nasties', but there is no reason why the majority cannot be taught by parents, teachers, siblings and peers to use the technology fruitfully, gaining access to vast areas of knowledge denied previous generations.

## Conclusion

The new information and communication technologies discussed in this chapter have raised issues and generated debates which are not in themselves new. Successive waves of 'information revolution', from the invention of the printing press to film and television, and now 'cyberspace', have each presented problems of control and regulation for our legislators; problems of adaptation and restructuring for the media industries; new challenges and temptations for audiences. We have, as human societies, dealt with these problems and challenges in the past, and we will surely do so with the latest wave. It is, as always, up to us.

## Questions

1   Evaluate the impact on either (i) the press, or (ii) broadcasting of the technological developments discussed in this chapter.

2   Is it possible, or desirable, to censor or otherwise restrict the dissemination of information on the Internet?

3   In your view, does 'real-time news' have a negative or a positive impact on public opinion and political decision-making? Illustrate your answer with examples.

# References

Curran, J. and Seaton, J. (1997) *Power without Responsibility: The Press and Broadcasting in Britain*, 5th edn, London: Routledge.

Elmer-Dewitt, P. (1995) 'On a screen near you: cyberporn', *Time* 3 July.

Fallows, J. (1996) *Breaking the News*, New York: Pantheon.

Gowing, N. (1994) 'Real-time television coverage of armed conflicts and diplomatic crises', Harvard University, Cambridge, MA.

Katz, J. (1995) 'Tomorrow's word', *Guardian* 24 April.

MacArthur, J. (1992) *Second Front*, New York: Hill & Wang.

McGregor, B. (1994) 'Crisis reporting in the satellite age', paper given to the European Film and Television Studies Conference, London, July.

McNair, B. (1996) *Mediated Sex*, London: Arnold.

Rimm, M. (1995) 'Marketing pornography on the information superhighway' (on-line version), first published in *Georgetown Law Journal Spring* 1995.

Tusa, J. (1996) 'A mission to destroy', *Guardian* 10 June.

# Further reading

Herbert, J. (2000) *Journalism in the Digital Age*, Oxford: Focal Press. Up-to-date guide to the impact of digital technologies on the production of news and journalism.

McNair, B. (1998) *The Sociology of Journalism*, London: Arnold. Contains a chapter on the implications of changing information technologies for the media industries, and news in particular.

McNair, B. (1999) *News and Journalism in the UK*, 3rd edn, London: Routledge. An accessible and comprehensive introduction to the political, economic and regulatory environments of press and broadcast journalism in Britain.

Yorke, I. (1995) *Television News*, Oxford: Focal Press. A practitioner's guide to the workings of TV news, with emphasis on technology.

**Part II**

# 'Outside' the Media

# Introduction to ' "Outside" the Media'

ADAM BRIGGS AND PAUL COBLEY

The chapters in Part II all deal with factors which might be considered 'outside' the media; however, this is not an entirely accurate formulation. Each factor is only 'outside' insofar as it can be conceived of as having some kind of independent existence apart from the media. In fact, each is so thoroughly a part of the fabric of the media that they can be understood to be 'inside'.

*Economics*, for instance, has a wider frame than just the media; yet media economics determines the production of representations as well as their consumption. *Policy* is made by governments and sets the parameters for models of media institutions' ownership and distribution and in this sense is also 'outside' the media; but like economics, it determines the kind of media that are offered to us. Audiences are clearly made up of people, large parts of whose lives are separate from media. Nevertheless, audiences also consist of consumers whose viewing/reading/listening activity is registered as feedback, whose engagement differs according to different 'forms' of media text, and whose behaviour is often attributed to the 'effects' of media.

In Chapter 14 on 'Economics' Patrick Barwise and David Gordon discuss the way in which representations found in the media are totally dependent on budgets. In short, no budget equals no media. Every media institution needs to raise cash in order that it may (a) produce representations and (b) reproduce itself (i.e. maintain its existence and even expand). Advertising, for example, has become crucial for many commercial media institutions as the primary source of revenue. Moreover, advertisers target consumers whose 'quality' and 'quantity' are measured by audience researchers (see Kent, Chapter 17). Such ratings research establishes who consumes what media and in what numbers, and therefore the likelihood of these audiences apprehending the advertising associated with these media. But media economics has numerous different guises so Barwise and Gordon go on to systematically outline the different funding issues relevant to specific media.

As Barwise and Gordon note, Lord Thomson described the setting up of commercial television as a 'licence to print money'. The making of large sums of cash out of the media has increasingly become a subject of government regulation. Those who have the most revenue to invest can, potentially, invest further and control large portions of output from different media within any one national market. With this, it is argued, comes a limitation on the diversity of media output. This criticism has frequently been lodged against the (once) Australian media mogul Rupert Murdoch by those who are hostile to his cross-media empire. The important question posed by Lord Thomson's statement is 'How can the activities of media owners be regulated in the public interest?'

Media activity is regulated by broadcast policy which is the subject of Sylvia Harvey's Chapter 15 and also frames Ralph Negrine's discussion in Chapter 16 of models of European media institutions. In general, for broadcast media, policy is applied to two traditions of operation: commercial and public service. Put simply, commercial media (as exemplified by ITV, Channel 4 and Channel 5) in Britain is funded primarily from advertising revenue; in spite of this it is not completely independent because it is subject to regulative bodies set up by government. Public service (such as the BBC in Britain) is set up by government but is relatively autonomous of it; although public service is subject to government-appointed regulative bodies many of its operations take place independent of government. The government do, however, set the licence fee which provides a major source of revenue and allows programming for many interests rather than simply those of ratings maximization. The government is also ultimately responsible for the renewal every ten years of the charter to broadcast and the appointment of the BBC's board of governors.

There can be no doubt that study of broadcast policy is essential to understanding media. However, it cannot account for everything. While policy study reveals the legal, economic and regulative underpinnings of the media that we consume, it can tell us very little about the key *raison d'être* for media text – the audience, the media's consumers. Approaches to an audience's activity are varied and sometimes conflicting. Frequently, all that we can say with certainty about an *audience's engagement* with media texts is that it took place. There is little that can be said definitively about the quality of that engagement. Raymond Kent in Chapter 17 looks at media research on audiences from what we have called, after Lazarsfeld (see Chapter 1), an 'administrative' standpoint. 'Administrative' research on audiences measures ratings, and this is as important for public service broadcasters as it is for commercial broadcasters, as the former have to seek to provide justification for their licence fees in an increasingly competitive environment. What such measurement cannot address are the complexities of actual audience members' 'reception' of media material. How do audiences make sense of media texts? With what 'effect' do they do this (if any)?

The three chapters which follow Kent's each address themselves to these questions. Moreover, each adopts a different perspective and poses different arguments which have been very much at the forefront of much media study, especially in the last fifteen years (see, for example, Morley 1992; Ang 1996; Hermes 1995). The question of media 'effects' is the subject of Guy Cumberbatch's Chapter 18. You will have noticed that throughout this book we have referred to 'effects' in inverted commas. The reason for this is that, although in everyday discourse it is often assumed that the media have powerful effects upon their audiences, there is little conclusive evidence that this is the case. As a social psychologist, Cumberbatch is sceptical about the evidence that has been used to support the media effects thesis. As he shows, this thesis has a very powerful grip on the popular imagination, so much so that it does not escape the attention of policy makers. Yet it is unsubstantiated.

Jenny Kitzinger's Chapter 19, on the other hand, while sharing Cumberbatch's scepticism towards crude stimulus–response models of media 'effects', introduces a number of arguments that the media, in fact, *do* have impacts and influences. She points to studies which suggest that some messages are conveyed particularly effectively because of features such as repeated key phrases and themes, coherence of narratives, use of metaphor, repeated formats and structures etc. As Kitzinger makes clear, one of the key reasons for controversies around the issue of media 'effects' concerns the nature of the audience's reception of media texts. Joke Hermes in Chapter 20 explores the *active* way in which audiences make sense of media messages. Different audiences, she emphasizes, can make different meanings from the same media message according to such factors as their pre-existing attitudes, values and experiences. Hermes goes on to explore how the 'active audience' has been conceptualized in different approaches to the reception of texts.

Media 'effects', however, are not simply a matter of what is contained in a media text but how those 'contents' are presented. What are the *forms* of representation with which audiences engage? How do they act to *frame* a specific 'content'? And what are the implications of different kinds of 'framing'? John Corner, in Chapter 21, shows that this can never be a simple issue. A content such as 'violence' can never be conceived as a straightforward category independent of the form in which it is presented. To say that certain texts are 'violent', for example, is to say too little.

This part, then, links issues of politics and economics to audiences and the impacts of different forms of media upon them.

## References

Ang, I. (1996) *Living Room Wars: Rethinking Audiences for a Postmodern World*, London: Routledge.

Hermes, J. (1995) *Reading Women's Magazines: An Analysis of Everyday Media Use*, Oxford: Polity.

Morley, D. (1992) *Television, Audiences and Cultural Studies*, London: Routledge.

**Chapter 14**

# Economics

THE ECONOMICS OF THE MEDIA

## PATRICK BARWISE AND DAVID GORDON

This chapter looks at the economic forces that shape the media. It is essential to have a good understanding of these forces because they help to determine what we read and what we see in the media. The chapter begins with an analysis of the key economic characteristics of the media in general and then describes the particular characteristics of the main print and broadcast media today. It then briefly discusses the Internet, and concludes by briefly outlining three scenarios for the future evolution of the media.

This chapter is concerned with the economics of the media. Once you have read this chapter, you might become more questioning about the media that you, as a reader and viewer, 'consume'. What made you watch this or that programme on this or that channel? What determines the scheduling of programmes on television? Why do newspapers have so many sections on Saturdays and Sundays? Since television, radio, teletext, and Internet-delivered news is so up to date, how can tomorrow's newspapers compete with them? How can the thousands of magazines that line the newsstands all stay in business? How much is it costing you per hour to read a book compared with watching a video compared with watching ITV compared with subscribing to Sky – and were you dimly aware of the relative costs before doing the exercise? Are you sensitive to the price of different media? How can so many Internet services provide so much, to so many, for so little money?

Of course there is much more to the media than economics, money and business. The media inform, influence, entertain and educate. Newspapers, magazines, television, radio, and other media are powerful forces in society shaping the way that we know about things, look at things, think about things. As other influences affecting the political and moral climate of the UK have receded, 'the media' have taken on an ever more prominent position as chief culprit for the ills of society. But apart from the BBC and Channel 4, the media – including the publisher of this book – are owned by companies that are seeking to make money.

Judging by the size of the media industries, it would seem that all tastes and all shades of opinion are catered for. Is this true? Do we get the media that we want, or do we get the media that others decide we want? Rupert Murdoch fashioned the *Sun*, which led the other tabloids downmarket in a search for circulation via sensation. If Murdoch had not done so, would someone else have spotted this gap in the market and filled it?

Are all the varied gaps and niches in the market being filled? Certainly, looked at as an industry, nearly every indicator shows an upward trend: there are increasing numbers of radio stations, television channels, magazines, books, CD-ROMS, cinema admissions, accesses to the Internet – and students enrolled on media studies courses. Some sectors show decline, such as tabloid newspapers, but overall, media growth is the story. Why? What are the factors underlying this trend?

- As consumers get richer, they spend an increasing proportion of their expenditure on leisure, pleasure, entertainment and information. So media get a bigger slice of the pie.
- As economies get richer, the pie gets bigger.
- Despite the increased working hours experienced by many sections of the workforce, the amount of time that people spend on media consumption seems to be growing. This is partly because many people do have more leisure time as a result of the impact in the office and at home of automation and new technologies. Also, for demographic reasons, the number of retired people is growing.
- Some media can be consumed while doing other chores – listening to the radio while ironing, listening to a CD while driving, having a Walkman blaring out while on the bus, even watching a miniature TV set while at a football match – and these consumption patterns are increasing.
- Cable, satellite, the spread of digital media, have had a dramatic effect on most aspects of existing media and have ushered in new media. More channels, enticing gizmos, lower costs, the ease of getting entertainment and information, all have empowered and excited consumers.
- The coming together of the telecommunications, computer and media industries has attracted investment from large companies and entrepreneurs who seek to build up competitive advantage on a worldwide scale by having a dominant brand, or great distribution power, or powerful content, or ideally all three. Many of these companies have expanded from one medium, such as newspapers, into another, such as television, so that it is accurate, though grammatically inelegant, to refer to the media (plural) industry (singular).
- Governments have been deregulating and privatizing, and allowing private capital into areas that were once state monopolies, such as broadcasting and telecommunications.

Money, time, technology and deregulation are the economic and industrial factors which, combined with the cultural and sociological factors dealt with elsewhere in this book, explain why media are likely to remain a growth industry for the foreseeable future.

## Who pays the piper?

Most media are paid for by the consumer and/or by advertisers wishing to reach the consumer. In some countries, some media are subsidized by the government either directly out of taxes or indirectly by giving certain media certain privileges. For example, the BBC is given the right to collect the licence fee from anyone with a television, whether or not they ever watch or listen to the BBC. (This works better than it sounds. In practice, everyone does watch or listen to the BBC, at an average cost of a few pence per hour. But it would be harder to justify if many people stopped using BBC services.)

A traditional example of getting money direct from the consumer is buying a book. A more recent one is pay-TV, which is mainly funded by monthly subscriptions supplemented by video on demand (VoD, mostly films) and, occasionally, pay-per-view (PPV) for major live events such as a top soccer or boxing match.

An example of advertisers paying for the privilege of getting their messages to consumers is ITV. To the viewer this is 'free', or at least, painless and invisible, to the extent that some of the cost is paid by buying the advertised products (Ehrenberg and Barwise 1983). It is the job of the ITV companies to put on good enough programmes to get a large enough audience to charge advertisers enough money to pay for the programmes, the overheads and a profit to shareholders. ITV's recent attempt to move its main evening news from 10 p.m. to 11 p.m. was aimed at boosting its total viewing figures for precisely this reason.

This, however, enraged the politicians, who see ITV as still having a public service role, part of which is to show the news (including the politicians!) during prime viewing time. The ITC, which currently regulates commercial television, has just negotiated a compromise with ITV, but the BBC, acting like a commercial operator spotting an opportunity, jumped in and moved its news from nine to ten, and made a virtue out of antagonizing the Media Minister in the process telling him it was none of his business.

An example of both streams of revenue is a newspaper, which charges its readers the cover price and also takes advertising. Newspapers are a 'joint product' like a sheep, which is both in the market for wool and in the market for lamb. A newspaper has to appeal in the market for readers. And it then has to sell those readers in the market for advertising.

All commercial media fall somewhere on a spectrum with charging consumers the full cost of the product at one end and all-advertising at the other end. In some cases, the media owner (or a joint venture in which it is a partner) uses its own advertising space to sell products or services. A typical example is the Sunday Times Wine Club. With the Internet and interactive digital television, 'transaction revenues' from these activities may become more than a sideline in some cases, blurring the distinction between electronic media and electronic retailing ('e-tailing').

## Advertising

The main reason that organizations advertise is to sell more of their particular brand – Coca-Cola or London Guildhall University – than they would have sold without the advertising. This does not necessarily mean selling more than before the advertising; a campaign for a long-established brand like Heinz baked beans could be cost justified if it helped to maintain sales and prices in the face of cut-price supermarket brands. You may remember a TV commercial a few years ago with dancing milk bottles. This was aimed at *slowing down the decline* in doorstep delivery. It succeeded in doing this, more than covering its costs, but did not cause doorstep delivery to start growing again.

Usually, increasing the sales of a brand means capturing a higher share of the market rather than increasing the total size of the market (Barwise 1994; Barwise and Ehrenberg 1988: Appendix A). An advertisement for London Guildhall University is unlikely to persuade many people to go to university – the aim is to increase the proportion of people applying to that particular university. Some campaigns are directly aimed at taking sales from the competition. One well-known example was Pepsi-Cola's long-running 'Pepsi Challenge', which showed many consumers that under 'blind' conditions they preferred the taste of Pepsi to Coke.

In some cases, advertising for a particular brand does increase the size of the total market. One aim of BT's campaigns with Maureen Lipman, Bob Hoskins, and ET has been to encourage us all to use the telephone more – partly because it costs less than most of us think. As an unwanted side-effect, those campaigns have probably increased the revenues of BT's fixed-line and cable competitors, and perhaps even the mobile phone companies. Advertising can also accelerate the growth of a new market like the Internet, although if a product or service is really new it can also benefit from a lot of free media coverage.

Advertising can help a brand sell at a higher price than competing brands. Coca-Cola, Absolut vodka, Levi's jeans, Nike trainers, Benson and Hedges cigarettes, and Andrex toilet tissue all sell at a higher price than their 'no-name' competitors and most consumers know this. Stella Artois has even been advertised as 'reassuringly expensive'.

For the economy as a whole, however, the effects of advertising on prices are complex. Advertising in some form is a necessary part of a competitive market economy. It does cost firms money, but without it, competition is reduced and prices can be higher. For instance, when opticians in the USA were allowed to advertise, the price of spectacles sharply decreased (see MacRury, Chapter 4 in this volume).

## How much money do advertisers put into the media?

Total UK advertising expenditure in 1998 was about £12.6 billion. This excludes direct mail but includes posters, directories such as *Yellow Pages*, and business and professional magazines. Excluding these, almost £10 billion was spent on advertising in the mass consumer media this book is about. This is about 1.9% of total consumer expenditure on goods and services. Most of this was spent on press and TV advertising, nearly 5% (and growing) went into radio, and 1% into cinema advertising (see Table 14.1).

It is not only big companies that advertise. If you place a small ad for someone to share your flat or your life, the money you spend will be included in the advertising statistics. Classified advertising – job vacancies, houses, second-hand cars, and so on

*Table 14.1* UK mass media advertising expenditure 1998

|  | £ billion | % |
|---|---|---|
| National newspapers | 1.95 | 20 |
| Regional newspapers | 2.60 | 26 |
| Consumer magazines | 0.82 | 8 |
| All newspapers/consumer magazines | 5.38 | 54 |
| Television | 4.03 | 40 |
| Radio | 0.46 | 5 |
| Cinema | 0.10 | 1 |
| Total | 9.97 | 100 |

Authors' estimates based on Advertising Association (1999). These figures include production costs but exclude advertising agency fees/commissions (typically an additional 10–13% of the figures shown).

– accounts for about 40% of total advertising expenditure among print media – as much as 65% in the case of regional newspapers, about 20% for national newspapers and consumer magazines.

Virtually all the money spent on classified advertising goes to the media themselves. For display advertising, about three-quarters of what companies spend goes to the media. The other quarter goes to the advertising agencies who develop the advertising and buy the time or space, and to the printers, photographers, actors, producers and technicians who produce the advertisements themselves. When Coca-Cola hires Michael Jackson for a commercial, or British Airways hires the director Ridley Scott and a large number of extras, the result can cost more on a per-second basis than even the most expensive Hollywood feature film. For the audience, great advertisements are an important genre in their own right (see MacRury, Chapter 4 in this volume).

## What advertisers want: numbers and demographics

In choosing which media to use, advertisers' main aim is to reach as many people as possible within their target market. Other things being equal, a media vehicle with a large readership or audience can charge more for the space or time it sells to advertisers.

For instance, in March 1999 the price of a full-page colour advertisement in the *Mirror* was £40,100. The *Mirror* had a circulation of about 2.2 million copies. That is, it sold about 2.2 million copies of each issue. Each copy was read by an average of 2.8 adults, giving a total adult readership of 6.3 million. This is the number of people who would have had an 'opportunity-to-see' your advertisement. Dividing the cost of the space (£40,100) by the number of readers (6.3 million) gives a cost per thousand (CPT) of about £6.40. This is equivalent to 0.64 pence for each adult reader.

As an advertiser, you could instead have bought a full page in the *Daily Star* for only £15,000. But in this case you would have reached only 1.7 million readers, not

6.3 million. The cost per thousand would have been higher than for the *Mirror*, about £9.00. The *Mirror* can charge much more than the *Daily Star* because it has many more readers. (Official 'list prices' from Advertising Association 1999.) The actual prices paid are usually lower and depend on many factors but these do not affect the main argument here.)

Size is not everything, however. The advertisements in the *Mirror* are for things like records, car and home insurance, disposable razors, cold sore cream, made-to-measure furniture covers, personal loans, and car parts – products and services aimed at the mass market. Most advertisers, however, want to reach a specific 'target segment' of people. In some cases this is extremely difficult. For instance, firms advertising dog food or dishwasher liquid have no major media for reaching customers efficiently. Instead they have to use mass media with a lot of wastage (that is, targeted in a manner which is more disparate than direct), or develop costly direct marketing channels such as direct mail.

Often, however, there are media whose readership/audience closely matches the advertiser's target market. The most general way of categorizing consumers is by demographics – age, sex and household income. Consumer magazines are highly targeted in terms of the age, sex or special interests of their readers. This is reflected in the types of products and services advertised in them and in the style of the advertisements. Radio stations can also have highly segmented audiences, especially in the big cities with many local stations including those for specific ethnic audiences. Nationally, Virgin Radio and Classic FM reach quite different audiences.

The most valuable consumers to advertisers tend to be those with the most spending power. For some media, notably the *Financial Times* (*FT*) and the business sections of the other quality national newspapers, this includes their influence on purchases by organizations as well as their own personal purchases. Advertisements in a typical day's *FT* are for commercial property, trade shows in Singapore, financial information services, business courses, cheap flights to Amsterdam ('finance director's dream ticket'), various personal financial services, and a lot of corporate publicity announcements such as one listing all the banks that have arranged a $75 million loan for a Hungarian investment fund. A half-page colour advertisement in the *FT* in 1999 (the same size as a full page in the tabloid *Mirror* or *Star*, but with arguably less visual impact) would have cost about £26,000, to reach a readership of just over 600,000 adults. This works out at a cost per thousand of about £42 – five or six times the CPT of the *Mirror* and *Daily Star* (see Curran, Chapter 7, and Kent, Chapter 17 in this volume).

Television audiences are largely unsegmented (Barwise and Ehrenberg 1988). Most people watch all five of the main channels in the course of a week or so and spread their viewing across most programme types. There are some differences: the average programme on ITV has somewhat more viewers who are downscale, older and watch a lot of television than for the average programme on the other channels; soap operas tend to be watched by women, soccer by men, news by older viewers and 'action' (i.e. violent drama) programmes by young males. But there is nothing like the strong segmentation of print media and radio. For instance, there is no TV audience with the same profile as the *FT* readership, which can therefore be sold to advertisers at a high cost per thousand viewers.

This is important as we move towards multi-channel television. Many of the new channels are 'narrowcasting' rather than broadcasting, in the sense that they show only one type of programme (films, sport, news, etc.) In some cases like MTV, which has a very young audience, the audience is strongly skewed towards the target segment, as you would expect. But this does not mean that advertisers will pay a premium price for this audience, even on a cost per thousand basis. This is partly because few of these audiences are from especially valuable segments; partly because they are available only in homes with satellite/cable (still only about one home in three) which limits their reach; and partly because their viewers are also heavy viewers of network television. They do not enable advertisers to reach viewers that other channels do not reach. Broadly similar arguments apply in the USA and other countries with high cable penetration. The overall effect is that air-time on so-called narrowcast channels sells at a lower price, even on a cost per thousand basis, than for the main commercial networks. For somewhat similar reasons, the CPT on daytime television is less than for prime time in the evening.

As well as efficiently reaching their target customers, advertisers also look for high impact. Television is usually the highest impact mass medium for advertising although it is, as just discussed, not efficient at reaching narrow segments, especially high-income segments. It is also unsuited to campaigns which need to communicate a lot of detailed information such as a list of 100 shops across the UK which stock the product. Advertisers are well able to compare the cost efficiency of different media of the same broad type – different television programmes, different mass market daily newspapers – but comparisons between different types of media – print versus television versus radio – involve more art than science.

## Issues to do with advertising

Advertising – like media in general – has had its fair share of criticism. In the past it has been seen as wasteful, as making people buy things they did not really want or need, and as anti-competitive. The view today is more balanced. Economists now recognize that advertising is a necessary part of competition. Few people today believe that advertising has a very powerful effect on how much we spend on broad categories such as cars, holidays, and fast food. But the extent of advertising's influence is still controversial.

If advertising is a big source of revenue for a media business this will strongly influence the content of the medium. Consumer media funded by advertising have to provide content which will attract a large readership/audience of high value to advertisers. In the case of print media and (with enough spectrum) radio, the result is to produce a wide range of vehicles suiting many different tastes and interests. In the case of television funded by advertising, this process works less well. Minority programmes which are relatively demanding to watch tend to be unable to generate enough advertising revenue to cover their costs. For those consumers willing and able to pay more for more, subscription TV can fill this gap. A cheaper and arguably more equitable alternative is the traditional policy in Britain which combined licence fee funding for the BBC with advertising funding for ITV, Channel 4 and Channel 5 and with all five main terrestrial channels required to show a wider range of programmes than is found on deregulated advertising-funded networks as in the USA or Italy.

Advertisers may also seek to influence programming policy directly. This especially applies to media in a small community where everyone knows everyone. This is why the news stories in local newspapers and in trade magazines tend to be bland: the local newspaper may be afraid to criticize important local business people in case they stop advertising in it. Even national mass media can be subject to pressure. In the USA, the Moral Majority, a pressure group for so-called 'family values', has successfully driven off air several programmes of which it disapproved (e.g. *Soap*) by organizing a consumer boycott of the brands advertised on the programme.

## Regulation and deregulation

As each medium comes in, and is at first scarce, those in power try to exercise control. Knowledge is power. Before the days of printing, the Church kept a tight control of manuscripts and copying them was a specialist occupation of monks. Then came the printing press and governments tried hard to keep control of what was printed. This process continues today in many countries.

In the UK, radio was made a monopoly and handed to the government-owned, if not government-controlled, BBC.

We take it for granted that the government should regulate parts of the media. The news media can have a huge impact on political views, the entertainment media on social attitudes. Ministers are asked in Parliament to do something about the level of violence on television. What has given governments the standing to exercise control has usually been the technical need to allocate scarce capacity. For many years that was the excuse given for the tiny number of radio stations in the UK compared with the USA. As became gradually clear, the truth of the matter was that the Home Office did not think it good for people to have a lot more radio. The retreat of the Nanny State together with technological developments led to the sudden discovery of more radio bandwidth. The government is now keen to get everyone onto digital broadcasting to free up more of the spectrum for mobile communications.

But there are also good reasons why governments think that media are different from sausages and that some care ought to be exercised in passing control over to the owners of bandwidth that has been in the past limited. In Britain, the idea is expressed as 'public service broadcasting': broadcasters have to broadcast certain things at certain times as a service to the public, even if it is unprofitable for them to do so, in return for their broadcasting licence. Even in the USA, Rupert Murdoch had to become an American citizen before he could be entrusted with the ownership of television stations.

As the number of channels of television is increased through cable and satellite, the degree of regulation will decrease. Many regimes control media for political reasons. The former Soviet government tried to control all access to photocopiers and did not give telephone directories to ordinary citizens. The Chinese government is trying to control access to the Internet. Numerous British politicians, from both left and right, have accused the BBC of political bias, although the public is largely unconvinced of this.

## The characteristics of particular media

### Television: broadcast, cable and satellite

The most famous quotation about the economics of television in Britain was made by the Canadian television and newspaper proprietor, Lord Thomson, ten years into his ownership of the main ITV franchise for Scotland: 'It is just like having a licence to print your own money.'

Until 1955 the BBC, owned by the state, had a monopoly of broadcasting, and put out one rather staid national television service and three radio services. The Conservative government of the day, after much lobbying, agreed to a new channel to be financed entirely by advertising, as in the US model.

Those hostile to 'commercial' television feared that the need to attract large audiences would lead to endless game shows, cheap sitcoms and American imports, and would sap national morals and morale. The concerned government obliged the new service, which its supporters termed ITV, for Independent (rather than 'commercial') Television, to satisfy a new authority, the Independent Television Authority (now the Independent Television Commission), that it was keeping up standards of production in drama and entertainment, producing enough documentaries and current affairs programmes, and so on. The licence conditions also laid down that ITV had to have its own high-quality news service, ITN, which, in the event, showed a clean pair of heels to the stodgy, complacent and over-respectful BBC news.

In a worthy attempt to spread the benefits of producing for this new channel around the country, and to foster some regionalism in the new television culture, the franchises were awarded on a regional basis. Hence Lord Thomson, who owned regional newspapers, became a major shareholder in Scottish Television.

What he and the other owners of the channel found was that viewers' appetite for popular programmes, and advertisers' appetite to reach this receptive mass audience, led to viewing and revenues much higher than anyone had anticipated. The regional companies did not in practice spend much on the less remunerative local programming. They spent most of their production budgets on programmes that were networked, i.e. shown nationwide. ITV rapidly established dominance and by 1962 had a 70% share of television viewing, leaving the BBC in the shade.

The BBC fought back. BBC2 was introduced to cater for the more highbrow tastes and as a showcase for the BBC's more public service endeavours, freeing BBC1 to respond to ITV with programmes that aimed to be not only distinctive – justifying its non-commercial stance – but also popular, on the grounds that licence-fee payers should be given something they enjoyed watching. The BBC has always been on the horns of this dilemma. By the late 1960s, the BBC (with two channels) and ITV were each attracting about 50% of viewing. The British system was widely admired as showing a wide range of programmes which were good of their kind ('making good programmes watchable and watchable programmes good') as well as for its political independence.

The slow release of television frequencies led in 1982 to the fourth nationally available broadcast network, Channel 4. It was a real innovation. Channel 4 was solely a broadcaster: it owned the airwaves but commissioned its programmes from newly formed independent production companies who were paid a fee on commission and the balance on delivery, in the same way as a book publisher commissions and pays authors. It had a charter from the regulator requiring it to meet the needs of specialist and minority audiences. It was financed by the sale of advertising – until 1993 sold by the ITV companies but since then by Channel 4 itself. Channel 5, another national channel also wholly financed by advertising, was launched in 1997 and has positioned itself younger and downmarket of ITV.

The effect of having the BBC and two of the advertising-financed channels (ITV and Channel 4) which have to meet quality terms laid down in charters and franchise agreements has been that the range and variety of television programmes has been greater than on the main networks in the USA which (despite having massive resources) all chase the same audiences with the same formulas and the same mix of pro-grammes. In an uncontrolled mass market like television or selling petrol there is a tendency towards sameness. There is an old joke in the USA that American television is like the film *Battleship Potemkin* – it shows what happens when the ratings take over. (Of course, this is not the whole story: a typical US home has plenty of good pro-grammes to watch – spread across many channels – but many of the best channels have to be paid for and the 'free' channels carry far more commercials and other 'clutter' than most Europeans would tolerate.)

The number of channels available on cable and satellite is mushrooming, and with digital satellite and cable TV the number of channels potentially available is now in the hundreds. This means that the market will fragment; given a fixed (or even declining) quantity of eyeball-hours, the audience for any one channel is likely to decline. How have broadcasters responded?

First, they have cut their operating costs. The controversial reorganizations of the BBC by its directors-general, John Birt and then Greg Dyke, have been designed to reduce the costs of programme-making and administration, and to generate more income by selling programmes more aggressively abroad as television follows other industries into becoming more global. The ITV companies, now freed (within limits) to buy each other up, have done so and been able to reduce the overheads of the old regional set-up. ITV is heading towards being organized as a single national company showing some regional programmes. In some cities, the headquarters of the local ITV company was the second most imposing building after the town hall and will now have to find other uses.

Second, the cost of making some programmes, especially factual programmes, is coming down, aided by new technology (smaller cameras, digital editing), higher productivity and lower salaries. In the days of the television duopoly the television unions were able to push salaries up to levels achieved by old Fleet Street print workers. On the other hand, the sums paid to 'the talent' – the on-screen faces and some of the writers – is going up fast as broadcasters try to attract audiences in a more competitive environment. Similarly, the cost of television rights for movies, sport, and popular shows like *Friends* has escalated.

Third, viewers are prepared to pay much more money for the programme of their choice. With the TV licence fee at £104 (2000), and an average total BBC viewing in each home of 1200 hours a year, BBC television is still excellent value at 9p an hour (with radio thrown in free). BSkyB has now signed up over 8 million cable/satellite subscribers paying some £250 a year, who on average watch about 1400 hours of cable/satellite-only programmes per year, or 18p an hour. This compares with a cinema visit for two people costing, say, £15 just for tickets, leaving aside transport, popcorn and baby-sitter. Even a £5 paperback which takes ten hours to read is costing the consumer 50p an hour if it is read only once. Reading a newspaper or magazine typically costs 20p to 50p per hour.

Technology is making it even easier and cheaper for television programmes to be delivered to consumers, at a time of their choosing instead of in a linear stream that obliges them to sit and watch or to remember (and know how) to set the video recorder. The indications are that viewers are prepared to pay a great deal more per hour to get what they want when they want it. Sports fans are a particularly strong niche audience. BSkyB began the process of bidding up the rights to sports (part of 'the talent') to win viewers for its specialist sports channels. These sports channels have the advantage that there are no anti-sport viewers who are being put off (although there may be tensions within households). They also generate some revenue from advertising targeted at an audience with more homogeneous characteristics than a general audience, including hard-to-reach young men. Football clubs have themselves become more sophisticated media players – and, in turn, broadcasting and cable companies are becoming part-owners of them.

It seems likely that the same viewers who are sometimes in search of specialist channels will most of the time want to relapse into couch-potato mode, with choices being made for them by channel controllers, and at a much lower price per hour, for much of their viewing. Stream-viewing does allow a skilful scheduler to some extent to build audiences although this 'audience inheritance' or 'lead-in' effect is only shortlived (Barwise and Ehrenberg 1988). The mainstream channels have tried to keep audiences with comedy nights and Sci-Fi weekends. The BBC is now planning to make BBC1 mostly entertainment and BBC2 mostly heavyweight.

All this implies that, for the time being, the existing mass-market broadcasters will continue to enjoy a substantial audience, retain the bulk of the advertising revenue, benefit from substantial economies of scale and coexist with specialist subscription channels and programmes delivered on a pay-per-view basis. In the longer term, they face a threat from personal video recorders (PVRs) like TiVo and Replay TV, which make it easier for viewers to find programmes they want on small channels (in multichannel homes) and to watch in 'almost real time' skipping the commercials. PVRs are already being marketed in both the USA and Europe. Depending on their speed of adoption, they may over time erode the audience for TV commercials, and therefore the revenue of advertising-funded channels. As yet, it is too soon to judge the speed and scale of this potential threat.

## *Radio*

Radio is the oldest electronic mass medium. The BBC began in 1922. For decades travellers would return from the USA telling of the plethora of radio stations in all large American cities, while in the UK there were only a handful of national stations, all BBC. Those with powerful radio sets listened to Radio Luxembourg to get the popular music they craved. In the 1960s pirate radio stations on ships within transmission distance of big cities founded the careers of many disc jockeys (DJs). The first reaction of the then government was to make illegal the selling of advertising on these pirates. It was only in 1973 that the first licensed commercial radio station, LBC, got on the air. Independent Local Radio (ILR) then gradually took off, and the BBC countered by launching its own local radio stations.

It is hard to believe that in the nationalized, regulated world that crumbled in the 1980s the attitude of the regulators was to restrict the amount of radio and television. The arguments were based on a supposed technical shortage of frequencies, but underlying them was the Reithian belief that more would mean worse and have a corrupting effect on the nation's mental and spiritual well-being. Radio shows the braking effect of excessive regulation on a media industry. There are now well over 200 local commercial radio stations in the UK and four national networks (Virgin, Classic FM, Atlantic 252, TalkSport). Advertising revenue is about £500 million and growing. Much of this could have happened much earlier (see Crisell, Chapter 9 in this volume).

Radio is still highly regulated; the Radio Authority issues a licence for a particular kind of station and the staff monitor the station to check that the owners are broadcasting what they promised. (In practice, the Radio Authority can be pretty liberal in its interpretation, e.g. most of the music on Jazz FM is not jazz.)

Commercial radio illustrates in simple form one general characteristic of media, especially broadcast media: most of the costs of radio are incurred before there is a single listener; each extra listener adds nothing to costs; therefore the aim is to get as many listeners as possible (while staying within the bounds of the licence promise), to generate the maximum amount of advertising revenue. Given the number of radio stations, most of which are music-based, each station has to carve out a loyalty based on a definite personality, expressed in its music policy, the kinds of presenters and DJs it uses, its jingles, and the predictability of its output at various times of day. Since the advent of television, radio has become a secondary medium. People are usually doing something else at the same time as they listen: getting dressed to Radio 4 or driving to Atlantic 252 or working to Classic FM or doing the washing up while listening to an ILR station.

A change in the Broadcasting Act 1990 allowed greater freedom in the ownership of stations. Once a licence is awarded, the station can be sold, and there are now a few large groups eager to buy up the minnows, which can dramatically reduce the operating costs of the acquired stations while still meeting the requirements of the licence. This illustrates another characteristic of media industries: media owners can often extract considerable value from 'horizontal integration', that is, buying other similar businesses.

The next big step will be digital radio, with excellent sound quality, capacity for many channels, and other new features. However, these benefits are not enough to justify the high current cost of receivers, except for enthusiasts and in new luxury cars. As the cost of receivers falls and the technology diffuses, we should see broadcasters investing in new digital content, reinforcing the diffusion process.

## *Newspapers*

National newspapers are the mirror of the nation. Britain has an unusually large number of national daily and Sunday newspapers, reflecting readers that are serious and balanced about matters affecting finance and industry (*Financial Times – FT*), critical of the government from the right (*Daily Telegraph, The Times, Daily Mail, Daily Express, Sun, Daily Star*) and from the centre and left (*The Independent* and *The Guardian*), transfixed by the Royals (most of them), obsessed by sex scandals relating to minor TV personalities and footballers (the tabloids – but not only the tabloids). It is interesting to note, however, that although traditionally party allegiances have been seen as fixed, the *Sun*, which was always a Tory paper, very publicly announced its support for the Labour leader, Tony Blair, in the run-up to the 1997 General Election.

The economic fundamentals of newspapers are that, unlike for radio and television, each extra copy sold does cost money for paper and distribution. The mass-market newspapers get about three-quarters of their revenue from the cover price and only one-quarter from advertising, whereas the quality newspapers get at least half of their revenue from advertising – up to three-quarters in the case of the *FT* – despite their higher cover price. This reflects their much higher advertising CPTs.

As already discussed, advertising is sold on the basis not only of the number of readers but also of their spending power: having 1000 rich readers will justify a higher advertising rate than 1000 poorer ones. Since advertising is so crucial to the quality newspapers, the need to appeal to the more affluent readers partly explains why traditionally there have been more newspapers on the right of the political divide than on the left. The other reason is that there are more right-wing than left-wing newspaper owners.

Still, there is a large number of titles, with a fair range of opinion, competing in an overcrowded and mature market. A variety of survival strategies have been deployed in this competitive market:

- merger
- price cuts
- adding sections
- promotions.

### Merger

Rupert Murdoch was allowed to side-step newspaper monopoly regulations (on the grounds that he was coming to the rescue of titles that would otherwise die) and assemble a large stable of titles (1970s). He took on the overweening print unions of his day and brought production costs down dramatically (early 1980s), from which all proprietors and newspaper readers benefited, and was also able to reap the benefits of having printing economics from one huge plant at Wapping. *The Guardian* bought the ailing *Observer* (1994). The Irish Independent Newspaper Group took over management control of *The Independent* (which had itself been launched as a result of the lowering of entry costs brought about by Mr Murdoch).

Mergers allow overhead, production and distribution cost economies, and also cross-promotion of other titles – or of BSkyB, in the newspapers owned by Rupert Murdoch.

## Price cuts

In a mature market, each manufacturer is tempted to increase market share by cutting prices. Other manufacturers have to lower their prices to retain their sales volume. The weakest are forced out of the market and once excess capacity has been removed, the remaining companies can then put prices back up again.

In newspapers this tactic has been attempted off and on by tabloids in periodic circulation wars, but until Mr Murdoch slashed the price of *The Times* from 45p to 30p in September 1993, the conventional wisdom was that the strong loyalties of the readers of the quality newspapers would overcome a cut of a few pennies in a product that does not in any case cost much. In the event, the circulation of *The Times* rose 85% from 354,000 in August 1993 to a peak of 656,000 in July 1995 when the price war abated. Even so, once a week on a Monday, *The Times* was still available at the nominal price of 10p. The idea was to build up such a commanding circulation and readership lead that what was lost in circulation revenue would be more than made up in advertising revenue, despite some drop in CPT (as the average 'quality' of the readership fell). It was also widely believed that the aim was to drive *The Independent* out of business. But true to form, a proprietor wanting the prestige of a national newspaper – Ireland's Mr Tony O'Reilly – came to the rescue. Other newspapers had to follow suit – except for *The Guardian*, which stayed resolutely at its old price of 45p, and lost few readers.

Recent price wars have been limited mostly to the quality newspapers because circulation revenue is far less important to them than it is to the tabloids, whose circulations are in the millions and for whom therefore a cut of 10p would be even more costly.

## Adding sections (which, sometimes, improve the product)

The *Sunday Times* was the pioneer in the UK in copying the *New York Times* in making a newspaper so voluminous, with endless sections appealing to many different interest groups, that it would drive out the competition by sheer volume of newsprint. Its advertising slogan is 'The Sunday Times *is* the Sunday newspapers'). Each newspaper used the savings from cheaper production following the disempowering of the print unions to add new sections and magazines, hoping to make itself the only game in town; to broaden the products to cover topics that had usually been left to magazines like health, food and lifestyle; and to sell advertising in each section aimed at those most likely to read it.

Promotions

Cheap videos, games, competitions – all designed to retain fickle readers whose traditional loyalties to an editorial position or style have weakened. No national newspaper – except *Today* – has recently disappeared and the overall effect of these various competitive stratagems has been to reduce the profits of all. The owners have deep pockets or deep pride. History shows that national newspapers rarely go out of business. Someone, usually a would-be newcomer to the establishment, comes to the rescue, hoping for the kudos and influence that come from being a newspaper tycoon and the invitation to take tea at Number 10. Currently, the Barclay Brothers are assembling a clutch of newspapers and have successfully launched *Sunday Business.*

## Regional newspapers

The regional and local newspaper segment of newspapers is large (over £3.5 billion in annual revenue, including cover price revenue), but unglamorous. Each local newspaper tries to become a local monopolist, and there are few areas of the country where two local newspapers survive. Where this does occur one is typically a 'free' (wholly advertising-supported) title. Local newspapers rely heavily on classified advertising which accounts for almost two-thirds of their advertising revenue. In the long term this makes them vulnerable to the migration of classified advertising to new electronic media such as the Internet. Local newspapers are therefore now getting together to provide an electronic service themselves.

The big media groups have been selling off their regional titles, but the builders of new regional newspaper empires might find a way of rejuvenating the industry.

## Magazines

There are some 15,000 consumer magazines in Britain, covering every imaginable subject and special interest under the sun. Magazines are versatile and flexible. Barriers to entry are low: it costs far less to start a magazine than to start a newspaper or television channel. Hundreds of new magazines are launched each year. Readers tend to have a strong loyalty to their magazine; this can be buttressed by turning casual readers into subscribers – who then pay a year's subscription in advance, reducing the need for outside funding. There is a wide range of formats, sizes, paper types, designs – all of which allow great distinctiveness to an original magazine idea.

Of all traditional old media, magazines allow the greatest ability to form a community of the like-minded, which can be reinforced using the Internet (especially for trade magazines as opposed to consumer magazines). Although there are large magazine companies, the magazine industry is more fragmented than for other media. This is because, although there are economies in owning a stable of magazines – shared overheads, skill in print buying, a 'feel' for starting new magazines based on an understanding of markets, the capital for launches – each magazine needs to have its own dedicated editorial, advertising and marketing staff in order to portray its distinctive character to readers and advertisers. There is always room for one more magazine (see Braithwaite, Chapter 8 in this volume).

## The Internet

The Internet is formed by linking personal computers to each other around the world. The main part of the Internet is known as the WorldWideWeb, or just 'the Web'. Web revolutionaries would argue that the Web is not just a new medium – it will eventually be the medium that encompasses all the others. What most Web users experience in 2000 is the freedom to trade text from one point on the globe to another quickly, cheaply and easily, and graphics and sound slowly and with more effort and cost. The Internet's capacity will increase. But it already has extraordinary characteristics:

- point-to-point communication, rather than one-to-many broadcast communication, for the one rather than for the many
- 'hyperlinking' from one server to another: by clicking on a highlighted word, the user is directly switched to another database, perhaps on the other side of the world
- ability to search vast amounts of data
- increasingly intelligent software agents that sift what they have learnt the user wants to get hold of
- instant and interactive community creation, on a global basis.

The Internet provides a model for the way we may receive television, telephony, magazines, newspapers, and music. The capacity in the form of wires, cables and satellite dishes, and mobile channels and the decoding boxes to turn the digital stream into text, sound and pictures – the digital superhighway – is gradually being laid by the cable companies, BSkyB, British Telecom and other telecom companies.

Once the digital highway is laid, the economics of all the media industries will change: the content suppliers will be able to choose the cheapest and best path into the home or office, and pay carriage to the highwaymen, and the competitive battle will be about (in order of importance) content (who has the best material to interact with, to see or read), marketing (how to tell viewers about the needles in the haystacks) and customer service. But in the years before the highway is completed, the battles will include distribution – who owns which pipe to the consumer.

The economics of the Internet, and Internet businesses, is a huge and controversial topic which goes well beyond the scope of media economics. The challenge for 'pure-play' Internet businesses, even the most successful like the top e-tailer Amazon, the portal Yahoo!, and the online auction house eBay, is to generate enough revenue to cover their enormous marketing costs as well as their other costs.

The Internet is a medium which putatively puts the Web surfer in control. This makes it limited as a 'push' medium for advertising. Nevertheless, a site such as handbag.com (currently the leading UK site aimed at women) is able to generate significant revenue from advertising and sponsorship, since it has created relatively high loyalty and 'stickiness' (how long users stay on the site) and high 'clickthrough rates' onto its partners' sites. In the long term, a site like handbag.com – essentially, a publisher – can expect to earn most of its revenue from sales commissions on users' purchases. Another revenue source in the short term is for the site to take a share of users' telecom charges while they are online. This was the model on which the Freeserve internet service provider was launched.

Overall, however, most pure-play business-to-consumer ('B2C') Web start-ups are struggling and have fallen out of favour with the financial markets since the 'Internet bubble' burst in spring 2000. The main focus of Internet development is now elsewhere: technology companies, business-to-business ('B2B') e-commerce, linking the Internet to advanced (third generation or '3G') mobile devices, and especially the use of the Internet by established businesses as an additional channel, in combination with existing channels ('clicks and mortar'). Some of these commercial developments are reviewed more fully in Barwise (2000) and Barwise *et al.* (forthcoming).

For three somewhat contrasting perspectives on the long-term impact of the internet on everyday life and society, see Negroponte (1995), Barwise and Hammond (1998), and Cairncross (forthcoming).

## Three scenarios

The media industry is dynamic, ever freer of regulation, and with the prospect of more and more creative competitors. But there are strong pressures for concentration within and between media.

With growing competition, there are three broad scenarios:

- more means worse as competition leads to lurid sensationalism and sex and the tabloidization ('dumbing down') of all media
- more optimistically, more means more diversity as each shade of taste and opinion is catered for by an appropriate medium able to target an interest group economically
- a hybrid with policies to ensure access by everyone to a basic tier of communication, but with an additional huge variety of services available to those willing and able to pay more for more.

With growing concentration, the issue is whether diversity is increased or whether there will be a tendency towards bland, inoffensive entertainment.

## Questions

1  Do the owners of media owe a duty of care for the state of society – or only one of profit to their shareholders? Is there a conflict between the two? Do they have to behave 'responsibly', and what does that mean in practice?
2  Analyse a media company. Look at not only which media it is in but also which activities within those media it carries out, and why.
3  Has the desperate race for readers improved or reduced the quality of the editorial in newspapers? Has there been a different effect on the qualities, mid-market newspapers, tabloids? What economic factors explain why one newspaper is different from another? Give specific examples.
4  Can public service broadcasting survive in an era of multiple narrowcast channels?

# References

Advertising Association (1999) *Marketing Pocket Book 2000*, Henley-on-Thames: NTC Publications.

Barwise, P. (1994) *Children, Advertising, and Nutrition*, London: Advertising Association.

Barwise, P. (2000) 'Business use of the Web in Europe', working paper.

Barwise, P. and Ehrenberg, A. (1988) *Television and its Audience*, London and Beverly Hills: Sage.

Barwise, P. and Hammond, K. (1998) *Predictions: Media*, London: Weidenfeld & Nicolson.

Barwise, P., Hammond, K. and Elberse, A. (forthcoming) 'Marketing and the Internet', http://www.marketingandtheinternet.com

Cairncross, F. (forthcoming) *The Death of Distance*, 2nd edn, London: Orion.

Ehrenberg, A. S. C. and Barwise, T. P. (1983) 'How much does UK television cost?' *International Journal of Advertising* 2(1): 17–32.

Negroponte, N. (1995) *Being Digital*, New York: Alfred A. Knopf.

# Further reading

Advertising Association (1999) *Marketing Pocket Book 2000*, Henley-on-Thames: NTC Publications. Excellent annual source of data on UK and international markets and media.

Barwise, P. (1994) *Children, Advertising, and Nutrition*, London: Advertising Association. Highly polemical. Argues that advertising (e.g. on children's TV) has minimal effect on children's diet.

Barwise, P. and Ehrenberg, A. (1988) *Television and its Audience*, London and Beverly Hills: Sage. Describes patterns of TV viewing behaviour (and audience appreciation), mainly in the USA and UK. Relates these patterns to the economics of TV and the debates about its effects.

Barwise, P. and Hammond, K. (1998) *Predictions: Media*, London: Weidenfeld & Nicolson. Short essay on the digital revolution and its impact on consumers and everyday life.

Barwise, P., Elberse, A. and Hammond, K. (forthcoming) 'Marketing and the Internet', http://www.marketingandtheinternet.com. Reviews the academic literature on marketing and the Internet.

Cairncross, F. (forthcoming) *The Death of Distance*, 2nd edn, London: Orion. Explores the likely impact of digital technology and almost-free international communications on geopolitics and society.

Davis, M. P. and Zerdin, D. (1996) *The Effective Use of Advertising Media: A Practical Handbook*, 5th edn, London: Century. Gives the background on advertising media from an advertiser perspective.

Ehrenberg, A. S. C. and Barwise, T. P. (1983) 'How much does UK television cost?' *International Journal of Advertising* 2(1): 17–32. Shows how cheap public service television is and discusses the not-so-straightforward question of how much advertising-funded TV costs the viewer.

Hirsch, F. and Gordon, D. (1975) *Newspaper Money*, London: Hutchinson. The economics of UK national newspapers – before Thatcher – focusing on the relationship between subscription revenue, advertising, market segmentation, and costs. (Post-Thatcher, the costs are lower but the revenue tradeoffs are the same.)

Negroponte, N. (1995) *Being Digital,* New York: Alfred A. Knopf. The clearest exposition of the promise of digital technology, by the head of the Media Laboratory at MIT.

Rosen, N. and Barwise, P. (2000) *Business.eu: Corporates vs Start-ups,* London: Protégé Group and Online Research Agency. A detailed survey of business use of the Web in Europe, focusing on differences between big businesses and Internet start-ups ('dotcoms').

# Chapter 15

# Policy

MAKING MEDIA POLICY

**SYLVIA HARVEY**

This chapter sets the topic of media policy within the broader context of the role of communications media within human society and human history. In examining the social and political priorities at work in the take-up and shaping of media technologies it asks what role media policy might play in this process. It is argued that media policy – how it is made and who makes it – matters in relationship to the broader debate about free trade in cultural commodities, on the one hand, and the theory of communicative rights, on the other. Examples are drawn from the last twenty years of media policy in Britain and in Europe.

## Introduction: technologies for communicating

It has become a truism to say that at the start of the twenty-first century we are living through a period of rapid change. These changes are driven in part by the economic pressures of a global corporate quest for new markets, cheaper labour and increased profitability and in part by the new information and communications technologies. These new technologies have transformed production and retail processes – from robots making cars to shop assistants ordering new stock – and have, in richer countries, extended the range of domestic services, from computer games, e-mail and electronic shopping to specialist satellite channels and on-line assistance for children's homework.

In countries which either host the headquarters or are connected to the branch offices of transnational corporations the new information technologies have transformed methods of working and of selling and the cultures of everyday life, though the benefits of these technologies have not been evenly or universally applied. The differential application of technological solutions reflects, as one would expect, the different economic, political and cultural priorities of different societies. In this regard the enormously complex but relatively perfectly functioning communications network of cash-dispensing machines might be compared with the relatively old and inefficient technologies applied (in some places) to the recording of votes in the close-run US presidential election of 2000.

While technological inventions cannot, of themselves, predetermine the method of their diffusion and use, we can trace over a period of several hundred years the ways in which technologies of communication have transformed human societies, from the invention of the printing press to the potential convergence of telephone, computer, radio and television in the digital era of the Internet. Media policy in the modern era is the arena within which governments, citizens, consumers, companies and, sometimes, religious organizations seek to manage the social or economic impact of these technological changes. There is a particular sensitivity in the debate about communications technologies since these technologies disseminate ideas and may therefore play a crucial role in the shaping and changing of the cultural and political realms. This added significance of the technologies of meaning-making is signalled by the saying that 'the pen is mightier than the sword' and by the caution against censorship given by John Milton: 'as good almost kill a man as kill a good book' (Milton 1927). As the technologies of broadcasting emerged and extended their reach to millions of people they began to be monitored and sometimes controlled in different sorts of ways – by religious bodies in theocracies, by governments in democracies, by unelected leaders in non-democratic states.

By the start of the twenty-first century we have come to take it for granted that the technologies of communication produce commodities – things and experiences that can be bought and sold; this has been called the industrialization of culture. Thus we subscribe to an e-mail or television satellite service, we buy a book, newspaper, CD or cinema ticket. In earlier periods of human history this 'buying of culture' was not assumed and much of cultural expression was (and to some extent still is) self- or community-generated, not bought. Over a long period of historical development the right to reason, to think for oneself, to express oneself, to generate ideas and stories (not as commodities) came to be seen as part of what it meant to be human. At the time of the French Revolution this was encoded as a general right: 'The free communication of thoughts and opinions is one of the most precious rights of man; hence every citizen may speak, write and publish freely.' By the middle of the twentieth century this Enlightenment tradition with its emphasis on the free exchange of ideas was codified in different parts of the world – in the European Convention on Human Rights as: 'the right to freedom of expression . . . to receive and impart information and ideas' (Craufurd Smith 1997: 249 and 245) and in the Constitution of India as 'the right to freedom of speech and expression' (Price and Verhulst 1998: 265).

As we shall see in the following sections of this chapter there is, in our own time, a possible tension between market freedoms (the right to trade cultural commodities) and communicative freedoms (the right to free exchange of ideas and to the expression of cultural identity). It is this tension which led the European Information Society Forum to note its concern that the process of globalization in trade might '. . . pose risks and challenges to cultural and linguistic diversity arising from the promotion of global cultural industries and international trade in cultural products'.

In a Declaration prepared for the heavily disrupted World Trade Organization (WTO) talks in Seattle in 1999 the Forum noted that the media have the potential to play a 'unique role' in the preservation of national heritage and in the 'promotion of diverse cultural traditions and indigenous cultural identities'. This observation was followed by an appeal to the member countries of the WTO to 'acknowledge that cultural goods and services are significantly different from other products' and that the preservation of, for example, public service broadcasting within a nation and any other national measures designed to 'ensure access to a variety of indigenous products and services' should be regarded as legitimate public interest objectives and exempt, therefore, from global agreements on free trade in services (Information Society Forum 2000: 68–69). Similar arguments have been developed in India where the 'adverse impact' of foreign television satellite channels on Indian values and culture has been noted, and new legislation recommended to 'preserve our national identity' (Price and Verhulst 1998: 224, 275).

The application and take-up of new communication technologies has been uneven, giving rise to concerns about a growing gap between 'information-rich' and 'information-poor' both within and between countries. Nonetheless the impact of these technologies is global and the threshold years of the twenty-first century have seen a range of countries with very different economic and cultural priorities all involved in framing new laws as a way of managing the perceived threats and opportunities of the digital age. Within these laws (or proposed laws) there is a variable emphasis on the principles of market freedom, cultural diversity and citizens rights. We may cite in this context the 1996 Telecommunications Act in the USA, the 1997 Broadcasting Bill in India and the Government White Paper, *A New Future for Communications*, published in Britain in December 2000 (Aufderheide 1999; Price and Verhulst 1998; Department of Trade and Industry 2000).

The following sections of this chapter will look in more detail at the purposes of media policy and at the development and implementation of such policies principally in Britain but with some reference to developments in Europe and the USA. The emphasis will be on broadcasting but with some mention of changes in cinema, telecommunications and press policy. Finally, although we still tend to think of media policy being shaped by the priorities of national governments it is important also to recognize the part played by citizens, consumers and, indirectly, by shareholders in the framing of corporate and public policy and to note the possibly increasing role of supra-national bodies such as the European Union, the Council of Europe and the World Trade Organization (WTO).

## Media policy – its makers and purposes

Media policy involves the making of plans for shaping media output developed by individuals, companies or governments. The word 'policy' is derived, ultimately, from the Greek term for citizenship and so it tends to be reserved for activities undertaken within the public sector by governments claiming to represent the interests of their electors. Political parties opposed to each other on matters of both principle and detail will nonetheless represent themselves as advancing the public interest in putting forward their legislative proposals and in attacking those of their opponents; it is for the electors to evaluate the purpose and consequences of such proposals. But this process also has implications for academic study. Thus the sometimes relatively hidden political and economic priorities present within particular policy proposals requires media policy students to have some understanding of political theory and of social and economic policy, with an additional willingness to engage in political debate and to make value judgements where necessary. In the 'Making policy' section which follows various examples will be presented in relationship to the two distinct political theories so far identified, namely of market liberalism or 'market freedom', on the one hand, and of public interest intervention designed to enable 'communicative rights', on the other.

In countries where the political system that we call democracy is either not present or exists in a fragile condition then media policies, legislation and regulation are likely to represent the views and interests of a ruling political or business elite. But even in those countries where democracy is thought to exist in a relatively vigorous form the specialist nature of debates about frequency allocation or the regulation of broadcasting content and standards tends to result in the involvement of only a small number of people, despite the fact that the quality and range of broadcast output is of practical and daily concern to millions.

In Britain there have been a number of small, policy-oriented groups seeking to represent the broader public interest, especially in periods when new legislation is proposed to change aspects of media content, ownership and control. These include the 'Voice of the Listener and Viewer', the 'Campaign for Press and Broadcasting Freedom' and most recently, in 2000, 'Public Voice' (Reading 1999). Similar public interest and campaigning organizations exist in the USA including the Center for Media Education (Aufderheide 1999: 45), the 'Cultural Environmental Movement' and 'Citizens for Independent Public Broadcasting'. In Britain the organizations named above together with a host of both politically neutral and politically affiliated bodies are involved in lobbying civil servants, ministers and Members of Parliament with a view to including or excluding particular provisions in law. The Consumers Association can be seen as an example of a politically neutral body involved in such lobbying, while the Adam Smith Institute is aligned with the principles of free market Conservatism and the Institute for Public Policy Research grew out of the social democratic tradition which favours state interventionism.

This sketch of the many organizations and interests seeking to exert pressure would be incomplete without reference to the 'industry lobby'. The best-resourced lobbyists are likely to be those paid by and representing various industry interests from broadcast licence holders and advertisers to newspaper owners, telecommunications providers and independent producers. However, it is important to realize that there is no one 'industry voice' and that different sectors of the industry may disagree on the desirability of particular rules.

It follows from this picture of competing interests involved in the framing of public policy, together with the difficulty of defining 'the public interest', that media policy is almost never a given. Rather, it is the outcome of a process of sometimes acrimonious disagreement and the result of a settlement or accommodation presided over by elected politicians.

## Making policy

The last twenty years of the twentieth century in Britain offer us a useful range of examples of the making and implementation of media policy. During this period

Conservative governments were in power for eighteen years (from 1979 to 1997) with a Labour government in power from 1997 to the time of writing in early 2001. During these two decades there has been an acceleration in the processes of economic globalization radically reducing (in Britain) the numbers employed in the traditional 'heavy industries' of steel, engineering and mining and increasing employment in the new leisure and service industries, after a period of very high unemployment in the mid-1980s. The expansion of the communications and audio-visual service sectors as a consequence of both new technologies and new public policies has already been noted.

During the 1980s and much associated with the political philosophy of 'Thatcherism' the broadly bipartisan commitment to full employment, cradle-to-grave welfare, high-quality public health and education, and the nationalization of key services (telecommunications, transport, gas, electricity, mining) came to an end. The Thatcherite revolution issued a challenge to public monopolies, welfarism and statism and proposed a new emphasis on the values of the free market, on individual entrepreneurship and on the necessity for individuals to 'stand on their own two feet', to provide for themselves and their families and to move away from dependency on the public purse. This radically pro-market philosophy sought to dismantle and replace the social democratic consensus that had, on certain key issues, linked Labour supporters to 'one nation' Conservatives since the Second World War.

## Conservative media policy, 1984–96

In matters of morality and cultural expression, Thatcherism tended to be traditional, censorious and authoritarian, introducing stringent controls for the censorship of video content in the Video Recordings Act of 1984, creating a new body – the Broadcasting Standards Council – to monitor 'sex and violence' on television in the Broadcasting Act of 1990, and developing an extraordinary and anti-libertarian prohibition on the 'promotion of homosexuality' in local government legislation. In economic and industrial matters, however, the government was open to radical change and, specifically, committed to the free market principles of competition and technological innovation. In the field of broadcasting the government was keen to challenge what it saw as the comfortable and inefficient duopoly of BBC and ITV. And it is this which in part explains the (relatively unsuccessful) encouragement of cable and satellite delivery systems in the early and mid-1980s and the (successful) creation of Channel 4 in 1982 (Goodwin 1998). It should be noted, however, that the Cable Act of 1994 and subsequent support for various satellite initiatives (including Rupert Murdoch's Sky Television) paved the way for the proliferation of television and telecommunications services in the 1990s.

Channel 4 was born out of a complex and contradictory process of lobbying which began well before the election of a Conservative government in 1979 (Blanchard and Morley 1982; Lambert 1982). The new television channel was brought into existence by Conservative legislation and yet its existence could not be seen in any simple way as fulfilling free market principles. The balance sheet here is a mixed one. From an ideological point of view the content of Channel 4 programming was often hostile to conservatism. But from an economic point of view it represented a new and innovative mode of industrial organization. Channel 4 commissioned or – in economic terms – 'subcontracted' large numbers of small independent producers to make programmes (Harvey 1996). From a Thatcherite perspective this process injected a new element of competition into broadcasting and challenged what were seen as the costly and inefficient production practices of the vertically integrated broadcasting duopoly of BBC and ITV. The Independent Television (ITV) network in particular with its long-standing monopoly over television advertising revenue, its strong trade union and what some saw as its unnecessarily large production teams had been famously referred to by Thatcher as the 'last bastion of restrictive practices'. Channel 4 offered a different model for production. And it was believed that the lower fixed costs of independents and their willingness to undertake unpaid development work would ultimately reduce production costs across the whole of the television sector.

Along with an 'uncompetitive' ITV, the BBC was also viewed with considerable hostility by those 'New Right' theorists who provided the theoretical and principled core of Thatcherism (Veljanovski 1989). This hostility stemmed partly from the belief that the BBC was improperly protected from the chill winds of the market through the device of the compulsory licence fee, and partly from the belief that it was run by cultural elitists and was the chosen home of left-wing journalists. Various attempts were made to destroy or to transform the Corporation and politicians of the radical right were assisted in this endeavour by the journalists of Rupert Murdoch's News International Group writing in the *Sun* and in *The Times*. There were also critics within the BBC who saw it (at worst) as backward-looking and economically inefficient; many of these left in the early 1980s to set up independent production companies. In the 1990s this was followed by a second wave of protestors who, unlike the 1980s generation disliked the internal market reforms brought in by BBC Director-General, John Birt and resented what they saw as the shift of power from programme makers to accountants and schedulers.

Following the pro-business lead offered by President Reagan in America and bent on rooting out as much 'red tape' and public interest regulation as possible, the Peacock Committee was charged to report to Parliament on the subject of replacing the BBC's licence fee with advertising revenue and with a full exploration of the potential for deregulation and the 'freeing of the market' within the broadcast sector. The Peacock Report, submitted in 1986, was thorough and authoritative though its membership had clearly been selected with a view to returning a series of pro-free market recommendations (Veljanovski 1989; Goodwin 1998). Perhaps surprisingly the Report did not recommend the adoption of advertising by the BBC and this, coupled with the fact that the BBC's Royal Charter was not due for renewal until 1996, removed the Corporation at least temporarily from the prime focus of government legislative attention.

There were, however, a series of what might be called politically motivated incidents (a Conservative Party complaint about the coverage of the American bombing of Libya; police a Special Branch raid on the BBC offices in Glasgow) which led to the enforced resignation of the BBC's Director General in 1987 (Milne 1988). Some of these incidents, vividly recounted in this Director General's autobiography provide useful evidence for the argument that effective media policy is not only developed through the legislative cycle but is also a matter of direct and indirect pressure being brought to bear upon key individuals.

For a more formal statement of free market media policy we can do no better than to turn to the Conservative government's White Paper of 1988: *Broadcasting in the '90s: Competition, Choice and Quality.*' In this document (as its subtitle suggests), the government expressed the belief that: 'a more open and competitive broadcasting market can be attained without detriment to programme standards and quality' (Home Office 1988: 1). There has been much debate since that time about the consequences of greater channel competition, with some public scepticism as to whether 'more channels' has meant 'more choice'. This has been accompanied by a concern that increased pressure on terrestrial broadcasters to maintain viewing figures has resulted in a move to the middle ground with a consequent reduction in range and choice. Others have argued that the new channels have greatly extended public choice.

The 1988 White Paper proposed that there should be competitive bidding for the allocation of independent television licences, that the commercial system should be managed by a new 'light touch' regulator, that satellite television should be set upon a firm footing (with a way being found for exempting Murdoch's Sky Television from continuing cross-media ownership restrictions) and that all terrestrial broadcasters should be required to commission a minimum of 25% of their original output from indepedendent producers. On this last point the industrial lessons of Channel 4, created at the beginning of the decade, had been learnt and were further advanced by being enshrined in law.

The 'light touch' regulator was to lose its powers to preview programmes and to control the schedule. Preview powers had given the regulator considerable opportunities for censorship (it could require programme changes in advance of transmission) and scheduling powers had given it the right to insist upon the presence of certain types of programmes in peak time. While there were few who mourned the disappearance of what the Peacock Report had criticized as 'pre-publication censorship', the loss of scheduling powers was seen by some to open the system up to much more aggressively competitive scheduling, ultimately placing at risk the future of less popular programme genres.

The proposal to award independent television (ITV) licences to the highest bidder evoked a storm of protest both within and outside the industry. In response to the White Paper an industry-funded lobbying organization, The Campaign for Quality Television, argued that the economic valuing of licences would put in jeopardy the cultural value of programming as companies sought to reduce their costs in order to pay their often quite substantial 'bid price' (Corner *et al.* 1994). One consequence of the very public protests made about the draft legislation was to strengthen the concept of a 'quality threshold'. This was the legal means by which the regulator might consider issues of programme quality as outlined in the applicant's service proposals, before considering the amount which the applicant had offered to pay for the licence. However, the government remained unrelenting in the view that, once this quality threshold had been passed, the licence must be awarded to the highest bidder.

In the event, with 40 applicants competing for a total of 16 ITV licences, only five of the licences went to the highest bidder; though there were also three regions where the presence of only one bidder meant that there had been no competition for the licence and the 'only bidder' won. Fourteen of the applicants were deemed to have failed the quality test which would suggest that the regulator was determined to use its full powers under the law (Davidson 1992: 297–8). The then new regulatory body, the Independent Television Commission (ITC), also seems to have been encouraged by the public debate prior to the legislation to set quite high programming standards in its tender document. Thus, for example, applicants were required to outline their weekly programme proposals in ten generic categories: drama, entertainment, sport, news, factual, education, religion, arts, children's and regional (Corner and Harvey 1996: 234–5).

The Broadcasting Act of 1990 (based on the 1988 White Paper) could be seen as a coherent statement of radical free market principles applied to broadcasting. And yet there were elements in this Conservative legislation which sought to maintain the traditions of British broadcasting and its commitment to quality programming. For example, the non-commercial BBC was recognized as the 'cornerstone' of the system and left relatively untouched; public service broadcasting survived for another decade as a consequence of this decision.

In addition, the traditional safeguards which ensured 'impartiality' in the coverage of controversial matters were maintained. Unlike the paper press (or the Internet) British television is not permitted to advance the views of station owners on controversial matters. And it has been suggested that public confidence in the accuracy of television news – as against newspaper news – is a consequence of this measure (Svennevig 1998: 49, 65). In the USA, by contrast, where a Reagan-appointed Federal Communications Commission suspended the operation of the American equivalent, the 'Fairness Doctrine', in 1987, a more radical deregulatory and pro-business approach was adopted. Business interests had argued that the Doctrine contravened the free speech rights of television owners. However the suspension of this form of regulation in the USA, with the obligation that it had previously placed on broadcasters to report disagreements on major issues, might be seen to contravene the rights of the audience, ignoring the communicative rights and information needs of the viewer (Harvey 1998).

The British legislation of 1990 retained fairly strict cross-media ownership controls but these were liberalized in the 1996 legislation and the way was opened up for further concentrations of ownership among the companies which formed the ITV network.

While the legacy of British Conservatism in the field of broadcasting policy has been radical and structural, broadly instating the principle of market competition above that of the maintenance of cultural standards, and downgrading the issue of communicative rights, its impact in other media sectors has perhaps been of less significance. The privatization of telephone services in 1984 introduced the possibility of competition and, arguably, greatly extended the range of telephone and then on-line services available to businesses and to the public. But there were few issues of cultural content at stake.

In the field of cinema the old forms of cultural subsidy and protection were removed in the Films Act of 1985, although subsidies for film production were reintroduced a decade later with the announcement of substantial funding from the National Lottery (British Film Institute 1995: 21). On the censorship front there were great increases in productivity. The British Board of Film Censors, established by the industry in 1912 as a means of self-regulation, was renamed the British Board of Film Classification and entrusted in 1985 with the statutory duty of classifying and issuing certificates for all videos as well as for all cinema films. The number of films being dealt with leapt from 400 to 4000 per year (Richards 1997: 176).

In the field of the press where self-regulation had traditionally been the norm, no significant legislation was introduced. However, public concern about issues of privacy and of unwarranted press intrusion led to the abolition of the old Press Council which had been regarded as relatively ineffective and to its replacement by a new Press Complaints Commission in 1991 (Hutchison 1999: 143).

## From Conservative to Labour policy: changes and continuities, 1997–2000

The fast pace of 'marketization' of the broadcasting sector, the proliferation of new television channels and intensified competition for audiences continued during the period of Labour government, though there were some modest shifts of emphasis in government policy. The Conservative 'Department of National Heritage' was renamed the 'Department of Culture, Media and Sport' (DCMS) and a new interest was taken in the economic value of the 'creative industries'. A DCMS report of 1998 suggested that this relatively modern industrial sector was worth £60 billion per annum and employed some one and a half million people. Thus, while the non-material value of culture was recognized this was accompanied by a forceful new emphasis on its economic potential.

In the field of film some moves were made to counter the 'hands-off' or *laissez-faire* approach of the previous government and new tax breaks were announced for film production in 1997. A new body, the Film Council, was launched in 2000 with the strategic responsibility for developing both the film industry and film culture.

In relationship to the BBC the new government offered more positive and practical forms of support than had been forthcoming in the previous period. Following the report of the Davies Committee in 1999, the Secretary of State announced that the BBC would be permitted above-inflation increases in the value of the licence fee, and that these increases would continue for the remaining seven years of the licence term. And while the BBC was required to become more transparent in the announcement of its programming promises and the minister responsible indicated an intention to give close scrutiny to any proposals for new BBC services (particularly in the light of competition issues), a new warmth was observable in the relationship between Westminster and White City.

The greatest challenge facing the new government in the media field was undoubtedly that of digitalization with the prospect of major increases in the number of both terrestrial and satellite digital television channels, an ever-growing Internet and the prospect of convergence between previously distinct telephone, television and computer services. New Internet practices were undermining established principles from the security of music copyright in the 'Napster' case to the operation of obscenity laws in the case of child pornography. While the availability of moving pictures (including video on demand) via the telephone network, the availability of radio and 'web-streaming' broadcasts on computer screens and the development of e-mail facilities connected to television sets suggested an end to many of the old technological boundaries and cultural certainties.

In December 2000 the government issued a White Paper, *A New Future for Communications*, designed to address some of these issues and to pave the way for new legislation. The Labour Party has strong links to the European tradition of social democracy with its attachment to the philosophy of state intervention in defence of social welfare and equality of opportunity. But this government document reflects and embodies the interests of businesses in the media sector at least as much as the interests of consumers and citizens. While this might be celebrated as an instance of the political 'Third Way' seeking to establish the conditions for the co-existence of public and private interests, of citizens and businesses, it is clear that a tension remains between these two sets of interests. The White Paper speaks of ensuring 'the widest possible access to a choice of diverse communications services of the highest quality' and of including 'every section of society in the benefits of these services'. There is equal emphasis on making Britain 'home to the most dynamic and competitive communications market in the world'. Public service broadcasting is designated as having a 'key role' in the digital future but the Paper's advocacy of the methods of industrial 'self-regulation' and 'co-regulation' give little sense of the powers that the proposed new regulatory body might have to maintain the quality of, in particular, television services, in the public interest (Department of Trade and Industry 2000: 3, 48, 83).

## Developments in European policy

In the twenty-first century many of the acts and artefacts of human expression exist as commodities, but it may also be important to assert their right to exist outside the realm of commodity form. Expression and information with their respective links to the formation of individual and social identity and the constitution of the informed citizen, have a social significance beyond that of a freely tradable commodity. It is for this reason that some countries subsidize cultural expression and the provision of high-quality information, from the public purse, and enshrine in law various forms of support for the arts and for indigenous cultural expression (in film, in television, in publishing, in oral culture). Such laws and practices, including the existence of national television licence fees (for the BBC, for example), subsidies for film production, national or pan-national quotas and regulatory interventions in the content and scheduling of television, can be seen to represent an alternative or addition to free market principles. In some instances these laws and practices have been seen by global cultural corporations to contravene their own interests; as such they have come under considerable pressure in recent years.

Thus, and in the name of free market principles, a number of private broadcasters have submitted complaints to the European Commission, objecting to the existence of national television licence fees, subsidies and special arrangements for public service broadcasters and arguing that these represent unacceptable, anti-competitive practices (Goldberg *et al.* 1998: 92). Similar pressures were brought to bear during the 1993 round of trade negotiations for the General Agreement on Tariffs and Trade (GATT), when the US entertainment industry argued that European quotas acted as an unacceptable form of restraint on free trade between countries (Venturelli 1998: 17; Goldberg *et al.* 1998: 62). The controversial European Directive of 1989 had introduced the principle that 'where possible' a majority of the television programmes transmitted in Europe (on all channels) should be of European origin, not imported. In the case of English-language satellite programming the Directive was more honoured in the breach than in the observance but was still seen to pose a threat to some business interests.

The argument against European cultural quotas and subsidies was not successful in 1993, but it has not gone away and powerful global corporations continue to argue the case against such measures. However, there has been some change in the political climate within which such lobbying takes place. Thus, for example, in 1996 the European Parliament passed a resolution in support of public service broadcasting, describing this as 'an aid to informed citizenship' and 'an agency of representative pluralism' with an obligation to: 'reflect and support the cultures of Europe's nations and regions', to 'serve minority interests' and to 'encourage understanding of the non-European cultures and ethnic groups present in the Union' (European Communities 1996). Such issues tend to be of little concern to media corporations though they have a close bearing on the prospects for democracy in Europe.

The European Parliament has relatively little power but its public service broadcasting resolution was followed up by a statement or 'protocol' added to the Treaty of Amsterdam in 1997. This Treaty is a key document for the European Union and Protocol 32 notes that 'public broadcasting in the Member States is directly related to the democratic, social and cultural needs of each society and to the need to preserve media pluralism'. The competence of Member States to provide funding for such broadcasting is acknowledged, but the powerful lobbying of commercial media interests is also reflected in the caveat that such funding should not have a negative effect on 'trading conditions and competition' (Duff 1997: 298).

The tension here between free trade principles and the notion that it is right for the state to intervene in order to enable and secure communicative rights (specifically, the provision of a wide range of types of programmes) remains unresolved. Students of media policy will see the drama of this conflict unfold in the years ahead; some may wish to contribute to its resolution.

## Conclusion

As the industrialization of culture enters the phase of globalization, and as cultural commodities (including films, television programmes, computer games) become an increasingly important element in the trading balances of some countries, there is an increased tension between the philosophy of communicative rights and the philosophy of free trade. How these two philosophies are to co-exist, and how one side or the other may be favoured in practice, is a key issue for students of media policy and for citizens.

## Questions

1  What are the implications of the theory of the 'free market' both for the communications industries and for the public interest?

2  What is the theory of 'communicative rights' and what is its relevance for the framing of media policy?

3  What is the difference (if any) between the interests of citizens and the interests of consumers in the field of media policy?

## References

Aufderheide, P. (1999) *Communications Policy and the Public Interest. The Telecommunications Act of 1996*, New York: The Guilford Press.

Blanchard, S. and Morley, D. (eds) (1982) *What's This Channel Four? An Alternative Report*, London: Comedia Publishing Group.

British Film Institute (1995) *BFI Film and Television Handbook 1996*, London: BFI.

Corner, J. and Harvey, S. (eds) (1996) *Television Times. A Reader*, London: Arnold.

Corner, J., Harvey, S. and Lury, K. (1994) 'Culture, quality and choice: the re-regulation of TV 1989–91' in S. Hood (ed.) *Behind the Screens. The Structure of British Television in the Nineties*, London: Lawrence and Wishart, pp. 1–19.

Craufurd Smith, R. (1997) *Broadcasting Law and Fundamental Rights*, Oxford: Clarendon Press.

Davidson, A. (1992) *Under the Hammer. the Inside Story of the 1991 ITV Franchise Battle*, London: Heinemann.

Department of Trade and Industry and Department of Culture, Media and Sport (2000) *A New Future for Communications*, Cmnd 5010, Norwich: The Stationery Office.

Duff, A. (1997) *The Treaty of Amsterdam: Text and Commentary*, London: Federal Trust.

European Communities (1996) *Official Journal of the European Communities*. Information and Notices, 28 October, Luxembourg: Office for Official Publications of the European Communities.

Goldberg, D., Prosser, T. and Verhulst, S. (1998) *EC Media Law and Policy*, London: Longman.

Goodwin, P. (1998) *Television under the Tories. Broadcasting Policy 1979–1997*, London: British Film Institute.

Harvey, S. (1996) 'Channel 4 television: from Annan to Grade' in J. Corner and S. Harvey (eds) *Television Times. A Reader*, London: Arnold, pp. 201–10.

Harvey, S. (1998) 'Doing it my way – broadcasting regulation in capitalist cultures: The case of 'fairness' and 'impartiality', *Media, Culture and Society* 20: 535–6.

Home Office (1988) *Broadcasting in the '90s: Competition, Choice and Quality*, London: HMSO.

Information Society Forum (2000) *A European Way for the Information Society*, Luxembourg: European Commission.

Lambert, S. (1982) *Channel Four. Television with a Difference?* London: British Film Institute.

Milne, A. (1988) *DG. The Memoirs of a British Broadcaster*, London: Hodder and Stoughton, Coronet Books.

Milton, J. (1927) *Areopagitica and Other Prose Works*, London: Dent.

Price, M. E. and Verhulst, S. (1998) *Broadcasting Reform in India. Media Law from a Global Perspective*, Delhi: Oxford University Press.

Reading, A. (1999) 'Campaigns to change the media' in J. Stokes and A. Reading (eds) *The Media in Britain. Current Debates and Developments*, London: Macmillan Press, pp. 170–83.

Richards, J. (1997) 'British film censorship' in R. Murphy (ed.) *The British Cinema Book*, London: British Film Institute, pp. 167–77.

Svennevig, M. (1998) *Television Across the Years. The British Public's View*, London: the Independent Television Commission.

Veljanovski, C. (ed.) (1989) *Freedom in Broadcasting*, London: Institute of Economic Affairs.

Venturelli, S. (1998) *Liberalizing the European Media. Politics, Regulation and the Public Sphere*, Oxford: Clarendon Press.

# Further reading

Barnett, S. *et al.* (2000) *e-britania: the Communications Revolution*, Luton: University of Luton Press. A series of articles commissioned by the BBC to explore the relationship between broadcasting and internet services.

Calabrese, A. and Burgelman, J.-C. (eds) (1999) *Communication, Citizenship and Social Policy. Re-thinking the Limits of the Welfare State*, Lanham, MD and Oxford: Rowman and Littlefield. Writers from three continents review the debate about welfare entitlements in the context of a changing global communications economy; the neo-liberal critique of public provision is assessed as a threat to democratic participation in the institutions of civil society.

Collins, R. and Murroni, C. (1996) *New Media, New Policies. Media and Communications Strategies for the Future*, Cambridge: Polity Press. Based on research undertaken at the Institute for Public Policy Research and contributing to the development of 'New Labour' thinking on the media during its period in opposition, the book offers an ambitious overview of changes and policy options across a range of different media in Britain.

Corner, J. and Harvey, S. (eds) (1996) *Television Times. A Reader*, London: Edward Arnold, Hodder Headline. The *Reader* includes a series of articles on aspects of television policy in Britain, the USA and Brazil as well as a selection of industry documents which may provide useful case study material for media policy research.

Curran, J. and Seaton, J. (1997) *Power without Responsibility: the Press and Broadcasting in Britain*, 5th edn, London: Routledge. A clearly written and often sharply critical account of the social and political role of the media, including valuable material on the early history of the press and broadcasting.

Department of Trade and Industry (DTI) and Department of Culture, Media and Sport (DCMS) (2000) *A New Future for Communications*, Cmnd 5010, Norwich: The Stationery Office. This Labour government White Paper heralds new legislation designed to recognize the convergence and to transform the regulation of broadcasting and telecommunications. The document proposes the creation of a new regulatory body (OFCOM) and manifests a contradictory attachment to the principle of public service broadcasting, on the one hand, and to the priority of expanding global markets in communications and culture, on the other.

Goodwin, P. (1998) *Television Under the Tories. Broadcasting Policy 1979–1997*, London: British Film Institute. A detailed review and analysis of the key features of British Conservative government policy in the field of communications.

Herman, E. and McChesney, R. (1997) *The Global Media. The New Missionaries of Corporate Capitalism*, London: Cassell. A bold and polemical account of what is seen as the negative impact of neo-liberal philosophy and capitalist economic practice on the prospects for global democracy and development. The book explores some examples of alternative media and advocates the creation of a 'global nonprofit public sphere'.

Home Office (1998) *Broadcasting in the '90s: Competition, Choice and Quality*, Cmnd 517, London: HMSO. Responding to technological innovation in the fields of cable and satellite and underwritten by a philosophy broadly hostile to public provision this Conservative government White Paper paved the way for increasing deregulation and competition in broadcasting while maintaining the key instrument of public service broadcasting: the BBC.

Hutchison, D. (1999) *Media Policy. An Introduction*, Oxford: Blackwell. An engaging, clear and comprehensive exposition of some of the key issues in contemporary media policy.

## Web site

www.culture.gov.uk This website of the British government's Department of Culture, Media and Sport covers the range of responsibilities of the Department. The broadcasting and arts sections of the site carry useful updates on current developments as well as references to key policy documents.

# Chapter 16

# Models of media institutions

MEDIA INSTITUTIONS IN EUROPE

**RALPH NEGRINE**

Broadcasting institutions in Europe developed at about the same time but their main features differed in significant ways. Different political and cultural traditions, and different political arrangements within each European nation, gave rise to a number of different models of broadcasting. In the 1970s and 1980s, most European broadcasting systems faced a similar set of issues: there was pressure to deregulate the systems of broadcasting, there was also pressure to open up the system to new broadcasting systems based around new technologies of cable and satellite broadcasting. The consequences of these pressures has led to the broadcasting systems across Europe facing a common set of problems: problems in respect of competition, problems in respect of funding, problems in respect of sustaining their traditional and prime positions in the broadcasting environment. These problems continue to challenge the traditional public service broadcasting organizations in Europe.

In studying media institutions, it is often unwise to take it for granted that similar forms of communication – television, newspapers, radio, etc. – will have similar characteristics in different settings. For example, though the nature of television as a medium of communication may be (more or less) identical across countries, the organization of that medium for the purposes of delivering a wide menu of content will vary quite considerably from one socio-political environment to another. In many respects, then, each national broadcasting system (and the same goes for newspapers) will represent a particular – sometimes a unique – arrangement; an arrangement which, in turn, reflects different socio-political traditions, economic forces, geographic features, and so on.

By making comparisons across countries, one can come to appreciate the extent to which there are similarities, and differences, and the possible reasons for either and/or both. Only by addressing the issue of similarities and differences and the significance of both does it become possible to develop a proper understanding of processes of communication in contemporary societies.

The aim of this chapter then is to explore briefly the historical development of broadcasting across Europe, and to identify some of the factors which account for significant differences across institutions. The last section of this chapter will identify technological and political changes in the 1980s and 1990s which have had, and which continue to have, a significant impact on broadcasting systems.

## The development of broadcasting across Europe

Three brief comments need to be made prior to exploring the various 'models' of broadcasting which have developed historically in some major European countries.

- The first is that Europe is made up of different political units (countries), with different dominant languages, different traditions, histories, memories, etc. Developments in the media to an extent reflect these differences. The economic and cultural repercussions of this are visible today in the light of the European Union's efforts to overcome these differences and so harmonize European media industries in order to meet the challenge from the much larger American media industry (see Collins, 1994).
- The second factor which played a part in the development of the broadcast media in Europe was the Second World War. This 'interrupted' processes of development; in the case of Germany, the post-1945 media were to a large extent shaped by the Allies on a completely different basis from their previous structures (Tracey 1998: Chapters 8 and 9); the Liberation of France in 1944 saw the establishment of many new newspaper titles and a restructuring of many newspaper groups which had been owned by proprietors who had been discredited because of their role in pre-war France (Kuhn 1995: 23–4).
- The third factor is that governments have regulated broadcasting systems (and the press) in ways which reflected different attitudes towards economic organization, the rights of individuals, political traditions, and so on. Governments committed to non-intervention in economic affairs have been less likely to consider state help for the media, whereas governments keen to sustain a plurality of media have tended to support an element of intervention. This has been the case with the press industry (see McGregor 1977: Chapter 12), although there has been a more common approach towards the broadcast media with a strong emphasis on control and regulation given the belief in the power of the media and the limitations of services possible via terrestrial means. Consequently, and unlike the US experience where radio broadcasting developed within a competitive framework with private commercially funded companies running the broadcasting services, European countries mostly favoured some form of state control over broadcasting as a way of avoiding the chaos in the airwaves which was characteristic of an unregulated system and also as a way of ensuring that the 'public interest' was not overlooked.

However, since the idea of the 'public interest' is ambiguous, the methods chosen to ensure that it was not overlooked varied according to the individual political and cultural traditions of European countries (McQuail and Siune 1986; Papathanassopoulos 1990). It is possible, nonetheless, to identify a number of characteristics which were taken to encapsulate the idea of a broadcasting organization working in 'the public interest' and not simply as commercial, profit-making organizations. These characteristics are often subsumed into a definition of public service broadcasting, a definition which is itself imprecise (see Home Office 1986).

The definition of public service broadcasting usually comprises the following characteristics:

- a universal service available to all irrespective of income or geographical location;
- a commitment to a balanced output and to balanced scheduling across different programme genres;
- a balanced and impartial political output; and
- a degree of financial independence from both governmental and commercial bodies (Kuhn 1985: 4).

A more elaborate definition would also identify broadcasting's cultural and social missions, including catering for minorities, a concern for 'national identity and community', competition in good programming rather than for audience numbers, and guidelines to liberate programme makers and not to restrict them. (Broadcasting Research Unit 1985: 2; Tracey 1998: Part I) In practice, no public broadcasting organization would claim that it has (always) adhered to all the values which these definitions embrace though they have probably been a guide to broadcasting practices.

The models of broadcasting which eventually developed in European states reflected both individual political, economic and cultural arrangements and attempts to uphold the 'public interest'. Generally speaking, three different European 'models' of public broadcasting can be identified.

## The 'integration' model of broadcasting

This model has its roots in the idea that broadcasting could be treated as a natural monopoly and in the belief that this sort of structure could uphold the 'public interest'. The services would be run by councils or committees which comprised representatives of various political, social and cultural groups in society; hence a measure of 'internal pluralism' existed in the organization of the service. In this way, the councils or committees would ensure that a wide variety of perspectives were represented by the broadcasting authorities. In the (then) Federal Republic of Germany, in the post-war period 'there was a common concern to secure broadcasting against capture either by the state or by sectional interests in society'. There was also a concern 'to regulate for pluralism' and to 'assure "balance" and "diversity" in broadcasting'. This would not be done by setting up competing broadcasting bodies but by ensuring that there was 'a balance of opinion and a fair representation of social diversity within each channel' (i.e. internal pluralism') (Humphreys 1988: 113–15; see also Hoffman-Reim 1996: 284–5).

Unlike the West German system, the French broadcasting structure was also a monopolistic one but there was less of an effort to ensure 'balance' and 'diversity' within it. Although in theory the broadcasters tried to be impartial in their approach to contemporary issues, partisan political control of broadcasting was the practice with each change of government bringing about changes to the system of control (Kuhn 1995). Both the French and German systems favoured a funding structure which mixed commercial revenue and licence fees (to be paid by radio and television set owners) within each broadcasting institution. Consequently, there was competition for audiences and advertising revenue within the state monopoly of broadcasting.

## The 'duopoly' model of broadcasting

Britain offers a good example of the duopoly model of broadcasting. The duopoly model requires the co-existence of public and private broadcasters who compete for audiences but not for the same sources of revenue: the BBC relies solely on the licence fee, while the commercial companies rely on commercial funding. Initially, the British broadcasting system was organized as a state monopoly with the exclusive rights to broadcasting given to the BBC (British Broadcasting Company (1922–6), later Corporation (1926 onwards)). After intense lobbying from private interests and advertisers, a Conservative government passed the Independent Television Act 1954, which allowed for the creation of a commercial television service. This became operational in the mid-1950s. The commercial television service (ITV) was overseen by a regulatory body, the Independent Television Authority (then ITA, now Independent Television Commission). In 1964, a second public service was introduced (BBC2) and in 1982 a second commercial channel (Channel 4) albeit with a very specific remit to cater for minority interests and tastes. In 1997, Channel 5 was launched using the last available terrestrial frequencies for television. In these ways, competing broadcasters came to provide for a degree of 'external pluralism' (Hoffman-Reim 1996: 284–5).

The authorities in charge of broadcasting – the BBC Board of Governors, and the ITC – oversee the broadcasters and ensure that they fulfil their obligations as public service broadcasters. Significantly, both private and public authorities pursue broadly similar public service broadcasting obligations. Although the British broadcasting system is considered to be heavily regulated, a great deal of the control exercised over it is indirect, informal and often through private contacts (unlike the more direct mechanisms common across continental Europe: see Negrine 1994).

## The 'private sector monopoly' model of broadcasting

One other model is worth taking into account because it has implications for the discussion of the processes of deregulation which swept across European broadcasting systems in the 1980s. This is the 'private sector monopoly' model of broadcasting in the Grand Duchy of Luxembourg. According to Dyson and Humphreys, 'as early as the inter war period, Luxembourg had seen the advantage of creating an appropriately lax regulatory environment so that its national private commercial operator (CLT/RTL) could cream off advertising from its neighbours' (Dyson and Humphreys 1988: 7). It was a policy which inevitably brought it into conflict with countries which wanted to preserve their cultural dominance and their programming policies (e.g.

the UK). Other countries, notably France, which were also likely to lose out financially as funds flowed to Luxembourg overcame the problem by acquiring stakes in CLT, the broadcasting company.

What problems did these systems encounter? Four stand out:

- Problems of how to organize and control the broadcasting system: these were particularly severe in countries which experienced major political dislocations or a readiness on the part of politicians to interfere in all aspects of broadcasting.
- Pressure, roughly from 1950 onwards, to introduce commercial broadcasting services: by the 1970s, and with few exceptions, most European broadcasting systems had embraced some element of competition, adopting commercial practices in terms of either funding and/or programming. One could in fact argue that in this period – a period before most of the contemporary technological and political changes powerfully challenged the status quo – broadcasting systems had begun to settle into a period of relative calm.
- Recurring funding problems, particularly for the public broadcasters whose funding from the licence fee never quite managed to match the resources of the commercial broadcasters: at the same time, there was often pressure to supplement (or entirely replace) licence funding with advertising revenue.
- Problems arising from the end of the 'scarcity' of frequencies which informed early policies on broadcasting: under conditions of scarcity, monopolies could be justified as 'natural' but once technological developments overcame scarcity, other justifications needed to be found, or the monopolies abandoned.

With the challenge from the new technologies of cable, satellite and, more recently digital, television and the advance of new ideas about how broadcasting systems could be organized in a different technological era, these problems became more acute. For example, could monopolies be justified when there was no longer a scarcity of frequencies? Should the state continue to determine what services should be available to viewers or consumers of broadcasting? How could one continue to justify the licence fee? How could one maximize consumer choice and yet maintain public services and the public interest?

## Towards broadcasting deregulation

The speed of technological and political change made leisurely discussions about broadcasting immensely difficult. But many of the other issues that had to be confronted were not in themselves new. The threat to established practices and structures from commercial bodies wanting to run broadcasting on commercial lines had always been there. Sometimes the challenges were successful and change came about; at other times, the challenges failed. What is therefore interesting is to begin to identify the points at which such pressures become irresistible.

By the 1980s the pressures for change became very real. On the one hand, governments began to change their attitudes towards the need for regulatory agencies and their activities. Those who advocated 'deregulation' questioned the view that regulatory agencies were in the public interest and saw them as distorting public desires through their regulatory activities. The aim of proponents of these views was to reduce or eliminate regulatory activity and simply let the marketplace dictate the level and the nature of services (see Tunstall 1986; Tunstall and Palmer 1990: Chapter 14; Veljanovski 1989). On the other hand, the new technologies of cable and satellite broadcasting, and increasingly sophisticated telecommunications systems, began to challenge the established terrestrial broadcasters by promising or creating the possibility of new broadcasting services. With governments showing interest in these new technologies as part of the development of 'information technologies' for economic and industrial growth, their development was usually encouraged in some way or other. Consequently, new privately funded, commercial cable and satellite television services came into being and began to compete with the established broadcasters. Perhaps the most obvious manifestation of that change took place in countries where public broadcasters had an effective monopoly, e.g. Greece, and where competition was introduced very rapidly and so undermined the monopoly.

Many of these changes – individually or together – have been described as the *deregulation* of broadcasting. This suggests the relaxation of the rules that govern the state-controlled broadcasting monopoly and the emergence of competition. But deregulation is more than the simple removal or relaxation of rules and regulations. According to Dyson and Humphreys (1990), deregulation is central to a neo-liberal strategy for modernizing the economy by privatization and the creation of an 'enterprise culture'. It is also seen as a response to increasing international competition in television by making it easier to create larger broadcasting organizations which are able to compete internationally. (Dyson and Humphreys 1990: 231–3)

Such changes were taking place at a time when public broadcasters were facing other difficulties. First, the position of public broadcasters was under attack from within. In 1981, in the then Federal Republic of Germany, the Constitutional Court ruled that 'private broadcasting was constitutional' within a model of 'external pluralism' between competing private channels. In France in 1982, the government abandoned the state monopoly of broadcasting partly as a way of redressing the weaknesses of the traditional system. Second, television penetration had reached saturation point in many countries and consequently funding from the licence fee levelled off. It could not be increased by the sorts of amounts desired by the broadcasters since politicians often feared the electoral consequences of large increases. Commercial broadcasters also suffered the effects of recession and this too highlighted the fact that funding for broadcasting activities would not grow indefinitely. Third, broadcasters were also finding it difficult to adapt to the cultural and moral pluralism which undermined the idea of universal service established in the early years of broadcasting. Fourth, governments were becoming aware of what their neighbours were doing and sometimes benefiting from. Finally, broadcasters now had to contend with the challenge of the new technologies of cable and satellite television. Though they were much slower to develop than initially promised, their high profile forced policy makers to act and broadcasters to respond to the challenge of having their control over the airwaves, and over key sources of funding, put into question.

In this changing environment, new commercial broadcasters came into existence. Some took advantage of the new technologies by broadcasting by satellite or cable, others took advantage of a more liberal approach to broadcasting which permitted the development of terrestrial television systems – but all took advantage, one way or another, of the more liberal set of rules which were now in place. Rules, for example, which did not prevent commercial broadcasters from carrying anything more than entertainment or from broadcasting large quantities of imported material. And so what had initially been a fairly closed, state-controlled system characterized by a small number of public broadcasters now became a large competitive environment, with a knock-on effect on the nature of the public broadcasters, on funding systems, on cultures, and on the media and cultural industries.

## Changes in regulatory policy

What forms did the change in regulatory policy take? Four main types of policy regimes in the deregulation of public monopolies stand out. (Scherer 1986) These also contain different phrases or words which are sometimes used interchangeably with 'deregulation' but which, in reality, describe different arrangements and policy consequences. The four types are as follows:

- *Denationalization or privatization*: the transfer of public property from the government-owner to the private-owner. The best example of this is the privatization of TF1 in France under the Chirac government (1986–8). Privatization is usually but not necessarily accompanied by a liberalization or relaxation of the rules which apply to those previously nationalized entities.
- *Privatization of tasks*: one or more (but not all) of the tasks previously protected by a *de jure* monopoly are taken away from the public entity and transferred to private enterprises. An example of this would be the requirements that the BBC and ITV in the UK adopt a 25% quota of programmes to be made by independent producers.
- *Demonopolization*: abolishing the *de jure* monopoly of the public institution by permitting competition. Thus commercial radio was introduced almost everywhere in Western Europe (Britain, France, Greece, Spain, Scandinavia) as a means of breaking the monopoly.
- *Organizational privatization*: some or all of the regulatory constraints under which public, as opposed to private enterprises, have to operate are abolished. This is similar to the process of liberalization since regulatory requirements are removed. The public entity concerned may also be privatized in the process.

If one applies the above typology to European broadcasting systems then it becomes clear that each and every one has adapted to meet different sets of circumstances, but in no case have regulations been completely abandoned. Pressure for new regulations often comes from politicians who fear complete liberalization, and sometimes the new broadcasters themselves seek protection by asking authorities to recognize their fledgling status. The deregulation of broadcasting can often therefore lead to new procedures or bodies, e.g. to the foundation of new regulatory bodies to oversee or license new broadcasters. It may thus be more appropriate to describe certain contemporary changes as bringing about the *re*regulation, rather than the deregulation, of broadcasting. In other words, processes of deregulation have usually been controlled in some way or other; 'savage deregulation', i.e. where no controls are put in place to lessen the 'undesirable' impact of liberalization and commercialization on domestic culture and productions has not taken place (Traquina 1995).

## Case study: the UK

The terrestrial broadcasting system remains heavily regulated although the nature of the regulatory regime has changed. This change has involved an alteration in the way that the commercial television regulatory body – the ITC – regulates commercial terrestrial television. In the past it oversaw all aspects of the system; from 1992 onwards, individual programme companies have been made responsible for meeting their licence obligations. Programme companies have thus gained a degree of autonomy. Other examples of change would include the 25% quota of programmes to be made by independent producers which must be carried by the terrestrial broadcasters ('privatization of tasks'), and the removal of the requirement that a certain amount of current affairs programmes has to be carried during peak-time on the commercial channels ('liberalization'). The system for awarding licences to cable and terrestrial broadcasters remains strictly controlled, e.g. strict rules apply with regards to 'erotic' services, and services have to meet guidelines established by the relevant authorities such as the ITC. (see www.itc.org.uk/)

The enormous increase in the number of channels available to households in the UK has come about as a result of the new technologies – cable, satellite broadcasting and now digital television. Even so, the terrestrial broadcasters continue to dominate the broadcasting scene and their audience share remains large: in 1999, BBC1 had 28.4%; BBC2 10.8%; ITV 31.2; Channel 4 10.3; Channel 5 5.4% – about 86.1% of all viewing, but down from 90.4% of all viewing in 1996/7 and down from 91.1% in 1995/6 (BBC 1999: 8). Nevertheless, the new competitive environment has had an effect on how the BBC, the public broadcaster, operates now and will operate in the future when its public funding will be reconsidered. As a way of retaining its hold on the audience, and of increasing it, the BBC has entered into a significant alliance with BSkyB over sports coverage and with other interests such as Discovery Channel Inc. to create new channels within which to distribute its material. It has also launched digital television services as part of a general commitment to making all its services available to the general public (see www.bbc.co.uk/info/news/2000/executive/index.shtml). Private commercial broadcasters have also consolidated their position by buying other companies so as to create larger, more competitive, commercial television companies, or by extending their interests into newspapers. The latter is a consequence of the liberalization of media cross-ownership rules (see Department of National Heritage 1995).

At present, the British media system – like many other systems across Europe – is guided by practices which have attempted to minimize the extent of media concentration within different media sectors as well as across different media sectors. Examples of such practices include the following: newspaper mergers involving large groupings can be referred to the Mergers and Monopolies Commission in order to investigate the potential for abuse of market position; no one organization can own more than two commercial regional (Channel 3) licences (and not both the London licences); newspaper groups are not permitted to control more than 20% of commercial regional (Channel 3) licences; and so on.

Under pressure from newspaper groups seeking to diversify into television the British government has moved to liberalize the media ownership rules but, at the same time, to retain an element of control over the system so as to ensure some measure of diversity and plurality across media markets. The 1996 Broadcasting Act will consolidate this trend. Under the new rules, it will become possible for newspaper companies with less than a 20% share of total circulation to control up to 15% of the total television market as defined by audience share. The reverse also applies: a television company which has less than a 15% share of the television audience will be allowed to own a national newspaper. Larger media groups such as News International or Mirror Group Newspapers which have over 20% share of total newspaper circulation will be prevented from controlling Channel 3 licences.

The above examples relate only to specific areas. There are numerous other proposals which cover many possibilities across different media sectors. Nonetheless, the central features of the Act have made it easier for media groups to move into other media sectors and to allow for the creation of larger groupings of media interests in line with their national and international commercial interests. However, in spite of the moves towards deregulation, there continues to be pressure to maintain a structure which would prevent a concentration of media ownership and which would lead to a loss of diversity, as can be seen in the restrictions imposed on the larger media groups such as News International.

## The effects of broadcasting deregulation

The overall change in the thinking surrounding the subject of broadcasting is significant. It replaces an approach to broadcasting which emphasizes social and cultural objectives with an approach which stresses the commercial and economic aspects of broadcasting. A liberalized or deregulated system of broadcasting thus imposes very different requirements on broadcasters from those which usually apply in a publicly regulated system.

Some of the effects of broadcasting deregulation are already being felt in diverse countries around Western Europe with new commercial players and forces coming into play. But, in the same way that national responses differ, the effects of changes in broadcasting systems (see below) will also differ depending on such factors as the strength of the national culture, the financial strength of existing and new broadcasters, language and cultural differences, political support for public broadcasters, and so on. In sum, then, there are different strategies which can be pursued (see Achille and Miege 1994).

## Effects on programmes and scheduling

As new channels develop:

- There is an increase in competition and an increase in demand for programmes.
- Existing broadcasters (private and state) are forced to meet the challenge of the newcomers in order to retain their audiences.
- The content of the broadcasting channels can often become more similar than dissimilar as each competes more vigorously for the attention of the audience.

In terms of scheduling, commercial channels appear to follow a common strategy: initially a reliance on (usually American) imports, a dependence on certain types of entertainment programmes (television games, talk shows, soaps and series) and a move away from informational and educational content. Whether that pattern alters in subsequent years as the new broadcasting systems 'matures' – leading, for example, to new domestic productions – is a topic that can now be investigated. Nevertheless, the concern over American imports in the light of the liberalization of broadcasting post-1980 is particularly noteworthy. Europe, as a whole, imports a considerable amount of audio-visual products from the USA but it exports a tiny fraction of that total. This has created an obvious cultural and economic imbalance which the European Union has battled long and hard to counter (see Collins 1992; David Graham Associates 1999; Lange and Renaud 1989; McAnany and Wilkinson 1992).

## Effects on financing

With more competition in television, advertising revenue has to be shared out among even more broadcasters. On the one hand, more competition for programmes increases the costs of programme acquisitions but, on the other, it also increases the power of advertisers to negotiate for better prices and a greater range of audiences. The merger between BSB and Sky TV in Britain in 1991 shows how television can be a very profitable medium in a monopolistic environment but less so in a fully competitive one. As a result, new broadcasters are eager to develop new streams of revenue, such as sponsorship and pay-per-view, in order to create profitable enterprises.

As far as the public broadcasters are concerned, their primary source of revenue remains the licence fee. Some, such as the BBC, Norway's NRK and Sweden's SVT, continue to be totally dependent on it. With governments usually unwilling to allow for large increases in the licence fee, these broadcasters have had to engage in radical restructuring so as to adjust (downwards) their costs. Broadcasting organizations which have been in the past partly dependent on advertising revenue have clearly experienced a loss in their advertising revenue share as a consequence of increased competition. In some countries, governments have accordingly granted increases in licence fees or have relaxed rules limiting the amount state broadcasters can raise from advertising. On the whole, though, public broadcasters face a continuing problem as the licence fee system comes under increasing scrutiny and pressure.

## Effects on state broadcasters

Although public broadcasters have faced an erosion of both their viewing share and their revenue, for some that erosion has been more severe than for others. While in Austria, Germany, Ireland, the Netherlands, Norway, Sweden, Spain and the UK a combination of public broadcasters has managed to retain a large share of the television audience, in some cases, as in Greece, public television's audience has decreased dramatically. The point here is that an erosion in the share of the audience has repercussions on the issue of public funding for public broadcasters.

## Effects on media ownership

Media entrepreneurs such as Murdoch, Berlusconi, Kirch, and Bertelsmann have taken advantage of the new possibilities that the new television environment has offered. The creation of larger and fewer dominant media groups has been well documented, as have the problems and issues which are associated with it, problems such as a loss of diversity, dangers of monopolization of information and perspectives, and the concentration of power in too few hands (see Mazzoleni and Palmer, 1992; Tunstall and Palmer, 1991). So far, though, the European Commission has not been successful in coping with this issue (CEC 1992). One of the main obstacles to drafting legislation to deal with a concentration of ownership across the audio-visual landscape is determining the market share of any particular media proprietor. Furthermore, with rapid technological change, and media entrepreneurs moving into, and out of, sectors very quickly, the picture is constantly changing.

## Summary

The changes described above have given rise to very different broadcasting systems from those in existence at the beginning of the 1980s. New technologies, new policies towards communication sectors and a willingness to question the then existing structures of broadcasting have led to the creation of a more competitive and international broadcasting industry. The old systems of broadcasting have had to adapt to newer systems and players in the increasingly competitive environment of broadcasting.

## Questions

1 Describe the main features of the broadcasting system of any *one* European nation and examine the consequences of deregulation.

2 Has competition in broadcasting led to a more diverse range of output?

3 Should public service broadcasters continue to be favoured by either government policies or financial support, e.g. through a licence fee?

## References

Achille, Y. and Miege, B. (1994) 'The limits to the adaptation strategies of European public service television', *Media, Culture and Society* 16(1): 31–46.

BBC (1999) *BBC Television and Radio Facts and Figures*, London: BBC.

BBC at www.bbc.co.uk/info/news/2000/executive/index.shtml

ITV at www.itv.org.uk/

Broadcasting Research Unit (1985, 2nd edn 1985) *The Public Service Idea in British Broadcasting, Main Principles*, London: John Libbey.

Burgelman, J. C. (1986) 'The future of public service broadcasting: a case study for "new" communications policy', *European Journal of Communication* 1: 172–201.

CEC (1992) Green Paper by the Commission of the European Communities, *Pluralism and Media Concentration in the Single Market*, Com (92) 480 Final.

Commission of the European Communities, *Television Without Frontiers*, Commission Com (84) 300 Final/2.

Collins, R. (1992) *Satellite Television in Western Europe*, London: John Libbey.

Collins, R. (1994) *Broadcasting and Audio-visual Policy in the European Single Market*, London: John Libby.

David Graham Associates (1999) *Building a Global Audience*, London: Department of Culture, Media and Sport.

Department of National Heritage (1995) *Media Ownership: the government's proposals*, London: HMSO.

Dyson, K. and Humphreys, P. (eds) (1988) *Broadcasting and New Media Politics in Western Europe*, London: Routledge.

Dyson, K. and Humphreys, P. (eds) (1990) *The Political Economy of Communications; International and European Dimensions*, London: Routledge.

Fiddick, P. (1995) 'TV share', *Guardian* G2 26 June: 10.

Fowler, M. S. (1982) 'Broadcast unregulation in the 1980s', *Television Quarterly* 19(1): 12–18; see also Fowler, M. and Brennan, L. D. (1982) 'A marketplace approach to broadcast regulation', *Texas Law Review* 207–57, 221.

Hoffman-Reim, W. (1996) *Regulating Media. The Licencing and Supervision of Broadcasting in Six Countries*, London: Guilford Press.

Home Office (1986) *Report of the Committee on Financing the BBC* (Peacock Report), Cmnd 9824, London: HMSO.

Humphreys, P. (1988) 'Satellite broadcasting in West Germany' in R. Negrine (ed.) *Satellite Broadcasting*, London: Croom Helm.

Kuhn, R. (1985) (ed.) *The Politics of Broadcasting*, London: Croom Helm.

Kuhn, R. (1988) 'Satellite broadcasting in France' in R. Negrine (ed.) *Satellite Broadcasting*, London: Croom Helm.

Kuhn, R. (1995) *The Media in France*, London: Routledge.

Lange, A. and Renaud, J. L. (1989) *The Future of the European Audiovisual Industry*, Manchester: EIM.

Locksley, G. (1988) *Television Broadcasting in Europe and the New Technologies*, Luxembourg: European Communities.

Mazzoleni, G. and Palmer, M. (1992) 'Crossing borders' in K. Siune and W. Truetzscler (eds) *Dynamics of Media Politics*, London: Sage.

McAnany, E. G. and Wilkinson, K. T. (1992) 'From cultural imperialists to takeover victims?' *Communication Research* 19: 724–48.

McGregor, O. (1977) *Royal Commission on the Press: Final Report*, Cmnd 6810, London: HMSO.

McQuail, D. and Siune, K. (1986) (eds) *New Media Politics*, London: Sage.

Negrine, R. (1985) *Cable Television and the Future of Broadcasting*, London: Croom Helm.

Negrine, R. (1994) *Politics and the Mass Media in Britain*, London: Routledge.

Negrine, R. and Papathanassopoulos, S. (1990) *The Internationalisation of Television*, London: Pinter.

Papathanassopoulos, S. (1990) 'Public service broadcasting and deregulatory pressures in Europe', *Journal of Information Science* No. 19: 113–20.

Porter, V. (1990) 'Broadcasting re-regulation in Europe – citizenship and consumerism', *EBU Review*, XLI(6): November.

Richeri, G. (1985) 'Television from service to business: European tendencies and the Italian case', in P. Drummond and P. Paterson (eds) *Television in Transition*, London: BFI.

Sanchez-Tabernero, A. (1993) *Media Concentration in Europe*, European Institute for the Media Monograph 16, Dusseldorf: European Institute for Media.

Sassoon, D. (1986) 'Political and market forces in Italian broadcasting', *West European Politics* No. 2: 67–83.

Scherer, J. (1986) 'Historical analysis of deregulation: the European case', paper presented at the International Symposium, La Dereglementation des Telecommunications et de l'Audiovisuel, Paris: Centre Nationale Researche Scientifique, March 1986.

Seymour-Ure, C. (1987) 'Media policy in Britain: now you see it, now you don't', *European Journal of Communication* 2: 269–87.

Seymour-Ure, C. (1991) *The Press and Broadcasting in Britain since 1945*, Oxford: Blackwell.

Siune, K. and Treutzschler, W. (1992) (eds) *Dynamics of Media Politics: Broadcast and Electronic Media in Western Europe*, London: Sage.

Syvertsen, T. (1991) 'Public television in crisis: critiques compared in Norway and Britain', *European Journal of Communication* 6(1): 95–114.

Tracey, M. (1998) *The Decline and Fall of Public Service Broadcasting*, Oxford: Oxford University Press.

Traquina, N. (1995) 'Portuguese television: the politics of savage deregulation', *Media, Culture and Society* 17(2): 223–39.

Tunstall, J. (1986) *Communications Deregulation*, Oxford: Basil Blackwell.

Tunstall, J. and Palmer, M. (1990) *Liberating Communications. Policy-making in France and Britain*, Oxford: Blackwell.

Tunstall, J. and Palmer, M. (1991) *Media Moguls*, London: Routledge.

Veljanovski, C. (ed.) (1989) *Freedom in Broadcasting*, London: Institute of Economic Affairs.

Weymouth, A. and Lamizet, B. (eds) (1996) *Markets and Myths: Forces for Change in the European Media*, Harlow: Addison Wesley Longman.

## Further reading

Blumler, J. (1992) (ed.) *Television and the Public Interest*, London: Sage. This book contains a full discussion of public service broadcasting systems across Europe and the possible impacts of competition.

DTI/Department of Culture, Media and Sport (2000) *A New Future for Communications*, White Paper, Available; www.communicationswhitepaper.gov.uk. This White Paper addresses issues of regulating communications in the twenty-first century and sets out the Blair government approach. See also www.culture.gov.uk for the department's position.

Burgelman, J. C. (1986) 'The future of public service broadcasting: a case study for "new" communications policy', *European Journal of Communication* 1: 172–201. A good discussion of old and new issues.

Richeri, G. (1985) 'Television from service to business: European tendencies and the Italian case' in P. Drummond and P. Paterson (eds) *Television in Transition*, London: BFI. A chapter that traces changes across European broadcasting systems.

Sanchez-Tabernero, A. (1993) *Media Concentration in Europe*. European Institute for the Media Monograph 16, Dusseldorf: European Institute for Media. Although out of date, it still provides much information that relates to the study of media, ownership and control in Europe.

Siune, K. and Treutzschler, W. (eds) (1992) *Dynamics of Media Politics: Broadcast and Electronic Media in Western Europe*, London: Sage. One of many overviews of change across Europe produced by a group of European scholars. Later volumes update information.

Syvertsen, T. (1991) 'Public television in crisis: critiques compared in Norway and Britain', *European Journal of Communication* 6(1): 95–114. A useful comparison between two European public service broadcasting systems.

Weymouth, A. and Lamizet, B. (eds) (1996) *Markets and Myths: Forces for Change in the European Media*, Harlow: Addison Wesley Longman. A useful overview of key issues and systems.

# Chapter 17

# Audience research

ADMINISTRATIVE RESEARCH OF AUDIENCES

**RAY KENT**

The purpose of audience research is to provide both quantitative and qualitative feedback on audiences to television, radio, newspapers, magazines, outdoor posters and cinemas. Audiences are measured using a variety of techniques including meters attached to television sets in a panel of 4700 homes selected to be representative of all homes in the UK, weekly diaries placed with a random samples of radio listeners, and a National Readership Survey that interviews some 38,000 people a year.

## Introduction

The producers of television and radio programmes, the makers of films and videos, broadcasters, newspaper and magazine editors, media owners and advertisers all require information about their audiences. Advertising agencies, media consultants and market research agencies also need data on the audiences to all the media in order to be able to advise their clients or to undertake work on their behalf. The 'ratings' achieved by individual broadcasters, television channels or radio stations, the circulations and readerships obtained by the print media, cinema attendances and passages of vehicles and pedestrians past outdoor posters are all crucial to those involved in the media industry since such measures are the basis for determining the success or failure of media outputs and, furthermore, constitute the 'currency' for negotiating advertising space.

The purpose of audience research is to provide both quantitative and qualitative feedback on the size, composition, usage, lifestyles and opinions of audiences to television and radio, readers of newspapers, magazines and books, and viewers of outdoor posters and billboards. For the purpose of this chapter, the term 'audience' will be taken to include not only viewers and listeners but also readers all of whom are users or consumers of the wide range of media considered in Chapter 1.

While editorial and creative staff in public service organizations such as the BBC will clearly be interested in the findings of such research (not least for the purposes of justifying the annual licence fee paid by viewers), the process of audience research is driven largely by purchasers and sellers of opportunities to target audiences through advertising. In the UK the total spending on advertising is currently over £7 billion per year and rising at about 7% a year. All the major sources of audience research are the product of cooperation between these buyers and sellers who finance carefully designed and expensive research into the viewing, listening and reading habits of the population. Having said that, in the UK it was the BBC that pioneered both radio and television audience research in the 1930s and 1940s. It needed to justify the licence fee being levied by demonstrating that the public was getting good value for money. It began what became known as the 'Daily Survey' in which interviewers asked a sample of people each day what they had listened to on the previous day. This was then used to estimate the entire audience size.

## Television audience research

It was only with the development of commercial television channels – those supported by advertising revenue – that the demand emerged for detailed and precise information on the audiences achieved. The UK was the first to introduce commercial television in Europe (ITV) in 1955. Other large European countries did not follow until the 1980s (Gane 1994). The technical characteristics of television lent themselves to the use of electronic meters, which were introduced in the UK as early as 1956. In France, Germany and the Netherlands, meters were installed in panel households somewhat later, but in advance of commercial television and at the behest of governments. Consequently, their development has tended to be controlled by official organizations.

The early development of meters to measure television audiences took place in the USA where the television industry began as a commercial venture from the outset. The original 'set meters' both in the USA and in Europe recorded only the status of the set (on or off) and the channel selected. The viewing of individuals was determined separately through self-completion diaries. However, as more and more channels became available and as increasing numbers of households had more than one set – and nowadays probably also a video recorder – so the demands on meters grew rapidly. In the UK, a market research agency known at the time as Audits of Great Britain (AGB) was the first to develop a 'peoplemeter', which not only recorded who was viewing but also allowed for the retrieval of data via the telephone. These were installed in panel homes in the UK and Italy in 1984 and in Ireland in 1985.

By the early 1990s, fully operational peoplemeters were in place throughout Europe (Gane 1994). There are, however, still considerable differences in the ways the meters are used, for example whether to include people who are on holiday, and whether 'viewing' means present in the room with a television set switched on, present in the room and able to watch, or actually watching. Attempts are being made to harmonize techniques across Europe, but progress is slow.

### *The administration of data collection*

In the UK a committee was set up in 1957 to represent the interests of both the advertisers and the ITV companies and to award a contract to a market research agency to measure television audiences. This was the Joint Industry Committee for Television Advertising Research (JICTAR). At the time the BBC had its own system, but in 1981 a joint system was established which involved creating a company jointly owned by the BBC and the ITCA called the Broadcasters' Audience Research Board (BARB). AGB held the contract to supply the quantitative audience measurement service exclusively until 1991, when BARB split the contract between two research contractors. Television audience measurement depends on peoplemeters being installed in panel homes that are representative of the country as a whole. Panel recruitment and quality control was passed over to a company established for the purpose by two market research agencies, Research Services Limited (RSL) and Millward Brown, called RSMB. This company was to be responsible for the design and execution of an Establishment Survey, the sample design for the main panel, the design and maintenance of the panel control scheme, the recruitment of panel households, the maintenance of details about panel households, panel household incentive schemes, and the design of weighting procedures. AGB (later Taylor Nelson AGB and now Taylor Nelson Sofres) was to supply and connect metering equipment, the nightly telephone polling of panel households, data processing and the publication of data to subscribers.

Establishment Surveys establish and track reception and viewing characteristics of television viewing households in the 17 ITV regions into which the UK is divided. The information is then used to design, monitor and control the composition of the main panel in each region, and to provide a pre-screened address bank from which homes may be recruited when they are required to meet control targets in their area. Information from the Establishment Survey is combined with basic population demographics from the Office of National Statistics (ONS) to produce universe size estimates for panel control purposes and to weight survey results.

### Data collection method

The main panel consists of some 4700 households. With an average of 2.56 individuals per household, the sample size of individuals is over 12,000. These individuals, aged from 4 upwards, are the basis for reporting viewing. The panel in each region is balanced by size of household, presence of children, age of housewife, presence of working adults, and socio-economic status and educational status of the head of household. The current peoplemeter, which is placed in every panel home, consists of a meter display unit and remote control handset for every television in the home plus a central data storage unit, which is connected to each display unit via the domestic mains supply. The central data storage unit records viewing on a second-by-second basis and has the ability to record up to 255 channels as well as the use of the VCR for time-shift viewing. It can track the viewing habits of eight members of any one household, plus up to seven guests. This it does by allocating a number to all household members who press their numbered button on the handset to indicate that they have started to view. It is pressed again when the person stops viewing. Demographic data on age and sex of the guests are entered via the handset, following prompts on the display screen on the peoplemeter. Viewers are prompted to check that the correct buttons are pressed every 15 minutes while they view in order to maximize the accuracy of the information being recorded.

The central data storage unit contains a modem and is located near a telephone point into which it is permanently plugged. During the night it is interrogated by means of a telephone call from the agency's central London computer (telephone ringing is suppressed) and information in its memory is downloaded. Audience figures become available the next day after data from all the panel homes are aggregated, adjusted for imbalances and projected to the total population.

### Audience ratings

The main currency for the measurement of television audiences is the 'rating'. The rating for a television programme is the size of its audience expressed as a percentage of the relevant population size. Thus the adult rating for *Coronation Street* in the Midlands ITV area is the proportion of all adults in that area who watched a particular episode. The 'relevant' population is those adults living in private households capable of viewing the appropriate station. Audience sizes vary throughout the duration of a programme and is measured for each individual minute. The minute-by-minute ratings are then averaged over the whole of the programme. A rating of, say, 37% would be typical for such a favourite programme. Some advertisers will call this 37 'rating points'.

Ratings are also calculated for advertisements by taking the minute in which the advertisement begins. Advertisers and their agencies then add these ratings over all the 'spots' (showings) for a given advertising campaign. The total is called either the total television rating or the Gross Rating Points (GRP). The figures will, of course, no longer be a true percentage since it can exceed 100, but it is taken as a measure of the 'weight' of the advertising campaign. If the audience sizes themselves rather than the ratings are added together, it measures total 'impacts' for the campaign, reflecting the actual sizes of the audience rather than the proportion of the total potential watching. Impacts are often the basis for charging differential rates for advertising air-time according to region.

Ratings are used by broadcasters, advertisers, advertising agencies and media specialists who need to know what proportion of the population watch each programme, and the regional and demographic characteristics of each audience. Not all programmes are expected to achieve high ratings, but there is a target depending on the type of programme and its place in the schedule. Commercial broadcasters also need spot ratings (for each commercial) and break ratings (for each commercial break) as a guide for selling air-time to advertisers. Highly rated spots (with large audiences) command a higher price and the broadcaster issues a rate-card giving the price of each spot.

Advertisers need reassurance that their advertising budgets are being spent effectively, so they require information on the size, frequency of exposure and demographic profile of the audience to their advertisements. Equally important is information on the cost per 1000 viewers.

## *Audience appreciation*

Qualitative assessment and the evaluation of television programmes was for many years undertaken by the BBC's Audience Reaction Service using a Television Opinion Panel (TOP). This has now been taken over by Research Services Limited (RSL), which maintains a national panel of individuals on which the 17 ITV regions are represented according to size. National panel members, of which there are 4600, are contacted weekly and, with a response rate of about 65%, gives the achieved sample of approximately 3000.

Panellists are given a 7-day booklet running from Monday to Sunday and is in three sections:

- a list of all programmes on a day-by-day basis asking respondents to give a score on a 6-point scale for each programme seen (see Table 17.1);
- more detailed questions are asked about selected programmes;
- questions about series that have just finished, long-running serials or questions of a more general nature.

From the first section an Appreciation Index (AI) is calculated. This is done by allocating a score out of 100 for each level of response (see Table 17.1). The AI is the average of all the responses. Most AIs are between 50 and 90, but they are not absolute numbers; rather they facilitate comparisons with programmes of a similar type, for example, 'feature films', 'sport', or 'news and current affairs'. Weekly AI reports list each category separately and are broken down by age, sex and social class.

It has been found that, overall, there is little correlation between AI scores and audience ratings – bigger audiences do not necessarily mean higher appreciation scores and vice versa. Audience size for any programme is determined largely by the time of day it is broadcast, and what the competing programmes are, irrespective of the quality of the programme. AIs are a crucial and necessary complement to estimates of audience size in evaluating channel and programme performance. AIs, furthermore, have a useful role in predicting, and later explaining, the audience delivery for a series of programmes.

*Table 17.1* The Audience Appreciation Index

|  | **Allocate score** |
|---|---|
| Extremely interesting and/or enjoyable | 100 |
| Very interesting and/or enjoyable | 80 |
| Fairly interesting and/or enjoyable | 60 |
| Neither one thing nor the other | 40 |
| Not very interesting and/or enjoyable | 20 |
| Not at all interesting and/or enjoyable | 0 |

## *The future*

The UK currently has what is probably the most sophisticated and accurate gauge of a nation's viewing habits in the world. However, advertising agencies have had to learn new skills in accessing the data in electronic form and in coping with more complicated data. With the rapidly developing use of video-recorders to time-shift viewing, viewing behaviour is becoming more complex, so there are more ways of measuring ratings. Thus 'consolidated' ratings consist of ratings achieved at the time of the broadcast plus any ratings accrued to the same programme if it has been recorded on a VCR and played back within a seven-day period. This may sound simple, but the combination and permutation of live and playback ratings with house-hold and guest viewing, adult and child ratings, people viewing only fragments of a playback or zapping chunks of it, or viewing it on several occasions, will facilitate vastly more complex analyses when users require them. Stored viewing is likely in future to outweigh live viewing and advertisers will need to rethink how they target their audiences, particularly since the ads will probably have been automatically edited out.

The BARB contract is now due for renewal with effect from January 2002, although tenders have already been received and the new contractor or contractors will be announced some time in 2000. The existing peoplemeter system will have problems in coping with digital compression, video-on-demand, and interactive television. A new meter system called Picture Matching is already being trialled by TNS. This will sample the content of the programmes being watched and match this with pro-gramme outputs. It will be able to handle digital television and interactive television in addition to satellite television, cable TV, video playback, digital video disk (DVD), along with the standard broadcasts from the BBC and ITV.

## Radio audience research

In many ways the measurement of radio audiences is more complex than for tele-vision. First, listeners are not always aware of, or can correctly identify, the station to which they are listening (for television this is automatically recorded by the peoplemeter). Second, radio listening is often casual and undertaken while other activities are being pursued, or it may be used just as background. Although there are problems, as we have seen, over what counts as 'watching' a television, at least presence in the room in which there is a television switched on (and peoplemeter attached) is clearer than the idea of 'presence' when a radio can be heard. Third, listeners tend to be mobile – some 20–35% of listening takes place outside the home, often on radios not owned by or tuned in by the listener. This creates problems either for recall or for diary-keeping. Fourth, radio is a highly fragmented and rapidly expanding service. At present there are over 200 radio stations using the airwaves in the UK. This number could expand considerably with the extension of digital audio broadcasting.

## The administration of data collection

Until 1992 the BBC and independent local radio undertook separate radio audience research. In 1992 a new company, Radio Joint Audience Research Ltd (RAJAR), was established to operate a single audience measurement system for the radio industry as a whole. This company is jointly owned by the Commercial Radio Companies Association (CRCA) and the BBC. It covers all BBC national and local stations, UK licensed stations and most other commercial radio stations. RAJAR research is currently contracted to Research Services Limited (RSL), which has since become part of Ipsos and is now Ipsos-RSL.

## Data collection methods

While it is, of course, technically feasible to use meters on radio sets, it has until recently been considered far too expensive for the industry to afford. Consequently, it has nearly always been done using either interview survey techniques or self-completed diaries. RAJAR uses a seven-day diary covering Monday to Sunday. Some 150,000 diaries are placed and collected annually by 200 interviewers who use prompt cards to determine which stations each respondent actually listens to. The diary is in two sections. The first covers media consumption including general radio listening, television viewing and newspaper readership. The second section records actual radio listening (see Figure 17.1). For any occasion when respondents listen to the radio for 5 minutes or more, they are asked to record their listening by drawing a line through the appropriate time segment boxes. Respondents are also asked to indicate where they listened – at home, in a car, van or lorry, or at work/elsewhere. The stations that the respondent listens to are listed across the top using stick-on labels.

All questionnaire and diary data are processed using optical scanning technology and undergo a series of checking procedures. The data are then adjusted and grossed up to give population estimates. The results measure:

- reach – the unduplicated number of different people listening to any specified service over a period of time expressed as a percentage of the total universe;
- total hours – the overall number of hours of adult listening to a specified service over a specified period of time;
- average hours – average hours per listener calculated from total hours divided by reach.

## Audience appreciation

In terms of audience appreciation, the BBC had its own Listening Panel until 1992 when it was replaced by the Radio Opinion Monitor (ROM), but it still covers only the BBC's networked programmes. Panel members are recruited from the RAJAR survey. Two panels, each of 2250 listeners, complete diaries once every four weeks. One of the panels is thus active every two weeks. The ROM collects Reaction Indices

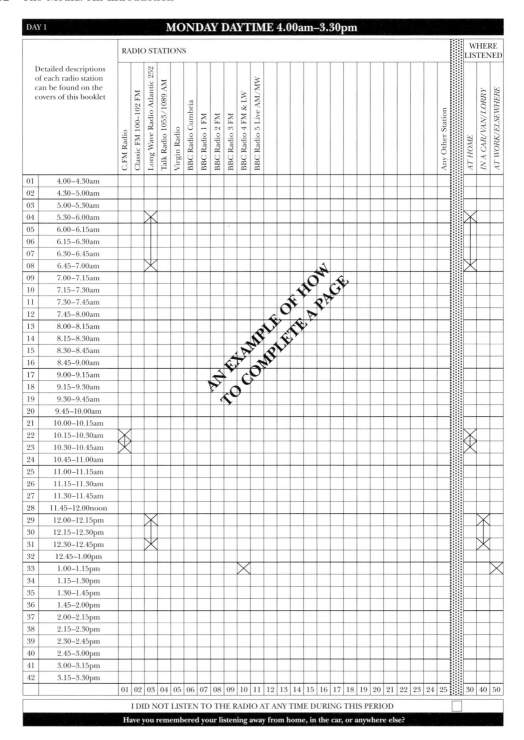

**Figure 17.1** A demonstration diary page

to each programme based on a 'marks out of ten' evaluation. There are also diagnostic questions that contain in-depth questions about selected programmes or series. The service is currently contracted to Ipsos-RSL.

## *The future*

The present contract runs to 2002, by which time digital audio radios will probably be widespread. To match the vastly expanding possibilities of this medium, interest is likely to focus on using meters. RSL, with its parent company Ipsos, France's largest independent market research agency, and Germany's Infratest Burke, is developing a Radio Watch. This contains not only a microphone with which to hear what the panellist's radio is playing, but also a radio receiver and antenna by means of which it can match panellists' choice of listening against the output of a variety of stations. As yet it is not down to wristwatch size and costs nearly £500 to manufacture. However, this and other competing meter systems could conceivably be developed to monitor television viewing as well as radio listening. This would totally change the way television viewing is recorded. It would mean, for example, a shift away from the household as the unit of measurement to the individual.

## Newspaper and magazine readership

As in other areas of audience research, the commercial importance of readership research stems from the fact that newspapers and magazines carry advertising and are often dependent – sometimes heavily dependent – on this source of revenue. At the same time, advertisers depend on readership research to determine the allocation of their spend between the many different titles available. Readership estimates have become the currency in which advertising space is traded. The data are also of relevance to editorial and circulation departments.

## *Measuring readership*

Measuring readership is quite possibly more difficult than measuring either television viewing or radio listening. Reading can mean anything from a cursory glance to a thorough study. Usually, it means that the reader has 'read' only those sections of interest and skipped or glanced at others.

Most readership research takes a complete issue of a publication as its focus of measurement rather than a section, a page or an advertisement. Personal interviews remain the favoured method of data collection since the number of questions that need to be asked is inevitably very large. In addition it is usually necessary to show visuals of mastheads or logos to help respondents to correctly identify publications. Since readership tends to be highly seasonal and subject to atypical events and circumstances, most readership research will be continuous, while the use of panels tends to be too expensive, so they will often be based on independent samples.

Readerships are usually measured in terms of what is called average issue readership (AIR) – the number of different people who read a single issue, averaged across issues. This measure has attracted some criticism – that it is a very bland measure, or that it seriously inflates estimates. It is based on asking respondents when they last saw a copy of a publication. If they claim to have done so in the last publishing interval, they are added to the AIR. The problem is that if the reader looks at the copy again outside the publishing period, then the reading event may be counted twice. This phenomenon of 'replication' can, according to Shepherd-Smith (1994), seriously inflate the apparent AIR estimate.

AIR identifies respondents as either readers or non-readers, but it is also necessary to estimate the frequency of reading. Again, this is very difficult to measure. It is usual to ask respondents about their claimed regularity of reading and to take their answers at face value. But, should we ask about actual past reading behaviour or what people 'usually' do? Should the alternative answers between which respondents must choose be couched in numbers, in verbal terms or in a mixture of the two? An example of a mixture would be: 'About how often do you see *The Economist* these days – frequently (three or four issues out of every four), sometimes (one or two issues out of four) or only occasionally (fewer than one issue out of four)?'

## Data collection

The current contractor for readership research is, once again, Ipsos-RSL. Research Services Limited has, in fact, operated the National Readership Survey (NRS) for over 30 years. The NRS is based on some 38,000 interviews a year covering nearly 300 newspapers and magazines. The results give 5-day, 6-day and Saturday average issue readership for national daily newspapers, plus frequency, recency, source of copy and how disappointed readers would be if the copy were not available for all publications. It also covers car ownership, holidays, consumer goods, financial arrangements and classification questions.

The NRS has sometimes been criticized for not providing enough information on the manner in which different titles are read, so a question has been introduced on whether respondents look at particular topics when they are reading newspapers or magazines, for example, 'UK/British news', 'Sport', or 'TV programmes'. This, however, still does not refer to the reading of specific sections in specific issues. Some users are frustrated that the survey does not go beyond 'reading frequency' and 'source of copy' to qualify the average issue readership score. Ideally, users would like to know the numbers and profiles of people exposed to a given advertisement. There is currently nothing on time spent reading, the reading of sections or specific issue readership.

Despite these criticisms the NRS has over the years been seen as the 'gold standard' for survey research, setting the standard not only for readership measurement, but also for demographics. Social grading as defined by the NRS has become the standard for the whole of the UK market research industry. Social grade quota setting and weighting of many surveys is often undertaken with reference to the findings of the NRS.

## The future

The current contract with Ipsos-RSL has been renewed until the end of 2002. Developments are likely to focus on abandoning hard copy prompts in favour of on-screen interviewing using lap-top computers.

## Other media

Other media that are currently subject to systematic audience research are outdoor posters and the cinema.

### Posters

Posters, unlike the media mentioned so far, are not embedded in information or entertainment. They are not consciously 'used' and contact with them is quite unintentional. This means that people cannot sensibly be asked to recall what posters they have recently seen. In the UK there are probably around 130,000 poster panels at 70,000 sites, all unevenly distributed about our towns and cities. In addition, there are over 400,000 panels of various sizes on buses, rail and tube trains and stations. Poster research is aimed at estimating how many people are likely to see or pass by a particular panel and with what frequency. Into this also has to go some measure of visibility.

At the end of the day the advertising value of each site has to be assessed so that advertising campaigns using combinations of sites can be planned. The current system called POSTAR (for Poster Audience Research) was launched in 1996. It is a complex system involving vehicular and pedestrian traffic models, a reach and frequency model, plus a visibility model. This takes into account:

- panel size and angle;
- illumination;
- visual clutter;
- duration, which depends on the speed of traffic and the distance over which the poster can be seen.

### Cinema

Interest in measuring the audiences for cinemas comes from a number of industry sectors, including:

- cinema advertising contractors, together with their clients and advertising agencies;
- cinema exhibitors, who have their own admission statistics, but they are also interested to know their share of the market, the composition of the audience and how particular films are doing;

- cinema distributors, who are keen to monitor through film tracking the progress of a new film as the publicity builds up;
- video distributors, who wish to study the success of cinema films as a guide to the video launch.

The basic measurements taken are:

- Cinema admissions. It is necessary to collect admission figures weekly in support of cinema advertising.
- Audience composition. This tells us on average who is going to the cinema, for example which age and social class groups.
- Audience by film. The audience composition for different films varies greatly and this needs to be plotted.
- Qualitative studies. Recall surveys can measure the impact of cinema advertising, appreciation of advertisements and so on.
- Film tracking. This is a weekly service for film distributors which, for example, plots the awareness of new films or the desire to see.
- Analysis of drive time. Cinema exhibitors plot the hinterlands of a potential new cinema to examine the possible audience.

The most accurate, comprehensive and widely used source of UK cinema admissions data is that commissioned by the Cinema Advertising Association (CAA). This provides weekly estimates of the total number of audience admissions to all circuit and independent screens that carry advertising. It is important that admission data be available on a regular basis with quick reporting of results.

The CAA sponsors a joint industry body called CAVIAR (Cinema and Video Industry Audience Research) which is supported by advertising agencies, cinema exhibitors, film distributors, video distributors and video retailers. The main CAVIAR survey is carried out in October/November each year with a quota sample of about 3100 covering all age groups over 5 years old. The questionnaire covers cinema, video films, television, satellite and cable, and newspaper and magazine reading. The interviews are conducted face-to-face by the British Market Research Bureau.

As far as cinema is concerned the main questions cover:

- frequency and recency of cinema going (similar to the NRS questions);
- detailed records of visits in the last two months including the cinemas attended and the films seen;
- attendance at any of a list of 60 films during the previous year. This list includes 48 main releases and 12 'art' films;
- a variety of questions about the film, who goes with whom, means of transport, interest in other facilities at the cinema site and reasons for going to multiplex cinemas.

## Conclusion

In the UK the average person spends about 3.8 hours a day viewing television, about 3 hours listening to the radio and about 20 minutes reading a newspaper or a magazine – some 7 hours per day in all. This is a high proportion of any person's wake time, but the relationship between the use of the media is something that has yet to be studied in detail, for example are those people who watch a lot of television also those who listen a lot to the radio? Patterns of media use also vary from country to country. Thus the UK, Poland and Italy have the lowest share of radio (about 30%) while Denmark, Flemish Belgium and Finland have very high radio shares (about 60%). Overall, however, certain trends can be discerned:

- a growing fragmentation of audiences;
- increased media choice for audiences;
- intensifying media industry competition;
- the development of pan-European and multi-country advertising;
- deregulation and privatization of the media;
- moves towards harmonization of research methodologies.

## Questions

1   Why is it so important for those in the media industry to agree on methods of data collection?

2   In what ways is digital broadcasting likely to change the need for audience research?

3   To what extent is the 'audience' to a particular medium a creation of the procedures used to measure it?

## References

Brown, M. (1994) 'Estimating newspaper and magazine readership', in R. Kent (ed.) *Measuring Media Audiences*, London: Routledge.

Gane, R. (1994) 'Television audience measurement in Europe. A review and comparison' in R. Kent (ed.) *Measuring Media Audiences*, London, Routledge.

Shepherd-Smith (1994) 'Something's wrong with average issue readership' *ADMAP* February 89–94.

## Further reading

Kent, R. A. (ed.) (1994) *Measuring Media Audiences*, London: Routledge. This edited book contains contributions by some of the top experts in the field. While some of the techniques described have since been overtaken by events, the basic principles and background are clearly explained in some detail.

McDonald, C. and King, S. (1996) 'Research and the media', in J. Goodyear (ed.) *Sampling the Universe. The growth, development and influence of market research in Britain since 1945*, Henley-on-Thames: NTC Publications Ltd. A clear and non-technical account of how media research developed in the UK since 1945.

Mytton, G. (1999) *Handbook on Radio and Television Audience Research*, UNESCO, UNICEF and the BBC World Service. Not limited to the UK, this source gives the most up-to-date account on television and radio audience research currently available.

# Chapter 18

# 'Effects'

MEDIA EFFECTS: CONTINUING CONTROVERSIES

**GUY CUMBERBATCH**

Concerns about media effects have a long history, changing little with the arrival of each new medium. They have focused on the media's potential to aggravate crime and violence in society. Despite the majority view that research evidence supports such concerns, these conclusions tend to be based on the selective use of rather weak data. In the last decade research appears to have become more closely aligned with demonstrating harm than in attempting to unravel the relationship between media and audiences.

## History of concerns

As Geoffrey Pearson (1983) has pointed out, there has been a long history of moral panics about the possible harmful effects of popular culture. In the sixteenth century 'popular songs too often presented criminals as heroes' while in 1776 Joseph Hanway suggested that 'debasing amusements' in newspapers were among the causes of 'the host of thieves' which 'have invaded us'. Similar concerns were raised about 'penny dreadful' comics and amusement houses in the mid-nineteenth century, expanding to embrace popular theatre, followed by cinema and television almost from their inception and then comic books again in the 1950s. Since then video and more recently computer games seem to have inherited the legacy of fears and anxieties about earlier media without altogether eclipsing them. Of course, the range of concerns raised about all the possible effects of the mass media is extremely wide – from the almost mythical phenomenon such as subliminal advertising/persuasion (Cumberbatch and Wood 1998) to more tangible issues such as the erosion of literacy in a televisual world (Neuman 1991).

While we know little about the extent of these various concerns, the annual ITC surveys: *Television: the Public's View* (e.g. Cumberbatch, 2000b) reveal that bad language, sex/nudity and violence are among the principal causes of offence and complaint. The Broadcasting Standards Commission identifies violence, bad language, sex and nudity and the representation of minority groups within its research on 'social concerns' (e.g. Cumberbatch *et al.*, 2000a, b). Other research suggests that there is more concern about the effects of violence. The majority of people believe that media violence inspires young people to behave violently while 76% think that it makes viewers insensitive or callouse (Lacay 1995, cited in Smith and Donnerstein 1998).

Research has revealed an interesting phenomenon in public perceptions of harmful effects where individuals seem to hold a simple magic bullet-like theory for media effects on others but assume they are themselves more sophisticated and less vulnerable (Eveland and McLeod 1999).

The most enduring of concerns is that crime and violence in the media fuel crime and violence in society. This provided the initiative for a wide variety of legislation to control the media including the establishment of the British Board of Film Censors as early as 1912. However, it also provided the focus for some of the earliest research in mass communications and helps to illuminate some of the many methodological and conceptual problems which pervade the study of effects.

## Early research

Perhaps the most notable of early studies were those by the Payne Fund which was set up in New York in 1928 to study the impact and influences of motion pictures on youth. This produced a series of twelve independent studies published in several volumes with a summary volume written by Charters (1933). Here the overall conclusions were that, despite public anxiety about the new medium, any influences were fairly modest and superficial in such things as fashion rather than on morals. Charters was unwilling to attribute criminal delinquency to film-going.

Somewhat similar conclusions were reached in Britain in 1951 by the Departmental Committee on Children and the Cinema (the Wheare Committee) which sponsored a very large survey of all juvenile offenders appearing before the courts over a six-month period. This produced an impressive sample of 38,000 young offenders. The committee considered that perhaps in 141 of these (i.e. 0.4% of cases) the offending behaviour might be related to cinema attendance (Home Office 1951).

The most broadly based studies of media effects were carried out as television was being introduced extensively to the UK (Himmelweit *et al.* 1958) and to the USA (Schramm *et al.* 1961). Both studies were able to compare areas which had begun to receive television with those which were still waiting for the new medium. They make fascinating reading, especially in how people found the time to accommodate television. Himmelweit *et al.* introduced the concept 'functional similarity' to explain why some activities declined (like cinema attendance and comic book reading) but left others untouched (such as teenage social activities and sports). However, the bulk of the time found for television seems to be drawn from essentially time-wasting activities (like watching raindrops run down a window pane).

In terms of harmful effects, very little support was found for popular concerns about television. Schramm *et al.*'s conclusion was a classic in circumspection:

> For some children under some conditions, some television is harmful. For other children under the same conditions, or for the same children under other conditions, it

may be beneficial. For most children under most conditions television is probably neither harmful nor particularly beneficial (Schramm *et al.* 1961: 13).

Despite the generally reassuring tone of much of this early research, the 1960s saw a rapid growth of psychological research into media aggression, largely stimulated by the laboratory experiments of Albert Bandura at Stanford University and Leonard Berkowitz at Wisconsin. Their contributions, along with some of the more notable theoretical developments since, are discussed below.

## Imitation

In the early 1960s Bandura published a series of experiments demonstrating that children exposed to a film clip of someone behaving aggressively were more likely to play in a similarly aggressive manner than a control group of children who had not seen the film. This research has become something of a classic and indeed is one of the most cited in psychology textbooks. Bandura soon became convinced that violence on television would lead to children imitating what they saw and became involved in various campaigns against violence on television.

Bandura's experiments were certainly impressive in the results obtained. Up to 88% of the children imitated the aggressive acts which they had seen 'on television' (see Bandura 1994). However, some details of the experiments are worth noting. Pre-school children were used – mostly recruited from the university crèche. They saw a film clip on television featuring a model (initially an adult but in later experiments another child) assaulting a large inflated plastic clown called a 'Bobo' or 'Bozo' doll which, due to its weighted base, would bounce back up again when hit. The model engaged in various 'aggressive' acts uttering various comments from a prepared script such as 'Whack it, eh!' After being exposed to the model's curious antics, the children were led from the viewing room to the laboratory to be observed. On the way they passed some very attractive toys, which they were invited to admire by the researcher who asked if they would like to play with them, only to be told 'well you can't'. The children, described by Bandura as 'frustrated', then entered the laboratory, which contained both the Bozo doll and various other toys. They were ostensibly left alone to play but were secretly observed through one-way mirrors.

Of course, one key observation might be that this kind of behaviour isn't really aggression since there isn't much else one can do to a Bobo doll except hit it. Indeed my own Bozo doll was wrecked due to the enthusiasm of an elderly professor who could not resist the temptation to kick it whenever he came to my office!

## Limitation

The simple notion of imitation as described above cannot do justice to the more sophisticated theory of social learning which Bandura developed and no-one can deny that this is an important part of socialization or that some children and even adults do sometimes imitate what they see on television. Indeed in one study of young people between 7 and 16 years old, almost six out of ten (58%) interviewees said they had seen somebody copying from video games and of these 77% spontaneously mentioned fighting. However *all* the young people thought that when children copied it was pretend and not serious (Cumberbatch *et al.* 1994). Thus, the crucial issue must be whether crime and violence in society are aggravated by people imitating the mass media.

A good authority on this subject is James Ferman who for more than a quarter of a century was Director of the British Board of Film Censors and now Film Classification. Whenever some crime occurred where claims were made that it was linked to film/video violence, he had to investigate. Does he think that there are cases – as routinely reported in the mass media – of such imitation? After all, Michael Ryan murdered 16 people in Hungerford, apparently imitating Rambo in *First Blood* didn't he? It said so in the newspapers.

When James Ferman was questioned about imitation by the House of Commons Home Affairs Select Committee in 1994, he replied:

> I do not know of particular cases where somebody has imitated a video and gone out and actually committed a serious crime as a result of what they have seen (Home Affairs Committee, Fourth Report 1994: 5).

Similar conclusions were reached in a *Panorama* programme in 1988 by the BBC's leading journalist Katie Adie and her team who researched six cases where a crime had been clearly 'linked' to the mass media. None of the cases, including the massacre in Hungerford, were supported by the evidence and turned on mere speculation.

### Priming aggression

Perhaps the strongest claims for harmful media effects have come from the laboratory experiments conducted from the early 1960s by Leonard Berkowitz (see Berkowitz 1993). He suggested that observing violence triggers or 'primes' aggressive thinking and emotions and encourages aggressive actions. Although the experimental designs evolved over time and his theoretical position became more sophisticated, essentially the studies involved showing either violent or neutral film clips to university students. They were then given the opportunity to give electric shocks to someone (who was a confederate of the experimenter and did not actually receive the shocks). Half of the participants were 'anger aroused' by the confederate insulting the participants and half were treated neutrally. Berkowitz concluded that violent film clips produced more aggressive behaviour (i.e. electric shocks) in those who were angry, especially when the violence in the film was justified.

Support for Berkowitz's theory is claimed from a variety of experiments including one where firearms were casually displayed in the laboratory. In this condition participants produced more aggression-related thoughts which led Berkowitz to conclude that, to some extent, 'the gun pulls the trigger' (see Anderson *et al.* 1998).

## Arousal or aggro?

Zillman (e.g. Bryant and Zillman 1994) has questioned whether the results obtained by Berkowitz are due to the violence *per se* in the film clips. He compared responses after *The Wild Bunch* (a violent film) with a neutral film (*Marco Polo's Travels*) with a no-film control group. Physiological measures of the participants revealed that the neutral film depressed arousal compared with the no-film condition. There were no differences between the no-film and the violent film group in the willingness of participants to deliver electric shocks to a victim.

Rather similar conclusions were reached by Gadow and Sprafkin (1993) in a review of twenty naturalistic field experiments where children were exposed to various film clips or television programmes. They note that, while aggressive film clips often produced elevated levels of anti-social behaviour, sometimes the control film produced even more. Even fast-paced pro-social educational programmes (like *Sesame Street*) produced more aggressive responses in the children. Perhaps one policy recommendation to reduce violence in society might be to show an endless diet of non-arousing films on television like *Marco Polo's Travels*!

## Time bomb . . .

Although laboratory experiments have featured largely in many reviews which have concluded that viewing television violence increases aggressive behaviour (e.g. Paik and Comstock 1994), their popularity has declined in recent years largely due to a concern that they measure only short-term effects and have low ecological validity (telling us little about how viewers behave in the real world).

The most cited of recent research is that by Huesmann and Eron (1986) who orchestrated cross-national comparisons in Australia, Finland, Holland, Israel, Poland and the USA of the long-term effects of exposure to television. These built on earlier research in 1972 by Eron and Huesmann who had measured aggression and television violence exposure in children aged between eight and nine and again ten years later. They claimed a 'Rip Van Winkle' or sleeper effect where early television viewing predicted later aggression. While this is true of one of their measures of aggression in boys, two other measures did not support the hypothesis and none of the measures were significant for the sample of girls. Stronger claims were made for their more modest cross-national study. Newson *et al.* (1994) describes the findings as 'robust'. But were they?

## ...Or damp squib?

On closer examination the results show a very mixed pattern:

- The Dutch researchers concluded that their results did not provide evidence of any effects of television and refused to allow their results to be included in the edited book (Wiegman *et al.* 1992).
- In Australia there were no significant correlations between early television violence viewing and later aggression.
- In the USA, after controlling for initial aggression, the relationship between early violence viewing and later aggression was only significant in girls.
- In Israel, significant effects were found in the city samples but not in the Kibbutz samples.
- In Poland, while the authors recognized that the house style of the book should concur that 'a greater preference for violence viewing was predictive of greater aggression' they also admitted 'nevertheless the effects are not large and must be treated cautiously'.
- In Finland the researchers conclude that 'our study in Finland can be taken to corroborate the previously obtained results that the amount of aggressive behavior in children is related to their viewing of violence on TV . . .' However the results were not significant for girls and it is apparent from the full report (Viemero 1986) that while there is indeed a relationship in boys, it is actually negative (−0.324). In other words, the more boys watched violent television, the *less* aggressive they were later!

Undeterred by this rather weak evidence, Huesmann (1998) developed an all-embracing theory of 'cognitive scripts' suggesting that children learn aggressive scripts from television to deal with problems. However, this theory is quite speculative since the 'scripts' are assumed rather than elicited. The ease with which such 'explanations' are thrown over real-world cases of violence cloaking understanding is illustrated below.

## The case of Ronnie Zamaro

Perhaps one of the best-known cases where the defence claim was that television had 'made' someone violent was that of 15-year-old Ronnie Zamaro who carried out the seemingly pointless murder of his 82-year-old neighbour in Miami, Florida. His attorney, Ellis Rubin, claimed 'subliminal television intoxication' while one expert witness, the psychiatrist Albert Jaslow, thought that television had 'blunted his awareness and his capacity to understand his actions'. One other witness, the psychologist Margaret Hanratty Thomas, argued that television violence had 'unbalanced' the boy. The public trial, lasting ten days, attracted larger television audiences than the popular *Johnny Carson Show*. Central to the defence was Zamaro's fascination with Kojak whom he so admired that he asked his father to shave his head to look like the detective. Perhaps the real flaw in this argument is that Kojak is a good guy, on the side of law and order. The jury were unimpressed by Rubin's defence and found Zamaro guilty as charged (see Fowles 1992).

## The murder of James Bulger

In England the abduction and murder of 2-year-old James Bulger by two 10-year-old boys in February 1993 was an event which not only shocked the country but was followed by the world's media. The abduction had been captured by security cameras in the shopping centre where James disappeared and thus the child killers were quickly captured. From the outset the whole affair received considerable media attention with clips of the abduction providing the lead story in television and newspaper stories. The trial was, unusually for such young offenders, a public one, providing pages of verbatim copy in all the press. In sentencing the boys to be detained during Her Majesty's Pleasure, the judge, the Honourable Mr Justice Moorland, commented:

> It is not for me to pass judgement on their upbringing, but I suspect that
> exposure to violent video films may, in part, be an explanation (e.g. *The Independent*
> 25 November 1993).

It seems clear that many journalists had expected the trial to produce some 'link' with media violence (a number had contacted the author for comment earlier in the year). Although this link emerged only as a throwaway line at the end of the trial, it was sufficient to launch major media coverage speculating that violent videos had created two children capable of committing an act of 'unparalleled evil and barbarity'. By the following day the witch hunt named *Child's Play 3*, a film which continued the adventures of Chucky, a doll possessed by the evil spirit of a child murderer. In a staged event reminiscent of the execution of witches in medieval times, the popular tabloid the *Sun* organized a public burning of the video *Child's Play 3*, urging readers 'For the sake of ALL our kids, BURN YOUR VIDEO NASTY' (*Sun* 26 November 1993).

Among the 'chilling links' between the film and the murder of James Bulger was the fact that Neil Venables, the father of one of the boys found guilty, had rented the video some weeks before. However, Albert Kirby, who directed the police inquiry, had specifically looked for any possible links and concluded that there were none. Jon Venables was not living with his father at the time and thus the police did not think it possible that he could have seen the film there. Moreover, the boy disliked horror films and was upset by violence in videos – a point confirmed by later psychiatric reports. Of course, such mundane facts could not be allowed to spoil a good story, or the campaigns calling for a 'crackdown' on video violence.

## Political pawns

One of the major players in this blame game was the Liberal MP David Alton who was convinced that the legislation controlling the supply of videos was ineffective and that children were gaining access to unsuitable and damaging films. With all-party support he tabled an amendment to the Criminal Justice Bill. This amendment proposed further penalties for trading in uncertificated films and videos, for supplying children with films inappropriate for their age group plus the removal of films which offered 'inappropriate role models' for children or those which could produce 'psychological damage'. The then Home Secretary, Michael Howard, was unconvinced of the need for such ambiguous and potentially draconian legislation, pointing out that the Video Recordings Act of 1984 already allowed tough fines (such as £20,000 for dealing with uncertificated videos). However, David Alton proved an effective campaigner. He invited a retired professor of child psychology, Elizabeth Newson, to support his case. Her report – *Video Violence and the Protection of Children* – was launched for Good Friday, 1 April 1994 via a press release. It became the lead story in almost all newspapers. 'VIDIOTS! At last experts admit: movie nasties DO kill' (*Daily Mirror* 1 April 1994) and ' "Naive" experts admit threat of violent videos' (the *Daily Telegraph* 1 April 1994) were typical headlines.

This report was a watershed in the long debates about media effects. Speculation that media violence might make people violent was now presented as uncontroversial fact. The Home Secretary reconsidered his position and – in what was widely seen by political commentators as a 'U'-turn – essentially adopted David Alton's amendment accepting that psychological harm could be caused by film and video and increased the penalties laid down by the earlier Video Recordings Act (e.g. 'Howard retreats on "video nasties"' was the lead story in *The Independent* on 12 April 1994).

## The Newson report

Newson's report is perhaps unique in the sympathetic publicity it received. It begins 'Two year-old James Bulger was brutally and sadistically murdered on 12 February 1993 by two ten-year-old children'. Harrowing details of the murder then set the scene for a different explanation than that the children were simply 'evil freaks': 'even the most cursory reading of news since then suggests that it is not a "one-off". . . .' In England, an adolescent girl was tortured by her 'friends' over days using direct quotations from a horror video (*Child's Play 3*) as part of her torment' (a reference to the recent murder of Suzanne Capper).

Part of the report's success was probably due to twenty-five 'experts' endorsing it. However, none of the signatories appear to have published any empirical or indeed clinical findings in the field. Moreover, the report, on closer examination, mentions only two secondary reviews of media effects and seems largely inspired by Michael Medved's 1993 book: *Hollywood versus America*. The focus of the report is provided by newspaper clippings (most from the *Nottingham Evening Post*) dealing with the Bulger murder and other cases of violence by young people which, it is argued, show that things have changed and this must be due to the easy availability of videos containing graphic violence. Astonishingly, more than one third of her report seems to be based entirely on press clippings (see Barker and Petley 1997/2001 for a full account of the report and Cumberbatch 1994 for a critical review).

# A matter of faith?

There would seem little doubt that Newson sincerely believes that film and video can be harmful to children. The issue is simply this: why does she believe so? Apparently it does not come from studying the effects of the media on children. Perhaps the most obvious clue is given in her evidence to the House of Commons Home Affairs Select Committee on Video Violence. During this, Newson was asked to explain the links between video violence and real-world violence:

> *Professor Newson:* 'The Suzanne Capper case is another example of very explicit imitation of video and the use of a video and that was *Child's Play 3.*'
> *Sir Ivan Lawrence* (chair): 'We were told this morning that that had been looked into and the Earl Ferries in the House of Lords has denied – I have not got the evidence we heard this morning – that there was a basis in the Capper case of *Child's Play 3.*'
> *Professor Newson:* 'The soundtrack was actually played.'
> *Sir Ivan Lawrence* (chair): 'Can I read from an analysis of this from Mr Ferman of the British Board of Film Classification of course. What was played to her was a rock version of the music from the first *Child's Play* film recorded on Manchester Piccadilly Pop Radio Station. That is all – music not video?'
> *Professor Newson:* 'In that case it depends. That has been widely reported in that case.'
> *Sir Ivan Lawrence* (chair): 'Yes, it has.'
> *Professor Newson:* 'That would depend on whether that particular girl had seen that film and whether she was able to identify the film from the music.'
> *Sir Ivan Lawrence* (chair) 'There were no videos in the houses that this young lady was held in, apparently. That was the evidence. However let us not argue about it'
> (Home Affairs Committee, Fourth Report, 1994: 12).

This exchange identifies one important issue in media effects: that even retired professors who should be experienced in evaluating evidential claims may slip into uncritical acceptance of media stories – especially when they are 'good' stories. However, perhaps the only goal of academic studies is that we should learn to discriminate sources of knowledge in terms of various criteria such as internal validity, logic, reliability of sources and so on.

Newson's report provides an illusory image of expert knowledge. Her description of the Bulger murder was that it was done with the 'expectation and satisfaction of deliberate and sustained violence'. However, this insight turns out to be no more than a reading of press coverage of the trial but implies a familiarity with the case as does her (later) use of the name 'Jamie'. Indeed, Kirby, the investigating officer in the case, confirmed that James's parents were upset by him being referred to as 'Jamie' and asked that the media should respect this.

All in all, the problem which we see above is that tenuously supported theories become applied to real-world tragedies which then take on their own existence as facts which support the theory. However, to make matters worse, the Newson report was released on a Good Friday when it would be most unlikely that her peers, who might be able to offer informed comment on the work, would be available.

All the above apply to the most recent press released report on 23 April 2000 – again an Easter weekend – which claimed 'Violent video games can cause aggression'. It went on to suggest that they were probably to blame for the school shootings by

Eric Harris and Dylan Klebold in Columbine High School in Littleton, Colorado in 1999 when 15 died and 23 were wounded. 'Official: video games make people violent' (*Observer* 23 April 2000) was typical of press coverage.

## Training kids to kill?

This press release was by the American Psychological Society to launch a publication by Anderson and Dill (2000) in one of the most prestigious American psychology journals. In contrast to customary styles of academic caution, the article opens with an anonymous quote from 'an investigator from the Wiesenthal Center' who claimed that one of the young killers, Harris, had customized the video game *Doom* to make it more violent. The boys had then made a video of this and when they began killing at the school, they were 'playing out their game in God mode'.

This is probably the first time that such a journal has carried 'hearsay' evidence but this might be considered the least of the sins the authors commit. Anderson and Dill claim that their survey of undergraduates found that 'students who reported playing more violent video games over a period of years also engaged in more aggressive behavior in their own lives'.

## . . . Or just torturing data?

Unfortunately the researchers did not seem to have asked whether the games students had played in earlier years were violent or not (asking only how much they played and what games they played now). Thus the above finding cannot be based on any results in their 43-page paper! In a separate experiment students played either a 'violent' video game (*Wolfenstein 3D*) or a 'non-violent game' (*Myst*). They then played a competitive game which if they lost they received a noise blast, but if they won they could send a noise blast to their 'opponent' (actually a computer). This was, of course, a ruse to measure aggression since participants could vary the amount of noise which they delivered. Anderson and Dill conclude that playing the violent game increased the aggressiveness of participants (notably in 'significantly longer' noise blasts they gave to their opponents). However, the 'significantly longer' noise blasts which they delivered turn out to be a mere 2% longer, which is hardly of psychological significance and seem to have been just one half of what they received (Cumberbatch 2000a). Perhaps a more obvious interpretation of these results is that video game playing encourages players to turn the other cheek rather than to aggress!

## Violence to the media

One notable feature of the vast research literature on media effects which can be only touched upon here is for strong conclusions about harm to be reached on rather weak data. The devil is always in the detail which reveals considerable discrepancies in the findings, eroding confidence in the 'media harm theses'. Of course, a practical problem lies in attempting to disentangle media effects when the media are so embedded in our culture. Much 'evidence' of media effect relies merely in establishing a link whereby, for example, aggressive children may be shown to enjoy media violence. But this can tell us little about how such individuals are changed by the process if at all. Indeed, in the UK at least, the pattern emerging from Hagell and Newburn's (1994) study of seventy-eight young offenders was that, compared with a school control group, the delinquents reported having fewer television sets, were less able to name favourite television programmes or characters they would like to be like and were less likely to go to the cinema. As Messner (1986) concluded, the pattern for delinquents is for them to be out on the streets offending rather than to be at home watching television – violent or otherwise.

As a final point, perhaps the largest deficiency in the various research lies in the oversimplified approach to both media content and media experiences. For example, Viemero (1986) categorizes the following programmes as having the same 'violence score': *The Benny Hill Show*; *Bergerac*; *Magnum*; *Dallas* and *Woody Woodpecker*. In most studies the old *Batman* series are considered 'violent' even though the heroes are portrayed as excessively moral beings. Whether children perceive these moral narratives is, of course, another matter (Buckingham 1996) but it is as much a disservice to research as it is to children or to the media not to ask. As Marvin observes 'Understanding how cultures circulate meanings about the exercise of physical force requires a richer background language and thicker description and appraisals than can be found in the simplifying presumption that such representations are inevitably coarsening, frequently dangerous and always to be avoided' (Marvin 2000: 148). Quite so.

## Acknowledgements

Thanks to Gary Wood for his assistance in preparing this chapter.

## Questions

1  In what different ways do we 'circulate meanings about the exercise of physical force' in our culture?

2  What would you say to a Home Secretary who felt that a 'crackdown' on media violence was necessary?

3  Taking any *one* social problem (such as crime; drink-driving; child abuse; racism; unsafe sex; unhealthy lifestyle) what various roles might the media play in aggravating or ameliorating it as a social problem?

# References

Anderson, C. and Dill, K. (2000) 'Video games and aggressive thoughts, feelings, and behavior in the laboratory and in life', Journal of Personality and Social Psychology 78(4): 772–90.

Anderson, C., Benjamin, A. J. and Bartholow, B. D. (1998) 'Does the gun pull the trigger: automatic priming effect of weapon pictures and weapon names', *Psychological Science* 9(4): 308–14.

Bandura, A. (1994) 'Social cognitive theory of mass communication,' in J. Bryant and D. Zillman (eds) *Media Effects: Advances in Theory and Research*, Hillsdale, NJ: Lawrence Erlbaum, pp. 61–90.

Barker, M. and Petley, J. (eds) (1997, second edition 2001) *Ill Effects: The Media/Violence Debate*, London: Routledge.

Berkowitz, L. (1993) *Aggression: Its Causes, Consequences and Control*, New York: McGraw-Hill.

Bryant, J. and Zillman, D. (eds) (1994) *Media Effects, Advances in Theory and Research*, Hillsdale, NJ: Lawrence Erlbaum.

Buckingham, D. (1996) *Moving Images: Understanding Children's Emotional Responses to Television*, Manchester: Manchester University Press.

Charters, W. W. (1933) *Motion Pictures and Youth: A Summary*, New York: Macmillan.

Cumberbatch, G. (1994) 'Legislating mythology: video violence and children', *Journal of Mental Health* 3: 485–94. http//www/crghq.com/publications/legislating_myths

Cumberbatch, G. (2000a) 'Only a game?' *New Scientist* 10 June, No. 2242: 44–5. http//www/crghq.com/publications/only_a_game

Cumberbatch, G. (2000b) *Television: the Public's View*, London: ITC.

Cumberbatch, G. and Wood, G. (1998) *The Evidence of Things not Seen: Television Images of Short Duration*, London: ITC.

Cumberbatch, G., Maguire, A. and Woods, S. (1994) *Children and Video Games: an exploratory study.* http//www/crghq.com/publications/children_and_videogames

Cumberbatch, G., Woods, S., Gauntlett, S. and Littlejohns, V. (2000a) *Content Analysis of Social Concerns on Terrestrial Television: Year on year comparisons*, London: Broadcasting Standards Commission.

Cumberbatch, G., Woods, S., Gauntlett, S. and Littlejohns, V. (2000b) *Content Analysis of Social Concerns on Satellite Television: Year on year comparisons*, London: Broadcasting Standards Commission and http//www/crghq.com/publications/bsc_contentanalyses

Eveland, W. P. and McLeod, D. M. (1999) 'The effect of social desirability on perceived media impact', *International Journal of Public Opinion Research* 11(4): 315–33.

Fowles, J. (1992) *Why Viewers Watch: a Reappraisal of Television's Effects*, Newbury Park, CA: Sage.

Gadow, K. D. and Sprafkin, J. (1993) 'Television violence and children with emotional and behavioral disorders', *Journal of Emotional and Behavioral Disorders* 1(1): 54–63.

Hagell, A. and Newburn, T. (1994) *Young Offenders and the Media*, London: Batisford.

Himmelweit, H. T., Oppenheim, A. N. and Vince, P. (1958) *Television and the Child: An Empirical Study of the Effect of Television on the Young*, London: Oxford University Press.

Home Office (1951) *Report of the Departmental Committee on Children and Cinema*, London: Home Office.

Huesmann, L. R. (1998) 'The role of social information processing and cognitive schema in the acquisition and maintenance of habitual aggression', in R. G. Geen and E. Donnerstein (eds) *Human Aggression: Theories, Research and Implications for Social Policy*, New York: Academic Press, pp. 73–109.

Huesmann, L. R. and Eron, L. D. (eds) (1986) *Television and the Aggressive Child: A Cross-National Comparison*, Hillsdale, NJ: Lawrence Erlbaum.

Marvin, C. (2000) 'On violence in media', *Journal of Communication* 50(1): 142–9.

Messner, S. F. (1986) 'Television violence and violent crime: an aggregate analysis', *Social Problems* 33(3): 218–35.

Neuman, S. B. (1991) *Literacy in the Television Age: the Myth of the TV Effect*, Norwood, NJ: Ablex.

Newson, E. *et al.* (1994) *Video Violence and the Protection of Children*, Mimeo University of Nottingham. Reprinted in M. Barker and J. Petley (1997) *Ill Effects: The Media/Violence Debate*, London: Routledge.

Paik, H. and Comstock, G. (1994) 'The effects of television violence on antisocial behavior: a meta-analysis', *Communication Research* 21(4): 516–46.

Pearson, G. (1983) *Hooligan: A History of Respectable Fears*, London: Macmillan.

Schramm, W., Lyle, L. and Parker, E. B. (1961) *Television in the Lives of our Children*, Stanford, CA: Stanford University Press.

Smith, S. L. and Donnerstein, E. (1998) 'Harmful effects of exposure to media violence: learning of aggression, emotional desensitisation, and fear', in R. G. Green and (eds) (1998) *Human Aggression*, San Diego, CA: Academic Press, pp. 168–202.

Viemero, V. (1986) *Relationships between Filmed Violence and Aggression*, Åbo Akademi, Finland: Akademisk Avhandling Monograph Supplement 4.

Wiegman, O., Kuttschreuter, M. and Barda, B. (1992) 'A longitudinal study of the effects of television viewing on aggressive and pro-social behaviours', *British Journal of Social Psychology* 31: 147–64.

Zillman, D. (1991) 'Television viewing and physiological arousal', in J. Bryant and D. Zillmann (eds) *Responding to the Screen: Reception and Reaction Processes*, Hillsdale, NJ: Lawrence Erlbaum, pp. 103–33.

## Further reading

Barker, M. and Petley, J. (eds) (1997, second edition 2001) *Ill Effects: The Media/Violence Debate*, London: Routledge. A lively account and critique of media violence as a moral panic. Especially useful in examining the logic of the discourse.

Cumberbatch, G. (2000) *Video Violence: Villain or Victim?* London: Brittania. http//:www/videostandards.org.uk/publications/videoviolence. A comprehensive and critical review of the various research evidence on media violence including video games.

Gauntlett, D. (1995) *Moving Experiences: Understanding Television's Influences and Effects*, London: John Libbey. A clear exposition of key research on effects including both anti-social and pro-social influences.

Goldstein, J. (ed.) (1998) *Why We Watch: the Attractions of Violent Entertainment*, New York: Oxford University Press. A fascinating collection of essays from a wide variety of disciplines covering a wide variety of forms of entertainment.

# Chapter 19

# 'Impacts and influences'

MEDIA INFLUENCE REVISITED: AN INTRODUCTION TO THE
'NEW EFFECTS RESEARCH'

## JENNY KITZINGER

This chapter summarizes debates about media effects and introduces readers to recent research around this issue. It briefly reviews historical developments and critically examines assumptions about direct media impacts while also challenging those who dismiss questions of media influence. The chapter then goes on to outline up-to-date qualitative studies which address the complexity of people's engagement with media coverage of contemporary events. Such studies, I argue, constitute a valuable body of 'new effects research' which demonstrates multiple ways in which mass media representation can influence how we understand, and engage with, the world around us.

## The effects of communication: a brief history of theoretical approaches

A long history lies behind questions about how communication affects or influences people.[1] Even in one-to-one conversations each of us implicitly mobilizes theories about how to influence our listeners. We communicate in order, for example, to seek cooperation or invite confidences, to reassure or to inform. We may wish to make others understand how we feel, invite debate, or simply want to entertain our friends. We tailor our words to different audiences, depending on our relationship and what we know about them. Sometimes we consciously alter what is said, or the *way* we say it, in order to maximize its impact.

Public speaking, and the printed word, involves a different type of relationship. In this case the communicator is often addressing many different people at the same time and may be separated from them by both time and space. It is not possible to know one's audience in the same way or, necessarily, directly to observe their response and tailor communication accordingly. Formal theories about how best to communicate to a wider audience have been consciously explored throughout history by political, religious and military leaders, as well as philosophers, playwrights and poets. The ancient Greeks, for example, developed highly sophisticated hypotheses about how to impress listeners through the spoken word. Aristotle's *Treatise on Rhetoric* (fourth century BC) was concerned with theorizing the art of speaking.

It examined 'the recesses and windings' of the human heart, in order to discover how to 'to excite, to ruffle, to amuse, to gratify or to offend it' (Copleston 1810 cited in Eldridge *et al.* 1997).

Today, mass communication studies has developed as a distinct discipline with a focus on television and newspapers and, to a lesser extent, cinema and radio. Mass communication technologies reach thousands or even millions of people simultaneously, and a single programme can now be viewed nationally, or even globally. Questions about effect have thus become all the more pressing, as well as complex. The origin of modern media studies is usually located in 1930s Germany associated with work by scholars such as Adorno, Marcuse and Horkheimer. It is these writers who coined the term 'mass culture' – a concept originally suggested by the Nazi propaganda machine. Their theories were developed in response to Germany's descent into fascism. This work, collectively known as 'The Frankfurt School', theorized that social disintegration left people vulnerable to propaganda. The Frankfurt School promoted a 'hypodermic model' of media effects whereby messages were directly absorbed into the hearts and minds of the people (rather like a drug injected directly into the bloodstream).

Many other theories and approaches to the media have developed since then. The Frankfurt School's 'hypodermic model' was challenged by subsequent work highlighting the importance of personal influence. These studies showed how social mediation and opinion leaders within communities filtered and shaped how messages were received by the general population (Katz and Lazersfeld 1955). Other researchers argued that people select from media messages for their own purposes and that the media is therefore more likely to be used to *reinforce*, rather than to change existing attitudes (Blumler and McQuail 1968).

More recently, audience-reception studies have revealed the diverse ways in which different people may respond to the same programme. These researchers highlight the fact that the messages 'decoded' by audiences are not necessarily those intended by the programme producers (Hall 1973). Meaning, it is argued, does not lie in the text (programme or newspaper article) alone; it is created in an encounter between text and audience. Research exploring how different groups of people engage with the media shows that we are not blank slates ready to absorb uncritically whatever we see or hear. How we respond to a particular programme or newspaper article may be influenced by class, gender, sexual and ethnic identity as well as wider cultural context. Programmes which might seem to promote one sort of world view may in fact be used, at least by some viewers, to support another and representations which seem 'negative' may be used positively. Fascinating data has been collected through comparing sub-cultural, cross-cultural and cross-national 'readings'. A traditional Western which casts cowboys as heroes and 'red Indians' as savages can still be enjoyed by some Native Americans who identify with the cowboy character and see him as representing a free and autonomous way of life akin to Native American values. An American soap opera understood by some viewers as a display of consumer capitalism will be seen by others as a critique of mainstream American values. (For further discussion see Eldridge *et al.* 1997, Chapter 12.)

The trajectory of media and cultural studies during the last fifty years increasingly insisted that we recognize audience diversity and see people as 'active' rather than passive consumers of media images (see Hermes, Chapter 20 in this volume). The hypodermic model of media effects has been thoroughly discredited.

## Straw-men, babies and bath water: discrediting the question of effects

The fact that the hypodermic model has been exposed as too simplistic should not mean that we totally dismiss the question of media effects. To do so risks, if I may mix my metaphors horribly, setting up a 'straw-man' and throwing out the baby with the bath water as well. Cross-cultural and cross-national work with diverse audiences, such as that mentioned above, has opened up important new avenues of exploration. It demands more sophisticated understandings of how media effects might operate. However, instead of *developing* our understanding of media effects, this research has often been used to side-line such areas of enquiry. Mainstream media studies, at least in much of Europe, has increasingly absented itself from the effects debate. This arena has been left to criminologists, psychologists, politicians, market researchers, and tabloid journalists. Within much of the media studies literature concerns about media effects are characterized as paternalistic and assumed to cast the general public as 'cultural dopes'. Effects research has become associated with a very narrow and methodologically weak strand of work. Indeed, it is even suggested that the very word 'effects' is problematic because it implies that media influence operates rather like 'a bat hitting a ball' (Hodge and Tripp cited in Gauntlett 1995: 12).

Gauntlett presents a thorough requiem for the traditional effects model in his book *Moving Experiences* (1995). He rightly condemns crude stimulus–response approaches and unreflective confusion of correlation with causation. He criticizes the over-simplistic way in which the traditional effects model categorizes influence ('good' and 'bad'), violence (often treated as a generic category regardless of context – see Corner, Chapter 21 in this volume) and audiences (e.g. 'heavy' and 'light' viewers). He also attacks the politics of the traditional effects model: its focus on children and negative outcomes and its tendency to scapegoat television for problems such as crime while ignoring other possible factors such as inequalities (Gauntlett 1995: 116). His review of the field concludes that:

> The cumulative 'message' of this monograph is not so much that there should be no concern about television content . . . but that, scientifically speaking, you're on your own . . . The search for direct 'effects' of television on behaviour is over, every effort has been made, and they simply cannot be found (Gauntlett 1995: 115, 120).

This conclusion is shared by many other commentators (see, for example, Cumberbatch and Howitt 1989; Cumberbatch 1998 and Chapter 18 in this volume).

The problem with such conclusions is that the lack of evidence for direct, observable effects on behaviour, similar to that of 'a bat hitting a ball' is used to imply that there is no evidence that media representation is important at all. Such conclusions also ignore a whole body of new research into effects and influence which *does* justify 'concern about television content' and clearly demonstrate how media images impact on viewers' perceptions. There is, in fact, a great deal of in-depth qualitative work with audiences which provides compelling evidence about the media's role in representing, and misrepresenting, key social issues and helping to shape public understandings. I would include in this category work by, among others, Jhally and Lewis (1992), Gamson (1992), Corner *et al.* (1990) and much of the audience reception work produced from the Glasgow Media Research Group. Such research, I argue, constitutes a significant body of evidence that might usefully be identified as 'the new effects research'.

## Evidence of effects and influence: 'the new effects research'

This section outlines a range of recent research projects which explore media influence and effects. These projects are quite different from those routinely reviewed in attacks on 'effects research'. They do not pursue a simplistic search for crude correlation or adopt a shallow stimulus–response model. They all also, to a greater or lesser extent, are sensitive to audience diversity and the broader cultural context of reception. There may, of course, still be weaknesses in the method or conclusions of such studies. However, in combination, they make an important contribution to debates about effects and influence. New kinds of critiques need to be developed if we are to argue that there is no evidence of media effects.

I cannot do justice to each study here. However, I hope that a brief outline of their approach and sample of their findings will stimulate students to read the primary texts on which these summaries are based.

## Jhally and Lewis's study of *The Cosby Show*

Jhally and Lewis studied audience reception of *The Cosby Show*, a situation-comedy which revolves around a black American middle-class family (the parents are a doctor and a lawyer). They were interested in this programme's role in a society where, in reality, most black people are not professionals and most are much poorer than white people. Their study was designed to 'delve into the complex interaction between the program and the viewer. . . . [to] look into the delicate ideological suppositions that inform the sites where program and viewer meet to create meaning and pleasure' (Jhally and Lewis 1992: 9). They conducted 52 focus groups with white and black viewers in the USA to explore whether 'television influences the way we think' (Jhally and Lewis 1992: xv). Through close attention to how people discussed the programme they conclude that there is clear evidence of influence. *The Cosby Show*, they argue, was used by white people to make judgements about the position and behaviour of black people, 'observations that their actual experience of black people did not equip them to make' (Jhally and Lewis 1992: 32). The growing image on TV of black middle classes helps to create the illusion that racism is 'a thing of the past' and fuels resistance to affirmative action. *The Cosby Show* and programmes like it, they argue, obscures the class–race nexus, diverting attention from class-based causes of racial inequality (Jhally and Lewis 1992: 70).

## Gamson's study of politics

Gamson's work is a similarly fascinating and in-depth study. Gamson bases his analysis on 37 focus groups in which people talked about four political issues: affirmative action, Arab–Israeli conflict, nuclear power, and troubled industry. He examined how people talk about such issues and how this related to media treatment, particularly media 'frames' (the overall conceptual approach). His writing is self-consciously respectful of his participants and certainly avoids the 'cultural dope' approach so criticized in relation to conventional effects research. He also thoroughly explores how people draw not only on the media but also on experiential discourse and popular wisdom and argues that 'people read messages in complicated and sometimes unpredictable ways' (Gamson 1992: 6). However, he points out '[f]rames . . . invisible in mass media commentary rarely find their way into [people's] conversations. Systematic omissions make certain ways of framing issues extremely unlikely' (Gamson 1992: 6). In his final chapter he also suggests a particular way of thinking about 'effects' as 'effects *in use*'. Media content, he argues, serves as:

> an important tool or resource that people have available, in varying degrees, to help them make sense of issues in the news. When they use elements from media discourse to make a conversational point on an issue we are directly observing a media effect . . . The causal relationship is complicated and bidirectional as the tool metaphor implies (Gamson 1992: 180).

## Corner, Richardson and Fenton's study of nuclear power

The third example I wish to draw attention to is work by Corner, Richardson and Fenton. They examined people's responses to different programmes about nuclear power. Again, this study has little in common with the traditional hypodermic effects model but does tell us a great deal about how media effects (influence or impact) can operate. Corner and his colleagues place themselves in a tradition of reception studies that examines 'the "creative" processes of interpretation' but are still concerned with audience 'responses' and 'understood meaning' (Corner *et al.* 1990: 47, 2).

Corner *et al.* examined four programmes about nuclear power and analysed discussions among nine groups of viewers. They looked in detail at how people respond to different images (such as steam rising from a pond next to a nuclear power plant), presentation of facts (such as information about leukaemia pockets) and also to programme structures. For example, one documentary programme was generally interpreted as suggesting that the Sellafield nuclear power plant was implicated in causing leukaemia. This was in spite of the programme's presentation of many explanations which problematized or even rejected this suggestion. Through close attention to their research participants' conversations, Corner and his colleagues suggest why the programme operated in this way. They argue that the documentary's imagery and structure, built around one family's search for answers about their child's leukaemia, was more powerful than the programme's abstract speculation about risk.

At one level, it [the programme] focussed on a particular instance of illness and the legal battle that was beginning around it. At another level, it engaged more broadly with questions of risk probability in the nuclear industry. But the sheer power of the depiction it offered of one family's tragedy, backed up by the programme's own 'dark' framing of the industry . . . tended to crystallise meanings at the lower level for our respondents, leaving the wider reach of speculation relatively unassimilated (Corner *et al.* 1990: 100).

These authors comment that their research engages with questions of influence by demonstrating how 'television images can exert a "positioning" power upon viewer imagination and understanding of a kind which may prove more resistant to counter-interpretation than the devices of commentary, interview and voice-over' (Corner *et al.* 1990: 105). They go on to comment that divergence between the groups in how they related to the programme 'should not be allowed to obscure the more import-ant *convergence* – the power of the affective dimension, even on groups who reject its legitimacy, comes through in many ways. This may be of considerable significance in the shaping of public opinion about the issue'. Corner and his colleagues conclude:

. . . though our findings suggest that, indeed, there is a good deal more at issue than many traditional approaches [e.g. the hypodermic effects model] have assumed, they also suggest that taking the power of television seriously is as important as recognising the considerable extent to which it falls well short of being omnipotent (Corner *et al.* 1990: 108).

## Audience reception work at the Glasgow University Media Unit

The final set of research projects which I want to highlight in this chapter are a series of studies developed by researchers at Glasgow University during the late 1980s and into the 1990s. These projects involved focus group discussions about contemporary issues such as industrial disputes, BSE, conflict in Northern Ireland, AIDS and breast cancer. In most of these projects the research participants were invited to write their own media scripts, such as a news report or dialogue from a soap opera. These scripts were then used as a basis for discussion and reflection (for descriptions of this technique see Kitzinger 1990 or Philo 1990).

These projects show how the media conveyed facts which influenced public beliefs, assumptions and actions. Concrete examples are located where misinformation had been conveyed, e.g. leading to inaccurate public beliefs about the shooting dead of three IRA members in Gibraltar (Miller 1994). This body of work demonstrates how patterns of media coverage, and routine associations can influence beliefs and assumptions, invoking, for example, fear of people with mental illnesses and impact-ing on people's willingness, or not, to believe that BSE was a threat to humans (Reilly 1999). Close attention to people's talk shows how images and themes from the media are used as rhetorical reference points to explain or justify a point of view (rather like the 'effects in use' discussed by Gamson). It also reveals how dramatic personal accounts may have greater impact than statistics, for example in assessing breast cancer risk (Henderson and Kitzinger 1999). More specifically some of this research examined how words, images, story lines or themes can become integrated into people's conversation and arguments and inform public understandings.

My own work while I was at Glasgow included an extensive study of audience understandings of AIDS. The 52 focus group discussions conducted for this project suggested that widespread media adoption of the phrase 'body fluids' contributed to some people's belief that saliva was a route of HIV infection ('because it is a body fluid'). This research also demonstrated the impact of vivid media images of people dying from AIDS on people's understanding of HIV (mass media images undercutting health education messages). And it revealed how health education advice such as 'If you're not 100% sure of your partner, use a condom' interacted with cultural conditions to produce, in some cases, an anti-safe sex message e.g. that using a condom implied distrust of your partner. More general cultural associations were also explored. For example, the media implicitly associated HIV transmission with 'unnatural' and 'perverse' acts – feeding into incorrect inferences that lesbians were a 'high-risk' group (Kitzinger 1993). This research project also showed how the media contributed to a racist formulation of associations between AIDS and 'Africa' (Kitzinger and Miller 1992) and highlighted the importance of 'social currency' in determining whether, and how, media accounts came to be reiterated through social networks (Kitzinger 1993).

Similar findings, around the significance of specific images, phrases, and the 'social currency' of particular stories, emerged from a subsequent study of audience understandings of child sexual abuse. Analysis of the 49 focus group discussions in this project also highlighted the significance of historical analogies which, I argue, operated as media 'templates'. Participants' discussions illustrated the way in which one scandal around allegations of abuse ('the Orkney case') was successfully associated with two previous scandals, cases already seen as proven examples of professional malpractice. The earlier scandals acted as templates for telling the story, and interpreting the meaning, of unfolding events in Orkney several years later (Kitzinger 2000).

Comparing this focus group data with interviews with incest survivors during the 1980s also highlighted the significance of media representation even in the interpretation of personal experience. The media's sudden and dramatic discovery of child sexual abuse, particularly incest, during the second half of the 1980s led many women to name and speak out about their abuse for the very first time. Prior to that, without any social recognition, their own experience seemed unspeakable, or even unbelievable. Interviewees and focus group research participants described how media recognition of sexual abuse during the 1980s and 1990s allowed them to confront their memories of abuse. It allowed some to 'put together pieces of a jigsaw' and others to identify what had been done to them as wrong or redefine it as abuse instead of a consensual affair. The media in this case played a crucial role in facilitating dramatic personal and social transformations (Kitzinger 2001).

## Conclusion

The mass media are an important site of influence. There is now an established body of research which demonstrates how the media help to define what counts as a public issue, organize our understandings of individual events, shape suspicions and beliefs, and resource memories, conversations, actions and even identities. Such media effects can not be dismissed simply because these processes are complex, multi-mediated, and sometimes successfully resisted.

Research on audience reception highlights how some messages are conveyed particularly effectively because of features such as: reiteration of key phrases and themes, coherence of narratives, use of metaphor or particular images. Patterns are evident across studies. Several different studies, for example, highlight the role of particular formats and structures (e.g. the impact of personalized accounts or family drama). Others emphasize the impact of story trajectory and timing (e.g. how a story is initially framed and first emerges into the mass media). Particular themes recur across studies such as the importance of 'social currency' (the value of an item of media information in conversation) and the power of tapping into pre-existing discourses or ways of thinking about the world. Detailed investigations of how people relate to media representations can thus help us to refine how we analyse media content and hypothesize about the meanings and likely impact of media coverage.

There is now a growing critical mass of 'new effects research' which shows that complex processes of reception and consumption *mediate*, but do not necessarily *undermine* media power. Acknowledging that audiences can be 'active' does not mean that the media are ineffectual. Recognizing the role of interpretation does not invalidate the concept of influence. A major task for the next generation of researchers is to further explore and consolidate our understandings of how media effects operate, both now and with the development of new communication technologies.

## Questions

1  What is wrong with the traditional model of media effects operating like a hypodermic syringe?

2  What do we know about media effects and influences?

3  How can analysis of how people *relate* to television programmes or newspaper articles inform our analysis of media content? What are the limitations of content analysis on its own?

## Exercises

1  Make a list of different countries or continents (such as Africa or the USA). Ask people to choose one about which they have no personal knowledge (e.g. through having lived or visited there, or having family who live there). Invite them to jot down their images of those places and then try to trace the source of their ideas.

2  Collect newspaper clippings and video tape news reports around a particular one-off event such as a crash, scandal or crisis. Several weeks later ask people to recount their memories and thoughts on the event. Compare what they say with your media archive. What were the images, explanations or phrases recalled by your interviewees? Were these directly taken from the media coverage, from a shared cultural repertoire, or from other specific sources? What facts have been forgotten or ignored? How did people come to the opinions they did?

3  Ask a group of friends to talk about an issue (perhaps one that you care about passionately, or simply one that has had a great deal of media coverage). Encourage them to assert their own beliefs and debate the rights and wrongs of the issue. Try to identify the source of the information, images and ideas that they use in the discussion. How difficult is it to determine the source of ideas? Pay close attention to the difference between people and the way in which they interact, share information, jokes and stories or challenge one another.

## Note

1 Synonyms for 'effect', according to my thesaurus, are words such as 'outcome', and 'consequence'. Synonyms for 'influence' include 'control', 'power', 'sway', 'rule', 'authority' (and 'effect') (Windows 97, tools). *Chambers Dictionary* defines 'influence' as 'power of producing an effect, especially unobtrusively' and 'ascendancy, often of a secret or undue kind'. Oddly, within the media studies literature the term 'effects' is sometimes used to imply crude models of media impact, whereas 'influence' is seen as a more sophisticated term. This allows for conceptual slippage when dismissing 'effects research', I therefore deliberately chose to use both terms.

## References

Blumler, J. and McQuail, D. (1968) *Television in Politics: Its uses and influences*, London: Faber.

Corner, J., Richardson, K. and Fenton, N. (1990) *Nuclear Reactions: Format and response in public issue television*, London: J. Libbey.

Cumberbatch, G. (1998) 'Media effects: the continuing controversy' in A. Briggs and P. Cobley (eds) *The Media: An Introduction*, Harlow: Longman.

Cumberbatch, G. and Howitt, D. (1989) *A Measure of Uncertainty: The Effects of the Mass Media*, London and Paris: John Libbey.

Eldridge, J (ed.) (1993) *Getting the Message*, London: Routledge.

Eldridge, J., Kitzinger, J. and Williams, K. (1997) *The Mass Media and Power in Modern Britain*, Oxford: Oxford University Press.

Gamson, W. (1992) *Talking Politics*, Cambridge: Cambridge University Press.

Gauntlett, W. (1995) *Moving Experiences: Understanding television's influences and effects*, Acamedia Research Monograph 13, London: John Libbey.

Hall, S. (1973) 'Encoding and decoding in the television discourse', in S. Hall, D. Hobson, A. Lowe and P. Willis (eds) (1981) *Culture, Media, Language: Working papers in cultural studies 1972–79*, London: Hutchinson.

Henderson, L. and Kitzinger, J. (1999) 'The human drama of genetics: "hard" and "soft" media representations of inherited breast cancer', *Sociology of Health and Illness* 21(5): 560–78.

Jhally, S. and Lewis, J. (1992) *Enlightened Racism:* The Cosby Show, *audiences and the myth of the American Dream*, Oxford: Westview Press.

Katz, E. and Lazersfeld, P. (1955) *Personal Influence: the part played by people in the flow of mass communication*, New York: Free Press.

Kitzinger, J. (1990) 'Audience understandings of AIDS media messages: A discussion of methods', *Sociology of Health and Illness* 12(3): 319–35.

Kitzinger, J. (1993) 'Understanding AIDS – media messages and what people know about AIDS', in J. Eldridge (ed.) *Getting the Message*, London: Routledge.

Kitzinger, J. (1999) 'Some key issues in audience reception research', in G. Philo (ed.) *Message Received*, Harlow: Longman.

Kitzinger, J. (2000) 'Media templates: patterns of association and the (re)construction of meaning over time', *Media, Culture and Society* 22(1): 64–84.

Kitzinger, J. (2001) 'Transformations of public and private knowledge: audience reception, feminism and the experience of childhood sexual abuse', *Feminist Media Studies* 1(1).

Kitzinger, J. and Miller, D. (1992) 'African AIDS: the media and audience beliefs', in P. Aggleton, P. Davies and G. Hart (eds) *AIDS: Rights, Risk and Reason*, London: Falmer Press, pp. 28–52.

Miller, D. (1994) *Don't Mention the War*, London: Pluto.

Philo, G. (1990) *Seeing and Believing*, London: Routledge.

Philo, G. (ed.) (1999) *Message Received*, Harlow: Longman.

Reilly, J. (1999) 'The media and public perceptions of BSE', in G. Philo (ed.) *Message Received*, Harlow: Longman.

## Further reading

Curran, J., Morley, D. and Walkerdine, V. (eds) (1996) *Cultural Studies and Communications*, London: Arnold. Includes a lively exchange between James Curran and David Morley about developments in audience research.

Dickinson, R., Harindranath, R. and Linné, O. (eds) *Approaches to Audiences: a reader*, London: Arnold. Includes a straightfoward attack on the traditional effects model.

Eldridge, J., Kitzinger, J. and Williams, K. (1997) *The Mass Media and Power in Modern Britain*, Oxford: Oxford University Press. An introductory text examining media power, this includes discussion of advertising, media images, and a review of different approaches to studying audiences.

Kitzinger, J. (1990) 'Audience understandings of AIDS media messages: A discussion of methods', *Sociology of Health and Illness* 12(3): 319–35. This short article is useful for anyone wanting to use group discussion to explore audience understandings, especially using pictures to stimulate discussion.

Philo, G. (ed.) (1999) *Message Received*, Harlow: Longman. The edited collection brings together recent work from the Glasgow Media Group, including research into audience understandings of contemporary issues such as immigration, AIDS, BSE, sexual violence and mental illness.

# Chapter 20

# Active audiences

THE ACTIVE AUDIENCE

**JOKE HERMES**

This chapter will discuss the academic debates on media in which the term 'the active audience' was introduced. It will become clear that discussion of the media was usually couched in terms of whether and how the media could influence media consumers or have specific effects on publics. Questions of influence and effect tend to assume that the audience is 'passive', no more than the recipient of a message produced elsewhere. Critical media scholars sought to challenge this (implicit) view, by arguing the case of audiences as meaning producers. Some proposed that audiences have agendas of their own that direct their media consumption (the uses and gratifications approach), but stayed within the (dominant) social-scientific framework. Others (media and cultural studies) argued a more radical case against mainstream media and communication research, by allowing for discussion of e.g. social power relation and the contextual nature of meaning production. Active, in that case, becomes almost synonymous with 'resisting (dominant ideology, or meanings)'.

'Active', according to my *Concise Oxford English Dictionary*, means 'energetic', or 'doing things'. In relation to audiences, 'the active audience' calls forth a vision of audiences who act upon what they see. The addition of 'active' suggests that normally audiences are passive. It is fairly easy to visualize what could be meant by the 'passive' audience, whether as a concept or as a description of an everyday practice. Someone on a sofa, perhaps, with crisps or cookies and a remote control, zapping from station to station. Here we run into a problem. The zapping would constitute an act. Perhaps the implicit 'passiveness' of audiences is not so much suggestive of total inactivity, as of a compliantly going along with whatever is on offer.

Mainstream media and communication research has not so much visualized audiences asleep on their couches in front of the television set, remote control on the floor, but hypnotized by what is on offer, out of contact with their critical faculties. The *raison d'être* of mass communication research has been to reconstruct how media influence works in order, assumedly, to be able to guard ourselves against it. Metaphors and concepts, such as hypodermic needle, or magic bullet, but also two-step-flow and spiral of silence all captured the scientific and the social imagination alike. Media scholars have been cast in a role of public and scientific responsibility, as keepers of our collective sanity in times in which the opium of the people has all but drugged most of us. However, it is well to remember that most of the eminent scholars in the field were wary of the popularized thesis of media influence. For there was one problem with the popular, alarmed view of the media: there was no evidence. Klapper (1960) famously concluded after reviewing all the then available research that it could not be proven that publicity or media exposure led to changes in, for instance, voting behaviour. We may love opinion polls, their suggestion of predictive value, and fear their possible influence on the outcome of elections: but all of that has never been proven beyond a doubt, and this remains the case to date.

In media and communication handbooks there is no entry for 'the passive audience'. Indeed, passivity of audiences is (still) seen as business as usual. Much research on the media has implicitly understood the researcher, and those others 'in the know' as enlightened, as ahead of the masses, aware of the possible dangers of the media. As a result 'the active audience' is part of a deviant view that needs to be named and is not the norm. Neither active nor passive refer to audience activity in a direct manner, nor was 'active' introduced in media studies theory as a twin to 'passive'. The term 'the active audience' is the product of critical interventions in the history of mass communication research that will be discussed below. 'Active' in these traditions means different things, varying from indeed using the media to accomplish specific goals (to be informed about what is happening in the world; to be able to have small-talk with colleagues; not to feel alone), to the basic act of making media texts meaningful, that is, to translate coded words and images into stories, ideas that are either are or are not relevant to how we understand the world around us.

The active audience is a phrase that can be dated back to different historical periods, but only to two academic paradigms. The best known of these is the uses and gratifications approach (1970s–), a body of empirical work that was said to ask 'not what it is that the media do with people, but what do people do with the media'. It questioned why there is such audience interest in staple media genres. An early example is Herta Herzog's research on radio soap opera. Later uses and gratifications research was interested in what exactly people use the media for: personal guidance, relaxation, adjustment, information (McQuail 2000: 387). It would take the interdisciplinary projects in what came to be known as cultural studies, the other paradigm, to really reconceptualize the audience in terms of subjectivity rather than individuality and in terms of meaning production rather than effects and influence (1980s–) which gave more room to think through the diverse and complex relations between media as texts and their users. Unlike uses and gratifications research, media and cultural studies research does not foreclose the possibility of fruitfully combining audience and text research.

## Uses and gratifications versus media and cultural studies

In the early 1970s McQuail, Blumler and Brown published results of research into the goals served by media use, not for society, but for media users. They assumed media and content choice to be rational and directed to specific goals and satisfactions. Audience members are conscious of the fact that they make choices. In general these choices, or as McQuail calls it later, personal utility, is a more significant determinant of audience formation than aesthetic or cultural factors. All these factors Blumler and McQuail assumed could be measured (McQuail 2000: 387–8). They do, in fact, offer a typology of media–person interaction, which lists: diversion, personal relationships, personal identity and surveillance (or information seeking) goals (McQuail *et al.* 1972). Market research took up the model and continues to use versions of it. Looking back, McQuail is critical of his own earlier work, and suggests that social origins and ongoing experience are important in understanding audience–media relations, which fell outside the initial behaviourist and functionalist leanings of the research. These however are not so easily measured (McQuail 2000: 389). Social origins, any person's class background, for example, can be translated into quantitative terms (as more or less formal and informal schooling), but ongoing experience may, for any one person, take a multitude of forms that need not even relate directly to one another: from what one learns from an individual film or article in a magazine, to witnessing everyday racism or parental neglect in the street, to boredom doing a job that had seemed so exciting.

Theoretically, uses and gratifications never really develops. Critics do not need much space to make clear that it is theoretically impossible to separate uses and gratifications, and that it is impossible to establish whether uses indeed precede gratifications in time, or whether gratifications are legitimized by inventing uses. If the last is the case, the uses and gratifications model cannot free us from the dominant paradigm: we are still seduced by the media, to such an extent even that we invent needs for what is basically imposed on us by capitalism (commercial media) or a paternalist nation-state (public broadcasting, state-sponsored serious news journalism). It is important to stress that 'gratificationist research' as it has also been called, was not initially understood to be a mainstream or conservative approach to media and society. On the contrary, it appeared to break with a tradition of only looking at effects (mass communication research) or at texts (such as the film criticism of the British journal *Screen*) in order to conclude something about audiences. Gratifications research at least asked people and made them part of the media–meaning–society equation. It is only when gratificationist research is used as a spearhead in debates about the possible convergence of quantitative and qualitative traditions in media research (the first seen as conservative and mainstream, the second as its challenger), that media critics such as Ien Ang offer a strong defence of 'ethnographic' method against individualistic quantitative research, and of taking a closer look at what we mean by the term 'active audience'.

In a critical essay written in 1989 Ang suggests that it is basically impossible to bring the two traditions in mass communciation research together. The social scientists who work with quantitative method in uses and gratifications research and have here been labelled 'mainstream' may superficially be seen to use the same terms the 'critical' scholars (Ang's term) use, but this does not mean that the two have consensus over the way in which the object of study needs to be conceptualized, or, in fact, over the goals and aims of science or social research as an enterprise (Ang 1989: 101). What is important here is that from the side of mainstream media research especially the term 'the active audience' was brought in as an argument for (the desirability of) convergence. After all, if everybody agrees that the (television) audience is 'active' (rather than passive) and that watching television or other forms of media use, is a social (rather than an individual) practice, is not, says Ang, saying all that much. But of course from the side of mainstream media research it was saying a lot. In line with McQuail's (self)criticism of the earlier uses and gratifications research, for mainstream media and communications research to give up such tenets as the basic measurability of audience behaviour, is tantamount to owning up to defeat.

The convergence discussion of the 1980s (Jensen 1987) bandied about 'the active audience'. In retrospect it would appear to be the case that it was seen as a magic key to convince cultural studies researchers that mainstream research was basically of good faith and willing to incorporate a number of terms that were alien to earlier work. 'Active', in this discussion, denoted the fact that the meaning of texts is always subject to negotiation. It suggested that researchers on both sides of the divide were aware of the role of ideological formations: the active audience did battle with media institutions from a formed background, the bastion of class position, of the values, ideas and perspectives that are part of being raised in a particular milieu. Ang's critical response to the convergence tradition makes clear that she, as one of the leading figures in qualitative audience studies, was not at all taken with the forceful invitation from the other camp. Though the audience might be labelled active, there still was no room for a conceptualization of context: mainstream social researchers were and are intent on measurement and therefore need to closely guard what they allow as variables in their models and what not. As will become clear, this is totally against the grain of qualitative audience research which was to take a turn to ethnographic method in precisely that period.

Characteristic of ethnographic approaches is that they start from the widest possible context and focus only gradually. Perhaps more importantly Ang pleads the incommensurability of the goals' audience research was to serve in both projects. Social scientists intent on scientific results, on finding truth and on predicting audience behaviour (a highly valuable type of knowledge in the media production marketplace), certainly were not highly interested in the political project that audience ethnography also was and is for critical researchers. The last speak of 'giving a voice' to respondents, of countering official knowledges that are used to monitor and control people, of countering apparatuses of dominance and of giving credence to forms of pleasure and resistance that have no place in mainstream media research.

Mainstream social research certainly was not to be defeated that easily. The work of Tamar Liebes and Elihu Katz (1986) is often quoted as the perfect counter-example for those who see no good come of converging research traditions. In their internationally comparative *Dallas* research (*Dallas* was a prime-time soap opera, or serial television drama made in the USA and sold to many countries outside the USA where it also captured large audiences) they use qualitative method to mainstream goals. Because their work illustrates Ang's argument against convergence perhaps even better than the better-known quantitative uses and gratifications research, it will be summarized here.

Liebes and Katz cannot, they write in a 1986 article about their research, accept content analysis as the basis for statements about the effects of a television text (1986: 151). Nor do they accept the procedure as used in Gerbner's cultural indicators research as adequate (in which respondents are asked to fill out questionnaires about television content and about 'real life' such as the crime rate. Their answers about television and 'real life' are compared to find out how much their view of reality has been influenced by television). Liebes and Katz would like to see 'the process of influence' in action in order to be able to determine whether American television programmes such as *Dallas* have a cultural imperialist effect. Thus, while audiences may in the end be duped by the media, they allow for some space for audience members to accord meanings to texts. They certainly do not believe that the media can influence audiences uniformly. Theirs is a mainstream vision of the active audience.

Liebes and Katz asked fifty small groups of befriended couples from five ethnic communities (four in Israel, one in the United States) to view an instalment of *Dallas* and afterward discuss a list of open questions. The sessions were tape-recorded by the respondents themselves. Neither Liebes nor Katz or their assistants attended these sessions. From the interview transcripts statements were selected that were analysed to trace patterns of involvement in *Dallas* of the five ethnic groups. Involvement is seen as the key to media effects and thus to the possible cultural imperialism of *Dallas*. A complex analytical structure is used to pattern the responses of the different groups. Liebes and Katz differentiate between critical and referential *frames* used in the interviews, between realistic or playful *keyings*, *referents* (I, we or they) and between value-free and normative *value orientations*. Together these rhetorical forms allow the researchers to assess the respondents' degree of involvement, which is seen as an indicator of influence. If there is no involvement in a text, presumably the text cannot influence viewers.

They conclude that the Americans and the kibbutzniks (the 'Western' groups) had the most complete set of distancing mechanisms. They address *Dallas* more critically, personally and playfully. Ironically, the authors conclude, the groups whose cultures seem most remote from the culture of *Dallas* seem most involved. The Arabs and Moroccans would seem to be challenged by the programme to 'defend' themselves, to respond reflexively by examining their own values in the light of what they perceive to be the 'real' but threatening option of 'modernity' (Liebes and Katz 1986: 166). Mechanisms of distance then do seem to inoculate against the influence of the programme. The more traditional groups lack the rhetorical mechanisms of defence and seem to be more vulnerable. Presuming that, stress the authors, involvement does make for vulnerability. It could also be the case that their normative rebuttals make the Arabic viewers less vulnerable, by virtue of their higher involvement. Likewise, the playful, Western viewers may be more influenced by virtue of their lowered defences. The critics of Liebes and Katz argued in response that the fact that the Western viewers also had access to more cultural knowledge and experience with this kind of television could count against such a conclusion. Let us now turn to Ien Ang's research, also on *Dallas*, to compare mainstream and critical research in more detail.

Ang invited readers of the Dutch women's magazine *Viva* to write to her about their *Dallas* viewing experience. 'I like watching the TV serial *Dallas* but often get odd reactions to it. Would anyone like to write and tell me why you like watching it too, or dislike it? I should like to assimilate these reactions in my university thesis. Please write to . . .' (Ang 1985: 10). She received 42 letters, most of them from women. Based on these letters Ang reconstructs what kind of pleasures watching *Dallas* offers for these Dutch viewers. Her goal was not simply to describe how viewers make sense of and find pleasure in watching *Dallas*, she also wanted to intervene in the then fierce debate in the Netherlands and in other European countries about the cultural imperialism of American televison shows as well as take a stand against the often-denigrating views of popular culture and its users.

Through qualitative method, inspired by ethnography, Ien Ang was able to access audience pleasures in viewing *Dallas* (and hating *Dallas*), and to identify how the dominant ideology of mass culture and its populist opponent organize social debate and individual evaluation of popular culture (even if they cannot determine audience pleasure in itself). Ang's choice to work with readers' letters also has a second political dimension. She helped to establish a new, more radical forum for feminist interest in popular culture, women's genres and women readers. The feminist work on popular culture at that time consisted primarily of text-based analysis. As has been implied above, text-based analysis that is used to also understand audiences, tends to not recognize audience activity and hence understand it, implicitly, as passive. In the early 1980s such a text-based view was offered in Tania Modleski's (1982) work on women's genres (which included soap opera). Modleski combines her decoding of the narrative structure of romances, Gothic novels and soap opera with psycho-analytical and clinical psychological views. As a result some critics see her work as ultimately contradicting its own goals. Instead of generating respect for female audiences she stigmatized them as hysterics (romance readers) or stereotyped them as housewives (soap opera) whose distracted frame of mind, crucial to their efficient functioning as cleaners and caretakers in the household, fits appropriately with the structure of daytime television soap operas, a characteristic of which are its multiple and fragmented plotlines.

In a nutshell, then, this debate about the prime-time soap opera *Dallas* and its daytime counterparts provides us with the positions taken on the subject of the audience in media and cultural studies research against social science and against textual analysis. On the one hand, social scientists gave little credence to the contextuality of audience negotiation with media texts, on the other, research in the humanities tended to focus especially on the text and exclude the audience altogether. Media and cultural studies research maintained that to understand how popular genres have meaning for audiences it is crucial to take the social context in which they are used into account. Analysis based on the text only, raises difficult questions about the status of the researcher. Is she the enlightened expert? Can she, contrary to the women she describes, withstand the enticements of the text? Modleski's analysis sets her apart from the people she writes about. Compare this to Ang's invitation to *Dallas* viewers to write to her about their experiences. ('I like watching . . . *Dallas*, but often get odd reactions to it.' Her position is totally different. Her 'authority' is of a more 'dialogical' nature, in tune with ethnographic work. Ethnographers, after all, tend to spend much time in the field, in contact with their respondents in order to get to know them well. They talk as well as observe. Ang's position is also very different from the approach of Liebes and Katz, who more than any other researchers in audience research managed to be flies on the wall: observers who are totally hidden from the participants and who therefore do not disturb 'naturally' occurring inter-action and meaning production. Their position derives from a deep-seated belief in objectivity and truth that Ang and other cultural studies researchers do not share because it tends to obfuscate very real power relations in research situations. What issues then are raised by our charting of the active audience so far, if we use these *Dallas* studies?

Although all three *Dallas* authors are concerned about American cultural imperialism, their concern is of a different order. Liebes and Katz try to find as fine-tuned a method as possible to determine possible effects. Ang, on the other hand, is not very interested in methodological issues nor is she much bothered by the question of media effects. She reconstructs her letter-writers' pleasures as well as their dislikes of the programme and identifies that which she labels 'the ideology of mass culture' as a frame via which a large number of *Dallas* haters account for their displeasure (Ang 1985: 95), or the way in which some *Dallas* lovers excuse their 'weakness'. Abhorrence of American cultural products and a show of great concern for their influence is a part of this ideology of mass culture, which is a vehicle for what Bourdieu called the 'bourgeois aesthetic' (Ang 1985: 116). Ang is thus interested in the ideological or discursive functioning of popular television as well as in how popular television becomes meaningful for viewers given such an ideological context.

In so far as the rhetoric of media effects would have a place in Ang's reconstruction, it would be in the ideology of mass culture itself when it professes concern for manipulable and vulnerable audiences. To some extent this is exactly what classical or mainstream mass communication research does. Indeed, in the conclusion of Liebes and Katz we find it stated that '(t)he more traditional groups . . . seem to be more vulnerable', and that 'the Western groups lack a normative defence' (1986: 169). Rather than give a voice to media consumers, Liebes and Katz aim to conclude something about them: the degree to which they are influenced by the programme and are 'victims' of American cultural imperialism.

Of course the Liebes and Katz project cannot be taken for uses and gratifications research because it is not. While Liebes and Katz offer a theoretical *tour de force* to account for how media influence works, uses and gratifications continues to have the more sympathetic view of the relation between audiences and media. What is it indeed that audiences do with the media? Media and cultural studies research offers the more complex and theoretically interesting argument as well as strong support for the view that audiences are not so much duped by the media, as have to operate within the constraints set by society, including mixed systems of state and commercial efforts to control publics: whether as fodder for advertisers, or as unruly subjects that should be disciplined to be fully rounded citizens. Counter to these disciplinary efforts, media and cultural studies poses the question of what is in it for audiences to comply with these roles. What pleasures, in short, are gained by being a media audience, and how are these contextually determined and enabled?

## Questioning media and cultural studies research on audiences

Above it has been made clear that the notion of the active audience was the intellectual property of two highly different research traditions: gratificationists from social science backgrounds on the one hand, media and cultural studies scholars from interdisciplinary backgrounds (involving both the humanities and the social sciences) on the other. Although uses and gratifications research would seem to offer an attractive prospect, it is very much part of a hard-nosed scientific community, in which the term 'active audience' in practice is reduced to a gimmick. That at least was the claim of media and cultural studies scholars in the convergence debate of the late 1980s, which in some fora still continues (Schroeder 2000). In practice the conceptualization of 'active' in traditional approaches, even in the monumental Liebes and Katz project, reflects strongly the underlying conviction that audiences are manipulated and duped by the media, and that they are willing but unwitting partners in their own downfall, that is, that they are ultimately better labelled 'passive'.

To concentrate solely on the difference between these two traditions that actually use the term 'active audience' would obscure the fact that in both camps there are major differences between practitioners, not just among the mainstream social scientists (as became clear above in the difference between uses and gratifications research and the Liebes and Katz project) but also in the media and cultural studies camp. To elucidate the full importance of the adjective 'active' let us return to Ang's criticism of gratificationist research and the convergence discussion (Ang 1989). In point of fact, Ang's piece is directed more against the work of David Morley, who is seen, like Ang, as one of the founders of audience research within media and cultural studies, than against the above-mentioned social scientists.

In 1980 David Morley published *The Nationwide Audience*, the audience part of a study of a popular British current affairs programme that he undertook together with Charlotte Brunsdon. The book is based on group interviews with students, workers and managers about *Nationwide*. Its most pressing question was whether audiences will repeat dominant ideology, or whether they will occupy a variety of positions as suggested by a model Stuart Hall had sketched in an occasional stencilled paper at the then Centre for Contemporary Cultural Studies at the University of Birmingham ([1974]1980). The variety of opinions and views that Morley gathered convinced him that audiences are not necessarily positioned or placed by a programme so as to reproduce the dominant ideology. The audience is not a puppet pulled by the strings of an individual text. Programmes become meaningful through a combination of the position offered by the text and the social background of its viewers, combined with the codes and discourses viewers are familiar with. Television programmes can therefore never be seen as an unproblematically shared referent for all members of the audience.

Six years later Morley published another audience study, this one called *Family Television* (1986). In Ang's review it is portrayed as a convergence study, in contrast to Morley's earlier work. Indeed, Morley pleads against 'unproductive form(s) of segregation'(1986: 13) between questions of interpretation and questions of use. To her dismay, Ang cannot locate Morley in his text at all. As writer he is a totally disembodied subject driven by a disinterested wish to contribute to scientific progress (Ang 1989: 107). The political thrust of his analysis does not become clear at all. In fact, like uses and gratifications research, Morley appears primarily interested in difference, in the range of audience experience. The experienced reader, however, will soon discern important differences. Where uses and gratifications are interested in drawing up typologies, Morley, as a media and cultural studies scholar interprets some differences as far more significant than others. Family television is also very much a book about the power structure in families. Reviewing Morley's interpretation and debate with Brunsdon, reported in the book, Ang concludes that: 'What emerges here is the beginning of an interpretive framework in which differences in television viewing practices are not just seen as expressions of different needs, uses or readings, but are connected with the way in which historical subjects are structurally positioned in relation to each other'(1989: 109). The concentrated viewing mode of many of the men in Morley's study and the distracted mode of watching television that characterized many of the women, are constituted in relation to one another. They are not individual choices, they are two sides of one coin. How television is used (literally) and how programmes are interpreted, the two dimensions of audience activity, need to be understood as questions of the social power relations in our society.

This debate between Ang and Morley, whose work is usually understood as closely related, shows how media and cultural studies scholars were less interested in the activities of audiences as such, than in how to come to a self-reflexive theoretical understanding of how people cope with the media. Although I started out this chapter by simply defining 'active' as 'meaning making', and by stating that 'the active audience' was a phrase coined by different research traditions, I now have to retract this. Media and cultural studies would seem to have very little interest in audience activity as such. Within this framework audience activity is only the beginning of an engaged trajectory of getting to know viewers, of interviewing them, of understanding their lives and backgrounds in order to develop critical theory. Whereas social scientists in a sense lament the unruliness of audiences, their unpredictable behaviour, the key to media and cultural studies research is political engagement and criticism. Styles of doing research and styles of writing are therefore key ingredients of ethnographic audience research. The key to its research practice has been to look not only for regularities as such but also for exceptions. If the designated readers of women's magazines are female, how do men read them? (Hermes 1995) Such strategies will take us beyond the assumption that audiences are active meaning producers, by allowing us to theorize *how* they are meaning makers, and also what the role of the text might be in all this.

## Conclusion

That single adjective 'active' stands for more than just 'doing things', or 'energetic'. In the context of mainstream media and communication research it is better translated as 'unpredictable' or 'uncontrollable'. Active as a description of what it is audiences do with the media or with media texts for me signals most of all a discussion between quantitative and qualitative audience researchers in the 1980s. This seems like far away. But the battle was won by no-one, nor have the issues of contention become void. It remains important to reflect on how we relate to those we do research on, whether or not we are part of those we do research on, and if so how? It remains important to think of the goals we wish our research to serve. Should they be a means to have even better programming, to net even more advertising revenue? Should they help support the identity struggles of paternalistic public broadcasters? Would it at all be possible to really make a difference in the lives of all those ordinary people out there through our research efforts? Difficult questions, that point that adjective 'active' back to ourselves. We need to be 'doing things', as the *Concise Oxford English Dictionary* tells us. I have opted for continuing my research in terms of cultural citizenship. If one thing has become clear in the discussion around the 'active' audience, it is that – notwithstanding the public and media-fed mourning of Princess Diana – media use seldom moves us to act collectively. Yet our media use can make us feel part of real or virtual communities: as readers of a particular genre or as discussants on a mailing list. Active for me still means: making meanings, and those meanings are potentially against the grain, and steps forward towards a better world, incorrigible optimistic that I am . . . , and critic of a dominant pessimism around the media and how they influence our lives.

## Questions

1  List the arguments for and against convergence of quantitative and qualitative audience research. Present a case for and against by focusing on the logic of both approaches, and on in what order the two would be conducted. Would they indeed be able to strengthen one another, or is it impossible to allow the audiences' own terms to emerge from such a study? (Tip 1: would it be possible to use interview material to phrase questions? Tip 2: what would the role of the researcher be in both parts of the research – would he or she be able to reflect on her or his role in dialogue with media consumers?)

2  Prepare an interview about everyday television use by interviewing yourself. How would you answer questions about the programmes you really like to watch (what makes them such fun to watch, or to talk about)? Which programmes irritate you but are you familiar with nonetheless? (Do you often watch programmes not of your own choice because you share your living space and TV set with others?)

3  Ethnographic audience study wishes to reconstruct media use from the perspective of the audiences themselves. To that end researchers try to find and use 'members' categories' (an anthropological term); and as evidence of the authenticity of their reconstruction they introduce large segments of interview texts in their academic publications. Some have argued that within such a framework asking so-called leading questions does little harm. After all, the ethnographer only uses them to provocate interviewees, in order to get them to talk back. Simple yes or no answers are no good in qualitative research. Also, we all have finite cultural capital and will use our own terms and categories to explain our point of view as media users. Argue why you do, or do not agree with this point of view.

# References

Ang, I. (1985) *Watching Dallas*, London: Methuen.

Ang, I. (1989) 'Wanted audiences. On the politics of empirical audience research', in E. Seiter, H. Borchers, G. Kreutzner and E. Warth (eds) *Remote Control. Television, audiences and cultural power*, London: Routledge, pp. 79–95.

Hall, S. (1980) 'Encoding/decoding', in S. Hall (ed.) *Culture, Media, Language*, London: Hutchinson, originally published in 1974, pp. 197–208.

Hermes, J. (1995) *Reading Women's Magazines. An analysis of everyday media use*, Cambridge: Polity Press.

Jensen, K. B. (1987) 'Qualitative audience research: towards an integrative approach to reception', *Critical Studies in Mass Communication* 4(1): 21–36.

Klapper, J. (1960) *The Effects of Mass Communication*, New York: Free Press

Liebes, T. and Katz, E. (1986) 'Patterns of involvement in television fiction: a comparative analysis', *European Journal of Communication* 1: 151–71.

McQuail, D. (2000) *McQuail's Mass Communication Theory*, 4th edn. London: Sage.

McQuail, D., Blumler, J. and Brown, J. (1972) 'The television audience, a revised perspective', in D. McQuail (ed.) *Sociology of Mass Communication*, Harmondsworth: Penguin, pp. 135–65.

Modleski, T. (1982) *Loving with a Vengeance. Mass-produced pleasures for women*, New York: Methuen, originally published in 1982.

Morley, D. (1980) *The Nationwide Audience*, London: BFI.

Morley, D. (1986) *Family Television, Cultural power and domestic leisure*, London: Comedia.

Schroeder, K.-C. (2000) 'Making sense of audience discourses. Towards a multidimensional model of mass media reception', *European Journal of Cultural Studies* 3(2): 233–58.

# Further reading

## *Classic studies*

Ang, Ien: Any of her books are well worth reading. Her *Watching Dallas* (London: Methuen, 1985) has become a classic in qualitative audience research. It reconstructs the attractions of this American prime-time soap for a Dutch audience on the basis of letters from viewers. *Desperately Seeking the Audience* (London: Routledge, 1991) documents the ideological background of different forms of quantitative audience research used in the television industry. *Living Room Wars* (London: Routledge, 1997) is a collection of articles that together present the ongoing discussion on the critical project of engaging with audience practices.

Morley, David: his *Nationwide* studies (London: BFI, 1980) (undertaken with Charlotte Brunsdon) and his *Family Television* (London: Comedia, 1986) are 'musts' for those interested in the actual work that launched such a fierce debate on the nature of audience activity and how that should be conceptualized. In *Television, Audiences and Cultural Studies*, articles are collected in which Morley also reflects critically on his own work.

## Examples of empirical work

My own *Reading Women's Magazines* (Cambridge: Polity, 1995) shows the delicate nature of working with audience material and the limited range of conclusions that can be drawn on the basis of such work. The book reconstructs the meaning of women's magazines as everyday media use solely from the viewpoint of readers, who cherish fantasies of ideal selfs and communities while reading that only to a small extent coincide with the expectations of the industry and of text-based research.

Marie Gillespie's *Television, Ethnicity and Cultural* change (London: Routledge, 1995) is perhaps the best example of a truly ethnographic project. Gillespie worked with Punjabi youngsters in London and did more extensive fieldwork than most of the qualitative audience research projects. She documents the use and meaning of different media and genres, such as the news, a soap and commercials.

An excellent overview of qualitative audience research from the perspective of the British cultural studies tradition is offered by Shaun Moores in *Interpreting Audiences* (London: Sage, 1997).

Those interested in quantitative audience research should consult Denis McQuail's *Mass Communication* Theory, 4th edn (Sage, 2000) which manages to lucidly map all the known work on audiences in all relevant traditions.

# Chapter 21

## Approaches

WHY STUDY MEDIA FORM?

**JOHN CORNER**

This chapter looks at how questions of form have figured in study of the media. It relates such questions to matters of content, interpretation and influence. Having outlined some key features and problems of formal analysis, it takes the perennial issue of screen violence in order to examine how further attention to form could clarify and focus debate.

In this chapter I want to look at why the study of form is of key importance in any programme of media studies or, for that matter, of media research. This aim will require some attention to be paid to definitions of 'form' (notoriously, in relation to 'content') and also to ideas about its analysis and to the way in which it is linked to other dimensions or phases in the whole process of mediation. I shall attempt to give the discussion exemplification and grounding by taking one area in which factors of form, for long overlooked, are now being recognized in their full complexity and importance – representations of violence on television and in films.

It is significant for my argument and examples, and for the evaluation and use of them by student readers, that the range of Media Studies and Communication Studies available in the UK and mainland Europe shows considerable variation in the scale and kind of attention given to formal analysis. On some courses, particularly those influenced strongly by Arts and Humanities perspectives, elements drawn from linguistic study are clearly seen as 'core'. On other courses, particularly those generated from a Social Studies base, such attention may be far less extensive, with few, if any, opportunities for going beyond a basic awareness. These variations are often a proper reflection of staff interests but they also indicate a tension within the whole field of Media Studies, a tension between Humanities and Social Science modes of enquiry and, at bottom, what I have elsewhere (Corner 1999) described as a tension between Media Studies as a form of 'criticism' (where the primary emphasis may be given to media output) and Media Studies as a form of 'sociology' (where primary emphasis may be given to history, institutions, production practices and audiences). I do not hold the view that the tension is an irresolvable one or, indeed, that it is necessarily unproductive as a play-off of one kind of approach against another. However, I do think that *one* way in which Media Studies might develop and progress is by more sustained dialogue between contributing disciplines precisely on issues to do with media form and its interconnection with media production and consumption (the introduction to Corner 1999 discusses this at some length).

Another good reason for giving formal issues close attention in any course of study is that both in broadcasting and the press there have recently been quite radical changes in form, occasioned by the stronger market need for mediations, as commodities, to appeal to specific viewers and audiences. A key process here has been that of 'hybridization', the mixing of elements from what were previously distinct conventions, thus breaking down some of the older genres, including those dividing off 'higher' from 'lower' forms or demarcating the 'serious' from the 'entertaining'. A quick walk around the magazine racks of a high street newsagent will show how this has affected the specialist publications sector, with its various and often strident attempts to construct a readership subculture around particular groups, hobbies and interests which have either newly emerged or which have undergone radical change. In broadcasting, one international shift has been towards a new kind of 'reality programme', drawing on documentary formats and dramatic techniques to provide either thrilling stories of real-life action (see the overview in Kilborn 1994) or, in the 'docusoap', diverting accounts of everyday occupational life and its mixture of the routine and the unexpected.

It is perhaps worth noting, as a final preliminary comment, that from the point of view of many teachers and researchers, Media Studies has already suffered from an overdose of enquiry into form (the term 'formal*ism*' has quite a long history as a label for distortion and limitation, especially in relation to literary and fine arts scholarship). I have some sympathy with this view, but I would want to argue that the problem, rather than deriving from formal analysis as such, lies with the way in which it has often been done. My basic claim about the study of form is that only by attending to formal issues can we engage with two things which it is vital for media studies to tackle. First, we require to have an analytic understanding of the range of ways in which the media industries produce cultural artefacts, whether these are 'fictional' or 'factual' by categorization. Questions of form are important in this process of design and fashioning. Second, any understanding of 'media influence', actual or potential, will come to grief if it is not sensitive to the way in which artefactual design is instrumental in cueing those various acts of knowing and feeling – of finding sense and significance and having emotions – which happen when we read newspapers, watch television and listen to radio.

## Form and content

By 'form' I mean the particular organizations of signification which constitute a given item *as communication* – for instance, an advertising hoarding, an episode of a situation comedy on television, an article in the local evening newspaper. Inevitably, such signification is *conventional*, drawing on what may well be a large and complex range of conventions for doing what it tries to do and for being what it is (the term 'genre' is often used to describe specific clusters of convention in media practice). These conventions will inform word choice and syntax (as, for instance, in a popular newspaper editorial column), and they will be behind the ways in which a particular image is lit and photographed and the ways in which items depicted in it are composed within a given frame and perspective (as, for instance, in an advertising hoarding). Even if the communication is designed to read, sound or look highly 'original', conventions of form will be an important constitutive element (perhaps informing decisions about what is omitted or what is done with a significant difference). The basic 'content' of any communication could, in most cases, be articulated by the use of any one of a number of different formal choices. So, for instance, there exists an extremely wide range of English syntactical and lexical variations by which to tell someone in one sentence that you wish them to shut the door through which they have just entered. And there exists a similarly wide range of visual techniques and styles by which to shoot, for the opening of a television programme, the main waterfront buildings of Liverpool. On the other side of the equation, the formal means used in telling people to shut doors and in depicting Liverpool will have a relative independence from their employment in these particular instances. Following the two different lines of possibility thus opened up is, in fact, a key feature of formal analysis – *noting how* **this** *instance might have been communicated differently and noting how* **different** *instances have been communicated similarly.*

One objection to what I have said so far might come from someone firmly committed to the view that it is impossible to separate 'form' from 'content', with the implication that even to use these terms at all is to slip into self-deception. This seems to me to be an over-reaction to those analysts who have gone on about 'form' without any apparent regard at all for 'content' and those who have studied 'content' without paying the slightest attention to 'form'. Certainly, we can agree that any study should connect with *both*, but it is quite legitimate (indeed, absolutely necessary to analytic progress) to see the two as separate, if only the better to understand the way in which they are tightly interconnected. Media analysts have a rather bad track record of claiming the fusion of things which, illogically, they also wish to claim are related (only separate things can relate). To make this point about separation clearer, take my own specialism. I have a particular academic interest in documentary film and television, its history and development. In pursuing this, I believe I can analyse documentaries in a meaningful way while paying primary attention to their particular visual and aural 'shape' and their use of distinctive mediating devices rather than to their content (see, for instance, Corner 1996). Their content may well be the factor which most directly 'sells' them to an audience (a documentary about drug abuse, for instance, connecting with very different expectations, interests and fears from a documentary about the growth of the sport of rock-climbing). However, I am enquiring into the kinds of 'communicational packages' that modern documentaries are, and this is not at all a topic-specific enquiry, even though one of the interesting things it may be able to do is to see how similar formal systems are modified when they are applied to different substantive themes. What about the reverse case? Is it possible as a viewer to take the 'content' of a documentary without regard to the form? This question poses the difference between analytic attention to a communication and 'normal' attention. For while it is certainly possible to watch and enjoy a documentary without consciously registering much if anything to do with its communicative design (this is in fact the intended and normative way in which most documentaries *are* watched), the 'content' is made available to meaningful consciousness only *through* the form, so the form is 'at work' even though the viewer (perhaps especially when the viewer) is unaware of it. This complicates the form/content relationship – content, like form, is still a 'separable' element but in any given media artefact it has a high level of form dependency; *it is rendered through the form.* At certain levels of (high) generality, its separability *may* be relatively trouble-free for the conduct of an argument (for example, the number of appearances in British television drama of Black police officers in comparison with Black criminals). Elsewhere, abstraction of content may be hazardous (for example, in discussing the frequency of depiction of acts of murder on television – where, as I shall argue later, the matter of the form of depiction is absolutely vital to what is at issue).

So, to summarize, my view is that while content and form indicate elements of communication which cannot usefully be considered in isolation from each other – in many instances the interconnections and dependencies are too close for that – they are analytically separable and, indeed, the consequences of their not being so would be extremely dire for media analysis. Certain studies of the media rightly place emphasis on content factors, others are more interested in questions of communicative design and construction. Although there is some truth in the charge that attention to form has often failed to get to grips with the *political and social embeddedness* of mediation, preferring instead to speculate about the complexities of signs, there is a long history of mass communication research which has rendered itself of limited value by its inattention to the details of language and depiction, to the *means* by which communication gets done. Despite some of the theoretical obscurities it has had a habit of falling into, one of the principal and continuing contributions of 'Cultural Studies' to international media research has been its refusal to foreclose on what, at the risk of sounding very unscientific, we might call the 'mysteries' of signification. It has always tried to remember that mediation is a matter of *symbolic exchange.* In fact, this exchange is, judged from one point of view, very one-sided. The media put out symbols and audiences and readerships 'receive' them. However, this is to miss the point that audiences and readerships invest their own symbolic resources (their ways of attaching meaning and value to word, image, narrative and character) in coming to terms with the media productions they encounter: enjoying some of them, disliking some and quite possibly not 'getting the sense' of quite a few too. This leads on to the links between form and interpretation.

## Form and interpretation

Other chapters in this book refer in more detail to the ways in which study of the variables of interpretation has figured in recent media enquiry. A realization of the extent to which meaning is contingent upon the act of interpretation rather than being a property somehow inherent to media artefacts themselves, simply projected outwards from them, has been the single most important point of development in recent media research. It has given rise to a number of challenging lines of study into the social conditions of interpretability as they vary among different readerships and audiences. It has also broken forever any direct linkage between media items and influence, since it has introduced variables of meaning into the research perspective. Research on influence has always been aware of the importance of variables but it has generally related these to a 'message' whose basic meaning was stable even if the 'use' made of it or its 'trigger' function in prompting behaviour were not. I have written on these issues elsewhere (Corner 2000), in the context of continuing debate over just what the implications of interpretation are for *any* theory of influence.

The scope of the debate exceeds this chapter's remit but what I would want to claim here is that an emphasis on the 'role of the reader' in giving meaning to what they see and hear in no way reduces the need for media research to pay attention to questions of signification. Far from it. We shall understand meaning-making 'from' the media as a social process only if we increase our understanding of significatory structures and their operation within the 'spaces and times' of media texts (both written and broadcast forms have spatial and temporal dimensions to their communicative character). Signification also needs to be traced back to specific authorial/ editorial/technical production practices too, many of which are self-consciously rhetorical in the sense that they intend to cause certain kinds of response in the viewer or reader. Think, for instance, of the formal properties required of photographs which are placed on the covers of outdoor sports magazines, what they are supposed to 'say' about the exhilaration and intensity of skiing, surfing or rock-climbing, quite apart from their literal depiction of a sporting act.

The scope of reader/viewers to interpret variably is, in any given case, constrained by the social and biographical factors informing the interpretative framework they mobilize in response to a mediated item. A fanatical surfer will 'read' an image of a big wave differently from someone who hates the sea, for instance. Someone who has been an unemployed machinist for 4 years may well understand a television news item on job centres differently from someone who is a successful banker. But interpretative limitations are not the only constraint. The significations themselves carry levels of determination which it would be extremely odd to find varying greatly in their interpretative uptake. At the most obvious level, this is sustained by the stability of signs themselves. If the news item I mentioned above finished with a shot of someone shaking their head as they looked at the 'jobs available' board and then promptly leaving the job centre, the visual cues of this little narrative would be hard not to interpret as indicating a *problem* – an under-supply of jobs – whatever information was carried elsewhere in the story. If the reporter went as far as to run a voice-over across this scene, along the lines 'But disappointment still awaits many who call here', it would be virtually impossible to imagine much interpretative latitude among viewers (although there would definitely be differences in social and political response, including the possibility of complaints being made to the broadcasters on grounds of bias). If we take the case of the picture of the big wave, the cultural connotations of waves with 'power' is securely enough established in our culture (reinforced as it is by advertising and packaging) to generate that reading, and its attendant emotional sense, for most viewers of the image, whatever their interest in, or experience of, the sea. Of course, the dedicated surfer may be able, at a quick glance, to place the depicted wave into a numerical category of power potential!

This general point needs making lest media artefacts end up being seen primarily as kinds of open invitation to create 'personal' meanings. A level of 'personal' meanings *is* created around media artefacts, grounded in our biographical individuality, and *all* meanings have to be *attributed* to artefacts by those who apprehend them. But meanings are attributed in response to powerful and often densely organized signifiers, whose job it is precisely to direct and organize meaning-making, to generate sense and significance and as far as possible to cue feelings too. Is it hardly surprising that, when it comes to discussing last night's news, film or comedy show with friends, we have a lot of meanings to *share* as well as to discuss, debate and perhaps contest?

## Elements of formal analysis

Analysis of communicative form has been undertaken in a wide range of disciplines; literary criticism, linguistics and art history have lengthy traditions of enquiry while film studies, cultural sociology, cultural studies and media studies have more recent bodies of work. One of the key factors differentiating the analytic approaches is their level of systematic formulation, that is, the degree to which they self-consciously follow procedures. Many literary critics analysing a poem, for instance, will do so with extremely close attention to its linguistic character, but probably with little by way of procedural explicitness. Linguists, on the other hand, often analyse language with careful regard to their own analytic scheme and its categories, which are made explicit in the analysis. Such a difference is partly a product of the different *aims* of enquiry – in the one case an artistic appreciation, in the other a description of language structures – but many types of communicative analysis combine a number of aims, so distinctions of this kind can prove troublesome. Semiotics, the science of signs developed in part by Ferdinand de Saussure in the early part of the twentieth century, has undoubtedly seemed to many to offer the most general and rigorous system for analysing communication. Its emphasis on structural interrelations provides a framework of procedures for use across a whole range of different media forms, including visual texts. Here, the work of Roland Barthes (especially 1972) has been exemplary and highly influential (in Media Studies, Fiske and Hartley 1978 was a key textbook). However, the very precision of semiotics in the tradition exemplified by Saussure and Barthes has been a problem insofar as it assumes too rigid and stable a communicative *system*, blocking out varieties, and frequently ignores that process of interpretation, described above, by which meaning is the product of specific, socially situated acts of reading and viewing. Despite some excellent and suggestive work, semiotics has by no means consolidated itself as the dominant perspective on formal analysis it once appeared well on the way to becoming. Another general problem for formal analysis has been posed by visual texts. Clearly, the study of visual depiction, whether in drawing, photography, film, television or whatever, requires different tools from the study of written and spoken language (see Messaris 1994). With language, the signifying units of words and the rules of combination (syntax) may not be immutable but they do have a degree of significatory stability. A dictionary and a grammar primer are indications of this. The units and combinatory rules of, say, photography are far harder to grasp as a formal system. For a start, in a photograph we have no obvious signifying unit to compare with the word. Second, we face the problem that while a sentence is clearly a communicative device capable of generating all sorts of propositional and evaluative information, a photograph of, say, a car in a street may just seem to be showing a car in the street. In other words, it may appear to have no communicative project apart from presenting us with a 'likeness'. Barthes' (1977) insightful discussion of the photograph as appearing to be 'a message without a code' takes up this very point. We may recognize that there is *more* communicative work going on than this, and that indeed the 'message' is 'coded', but specifying the visual code system and its particular local application has often proved, not surprisingly, to be a formidable and controversial task.

All I will say here on this question is that any serious project of formal analysis must have reasonably consistent, and preferably explicit, criteria for *identifying* distinctive components of communication. It must have a way of providing a *description* of communicative organization which registers these components in rule-based combination (the rules can't be 100% tight but they must show good consistency across instances). The project should then be able to offer *explanations* that can address the link between particular significatory elements and levels of relative stability in socially ascribed meaning. It should, in short, be able to match 'sign' to 'sense'.

Say, for instance, I wanted to look at how elements from 'camcorder culture' had become inscribed within mainstream media output (which they have, in advertising and a range of documentary and magazine programmes). I would need to identify those elements, their combination across a range of instances with other elements, and the kinds of social meaning which they were designed to generate. Some clues as to intentions here might be obtained from context of use. Of course, it could turn out that rather different aspects of 'camcorderism' (e.g. authenticity, domesticity, ineptness, expectations of comedy) were being deployed and that analysis needed to move to a *typology* of usage, indicating the range of variants and their associated formal properties. As I noted earlier, ignoring specific 'content' here is likely to lead to elaborate speculation, the subsequent value of which may be very questionable. Alertness to form in relation to specific themes and contexts (and perhaps to production practices and/or the sampled responses of viewers) might help us make useful headway into charting how the terms of mainstream televisuality are being modified by non-professional practice.

There is a great deal more to be said about formal analysis at the level of theory and method. However, having drawn attention to at least some of the issues, I want to look at how much of what I have said so far in this chapter comes to bear on one particular area of concern – screen violence.

## The screen violence issue

The issue of 'screen violence' has generated much debate in recent years, both in respect of feature films and of broadcast television. Fears of a negative connection between depictions of violence and real behaviour have been widely expressed. Generally speaking, there have been three kinds of fear. First, there has been fear of depicted violence stimulating real violence. Second, there has been fear of depicted violence reducing sensitivity and proper concern for real violence. Third, there has been fear of depicted violence inducing excessive and unwarranted levels of anxiety among sections of the population about being the victims of violence. However, the first two kinds of fear are the ones most evident in the UK, and they have been developed in respect both of fictional and non-fictional material, with particular attention being paid to the vulnerability of young viewers.

Elsewhere (Corner 1995) I have explored some of the broader issues surrounding 'screen violence', including the basic cultural paradox that forms of behaviour which are widely considered to be wrong in reality constitute the basis of a broad range of popular culture. It is necessary, I believe, for analysis to come to terms with the wide-spread *enjoyment* of depicted violence (violence as 'play') across most age-groups and social groups before much progress can be made on the question (see Hill 1997 for a suggestive approach to viewer studies). In earlier writing, I used the terms 'turn-on' and 'turn-off' violence to indicate two basic ways in which depictions might differ. In 'turn-off' depictions (and the portrayals of most serious TV drama would fit here, as would the majority of violent incidents in soap operas), the aim is to portray the violence within terms of the moral framings of everyday life. So a degree of un-pleasantness, disturbance and even distress will accompany the viewing (directors have to be careful: *too* much distress may bring a problem for the viewers and then for the broadcasters and the regulating authorities). In 'turn-on' depictions by con-trast (and a whole range of popular drama formats, including thrillers and many 'cop shows' would fit here) the aim is to portray violence in a way which provides excite-ment by heightened action, intensified character performance and, perhaps, by spectacular visual effects. Of course, even allowing for the difficulty of applying my categories with consistency and precision, it is quite possible for an item to shift between 'turn-off' and 'turn-on' depictions. In fact, it seems pretty clear that a number of recent films structure this shift into their basic design, often giving rise to a debate about their moral ambivalence.

But it should immediately be obvious how quickly this whole debate turns into a set of questions about *form*, and cannot be properly addressed using items of extracted *content*. So, for instance, it is almost (not entirely) beside the point to note how many murders there are each week on network television. What we need to know is the dramatic context for the incidents and the ways in which the murders were portrayed. It is clear that a murder done in a certain way on television can leave the viewer relatively unmoved whereas a lower-level act of violence, like repeated blows to the body, can be deeply disturbing but can also be exciting or even comic.

On the basis of these general points, we might formulate a rule along the following lines – the more that violence which is judged to be 'turn on' involves sustained, graphic depiction of physical injury, the more worry is likely to be generated around it. We could even go further – the more that this violence lacks obvious action-values (chases, fights etc.) and therefore depends on the violence itself to generate viewing intensity, the more likely it is that it will be judged controversial.

As I shall indicate, these 'rules' tend to hide some considerable complexities, but they do seem close to the ones which have been applied in recent years, particularly in relation to the newer stylizations of violence to be found in cinema (on this, see the discussion in Hallam 2000). What specific questions of form do they raise? And how is form related to the particular psychology of viewing, with its broader cultural interconnections, which comes into play when watching violent depictions?

We might initially work with a checklist of factors that, in combination, could be seen to constitute key features of depiction. On it, we would need such items as:

- Strength of prior identification with characters (both those to whom violence is done and those who are violent).
- Links within the narrative to notions of justness and unjustness in relation to specific, violent events. The indication of general and local causation would be important here. Clearly, war films tend to have a radically different structure from crime films, but there are variations within the categories.
- The levels of 'realism' (themselves, posing well-attested problems of definition) and of 'entertainment' at work within the surrounding narrative. Themes and characterization would in part reflect these levels.
- The terms in which the violent scene was *acted*; for instance, expressions of pleasure and of pain, the relationships established between act and persons.
- The terms in which the violent scene was *shot* and *edited*; for instance, proximity to action, camera angles, camera mobility and variable viewpoints, duration of shots, explicit indications of physical injury. There would also be the question of the presence, and type, of sounds and music on soundtrack.

Such a list might quickly be able to make important distinctions. For instance, scenes designed to have a turn-off effect will not usually be accompanied by an exciting musical score. And the kind of cartoon violence and old-style Western violence which (while clearly 'turn-on') appears not to bother many people, will have nothing like the degree of explicit indications of injury of more recent productions. Incidentally, we might wonder why 'sanitization' of this kind is thought so culturally acceptable! However, at other points the scheme would be challenged and perhaps even thrown into question. Just *how* subjective in their significance are the workings of the various formal factors which are under review? It is certainly possible for someone to find a scene intended as 'turn-off' to work as 'turn-on' (this comes up frequently when directors defend themselves against a 'turn-on' charge) and the reverse is true too. But how varied, for instance, are our criteria for finding given acts of depicted violence comical, and what adjustments to depiction can make acceptable the previously unacceptable and vice versa?

Here, it would be useful to have the means to produce depictions designed precisely to test depictive factors with sample audiences. A much-cited study (Docherty 1990), although it could not run to this, had respondents do editing and sequence work on scripts containing violent scenes, observing how 'producerly' criteria related to the 'consumerly' ones normally used in discussion of responses. In the process, it identified a number of areas of tension and potential conflict in people's relation to the violent.

All these procedures of analysis have limitations on their reliability. But they take us to the heart of this vexed issue, raising questions about culture, imagination and fantasy – as well as about attitudes and behaviour – much more quickly than is achieved by holding up a set of moral norms against statistics showing simply the frequency of certain depicted acts. See the essays in Barker and Petley (1997) for further discussion of these questions.

## The future of form in media study

This has been no more than a brief opening-up of some questions about media form and its study. Students using this book will probably be doing concurrent work on a range of specific issues involving form and the various questions it poses (for instance, in advertising, television drama, news and current affairs, popular press reporting and feature cinema). I have wanted to stand back a little and address the matter directly at a general level. My fundamental argument is that symbolic exchange is the pivotal moment in mass communication processes, the moment around which both production capacities and intentions and consumer expectations and interpretations gather. This is true for all media. Studies of the Internet are showing a greater recognition of the Web as a symbolic not merely informational medium and we can look forward to more attention being paid to the formal organization of web sites and the kinds of experience – linguistic, iconic, spatial and temporal – that they offer (see the excellent commentaries in Gauntlett 2000). If media systems exert power, then it is primarily through the mediations which appear on page and screen (and, by implication, through the absence of those which do not) that such power is exercised. To this process, form is central and it is therefore a factor in any proper consideration of media history, media institutions, media policy and media audiences.

The analysis of form poses problems for the analyst, and some work has slipped into obscurity and inconsequentiality, but this is no good reason for displacing attention on to other factors that are perhaps thought more reliable as foci of study. Given their role as the very mechanisms of mediation, we need to engage with the elements and processes of form as directly as we can.

## Questions

1   How do formal factors contribute to the overall meaning of an item? Tape television news of the same lead story from two channels and by examination of visual and verbal organisation (e.g. sequencing of segments, visualization, phrasings, captions) consider the differences produced in the understanding of the news event.

2   How varied are the ways in which violence can be depicted? Take six examples of 'violent scenes' (two from written accounts) which you feel to be as different as they could be and examine them in the light of the list of factors outlined in this chapter.

3   How does form relate to variations in interpretation and evaluation? Take a magazine advert which you think works well and one which you think does not and briefly list the reasons for your judgements. Ask a friend to assess the same examples without knowing your opinion and then compare the results.

# References

Barker, M. and Petley, J. (eds) (1997) *Ill Effects*, London: Routledge.

Barthes, R. (1972) *Mythologies*, London: Jonathan Cape.

Barthes, R. (1977) 'The rhetoric of the image' in his *Image, Music, Text*, London: Fontana.

Corner, J. (1995) *Television Form and Public Address*, London: Arnold.

Corner, J. (1996) *The Art of Record*, Manchester: Manchester University Press.

Corner, J. (1999) *Studying Media: Problems of Theory and Method*, Edinburgh: Edinburgh University Press.

Corner, J. (2000) 'Influence: the contested core of media research', in J. Curran and M. Gurevitch (eds) *Mass Media and Society*, 3rd edn, London: Arnold, pp. 376–97.

Docherty, D. (1990) *Violence in TV Fiction* (BSC Annual Review), London: Broadcasting Standards Council.

Fiske, J. and Hartley, J. (1978) *Reading Television*, London: Methuen.

Gauntlett, D. (ed.) (2000) *web.studies*. London: Arnold.

Hallam, J. (with Marshment, M.) (2000) *Realism and Popular Cinema*, Manchester: Manchester University Press.

Hill, A. (1997) *Shocking Entertainment*, Luton: Luton University Press.

Kilborn, R. (1994) 'How real can you get: recent developments in "reality television"', *European Journal of Communication* 9(4): 421–39.

Messaris, P. (1994) *Visual Literacy: Image, Mind and Reality*, Boulder, CO: Westview.

# Further reading

Books with good introductory material on matters of form, together with examples of detailed formal analysis, include:

Bordwell, D. and Thompson, K. (1993) *Film Art: An Introduction*, 4th edn, New York: McGraw-Hill. This is a widely used and comprehensive introduction to film analysis, which offers clear guidelines through a sequence of discussion with examples. Much of it can be adapted for work on television.

Corner, J. (1995) *Television Form and Public Address*, London: Arnold. A review of television as a public medium, which pays close attention to questions of audio-visual form and draws on detailed examples.

Deacon, D., Pickering, M., Golding, P. and Murdock, G. (1999) *Researching Communications*, London: Arnold. A very helpful account of some of the principal approaches to studying communication, addressing questions both of concept and method. Good chapters on still and moving images and on various types of media language use.

Ellis, J. (1982) *Visible Fictions*, London: Routledge. A stimulating study of television and cinematic modes of depiction, partly comparative, with strong chapters on narrative and the basic organization of sound and image.

Keeble, R. (1994) *The Newspaper Handbook*, London: Routledge. A useful attempt to provide students with a sense of the complexity of newspaper layout and language use, among other things. Lots of excellent examples and an appeal that extends to trainee journalists as well as to those on media studies courses.

# Part III

**In the Media**

# Introduction to 'In the Media'

ADAM BRIGGS AND PAUL COBLEY

That which appears 'in' the media is a fraught issue. It is clearly a result of factors 'outside' media such as policy; it is also received by audiences who lead lives beyond their engagement with media. But, importantly, media texts, for many people, *do* seem to permeate all aspects of our lives. By looking at the forms and contents of media, but without proposing direct unitary 'effects', the contributors to Part III explore the vexed issue of representation.

This part conceives of the media as a set of 'representations'. Whereas Parts I and II dealt with the media as a collection of institutions, economic entities and determined practices, this part looks at the media as an ensemble of texts. These texts are important as a result of their ubiquity and because there is widespread belief that they contribute to the production of our 'commonsense' understandings of the world. As such, media texts are thought to affect, in a very real sense, the way in which we understand ourselves/others and the way we lead our lives.

This is a different approach to media 'effects' from those 'scientific' studies which create so much controversy and are analysed by Guy Cumberbatch in Chapter 18. The 'effects thesis' often serves to swamp more subtle understandings of how media representations contribute to our *shared* systems of belief and are related to the power relations of our cultures. The chapters in this part all work from the assumption that representations at least partially construct the social fabric of peoples' lives. The reason that *re*presentations are considered such an important issue is that they do not entail a straightforward *presentation* of the world and the relationships between people in it (Hall 1997). As one commentator has noted, 'Representation is a very different notion from that of reflection. It implies the active work of selecting, and presenting, of structuring and shaping: not merely the transmitting of already existing meaning, but the more active labour of *making things mean*' (Hall 1982).

Moreover, not only are representations thought to be a flawed and limited 'reflection' they are also considered to be a 'cause' of our social relations. One way in which this is signalled in the chapters is by the recurrent use of the term 'ideology', a term which has been the subject of some debate in numerous fields and, consequently, carries a range of different (and contested) meanings (Eagleton 1991; Hawkes 1996; Thompson 1984; Strinati 1995). It is worth considering some of the general ways in which ideology has been conceptualized. This will help you to develop a working knowledge of its applications, implications and limitations.

The influential British theorist, Raymond Williams, identifies 'three common versions of the concept':

(i)   a system of beliefs characteristic of a particular class or group.
(ii)  a system of illusory beliefs – false ideas or false consciousness – which can be contrasted with true or scientific knowledge.
(iii) the general process of the production of meanings or ideas (Williams 1977).

Ideology can also be understood as

- Sets of ideas which give some account of the social world, usually a partial and selective one.
- The relationship of these ideas or values to the way power is distributed socially.
- The way that such values are usually posed as 'natural' and 'obvious' rather than socially aligned (Branston and Stafford 1999).

As you will notice, all the above formulations treat ideology as existing in the realm of 'ideas' and 'values'. It is this concept of 'ideology as ideas and values' which highlights the connection with the term 'representation'.

Representation – as the 'active labour of *making things mean*' – necessarily embraces ideas and values. As such, representations are ideological. However, ideology operates beyond the realm of representation; it does so by occupying the space of people's concrete experience, donating a sense of coherence, consistency and 'naturalness' to our lived existence. Ideology, it is argued, functions to 'naturalize' our actual modes of living and working. In so doing, it serves to perpetuate and extend existing power relations which may serve the interests of some at the expense of others (for example, in the classic Marxist version of this formulation, ideology advances the capitalist bourgeoisie at the expense of the proletarian workers – see Marx and Engels 1970).

Ideology, therefore, frequently attempts to make that which is historically and culturally determined not only *appear to be* but *also be experienced as* the product of 'human nature'. Yet, it is important to stress, as Terry Eagleton does, that ideology cannot simply be equated with 'falsity' alone:

> Much of what ideologies say is true, and would be ineffectual if it were not; but ideologies also contain a good many propositions which are flagrantly false, and do so less because of some inherent quality than because of the distortions into which they are commonly forced in their attempts to ratify and legitimate unjust, oppressive political systems (1991: 222).

The emphasis given to ideology in this part, however, is less to do with the unjust and oppressive political systems *per se* than with the manner in which ideology underpins and endows with meaning the constituent components of our identities and what these entail: i.e. what it is to 'belong' to a particular nation, social class, age group; 'race', gender, sexuality, (dis)able(d) group, etc. As such, ideology precedes media representations but it also charges them with the task of disseminating nutshell versions of the complex configurations of our identities. Media representations reduce, shrink, condense and select/reject aspects of intricate social relations in order to *re*present them as fixed, 'natural', 'obvious' and ready to consume. In brief, media representations, as the bearers of ideology, (sometimes necessarily) trade in *stereotypes*; thus, ideology, for instance, tells us through representations who should change the baby's nappy.

But it is misleading to talk of just one ideology; there are, in fact, many possible competing ideolog*ies*. Different ideologies of childcare might promote nappy-changing as a practice that is not the responsibility of just one gender. Representations, too, are subject to the same kind of contestation. Because they often offer stereotypes, many representations conflict with our own experiences and ideologies. In fact, representations in general can be considered to be ideological because the very processes of selection and condensation serve not only to stereotype but also to *exclude* many features and ways of understanding the social world. The ideological nature of selection/condensation means that ideology is materialized in all manner of representations where selection/condensation occurs, for example sport, 'news', pornography, etc.

As we have noted, ideology has been the focus of heated debate. One reason is that, in its very definition, ideology is opposed to some notion of essential 'truth' or fixed 'reality' (Foucault 1980: 118); it is argued that ideology acts to prevent humans from apprehending the 'real', 'objective', social conditions of life. But *if* there are some that can unmask the workings of ideology and recognize 'objective' conditions, and some that cannot, on what basis do the former claim privileged access to 'truth'? Can ideology be understood as the means of reproducing the conditions by which inequitable distributions of wealth and power in society are maintained? Is it correct to assume that the vast majority of us fail to recognize the ideological nature of representation? Is it, alternatively, the case that we do recognize this even if we may not use the word 'ideology'? Does the recognition of ideology within representations indicate that one has moved beyond ideology (to 'truth') or that one is simply operating from a different ideological position? Is it possible that everything is ideological, through and through?

Given this list of questions (and there are many others), ideology is clearly a very problematic concept. Since the 1980s, the concept of ideology has been complemented (as you will see in this part's contributions), absorbed or replaced by the term 'discourse', a slippery concept with numerous definitions (see Schiffrin 1993; Macdonell 1986; Coupland and Jaworski 1999, 2001; Fairclough 1992; Mills 1997). The chief reason for this substitution is that the notion of ideology as separate from – and *preceding* – the act of representation while nevertheless still playing an influential role in it, runs into difficulties. It implies that representations disseminate an ideology which, supposedly, has an independent existence. The term 'discourse', on the other hand, suggests that the very act of communicating about the world should be the focus of any investigation into the workings of representation. It suggests that, referring to the world is also 'making' the world about which it is possible to refer. 'Discourse', as it is used here, can be defined as 'A way of constructing meanings which influences and organizes both our actions and our conceptions of ourselves' (Hall 1992: 292–3). In this formulation, the very act of communicating actually *produces* the objects about which one can have an ideological understanding.

Many of the chapters in Part III concern representations of specific components of our identities (e.g. age, class, sexuality, gender). The status of representations as discourse allows us to think of them not just as representing or contributing to pre-existing categories but actually creating the parameters of those categories. Such categories are the shorthand means of labelling deeply felt aspects of our identities – whether we are 'straight', 'gay', 'polysexual', 'perverted', 'middle class', 'English', 'Scottish', 'Jamaican', 'Black British', 'old', 'middle-aged', 'young', 'teenaged', 'male', 'female', 'trans-sexual', etc. Representations not only promote and circulate an understanding of these and other categories, but can often generate them. The concept of discourse enables an understanding of representation as creating and giving meaning to the significant differences between people.

It is worth remembering that such classification of identities and differences is invariably the basis of *power relations*. Media representations do not only act to tell 'other people' about 'us'. They also tell us about other people. And tell us what it means to be ourselves: for instance, what it means to be – what is appropriate behaviour for – the category 'man'. Representations therefore play out the repertoire of some identities extensively (e.g. what it is to be heterosexual or able-bodied or middle-class); conversely, they play out of the repertoire of others in a very limited way (e.g. what it is to be lesbian or disabled or upper-class).

The theory of ideology, then, takes communication or representation as a 'vehicle' for transmitting ideologies in the service of maintaining/extending power relations. 'Discourse', on the other hand, conceives the act of representation *itself* as the very stuff of power relations. Rather than carrying ideology in the content of a representation, 'discourse' indicates that the mere fact of representation shapes our relations to the world, ourselves and others. This argument holds that there is nothing 'outside' a given 'discourse' – no 'reality' as such – except other 'discourses'. Power struggles do not therefore take place between different components of the social world, each of which exist as 'naturally' preconstituted entities. 'Black', defined as a feature of nature such as 'skin colour' or 'natural rhythm', cannot simply be opposed to 'White' as 'Nordic' and lacking rhythm. Something like 'natural rhythm' is a discursively constructed quality.

Power struggles take place, then, in the competition between and within different discourses. These power struggles take place in two ways. First, they challenge the stereotypes that are often a result of certain categories (e.g. race, class, gender) but retaining the idea that these categories are definitive of the person to whom they are applied. Second, power struggles can take place by a questioning the validity of categories as being definitive. For example, the statements 'Black is beautiful', 'Welsh is wonderful', 'Gay is great', while challenging pejorative versions of Blackness/Welshness/Gayness do not abandon the categories themselves. Whereas, statements such as 'I cannot be defined by my "race"/"nationality"/"sexuality"' do. As such, the latter statements recognize that it is not enough to argue *within* a particular discourse about a category. They imply that *all* categories are discursively constructed and that they compete to define the person.

A person does not exist, for example, as a member of a specific 'racial' identity as if 'race' was a quantifiable biological category inherent in him or her from the moment of birth; there have to be discourses of 'race', operating on many different levels, which 'constitute' him or her as belonging to a 'racial' identity. To begin with, a discourse of 'race' has to identify the following:

- the person's own 'racial' identity (e.g. 'White')
- other 'racial' identities to which that person's 'racial' identity can be opposed in a power relationship (e.g. 'Black' versus 'White')
- a discourse that asserts the centrality of race as a defining feature of a person's identity (e.g. racism)
- other (non-'racial') identities to which that person's 'racial' identity can be opposed/complemented in a power relationship (e.g. 'race' may be outweighed by 'gender').

In addition. 'race' may feature in other prominent discourses which, in turn, contribute to the idea of a 'racial' identity; for example, the discourses of biology, law, media studies, sociology, criminology, demography, sport, music, etc.

So 'race', in this way of understanding it, is not a simple biological given, nor is it an ideology which precedes the act of communication. Instead it is constructed in and through the working of discourse. Moreover, it is not the only constituent of a person's discursively constituted identity. In this theory a Black Male Liverpudlian Catholic from a working-class background who works in a managerial position and is heterosexual cannot simply be defined in relation to 'race'. He is a participant in the *competing* and, sometimes, *complementary* discourses of 'race', ethnicity, gender, region, religion, social class, occupation and sexuality (at least). Some of these discourses, in different combinations, will be to the fore at some moments and others, in other combinations, will be to the fore at different moments (Hall 1992; Rutherford 1990).

The emphases which we have taken in this introduction will be found reflected especially in those chapters that deal with specific facets of our identities. Equally, in the chapters which are not directly concerned with identities – those on news representations, sport and pornography – there is a focus on the manner in which representation may contribute to a shaping of the many categorizations we use in the world of discourse.

## References

Branston, G. and Stafford, R. (1999) *The Media Student's Book*, 2nd edn, London: Routledge.

Coupland, N. and Jaworski, A. (eds) (1999) *The Discourse Reader*, London: Routledge.

Coupland, N. and Jaworski, A. (2001) 'Discourse', in P. Cobley (ed.) *The Routledge Companion to Semiotics and Linguistics*, London: Routledge.

Eagleton, T. (1991) *Ideology: An Introduction*, London: Verso.

Fairclough, N. (1992) *Discourse and Social Change*, Oxford: Polity Press.

Foucault, M. (1980) 'Truth and power', in C. Gordon (ed.) *Power/Knowledge: Selected Interviews and Other Writings, 1972–1977*, New York: Harvester.

Hall, S. (1982) 'The rediscovery of ideology: the return of the repressed in media study' in M. Gurevitch, J. Curran, T. Bennett and J. Woollacott (eds) *Culture, Society and the Media*, London: Methuen.

Hall, S. (1992) 'The question of cultural identity', in S. Hall, D. Held and T. McGrew (eds) *Modernity and Its Futures*, Milton Keynes, Cambridge and Oxford: Open University Press, Blackwell and Polity Press.

Hall, S. (1997) 'The work of representation', in S. Hall (ed.) *Representation: Cultural Representations and Signifying Practices*, London: Sage.

Hawkes, D. (1996) *Ideology*, London: Routledge.

Macdonell, D. (1986) *Theories of Discourse: An Introduction*, Oxford: Blackwell.

Marx, K. and Engels, F. (1970) *The German Ideology*, ed. C. J. Arthur, London: Lawrence and Wishart.

Mills, S. (1997) *Discourse*, London: Routledge.

Rutherford, J. (ed.) (1990) *Identity: Community, Culture, Difference*, London: Lawrence and Wishart.

Schiffrin, D. (1993) *Approaches to Discourse*, Oxford: Blackwell.

Strinati, D. (1995) *An Introduction to Theories of Popular Culture*, London: Routledge.

Thompson, J. B. (1984) *Studies in the Theory of Ideology*, Cambridge: Polity Press.

Williams, R. (1977) *Marxism and Literature*, Oxford: Oxford University Press.

# Chapter 22

# Sexuality

TRACING DESIRES: SEXUALITY IN MEDIA TEXTS

## ANDY MEDHURST

This chapter surveys the question of sexuality and representation by exploring five key questions. First, what are the mechanisms by which media stereotypes of sexual minorities come into being, and what do those stereotypes reveal about how sexuality is culturally perceived? Second, is it feasible or desirable to try to counter stereotyping with representations that can be seen as 'positive images'? Third, should minorities (in this case, lesbians and gay men) seek to bypass mainstream media institutions in order to produce media images and images from their own perspectives? Fourth, what happens to questions of sexuality and representation if the focus is shifted away from representations of minorities to look at powerful, dominant identities? Finally, what techniques of understanding media representations have been developed and practised by sexual minority audiences when confronted with a media world that largely excludes or marginalizes them?

*How we are seen determines in part how we are treated;*
*how we treat others is based on how we see them;*
*such seeing comes from representation (Dyer 1993: 1).*

## An invisible identity

Analysing media representations of sexuality involves many of the same issues, concepts and processes as the analysis of any other form of identity – issues of power and politics, concepts like stereotyping and ideology, processes of production and consumption. There is one crucial difference, however, when sexuality is the focus of study, a difference that complicates Richard Dyer's claim quoted above that the politics of representation are based on the power-relations of 'seeing', and that is the fact that sexuality is one of the most invisible of cultural identities. If (heaven forbid) there was a photograph of me accompanying this chapter, you would see that I am white and male, but you would not be able to know about my sexuality. You might make assumptions, based on whatever preconceptions you carry about how visual codings might be taken as signs of certain sexual identities, but you could not know for sure. The only way to be sure would be for me to declare myself, to say 'I am a homosexual'. Like I just have.

Making that kind of statement might strike you as unnecessarily personal, hardly in keeping with the dispassionate tone often expected in academic writing, but making it has three benefits as far as I am concerned. It helps me to establish, concisely and directly, the point that sexuality is not visually evident in the way that other identities like gender and ethnicity almost always are. Second, it lets you know that I have a particular stake in and a particular take on debates around the representation of sexuality, which is important because representation is a battlefield on which none of us can be neutral. Third, it enables me to go on and say that I don't see a statement of my sexuality as a personal issue, since it is my conviction, and the conviction of those theorists and critics who have addressed this topic, that sexuality is not just a matter of personal desires but also a site of political conflicts. Perhaps that sounds odd, since we are culturally encouraged to think of sexuality as something intrinsic, inner, concerned with deeply private emotional investments, but emotions are not devoid of social contexts and desires only exist within ideological frameworks – and one of the most important of those ideological frameworks is the sphere of media representations. Daily, endlessly, media texts and discourses endorse certain sexual options while stigmatizing others.

There is already a contradiction here. If sexuality is invisible, how can it be identified in order for those ideological judgements to proceed? That question is all the more pressing once we realize that not only is sexuality invisible, it is multiple, unstable and fluid. Heterosexuality and homosexuality are not the only players in the game, though they tend to receive most of the attention. What about bisexuals, transgendered people, or people who move between sexual identities at different stages in their life? Even within the category of homosexuality, there are enormous differences between individuals placed in that category – what on earth could a working-class teenage Asian lesbian in Southampton have in common with a wealthy middle-aged gay Scotsman? Furthermore, there have been many disputes among people who belong to sexual minorities over what label they should choose to identify themselves – homosexual, lesbian, gay, lesbian-and-gay, dyke, queer. These are important questions, which a fully nuanced account of this topic would have to take into account,[1] but this chapter will have to rely on simplifications and generalizations. That isn't entirely inappropriate, since the prevailing media representations of sexuality available to us depend precisely on simplified and generalized versions of the multiple complexities of lived experience. After all, simplifying and generalizing are what ideology is all about.

## Stereotypes, boundaries and power

The prime device through which ideological positions about sexuality are circulated in media texts is the stereotype. That's a word which only ever seems to have negative connotations, as if representations would be better and fairer if all stereotypes vanished. Unfortunately, stereotyping is inevitable in any form of immediate, accessible communication. Since there is never enough time or space to describe people in all the rich complexity that their individuality deserves, short-cuts have to be taken, comparisons made, generalizations risked, labels attached. Stereotyping is a process of selection, magnification and reduction: it takes one perceived attribute of a social group, blows up that attribute until it obscures all others, then boils it down until it comes to stand for that group, summarizing that group in a kind of cultural short-hand. To take an example of a sexuality stereotype, film and television comedies are full of images of gay men as effeminate screaming queens. Such images are not fabricated out of nothing – some gay men are just like that some of the time, but what the stereotype does is to take out those 'somes'. It chooses that one aspect of gay male behaviour (selection), inflates it into the defining characteristic of male homo-sexuality (magnification), then establishes it as the most easily recognizable image (reduction).

The ideological implications of stereotyping are obvious, since the groups most liable to be stereotyped are those with less social and cultural power – indeed one crucial distinction between powerful and less powerful social groups is that the former hold the ability to stereotype the latter. Stereotyping becomes ideological the moment it stops being simply a method of description and becomes a vehicle for values: the image of the screaming queen does not just mean 'all gay men are like that', it means 'all gay men are like that and aren't they awful', which in turn means 'and they are awful because they're not like us'. Here it's important to remember the invisibility and fluidity of sexuality, since if an ideological hierarchy between 'us' and 'them' is what a stereotype serves to perpetuate, it has to work that much harder if the bound-aries between us-ness and them-ness are so treacherously vague and mobile.

This is why stereotypes of sexuality strive so vigorously to create two, polarized sexualities, hetero and homo, and to insist with such obsessive reductiveness that people who belong to those poles are easily identifiable – hence the recurring pres-ence across media texts of the screaming queen (so **obviously** gay) and his female equivalent the butch dyke (so **obviously** lesbian). As Richard Dyer has said, such stereotypes exist in order to 'make visible the invisible, so that there is no danger of it creeping up on us unawares, and to make fast firm and separate what is in reality and much closer to the norm than the dominant value system cares to admit' (Dyer 1993: 16). Given the invisibility of homosexuality, homosexuals could be anyone, could be everywhere, and of course happily we are, but such a realization seriously chal-lenges heterosexuality's idea of itself as natural and universal. Traditional stereotypes of lesbians and gays are one way of defusing that challenge, since they construct images that few actual lesbians and gays would wish to align themselves with, thereby discouraging them from coming out and affirming their sexual identities. Those sexualities outside the homo–hetero binary are even more troubling for the hetero-sexual hierarchy, to the extent that they rarely figure in media representation at all, except as quite literally murderous – examples of these particularly extreme and unforgiving stereotypes would include the transsexual serial killers in films like *Dressed To Kill* or *The Silence of the Lambs* or the bisexuals blamed for 'spreading' AIDS into the heterosexual community in some tabloid accounts of the HIV epidemic.

Lesbians and gays who could not be corralled into one of the polarized stereotypes of effeminate queen or butch dyke were, until quite recently, simply not representable in mainstream media texts – not, that is, if their sexuality was to be made unambiguously evident. There are many characters in film and television fiction, however, who while not crudely labelled as queer were sufficiently different from heterosexual norms to offer the possibility of being interpreted in ambiguous ways, and trawling back through media history to uncover and assess these intriguing representations has become one important area of lesbian and gay media scholarship.[2] There are important questions here about the relationship between representations and audiences, since these less-stereotyped characters may well have been understood in very different ways by mainstream heterosexual audiences, accustomed to seeing homosexuality only in terms of the crassest stereotyping, than by lesbian and gay viewers more attuned to the subtle inflections of subcultural coding.

More recently, as part of a gradual change in social attitudes towards homosexuality, media representations have become more varied; the simplistic stereotypes have not vanished, but they have been supplemented by alternatives which might suggest progression towards more enlightened attitudes. Television talk shows, for example, frequently feature studio debates on matters of sexuality, and these at least give the impression that lesbians, gays and other sexual minorities are free to speak on their own terms rather than being filtered through fictional codes. That is not an impression to be seduced by, however, since shows like *Oprah* and *Ricki Lake* are just as codified, just as bound by genre conventions, as any Hollywood drama or British sitcom. Lesbian or gay guests on talk shows may feel they can escape stereotyping by speaking directly from their own experience, but that aspiration towards truthfulness runs aground on the gladiatorial organization of the studio space, the role of the host, the audience and the inevitable 'experts' in contextualizing the guests' testimonies in discursive frameworks beyond their control, and the narrative drives of scandal, interrogation and confession that give daily continuity to such series whatever the subject-matter under discussion.

Another response to the problem of stereotyping is to create, with a consciously didactic intention, positive images to counter the negative misrepresentations found elsewhere. Though well intentioned, the call for positive images rests on several shaky foundations. Such a project prides itself on rejecting stereotypes but aims to do so by creating another stereotype, it would do away with 'gay men are effeminate' only to replace it with 'all gay men are masculine': a positive image is really only a stereotype that suits my ideology rather than yours. It also assumes that all members of a social group can agree on what might constitute a positive image of themselves, ignoring differences between lesbians or gay men, some of whom may well feel much more in tune with the characteristics implicitly or explicitly rejected as 'negative'. Connected to this is the suspicion that positive images are primarily concerned with reassuring heterosexual audiences, unable to counter prejudice with anything more than unthreatening blandness. The Hollywood film *Philadelphia* would be a typical example of this ploy, encouraging heterosexual spectators to feel sympathy and tolerance for homosexual characters, but lesbian and gay audiences are increasingly impatient with the condescension built into such approaches, even going so far as to re-examine the old, discredited stereotypes of polarized homosexuality to see whether they may have been unfairly dismissed in the positive-image rush to court heterosexual approval and may, in their unapologetic if ostensibly ridiculed queerness, be ripe for reappropriation.[3]

   The factor which underpins all these debates over stereotyping is the sheer paucity of homosexual representations, the fact that there are simply so few images of sexual variety in media texts. Crude stereotypes might be easier to condone if they were part of a spectrum, and the urge to generate positive images would be superfluous if there were a larger number of lesbian or gay characters through whom the diversity of our experiences could be expressed, and this is indeed slowly beginning to happen, but it still remains too often the case that drama series feel able to sum up homosexuality with a single plot line or cast member. Such characters are forced to shoulder the weight of speaking for entire communities, a load no heterosexual figure would ever be asked to bear. A telling example of that problem was the first gay character in *EastEnders*. Colin was introduced in 1986 and stayed for three years, but he remained a middle-class outsider in a working-class milieu, and was never involved in any of the pivotal storylines. Consequently he stood detached from the soap's centre, all too obviously embodying the well-intentioned positive image, politically praiseworthy but dramatically uninvolving. Colin's mild presence did, however, pave the way for subsequent lesbian and gay characterizations to become textually richer and more emotionally engaging. Soap homosexualities are no longer the novelty they once were, and there has been an increasingly broad range of such images within the genre.

   Examples worth noting (and which you may want to discuss further) include the young lesbian couple Gina and Emily in *Hollyoaks*, the storyline in *Emmerdale* where the Australian half of a gay male couple married a heterosexual female friend in order to gain British citizenship, and the gay Asian doctor in *EastEnders* who came out to friends during a trip to Brighton (but left the series swiftly afterwards). *Brookside* has even dared to flirt with dangerous stereotypes, in the shape of the camp barman Lance and the predatory lesbian Shelley, who slept with a previously heteroexual female character in order to get closer to that character's mother, the woman she secretly desired all along. Ten years ago, I would have been scandalized by Shelley and Lance, accusing them of 'negative portrayals', but today I see them differently. First, *Brookside* has had earlier, more 'positive' lesbian and gay characters, so it has earned the right to move on and offer more complex portrayals. Second, neither Lance nor Shelley are as simply stereotyped as they might first appear. Lance may be a gossipy, fluttering queen, but he is also a loyal friend and a welcome source of wit (and, at the time of writing, about to be the centre of a story addressing the important issue of immigration rights for overseas partners of gay Britons). As for Shelley, she has been used to raise intriguing questions about bisexuality and desire in her seductive rampage through the women of the Corkhill family. *Coronation Street* still awaits its first full-time lesbian or gay character, but it has taken the even bolder step of not only introducing a transsexual but also making her one of the series warmest and most-liked figures. Hayley's presence in the *Street* shows beyond doubt that the repertoire of sexualities depicted in British soaps is far broader than would have been conceivable until recently. This is not said in order to paint a wholly rosy picture (these characters are, for example, almost always denied the chance to show affection in the ways that heterosexual characters take for granted), but an awareness of the limitations of these representations should not blind us to the progress that has been made.

## In our own voices?

> The most effective form of resistance to the hegemonic force of the dominant media is to speak for oneself (Gross 1991: 144).

Integration, of course, is not the only option. Many lesbians and gays have felt that expecting equality or accuracy in representations produced by the mainstream media is pointless, favouring instead the setting up of smaller-scale, community-based media projects. In the early 1970s, the Gay Liberation Front, Britain's first radical gay organization, dismayed by the lack of coverage they had received in the press, decided 'there was only one thing to do and that was to have a newspaper of our own' (Power 1995: 51). Their belief was that in such a forum, lesbian and gay concerns would be unfettered by the constraints encountered when those concerns were represented through heterosexual-dominated media institutions. The GLF path offered one way of minimizing those constraints, setting up a publication that was by, for and about lesbians and gays, creating, at least in principle, a rare unity of production, audience and content. There are inevitable obstacles impeding any such project, not least the dangers, already mentioned above, of homogenizing the multiplicities of lesbian and gay lives into one rather nebulous 'community', the 'oneself' spoken of by Larry Gross in the quote at the beginning of this section. There are some who believe those dangers are exaggerated, that the solidarity of a shared sexuality overrides other social differences: the gay broadcaster Paul Gambaccini has written of visiting a club and seeing 'a middle-aged white man and a teenage black boy wrapped around each other . . . same-sex passion across age, racial and economic divides. I quickly learned that these gaps simply do not exist for gay people' (Gambaccini 1996: 158), but such a claim is either naive utopianism on a somewhat heroic scale or a worrying blindness to power-relations of class, age and ethnicity which even if they miraculously evaporate in the heat of the moment will certainly return with the following dawn.

The GLF's magazine *Come Together*, irregularly produced and politically confrontational, collapsed after three years partly under the weight of factional infighting and partly because it was eclipsed by *Gay News*, a fortnightly paper which found a much more marketable balance of politics and what would later become known as lifestyle coverage (reviews, interviews, features). The brief dream of *Come Together* was to speak with one radical voice for all lesbians and gays,[4] but the first specialization *Gay News* undertook, detonating that dream along gender lines, was to become a publication predominantly concerned with gay men rather than lesbians, a direction even more eagerly pursued by its successor *Gay Times*. Now a range of diverse and often contradictory magazines cater for different niches of the varied complexity of contemporary queer lives. Larry Gross's vision of 'speaking for oneself' rest on a degree of unity, a shared common purpose, unsustainable in today's climate, where designer dykes can buy *Diva*, separatist lesbians can subscribe to *Trouble and Strife*, and *Attitude* (an even more lesbian-free zone than *Gay Times*) is aimed at gay men who'd rather not buy a magazine with 'gay' on the cover. Whether such a state of affairs reveals a welcome kaleidoscope of representations or a fragmentation that weakens the potential for coherent sexual politics remains an open question.

Television, at least in its pre-digital era, has never been able to match the choice of texts offered by the publishing industry, meaning that the handful of programmes made by and for lesbians and gays have had particular difficulties negotiating the competing demands of representativeness and diversity. If there is only one programme being broadcast that specifically targets a lesbian and gay audience, it runs the risk of turning into a token presence in the schedules, hovering apologetically on the margins like Colin in *EastEnders*. The first nationally broadcast series to take that gamble was Channel 4's *Out on Tuesday*, first aired in 1989 (Channel 4's stated remit to cater for minorities was crucial in allowing the programme to reach the screen). It sidestepped the trap of definitiveness, of saying this and only this is what homosexual life is like, by adopting a magazine format, featuring items of different length and seriousness, and never shying away from conflicts and debates. *Out* conceptualized its audience as plural, overlapping, not always easily co-existing communities, never reducing it to the impossibly simplified fiction of a single community. Although opinions were sharply divided among its target viewers,[5] *Out*'s greatest strength to me was in taking homosexualities for granted, placing them centre-stage but never on display as the object of voyeuristic scrutiny that they would have been in programmes made by and for heterosexuals. With considerable verve and panache, *Out* reversed the standard power relations of media texts concerned with sexuality, in which heterosexual identities remain unquestioned while homosexual ones go under the microscope.

The two successors to *Out* have learned from its pioneering efforts but have adopted different strategies. *Gaytime TV*, the BBC's first series aimed at lesbian and gay audiences, uses the magazine format but has snipped out all the pages except those concerned with gossip and gloss. Mindful that many had criticized *Out* for its commitment to a politicized representation of sexuality, *Gaytime TV* has emphasized an unashamedly consumerist version of being queer, featuring items on holidays, fitness and interior decor, representing sexuality wholly as a source of individual pleasure and never as a site of social conflict. The ability to represent it as both, and to walk the tightrope between them, seems on that evidence to be a skill that died out with the best editions of *Out*, though it has sometimes been managed by *Dyke TV*, Channel 4's most recent offering for lesbian audiences. *Dyke TV* is not a programme as such, but, in the currently fashionable jargon of television, a zone, where a string of discrete programmes are broadcast under one umbrella title. This has the benefits of range and the dangers of incoherence, but it at least makes possible a more sustained representation of the contradictions of contemporary sexuality than has been achieved on the debilitatingly cheery, complexity-free *Gaytime TV*.

## Scrutinizing dominance

Studies of media representation have almost always had as their chief focus the representation of 'minorities', a term used as shorthand for social groups at the less powerful end of the power spectrum. This is not surprising, since the political impetus behind such studies stems from a perception that media representations of less powerful groups play a key role in sustaining the social hierarchies which keep those imbalances of power in place. That focus is now beginning to change, broadening to incorporate studies of how 'majorities', or powerful social groups, are represented (work on the gender construction of masculinity, for example, or the cultural meanings of whiteness), but in general the equation between studying representation and studying 'minorities' still holds. That is one of the reasons why the bulk of this chapter has been about homosexualities, and why neither I as its writer or you as its reader are probably surprised by that emphasis, but I want to suggest now that analysing the codes and conventions through which media texts depict heterosexualities could prove a productive future direction for study and research.

The first barrier such an investigation runs into is the recurring issue of invisibility and sexuality with which this chapter began. Heterosexuality is not exactly invisible, in fact to my queer eyes it is utterly omnipresent – just look around a high street shop display of greetings cards to see how heterosexuality is privileged or watch how many television game shows group their contestants in terms of heterosexual domestic units – yet it is not really visible either, in terms of being a category in regular everyday social use. The word 'heterosexual' itself is used incredibly rarely in media texts, a fact which can lead to some pernicious inequalities: if a gay man is involved in committing a sexual crime, for example, news bulletins will routinely refer to his sexuality, but when did you last hear of a 'heterosexual rapist', even though that is what the overwhelming majority of rapists actually are?

The paradox of heterosexual representations is that heterosexuality is both everywhere and nowhere: everywhere, because it is taken for granted as the sexual norm, the centre against which other sexual options are obliged to define themselves, yet nowhere, because it is never required to identify itself, to acknowledge its particularity, to submit to the indignity of a label. Heterosexuality in media texts is only flushed into the open when it does not have the field to itself, when it is placed amid representations of other sexualities: in articles in lesbian and gay magazines, for example, or on Channel 4's parodic game show *Sticky Moments*, where the gay host Julian Clary found much comic mileage in mocking heterosexual lifestyles and dismissively summing up the inadequacies of his stooge by saying 'well, that's heterosexuals for you'. There the straight man truly was the straight man, but with the exception of such isolated examples heterosexuality remains serenely assured of its own centrality, luxuriating in its taken-for-grantedness.

Since heterosexual people almost never have to think of themselves **as** heterosexual, preferring instead to categorize themselves in terms of gender, ethnicity or age, it should come as no surprise that those critics who have begun to analyse the ways in which heterosexuality is culturally constructed are themselves lesbian or gay.[6] Those of us who live outside the mainstream find it much easier to see that although that mainstream may be dominant, it is certainly not universal, and that heterosexuality is not the sum total of human sexual experience. That knowledge enables us to turn some of the standard questions about media representation upside down and gain a usefully fresh perspective by doing so. An analytical model centred on the critique of stereotypes or the hunt for positive images might lament the absence of strong lesbian and gay characters in *Coronation Street*, for example, but if we reset our agenda and ask what that soap has to say about heterosexuality, such a question might yield unexpected answers and help to account for that soap's enduring popularity with non-heterosexual audiences, since the preponderance of happily single women and patently ludicrous married couples could be taken to suggest that *Coronation Street*'s representation of heterosexuality is not a particularly favourable one. It could be argued that my homosexuality inclines me towards making such a reading, and I wouldn't disagree with that accusation, but the point I want to underline here is that a heterosexual viewer's reading would be just as partial, just as slanted, just as rooted in his or her cultural identity, the only difference being that a heterosexual viewer would be far more reluctant to acknowledge this fact than I am. In much the same way that some men think questions of gender apply only to women, most heterosexuals think sexuality is something only non-heterosexuals have. Once they shed that misconception, heterosexuals' readings of heterosexual images will certainly prove fascinating.

## Trying to put yourself in the film situation in some way

The final issue I want to raise is perhaps the most amorphous of all, the ways in which media consumers belonging to sexual minorities might specifically interpret texts which appear to contain nothing but images of dominant heterosexuality. Lesbian and gay viewers are particularly skilled in reading texts against the grain, for the simple reason that we have only ever had a tiny number of texts offered to us that depicted versions of our own lives and experiences, and even then, as discussed earlier, those versions tend to cause controversy by imposing a false unity on our multiple diversities. Faced with a media world where heterosexuality reigns virtually unchallenged, queer audiences have rapidly learned the survival skills of refashioning heterosexual images to suit our own purposes, reworking them with an adroit subversiveness until they speak to our needs and desires.[7] Those skills were especially invaluable in earlier decades where recognizable lesbian and gay representations were impossible to find in mainstream texts, forcing those in search of such images to resort to the more private realms of fantasy: a survey of Britain's film audiences in the 1940s included the revelation of one schoolboy that 'My film idol is Errol Flynn and I fell madly in love with him after seeing *Dawn Patrol.* I think about him at nights, pretend I am with him and dream about him. I have never felt about a film actress in this way' (Mayer 1948: 49), while an interview with lesbian film fans who grew up having to negotiate their way through the relentlessly heterosexual regime of Hollywood contained this evocative recollection of

> trying to put yourself in the film situation in some way. . . At times I'd identify with a character. Other times I'd float outside the situation, sort of watching the effect this attractive woman was having on me. I'd imagine Katharine Hepburn and Spencer Tracy together, or sometimes I'd be Katharine Hepburn. And I might be sort of behind Spencer Tracy but I wouldn't **be** Spencer Tracy. I felt a tug of war with that (Whitaker 1985: 109).

Those kinds of subversive reappropriations continue even today (plenty of schoolboys dream of Brad Pitt and many young lesbians want to place themselves somewhere near Catherine Zeta Jones), and they are feasible because the sexuality of an image can never be fully secured by those that produce it – the pin-up in *Smash Hits* or the bodies in *Baywatch* may be primarily intended for heterosexual consumption, but there are no stickers on the posters or warnings on the television screen saying 'lesbians and gays keep out'. I began this chapter by stressing the fluidity and instability of sexuality, those factors which can frustratingly make its representation so hard to track and trace, so resistant to definitive summarizing, but those qualities don't just lead to frustration, they can also invite, enable and empower, opening up multitudinous possibilities for text–audience relationships that are subtle, creative and politically dynamic.

## Questions

1 Monitor a range of television programmes and note where and how representations of lesbians and/or gay men appear. Are there any characteristics in common across those representations, whatever kind of programme they appeared in, or do different types of television text treat sexual minorities differently?

2 How would you identify a stereotype of a lesbian or gay man in a film, television programme, newspaper or magazine? What codes, clues and conventions are used to establish the stereotype? What responses is it supposed to produce in its target audience? What responses does it produce in you?

3 Look at one of the magazines produced for lesbian and gay readers (*Gay Times, Attitude, Diva* and – if you live there – *Gay Scotland* are the most widely available). If you have never seen one before, does it conform to your expectations of what such a magazine might or should include? Would it be feasible to publish a magazine which addressed readers on the basis of their shared *heterosexuality* (possible title: *Het Gazette*), and if so what issues and features should it cover?

## Notes

1 The amount of literature covering the questions raised in this paragraph is intimidatingly vast, but here are some good starting points. On the diversity of lesbian and gay identities and lifestyles, see Ainley (1995), National Lesbian and Gay Survey (1992) and Plummer (1992). For bisexuality see Rose *et al.* (1996), for transgender see Prosser (1997) and Stone (1991). For the controversies surrounding the term 'queer', see Smyth (1992) and Warner (1993).
2 Excellent historical surveys detailing lesbian and gay representations in mainstream film and television are Howes (1993), Russo (1987) and Weiss (1992).
3 For a more extensive critique of positive images, see Medhurst (1994).

4   Walter (1980) both reprints many of the original *Come Together* articles and provides a perceptive overview of the historical and political contexts surrounding the magazine's formation, ambitions and demise.
5   Conflicting evaluations of *Out* can be found in Hamer and Ashbrook (1994), Richardson (1995), and Spry (1991).
6   See the chapter 'Straight acting' in Dyer (1993) and the essays in Wilkinson and Kitzinger (1993).
7   More detailed accounts of such subcultural re-readings can be found in Medhurst (1991), the chapter 'A queer feeling when I look at you' in Weiss (1992), and Whitaker (1985).

# References

Dyer, R. (1993) *The Matter Of Images: Essays on Representation*, London: Routledge.

Gambaccini, P. (1996) *Love Letters*, London: Michael O'Mara.

Gross, L. (1991) 'Out of the mainstream: Sexual minorities and the mass media', in E. Seiter *et al.* (eds) *Remote Control: Television, Audiences and Cultural Power*, London: Routledge.

Mayer, J. P. (1948) *British Cinemas and their Audiences*, London: Dobson.

Power, L. (1995) *No Bath But Plenty Of Bubbles: An Oral History of the Gay Liberation Front 1970–73*, London: Cassell.

Smyth, C. (1992) *Lesbians Talk Queer Notions*, London: Scarlet Press.

Spry, C. (1991) 'Out of the box', in T. Kaufmann and P. Lincoln (eds) *High Risk Lines*, Bridpoint: Prism.

Whitaker, C. (1985) 'Hollywood transformed: interviews with lesbian viewers', in P. Steven (ed.) *Jump Cut: Hollywood, Politics and Counter-Cinema*, Toronto: Between The Lines.

# Further reading

Ainley, R. (1995) *What Is She Like? Lesbian Identities from the 1950s to the 1990s*, London: Cassell. A series of interviews that builds up a fascinating and varied picture of lesbian lives in the 1990s.

Bad Object-Choices Collective (ed.) (1991) *How Do I Look? Queer Film and Video*, Seattle, WA: Bay Press. One of the first collections of analytical essays that adopted a self-consciously 'queer' perspective. Discusses mainly independent and non-mainstream texts.

Collis, R. (1994) 'Screened out: lesbians and television', in L. Gibbs (ed.) *Daring To Dissent: Lesbian Culture From Margin To Mainstream*, London: Cassell. A brief but perceptive overview of how lesbians have been represented in mainstream British and American television.

Doty, A. (1993) *Making Things Perfectly Queer: Interpreting Mass Culture*, Minneapolis: University of Minnesota Press. Analyses American popular culture (including TV comedy and Hollywood cinema) from a queer perspective.

Dyer, R. (1991) *Now You See It: Studies on Lesbian and Gay Film*, London: Routledge. A critical history of films made by and for lesbians and gays.

Dyer, R. (1993) *The Matter Of Images: Essays on Representation*, London: Routledge. Accessible and important, a collection of essays from the most influential of British gay film and media scholars.

Florence, P. (1993) 'Lesbian cinema, women's cinema', in G. Griffin (ed.) *Outwrite: Lesbianism and Popular Culture*, London: Pluto. A good introduction to the study and analysis of lesbian representation in film.

Gross, L. (1991) 'Out of the mainstream: Sexual minorities and the mass media', in E. Seiter *et al.* (eds) *Remote Control: Television, Audiences and Cultural Power*, London: Routledge. An influential article that clearly maps out many of the most important issues related to the relationships between sexual minority audiences and media texts.

Hamer, D. and Ashbrook, P. (1994) 'OUT: Reflections on British television's first lesbian and gay magazine series', in D. Hamer and B. Budge (eds) *The Good, The Bad and The Gorgeous: Popular Culture's Romance with Lesbianism*, London: Pandora. An interesting account of the successes and problems associated with the development of 'Out'.

Howes, K. (1993) *Broadcasting It: An Encyclopaedia of Homosexuality on Film, Radio and TV in the U.K. 1923–1993*, London: Cassell. Lively, revealing, witty and sharp, this is a dictionary of homosexual characters, texts and themes in the British media. An invaluable reference book, but much more fun that that sounds.

Medhurst, A. (1991) 'Batman, deviance and camp', in R. Pearson and W. Urricchio (eds) *The Many Lives of the Batman*, London: British Film Institute. Uses the case study of Batman to explore how gay audiences might make their own particular readings of mainstream media images.

Medhurst, A. (1994) 'One queen and his screen: lesbian and gay television', in E. Healy and A. Mason (eds) *Stonewall 25: The Making of the Lesbian and Gay Community in Britain*, London: Virago. Partly an autobiographical account of growing up gay but watching very straight television; partly a (very) potted history of queers on British TV; partly a critique of the idea of 'positive images'.

National Lesbian and Gay Survey (1993) *Proust, Michelangelo, Marc Almond and Me*, London: Routledge. Autobiographical accounts from young gay men about how they dealt with their sexuality in a homophobic environment.

Plummer, K. (ed.) (1992) *Modern Homosexualities: Fragments of Lesbian and Gay Experience*, London: Routledge. Academic essays that address the huge diversity of contemporary sexual minority lives and lifestyles. An invaluable corrective to any notions of a unified 'lesbian' or 'gay' identity.

Prosser, J. (1997) 'Transgender', in A. Medhurst and S. Munt (eds) *Lesbian and Gay Studies: A Critical Introduction*, London: Cassell. An excellent introductory overview of the issues around transgendered identities and representations.

Richardson, C. (1995) 'TVOD: The never-bending story', in P. Burston and C. Richardson (eds) *A Queer Romance: Lesbians, Gay Men and Popular Culture*, London: Routledge. A more sceptical account of 'Out' than that given by Hamer and Ashbrook (see above).

Rose, S. *et al.* (eds) (1996) *Bisexual Horizons: Politics, Histories, Lives*, London: Lawrence and Wishart. A comprehensive collection that introduces a range of bisexual voices and viewpoints into discussions about sexual identity.

Russo, V. (1987) *The Celluloid Closet*, New York: Harper and Row. The first (and although now dated, still the best) history of homosexualities in Hollywood cinema.

Stone, S. (1991) 'The empire strikes back: a posttranssexual manifesto', in J. Epstein and K. Straub (eds) *Body Guards: The Cultural Politics of Gender Ambiguity*, London: Routledge. A polemical account of transgender politics, drawing heavily on contemporary critical theory.

Walter, A. (ed.) (1980) *Come Together: The Years of Gay Liberation 1970–73*, London: Gay Men's Press. An invaluable anthology of the material first published during the early 1970s in the Gay Liberation Front journal, *Come Together.*

Warner, M. (ed.) (1993) *Fear Of A Queer Planet: Queer Politics and Social Theory*, Minneapolis: University of Minnesota Press. A good starting point for unravelling the complex theoretical and political issues raised by the use of the term 'queer' by 1990s sexual minority activists and thinkers.

Weiss, A. (1992) *Vampires And Violets: Lesbians in the Cinema*, London: Cape. A detailed and comprehensive history of lesbian representation in Hollywood and European cinema.

Whitaker, C. (1985) 'Hollywood transformed: interviews with lesbian viewers', in P. Steven (ed.) *Jump Cut: Hollywood, Politics and Counter-Cinema*, Toronto: Between The Lines. A revealing, funny and often moving account of how lesbian audiences managed to find their own ways of understanding and interpreting Hollywood films.

Wilkinson, S. and Kitzinger, C. (eds) (1993) *Heterosexuality*, London: Sage. A pioneering attempt to place heterosexual sexual identities under an analytical microscope.

Wilton, T. (ed.) (1995) *Immortal Invisible: Lesbians and the Moving Image*, London: Routledge. Innovative and enlightening, a collection of film analyses from leading lesbian critics and theorists.

# Chapter 23

# Gender

FROM BRITNEY SPEARS TO ERASMUS: WOMEN, MEN AND REPRESENTATION

**IRENE COSTERA MEIJER AND LIESBET VAN ZOONEN**

In this chapter we will examine the representation of women and men, show the asymmetry of the social relations of looking and discuss whether and how they are changing in contemporary (youth) culture. We will illustrate our arguments with those media and images which we do not consciously seek to use and consume, but which we inevitably do run into in the course of an ordinary day: outdoor advertising, magazine covers, music video's, news, sports television and popular series.

It is eight o'clock on a cold winter morning. I am waiting for the bus to the city-centre, hardly awake and shivering. The bus stop is lit by a huge billboard just behind me. On it is Jennifer Lopez, one of the biggest stars of contemporary pop music, throwing a defiant glance at me and flaunting her luscious body and beautiful hair for the international cosmetics firm L'Oreal. Thanks to L'Oreal's policy to distribute its posters freely among fans, the poster is still there, undamaged. Next to me, unaware of Jennifer's overwhelming presence, an old man is leaning on the billboard, his head resting against her shapely buttocks. A young man comes along and catches the picture of the old man in a paradisal position. He winks at me, as if we both would see a common meaning in this scene. I start to feel uncomfortable. It is a bit much for the early morning: the obtrusive presence of the Latin star Lopez and her impeccably made-up face and body, the conspiratorial invitation of the young man to share in the voyeuristic irony created by the picture in the bus stop. Fortunately the bus arrives in time.

Huge, well-lit billboards in well-protected thick glass frames have become a very fashionable advertising outlet in the city of Amsterdam, where we live and work. They are exploited by a private company which has a contractual obligation to their customers to repair or replace a damaged billboard within 24 hours, thus ensuring Amsterdam citizens of a continuous, perfect and inescapable flow of advertising images. Women, as the ultimate symbols in advertising and other forms of consumer culture figure prominently on these billboards. In the course of one bus ride to work, we not only meet L'Oreal's Jennifer Lopez, but also L'Oreal's beautiful and ageless actress Heather Locklear (from *Dynasty* to *Melrose Place*) and more anonymous but just as stunning and inviting women who put their bodies on display to promote certain kinds of products like bras, underwear, perfumes, cars, candy bars, ice cream, beer, chewing gum and so on. The intimate parts of women's bodies have thus become inescapably public in the symbolic city landscape of Amsterdam. Men also figure on these billboards, but less frequently. Although we do see their nude bodies often enough, their private parts are never as obtrusively pushed in our faces as those of Jennifer Lopez, Heather Locklear and their anonymous clones. The billboard campaigns hardly ever last longer than a week, making it impossible to get used to them and thus become able to ignore them. An incessant stream of continuously but only superficially changing images of women and some men forces itself on the ordinary person with no escape.

The ever-increasing ubiquity of visual images in our daily lives, of which these billboards are the latest exponents, keeps the issue of the representation of women and men high on feminist and scholarly agendas (e.g. Dines and Humez, 1995; Geraghty, 1996; Van Zoonen 1994). In this chapter we will examine the representation of women and men more closely, show the asymmetry of the social relations of looking and discuss whether and how they are changing in contemporary youth culture. We will illustrate our arguments with those media and images which we do not consciously seek to use and consume, but which we inevitably do run into in the course of an ordinary working day. Before we continue on our way to work, however, let us first consider some aspects of representation in greater detail.

## Representation and the reflection of reality

Looking at Jennifer Lopez we may only see a picture of a world-famous Latin singer/ actress: an artificially produced reflection of a great, but equally artificially produced body. In fact, that is how media representations are often looked upon: as a distorted reflection of a certain aspect of reality. Many research projects on women in the media, especially those carried out in the social sciences, claim that their images are not very realistic or 'not representative of women's position in our highly differentiated and complex society' (Cantor 1978: 30). It is indeed easy to see that real women are much different and more diverse than their representations in the media seem to suggest. If media images would indeed be a reflection of reality, women would be relatively rare in most parts of the real world yet overwhelmingly present in other areas, whereas black, older, disabled, lesbian, fat, poor or Third World women would be virtually non-existent. Men, on the other hand, seem to be abundantly visible on the front pages of newspapers or the screens of sports channels (Carter *et al.* 1998). One look at the front pages of a Dutch leading sports weekly (*Sportweek*), for instance, reveals that men feature on the cover of 48 out of 51 issues, hiding the bleak reality of their deeply humiliating loss in the European Football championship and ignoring the enormous contribution of women to Dutch sport, for instance in their golden achievements at the Olympics of 2000. (*Sportweek*, No. 51, December 2000).

Whereas both the images of women and men do not reflect reality very accurately then, Goffman (1979) in his classic study on gender advertisements, suggests that nevertheless for most people images of men seem to have a closer link with 'reality' than images of women. In addition to the fact that many images of men occur in the context of 'realistic' genres such as news and current affairs, male models have a certain amount of credibility that is lacking in images of female models. Goffman claims that when we see a man in an advertisement wearing a business suit and carrying a briefcase we believe that he is seriously representing a business man; if the same man is seen wearing shorts and carrying a racquet we believe, likewise, that he is representing the same man playing tennis. Yet, according to Goffman, when we see a woman wearing business or sports clothes it is as if we are watching a model play-acting at a perpetual costume ball trying on different things, instead of someone whose clothes indicate a real and serious person. In fact, an unpublished study conducted by Meijer in 1999 suggests that what people deem realistic for women is that of the young and attractive advertising model. Meijer's survey of 120 women and men exposed to two similar billboards – one showing a young semi-nude female model, the other one showing a young semi-nude male model – revealed that both women and men considered the female model to be represented in a realistic way, whereas the male model was thought to be portrayed in an unrealistic manner. What is *considered* 'realistic' and what is not, therefore, does not seem dependent on the qualities of the bodies or the picture itself – both pictures were in black and white documentary style, and represented relatively realistically beautiful bodies. We're simply more used to representations of women as objects, therefor they seem more realistic to us. At stake are as much our cultural understandings of what the female and male body can be used for, and what their representations mean. This brings us to the second dimension of representation; as an expression of cultural values.

## Representation and cultural values

Let's return to the Lopez picture. Reflection is not the only issue when looking at it. One may not immediately think of the connection between her beautiful body and shiny brown hair and those of earlier female icons of Western societies like Elizabeth Taylor, Romy Schneider, Audrey Hepburn and Joan Collins. Until recently, Jennifer Lopez's Latin background might have prevented her to stand as a general symbol for all women (Shohat and Stam 1994). The billboard's implicit reference to other images and texts of women, however, is a form of what is usually called 'intertextuality', i.e. a more or less explicit relation between different texts. Thus, following an argument made by Fiske (1987: 108), the billboard's 'intertextuality' refers rather to our culture's image bank of the sophisticated star who plays with men's desire for her and turns it into her advantage. Thus, how Lopez's real body and persona are reflected is not what is primarily at stake in her representation; it is the reflection of a common cultural understanding of dark-haired femininity that produces the *signifying* potential, the range of possible meanings, of her image. Many feminist studies of the images of women, especially those from the humanities, have examined how images of women are used to convey meaning to gender and other values. Although these studies differ widely from each other, one inescapable conclusion of this work is that women are usually related to (hetero)sexuality, nature and tradition (Coward 1982).

Colour makes many kinds of differences to the meanings of female bodies. Whereas fair-haired women (think of Brigitte Bardot, Marilyn Monroe, Doris Day, Pamela

Anderson and even Britney Spears) are used and perceived to express innocent female sensuality, dark-haired white women like Elizabeth Taylor, Katharine Hepburn, or Audrey Hepburn tend to be associated more with sophistication, style and sexuality. Similarly, white women are constructed as symbols of virtue and prudity, in contrast with the knowledgeable and sexually active allure of black and Latin women (Shohat and Stam 1994; Costera Meijer 2001). Masculinity, on the other hand, might understate differences in colour. White and black men alike are connected to muscularity. This is apparent in the male sports subculture, where size and strength are valued by men across racial and even class boundaries (Katz 1995: 139). Many advertisers use images of physically rugged or muscular male bodies to masculinize products and services geared to elite male consumers (Wernick 1991). The powerful male body is at one time a metaphor for the financial security offered by an insurance firm, at others for powerful cars. Violence is another vital part of the construction of masculinity. Katz stresses that violence on-screen, like that in real life, is perpetrated overwhelmingly by males. Males constitute the majority of the audience for violent films, as well as violent sports such as football and hockey. What is being sold, however, is not just 'violence' but rather a glamorized form of masculinity (Katz 1995: 140).

Race has also been seen to be an issue in depicting males. It has been argued that black men seem to be much more 'on display' than white men. Kobena Mercer and Isaac Julien (1988) compared the aesthetic presentation of black nude bodies in the work of the famous photographer Robert Mapplethorpe with the generic codes that govern the presentation of the conventional subject of the nude: the (white) woman.

> Mapplethorpe appropriates elements of commonplace racial stereotypes to prop-up, regulate, organise and *fix* the aesthetic reduction of the black man's flesh to a visual surface charged and burdened with the task of servicing a white male desire to look, – more importantly, assert mastery and power over the looked-at (Mercer and Isaac: 1988: 145).

The circulation of mass media images of black male bodies then, bears witness to a 'dominant 'colonial fantasy' in that there is distinct preference for a set of guises in which black males become visible: as sexualized and idolized 'others' in advertising, sports and pornography, much like female bodies are represented.

## Traditional ways of seeing

Both approaches to representation – as referring to a particular reality, or as referring to a culture's values – seem relevant for the analysis of visual images, but pose rather unresolvable issues. The main problem is the question of which or what kind of 'present' is actually *re*presented by media images. What does the Lopez billboard refer to: a particular Latin woman or a general western understanding of femininity (cf. Geraghty 1996: 267)? In thinking through and debating such issues, we will inevitably end up making assumptions or claims about the way audiences will interpret representations. Meaning, as so many authors have asserted by now, does not reside in images but arises from the interaction between images and audiences, producing a variety of 'texts' – i.e. the various interpretations by audiences – in the process. Fiske (1987: 154) suggests audiences shift between two different interpretative strategies that can be considered as the far ends of a continuum: a realistic interpretation takes images as reflections of real persons or real situations and enables identification. Discursive interpretations however, consider images as the 'embodiment of social values . . . and discourage identification'. Which of these interpretative strategies will be activated depends, according to Fiske, on the particular social, cultural and ideological position of audiences. Taken this view to the extreme, representation in fact becomes a non-issue, because the ultimate production of meaning is placed on the side of the audience, regardless of what is represented (cf. Hermes, Chapter 20 in this volume). In our approach, however, we see texts as containing significant meanings by the way they invite audiences to make sense of them, by the way they 'speak' to audiences, in other words by their mode of address.

> I get off in the city centre and begin my five-minute walk to work right through the red light district and other more down market features of inner city life in Amsterdam. Women of all kinds, sitting barely dressed on pink satin cushions, scan me from behind their well-lit windows. Suddenly I recognize the representational similarity between the L'Oreal posters and the prostitutes. This makes me understand a bit more of the uneasiness caused by the scene at the bus stop earlier this morning. Lopez, Locklear and other advertising models in the billboards are framed just like the prostitutes in the windows I am passing. They all seem to display availability. There is, however, an important difference in their respective attitudes: the prostitutes actively seek out who to 'address', unlike the L'Oreals in their equally well-lit frames who passively interpellate anyone, regardless of their posture or gender. The billboards seem to mean something for both women and men. But what?

In a classic and often-quoted work, *Ways of Seeing,* Berger (1972: 42) notes:

> Men act and women appear. Men look at women. Women watch themselves being looked at. This determines not only most relations between men and women but also the relation of women to themselves. The surveyor of woman in herself is male: the surveyed female. Thus she turns herself into an object – and most particularly an object of vision: a sight.

Barthel (1988) argued that men create a sense of identity by extending out from their body, using its and their evident *power* to control objects and others. This we see clearly in advertisements for cigarettes, alcohol, stereos, and, especially, cars. Women, by contrast, work with and within the body. The female body communicates not the woman's power over others, but her *presence,* how she takes herself (Berger 1972: 45–6). Berger positions both women and men as male heterosexual spectators of the female sight. Applying this logic, Kurtz (1986) goes so far as to argue that practically all advertising is on behalf of the masculine image, either showing him what kind of status he can hope to attain, or showing a woman what kind of man she can hope to attract. The problem is that the codes of possession still work when men are invited to look at other men in e.g. car commercials or perfume ads. This can threaten men's (hetero)sexual identity: they may *want* the (male) image. To foreclose this possibility, Costera Meijer (1993) noted that in more than half of the Dutch advertisements for perfumes aimed at male consumers, the threat of homosexual associations was countered by including a woman in the photograph.

The L'Oreal billboards and similar images of women invite us to look at them with a prospective male viewer in mind. The display of women for the pleasure of men has a long-standing tradition in Western patriarchal culture. Pornography is the most obvious expression of the use of women's bodies as objects of desire and fantasy. In advertising, cinema and other popular genres, similar textual strategies construct women's bodies as objects to look at and desire (Mulvey 1975). The codes of porn have been easily transferred to mainstream culture: the direct and inviting look at the camera indicates willingness and readiness to submit to the male consumer. The fragmentation of the female body into close-ups of breasts and buttocks reduces women to depersonalized body parts; particular camera angles construct women as powerless and submissive (Coward 1982). Despite the increasing usage of male nudes in a variety of genres there is no such widespread tradition for the male body (Craig 1992). Even in gay male pornography, the object of desire displays as much the will to conquer as to be conquered. Richard Dyer (1992) observed that the masculinity of male subjects might be undermined when they are the objects of the gaze, therefore numerous supplementary codes and conventions feature in gay porn and the male pin-up genre – such as the taut rigid and straining body pose; clothing details; narrative plot – in order to stabilize the gendered organization of the look.

Femininity is thus usually encoded as passive (to be, to appear); masculinity as active (to have, to possess) (Barthel 1988). This system, of course, is not watertight: It 'leaks' so to speak, and it does so in at least three ways:

- Women are active in their ways of looking at women.
- Women are active in their ways of looking at men.
- Women construct themselves as objects as well as subjects in the relations of looking.

> I stop at the news-stand and buy a couple of magazines. Women look at me from the covers of almost all the magazines, regardless of their readership. The cover of *Playboy* hardly seems to differ from the cover of *Cosmopolitan*: yet I don't think of buying *Playboy* whereas I do consider *Cosmo*. It would give a very strange impression if I were to walk away with *Playboy* instead of *Cosmo*, given the temporary public identity one takes on by buying a magazine. Most 'cover-boys' I see are well-known politicians or other male public officials, who obviously are on display not because their bodies matter. Even when football players are on the cover, it's not their beautiful bodies that count, but their power and their representation of more abstract values. Some men's magazines put more anonymous figures on the cover, but their anonymity doesn't seem to obstruct their radiation of individuality, power, success and control. On closer examination I also discover a couple of body building magazines in which male bodies do figure as object of the look, but it doesn't resemble the depiction of women's bodies at all, or does it?

## Women looking at women

All texts can be interpreted in a variety of ways: they offer dominant cultural interpretations as well as possibilities to read against the grain (Evans and Gamman 1995). Feminist and cultural studies suggest that the objectification central to the dominant male spectator position is hardly relevant in the oppositional meanings dug up by female audiences. On the contrary, it is the pleasure evoked by the particular subjectivity of both female and male characters on display and the relations between them that distinguish the oppositional female spectator position. Watching, for instance, a replay of an old movie like *Gentlemen Prefer Blondes* (1953), it is immediately clear how the female stars Marilyn Monroe and Jane Russell are framed as objects of male desire (which for that matter was also their public image) and the narrative is driven by their quest for heterosexual romance. Two feminist authors have pointed out that underneath this dominant patriarchal meaning, there is a story of resistance to male objectification and female love and friendship (Arbuthnot and Seneca 1982). Monroe and Russell never let themselves be looked at passively, they always return the gaze of men defyingly. In their dress and stature they resist objectification which is furthermore prevented by particular camera angles and lighting. We hardly ever see them filmed from the side which would emphasize their body contours. The narrative could also be read as a story of female friendship instead of heterosexual romance: when Monroe and Russell have finally succeeded in finding a husband, in the final double wedding scene they look at each other as much as at their husbands suggesting the equal importance of their relationship with each other. Other authors have found similar alternative reading possibilities in other media texts. Lewis and Rolley (1996) observed, for instance, that girls and women consume fashion images much like boys read biking or computer magazines. Like shopping together and experimenting with hair, dress and make-up, reading magazines plays an important part in female bonding. As a group activity, such reading resembles the erotic pleasures boys obtain from consuming porn. The common ground in all such analyses is the attempt to reveal the female pleasures evoked by popular genres and 'to hear the strong feminine resisting voices even within mainstream cultural artefacts' (Byars 1991: 20, see also Brunsdon 1986, 2000; Doane 1982; Johnson 1993; Kuhn 1982; Stacey 1987; White 1991).

## Women looking at men

Historically, mainstream culture has always provided possibilities for women to look at men, be it not in a very public way. The music and soccer stars that cover girls' bedrooms are enjoyed in their private space. In melodrama and soap operas that are watched inside the home it had also not been uncommon to see the male body constructed as an object of the female gaze. Their bodies, however, are hardly ever simply objectified and presented as desirable in themselves, but they usually figure in a romantic instead of a sexual narrative. Even the way male bodies are displayed in magazines aimed at women like *Playgirl* supports fantasies of romance rather than of female heterosexual desire (Ang 1983). The models look at us as if we are close friends; the aesthetic photography draws attention to the constructedness of the image rather than suggesting the representation of an available and submissive willing men as in male pornography; and finally accompanying texts focuses on personalities rather than on sizes thus preventing objectification. This strategy seems to be following women's wishes. Porn magazines for women such as *For Women* and *Women Only*, (founded in 1992 and 1993 respectively) created eroticized images of men specifically for women to consume. Yet, even in the 1990s, their founding editor Isabel Koprowski says that women do want to see:

> The Chippendale type, very muscular, oiled bodies. They also want to see men who look as though they've got personality: men who perhaps aren't as well 'developed: and they want, you know, dark men, fair men, red-headed men – all kinds of men. The thing that really impressed me was that for a men's magazine you could fill it with busty blondes and with very little editorial and men would buy it. You cannot do that with women (Evans and Gamman, 1995: 31).

The appeal of a variety of male television stars also seems to be located in the convergence of physical, personal, romantic and narrative qualities. The eponymous British detective *Inspector Morse*, running in the late 1980s and early 1990s and repeated regularly since, appears a source of pleasure for many men and women because of his passionate pursuit of justice, his narrative position of complete control and his nurturing and caring qualities. By representing Morse as a hero who is both ideal mother and ideal father the series secures a large (female) audience. Unlike other male detectives, emotion and intuition rather than intellect and deduction are Morse's trademark (Thomas 1995). On top of that, Morse remains, because of his lack of a steady relationship, the ideal lover, 'always more involved than the women in question, and not afraid to admit it'. King (1990) built much the same argument to account for the popularity of an earlier American police hero Sonny Crockett (Don Johnson) of *Miami Vice*. Nowadays, *The X Files'* agent Mulder (David Duchovny) not only exhibits the hard-boiled masculine qualities expected of a tough special agent but also is presented with qualities usually reserved for women on TV: physical attractiveness and a caring and sensitive nature. Visual and narrative codes in *The X Files* construct Mulder as predominantly 'feminine'. Unlike the fierce criticism many men expressed at *Miami Vice*, the overwhelming praise of *The X Files* uttered by female and male fans alike can be interpreted as the successful overcoming of the fear of the 'effeminate' man. Like women, more and more men seem to be able to cope with the pleasures of an attractive, romantic and caring male sight (Mort 1988).

## Objects and subjects of looking

Certainly, in contemporary girl culture images of men function as objects of desire. (de Bruin 1999; Moore 1988, 1991). Football teams, for instance, deliver a continuous stream of young male sex symbols like David Beckham and Michael Owen that cover many a girl's bedroom. Also, the overwhelming popularity of bands like The Backstreet Boys, Five, 'n Sync and Westlife, which contain a deliberately constructed variety of male sexualities embodied in the band members, suggest that men can be an object of the gaze and girls are perfectly capable of voyeurism.[1] As never before, young girls are more likely to participate in an active, even violent, role (cf. Hartley 1999). In music videos of the Backstreet Boys, one of the member's girlfriends takes revenge for him not being faithful to her by trying to kill all the group members. Another example is the ironic play with gender in a video clip from Boyband 'n Sync, where the guys were presented as small Barbie-dolls in a toy store, trying desperately to get some attention from a – much larger – female customer. Just as interesting is the exploitation of young girls' ambiguous sense of sexuality and subjectivity. World-famous teenage singer Britney Spears sang at one time: 'sometimes I run, sometimes I hide, sometimes I'm scared of you, but all I really want is to hold you tight, treat you right, be with you day and night, baby all I need is time' ('Sometimes' 1999). Three music videos later she appeared in a rubber outfit and sang: 'oops, I did it again, I played with your heart, got lost in the game, oops you think I'm in love, that I'm send from above, I'm not that innocent' ('Oops! I did it again' 2000). Her girlish ambival-ent relation to innocence and sexuality, however much reserved for fair-haired women these days, has been understated by a notorious and much-discussed photograph of a naked Britney posing in the middle of a heap of teddy bears.

The organization of the look in the younger segment of the market also seems to cross the traditional gender lines. Advertisements for perfumes, traditionally directed at separate audiences, are focusing on both boys and girls. Fashion statements in magazines like *Arena*, *The Face*, transcend gender and cause so-called 'gender trouble' (Butler 1990). Sometimes it is impossible to detect whether a model is male or female. Is it time to distance ourselves from Berger's clichés? Is it time to make space for new relations of looking?

> One of my students graduates this afternoon and I have to deliver a speech for her. The Graduation Hall, a former chapel of more than three centuries old, is filled with family, friends and fellow-students. On the walls, almost right under the ceiling, there are rows of eighteenth-century oil paintings of famous academics whose pictures have been painted a long time ago to honour them as benefactors and deans of the university. They look very much alike and I have some difficulty to keep them apart; the classic pictures seem interchangeable. The aura of power, authority and learnedness that is with all of them reminds me in a way of the also very interchangeable public officials on the cover of the magazines in the news-stand. I ask the graduation audience to look up to these men and realize that they are not so much there for their own persons but to symbolize the academy and to confer on us the appropriate awe and respect. The family and friends too, I think, have had to pass the red light district to get to the ceremony, but I wonder whether they realize the striking differences and resemblances between male and female symbols. It is not such a long way from the women of L'Oreal and teenage idol Britney Spears to ancient Desiderius Erasmus.

## Conclusion

Summarizing our analysis, we conclude that the representation of gender in main-stream culture is profoundly asymmetrical. This asymmetry appears in various dimensions of representation. If we think, first, of representations as a reflection of real persons, Goffman (1979) argues that pictures of men have a closer link to reality than pictures of women: they occur more often in non-fictional genres like news and current affairs and – as Goffman claims – their images in advertising have a more direct reference to reality than images of women. Behind the pictures of men audiences will imagine real persons, says Goffman, whereas behind the pictures of women, audiences will see models pretending to be real persons. The 'realistic' qualities of images of men, however, do not preclude a second, symbolic dimension in their representation. As the portrait gallery in our Graduation Hall revealed, pictures of men may also refer to more abstract cultural values such as power, rationality, wisdom and learnedness. Such so-called iconic features are not reserved to old paintings but are part of contemporary images of men as public officials as well; the pictures of world leaders meeting each other in the news or facing us from magazine covers are partly as interchangeable as the paintings on the wall. But the iconic elements of the representation of men are again different from the iconic qualities in the representation of women. It's not so much that male icons can be seen to refer to actual social positions of men, whereas female icons mainly refer to social fantasies about women – for power and its associated values are both male and female options nowadays. Still, a picture of a fully clothed businessman still *looks* more real than one of a naked model. The L'Oreal women of this world and their historic, contemporary and future counterparts imply a fantasy of global femininity which is characterized by sexuality and seductiveness, a status as available object presented as personal choice ('because I'm worth it'). This referential difference between male and female icons has consequences for the mode of address – a third element of representation – too: the public official positions audiences at a distance and invites respect and admiration; the sexy L'Oreal women welcome closeness and invite desire for male audiences (to have) and identification or envy (to be) for female audiences. Although some representations of men and women, especially those currently fashionable in advertising and fashion magazines, try to subvert this pattern by inviting more fluid gender-identifications, asymmetrical gender patterns occur here too. The way that female spectators are positioned by pictures of the male body is characterized by personification and subjectivity, as opposed to the objectification invited by the female body on display; the fantasy evoked by the male pin-up is often one of romance rather than of sex, as with the female pin-up.

Mainstream gender culture as expressed in representation, however, is continuously contested and undermined, by textual characteristics and audience activities alike. It is in the nature of texts to offer multiple meanings and even the ostentatious traditional images of the L'Oreal women are seen to invite oppositional readings, for instance by 16-year-olds who recognize and try to withstand the values being sold to them, or by lesbian women who lust after them. Whereas gender representation is a powerful and unavoidable part of mainstream culture that we can hardly escape, its effectiveness is contested.

> It is running late and I decide to go home. On my way out of the office I pick up my mail hoping to read it on the bus. But it is rush hour and the bus is crowded. I try to find a place to stand comfortably and see space next to the driver. A sign says it is prohibited to stand there. I decide to ignore it and move to the free space . . . nothing happens; the driver doesn't seem to mind. I wonder whether all the gender images and signs we see on a day-to-day basis may function in similar way. When we decide to ignore them and move into the free space, what would happen?

## Questions

1 This chapter mentions two approaches to representation. Which two are they and how are they related to realistic and discursive reading strategies?

2 How does the representation of gender in various expressions of contemporary youth and consumer culture seem to differ from traditional gender portrayals?

3 Which representational strategies are often used to construct the female and the male body as objects of the gaze? Which differential modes of address are the results?

## Note

1 Thanks to Joyce Heisen for sharing her knowledge on music videos with us.

## References

Ang, I. (1983) 'Mannen op zicht: Marges van het vrouwelijk voyeurisme', *Tijdschrift voor vrouwenstudies* 4(3): 418–35.

Arbuthnot, L. and Seneca, G. (1982) 'Pretext and text in *Gentlemen Prefer Blondes, Film Reader 5*', reprinted in P. Erends (ed.) *Issues in Film Criticism*, Bloomington: Indiana University Press, pp 112–26.

Barthel, D. (1988) *Putting on Appearances. Gender and Advertising*, Philadelphia, PA: Temple University Press.

Berger, J. (1972) *Ways of Seeing*, London: Penguin Books.

Bruin, J. de (1999), *De spanning van seksualiteit. Plezier en gevaar in jongerenbladen*, Amsterdam: Het Spinhuis.

Brunsdon, C. (ed.) (1986) *Films for Women*, London: British Film Institute.

Brunsdon , C. (2000). *The Feminist, the Housewife and the Soap Opera*, London: Television Studies.

Butler, J. (1990) *Gender Trouble*, London: Routledge.

Byars, J. (1991) *All That Hollywood Allows. Re-reading Gender in 1950s Melodrama*, Chapel Hill, NC: University of North Carolina Press.

Cantor, M. (1978) 'Where are the women in public broadcasting?', in G. Tuchman (ed.) *Hearth and Home: Images of Women in the Media*, New York: Oxford University Press, pp. 78–90.

Carter, C., Branston, G. and Allen, S. (eds) (1998) *News, Gender and Power*, London: Routledge.

Costera Meijer, I. (1993) 'Seksualiteit in reclame. mannengeur en homo-erotiek', in A. Kaiser and L. van Zoonen (eds) *Blikvanger. Reclame: het spel van kijken en bekeken worden*, Amsterdam: Uitgeverij In de Knipscheer, pp. 69–91.

Costera Meijer, I. (1998) 'Advertising citizenship: an essay on the performative power of consumer culture', *Media, Culture and Society* 20(2): 235–50.

Costera Meijer, I. (2001) 'The colour of soap opera. An analysis of professional speech on the representation of ethnicity', *European Journal of Cultural Studies* 4 (2) (forthcoming).

Coward, R. (1982) 'Sexual violence and sexuality', *Feminist Review* 11 (Summer): 9–22.

Craig, S. (ed.) (1992) *Masculinity and the Media*, London: Sage.

Dines, G. and Humez, J. M. (1995) *Gender, Race and Class in Media. A Text-Reader*, Thousand Oaks, CA: Sage.

Doane, M. A. (1982) 'Film and the masquerade: Theorizing the female spectator', *Screen* 23(3–4): 74–87.

Dyer, R. (1992) *Only Entertainment*, London: Routledge.

Easthope, A. (1990) *What a Man's Gotta Do. The Masculine Myth in Popular Culture*, London: Routledge.

Evans, C. and Thornton, M. (1989) *Women and Fashion. A New Look*, London: Quartet Books.

Evans, C. and Gamman, L. (1995) 'The gaze revisited, or reviewing queer viewing', in P. Burston and C. Richardson (eds) *A Queer Romance. Lesbians, gay men and popular culture*, London: Routledge, pp. 13–57.

Fiske, J. (1987) *Television Culture*, London: Methuen.

Frankenberg, R. (1993) *White Women, Race Matters. The Social Construction of Whiteness*, Minneapolis: Routledge/University of Minnesota Press.

Geraghty, C. (1996) 'Representation and popular culture', in J. Curran and M. Gurevitch (eds) *Mass Media and Society*, 2nd edn, London: Arnold.

Goffman, E. (1979) *Gender Advertisements*, New York: Harper and Row.

Hartley, J. (1999) *Uses of Television*, London, New York: Routledge.

Johnson, B. (1993) 'Lesbian spectacles: Reading *Sula, Passing, Thelma and Louise*, and *The Accused*', in M. Garber, J. Matlock and R. L. Walkowitz (eds) *Media Spectacles*, New York: Routledge, pp. 160–66.

Katz, J. (1995) 'Advertising and the construction of violent white masculinity', in G. Dines and J. Humez (eds) *Gender, Race and Class in Media*, London: Sage.

King, S. B. (1990) '"Sonny's virtues": the gender negotiations of *Miami Vice*', *Screen* 31: 281–95.

Kuhn, A. (1982) *Women's Pictures. Feminism and the Cinema*, London: Pandora.

Kurtz, I. (1986) *Malespeak*, London: Jonathan Cape.

Lewis, R. and Rolley, K. (1996) 'Ad(dressing) the dyke: lesbian looks and lesbians looking', in P. Horne and R. Lewis (eds) *Outlooks. Lesbian and gay Sexualities and Visual Cultures*, London: Routledge, pp. 178–90.

Lury, C. (1996) *Consumer Culture*, Cambridge: Polity Press.

Mercer, K. and Julien, I. (1988) 'Race, sexual politics and black masculinity: a dossier', in R. Chapman and J. Rutherford (eds) *Male Order: Unwrapping Masculinity*, London: Lawrence and Wishart, pp. 97–164.

Moore, S. (1988) 'Here's looking at you, kid!', in L. Gamman and M. Marshment (eds) *The Female Gaze*, London: Women's Press, pp. 44–59.

Moore, S. (1991) *Looking for Trouble: On Shopping, Gender and the Cinema*, London: Serpent's Tail.

Mort, F. (1988) 'Boys own? Masculinity, style and popular culture', in R. Chapman and J. Rutherford (eds) *Male Order: Unwrapping Masculinity*, London: Lawrence and Wishart.

Mulvey, L. (1975) 'Visual pleasures and narrative cinema', *Screen*, 16(3): 6–18.

Shohat, E. and Stam, R. (1994) *Unthinking Eurocentrism. Multiculturalism and the media*, London: Routledge.

Stacey, J. (1987) 'Desperately seeking difference', *Screen* 28(1): 48–61.

Stacey, J. (1994) *Star Gazing. Hollywood cinema and female spectatorship*, London: Routledge.

Thomas, L. (1995) 'In love with Inspector Morse: feminist subculture and quality televison', *Feminist Review* 51 (Autumn): 1–25.

Wernick, A. (1991) *Promotional Culture. Advertising, ideology and symbolic expression*, London: Sage.

White, P. (1991) 'Female spectator, lesbian specter: *The Haunting*', in D. Fuss (ed.) *Inside/Out Lesbian Theories, Gay Theories*, London: Routledge.

Wolff, N. (1990) *The Beauty Myth*, London: Chatto and Windus.

Zoonen, L. van (1994) *Feminist Media Studies*, London: Sage.

## Further reading

The subject 'gender and media' is covered widely in libraries, bookshops and on the internet. This selection of texts is therefore extremely arbitrary.

Barker, C. (1999) *Television, Globalization and Cultural identities*, Buckingham: Open University Press. An introductory text that examines how race, nation, sex and gender are constructed and represented on television.

D'Acci, J. (1994) *Defining Women. Television and the Case of Cagney and Lacey*, Chapel Hill: The University of North Carolina Press. Construction of and struggle over femininity in and through an extremely popular police series of the 1980s.

McKinley, E. G. (1997) *Beverly Hills, 90210: Television, gender, and identity*. Philadelphia: University of Philadelphia Press. Audience study of young women's construction of identity through talk on one of the most popular North American teenage series of the 1990s.

Heide, M. J. (1995), *Television Culture and Women's Lives: Thirtysomething and the contradictions of gender*, Philadelphia: University of Pennsylvania Press. The book explores the complex relationship between gender conflicts played out in the scripts of the television show 'Thirtysomething' and the real-life conflicts experienced by 'baby-boomer' women viewers.

Hermes, J. (1995) *Reading Women's Magazines*, Cambridge: Polity. What does 'reading' popular magazines mean to women? A repertoire analysis.

Holtzman, L. (2000) *Media Messages: What film, television, and popular music teach us about race, class, gender and sexual orientation*, Armonk, NY: M.E. Sharpe. Popular introduction into the potential impact of media culture on peoples' views on race, class, gender and sexual orientation.

McCracken, E. (1993) *Decoding Women's Magazines. From Mademoiselle to Ms*, London: MacMillan. Everything you want to know about the production of women's magazines with special attention to covers and advertising.

Spigel, L. (ed.) (1992) *Private Screenings: Television and the female consumer*, Minneapolis: University of Minnesota Press. How has electronic media, particularly television culture, invaded the lives of women and shaped both male and female perceptions of society?

Tasker, Y. (1993) *Spectacular Bodies: Gender, genre and the Action Cinema*, London: Routledge. One of the first books to delve into questions of masculinity and the 'masculine' genres of the action cinema.

Woodward, K. (ed.) (1997) *Identity and Difference*, London: Sage. Textbook on the address of identity in media coverage.

# Web sites

www.bbc.co.uk/education/archive/fe/summary/sum20.shtml This compilation takes a critical look at television's images of women. It aims to provide a valuable resource for social studies and media courses. A historical look at how the images have changed gives insights into changes in society. The other sections deal with women's roles and again provide a commentary on social attitudes.

www.aber.ac.uk/media/Functions/plaudits.html A site with numerous topics, links and information about a variety of issues, including gender and ethnicity.

www.uiowa.edu/~commstud/resources/GenderMedia/ Resources for communication studies: 'gender, race and ethnicity in the media'.

www.cis.vt.edu/ws/wsmodules/MediaIndex.html Index to gender and media resources on the Web.

# Chapter 24

# Social class

IDENTIFYING CHARACTERISTICS OF CLASS IN MEDIA TEXTS

## JOANNE LACEY

Why is it important to think about the relationships between the media and class? How can class be theorized in relation to media production, media consumption and media representation? How might we go about analysing images of the middle classes, or indeed the upper classes? This chapter looks specifically at the connections between class and the politics of media representation. It provides an introductory exploration to the ways in which class has been defined in media and cultural theory, and applies class to the analysis of a number of contemporary media images.

## Introduction: class matters

The fact that a chapter on class has been commissioned for this edition of *The Media: An Introduction* (the first edition did not have one) marks a cycle of theoretical fashion. Class is now considered to be worth giving attention to once again. This would suggest that at particular historical moments class has not been given serious attention. In other words, media theorists did not consider class to be an important issue to discuss in relation to the analysis of media industries, media texts and media representations. The question of social class and media politics, practices and representations has an interesting history, coming in and out of focus alongside theoretical, political, social and cultural changes. In this chapter I will trace some of the reasons why class has come in and out of view at particular historical moments. I will look at the status of social class as a concept now, why it's important, and consider how class might be applied to an analysis of particular media texts. The chapter will of necessity provide a simplified overview of complicated debates. I hope that it will enable you to think about the importance of class in relation to the study of the media, particularly the politics of media representation.

According to Raymond Williams (1988), a key theorist on social class, the etymology of the word 'class' can be traced back to the late eighteenth, and early nineteenth centuries, where processes of industrialization led to the construction or demarcation of separate social classes, the capitalist class and the workers. Andrew Milner argues that 'the novelty in the later usage consists, not so much in the recognition of the simple fact of social inequality, for this had long been designated by other, older terms, rank and order, estate and degree – as in the new sense of its social constructedness' (1999: 8). Why is it important to explore the place of the media within changing constructions of social class? First, because the media plays a complex and critical role in the creation/maintenance/representation of social divisions? Second (and relatedly), because the media is ubiquitous. Roger Silverstone's recent contribution to the question, 'why study the media?' places at the centre of his analysis the involvement of the media in every aspect of our daily lives. 'The media are an essential dimension of contemporary experience. We cannot evade media presence, media representation' (1999: 1). Silverstone places the media at the core of experience, 'at the heart of our capacity or incapacity to make sense of the world in which we live' (ix). Media representation then is everywhere, 'a battleground on which none of us are neutral' (Medhurst 1998: 283). We use it to make sense of who we are, and to make sense of each other. We use it to map our place in the world. We construct meanings around media representations that enable us to form social identities that are determined not only by gender, sexuality and ethnicity, but also by class.

If the media is ubiquitous, then so too is class. Class is always there, is always here in our daily lives, our daily interactions. It is a landscape that we are all part of. How we understand our classed identities, however, is a contentious issue. Are you working class, middle class or upper class? How do you define class? Is it to do with education, occupation, money, what your parents do for a living, where you live, the newspapers you read, the TV you watch, the food you eat? Are you neither one class, nor the other? Do you prefer to define yourself in relation to ethnicity, sexuality, gender? How does classed identity relate to the other identities that define us, and that are constructed for us in and through media?

## The theoretical life of class and the media

In order to pose some answers to these questions, this section will briefly chart a chronology of the theoretical life of class as a concept in relation to the study of the media. It will of necessity be a whistle-stop tour, pausing along the way at some of the major theoretical players and conceptual moments. The point of the journey is to give you a historical grounding, and to help you to realize that the meaning of class has shifted over time and in relation to various social and political changes. Thus, when you use class to examine the politics of media representation, you need to be aware that it is a complicated category. As a critical concept, it is itself a discursive construct. It represents particular things, orders particular kinds of knowledge and embodies particular ways of seeing in all kinds of texts. It is also important that you realize that the study of class is not just about looking at the working class. The study of class ought to involve an analysis of what it means to be middle class or indeed upper class. The study of media representations should look at the ways in which the middle classes and the upper class are represented. Historically this has rarely been the case. (There are some useful studies on middle class culture. See Ehrenreich 1990 and Silverstone 1997). To study class in relation to media has largely involved three options: studying the effects of the media on the 'masses', studying the representation of the working class in the media (particularly in relation to soaps and film), or considering the political economy of media industries as part of a capitalist mode of production, in which the concept of class struggle is implicated. The reasons for these options are complex, and a full exploration is beyond the scope of this chapter. Certainly, one of the reasons why class was for so long associated with the *working* class was through the dominance of Marxist theory.

More than any other social theorist, Marx's name is connected to the concept of class, yet he displayed relatively little interest in formal definitions of class categories. Milner (1999) provides a useful overview of the main theoretical components of Marx's understanding of class. For Marx, human societies were classifiable according to the predominant structural characteristics of their modes of production, that is, very loosely their economic systems. It is for this reason that Marxist theory has been called economically deterministic. For Marx it is the mode of production of any given society that generates its characteristic forms of class inequality. The main reference point for Marx was the modern bourgeois mode of production and the capitalist relations that accompany it. Capitalist relations of production generate a particular class structure in which the owners of capital buy labour-power from propertyless wage earners that are then obliged to sell it on the labour market in return for wages. The central social actors in Marx's account of capitalism are the capitalist class, or the bourgeoisie, on the one hand, and the proletariat, or working class, on the other. The Marxist mode of production model has been used by media theorists to attempt to understand and explain the power of media ownership and control. Political economists of the media attempt to understand the ways in which the media produces meanings that are made available in structurally determined ways through the institutions and circuits of commodified cultural production, distribution and consumption. Nicholas Garnham (1997) has provided a useful agenda of questions that can give students new to the field a much needed hook. For him, the media mediate and the media manipulate:

> How is it possible to understand soap operas as cultural practices without studying the broadcasting institutions which produce and distribute them, and in part create the audience for them? How is it possible to study shopping and advertising, let alone celebrate their liberating potential, without studying the processes of manufacturing, retailing and marketing that make those cultural practices possible? How, at this conjuncture, is it possible to ignore in any study of culture and its political potential the development of global cultural markets and the technological and regulatory processes and capital flows that are the conditions of possibility of such markets (Garnham 1997: 72).

There is an important place for political economies of the media, especially when, as Roger Bromley argues 'the alliance of class fractions which represents the dominant power bloc is almost entirely invisible' (2000: 53). He goes on to argue that the media now appears to be 'dispersed, international, corporate and impersonal, it eludes figuration other than through the odd fat cat caricature or the spectacular hyper-real grotesque like Robert Maxwell'. Beginning in the 1980s media studies turned to the analysis of what has been termed the 'readers rights' (see Moores 1993 for a useful summary of developments in the theorization of media audiences) school of analysis, where the meanings that groups of consumers made of media texts became the object of study rather than the political and economic power relations implicated in the production of media texts. Often this meant that media studies lost sight of questions of politics, economics and class in the celebration of audience's freedom. (David Morley and James Curran have engaged in important dialogue on this issue. These conversations are reprinted in Curran *et al.* 1996.) A number of key theorists (Kellner 1997; McGuigan 1994) have urged media and cultural studies not to lose sight of the political and the economic in the face of the celebration of consumer freedom.

## Ideology and the masses

In order to recap and expand on some of these points, the following section will explore the ways in which class in media studies has been linked to questions of either capital and cultural production (the structural forms of the media if you like) or of ideology (the masses being manipulated into political inactivity by the content of the media). Marx's notion of class consciousness, which broadly relates to a set of social beliefs that belong to a particular class, is important because it pertains to Marx's theory of ideology. His theory of ideology maintains simply that: 'Life is not determined by consciousness, but consciousness by life' (Marx and Engels 1948: 47). The ideas of the ruling class are the ruling ideas. Culturally dominant ideas are the ideal expression of dominant material relations, produced in the interests of the ruling class. The media as mass culture have been seen by many cultural critics as the ideological instruments of the ruling class – serving the interests of dominant social groups. One of the influential schools who took this position on the role of the media in society was The Frankfurt School, a body of thinkers who emphasized the importance of 'ruling ideas' within capitalism.

Indeed, since the 1960s it has been possible to set up a crude chronological shift in Western Marxism. It has shifted from 'class practice Marxism' to 'ruling ideas Marxism'. Capitalism appeared to be working, what could cultural theorists say about that? Ruling ideas Marxism focuses in particular on questions of ideology. Some of the key theorists are Louis Althusser and Antonio Gramsci. Ruling ideas theorists worked variously with the concept of ideology to 'generate very clear explanations for the proletariat's failure to consign capitalism to the dustbin of history: in short, some version or other that it had been ideologically duped' (Milner 1999: 47).

Beginning in the 1970s Western Media Studies, Cultural Studies and Film Studies came to be dominated by Althusserian theories of ideology. Althusser developed a highly significant conceptualization of ideology as interpellation. At the core of this was the idea that the subjects of ideology (you and I) have an imaginary relationship to our real (material) conditions of existence. This imaginary (ideological) existence is mediated on both a conscious and an unconscious level. (Althusser developed his theory of interpellation very loosely through psychoanalyst, Jacques Lacan's theory of the Imaginary.) We are 'hailed' by ideology. Ideology 'interpellates'; it calls us to order, it fixes us into a place. For example, when you switch on your favourite soap, it is as if it is saying, 'hey you' and you recognize and respond to its call for attention. Answering ideological calls for attention sustains our imaginary relationship to our real conditions of existence. The problem with Althusser's theory of interpellation was that the subject of ideology was trapped like a rat in a maze. While there was no outside of ideology, of interpellation for any of us, some of us were more vulnerable than others to the manipulation of ideology. It does not take a lot to guess who the vulnerable were: the masses. The shift to Althusser had an important and lasting effect on the study of working-class culture. Valerie Walkerdine identifies 'the moment of Althusser' as part of the continuing effort to explain the problem of class consciousness, that is its perceived failure:

> For Althusser, the working class was constructed not in the real relations of production, but in a set of imaginary relations in which bourgeois fantasies, especially those in the mass media, had produced the very mirrors in which the workers identity was formed. By referring to Lacan's psychoanalysis, the way the work was taken up clearly implied an account in which working-class identity was an ideological product down to the very unconscious meanings of the original fantasies (Walkerdine 1996: 103).

Walkerdine goes on to argue that the infantilizing location of the working class as being totally formed in ideologies of the mass media at *both* a conscious and an unconscious level paved the way for dropping the working class as an object of study. As Carolyn Steedman (1986) has argued, the key to analysing the working class was and is the attribution of psychological simplicity. If the masses had become increasingly difficult to handle at the level of their consciousness, then how much more difficult were they to handle at the level of their unconscious? As complicated as Marxist theory may be, historical materialism gave the masses a clear and simple revolutionary purpose. It had a revolutionary mission to fulfil, and it had not fulfilled it. Either this had to be explained or ignored, or questions had to be asked about the usefulness of class as a concept at all in the face of lived social realities and non-events.

## Studying the masses after the masses

Another significant critical turn took place in Western Media and Cultural Studies towards the mid-1970s. It continues to hold ground today. Antonio Gramsci, an Italian Communist, developed a theory of hegemony in the 1930s which was later taken up by cultural theorists as 'offering the possibility of a mid way position, somewhere between class practice Marxism and ruling ideas Marxism, where working class consciousness could be analysed as neither necessarily virtuously heroic, nor necessarily hopelessly duped' (Milner 1999: 49). Hegemony denotes those processes by which a system of beliefs and values supportive of the existing ruling class permeates the whole of society. What marked out Gramsci's theory from the Althusserianism, which had dominated, was the idea that hegemony is never an absolute structure. Hegemonic control is exercised as an unstable equilibrium, and in relation to counter-hegemonic forces. In other words hegemonic control is exercised through complex processes of negotiation. This idea was taken up by cultural theorists as a way out of the rat in a maze scenario. Hegemony underpinned much of the 'readers' rights' school of analysis that I mentioned earlier. Hegemony was used as a method to celebrate readers' and consumers' abilities to undermine the intended (authoritarian/ authorial) meanings of cultural texts and practices and make their own uses and meanings. In other words consumers negotiated their own meanings of the media through the negotiation of structures of control and power.

In this theoretical landscape class soon became wiped from the agenda to be replaced by a socially unspecified subject, or a subject whose cultural play was determined by gender, sexuality or race. Once the political and the economic structures of popular media culture fell from analytical grace in the face of the celebration of the ability of consumers to negotiate their own meanings as those not preferred by the dominant ideology, then class went out of the window. Connected to this also is the cultural and political context in Britain of Thatcherism and what was happening to the wider social understanding of the working class on a larger scale. I will explore some of these relationships in the next section.

## New times, Thatcher's Britain and the new middle class

By the 1980s the mention of class tended to 'stick in the throat like a large chunk of Hovis' (Anthony 1998: 2). The grid references of race, sexuality and gender plotted the maps of post-modern identities. Class was outmoded, conjuring up lost images of community, political unity and revolutionary fervour. In Britain during the period of Mrs Thatchers governments (1979–90) 'New Times' had arrived, and the old working class was swept up in a sea of consensus politics. The rise of Thatcherism convinced many cultural critics that public opinion had shifted decisively towards the right, and that the combination of post-Fordist economic policies and post-modernist cultural politics made fundamental change impossible. These are extremely complicated historical processes. However, it is important to note at this stage that a new kind of society was seen to be being built up. This society was rooted in post-industrial modes of production, the massive increase in the capabilities of information technology and its impact on the economy, the media and everyday communication. Critics like Fredric Jameson (1991) talked about the advent of 'late capitalism' where high-tech, post-industrial societies were governed by a post-modern logic of surface, irony and play. Capitalism's quest for profit and control marched on relentlessly.

In Britain the New Right's campaigning zeal was championed by the social crisis that began to grip the country in the late 1960s. Stuart Hall (1988), an important figure in the discussions around the social, economic and political plight of Britain during Thatcher's governments, identifies a 'conjunctural crisis' in the country at the time which forced establishment groups to redouble their efforts to maintain support for capitalist society. This 'conjunctural crisis' came about through a long economic downturn with high unemployment, the erosion of the manufacturing base of traditional industries, the renewed militancy of the trade unions, the threat posed to suburban values by a rise in crime, the worsening of the situation in Northern Ireland

and discontent among ethnic minorities. Margaret Thatcher was seen to be deeply attuned to 'the key preoccupations of the working class mind' (Bounds 1999: 32). The working classes were seen to be particularly vulnerable to the government's authoritarian promises of a better Britain that were filtered through right-identified newspapers like the *Daily Mail*, the *Sun* and *The Times*. Valerie Walkerdine has examined stereotypes of the working class that she believes to have endured during Mrs Thatcher's time in office:

> We are the salt of the earth, the bedrock of the revolution; we are working class women with big hearts, big arms, big breasts; we are stupid and ignorant, deprived and depriving; we are repressed, authoritarian, and above all *we* voted Thatcher into her third term of office. We are revolting, anti-democratic (1990: 206).

## 'Pukka': Tony Blair's bourgeois Britain

If some of this sounds strikingly familiar to some of the incantations of Tony Blair's bourgeois Britain then it ought to. Class differences are seen by many as irrelevant to Blair's cool Britannia; 'since the death of Di, we are a New Britain, cobbled together in a new national truce of participatory politics' (Munt 2000: 2). More of us will be made middle class. Middle class is no class, therefore, nothing to talk about, nothing to see. In December 1998 the Office for National Statistics spelled out the eight new categories for measuring social class by occupation, which for the first time made the majority of those designations middle class/professional. This was despite the fact that in an ICM poll commissioned by Radio 4 in 1988 55% defined themselves as working class.

It is fascinating to examine how class is represented across various media when there are seen to be no homogeneous classes to represent, when class isn't seen as an issue. How is class being represented when it seems that it isn't being represented at all? One possible answer: Delia Smith and Jamie Oliver. Food programmes and their surging popularity are fascinating texts through which one can examine the workings of various discourses around taste and class or taste and the eponymous 'lifestyle' category that has become a convenient catch-all for social differentiation in the new millennium. Delia Smith was an acceptable face of Thatcherism, beaming apparently benign conservative values of cosy good health and decent living from her middle-England suburban kitchen. A port in a storm. She has also become a powerful cipher for the aspirations of Blair's Britain. Delia, 'the lady next door', has become such a powerful media figure and dictator of lifestyle that if she recommends a particular product on her *How to Cook* series it flies off the supermarket shelves the next day. She has also been a corporate identity, linked to the 'helpful' 'caring' tag lines of Sainsbury's supermarkets. (Smith also has family connections to the Sainsbury's empire.) Jamie Oliver, the new face of Sainsbury's advertising campaign, has put the rough and ready back into cooking. An Essex lad (enough seemingly said) this 'lad' drags street slang into the domain of pecorino cheese and balsamic vinegar, making it seemingly democratic. Jamie Oliver espouses and embodies the values of Blair's bourgeois Britain. It matters little whether Jamie Oliver can be quantifiably defined as 'genuinely' working class or middle class. What matters is what he appears to represent, and what he appears to represent are the mixed metaphors of rough Essex lad with the aspirational values of white, heterosexual, loft living. His tastes and his culinary skills are apparently unfettered by his Essex background. He can be seen as a 'classless' 'geezer', a cipher, therefore, of the blurred boundaries of social classification in Britain today. Lifestyle eclipses class differences. But whose tastes does *The Naked Chef* represent? Whose lifestyle is on display? Who might the audience be? These are important questions for students of the media because, as Jon Cook argues, 'taste is what is being watched' and taste 'expresses our classed difference from others' (2000: 105).

The glut of home and garden make-over programmes on British television (other countries in Europe and other parts of the world are experiencing a similar media turn) speak again to the replacement of class with the category of lifestyle. With a slice of MDF, a lick of paint and a lot of styling, homes are given a window onto another lifestyle, other possibilities, other tastes. There are taste parameters around these programmes that speak to different kinds of audiences, audiences with different lifestyles, different incomes. In fact they speak to different classes. If you choose to watch *Charlie's Garden Army* over *Home Front in the Garden*, or if you watch both, but laugh at Charlie Dimmock in one, and long for the gardens of Diarmuid Gavin in the other then that may well say quite a lot about your class. It certainly says a lot about mine. Taste and lifestyle are merciless betrayers of social attitudes and markers of social differentiation. As much as class has been identified quantifiably (by income or occupation) it has also always been defined qualifiably by taste and lifestyle. I can remember vividly the first middle-class home that I ever entered. I defined it as such by the food in their cupboards, the pictures on the walls, their huge potted plants, their shabby antique rugs, the manners at the dinner table. With the shifts and changes in occupations, I doubt that the family earned more money at that point than mine, given that my father, like the father of that house, were now in middle management. Quantifiably there wasn't much in it, but qualifiably we were miles apart.

## Representing the underclass in recent British films

The emergence of the representation of a British underclass in recent British films poses an interesting agenda of questions and issues around ways of seeing and knowing the working class. The discourse of the underclass attempts to strike out at bourgeois Britannia. I do not have the space here to discuss the politics of class representation of individual films. I am thinking in general terms about *The Full Monty, Nil by Mouth, Ladybird Ladybird, My Name is Joe, Brassed Off,* and *Trainspotting.* It is interesting that at the moment when class is seen to be an outmoded category as more of us are swallowed into the milieu of the middle class, representations of the British underclass should become such a prevalent mode of representing class in film. The underclass is the extreme end of the class spectrum. It is a type of poverty linked to criminality, the breakdown in family structures, poor education, and long-term unemployment. Chris

Haylett argues that 'visions of "underclass" (have) become part of the personal, public and political imaginations of British culture in the 1990s. These are presented as entertainment in crime genre television programmes, as CCTV evidence in factual documentaries or news items as the backdrop for announcements of new social policy initiatives' (Haylett 2000: 72). In other words there is already a regime of representation of 'underclass' as Other.

Certainly in British film history there is a long tradition of representing working-class life. Who are these representations for? How are they seen? A student of mine a couple of years ago wrote a dissertation for a film audience's course on *Nil by Mouth*. She grew up on the estate where the film was shot, but watched the film with a group of middle-class students. She was made uncomfortable by their voyeuristic anthropological gaze at 'white trash' life – how could they live like that? Is it really like that? This student lived out her own class identity as a contradiction between the estate and the institute. She decided to use this to attempt to understand the ways in which working class (both white and black, male and female) and middle class (both white and black, male and female) audiences read the film. What difference did it make to audiences if they were looking at representations of themselves or of the Other? It seems to me that this kind of complex approach to class as a regime of representation and as lived reality that may determine particular ways of seeing is one way forward. Class analysis is not just about images of the working class, but about representations of the middle classes, and indeed the upper class; it is also about examining the ways in which audiences consume different images of class. How do we understand what it means to be working class, to be middle class or to be upper class? Is it rooted in experience, or is it rooted in mediated modes of seeing and knowing the classed Other?

## Making class matter again

How and why has class been made to matter again in cultural theory? This is a complex question that would require more space than I have available to address it more fully. However, what is significant is that class has been placed back on the agenda through narratives of personal experience (see Walkerdine 1990; Steedman 1986; Lacey 2000; Kuhn 1995). The point of much of this work is to bring class back into question by attributing to working-class identity and classifications of social class, a psychological complexity and fluidity that moves us beyond the stranglehold of economic determinism and economically determined invisibility. Media and cultural theorists have used their own often contradictory experiences of class and class move-ment to address the centrality of media representations and our identifications with media texts as part of the formation of identity. What do the working classes look like in the media? What do the middle classes look like? How is the upper class represented? What does it mean to experience class? How do we use the media to socially differentiate ourselves? Identity is a difficult theoretical concept. Think about what makes you who you are. If as John Berger says, 'I am includes all that has made me so' (1984: 2) then I am a woman, heterosexual, white, a mother, a working-class child, a middle-class adult, a Liverpudlian, a lapsed Catholic, 32. I am also what I buy, what I watch on TV, what I eat, where I holiday, where I go for coffee, the magazines that I read, the music I listen to. As Silverstone puts it:

> We consume objects. We consume goods. We consume information. We consume images. But in that consumption, in its daily taken for grantedness, we make our own meanings, negotiate our own values, and in so doing we make our own world meaningful. I am what I buy; no longer what I make or indeed think. And so, I expect are you ( Silverstone 2000: 80).

## Posh and Becks: you can't buy class

This section will seek to apply some of the ideas that I have discussed on the politics of the representation of class to the media coverage in the British press of the wedding of Spice Girl, Victoria Adams to footballer, David Beckham. The wedding was one of the biggest celebrity events of 1999. This chapter has introduced you to theories on social class. The point of this is to provide you with the analytical tools to examine particular representations of class in media texts. In an effort to show you how this might be done, I will examine the ways in which the reporting of the spectacle of Posh and Becks's wedding can be seen to embody particular stereotypes of class that are written around issues of taste. The point is not to offer you an opinion of whether or not I thought Posh and Becks' wedding was a trashy affair, but to explore the ways in which the coverage of the event as trashy or not can be seen to represent particularly classed points of view. In examining this, a number of factors must be taken into account. First, the context of the publication that is reporting the event. What kind of publication is it? Who is the target audience? What political affiliations does the publication have? Second, the social, cultural and economic context of Britain at the time of the event. In what way might the aspirations, anxieties and politics of the country feed into the reporting of the celebrity spectacle?

Posh and Becks are hyper-celebrities facing media meltdown on a daily basis, and currently occupy a unique place in British public life. I followed the build-up to this wedding, and the event itself through *OK!* magazine which I read every week, and which describes itself as being 'popular with celebrities who like their lifestyles reported and photographed in English good taste and sensitivity'. *OK!* have always gone to great lengths to paint Adams and Beckham as down to earth, not snobs. In its special on the inside of Beckham's parents home described as 'modesty itself', the magazine points out in the opening paragraph that his dad Ted is a gas engineer, and his mother, Sandra, 'a hairdresser in a retirement home'. Given the readership profile of *OK!* it makes sense that Posh and Becks would be aligned with the respectable working class. This is more difficult with Adams, who grew up with money, and was taken to school in her dad's Rolls-Royce, but her parents are classed as 'working class made good'. They occupy the ranks of the *nouveau riche.* Victoria Adams is often painted in the same light. She was a girl who like lots of girls in my working-class school (including myself) made sure that we went to school with designer carrier bags even if we didn't have the designer goods to go in them.

*OK!* paid out £1 million to get exclusive rights to photograph Posh and Becks £500,000 wedding at Luttrellstown Castle in Dublin. Victoria Adams describes the *OK!* magazine people as 'friends that have supported her for a long time' (*Vanity Fair* September 1999: 138). I admit to a fascination with Victoria Adams that I find difficult to understand. My own obsessive pursuit of their wedding and its media post-mortem made me think about how I was using the media analysis of the event with their attendant taste and value judgements to situate my own taste and values – in other words to socially differentiate myself. What fascinated me about the coverage of the wedding was the way in which different discourses of class, taste and lifestyle were lashed across these two people and this one event. It seems to me that Posh and Becks have come to signify the complexities of social classification in contemporary Britain. They are neither working class made good, *nouveau riche* or upper class. They are any of these things depending on the text in which they are being represented. The social classification of Posh and Becks runs the gamut from positionality in the conventions of the media's representation of royalty to 'not so posh spice' white trash.

The category of celebrity and celebrity lifestyle, or in this case hyper-celebrity, both eclipses and intensifies social classification through the visual and narrative possibilities of taste and value judgements represented through private lives made for public consumption. Beckham and Adams play the media in a professional and thoroughly post-modern way. Adams is certainly aware of the parasitic relationship between press and celebrity. 'As much as you say the press have done this and the press have done that, at the end of the day, right at the start of your career you need each other' (*Vanity Fair* September 1999: 192). Adams and Beckham executed something of a coup when they shut the press out of the wedding itself. It was a case, perhaps, of them mediating the mediators.

It was unsurprising that the *Daily Mail* should take an unfavourable stance to the perceived excesses of the Posh and Becks wedding. What was surprising was the extent to which their coverage of the wedding 'heritage' theme should be so rooted in a critique of aspirational bad taste working-class culture. You can't buy class, underwrote the *Daily Mail*'s A-Z of Posh and Becks.

The article entitled 'A truly posh bash' was affixed with '(that is if you like Rottweilers, a groom whose fussier about his hair than his bride and the theme to "It's a Knock-out")'. The piece trafficked in the circulation of stereotypical images of working-class culture designed to undermine and ridicule any aspirations that the couple might have to taste and respectability. The perceived grotesque excesses of working-class carnival were written across every aspect of the wedding from the food to the music. 'E is for EEUGH. Posh is said to have decreed that the meal should be composed of wholesome, no nonsense English food that everyone can enjoy, so it's probably sausage and chips.' This was followed by 'T is for tacky. Unless you happen to think that an 18 piece symphony orchestra playing classical adaptations of Spice Girl Hits which will blare out at the reception is Tasteful.' The article also defined 'F for "fick"', alluding to Beckham and Adams' alleged stupidity and ('W for "Wonga", soccer speak for money'. For the *Daily Mail* this was clearly a working-class wedding, and therefore a grotesque display. In a country where class is seen as an outmoded category, curiously/typically, Posh and Becks' wedding was analysed through stereotypical discourses of class. Class is clearly, according to the middle-England market

*Mail* something that you are born with and into, and not something that you can buy or perform. The *Mirror,* variously champions and critics of Adams and Beckham, were more contradictory in their coverage. Posh and Becks were to be applauded for having the guts to 'do it their way'. The problem lay with the working-class counterfeits that would follow in their wake:

> Soon village halls will be festooned with plush velvet drapes, star studded voile hangings and tiger print sofas. Naked statuettes of Wayne and Waynetta will adorn wedding cakes, while Holiday Inns will be transformed into decadent gardens of Eden with plastic red roses and ivy. Happy couples can sit in splendid isolation on gold-sprayed chairs called thrones as flags bearing their initials flutter from the trumpet section of the local brass band.

I would have felt compelled (as a loyal former working class, now tastefully restrained middle-class academic) to defend this charge of imminent duped bad taste until I read a recent article in *Marie Claire* about the visual and material culture of Irish travellers' weddings which are lavish and hugely expensive spectacles. One of the brides had in fact had copied for her own wedding each of Posh Spice's wedding outfits (Figure 24.1). She had not, however, copied the whole wedding theme. We are all bricoleurs; we pick and choose according to the parameters of our own tastes and our cultural locations. The Irish travellers' wedding was as much a post-modern event as Posh and Becks', stitched together with references to a range of other cultural texts.

The *Mail's* cynical position was determined in part by the linking of Posh and Becks' wedding in July to the other big royal wedding of the summer of Sophie

**Figure 24.1** Mary even had Posh Spice's wedding reception dress copied (*Marie Claire* August 2000, © Neelakshi Vidylankara)

Rhys-Jones to Prince Edward. The Royal wedding was a good taste, low-key affair (by relative standards), and the press went to great pains to try to inject some glamour and excitement into a thoroughly unglamorous event. Posh and Becks are continually referred to as the New Royals. Following the death of Diana the Royal Family have lacked a key celebrity figure, and the conventions saved for the coverage of Diana's life have been transferred onto Adams and Beckham. 'There are no paparazzi risking their lives for pictures of Edward Windsor and Sophie Rhys-Jones' (*Vanity Fair* 1999: 142) Their wedding florist, Jane Packer, has said, 'In a sense Victoria and David are the new royalty, and because they are not trapped by tradition, you can be more creative'. Their new mansion was referred to as 'Beckingham Palace' in more than one publication. The *Daily Mail* refers to Adams as 'The Queen of Herts' linking her hyper-celebrity status to Diana's and referencing her parents' home in Goff's Oak, Herts, reputedly one of the poshest parts of the country.

Posh and Becks' choice of wedding theme – a romantic Robin Hood woodland glen complete with Posh and Becks' coat of arms (their embossed gold initials read VD), gold thrones for the bride and groom and a crown for the bride – was a parody on their own status as the new royalty. It was a playful text designed to entertain. It was in the end what was expected of them as hyper-celebrities, and like them or loathe them, they do know how to deliver the goods. Adams has commented on the criticism of the crest of arms that the swan was the wrong way round:

> 'So what if the poxy swan is the wrong way,' snaps the woman who was once dubbed 'Relatively Posh Spice'. 'Does anybody really give a shit – d'you know what I mean? Having your own crest – it's one of them, innit?' Adams pokes her tongue into her cheek. 'We're just thinking, this is the biggest day of our lives – we're just going to go over the top and make it entertaining for everybody. Much as we want to, it's still one of those'. Tongue meets cheek again (*Vanity Fair*: 38).

The *Mirror* reported the wedding of Posh and Becks as 'The People's Royal Wedding'. It displayed its allegiance to a couple who knew how to stage 'a proper royal do'. In 'I Queen Posh, take thee, King Becks,' The *Mirror* reports, 'from the regal thrones at the reception to the imperial purple carpets and rows of liveried attendants, the sheer spectacle of yesterday's event could not have been more of a contrast to the real royal wedding last month'. They also comment, 'her crown, made by Slim Barratt, the jeweller who made pieces for the Princess of Wales, was fashioned out of 18 carat gold. It rather outshone the diamond tiara lent to Sophie Rhys-Jones by the Queen at that other summer wedding.'

If you look for it, discourses and stereotypes around class flow through the media all of the time. Michael Billig (1995) includes a useful media exercise in relation to constructions of national identity in the newspapers. He asks readers to take a selection of newspapers on any given day, and to analyse them for examples of banal nationalism. By this he means that you should look for the quiet, unassuming, taken for granted examples of constructions of nationalism, and not the screamingly jingoistic headlines.

This is a useful exercise to do in relation to representations of class. How prevalent are stereotypes of class in the press? What kinds of features contain particular stereotypes? Do stereotypes figure differently across different publications? What is the

**Figure 24.2** The *Sun* newspaper puts a spin on the 'regal' nature of the Beckhams' fairy-tale wedding (courtesy Dave Gaskill, the *Sun*)

relationship of the representation of class to questions of national identity, ethnicity, sexuality, and gender? Perhaps the choice of Posh and Becks' wedding is an obvious representation, an easy target. However, what struck me in the coverage of this event was the fact that the nowhere land, the seeming non-representability of middle-class culture was left out of the equation. Either this was a display of white trash carnivalesque or the usurping of the modes of royal representation by the footballer and the Spice Girl (Figure 24.2). The extremes of British social classification were applied in this culture of no class. There was absolutely, resolutely nothing middle class about this wedding. This, in the end, was why I liked it so much. This, in the end, was why I liked Edward and Sophie's wedding so little because it conformed to the rigidities, the tastefulness, the restraint and lack of spectacle of decent middle-class culture. The resolutely middle-class *Wedding Dresses Magazine* haughtily dismissed the event as 'vulgar and ostentatious. I don't think our readers would emulate any of that' (August 1999: 21). Is that what it means to be middle class? Is that what it means to be seen as middle class? The only 'non-class' it seems to me is the middle class. In as much as contemporary theorists have tried to deconstruct the unrepresentability of whiteness in terms of race and ethnicity (Dyer 1997) so too must we begin to deconstruct the unrepresentability of middle classness.

The way forward for class analysis in relation to media representations is to look at class as the most complex classification that embodies the variations and contradictions of what it means to be and to be seen as middle and indeed upper class (which I forget that some of you are), as well as working class. It also means taking account of the other aspects of identity formation, which cross social classification, like sexuality, ethnicity, disability, generation and gender.

## Questions

1   How do you understand your own class identity? How do you define it? How and where do you see your class identity represented in the media?

2   How do you understand the relationship between lifestyle and class? Choose a television programme or advertisement and examine the ways in which a discourse of class and lifestyle operates through it.

3   Choose three different media texts, one representing a stereotype of working-class culture, one representing a stereotype of middle-class culture and one representing a stereotype of upper-class culture. What codes, clues and conventions are used to establish the stereotype? Who is the intended audience?

## References

Anthony, A. (1998) 'What about the workers?' *The Observer Review* 13 December, 2–3.

Berger, J. (1984) *Ways of Seeing*, London: Routledge.

Billig, M. (1995) *Banal Nationalism*, London: Sage.

Bounds, P. (1999) *Cultural Studies*, London: Studymates.

Bromley, R. (2000) 'The theme that dare not speak its name: class and recent British film', in S. Munt (ed.) *Cultural Studies and the Working Class. Subject to Change*, London: Cassell.

Carroll, S. (1999) 'Tacky, tasteless . . . so at least they did it their way', *Mirror* 7 July, 9.

Cook, J. (2000) 'Culture, class and taste', in S. Munt (ed.) *Cultural Studies and the Working Class. Subject to Change*, London: Cassell.

Curran, J., Morley, D. and Walkerdine, V. (1996) *Cultural Studies and Communications*, London: Arnold.

Daly, S. (1999) 'Posh and Becks', *Vanity Fair* September, 138–9, 192–3.

Dyer, R. (1997) *White*, London: Routledge.

Ehrenreich, B. (1990) *Fear of Falling: The Inner Life of the Middle Class*, New York: Harper Perennial.

Garnham, N. (1997) 'Political economy and the practice of cultural studies', in M. Ferguson and P. Golding (eds) *Cultural Studies in Question*, London: Sage.

Hall, S. (1988) *The Hard Road to Renewal*, London: Routledge.

Harris, P. and Clark, N. (1999) 'A truly posh bash', *Daily Mail* 1 July, 13–15.

Haylett, C. (2000) 'This is about us, this is our film. Personal and popular discourses of the underclass', in S. Munt (ed.) *Cultural Studies and the Working Class. Subject to Change,* London: Cassell.

Jameson, F. (1991) *Postmodernism or the Cultural Logic of Late Capitalism,* London: Verso.

Kellner, D. (1997) 'Overcoming the divide. Cultural studies and political economy', in M. Ferguson and P. Golding (eds) *Cultural Studies in Question,* London: Sage.

Kuhn, A. (1995) *Family Secrets,* London: Verso.

Lacey, J. (2000) 'Discursive mothers and academic fandom', in S. Munt (ed.) *Cultural Studies and the Working Class. Subject to Change,* London: Cassell.

Marx, K. and Engels, F. (n.d., first published 1948) *Manifesto of the Communist Party,* Moscow: Foreign Language Publishers House.

McGuigan, J. (1994) *Cultural Populism,* London: Routledge.

Medhurst, A. (1998) 'Sexuality. Tracing desires: sexuality and media texts', in A. Briggs and P. Cobley (eds) *The Media: an Introduction,* London: Arnold.

Milner, A. (1999) *Class,* London: Sage.

Moores, S. (1993) *Interpreting Audiences: The Ethnography of Media Consumption,* London: Sage.

Munt, S. (2000) 'Introduction', in S. Munt (ed.) *Cultural Studies and the Working Class. Subject to Change,* London: Cassell.

Silverstone, R. (1997) *Visions of Suburbia,* London: Routledge.

Silverstone, R. (1999) *Why Study the Media,* London: Sage.

Steedman, C. (1986) *Landscape for a Good Woman,* London: Virago.

Walkerdine, V. (1990) *Schoolgirl Fictions,* London: Verso.

Walkerdine, V. (1996) 'Subject to change without notice', in J. Curran, D. Morley and V. Walkerdine (eds) *Cultural Studies and Communications,* London: Arnold.

Williams, R. (1988) *Keywords,* London: Fontana.

# Further reading

Bennett, T. *et al.* (eds) (1981) *Culture, Ideology and Social Process,* London and Buckingham: Batsford, Open University. An important book that examines the relationships between ideology, cultural production and cultural consumption. It is not a particularly easy read, but it is worth your attention as it gives a good feel for the language of existing theoretical debate and application.

Dodd, K. and Dodd, P. (1992) 'From the East End to *EastEnders*, representations of the working class 1890–1990', in D. Strinati (ed.) *Come on Down: Popular Media Culture in Post War Britain,* London: Routledge. This accessible essay looks at the politics of representation of class across a range of texts, both historical and contemporary. It provides a useful approach to the historical analysis of representations of class.

Hebdige, D. (1979) *Subculture: the Meaning of Style,* London: Methuen. A classic text still referenced extensively despite its age. Hebdige draws out important relationships between style, masculinity, national identity and the formation of working-class youth culture.

Hoggart, R. (1957) *The Uses of Literacy*, Harmondsworth: Penguin. One of the founding texts of British cultural studies in the 1950s. Semi-autobiographical account of a working class community. Very readable.

Mahony, P. and Zmroczek, C. (eds) (1997) *Class Matters: Working Class Women's Perspectives on Social Class*, London: Taylor & Francis. Very readable collection, much of it written from the personal. Looks at the different ways in which class can be defined.

Williams, R. (1958) *Culture and Society*, London: Chatto & Windus. Again, another key text in British cultural studies. Williams is a very important writer on class whose ideas have been formative across a range of academic disciplines. His work is well worth reading first-hand.

Wray, M. and Newitz, A. (eds) (1997) *White Trash: Race and Class in America*, New York: Routledge. This is a great book that examines the construction of images of white trash in American popular culture. It looks at representations of race and class across a range of texts from Elvis to country music to film.

# Chapter 25

# Race and ethnicity

RACE AND ETHNICITY: THE CONSTRUCTION OF BLACK AND
ASIAN ETHNICITIES IN BRITISH FILM AND TELEVISION

**SARITA MALIK**

This chapter outlines some of the key ways in which Black and Asian people
have been represented in British film and television. By tracing back early on-screen
images of 'Blackness', it reflects on the complex issues around race, ethnicity
and cultural identity. It takes us up to the present day by addressing issues around
new media technologies and the impact that they are having on Black and Asian
audiences.

Britain has recently witnessed a number of debates about race, national identity and
'institutional racism'. The key finding in William Macpherson's 1999 Report (following the unprovoked murder of Black British teenager, Stephen Lawrence, in 1993)
that Britain is 'institutionally racist' has triggered a new set of public debates about
the racism that exists within institutions (the police, the government, the media, and
so on). The British media has always been a key site of contestation in matters of
race and ethnicity. On the one hand, it has been seen as a problematic arena where
Black people are marginalized, excluded or stereotyped, but on the other, it has
been recognized as a critical space in terms of how social relations are developed and
in how ideologies around race and ethnicity are produced. Here we are talking not
just about how Black and Asian diasporas are represented, but also about how 'Whiteness', 'Englishness' and 'Britishness' are portrayed. (I shall use 'Black' as a collective
political term to refer to those of African, Caribbean and South Asian descent. I will
also use the term 'Asian' for those specifically from the Indian subcontinent. 'Diaspora'
refers to (the situation of) a group of dispersed people, so in this instance it indicates
Black and Asian people within the British context.) The term 'race' in the cultural
and political terrain, has almost universally been aligned with Black and Asian people,
as though they are the only racial groups that 'own' an ethnicity. There have been
very few occasions when 'Whiteness' itself, and more specifically English people, have
been depicted as a racial group with their own distinct culture, ethnicity and identity
(Dyer 1988).

## Different approaches to reading race in the media

The analysis of race and representational practice (not unlike studies of gender, sexuality or disability, for example) has generally taken three forms. The first has examined issues of production and consumption (the relationship between audiences and 'images of Blackness' or what audiences 'do' with images of race once they have watched them); the second refers to textuality and content (an analysis which usually considers stereotyping and ideology and looks at the types of images which are used to represent Black people); and the third has focused on power and politics (who 'controls'/is 'controlled by' the images).

Most media theorists in the field of race and representation have tended to focus on issues around *textuality* and *content* by analysing how various media forms choose to select and present information on different racial groups. For example, in the late 1970s, the Centre for Contemporary Cultural Studies (CCCS) introduced the issue of 'agenda setting' particularly in relation to news and documentary reports on race. It argued that the media set the agenda/public debate on race, and denied space and access for competing ideologies and images.

Few academics have disputed that the media, in general, have been very selective in their portrayal of Black and Asian people. Many have attributed this to the lack of ethnic minority people in key decision-making positions within media industries. (This was discussed at a Commission for Racial Equality (CRE) Conference on Channels of Diversity in March 1996.) Some of those who advocate 'equal opportunity' in the media industries argue that by employing more Black writers, actors, producers, directors, etc. richer and more diverse portraits of Black people will naturally follow. Although it is difficult to dispute that access to the media is desperately needed in employment terms (particularly in key decision-making positions) this, in itself, is no guarantee that a particular set of images will subsequently be produced. To suggest this would be to assume that all Black people (regardless of age, gender, sexuality, etc.) share the same political ground. In addition, it encourages a 'siege mentality which says that anything we do must be good' (Henriques 1988: 18).

Within this diverse range of theoretical and methodological approaches, a number of different arguments, views and positions on Black representation have emerged. Recent discussions have focused on how a multiplicity of views, of and from Black people, can be transmitted via the media and on how it can depart from what Stuart Hall has defined as the 'grammar of race'. This, Hall argues, is the traditional diet for the British media, based on three standard images of 'Blackness' – the native, the entertainer and the social problem (Hall 1981). There have also been new sets of debates, triggered by technological advancements such as digital, satellite and the Internet, which have considered how terrestrial television and the British film sector will renegotiate its relationship with Black British audiences as they increasingly engage in new types of media lifestyles.

## Stereotypes: positive and negative images

Much of the debate in the area of race and representation has revolved around the issue of 'stereotyping'. Since the 1960s, the sociological term has been widely used to refer to the process by which a reductive image/impression is produced of a given social experience. During the 1970s and 1980s, many of those who were dissatisfied with representations of Black people in the cultural arena called for 'positive images' in order to balance out the 'negative images' which were all too often packaged by the media. The mid- to late-1980s, in particular, brought a series of debates in which many argued about the limitations of discussing race and representation in these terms (for example, at the Black People in British Television event which was held at Cinema City, Norwich in May 1988 and the Black Film British Cinema Conference at the Institute of Contemporary Arts in February 1988).

Given the importance of stereotyping (since it is the primary device through which representations of race circulate in media texts), it is useful to make some comment about the ways in which 'typing' functions as a representational practice. Stereotypes are shorthand; they are palatable because they help us to decode people. They appear to simplify the world and its subjects, but they are often complex in that we can associate one aspect of a stereotype with many other things; creating a complex web of beliefs from a seemingly glib categorization. Thus the 'Asian immigrant', the 'Black mugger', or the 'bogus asylum-seeker' tells us more than just that; our associations encourage us to build on the basic information (issues of language, cultural values, social background etc. automatically follow) to create a quite detailed (though not necessarily accurate) profile of what that person constitutes. Stereotypes are social constructs designed to socially construct. They do not simply come into being from nothing and they are not 'used' in the same way by everyone. The way in which we use stereotypes in cultural production is as revealing as which stereotypes we select to represent. Stereotypes, in themselves, are not necessarily offensive or harmful, but the interests they can serve and the context in which they *can* be used have the potential to be precisely that.

Although it is useful to acknowledge the contexts, processes and interests that stereotypes might serve, leaning too heavily on the 'stereotypes/positive and negative image' rhetoric can be limiting (Malik 1996: 208–9). This is for three main reasons. In the first place, 'typing' has to be recognized as an inevitable and necessary system of representation; in the second, there can be no absolute agreement as to what 'positive' and 'negative' definitively constitute (can the image of a gold-medal-winning Black sportsman only be considered as 'positive'?); and in the third, the validity of 'positive' and 'negative' as racial categories of representation themselves need to be questioned since they do little to displace the assumptions on which the original stereotypes are based. 'Positive images' can also be stereotypes, and stereotypes can, in fact, be knowingly reproduced as forms of resistance (for example, in programmes such as *Goodness Gracious Me* (BBC) where the British-Asian comedy team rework well-versed stereotypes of Asians).

## Images of Blackness on British television in the 1950s and 1960s

Although the BBC first transmitted television on 2 November 1936, the 1950s were, in real terms, the decade when the medium was installed on a wide-scale basis. This, together with the mass migration of people from Asia, Africa and the Caribbean, was to produce a historically complex relationship between art and life, between the media and Black-British ethnicity. Although there had been many Black people in Britain prior to the 1950s, the rumblings of hostility towards New Commonwealth Black colonial migrants was to manifest itself in complex ways and the UK soon convinced itself that it had a 'race relations problem'. This was reinforced by incidents of 'racial tension' in Camden (London 1954), Nottingham and Notting Hill (London 1958). Immigration was perceived only in terms of Black people and they, in turn, began to be seen as a social problem. (This was despite the fact that 350,000 European nationals came to the UK between 1945 and 1957 to alleviate the chronic shortage of labour that Britain faced during the post-war period.). Where immigrants were desperately needed to provide labour, they were also seen to be causing problems in terms of 'numbers' particularly in housing and education.

The difficulties in balancing the 'pros and cons' which Black people were perceived to have brought with them resulted in confusion. This was perfectly embodied in the British media's ambivalent approach to the treatment of Black ethnic communities. Different 'moral panics' circulated concerning Asians and African-Caribbeans and each were seen to posses their own set of problems. Asians were often seen as overly traditional, unwilling/unable to integrate, having 'language problems' or oppressed by their own communities (often in the form of 'arranged marriages'). African-Caribbeans, by contrast, were often depicted as troublemakers, as muggers or rioters, or were seen to possess 'all brawn and no brains' (thus having the 'natural attributes' of athletes or entertainers). However they were located, it was always in relation to 'Englishness' which was assumed to be central to 'normal' patterns of behaviour.

A key feature of post-war programming was the construction of the image of Black people as a social problem. Documentary became the preferred genre for discussions around 'race', and documentary realism became the principal discourse through which 'Blackness' was framed. This alone implied that Black people and 'race relations' needed to be considered as social problems. The first full-length television documentary programme to examine the problems faced by Black immigrants in Britain was *Special Enquiry: Has Britain A Colour Bar?* (31 January 1955). The programme implied that the primary reason for discrimination and a colour bar was 'cultural difference' rather than racism. Nevertheless, it provoked emotive responses from many White viewers who felt that it was a defence of Black people in its acknowledgement that racial discrimination existed in Britain. Many documentaries at this time such as *Black Marries White* (1964), *The Negro Next Door* (1965) and *People in Trouble: Mixed Marriages* (1958) focused on 'racial problems' in British society from 'our'/the (White) audience's point of view. Black people were not assumed to come within the 'our' category and were regularly located as the troubled subjects 'stuck between two cultures'. The classic liberal technique of *talking on behalf of* 'the victims' while simultaneously arguing that they are silenced, marginalized and denied access was a key point of contradiction in the social-democratic discourse of many of these early programmes. These early actuality programmes attempted to depict the 'real-life' experiences of Black people, and show 'how they really were' (mostly within established, hybrid formats of interviews, observation, exposition and dramatization). This overwhelmingly anthropological approach is what we can refer to as 'social realism', usually produced in an attempt to make us, the viewer, understand Black people better – to de-alienate them. These early documentary forms largely worked with a self-image of neutrality and balance and of holding the 'middle ground' in documenting the Black experience and 'race relations'.

Enoch Powell was regularly called on as an 'expert' in programmes about British race relations. The focus on numbers and statistics in many of these early actuality programmes supported Enoch Powell's fears that White British people would be invaded by their racial Others. (Enoch Powell, a Conservative MP, supported New Right views in the post-war period and articulated his fear of Britain being 'swamped by alien cultures' in his notorious 'Rivers of Blood' speech in April 1968.) Pre-Powell, the media had generally restrained from tackling matters of race 'head-on' and disassociated itself from any 'extreme' views on race. The more usual approach was what Stuart Hall has called 'inferential racism' (Hall 1981: 37); always starting from the premise of White superiority and tolerance and the assumption that Blacks were 'the problem'. Within this context, Powell was a maverick voice who, during the 1960s, influenced public awareness and approaches to 'race' in unprecedented ways. The 'numbercentric' approach to analysing race implied that the presence of Black people in Britain needed to be read in terms of the problematic.

> You simply have to look at the programme with one set of questions in your mind: Here is a problem, defined as 'the problem of immigration'. What is it? How is it defined and constructed through the programme? What logic governs its definition? And where does that logic derive from? . . . The *logic* of the argument is 'immigrants=blacks=too many of them=send them home'. That is a racist logic (Hall 1981: 46).

The advent of Black programming in the mid-1950s operated as an extension of the BBC's core ideals of liberalism and public service broadcasting. The first programme to recognize that a space should be created for a specific racial audience was *Asian Club* (BBC, 1953–61), but this was basically an integration service where the *difference* of the Asian immigrant was always central to the discourse. *Apna Hi Ghar Samajkiye* (BBC, first transmission 10 October 1965) and *Nai Zindagi Naya Jeevan* (BBC, November 1968–82) had similar objectives but slightly broader repertoires. The dominant assumption behind most of these programmes was that any problems which Asian people faced in Britain could be eradicated by the assimilation of 'Asianness' into 'Englishness'. Nevertheless, at a time when many Asians inevitably felt alienated from the primary sources of information and entertainment in Britain, these programmes did indicate that efforts were being made to address non-English viewers.

In general, light entertainment and variety was where British television audiences were most likely to see Black, and usually Black-American, artists. There were some exceptions in dramatic productions, but not as many as you might expect given the great resource of aspiring Black actors in Britain (such as Norman Beaton, Carmen

Munroe, Horace James, Lloyd Reckord and Edric Connor). Nevertheless, there were a handful of notable dramas on television (mostly written by White male playwrights) that addressed the issue of British race relations in a quite unique way. One such example was John Hopkins' British-based anti-apartheid play *Fable* (BBC1, 1965) which marked a radical use of form and content compared to the dominant representations of 'race' and hallmark of documentary realism hitherto deployed in race relations discourses. Usually however, when Black people were consciously written into scripts, it was in the context of dramatic conflict because of the problems their colour was assumed to bring (e.g. the White girl bringing home a Black boyfriend, or the problem of a mixed marriage). In this sense, the Black televisual presence in drama was often about a Black person's colour, rather than about their character. One key pattern (long familiar to us from American cinema) which began to emerge in the 1970s was of Black characters in 'service' roles; as nurses, chauffeurs, waiters, hospital orderlies, and so on. Within the political context of mounting pressure in Britain for more Black representation, this made it *look* as though Black people had been included in the drama, although their roles were rarely developed into 'characters' or written in interesting ways.

One of the most offensive recurrent images of Blackness could be seen in *The Black and White Minstrel Show* (BBC, 1958–78), a nostalgic return to the days of the Deep South when the good Black slaves would serenade innocent White roses. Like other emblems of Blackness such as the Golliwog, the 'Nigger Minstrel' debased Black people and pertained to a particularly racist tradition of popular entertainment. During the two decades in which the Saturday-night phenomenon was transmitted, there were very few alternative images of Black and Asian people on British television. Despite (or perhaps because of) its widespread popularity, some such as the Campaign Against Racism in the Media petitioned (as early as 1967) for its removal from our screens and the BBC finally stopped producing the programme in the late 1970s.

Another programme which raised the public debate about race and representation was the popular sitcom *Till Death Us Do Part* (BBC, 1966–74) created by Johnny Speight. The comedy was either understood as stridently racist, or anti-racist, or something in between – depending on your point of view. Centred on Alf Garnett, a blatantly racist bigot, Speight argued that it was precisely Garnett's bigotry that he was working against. However, members of the public routinely told Warren Mitchell (who played Alf) that they loved it when he 'had a go at the coons'. Among other things, the series demonstrated the potential gap between (liberal) intention and impact (i.e. Speight could not guarantee that all members of the TV audience interpreted the programme in an anti-racist way). It also showed how representation can produce and circulate a number of different (and often competing) ideologies and meanings.

## Issues of access: 1970s

It was not until the 1970s that Black people began to use the media as a forum to 'answer back' to years of verbal negation and visual absence in the British media.

Many different groups in society (women, gays, disabled and elderly people) began to demand better rights and access to institutions such as the media, and to pinpoint the media's limited representation of restricted voices and viewpoints.

Some ITV companies such as London Weekend Television (LWT) began to experiment with schedules by using low-risk off-peak slots to respond to calls to improve minority programming. *Babylon* (LWT, 1979) for example, was a short series specifically targeted at young Black Londoners and the London Minorities Unit was subsequently set up under John Birt (then Head of Factual Programmes at LWT). This was followed by *Skin*, a 30-minute documentary series aimed at Asian and African Caribbean communities who were generally seen to be united by discrimination in housing, education and employment. Many criticized the series, however, for explaining the Black minority to a White majority, for being *about* not *for* Black communities and for always discussing Black people in relation to White people.

By the 1970s, analysis of the media (particularly television), its functions and its effects became central to cultural criticism and many Black and Asian people became more vocal and cohesive in their criticism of the media's racial bias. Slots such as the BBC's *Open Door* attempted to 'redress the balance' by expressing otherwise under-represented viewpoints. For example, the Campaign Against Racism in The Media used one such slot to make *It Ain't Half Racist Mum* (1 March 1979), 'a programme *about* the media and racism, *on* the media, *against* the media' (Hall 1981: 47). Such precious slots triggered debates about strategy and about *how* to approach form and content. They also prompted many to voice their concerns about the pressure which limited space (on 'their' public service broadcaster) brought – not only the pressure to say 'everything' in one slot, but also the pressure to please all sectors of Black communities at the same time (Gardner 1979). This impossible task has been termed 'the burden of representation' (Mercer 1994: 81).

## The emergence of Channel 4 and multicultural departments

In response to a growing debate about the role of television in social life, the BBC set up the Independent Programmes Complaints Commission in October 1977 to consider viewers' complaints about particular radio and television broadcasts. In the same year, the Annan Committee promoted the concept of 'liberal pluralism', a free marketplace in which balance could be achieved through the competition of a multiplicity of diverse and independent voices. This reconceptualization symbolized a shift in terminology and an erosion of the very principle of 'public service broadcasting' on which British television had traditionally been founded. The Committee suggested that 'Good broadcasting would reflect the competing demands of a society which was increasingly multi-racial and pluralist'. Discussions about the fourth channel subsequently began. British broadcasting was soon to witness one of the most radical moments in the medium's history in relation to Black British audiences, with the formation of Channel 4.

Black programming was built into the structure of Channel 4 and it was the first time ever that someone had been specifically appointed to commission programmes for a non-White British audience (Farrukh Dhondy replaced Sue Woodford as Commissioning Editor for Multicultural Programming in 1984 and maintained this position until 1997 when it was taken over by Yasmin Anwar). By the mid-1980s, Channel 4 had built up a large number of 'Black programmes', which formed a significant part of its weekly schedule. These included *Black On Black* and *Eastern Eye* (1982–5), Black magazine programmes which were targeted towards African-Caribbeans and Asians respectively. The regularity with which the programmes were screened was unique in that there was an ongoing weekly presence of Black people on British television. Since then, no terrestrial television channel has matched that consistency in terms of a specifically targeted Black programme, although there have since been a number of documentary series such as the BBC's *All Black, East* and *Birthrights* and Channel 4's *Black Bag, Bandung File* and *Ba Ba Zee*. Channel 4 also screened specifically Black-targeted sitcoms such as *Tandoori Nights* and *No Problem!* which, although they came under criticism for lampooning Black characters and perpetuating stereotypes of Black and Asian people (Gilroy 1983), represented a shift away from the crude racist 'name-calling'-style sitcoms of the 1970s such as *Love Thy Neighbour, Mixed Blessings* and *Mind Your Language*. Many of the BBC Multicultural Department's (which was split into the African-Caribbean Unit and Asian Programmes Unit in 1995) Black and Asian programmes such as *All Black* and *East* have also been criticized for reiterating problem-oriented discourses and for focusing on issues such as rent boys, prostitution, Asian pornography, girl-baby killing and Asian female self-mutilation. Both Channel 4 and the BBC have continued to produce mostly factual, usually poorly scheduled programmes. Just as the BBC have been accused of having a narrow conception of the British public it claims to be serving, Channel 4 has been accused of relinquishing its commitment to Black and Asian audiences and programme-makers by relying on guaranteed audience-pullers (such as US sitcoms and films) which have very little to do with the actualities of British multiculturalism.

The very presence of specialist units and racially targeted programming has sparked off disparate opinion about whether/how they can provide for Black audience needs. The main worry that some have about the existence of multicultural units is that they encourage the 'ghettoization' of Black programmes, experiences and programme-makers by containing them at the margins, and thus always ensuring they remain peripheral to mainstream television developments and portrayals. Furthermore, there is the fear that the existence of minority units allows other commissioners/departments 'off the hook' since they rely on the specialist units to have a conscience about Black audience needs.

## Channel 4 and Black British independent film practices

The radical impact of Channel 4, the development of Black British independent film workshops and the centrality of debates around Third Cinema, identity and diasporic experiences are central to any discussions of race, ethnicity and the media. All occurred in the 1980s, a period where contestation over national identity increasingly developed as a central political and social issue and as a preoccupation of emergent forms of representation.

In 1978, the soon-to-be-elected Prime Minister, Margaret Thatcher, echoed Enoch Powell's infamous 1968 'Rivers of Blood' speech when she spoke of the threat of being 'swamped by alien cultures'. In 1981 there were uprisings in St Paul's (Bristol), Toxteth (Liverpool) and Brixton (London). The politically stifling atmosphere of the 1980s acted as a catalyst, triggering off creativity and a strong desire to express and find a cohesive voice. Echoing the Black Power movement in the 1960s in the USA, many Asian, African and Caribbean people in 1980s Britain began to use the collective term 'Black' as a political term.

One of the most innovative interventions to emerge out of this socio-political context was Black British film, mostly in the form of grant-aided regional film collectives. In the 1980s independent workshops such as Black Audio Film Collective, Ceddo, Sankofa and Retake Film and Video Collective were created within a specific and rapidly changing social, political and economic framework. Many films made by these Black British cinematic practitioners signified a shift from the dominant linear forms of narrative towards a more experimental, non-linear and eclectic film style and, as such, challenged the Hollywood conventions of 'how to tell a story'. In terms of content, documentary films such as *Handsworth Songs* (John Akomfrah, Black Audio Film Collective, 1986) and *The People's Account* (Ceddo, Milton Bryan, 1988) and fictional features such as *The Passion of Remembrance* (Sankofa, Isaac Julien and Maureen Blackwood, 1986) and *Majdhar* (Retake, Ahmed A. Jamal, 1985) tenaciously invested in the notion of identity. *Handsworth Songs*, in particular, with its innovative, unsettling interrogation of the 1980s Brixton 'race riots', prompted a number of debates about how to address Black and White audiences, about the documentary form and about dealing with issues of history and memory.

Many Black British films of the 1980s continued the tradition and extended the framework established by film-makers such as Horace Ove (*Baldwin's Nigger*, 1969, *Reggae*, 1970, *Pressure*, 1975), Lionel Ngakane (*Jemima and Johnny*, 1963) and Lloyd Reckord (*Ten Bob In Winter*, 1963) in the 1960s and 1970s. If one were to identify a key difference between the two sets of films, then it is possible to notice a general drift from a concern with the 'politics of race' in the earlier films (often focusing on notions of belonging and identity for the Black British subject) to an experimentation with form in the films of the 1980s, where the politics of representation was privileged. Black film-makers in the 1980s approached the spaces they struggled for in a creative way, and worked towards reconceptualizing notions of what constitutes British film and Britishness. Despite this truly exciting moment in Black representation, towards the end of the decade (and for a range of complex social, political and economic reasons and as part of a more general closing up of 'minority' art spaces), many public institutions ended their commitment to the workshops, and the beginning of a single project-led commissioning structure began to arise. Since then, some of the films to emerge from Black British film-makers and scriptwriters such as *Bhaji on The Beach* (1993, dir: Gurinder Chadha) and *East is East* (1999, dir: Damien O'Donnell) have successfully emulated the 'crossover' (from art-house to mainstream) pattern of earlier films such as *My Beautiful Laundrette* (1985, dir: Stephen Frears). In general though, money and the 'burden of representation' continue to affect the majority of Black and Asian people involved in film production in Britain.

## Conclusion: the future for Black British audiences

It is useful for us to end where we began, with Macpherson's Report, which defined 'institutional racism' as 'unwitting prejudice, ignorance, thoughtlessness and racist stereotyping which disadvantage minority people'. The British media is not exempt from such processes, and indeed, must be recognized as a massively influential site where ideologies about race (both Whiteness and Blackness) are shaped. Television, as a principal signifying system for example, has considerable and critical powers in shaping the ways in which we *all* understand the meaning of 'race'.

Recent changes in the television infrastructure (the impact of cable, satellite, Channel 5, deregulation and the Broadcasting Acts 1990 and 1996, for example) have meant that, generally speaking, commercialism, ratings and revenue are being prioritized over what are assumed to be 'minority' needs. Many feel that Black and Asian audiences are still not sufficiently catered for and that insensitivity towards issues of race and ethnicity still exists. The reality of a lived multiculturalism is not represented on British television and the media in general can by no means be seen as ethnically neutral. Although it is now common to see Black and Asian people on British television who do not necessarily function to solely 'carry' the race theme, the repertoire of imagery still remains limited. We rarely see strong Asian women (Gita in *EastEnders* and Milly in *This Life* were notable exceptions) or Black factual commentators outside sports programmes and there are still too few Black people actually reaching the industry's boardrooms. Television is still far too 'White'; an admission made by the BBC's newly appointed Director General, Greg Dyke, following his visit around BBC departments (Dyke said this in a speech delivered at the CRE's Race in the Media Awards in April 2000).

These are issues now confronting terrestrial programme-makers as competition from non-terrestrial suppliers rapidly increases with a plethora of 'specialist channels' marketed towards niche audiences of which Black and Asian people are an integral part. There is increasing evidence that minorities are turning to extra-terrestrial channels to get the media they want. Many Asians, for example, are tuning into dedicated Asian channels via cable and satellite, and going to cinemas in droves to watch Asian films 'imported' from the Indian subcontinent. Attracting the Black and Asian television viewer and cinemagoer is speedily becoming not just a moral but an economic imperative. In the light of these changes, television itself – its programmes, its role, its value, its past, its future, its economics, its relation to nationhood, citizenship and the public – is being re-evaluated and strategically modified. On the one hand, there is a belief that the rise of new media technologies and processes (cable, satellite, digital compression, pay-per-view, etc.) will serve as one possible avenue through which each person can be granted their 'cultural rights' in more specific and varied ways. On the other, there is concern that an increasingly global future can, in fact, mean a 'downgrading of cultural specificity in themes and settings and a preference for formats and genres which are thought to be universal' (McQuail 1994: 112). However things develop, there is little doubt that British broadcasting's traditional legislative and ideological framework is, as a result of these and other shifts, under (commercial) threat. As Trevor Phillips notes

> The greatest irony in the TV landscape may well be this: the paternalistic, regulated environment of the terrestrial channels may increasingly force minorities off their agenda, whilst the buccaneering free marketeers of the cable and satellite channels could well begin to offer the chance of a presence hitherto unheard of (Phillips 1995: 20).

## Questions

1   Identify some common stereotypes of Black and Asian people in the British media and discuss how they have been perpetuated or deconstructed in various media texts.

2   What are the arguments for and against having specialist 'minority' programmes targeted at specific ethnic minority audiences on British television?

3   What impact do you think satellite, cable and other technological developments are having on terrestrial television's relationship with Black British and British Asian audiences?

## References

Dyer, R. (1988) 'White', *Screen: The Last 'Special Issue' on Race?* 29(4): 44–65.

Gardner, C. (1979) 'Limited access', *Time Out* 23 February.

Gilroy, P. (1983) 'C4 – Bridgehead or Bantustan?' *Screen* 24(4–5): 130–36.

Hall, S. (1981) 'The whites of their eyes: racist ideologies and the media', in G. Bridges and R. Brunt (eds) *Silver Linings: Some Strategies for the Eighties*, London: Lawrence & Wishart.

Henriques, J. (1988) 'Realism and the new language', *Black Film, British Cinema*, ICA Document 7, London: Institute of Contemporary Arts.

Macpherson, W. (1999) *The Stephen Lawrence Inquiry: Report of an Inquiry*, The Stationery Office.

McQuail, D. (1994) *Mass Communication Theory: An Introduction*, London: Sage.

Malik, S. (1996) 'Beyond "the cinema of duty"? The pleasures of hybridity: Black British film of the 1980s and 1990s', in A. Higson (ed.) *Dissolving Views: Key Writings on British Cinema*, London: Cassell.

Mercer, K. (1994) *Welcome to the Jungle: New Positions in Black Cultural Studies*, London: Routledge.

Phillips, T. (1995) 'UK TV: a place in the sun?' in C. Frachon and M. Vargaftig (eds) *European Television: Immigrants and Ethnic Minorities*, London: John Libbey.

## Further reading

Daniels, T. and Gerson, J. (1989) *The Colour Black: Black Images in British Television*, London: British Film Institute. Provides a range of debates and reviews of Black representation in British television drama series, comedy and soap operas in the 1970s and 1980s.

Donald, J. and Rattansi, A (eds) (1992) *'Race', Culture and Difference*, London: Sage. Focuses on debates about ethnicity, identity, culture and difference in contemporary society, particularly in relation to educational and social policy.

Hall, S. (1981) 'The whites of their eyes: racist ideologies and the media', in G. Bridges and R. Brunt (eds) *Silver Linings: Some Strategies for the Eighties*, London: Lawrence & Wishart. A seminal essay outlining the key approaches to representing Black people in the British media, which identifies a dominant 'grammar of race' based on three stereotypes: the native, the slave and the entertainer.

Malik, S. (2001) *Representing Black Britain: Black and Asian images on television*, London: Sage. A discursive analysis and historical reflection on images of Blackness on British television, bringing the story up to date to outline the new pressures on traditional broadcasting to address the various needs of its culturally diverse audiences.

Mercer, K. (1988) *Black Film, British Cinema*, ICA Document 7, London: Institute of Contemporary Arts. An essential introduction to debates around Black British film taken from the 1988 'Black Film, British Cinema' Conference at London's Institute for Contemporary Arts.

Pines, J. (1992) *Black and White in Colour*, London: British Film Institute. A book of interviews with key players in the history of Black representation on British television.

Rutherford, J. (ed.) (1990) *Identity: Community, Culture, Difference*, London: Lawrence & Wishart. A collection of essays about society and its complex and overlapping identities.

## Web sites

www.raceandethnicity.com

www.newsunlimited.co.uk/racism

www.bbc.co.uk/asianlife

www.bbconline

www.cre.gov.uk

www.blackbritain.co.uk

# Chapter 26

# Youth

'THE GOOD, THE BAD AND THE UGLY': POST-WAR MEDIA
REPRESENTATIONS OF YOUTH

**BILL OSGERBY**

Surveying the British media's representation of youth and youth culture since 1945, this chapter explores the way in which the 'youth question' has functioned as a medium through which fundamental shifts in social boundaries and cultural relationships have been explored, interpreted and made sense of. Charting key shifts in the media's responses to the social behaviour and cultural expressions of young people, it is argued that representations of youth possess a powerful metaphorical dimension – commentary on young people functioning as an important ideological vehicle for the discussion of wider shifts in social, economic and political relations.

## Mixed metaphors: the dual stereotyping of 'youth'

Reading the British press in the late 1950s it often seemed as though the nation was teetering on the edge of a moral abyss. Provincial newspapers warned of a 'new disease' – 'that of the maladjusted young men who don special clothes and rebel against any form of discipline' (*Brighton and Hove Herald* 28 February 1959), reporters conjuring with images of a new brand of vicious hooligan. The perpetrator of a violent street robbery, for example, was described as wearing 'the uniform of the "Wild Ones", youths who ape the dress worn by Marlon Brando in the film of the same name' (*Brighton and Hove Herald* 11 January 1958) and readers' attention was drawn to the effrontery of a young tearaway who had appeared in court sporting the racy ensemble of 'black shirt, pink tie and pink-trimmed jacket' (*Evening Argus* 23 November 1960). Local anxieties reflected a broader sense of alarm. Subcultural style was seen as a symptom of spiralling juvenile criminality which, in turn, was taken to exemplify a more wholesale state of moral debasement and cultural malaise.

Yet there was nothing especially new about these images of juvenile depravity. Geoffrey Pearson (1983) shows that since the nineteenth century Britain has regularly witnessed periods in which public opinion has been outraged by a seemingly unprecedented wave of hooliganism and debauchery among the nation's youth. At the turn of the century, for example, the 'scuttling' gangs of Manchester and the 'Peaky Blinders' of Birmingham were subject to a degree of social disapproval and official opprobrium akin to that which has attended groups of post-war youngsters.

On one level these concerns have related specifically to the demeanour and behaviour of young people, but more generally (and perhaps more significantly) they have also condensed a much wider set of apprehensions. An important 'metaphorical' dimension exists to media representations of young people. A crucial facet to the 'youth' debate is its capacity to function as a kind of 'ideological vehicle' that encapsulates more general hopes and fears about shifts in social relations and the condition of cultural life.

It is, perhaps, inevitable that conceptions of 'youth' and chronological age will figure in attempts to make sense of social change. Nevertheless, many theorists (Smith *et al.* 1975; Clarke *et al.* 1976; Davis 1990; Austin and Willard 1998) have pointed to the way in which youth's metaphorical capacity becomes powerfully extended at moments of particularly profound transformation. The twilight years of the nineteenth century were one such episode – concerns around hooliganism and delinquency embodying wider qualms about the stability of the social order and the vitality of the British economy. The decades following the Second World War were another. After 1945 the themes and imagery of 'youth' featured within the mass media and impinged upon the public consciousness as never before – the youth 'question' functioning as a medium through which fundamental shifts in social boundaries and cultural relationships were explored, interpreted and made sense of.

One does not need to search too hard to find negative representations of youth in post-war Britain. Crime, violence and sexual licence have been recurring themes in the media's treatment of youth culture, the degeneracy of the young depicted as indicative of a steady disintegration of the country's social fabric. Yet representations of young people have never been entirely pessimistic. Media coverage of youth has been characterized by a recurring duality. This Janus-like quality has seen youth culture both celebrated as the exciting precursor to a prosperous future and, almost simultaneously, vilified as the most deplorable evidence of cultural bankruptcy. These contrasting images – which Dick Hebdige (1988: 19) terms 'youth-as-fun' and 'youth-as-trouble' – are obviously distorted and exaggerated stereotypes which bear a tenuous relation to social reality. Nevertheless, their connotative power has been potent and throughout the post-war era this dual imagery of youth has been a key motif around which dominant interpretations of social change have been constructed.

## 'The teenage revolution'

Although Britain was no stranger to crisis and scandal during the 1950s and early 1960s, optimism and confidence were never far away. The nation, it seemed, had 'never had it so good'. As David Dutton (1991) contends, Labour and Conservative governments generally shared a set of key social and economic assumptions that embraced a commitment to the welfare state, a mixed economy and the maintenance of high levels of employment. This sense of political consensus arose in a context of economic growth and a sustained rise in real earnings which, taken together, laid the basis for a steady growth in consumer spending. The working class, in particular, benefited from these changes as enhanced incomes delivered an ever-growing range of consumer products to working-class homes. The substance and texture of working-class culture was transformed and recast during this period, though the British working class did not, in any sense, decompose or disappear and structured inequality remained pronounced. Nevertheless, the dominant imagery of the period was of a dawning 'classlessness'. Political rhetoric held that the pace of economic growth was ushering in a new era of 'post-capitalist' prosperity in which social divisions would be steadily ameliorated and traditional class antagonisms would evaporate. And within this discourse the image of 'youth-as-fun' found a prominent place.

Post-war mythologies of affluent harmony found their purest manifestation in the imagery of youth. Young people seemed to embody all that the consumer dream stood for and throughout the 1950s and early 1960s advertisers habitually used images of young people to associate their products with dynamic modernity and 'with it' enjoyment. Representations of youth, therefore, were deployed as a shorthand signifier for unbridled pleasure in the new age of hedonistic consumption (see Figure 26.1). Above all, this equation of youth with consumption was exemplified by the addition of the term 'teenager' to everyday vocabulary. A label first coined by American market researchers during the mid-1940s, the 'teenager' was quickly imported into British popular discourse, 'teenagers' being taken as the quintessence of post-war social transformation. Distinguished not simply by their youth but also by a particular brand of conspicuous, leisure-oriented consumption, teenagers were perceived as being at the sharp end of the new consumer culture. As Peter Laurie contended in his 1965 anatomy of *The Teenage Revolution*, 'The distinctive fact about teenagers' behaviour is economic: they spend a lot of money on clothes, records, concerts, make-up, magazines: all things that give immediate pleasure and little lasting use' (1965: 9).

The 'teenager', then, was far more than a simple descriptive term. Rather, the 'teenager' was an ideological terrain upon which a particular interpretation of post-war change was constructed. Central to the concept of the 'teenager' was the idea that traditional class boundaries were being eroded by the fads and fashions of a newly affluent 'gilded youth'. (*The Economist* 11 January 1958) 'Teenagers' were presented as a class in themselves, a 'solidly integrated social bloc' (Laurie 1965: 11) whose vibrant, leisure-oriented lifestyle seemed to offer a foretaste of the kind of prosperity that would soon be within everyone's grasp.

The image of the 'affluent teenager' owed a large debt to research conducted by Mark Abrams (1956, 1959, 1961) on young people's spending patterns during the late 1950s. According to Abrams (1959: 9) youth, more than any other social group, had materially prospered since 1945 – with young people's earnings rising by 50% (roughly double that of adults) and youngsters wielding an annual spending power of around £830 million. Abrams' figures were widely publicized and went a long way towards sedimenting notions of a newly affluent group of young consumers patronising a leisure market of unprecedented scale. Though exaggerated, his figures were not without foundation. Changes in production processes and shifts in employment markets had created a high demand for youngsters' labour and their earning power had been enhanced as a consequence. The range of products geared to this growing market was literally boundless, consumer industries interacting with and reinforcing one another as they sought to cash-in on youth spending.

Invitation to a world of pleasure

It's a drink to grace your best cups, to humour your best company. The very sight of it is an invitation to a perfect pleasure. For that's what Cadbury's Drinking Chocolate is. It's pleasure, pleasure all the way from the first tempting whiff to the last delicious drop. Wonderfully rich. Velvety smooth. Truly chocolaty.

Because Cadbury's Drinking Chocolate is all these luxurious things, it is the aristocrat of evening drinks. It belongs among the really good things of life you treasure for the rare enjoyment they bring you. And yet, surprisingly, Cadbury's Drinking Chocolate costs far less than you'd expect. Only 1/7d the half pound

**CADBURY'S
DRINKING CHOCOLATE**
*the luxury evening drink*

**Figure 26.1** 'Invitation to a world of pleasure . . .' Cadbury's Drinking Chocolate 1955 (courtesy Premier International Foods)

The prime example, of course, came in 1956 with the arrival of rock 'n' roll, a genre of popular music tied much more closely than its predecessors to processes of mass marketing and youth demand. The film industry also began to orient itself to the youth market. John Doherty (1988) has documented the post-war rise of the American 'teenpic', exemplified in the films of Roger Corman and Sam Katzman, but the British film industry also began to seek out youth audiences with greater vigour – the 1950s and early 1960s seeing the release of a host of films featuring pop idols such as Cliff Richard, Tommy Steele and the Beatles. Developments in British radio were more faltering. Restricted by limits on 'needle time' (time permitted for the broadcast of recorded music) and official distrust of the 'Americanizing' influences of rock 'n' roll, it was only with the launch of 'pirate' stations in the early 1960s that British radio began broadcasting programmes specifically geared to a 'teen' audience. Television, in contrast, responded relatively swiftly as BBC and ITV both made numerous forays into the field of 'youth' television. However, while the cinema was able to seek out age-specific audiences, John Hill (1991) has shown that early television programmes had to allow for the domestic environment of their viewers, shows like *Six-Five Special* and *Juke Box Jury* having to embrace a heterogeneous, 'family' audience. Nevertheless, by the early 1960s concessions to adult viewers had diminished, programmes like ITV's *Ready, Steady, Go!* revelling in an atmosphere of teen-exclusivity.

'Youth-as-fun' was a central motif within all these texts. Cliff Richard's films of the early 1960s are exemplary. Sprightly musicals *The Young Ones* (dir. Sidney Furie, 1961) and *Summer Holiday* (dir. Peter Yates, 1963) are both tales of ebullient youngsters liberating themselves from the dull conformity of their work-a-day lives. The young people here are not rebels but responsible and enterprising citizens, the films' unquestioning sense of freedom and optimism epitomizing the notions of prosperity and dawning social harmony that lay at the heart of dominant political ideologies during the early 1960s. Indeed, politicians were well aware of this and were keen to associate themselves with the positive attributes of such imagery. In these terms Harold Wilson's presentation of Variety Club awards to the Beatles in 1964 and his award of MBEs to the Fab Four in 1965 can be seen not as good-natured gestures by a warm-hearted 'man of the people', but as a calculated attempt to harvest political capital from the 'language' of youth and modernity.

## 'Teenage rampage'

During the 1950s and early 1960s the media coverage lavished on young people was often up-beat and laudatory. Newspapers and magazines – especially the *Daily Mirror* and *Picture Post* – helped popularize notions of 'youth' as an excitingly new social force, a vibrant contrast to the dull and wearied social order of the past. However, representations of youth have never been unanimously enthusiastic. Even when the cult of the 'affluent teenager' was at its height, images of 'youth-as-fun' co-existed alongside much darker representations in which young people came to epitomize the worst excesses and direst consequences of social change.

As Dick Hebdige (1982) has shown, critical representations of youth have often been a locus for elitist fears of a 'levelling-down' or 'Americanization' of culture – America, the home of monopoly capitalism, coming to epitomize processes of cultural debasement. Typical of such an approach was Richard Hoggart's critique of post-war popular culture, Hoggart's attack on 'canned entertainment and packeted provision' reaching a crescendo in his denouncement of the 'juke box boys' with their 'drape suits, picture ties and American slouch' who spent their evenings in 'harshly lighted milk bars' putting 'copper after copper into the mechanical record player' (1958: 248–50).

Related to this critique of youngsters' cultural preferences has been the stereotyping of young people as a uniquely delinquent generation. This line of argument has often taken subcultural style as its target. During the early 1950s, for example, these anxieties cohered around the figure of the Teddy boy. First identified by the media in the working-class neighbourhoods of south London in 1954, the Ted was soon presented as a shockingly new spectre haunting street corners all over the country, his negative image compounded in the sensational press coverage of cinema 'riots' that followed screenings of the film *Rock Around the Clock* in 1956. By the end of the decade the Ted's drape-suit had been superseded by the chic, Italian-inspired styles of the mods. However, like the Teds before them, the mods' appearance was often presented by the media as not simply a mode of dress but as a symbol of national decline. This approach reached fever-pitch in press responses to the mod 'invasions' of several seaside resorts in 1964, events given front-page prominence by national newspapers who spoke of a 'day of terror' in which whole towns had been overrun by a marauding mob 'hell-bent on destruction'.

Such spectacular reportage is invariably exaggerated and overwrought. In the case of the mod 'invasions', for instance, the initial acts of violence and vandalism were slight and it is likely that press coverage actually engendered and amplified subsequent disturbances. Stanley Cohen has termed such occasions of sensationalized media alarm 'moral panics', a situation in which:

> A condition, episode, person or group of persons emerges to become defined as a
> threat to societal values and interests; its nature presented in a stylized and stereotypical
> fashion by the mass media, the moral barricades are manned by editors, bishops,
> politicians and other right-thinking people; socially accredited experts pronounce
> their diagnoses and solutions; ways of coping are evolved or (more often) resorted to;
> the condition then disappears, submerges or deteriorates and becomes more visible
> (Cohen 1980: 9).

In these terms distorted media coverage plays an active role in shaping events. Media attention fans the sparks of an initially trivial incident, creating a self-perpetuating 'amplification spiral' which generates phenomena of much greater magnitude and social significance.

Cohen's case study focused on media representations of the 1960s 'battles' between mods and rockers, charting how media intervention gave shape to these groups and crafted them into threatening 'folk devils'. However, his arguments could easily be applied to media treatment of the procession of subcultural groups that have since appeared. From the skinheads of the late 1960s, through the punks of the 1970s, to the 'new age travellers' and 'acid house ravers' of the late 1980s and early 1990s, youth subcultures have been subject to processes of stigmatization and stereotyping – which, paradoxically, have also worked to popularize and lend substance to styles that were initially indistinct and ill-defined. Media intervention, therefore, gives youth subcultures not only national exposure but also a degree of uniformity and definition. Indeed, without the intercession of media industries it is unlikely that subcultures such as the Teddy boys, punks or ravers would have cohered as recognizable cultural formations, instead remaining vaguely defined and locally confined stylistic innovations.

Young women have been generally marginal to those moral panics related to public order. Alarm associated with the mods and rockers' lawlessness, the punks' outrageousness or the violence of football hooligans has generally (though not exclusively) focused on the behaviour of young men. In contrast, young women have figured much more visibly in moral panics related to sexual behaviour and 'permissiveness'. The post-war period, for example, has been punctuated by anxieties regarding perceived rises in the number of teenage pregnancies. Typical was the *Daily Mirror*'s 1991 revelation of 'the startling truth about teenage sex', the newspaper ominously announcing that Britain was 'in the grip of a teenage pregnancy crisis' (*Daily Mirror* 24 November 1991). In 1996, meanwhile, concern over the explicit discussion of sex in young women's magazines such as *19, J-17* and *Sugar* prompted Peter Luff, Conservative MP for Worcestershire, to propose the Periodicals (Protection of Children) Bill – with the objective of tightening legal controls over the sexual content of magazines aimed at young readers. The Bill itself was ultimately withdrawn, though only after magazine publishers had agreed to the introduction of a voluntary code of conduct (Gough-Yates 1999).

Again, however, this view of 'corrupted' youth was hyperbolic. Certainly, the period since 1945 has witnessed major change in young people's sexual attitudes and behaviour. Empirical evidence, however, indicates that 'casual' promiscuity among British youth has been considerably less than suggested in salacious media accounts, young people's sexual activity generally taking place within single, 'serious' relationships (Schofield 1965, 1973; Leonard 1980).

A parallel can be drawn here between the media's stereotyping of youth and its treatment of sexual behaviour more generally. Just as 'youth' has functioned as an 'ideological vehicle' for the discussion and interpretation of more general social issues, Jeffrey Weeks (1985) argues that developments in the field of sexuality have been taken as symbolic of wider patterns of social transformation. Debates around sexuality have been used to condense broader anxieties and to mobilize opinion and energies – increasingly on behalf of the political Right as the post-war political consensus disintegrated and gave way to a more confrontational and abrasive form of political order.

## 'Where did our love go?'

The media's representations of 'youth', then, tell us relatively little about the actual realities of life as experienced by young people. They reveal much more about dominant social and political preoccupations. Both lauded as the shape of wonderful things to come *and* reviled as the incarnation of malevolent forces menacing established ways of life, young people serve as a canvas on which debates about more general patterns of social change are elaborated.

During the 1950s and 1960s media representations of young people became a repository for misgivings about the 'state of the nation'. Spectacular subcultures, in particular, were presented as the neurosis of the affluent society – the alienated product of unfettered consumption and cultural decline. At the same time, however, the image of 'the teenager' encapsulated a more positive reading of change – one in which a new era of growth was fast ameliorating inequality and the generation gap was supplanting the class war as the nation's foremost social division. Indeed, while Britain enjoyed a period of sustained economic prosperity it was this positive stereotyping of youth that was most prevalent. Even subcultural 'folk devils' could be embraced in these feelings of optimism. The mod's superficially clean-cut and well-dressed appearance, for example, was easily co-opted within notions of post-war dynamism and mods were fêted as classless consumers *par excellence*, the media eagerly charting changes in the minutiae of mod dress and musical preference.

By the late 1960s, however, the rhetoric of prosperity and optimism was proving difficult to sustain as deep-seated problems within the British economy became evident. Social and political divisions intensified as industrial decline, unemployment and worsening labour relations steadily undercut notions of consensus and affluence. Stuart Hall and his associates (1978, 1983) have argued that this period saw a key shift in British political life, the state increasingly dispensing with attempts to rule by consent, embracing instead political strategies that were more visibly repressive and confrontational. In this context the negative stereotyping of youth became more pronounced. The 1960s counterculture, especially, was cast as part of a more pervasive 'enemy within'. Whereas earlier subcultures such as the Teds or mods had been depicted as *symptoms* of decline, the counter-culture was presented as actively *causing* a collapse of law and order and social stability. Media coverage of episodes such as university sit-ins and demonstrations against the Vietnam war cast student radicals and hippies as a minority of subversive extremists who deliberately sought to undermine the social and moral mainstays of the nation.

The counterculture, however, was not universally denounced. Its largely middle-class composition worked to temper criticism and media coverage was sometimes ambiguous, occasionally even positive. Hence the hippies' hedonistic lifestyle, even their drug-taking, could be treated with fascination and a degree of respect. In 1968, for instance, in its series 'The Restless Generation', *The Times* praised hippy communes such as the Tribe of the Sacred Mushroom for generating 'a fresh approach to living' that provided its members with 'livelihood and fulfilment' (*The Times* 18 December 1968). Similarly, when Rolling Stones Mick Jagger and Keith Richards were found guilty of possession of illegal drugs in 1967, *The Times* leapt to their defence in an editorial that attacked their sentences as unreasonably draconian. Indeed, on leaving court Jagger did not face a barrage of media criticism, but was whisked by helicopter to appear on Granada Television's *World in Action*, joining church leaders and politicians in a roundtable discussion on the nature of personal liberty.

The fragmentation and decline of the counter-culture during the early 1970s saw the negative stereotyping of youth return to more 'traditional' subjects. Throughout the 1970s and 1980s groups of working-class youngsters were once again paraded as baleful indices of growing lawlessness and social breakdown. Moreover, media preoccupation with street crime in the early 1970s, followed by the spectre of the 'inner-city rioter' in the 1980s, saw the addition of a powerful 'racial' dimension to the imagery of 'youth-as-trouble', while a seemingly endless series of moral panics grafted new terrors (lager louts, acid house parties, joy-riding) onto older and more established themes of decline – the collapse of the family, moral laxity, crime, and urban disorder (see Figure 26.2).

**GRIFFIN'S EYE**

"And if your dad comes home from work before midnight, don't go telling him who I've gone out with."

**Figure 26.2** 'I'll kick your head', *Daily Mirror* 13 July 1988 (courtesy of Mirror Syndication)

## 'Whatever happened to the teenage dream?'

The resurgence of the media's negative stereotyping of young people during the 1970s and 1980s was commensurate with broader political shifts. Trading on public fears and apprehensions the New Right managed to enlist support for an 'authoritarian populism' (Hall 1983) which successfully married a 'populist' appeal with the enforcement of a more coercive brand of authority and order. However, the ensuing 'law 'n' order' bandwagon did not entirely displace images of 'youth-as-fun'.

Governments of the 1980s galvanized popular support not simply through the promise of 'order'. Also important was the mobilization of people's concrete aspirations and desires via the promise of consumer empowerment in a 'property-owning democracy'. In the rhetoric of 'enterprise' and the 'free market', the positive stereotyping of youth found a new lease of life. In 1988, for example, the popular press acclaimed 'The Young Revolution' in which 'Britain's youngsters are riding the roller-coaster boom of Mrs. Thatcher's economic recovery. They have seen a new kind of revolution – giving power to the consumer – and they want to join the action before it ends' (*Daily Star* 11 May 1988). Advertisers also eulogized a 'new' brand of youth consumption. In their report *Youth Lifestyle*, market analysts Mintel claimed to have discovered among young people a 'new consumption and success ethic' that had been generated by 'the sustained economic growth of the enterprise culture', while McCann-Erickson's comprehensive survey, *The New Generation*, identified a 'New Wave' of 'post-permissive' youngsters who were committed to a new spirit of possessive individualism and who exhibited 'the most highly developed form of the new multi-profile consumption in our society' (McCann-Erickson Worldwide 1989: 25).

Nevertheless, representations of youth made only a cameo appearance within 1980s ideologies of 'consumer empowerment'. Compared to their ubiquitous presence within discourses of affluence and dynamism during the 1950s and 1960s, images of 'youth as fun' were relatively marginal to the rhetoric of the 1980s 'boom'. By the 1980s the concept of the 'teenager' as the embodiment of hedonistic consumption had become untenable. The commercial market that provided the basis for the 'teenage revolution' had been undercut by a combination of the demographic contraction of the youth population and growing levels of youth unemployment. The youth market became a shadow of its former self, retailers' and manufacturers' obsession with youth fading as young people's spending power decreased. In place of the youth market new growth areas emerged – the fashion, film and music industries all increasingly realigning to the consumer appetites of 'empty nesters' and the 'thirty-something' generation. Rather than the 'swinging teenager', therefore, it was the image of the more mature and cosmopolitan 'yuppie' that captured the mood of the 1980s 'good times'.

Indeed, growing levels of youth unemployment may have fundamentally transformed the connotations of the term 'teenager'. Simon Frith has argued that while the term was originally associated primarily with working-class youngsters and their consumption patterns, by the 1980s it had come mainly to refer to middle-class youth – 'the only young people for whom the problems of consumption remain paramount' (1981: 13). Certainly, there was more than a degree of truth to this. By the 1990s, in both Britain and America, representations of 'youth as fun' seemed to relate almost exclusively to youngsters from green-lawned, well-to-do suburbs. The American television series *Beverley Hills 90210* (1990–2000) was archetypal – its designer-clad adolescents lounging around luxurious swimming pools and cruising the streets in expensive convertibles. By the mid-1990s, however, the harsh realities of the contemporary economic environment were beginning to extend upwards (Rutherford 1998). Falls in student income and the contraction of the graduate job market meant that even middle-class youngsters were beginning to be excluded from the 'teenage' experience.

During the 1990s, then, it seemed as though the concept of the 'teenager' was not so much being redefined as gradually disappearing from view. Indeed, the term now seems strangely dated, even anachronistic. In place of the 'teenager' images of a 'lost generation' came to the fore. From Douglas Coupland's (1992) novel of the same name the term 'Generation X' entered the popular vocabulary. Coupland's quirky, anomic characters were born in the early to mid-1960s, yet Charles Acland (1995: 145–6) argues that 'Generation X' came to denote a younger cohort of overeducated and underemployed juveniles leading an apathetic and largely aimless existence. Films such as *River's Edge* (dir. Tim Hunter, 1986) and *Kids* (dir. Larry Clark, 1995) developed a similar motif, painting a picture of an adolescence that is not necessarily delinquent or depraved but is desolate and alienated. Though these texts were American, their themes were matched by British films such as *Trainspotting* (dir. Danny Boyle, 1995) and novels such as John King's *The Football Factory* (1996) – all of which articulated images of bleak and meaningless young lives.

Towards the end of the decade, however, it looked as though more positive representations of youth were set to be revived. The election victory of Tony Blair's ('New') Labour Party, in May 1997, ushered in a government whose proclaimed mission was to 'modernize' Britain. With more than a faint echo of Wilson's 1964 administration, New Labour's rhetoric deployed the iconography of 'vibrant youth' as the government scrambled to cash-in on the kudos of 'Cool Britannia' – a phrase that seemed to capture the renaissance then taking place in Britain's fashion, design and pop music industries. During the 1990s change also appeared to register in the character of moral panics, with many agencies and experts seemingly more willing to contest the media's demonization of youth and counter the vocality of the traditional moral crusaders (McRobbie 1994). Additionally, those groups of young people once reviled within dominant discourse and confined to the periphery of cultural life were increasingly successful in elaborating prominent and empowered cultural identities. Black and Asian British youth, in particular, emerged as a potent force in national popular culture – their subcultural expressions exercising an increasingly significant influence in the pop and fashion 'mainstream' (Back 1996; Sharma *et al.* 1996).

By the end of the 1990s, then, it was possible that the traditional stereotypes of 'youth-as-trouble' and 'youth-as-fun' were beginning to lose their relevance. Instead, a more ambiguous and open-ended set of images seemed to have emerged. Moreover, the media's understanding of 'youth' seemed, in some respects, to have become increasingly divorced from the lives of young people themselves. At the close of the century the television, film, music, fashion and advertising industries were gearing themselves less to specific generational categories than to particular 'mind-sets' and attitudes. As Frith observed of trends in music television during the 1990s. '"Youth" no longer describes a particular type of viewer, who is attracted to a particular type of programme but, rather, describes an attitude, a particular type of *viewing behaviour* (1993: 75)'. In these terms media representations of 'youth' have come to be characterized not by generational age but by a particular lifestyle. Indeed, 'youth' may have become simply a mode of consumption.

## Questions

1   How do the dimensions of gender and 'race' influence and mediate representations of 'youth' in the media?

2   How far, and in what ways, does the media exercise an influence over youth subcultures?

3   How are other generational groups represented in the media? Are there particular kinds of social meaning associated with these images?

## References

Abrams, M. (1956) 'The younger generation', *Encounter* 6(5): 35–58.

Abrams, M. (1959) *The Teenage Consumer*, London: Press Exchange.

Abrams, M., (1961) *Teenage Consumer Spending in 1959*, London: Press Exchange.

Acland, C. (1995) *Youth, Murder, Spectacle: The Cultural Politics of 'Youth in Crisis'*, Oxford: Westview.

Austin, J. and Willard, M. (eds) (1998) *Generations of Youth: Youth Cultures and History in Twentieth-Century America*, New York: New York University Press.

Back, L. (1996) *New Ethnicities and Urban Culture: Racisms and Multiculture in Young Lives*, London: UCL.

Clarke, J., Hall, S., Jefferson, T. and Roberts, B. (1976) 'Subcultures, cultures and class: a theoretical overview', in S. Hall and T. Jefferson (eds) *Resistance Through Rituals: Youth Subcultures in Post-War Britain*, London: Hutchinson, pp. 9–74.

Cohen, S. (1980) *Folk Devils and Moral Panics: The Creation of the Mods and Rockers*, Oxford: Blackwell.

Coupland, D. (1992) *Generation X: Tales for an Accelerated Culture*, London: Abacus.

Davis, J. (1990) *Youth and the Condition of Britain: Images of Adolescent Conflict*, London: Athlone.

Doherty, J. (1988) *Teenagers and Teenpics: The Juvenilization of American Movies in the 1950s*, London: Unwin Hyman.

Dutton, D. (1991) *British Politics Since 1945: The Rise and Fall of Consensus*, Oxford: Blackwell.

Frith, S. (1981), 'Youth in the eighties: a dispossessed generation', *Marxism Today* 25(11): 12–15.

Frith, S. (1993) 'Youth/music/television' in S. Frith, A. Goodwin and L. Grossberg (eds) *Sound and Vision: The Music Video Reader*, London: Routledge, pp. 67–84.

Gough-Yates, A (1999) 'Sweet sell of sexcess: The production of young women's magazines and readerships in the 1990s', in D. Berry (ed.), *Ethics and Media Culture: Practices and Representations*, Oxford: Focal Press.

Hall, S., Critcher, C., Jefferson, T., Clarke, J. and Roberts, R. (1978) *Policing the Crisis: Mugging, the State and Law and Order*, London: Macmillan.

Hall, S. (1983) 'The great moving right show' in S. Hall and M. Jacques (eds) *The Politics of Thatcherism*, London: Lawrence and Wishart.

Hebdige, D. (1982) 'Towards a cartography of taste, 1935–1962', in B. Waites, T. Bennett and G. Martin (eds) *Popular Culture: Past and Present*, London: Croom Helm, pp. 194–218.

Hebdige, D. (1988) 'Hiding in the light: Youth surveillance and display', in D. Hebdige, *Hiding in the Light: On Images and Things*, London: Routledge, pp. 17–36.

Hill, J. (1991) 'Television and pop: the case of the 1950s' in J. Corner (ed.) *Popular Television in Britain: Studies in Cultural History*, London: BFI, pp. 90–107.

Hoggart, R. (1958), *The Uses of Literacy*, Harmondsworth: Penguin.

King, J. (1996) *The Football Factory*, London: Jonathan Cape.

Laurie, P. (1965) *The Teenage Revolution*, London: Anthony Blond.

Leonard, D. (1980) *Sex and Generation*, London: Tavistock.

McCann-Erickson Worldwide (1989) *The New Generation: The McCann-Erickson European Youth Study, 1977–87*, London: McCann-Erickson.

McRobbie, A. (1994) 'The moral panic in the age of the postmodern mass media', in A. McRobbie, *Postmodernism and Popular Culture*, London: Routledge, pp. 198–219.

Pearson, G. (1983) *Hooligan: A History of Respectable Fears*, London: Macmillan.

Rutherford, J. (1998) 'Introduction', in J. Rutherford (ed.), *Young Britain: Politics, Pleasures and Predicaments*, London: Lawrence and Wishart.

Schofield, M. (1965) *The Sexual Behaviour of Young People*, London: Longman.

Schofield, M. (1973) *The Sexual Behaviour of Young Adults*, London: Allen Lane.

Sharma, S., Hutnyk, J. and Sharma, A. (eds) (1996) *Dis-Orienting Rhythms*, London: Zed.

Smith, A. C. H., Immirizi, E. and Blackwell, T. (1975) *Paper Voices: The Popular Press and Social Change, 1935–1965*, London: Chatto and Windus.

Weeks, J. (1985) *Sexuality and Its Discontents: Meanings, Myths and Modern Sexualities*, London: Routledge and Kegan Paul.

# Further reading

Bennett, A. (2000) *Popular Music and Youth Culture*, London: Macmillan. Bennett provides a comprehensive survey of the relationship between youth culture and popular music. Original ethnographic research on Bhangra and European hip-hop offers fresh insights on the way young people appropriate pop music as a cultural resource. The initial chapters also provide a clear and concise survey of existing critical work on youth culture and popular music.

Fornäs, J. and Bolin, G. (eds) (1995) *Youth Culture in Late Modernity*, London: Sage. Produced by a group of Swedish social theorists, this innovative and stimulating collection of essays outlines a range of contrasting theoretical approaches to the nature, formation and dynamics of youth culture and subculture. Especially valuable are the numerous contributions that explore the relation between youth culture and the commercial market. Though many of the case studies specifically relate to Swedish cultural history, many of the themes and issues explored are deeply pertinent to the wider analysis of youth culture and its place within contemporary social life.

Furlong, A. and Cartmel, F. (1997) *Young People and Social Change: Individualization and Risk in Late Modernity*, Buckingham: Open University Press. Furlong and Cartmel present a meticulously researched survey of the impact of socio-economic change on the lives of young people during the closing decades of the twentieth century. This wide-ranging overview provides an indispensable account of the shifting patterns of education, employment and political participation that have framed young people's social and cultural experiences and the media's responses to the 'youth question'.

Hebdige, D. (1979) *Subculture: The Meaning of Style*, London: Methuen. Part of the original canon of 1970s subcultural theory, this account of the emergence of the punk rock subculture in Britain during the late 1970s saw Hebdige emerge as the high priest of style analysis. Since its original publication, numerous critics have justifiably taken issue with many aspects of the book's approach, not least its portrayal of 'authentic' youth subcultures as being 'incorporated' by a predatory commercial market. Yet it remains useful as an informed and insightful history of British youth style from the 1950s to the 1970s.

McGuigan, J. (1992) 'Youth culture and consumption', in J. McGuigan, *Cultural Populism*, London: Routledge, pp. 89–123. Generally, this volume sees McGuigan squaring up to trends within cultural analysis during the 1980s which he presents as a drift towards a simple celebration of consumer sovereignty in the marketplace. Advocates of 'active audience' theory will inevitably take issue with McGuigan's account, yet he makes a persuasive case for theorists to accord greater attention to the importance of political economy. The chapter on youth culture and consumption represents a thorough-going and thought-provoking critical survey of theoretical approaches to youth culture and its relation to commercial media.

McRobbie, A. (2000) *Feminism and Youth Culture*, London: Macmillan. This collection brings together a selection of essays produced by Angela McRobbie at various points in her career as one of Britain's pre-eminent cultural theorists. The anthology not only represents a thorough-going engagement with the construction and experience of gender within youth culture, but also bears testimony to important shifts in emphasis within cultural studies – away from the 1970s focus on the 'ideological power' of the text, towards a growing emphasis on polysemy and the active agency of audiences.

Muggleton, D. (2000) *Inside Subculture: The Postmodern Meaning of Style*, Oxford: Berg. Drawing on a series of interviews and ethnographic research, Muggleton analyses the nature and significance of subcultural style in contemporary society. An eloquent and persuasive study, it challenges notions of the existence of discrete boundaries and categories within the field of modern youth culture, instead highlighting dimensions of stylistic fragmentation and fluidity between different subcultural identities.

Osgerby, B. (1998) *Youth Culture in Post-war Britain*, Oxford: Blackwell. A wide-ranging introduction to the major changes that have taken place in the lives and cultures of British youngsters since the Second World War. Attention is given both to the transformation of young people's experiences in modern Britain and to the key shifts in the ways that youth has been socially, economically and politically represented and responded to.

Redhead, S. (ed.) (1993) *Rave Off: Politics and Deviance in Contemporary Youth Culture*, Aldershot: Avebury. An anthology of critical writings on various aspects of 1990s youth culture, this collection combines description and theory in a series of fascinating case studies. Essays on such varied topics as the gendering of punk subculture, the layout of record shops and the cultural dynamics of Northern Soul all highlight youth culture as a complex and challenging field of social, economic and cultural relations.

Springhall, J. (1998) *Youth, Popular Culture and Moral Panics: Penny Gaffs to Gangsta Rap, 1830–1996*, London: Macmillan. This is an engaging and insightful study of the history of controversy surrounding the commercial media's putatively negative effects on young people. A history of anxiety is traced from the fears that attended the penny 'gaff' theatres of Victorian Britain to the hand-wringing responses to contemporary 'gangsta' rap and computer games. Springhall examines why emergent media forms become the locus for wider social anxieties and explores why critics so frequently portray the media as a corrupter of the rising generation.

# Chapter 27

# Disability

MAKING UP DISABLED PEOPLE: CHARITY,
VISIBILITY AND THE BODY

**JESSICA EVANS**

Why is representation important for the study of disability? What models of disability do the dominant representations of disability support? To answer these questions, this chapter focuses on the campaign posters widely produced by disability charities from 1980 to the early 1990s. It places this publicity in its historical and social context and compares the psychoanalytic and social constructionist approaches to the images it uses. Finally, it suggests that these campaigns should now be seen as belonging to an historical moment, and that the marketized economy of welfare provision has necessitated the demise of this kind of advertising strategy.

## Representation and the authority of the investigator

Why does representation matter to people with disabilities? Why is the politics of representation now central to the politics of disability? How does representation play a role in popular conceptions of disability? How do representations help shape the categories of person – 'the disabled' or 'the mentally handicapped' – that appear to us? These questions are central to this chapter. They also go to the heart of our own sense of self; whether you are disabled or not is likely to affect what disability means to you personally. If you are not disabled your image of what 'disability' means might be quite specific. A simple photograph of a wheelchair may conjure up in your mind images and words such as lack of mobility, physical impairments, needing others, helplessness, unattractiveness, asexuality. However, if you are disabled your association to the image of the wheelchair – what it signifies – will probably be different: 'wheelchairs are there to get me around'. You can see that both of these are chains of associated ideas that are also states of feeling, suggesting a particular disposition to the subject matter. The point is that the debate on cultural representation, in this case the mass media images of disabled people, is not merely a matter of academic interest, but one which touches upon our very sense of 'self': who we think we are and what others define us as being, and the relationships between the two. Images are at one and the same time material objects, placed in certain concrete places (billboards, magazines, books and so forth) and collections of signs that manufacture particular versions of the world to us, which we use to think and feel that world. The word 'representation' is complex: it refers to a process in which the world is not just mediated but actively 'made up', assembled in images and in words which do not just reflect that world but transform it in a distinctive way.

In this chapter I want to highlight something that is often taken for granted: how the power of non-disabled people lies hidden while the representational spotlight, i.e. *what is made visible* to the viewing audience, is focused on the impaired body. If you were shown a picture of a person in a wheelchair you may well define him or her as 'disabled' or 'handicapped' first and foremost. But if you looked at a picture of a person who has no visible impairments, you may first categorize that person in terms of gender or age, for example, and be oblivious of his or her apparent status as a *non-disabled* person. Awareness of a non-disabled identity did not even enter the picture! In fact the vast majority of still images, films and television programmes feature people and characters who are not only not disabled but who are not recognized as such. What does this tell us? It tells us that for people who do not identify as disabled there is at the present time no need for a publicly declared sense of affinity or shared identity with other non-disabled people. There is a parallel to this in the highly coded way in which white people speak about white society. Think, for example, about the conservative nostalgia for a rural village-orientated society: it is always implicitly pictured before 'foreigners' arrived, as if 'English' society achieved organic unity – and was thus complete – in the past. The (white) place *from where* this yearning must be spoken is only ever implicit and hidden. Whites are not called upon to think about themselves as whites; it is only *other* people who can be described and they are non-white. Representation thus has a central role to play in shaping individuals' sense of allegiance – or not – to a wider group identity.

One of the most powerful models of disability, one that still dominates professional policy and institutional practices as well as existing at a popular level, is the *legal–medical model*. Characteristically, as part of a conservative tradition of political thought, this emphasizes individual loss or incapacity, implying that the impairment is what essentially limits – and thus defines – the whole person. The focus here is on the failure of the individual to adapt to existing social relations, and so the impairment is regarded as the 'cause' of disability. Accordingly, the difference between 'the disabled' and the rest of 'us' appears to be simply the reflection of 'naturally occurring distinct types of human beings' (Burr 1995: 3). Smuggled into the medical model is the normative assumption that it is the disabled person whose incapacity is a natural, inevitable result of impairment, and who is thus not the healthy, normal majority. The history of disability in the UK since the late nineteenth century demonstrates the interwoven but discontinuous relationship between this medical model and the legal categorizations of the person. For example, in the 1913 Mental Deficiency Act the concepts of 'the idiot', the 'imbecile', the 'feeble-minded', and the 'moral imbecile' were legally distinguished for the first time in English law. With regard to the moral imbecile, his or her 'mental defect' would involve 'strong vicious or criminal propensities'.

The 1959 Mental Health Act made a significant break with this taxonomy in separating medical issues from moral ones and presented the medical model of mental disorder as pure scientific description: 'mental disorder', 'severe subnormality', 'psychopathic disorder', and so on. The most recent phase in the policy response to disability was the shift from institutionally based care to community care after the

1970s. Individuals previously understood variously as 'idiots', 'mentally handicapped' or 'subnormal' were increasingly regarded as having special needs or 'learning difficulties'. Education and the capacity to learn, integration, normalization and independence were, and remain, the watchwords, particularly since the Education Act (1980).

Now, although these definitions of disabled persons are certainly not continuous, they do cohere around an individualizing medical model in which incapacity is seen as an individual pathology. The impairment is the focal point for diagnosis and treatment, rather than the person. In the last two decades the Disabled People's Movement (see Campbell and Oliver 1996) and academics writing largely from a social constructionist perspective have countered this legal–medical model with a *social model* of disability. This emphasizes how powerful and dominant groups have defined the identity of the disabled person through the lack of provision of accessible environments, such as lack of provision of sign language subtitles on television, braille and so on. So, while impairment is just one limited fact about a given individual, an individual becomes disabled because of the failure of the social environment to adjust structurally to the needs and aspirations of citizens with impairments (see Barton 1996). According to the social model a fixed notion of normality would no longer be an ideal to aspire to – such as trying to make someone with spinal injuries relearn to walk so as to return the invidual to 'normal life', when a wheelchair would in fact vastly increase the quality of life. Social constructionism is a theoretical position currently ascendant in the social sciences and, in terms of disability, it takes the social model in a particular direction (see Saraga 1998).

As a general position, social constructionism observes the changing historical constructions of persons, specifically the way that, as described above, different (in)capacities are attributed to individual subjects within each historical moment, leading to different kinds and combinations of treatment and care (moral, medical, educational). *What* disability is, and *who* is construed as disabled, is, at any one time, therefore subject to its historical, legal, economic and social context. 'People with disabilities' (the quotation marks indicate that we can't assume this is a neutral term of reference, it is simply the currently preferred generic phrase), they argue, are not a homogeneous group existing in nature, whose individuals have more similarity to each other than to those without disabilities. Instead, they are defined, classified and thus constructed as a social group through the very process of identifying disability as a 'social problem' that requires intervention.

If we now return to the concept of representation then, it should be clear by now that it has a key role to play for those who advocate the social model of disability and the social constructionist approach more generally. It is instructive, for example, that fans of the television series *Ironside* (1967–75), which starred Raymond Burr as a wheelchair-using detective, report that they were not conscious of his impairment since it was never made significant in the narrative of the series (see Morris 1991). Thus representations may support different models of disability. With reference to the social model of disability, it seems clear that the character Ironside was not in effect disabled (though he did have an impairment), since no access appeared to be barred to him within the particular social environment in which he operated.

## Key themes in the portrayal of the disabled person: status, sexuality, gender

Studies of the representation of disabled people have shown that disabled people are habitually screened out of television fiction and documentary programmes or else occur in a limited number of roles. (For a 'content' analysis of British TV see Cumberbatch and Negrine 1992; see also Barnes 1992; Longmore 1987.) It is as if having a physical or mental impairment is the defining feature of a person to such an extent that it makes a character less than a whole character: it subtracts from personhood and undercuts one's status as a bearer of culture. Writers over many years have used mental and physical impairment or ugliness to signify badness, evil or moral ambivalence in a character – Shakespeare's *Richard III*, Captain Hook in *Peter Pan*, the *Phantom of the Opera*, the villains in James Bond films, *The Hunchback of Notre-Dame*. Where impairment is used as a cipher in this way, it represents the continuation of Judaeo-Christian archaic, pre-scientific and cosmological systems of thought in which biological wholeness is divine, its opposite cast out as legal impurities (see Parkin 1985).

Status and authority in images are implicitly associated with an absence of disability. For example, Franklin D. Roosevelt was never seen in a wheelchair although his legs were paralysed. Being President of the USA was felt to be incompatible with being physically damaged – the wheelchair is the ultimate symbol of lack of power. Representations of disability are, however, principally bifurcated by gender. In recent years, for example, the disabled man has been a central character in a number of Hollywood films. The body, its physical aspects and demeanour, are the concrete signifiers that carry associations and concepts of femininity and masculinity. Film-makers rely upon an audience's knowledge of these codes in order to make damage to the body of a character operate as a statement about that character. If masculinity is signified by strength and resolve, independence and will power, then dramatic power can be derived from constructing a narrative around a man who has lost power over his body, for example in the 1990 films *My Left Foot* (1990) and *Born on the 4th July* (1990). In the Multiple Sclerosis (MS) Society's campaign 'Tears Lives Apart' in the late 1980s, posters showed beautiful young bodies being ripped apart by the scourge of MS, a campaign known colloquially by the advertising agency that produced it as 'Beauty and the Beast' (see Hevey 1992: 43). The series of posters is photographed in and out of focus, pictorialist style; bodies intertwine against a black background with the sculptural drama of Rodin's *The Kiss* (see Hevey 1992: Plate 3). One shows a 30-year-old man being bathed by a sexualized woman – her sleeves rolled up, their heads bowed together. Here, the implication is that disability for men means a loss of (hetero) sexual virility, for where once the woman might have been his girlfriend, the narrative suggests she is now his mother. The text reads 'How does it feel to have a mental age of thirty and a physical age of one?' as if to anchor the meaning of the poster finally in a sense of childlike dependency. The fear portrayed is that physical impairment inevitably means the final triumph of the body over the mind: to be disabled is to be stripped of fundamental human capacities – such as thinking, acting, willing and taking responsibility – and being condemned to endlessly re-enact the 'horror' of one's earliest dependency on a woman in the role of mother.

Representations of disabled women in film have been significantly different. Since the traditional meaning of femininity is often synonymous with dependency and vulnerability, disability cannot be used to pose a threat to women's autonomy. Disability is therefore more commonly used as a sign of women's excessive vulnerability and so blindness is the central signifier in storylines which create a sense of cumulative foreboding, often ending in physical attack (in films such as *Wait Until Dark* (1967) with Audrey Hepburn, *Blind Terror* (1971) with Mia Farrow, and *Blink* (1994) with Madeleine Stowe).

But it is noticeable that, opposed to this, wheelchair-using fictional women characters have been embittered, aggressive, or assertive of their needs (for example, *What Ever Happened to Baby Jane?* (1962) with Joan Crawford and Bette Davis). In these cases my interpretation is that it represents a cultural fear that a physically damaged woman is incompatible with the requirement to be nurturing and caring (i.e. a good and protective mother). Her assertiveness is a direct threat, portrayed in revenge scenarios and perhaps even destructive of life. Impairment in representation is seemingly transgressive; pointing to the boundaries of taken-for-granted sexual difference and producing transgressive women who are more masculine and tough and conversely making men dependent and vulnerable.

## All in a good cause? the culture of charity

The 1980s and first half of the 1990s can now be regarded as the highpoint of disability charity publicity output in the UK. As I will suggest in my conclusion, the social conditions that brought about these kinds of campaigns have fundamentally altered. Furthermore, most charities now balk at the memory of the images they used to promulgate and are ostensibly desperate to distance themselves from the 'bad old days', since they now understand that they must take into account the virulent criticism of these images from disabled people themselves and their advocates (see Mack 2001). Nonetheless, charities still dominate the public sphere in terms of being the major institution involved in the circulation of images – in the widest possible meaning of the term – of people with disabilities.

From the early 1980s through to the mid-1990s, image-based publicity published by charitable organizations as part of their fund-raising activities were a taken-for-granted feature of the public sphere. Their apparently innocent invocation of civic virtue – the 'ethical' side of public life – was seemingly strengthened by the aesthetic shortcomings of the naive realism they deployed in contrast with the sophistries of modern commercial advertising. I shall argue that these images undermined disabled people as autonomous civic agents with all that that implies – will, purpose, rationality. In them, 'The Disabled' achieve a collective character – they are the eternally grateful and indebted recipients of others' good will; the charitable ethos *per se* actively structures a mental and social gap between the donor and the disabled recipient. Furthermore, as we shall see, charities invariably reproduced a medical model of disability and undermine the political struggle for citizenship that is being waged by disabled people themselves under the banner of 'rights, not charity'. Let us now trace the historical lineage of these images.

During the 1980s the balance between public and private aid for the poor and disadvantaged as a whole shifted towards greater reliance on the private charity organizations. Their traditional role of supplementing state provision was increasingly transformed into one of replacing it, in areas where state support had been withdrawn or decreased. In the area of disability, notions of community care and integration were the watchwords as government policy shifted towards the closure of long-stay subnormality hospitals and the 'return' of patients into the 'community'. This in fact meant a renewed pressure on the 'informal' sector of care, that is, voluntary organizations and relatives, taking over major responsibility for care. The publicity images that will form the subject of our case-study were commissioned not so much to raise money but to challenge what was considered to be the likely prejudicial public attitude towards people with learning difficulties. It needs to be remembered that these are people who had hitherto been publicly invisible in the post-war years through being largely institutionalized. Since the National Lottery was launched (November 1994), on the back of 24-hour television charity 'telethons', the mantra of 'good causes' has helped to drown out any public debate about the privatization of public services and the mixed economy of 'care' for disabled and other disadvantaged people. It subsequently feels like bad faith or just plain cynicism to criticize the whole edifice of a culture increasingly dominated by charitable practice and ethos, cast as permeated by unimpeachable motives. Nevertheless, there is good reason to be sceptical about the innocence of charities. Jacques Donzolot has written of the way that, in the nineteenth century, charitable motivation could 'only be kindled by the fires of extreme misery, by the sight of the spectacular suffering, and then only by the feeling of inflated importance accruing to the giver through the immediate solace his charity brought to the sufferer' (1977: 45). There remains a structurally necessary relationship between the portrayal of disability as a disaster or a tragic loss, and the function of raising money.[1] This means that any serious critique of representation must take into account the institutional practices and social contexts of charity.

Since the 1980s, the charity sector has become a rapaciously competitive big business (Drake 1996: 150). Impairment charities go about the business of constructing publicity campaigns in much the same way that any other business markets its product. But the difference is that unlike other companies, charities are advertising products that happen to be people, whose impairment then becomes the 'unique selling proposition' for the charity brand. In the taxonomy of charity posters, people with disabilities are characters cast into their various medical typologies, be it a person with Down's Syndrome, with spinal paralysis, Asperger's Syndrome, cerebral palsy and so on. But charities go to some lengths to play down the fact that they are in the business of marketing their wares as this may not be seen as compatible with voluntary giving. Their byline and logo are often discreetly placed at the bottom of the poster. But more importantly, charities seek to differentiate themselves from the whole world of public commercial advertising by adopting different visual conventions for their posters. One common difference is the use of black-and-white naturalist photography, photographs of 'real' disabled people – although some charities have in the last few years begun to introduce colour and to produce more obviously constructed, graphically based posters. Deploying monochromatic naturalism allowed the charity to associate itself with the tradition of social documentary that is embedded in a British tradition of philanthropic paternalism, and to distance itself in a protestant fashion from the commercial world of advertising with its promise of instant gratification and its narratives of the pleasure of acquisitiveness.

The marketing success of each charity depends upon it becoming synonymous with a particular impairment, and it is the impairment that the charity constructs as defining that person. The interests of learning-disabled children and adults are assumed to be represented by Mencap; those children who have Down's Syndrome by the Down's Syndrome Association; those of people with cerebral palsy by SCOPE; those with multiple sclerosis by the MS Society; blind people by the RNIB (Royal National Institute for the Blind), and so on. In a report on charity advertising commissioned by the King's Fund, Susan Scott-Parker says 'As it stands now, charities tend to commission campaigns as though they owned their particular model of disabled person, in much the same way that Ford owns Fiesta cars. . . . The aim of the campaign is to raise brand awareness for the charity' (1989: 11). The Multiple Sclerosis Society's 'Tears Lives Apart' rip (the corporate logo of ripped paper) has become the sign by which it and multiple sclerosis have become branded, connected together in the public consciousness. The relationship between branding and stigma is historically an absolutely literal one; the concept of stigma is derived from ancient Greece where it was a sign, cut or burned into the body, and advertising that its bearer was a slave (see Goffman 1963: 19). As we shall see, it is the body of the disabled person that bears the mark of essential and immutable difference.

## A case study: charity advertisements 1980–1995

A Mencap poster of the early 1980s, widely distributed via public billboards, has a photograph of a young girl ('Nina' in real life) with the words 'Twenty children born on Christmas Day will always have a cross to bear'. A headline on the front cover of *Parents Voice* (the Mencap magazine for its members) in the early 1980s, accompanying a photograph of a smiling baby with Down's Syndrome, read 'Sometimes late is as bad as never'. And on Mencap posters in the late 1980s the following slogans accompanied black-and-white studio portraits of learning-disabled people: 'Joanne can't get better. Her future can'; 'She's different. Her life doesn't have to be'; 'A mental handicap is there for life. So is Mencap' (see Hevey 1992: Plate 5). The charity is bent on informing the public and its own members that the disabled person is inherently damaged goods but that, at the same time, the charity itself is vital for the future of that person. It promises that it can add value to that person's life. 'Mental handicap' is presented as a fixed entity residing in a body from birth, furnishing an individual with predictable limits on life opportunities.

Let us unpack one particular, now notorious, 1985 poster, entitled 'No Sense, No Feelings?' This headline presents us with the attitude of the prejudiced viewer (indicated by the question mark), which the photograph and the rest of the text are supposed to refute (for the image, see Evans 1988: 44). Thus, 'No Sense, No Feelings?' is what the charity is imputing to the prejudiced audience; this is rebutted with 'They may not think as fast but they feel as deeply', representing the authoritative voice of the charity speaking the truth about people with learning disability. But, as we look at the poster, it can only confirm assumptions we might already have about 'mentally handicapped people' as abnormal, inferior, and slaves to their instincts. We are shown a man and a woman with their arms locked together in a heart shape, connoting the wedding or engagement portrait. But although they appear at first to be aspiring to this institution of normal culture, the cumulative effect of the poster is that of a parody of the ideal couple which is apparent when we compare this to the stock conventions of the High Street photographer. The image is a contradictory cohesion of this tradition of honorific portraiture (which continues today in the familial portraits of *Hello* magazine) with the denigratory tradition of nineteenth-century social scientific portraiture. The latter, taken in the prisons and psychiatric institutions, was a form of physiognomic practice, subjecting the individual to the interrogative gaze of the camera in order to establish evidence of innately degenerate types (see Green 1984).

Here we look at two models: joined together but otherwise isolated they emerge as if specimens from a black background; they are photographed with a wide-angle lens which when used in close-up projects lips, noses and hands forwards into the viewer's space. The use of top lighting from a small source casts deep shadows into their eyes and under their chins and emphasizes the creases in their clothes. The choice of heavy contrast, small source lighting (which throws deep shadows) and the wide-angle lens creates the effect used in expressionist or gothic horror films. Moreover, as if to underline this madhouse, the man has a pocketful of combs, implying an obsessional activity – but this is paradoxically offset by both heads of hair being untidy and uncombed. Such is obviously the innate handicapped character: persons who are perhaps mad, certainly very peculiar, who are masquerading as normal by aspiring to the conventions of the honorific portrait and the institution of marriage. The text is similar to the way in which animal lovers seek to defend animal protection – they may not be intelligent (like humans) but they have feelings none the less. Imagine if the text was to be placed against a picture of another social group: it would be denounced as offensively sexist or racist, for example. That a statement such as this can be publicly endorsed by a major organization (one that purports to act in the very interests of disabled people) is an indication of how little power learning-disabled people have.

It is also important to note the use of the charity's corporate logo, 'Little Stephen' as he was called, on the bottom right. Little Stephen, a forlorn and lonely little boy, was abandoned in 1992 after the charity finally capitulated to years of charges from 'People First' advocacy groups and the disability rights movement that it infantilized disabled people. The impact of the poster, from the point of view of the charity, relies upon it being seen as a truthful portrait of 'real' handicapped people – as if they have just walked off the street and into the studio. I have been challenged about this in lectures – how do I know they are models? Of course, the viewer cannot know for certain, but from the point of view of the effectivity of the image, whether they are technically models is beside the point. For *these* 'models' have been selected and their 'look' has been *assembled* by making selections from all the various paradigms of the signifying toolkit – clothing, lighting, camera angle, facial expression, etc. What is interesting is that people never question whether in regular 'commercial' advertising models are 'real people' or models! To believe that the models in this and other charity posters are somehow untampered with and authentically 'real' is to fall into the trap of thinking that we can have a direct experience of the truth and then find evidence for it in a photograph. It assumes one knows what a 'real' disabled person does, or should, look like, and that the purpose of the photograph is simply to reflect this. Oscar Wilde's point is instructive here: 'External nature imitates art. The only effects that she can show us are effects that we have already seen through poetry or in paintings' (Gilman 1982). In this way, this poster is the legacy of the social realism of the nineteenth century, in its barely concealed references to the social surveillance practices of physiognomy. It combines this with the mythological narratives of a pre-Enlightenment age of monsters and a religious sensibility of pity for those who, though seemingly like us, are innocent and childlike.

In another advert from the mid-1980s Mencap bases its truth claim upon an appeal to the visual paraphenalia of medical science: the text says 'On Friday May 6th 1983 these babies were born mentally handicapped' (see Evans 1988: 46). Below this are laid out geometric and clinical-looking rows of medical labels with dates and surnames attached, the kind that newborn babies wear. Then the voice of the charity continues – 'It was an average day'. There is here an ambiguous reference to labelling – the connotations of the medical labels in conjunction with the text which ascribes identity at birth allows the poster to refer at a less conscious level to social labelling and stigmatizing. The advert makes no bones about its position – it discloses a deliberately pessimistic, disparaging attitude to the existence of these babies as if they have absolutely no potential, as if everything that can be known about them is determined at birth. For Mencap this is an apparently natural not a social event – 'mental handicap' is established from birth as an entity residing in a body, rather than a matter of social construction and evaluation. This poster invokes fear, implying that there is no protection (except perhaps that of donating to charity in an echo, perhaps, of paying indulgences to the Catholic church) from the randomness of fate which can deal anyone a dud card – it could happen to YOU. The dread of bearing monsters is one of the perils of parenthood, a staple of nineteenth-century eugenic ideology (see Ryan and Thomas 1987).

However, in the late 1980s, as if to show it had learnt from the avalanche of criticisms from advocacy groups and critics, Mencap departed from documentary naturalism, and produced a series of posters using colour graphics rather than photographs. One poster showed a blank easel with the caption 'Life with a mental handicap', underneath which is a tin of paints labelled 'Mencap'. Another had the same captions but displayed an empty canoe on a river, below which is a paddle. The implication here is that the meaning and the life of a learning-disabled person is incomplete and empty without the charity to provide it. He or she is a 'tabula rasa' waiting to be filled up with the beneficence of the charity; the 'career' of the disabled person is but a shadow of the organization.

Mencap altered its brand image dramatically in 1992, although it retained the label 'mental handicap' (and a patronizing byline 'making the most of life') against the demands of People First, the disabled-led organization attending the launch event. The five new photographic images forming the new brand image were only ostensibly different. Using people with learning difficulties as models, they remained firmly in the portraiture tradition, deployed the signifiers of documentary naturalism but showed their subjects in colour, and used various poses heavily stereotyped as 'positive'. It should suffice to point out, with reference back to my interpretation of the 'No Sense, No Feelings?' poster, that the central poster was based entirely on a cut-out photograph of model Bobby Thompson, aged 55, wearing an old fashioned tank-top, grinning toothlessly at the camera with arms raised in a pose of child-like excitement. I return to this image at the end of the chapter.

It does seem, then, as if any attempt to deliver a new approach, even with best intentions, is continually hampered by the residue of historical baggage written into the very culture of charitable organizations. This is not only the case with disability charities; only very recently the Imperial Cancer Research Fund provoked widespread consternation, including from some of its own scientists, when it published a campaign poster in a number of UK newspapers (see *The Observer*, 9 July 2000). Using the visual rhetoric of 'labelling' very similar to the Mencap advert described above, it showed three young girls joined in an embrace, each with a label – 'lawyer', 'teacher', 'cancer'. In reducing the person with cancer to their disease, the charity continues the medical model of disability.

Disabled people have been regarded as a homogeneous group of people who are more similar to each other than to anyone else through the unifying factor of a shared nature; and therefore, whose situation, behaviour, actions, thoughts and needs are simply expressions of the truth of a deeper biological pathology. As we have seen, photographic naturalism, certainly in the way it has been deployed in the images produced by charities, appears to supply the evidence for this supposed 'truth' of the impaired person as someone whose 'difference' from everyone else derives from their body.

## The charitable state of mind: psychoanalysis and disability

My argument so far has deployed a social constructionist approach for the purpose of dissecting images of disabled people. In this section I introduce a psychoanalytic dimension into the argument. But, and I will return to this in the final section, it is not such a simple matter as at first appears to conjoin the social constructionist approach with the psychoanalytic and this should be born in mind while reading this section. Why is a psychoanalytic approach necessary? It is my contention that the naturalism employed in charity posters must also be a project of constructing a belief on the part of viewers in the illusion of objectivity. To believe in something being real is always also a psychical and emotional investment – there is always some trade-off for the viewer and a motivation at stake: why *should* anyone believe in the reality of the image, and what does it do for them? I should point out that there is a body of psychoanalytical work on visual representations which analyses how advertisements act as a catalyst for unconscious desire in their construction of pleasurable scenarios. There is an incitement of narcissistic identificatory processes for the viewing subject. But naturalism or documentary genres, whose codes are recognizably the construction of the non-ideal, gritty 'real' world have usually been exempt from a psychoanalytic form of analysis. The debate has focused on how far the realist image distorts 'reality' or generates consensus for ideological views about the world. However, to exclude questions of fantasy and identification with the realist image is, I suspect, partly a result of collusion with the premise of realism, expressed in the mistaken belief that the realist image *is* somehow less constructed and therefore less susceptible to the operations of unconscious process – and therefore less likely to be distorted by the irrational aspects of subjective life.

Charitable giving is both a monetary and a psychological transaction, one of social insurance against the prospect of damage to the viewer's own body. Presented, as so often is the case, with an aggressive image of pain or debility, the viewer feels relief (that they are not like that), guilt (for feeling relieved), and hatred (for being made to feel guilt). What I want to argue is that pity and altruism, which is the conscious aspect of reacting to disabled posters, are more closely linked to hatred and aggression than one might at first think. Giving to charity is at the same time an act of kindness and an act of rejection, making the giver feel whole and separate; these contradictory values at the heart of the charitable ethos makes disability into an arena for psychic conflict.

What I call the 'separating devices' (the way images portray 'them' and therefore imply a majority 'us') of charity posters can be understood as defensive strategies, colluded in by both the charity and intended to be colluded in by the audience. We need to examine the way in which fears about dependency, incompetence and debility are projected on to disabled people, who are then denigrated for what people cannot accept in themselves. Freud and other analysts such as Klein (2000) used the concept of projection to refer to the operation by which the qualities, feelings and wishes which the subject refuses to recognize or rejects in themselves are expelled from the self and located in another person or thing. Projection, then, is a denial of 'bad' parts of the self that are then 'split off' and externalized. A psychoanalyst would argue that strong expressions of hate can be a defence against feelings of love or desire which cannot be acknowledged. For example, those who feel so much fear and hatred of homosexuality that they will attack gay men may be driven by an excessive need to disown difficult and intolerable feelings towards their own sex (whether this be based on an association with a bad experience in the past or on a desire that is impossible to acknowledge). In some of the portrait-based posters that have been discussed, it can be seen that the visible differences of people become exaggerated and/or entirely invented – a sign of the unconscious defences at work. Thus these images construct an object of fear which is at the same time a source of fascination. Viewers and disabled people are, in terms of fantasy, deeply bound together and implicated in each others' characteristics, and the exaggerations and separation devices common in charity posters (such as the 'They' in the 'No Sense, No Feelings?' poster) are a manifestation of this.

What are the fears of – and the desire to look at – the disabled person about? It is my contention that the repressed infantile characteristics and feeling-states are projected on to disabled people who are seen as childish, dependent and underdeveloped and who are then regarded as 'other' and dissociated from the mature adult self. Popular images and rhetoric abound of disabled people that confront us with people who are imperfect and out of control: helpless, disgusting, shitty, dribbling – a threat to rigid ego boundaries. During the socio-developmental processes of early infancy, a range of strict rules of decorum involving standards of privacy, decency and dignity (for example, in potty training) effect a repression of these taboo activities. These codes are enforced to protect us from the disorder, chaos and dependency that, Freud argued, are characteristic of our experiences in the early stages of our development (Freud 1905). Infants will learn to repress what is 'unpleasant' and one mechanism for effecting this will be the 'projection' on to, or attribution of these unpleasantnesses to, the body of another. Yet, the posters in question not only encourage us to expel that which causes *un*pleasure and difficulty to the self, but also represent the resultant process of 'projection' on to the other as a process that is *already completed* – as if it is a *fait accompli*. In the splitting that is necessarily part of 'projection', as both Freud and Melanie Klein understood it, we become literally alienated from (and cannot identify with) the object/person we observe; the viewer is idealized in order to keep him or her apart from the persecutory and feared object.

The paradox that the disabled person as 'other' is seen as *feeble* and *fearsome* at the same time is unlikely to become evident to the producers of the image nor therefore to the imputed viewer. But the deeply contradictory nature of the beliefs held simultaneously about the 'other' and implicit in the images such as the ones we have considered is an important sign of the unconscious at work. Fantasies of disabled people as dangerously bad and threatening (fearsome) and excessively good and deserving (innocent, feeble, dependent) – the very fantasies we see in charity discourse – are products of an unconscious 'projective splitting' (see Klein and Rustin in du Gay *et al.* 2000).

The prevailing feeling-state associated with the dominant images of disability, then, is that of a child-like dependency. Freud, Klein and other psychoanalysts have elaborated on the experiences that all small babies have of being in a state of complete dependency on their mothers. The lack of control over their body and the feeling of being unintegrated can be felt as bewildering or even terrifying. In early development anger against the mother and consequent feelings of guilt about the destructive effects of that anger can lead to a bad body image which is carried forward into adult life as a revulsion against dependency and a flight from dependency in relationships. This 'badness' can be projected on to others as in the construction of femininity as extreme vulnerability, and particularly on to those who are dependent through disability, such as old people in our culture who are segregated and treated as people waiting to die. There are very close associations between dependency, illness, dying and death, associations we have already seen operating in the charity adverts that, as we have seen, are based on a medical model of disability.

## Conclusion

I have argued that the charities' historical obsession with the bodily mark betrays an irrational and even sadistic impulse which goes far beyond their humanist claims to be the defenders of disabled people. The case study of charity representation under consideration in this chapter demonstrates how a social issue gets reduced to individualized pathology and the spending priorities of disability charities conspire with this. So, instead of ensuring that all buildings are accessible for wheelchair users, or that sign language becomes integral to all television programmes, millions are poured into finding a 'cure' for congenital forms of disability. The research departments of impairment charities spend a large part of their income on research to remove the source of the impairment: their priorities are weighted heavily toward 'cure' rather than 'care'. For example, in the early 1990s the Muscular Dystrophy Society spent £2.3 million per year on research, £276,000 on welfare (and £286,000 on advertising) (see Hevey 1992: 31). This fantasy of eradication is based on a denial of the fact that there will always be disabled people and increasingly most of us will at some point in our lives be disabled – through old age and the illnesses that come with it.

Psychoanalysts point out that bodily difference and the specificity of bodily experience is repressed, or denied, at a cost. In particular, psychoanalysts have shown us that dependency should not be assumed to be avoidable, even if avoidance is widely seen as desirable. Furthermore, the most extreme depensive reactions against dependency – such as the denigration of the dependent person that is part of splitting and projection – could be better contained than they are at present by cultural mechanisms and social institutions such as charities. In this vein, Ian Craib (1994) has argued that we need to recognize the social and psychical 'importance of disappointment'. He thinks that our culture is dangerously close to denying the inevitability and necessity of suffering, of actual, intractable, differences between people, and of messy or 'negative' feelings, as part of normal life. Unless this dependency is consciously thought of as an experience we have all had earlier in our lives (and as something we will very likely experience again as a normal part of human life) it will continue to be parcelled off and projected outwards, to become the specialized attribute of people who, by the terms of our culture, are useless and need 'special' and paternalist treatment. Dependency and suffering, painful as they are, have to be acknowledged as a part of life itself, and particular groups should not be made to carry their associations for everyone else. At times there is, inevitably, a danger of over-compensation in the 'we are strong' mentality of the social constructionist advocates of the social model that verges on an overplayed omnipotence. The vision of simple equality that is sometimes offered can gloss over the losses that can be felt by those with any impairment and the relations of dependency that must be seen as part of life for all of us, not an aberration from it.

In the last few years, in the context of what has now become a well-embedded marketized welfare economy, it appears that charities do not see the need to produce publicity campaigns of anything like the scale of the 1980s. By the mid and certainly the late-1990s, the old paternalist role of charities in this field, with their appeal to individual donors and their protective approach to their user-groups as passive recipients of charitable munificence, was under threat, and from a number of directions. The charity images we have discussed belong to a period in which charities were grant aided by local government agencies but remained relatively autonomous, independent providers of services to their clients. The community care reforms of the early 1990s separated the roles of local authority as purchasers and providers of community care, one component of an emerging government strategy over the past ten years to become an 'enabling state' rather than a 'social state' (see Rose 1999: 142). Instead of national and local government agencies granting aid to voluntary sector organizations as they did in the past, they now directly contract with them for the provision of specified services, with closely defined performance standards. Charities and other voluntary organizations are highly professionalised, bidding for contracts and so competing in a 'quasi-market' (Le Grand 1991: 1259–60) as not-for-profit private delivery agents for the provision of social services as part of community care (see Butcher 1995). At the same time, many charities are now far more likely to allow their clients to participate at all levels of the organizational structure. This is not simply a result of the pressure to democratize that has been brought to bear on charities over the years by their own service users. It is also a result of the renewed life that has been breathed into the concept of 'community' since Clinton and Blair, infused as it is with notions of self-organized, rather than bureaucratic and elected provision, and the ethos of voluntarist service.

But what does this increased marketization of service provision mean for those who are recipients of care – the clients, or 'customers' of the charities? What does it mean for the image of people with disabilities? If the 'enabling state' in general (Rose 1999: 142–6) means that individuals – as customers or clients – must enhance their own well-being by becoming active participants in, and consumers of, the services provided them, then we can expect that disabled persons as social partners will become implicated in, and ultimately made responsible for, the care programmes designed to manage them. They will be represented as the active agents of social programmes, as now potentially useful persons who must offer something in return for being recipients of a service, rather than as voiceless victims existing on the margins of the social. We can perhaps detect the stirrings of this transformation in the 1992 Mencap relaunch images discussed earlier in which people with learning difficulties were represented as excessively active and innately 'positive' kinds of person.

## Questions

1   Find an advertisement produced by a disability charity. Discuss the components of the advertisement, including the text. At whom is it aimed? What model of disability does it support? What does it say about the charity's view of people with disabilities?

2   Look at the television scheduling for a whole week's viewing. What signals are used to indicate that a programme has reference to disability or a disabled person? What does this say about the current status of people with disabilities and their relationship to non-disabled persons? Are we to assume that the rest of the programming is for or about non-disabled people?

3   What image of disabled people, in terms of their identity and status, is provided by events such as the Para-Olympics and by 'minority' broadcast programmes such as Radio 4's '*Does He Take Sugar*'? Why do they exist, as specialist events and programmes?

# Notes

1   David Hevey (1992: 44) has argued that the purpose of charity advertising is not to appeal to a general public, for the income generated by this process is negligible compared to that of legacies and other donations. Its central purpose is to appeal to the internal army of volunteers, a kind of mission statement from the leaders.

There have not been many empirical investigations of actual viewer-response to disability images; however, one study in 1990 found that posters which generated feelings of guilt, pity, and sympathy were those than generated the greatest desire to donate (Eayrs and Ellis 1990; see also Doddington *et al.* 1994). My own view is that the kind of research which sets out to measure 'the public's attitudes' is problematic for three reasons: first, that it is limited to people's conscious response which may be in deep conflict with their unconscious feelings; second, that this conscious response is likely to be modified by what the interviewees think they ought to say, for many people do not want to appear to be prejudiced; and third, that it assumes a one-to-one cause–effect relationship between a single text and attitude-formation and thus neglects both the cumulative effects of certain kinds of images, and how their meaning is a consequence of their articulation with cultural values and discourses and with developments and transformations in social relations – all of which provide a structuring context for the ways in which people may think about disability, which, for example, may be closely linked to the way they think about ageing or the welfare state.

# References

Barnes, C. (1992) *Disabling Imagery and the Media: An Exploration of Media Representations of Disabled People*, Belper: British Council of Organizations for Disabled People.

Barthes, R. (1973) *Mythologies*, London: Granada.

Barton, L. (ed.) (1996) *Disability and Society*, Harlow: Addison Wesley Longman.

Bogdan, R. (1988) *Freakshow: Presenting Human Oddities for Amusement and Profit*, Chicago: University of Chicago Press.

Burleigh, M. (1994) *Death and Deliverance: 'Euthanasia' in Germany 1900–45*, Cambridge: Cambridge University Press.

Burr, E. (1995) *Introduction to Social Constructionism*, London: Routledge.

Butcher, T. (1995) *Delivering Welfare: the governance of the social services in the 1990s*, Buckingham: Open University Press.

Campbell, J. and Oliver, M. (1996) *Disability Politics: Understanding Our Past, Changing Our Future*, London: Routledge.

Craib, I. (1994) *The Importance of Disappointment*, London: Routledge.

Cumberbatch, G. and Negrine, R. (1992) *Images of Disability on Television*, London: Routledge.

Doddington, K., Jones, R. S. P. and Miller, B. Y. (1994) 'Are attitudes to people with learning disabilities negatively influenced by charity advertising? An experimental analysis', *Disability and Society* 9(2).

Donzolot, P. (1977) *The Policing of Families*, New York: Pantheon.

Douglas, M. (1966) *Purity and Danger*, Harmondsworth: Penguin.

Drake, R. (1996) 'Disability, charities, normalisation and representation', in L. Barton (ed.) *Disability and Society*, Harlow: Addison Wesley Longman.

Du Gay, P., Evans, J. and Redman, P. (eds) (2000) *Identity: A reader*, London: Sage.

Eayrs, C. B. and Ellis, N. (1990) 'Charity advertising: for or against people with a mental handicap?' *British Journal of Social Psychology* 29.

Evans, J. (1986/7) 'The imagined referent', *Block* 12 (Winter).

Evans, J. (1988) 'The iron cage of visibility', *Ten: 8 International Photography Magazine* 29.

Evans, J. (2000) 'Psychoanalysis and psycho-social relations: introduction' in P. du Gay, J. Evans and P. Redman (eds) *Identity: A reader*, London: Sage.

Foucault, M. (1980) 'The politics of health in the eighteenth century', in C. Gordon (ed.) *Michel Foucault: Power/Knowledge*, Brighton: Harvester.

Freud, S. (1905) *Three Essays on the Theory of Sexuality*, Pelican Freud Library, Vol. 7, A. Richards (ed.), Harmondsworth: Penguin.

Gartner, A. and Joe, T. (eds) (1987) *Images of the Disabled, Disabling Images*, New York: Praeger.

Gilman, S. L. (1982) *Seeing the Insane*, New York: Wiley.

Goffman, E. (1963) *Stigma*, Harmondsworth: Penguin.

Gould, S. J. (1981) *The Mismeasure of Man*, Harmondsworth: Penguin.

Gould, S. J. (1983) *The Panda's Thumb: More Reflections in Natural History*, Harmondsworth: Penguin.

Graham, P. and Oehlsclaeger, F. (1992) *Articulating the Elephant Man: Joseph Merrick and his Interpreters*, Baltimore, MD: Johns Hopkins University Press.

Green, D. (1984) 'Veins of resemblance', *Oxford Art Journal* 7(2).

Green, D. (1996) 'On Foucault: disciplinary power and photography', in J. Evans (ed.) *The Camerawork Essays*, London: Rivers Oram.

Haffter, C. (1968) 'The changeling: history and psychodynamics of attitudes to handicapped children in European folklore', *Journal of the History of Behavioural Studies* 4.

Hall, S. (ed.) (1997) *Representation: Cultural Representations and Signifying Practices*, London: Sage.

Hevey, D. (ed.) (1992) *The Creatures Time Forgot: Photography and Disability Imagery*, London: Routledge.

Jordanova, L. (1989) *Sexual Vision*, New York: Harvester.

Le Grand, J. (1991) 'Quasi-markets and social policy', *Economic Journal* 101, 1256–67.

Longmore, P. K. (1987) 'Screening sterotypes: images of disabled people in television and motion pictures', in A. Gartner and T. Joe (eds) *Images of the Disabled, Disabling Images*, New York: Praeger.

Mack, T. (2001) 'We'll do it our way', *The Guardian Weekend*, Saturday 14th April.

McKie, R. and Thorpe, V. (2000) 'Cancer charity attacked over "shock" advert', *The Observer*, 9 July.

Morris, J. (1991) *Pride Against Prejudice: Transforming Attitudes to Disability*, London: Women's Press.

Parkin, D. (1985) 'Entitling evil: Muslims and non-Muslims in coastal Kenya', in D. Parkin (ed.) *The Anthropology of Evil*, Oxford: Basil Blackwell.

Pfeiffer, D. (1994) 'Eugenics and disability discrimination', *Disability and Society* 9(4).

Proctor, R. (1988) *Racial Hygiene: Medicine under the Nazis*, London: Harvard University Press.

Rose, N. (1989) *Governing the Soul: the shaping of the private self*, London: Routledge.

Rose, N. (1999) *Powers of Freedom: Reframing political thought*, Cambridge: Cambridge University Press.

Ryan, J. and Thomas, F. (1987) *The Politics of Mental Handicap*, revised edn, London: Free Association Press.

Saraga, E. (ed.) (1998) *Embodying the Social: constructions of difference*, London: Sage.

Scott-Parker, S. (1989) *They Aren't in the Brief: Advertising People with Disabilities*, discussion paper, London: King's Fund Centre.

Shearer, A. (1981) *Helping to Live or Allowing to Die?* London: CMH (Campaign for People with Mental Handicaps), now called VIA (Values into Action), Oxford House, Derbyshire Street, London, E2 6HG.

Shearer, A. (1984) *Everybody's Ethics: What Future for Handicapped Babies?* London: CMH (Campaign for People with Mental Handicaps), now called VIA (Values into Action), Oxford House, Derbyshire Street, London, E2 6HG.

Tagg, J. (1988) *The Burden of Representation*, London: Macmillan.

Taylor, M. (1992) 'The changing role of the non-profit sector in Britain: moving towards the market', in B. Gidron, R. Kramer, L. Sulaman (eds) *Government and the Third Sector: emerging relationships in welfare states*, San Francisco: Jossey-Bass Publishers.

# Further reading

Barnes, C. (1992) *Disabling Imagery and the Media: An Exploration of Media Representations of Disabled People*, Belper: British Council of Organizations for Disabled People. Critical discussion of wide range of images of disability in the UK.

Barton, L. (ed.) (1996) *Disability and Society: emerging issues and insights*, Harlow: Addison Wesley Longman. Adds to Oliver's sociological introduction with this collection of critical essays.

Campbell, J. and Oliver, M. (1996) *Disability Politics: Understanding Our Past, Changing Our Future*, London: Routledge. A useful introduction to the history of the disability movement in the UK.

Cumberbatch, G. and Negrine, R. (1992) *Images of Disability on Television*, London: Routledge. UK-based content analysis.

Doddington, K., Jones, R. S. P. and Miller, B. Y. (1994) 'Are attitudes to people with learning disabilities negatively influenced by charity advertising? An experimental analysis', *Disability and Society* 9(2). An attempt to measure the actual 'effects' of charity advertising by interviewing individual viewers. See note 1 above.

Evans, J. (1988) 'The iron cage of visibility', *Ten: 8 International Photography Magazine* 29. Analysis of the categorization of people with learning difficulties as pre-verbal animals in charity advertisements, taking a Foucauldian perspective. Includes some of the charity advertisements discussed in this chapter.

Gilman, S. L. (1982) *Seeing the Insane*, New York: Wiley. Fascinating archival collection of images of 'mental illness' over the centuries, accompanied by historical analysis including a psychoanalytic dimension.

Gould, S. J. (1981) *The Mismeasure of Man*, Harmondsworth: Penguin. Important collection of essays about the (mis)use of science in support of social scientific conclusions. Includes essay about the Victorian scientist Dr Down.

Green, D. (1984) 'Veins of resemblance', *Oxford Art Journal* 7(2). Foucauldian consideration of the ways in which photography was enlisted for the purposes of eugenic policy in the nineteenth century.

Hevey, D. (ed.) (1992) *The Creatures Time Forgot: Photography and Disability Imagery*, London: Routledge. Challenges, partly through visual imagery, the dominant portrayal of people with disabilities and includes useful research on contemporary disability charities. Also contains reproductions of charity publicity from the 1980s.

Mack, T. (2001) 'We'll do it our way', *The Guardian Weekend*, Saturday 14th April. Insightful account of the complexities and contradictions of the populist self-advocacy groups for people with learning difficulties.

Morris, J. (1991) *Pride Against Prejudice: Tranforming Attitudes to Disability*, London: Women's Press. Accessible and thoughtful on the relationship of women to disability and the gendering of disability.

Oliver, M. (1990) *The Politics of Disability*, London: Macmillan. Excellent introduction to the sociological accounts of disability.

Ryan, J. and Thomas, F. (1987) *The Politics of Mental Handicap*, revised edn, London: Free Association Press. Still unrivalled in its scope, it provides a pre-history of 'mental handicap', looking at the treatment of, and mythology surrounding, people with learning difficulties over a number of historical periods.

Saraga, E. (ed.) (1998) *Embodying the Social: constructions of difference*, London: Sage. Taking a generalist social constructionist position on social policy, this volume from a series of Open University course texts includes chapters on race, sexuality and disability. It also includes some reproductions of disability charity posters.

Tagg, J. (1988) *The Burden of Representation*, London: Macmillan. Written from a Foucauldian perspective, this has important arguments about the realist uses of photography within penal and mental health institutions as part of the application of the social sciences.

# Chapter 28

# Nationality

NATIONAL IDENTITY AND THE MEDIA

**ANDREW HIGSON**

Using British cinema as a case study, this chapter explores the role the media play in constructing and reproducing a sense of national identity. Starting with an attempt to define national identity, the chapter goes on to read selected British films in terms of how they imagine the nation and its inhabitants. Some films seem to promote an image of consensus, others, especially more recent films, to stress the hybridity and instability of national identity.

## What is national identity?

National identity is generally understood to be the shared identity of the naturalized inhabitants of a particular politically and geographically defined space – that is, a particular nation. But how is that identity generated? How do the members of a particular nation come to take on that identity? Is national identity something we are born with as subjects of a particular nation? Or is it something we learn?

If we were to consider national identity as in part a question of appearance, of physical attributes, then we might conclude that national identity is something we are born with. Most Italians have dark hair, most Swedes have light hair; most Zimbabweans are Black, most Britons are White. But this will clearly not do, since not all Italians have dark hair, and there are many Black Britons. Similarly, it would be difficult to distinguish between the Belgians and the Dutch on the basis of physical attributes, yet for various political and historical reasons, national boundaries have been drawn around the proximate geographical spaces we call Belgium and the Netherlands, legally dividing into two a body of people who have many shared physical attributes.

This suggests that it would be inadequate to define national identity on the basis of physical attributes. We might therefore conclude that national identity is not biological but cultural, and to that extent something that is learned, often subconsciously. The purpose of this chapter is to explore the role of the media in this process of learning. What part do the media play in promoting particular ideas of national identity? What part do they play in helping us to learn how to be British, or Australian, or American? What part do they play in developing the culture of nationality?

Although I'll be addressing general issues, most of my examples, because of my own particular interests, will be drawn from British cinema. One of your tasks will be to explore the extent to which the issues I raise are applicable to other media, and other national identities.

## Imagined communities

One influential argument about the formation of nations and identities in recent years has developed out of the work of Benedict Anderson (1983). Anderson explores the historical development of the modern nation, in an effort to explain how such nations have emerged, and how they have maintained their status as nations. If we compare the modern nation to more archaic or traditional social formations, it becomes clear that the nation is far too vast an entity for all its members to know each other. Yet vital to the sense of a nation is that its members form a unified community of people with shared interests and concerns. Anderson argues that the unification of people in the modern nation is achieved not by military means (though they will often play a part) but by cultural means. In particular, Anderson looks at the role of national media and the education system in enabling a nation to imagine itself as a coherent, meaningful and homogeneous community.

This imaginative process takes place all the time, but it comes into increasingly sharp focus at times of crisis, and especially during wars which threaten the stability and sovereignty of the nation. Historians of British cinema, for instance, have demonstrated how many British films made during the Second World War, whether specifically promoted as propaganda or not, can be read as representations of a nation of people with common interests pulling together for the common good (Barr 1998; Higson 1995; Hurd 1984). Thus Charles Barr's work on Ealing Studios shows how several Ealing films of the period tell the story of a group of relatively diverse people, thrown together by circumstance, but then pulling together to achieve a common goal (Barr 1998). In *San Demetrio, London* (1943), for instance, the diverse members of the crew of a ship work collectively to ensure the safe arrival of the ship in a British port.

Social and cultural differences, from this point of view, seem less significant than what is shared. The common purpose pulls the individual characters of the drama together, forges them into an organic, self-functioning community, and ensures that each person has a clear role within that community. This small, self-contained functional community can then be read as standing in for the nation, which is thereby imagined as a consensual gathering together of the diverse interests and concerns of the individuals that make up that community.

Such consensual images of the nation are vital to the state machinery during times of war. So what happens in peacetime? It is of course still possible to find plenty of consensual images of communities in media texts at such times, and it is still possible to read those representations metaphorically: the tight-knit, microcosmic community stands in for the nation. The British musical comedy, *Sing As We Go* (1934), for instance, deals with representatives of different classes pulling together for the common purpose of putting a cotton mill back in business during the Depression. The final scene sees Gracie Fields leading the massed ranks of the workers back into the factory, all waving Union Jack flags. In other words, the imagined community is explicitly 'nationalized' in the final scene (Higson 1995).

It is also possible to read British television soap operas like *Coronation Street* and *EastEnders* in the same way. Both series deal with relatively small, tight-knit and clearly local communities that can be read as metaphoric representations of the nation. But is the image of consensus in media texts made in the last two decades as strong as it was in films made during the Second World War? Let's have a look at the seminal film *My Beautiful Laundrette* (1985).

## Hybrid identities

*My Beautiful Laundrette* tells the story of Omar, a young British-Asian man living in South London. He is situated as a member of the local Asian community, which provides him with work. But he is also friends with Johnny, who is white, and who spends most of his time with a street-wise gaggle of youths with racist inclinations. Omar employs Johnny to help him run a laundrette that a local Asian businessman has asked him to take care of. Omar and Johnny also become lovers.

The film therefore sets out quite clearly to offer a vision of contemporary multi-cultural Britain (Figure 28.1). But it can also be read as suggesting that identity

**Figure 28.1** A vision of contemporary multi-cultural Britain: *My Beautiful Laundrette* (Working Title/Channel 4 (courtesy Kobal))

is always fluid, unstable, dependent upon circumstances (Corrigan 1992). There is little sense of consensus here. Allegiances are forever being made, unmade and remade; communities cannot be taken for granted: they are insecure, and often self-destructive. The tensions within the Asian community are manifold, with young and old generations pitted against each other, as well as tensions at the level of gender, sexuality, and the family, and clear differences of opinion about business ethics. The White street gang is similarly at odds with itself, especially when Johnny 'defects' to the other side, to work for the immigrant Asian community.

In this case, then, the nation is represented not simply as multi-cultural, but in disarray. Images of social and cultural disturbance and fragmentation are more prominent than images of consensual community. Yet this is still a representation of the nation, which raises profound and challenging questions about what it is to be British. National identity in such texts is imagined not as consensual but as hybrid, not as pure but as variegated, not as natural but as something that is constantly fought over.

What is new about such representations by comparison with many films made in the 1940s is the much clearer recognition of social and cultural tensions, the shift from consensus to dissent. Of course, we can go back to earlier 'national' representations and argue that the image of consensus was always precisely no more than an image, a powerful cultural myth important to the nation's sense of its own identity. The function of such texts, it might be argued, is ideological: to win the consent of the people to a shared image of the nation and identity.

We can also go back to representations of Britain in the 1930s and 1940s and argue that the image of national identity as hybrid was just as strong then as it is now (Higson 2000). Britain has always been multi-cultural, even if the dominant cultural strands have changed. Films like *San Demetrio, London* always made room for cultural differences, particularly in terms of class, regional and sub-national identities. And the sense of community being forged in the circumstances of the moment out of a very hybrid group of people (rather than being taken for granted as a long-standing fact) is just as strong in this film as it is in *My Beautiful Laundrette* – or at least, it is perfectly possible to read the film in this way. Perhaps the sense of a core national identity is more difficult to find in a more recent non-consensual film like *My Beautiful Laundrette*. In wartime films, on the other hand, there is a much stronger sense of a core middle-class Englishness, with more peripheral identities gathered around that core. In *My Beautiful Laundrette*, all identities seem equally marginal and central.

*My Beautiful Laundrette* and other such films of recent times perhaps more sharply stress cultural diversity and difference, hybridity and heterogeneity. The idea that the nation – the body of people that collectively constitute the national – is not simply diverse but also inconstant, fluid, changing, is something that has been increasingly central to recent debates about the formation of contemporary Britain. As the UK becomes visibly more multi-cultural, so the makers of media texts have attempted to deal with plurality, to find space in representation for cultural minorities, ethnic or otherwise. In so doing, the cultural boundaries of the nation have been redefined, and a wider more extended and hybrid national 'community' imagined.

The emergence of Black British and British-Asian films in the 1980s and 1990s, from *My Beautiful Laundrette*, through *Young Soul Rebel* (1990) and *Bhaji on the Beach* (1993) to *Babymother* (1998) and the highly successful *East is East* (1999), is a vital sign

**Figure 28.2** The clash of cultures as comedy: *East is East* (Assassin Films (courtesy Kobal))

of such shifts in the national imaginary. Parallel developments can be seen on television too, with the Black sit-com *Desmond's* making the ratings charts in the 1980s, and several Black and British-Asian comedy shows achieving success in the 1990s, including *The Real McCoy* and *Goodness Gracious Me* (*Da Ali G Show* would also be worth considering in this context).

*East is East* explores very similar themes to *My Beautiful Laundrette*, this time in the form of an often uproarious comedy, set in Salford in 1971 (Figure 28.2). It tells the story of a family whose father is a violent, authoritarian and conservative Moslem Pakistani but whose mother is a White working-class woman born and bred in Salford. Their seven children rebel in their different ways against their father's attempts to bring them up to be good Moslems and to adhere to Pakistani customs such as arranged marriages. The family is presented as belonging to two distinct but overlapping communities. On the one hand, there is the local working-class community who live in and around their inner-city terraced street, and who include both salt-of-the-earth White friends and bigoted racists. On the other hand, there is the more dispersed Moslem community, with the mosque at its centre. If an image of the nation is offered here, it is an image of the nation as made up precisely of distinct but overlapping communities, in which identities are constantly being fought over, challenged and re-forged.

The television company Channel 4 has in many ways played a crucial institutional role in underpinning the development of Black British and British-Asian film and television activity in the 1980s and 1990s. The channel was created in 1982 in the wake of the Annan Report on the *Future of Broadcasting* (Home Office 1977) as a means of responding more sensitively to the plurality and multi-culturalism of contemporary Britain. This sensitivity was to be built into the organization of the television channel. Where existing British television companies were highly centralized institutions bringing together the functions of both programme-making and broadcasting, Channel 4 was set up as a broadcaster only. It would not make its own programmes, but would draw them from diverse sources, including independent programme-makers. Its remit was to address interests not otherwise catered for on the mainstream commercial channel, ITV. Channel 4 can then be seen as an attempt to encourage new representations of the nation and its place in the global village, and new representations of national identity – or rather, of the diverse identities that make up modern Britain. To some extent, this institutional experiment has been successful in this way, with British television now opened up to many more voices and images than were available in the 1970s: it has indeed been a force for plurality.

## Constructing images of national identity

If representations of national identity are partly imagined in relation to some idea of a shared community, the process of constructing images of national identity should also be understood in two other ways. The first involves an inward-looking process, defining the nation in terms of its own internal cultural history. The second is a more outward-looking process, defining the nation in terms of its difference from others (Higson 1989).

National identity is not just about sharing in a sense of community, however contingent. National identity is about belonging – to a community, yes, but also to a place, a homeland. And it is about recognizing as familiar the established indigenous cultural traditions of that homeland and community.

Media texts can invoke indigenous traditions in various ways: they can, for instance, quite self-consciously explore and innovate within national cultural traditions, or they can simply work with those established traditions. What we recognize as national in any given media text is, then, in part the extent to which that text deals with cultural material which we recognize as distinctively British, or French, or American, or whatever. The Hollywood Western, for instance, is clearly working with some very specific cultural-historical reference points that are unique to the USA. And of course each successive Western further reinforces the sense of that material as indigenous and distinctive.

Representations of the nation thus work to imagine the nation as a community partly by invoking this sense of a distinctive and familiar cultural history and indigenous tradition. To this extent, then, the sense of a shared national identity is established through an inward-looking process, through conjuring up a particular vision of the internal history of the nation.

The other important way in which nationality is imagined is in terms of difference. The national identity of the subjects of a particular nation is this time defined not by the nation's own internal history, but in terms of the presumed difference of those national subjects from others residing outside the national borders. What it is to be British is thus defined partly in terms of what it is: another version of a familiar indigenous identity; and partly in terms of what it is not: it is not French, it is not German, it is not African. If we apply this to films, we might say that a British film seems British because it works with distinctively British material – it reproduces what we already recognize as established British cultural traditions. On the other hand, a British film seems British because it is not French, or Irish, or American – that is, because it is different from films from other national cinemas. Distinctiveness in this case is forged in a system of differences. Britishness from this point of view is quite different from all other national identities.

Except of course that it isn't! If we were to proceed on these lines, and take these notions of cultural distinctiveness and national difference for granted, we would be eliding all sense of the hybridity and instability of identity, as discussed above. Culture, the nation, and national identity would all appear as homogeneous and monolithic entities, when in fact this is far from the case, as we have already noted. Think, for instance, of the extent to which British people, especially young people, have adopted aspects of American culture as part of their identity, from Levi's jeans and baseball caps to manners of speech and preferred food and drink. Think too of the internal differences within the UK, the differences between Englishness, Scottishness and Welshness, for instance, or between White British, Black British and British-Asian.

National identity is in part about the experience of belonging to a particular nation. The question is, who 'rightfully' belongs to that nation, who actually shares in that experience of national identity? To ask such a question is to recognize that defining a nation and its identity is in part about inclusion and exclusion. Who is to be included as British? Who is to be excluded as not-British, as different? The answers to such questions are historically specific – and often politically explosive. Nationality is not natural but contingent: it changes with historical circumstance. National cultural traditions too are always in flux, always subject to a struggle for recognition over against other traditions.

Thus while it is possible to look at films like *Trainspotting* (1995) or *The Full Monty* (1997), for instance, as British national films, it's also clear that they deal with quite specific cultural traditions which compete for attention with anything we might define as a British cultural identity. Thus in both films, there is a strong sense of local identity, gender-specific identity and working-class tradition. In *Trainspotting*, youth subcultural identity and a different national identity – Scottishness – are also very much to the fore. On the one hand, all these different identities and traditions can be subsumed under the umbrella term Britishness. On the other hand, they all also pull in different directions. Period costume dramas like *Sense and Sensibility* (1996) or *The Wings of the Dove* (1997), which tell stories about love and inheritance among the English upper classes, also of course deal with quite specific cultural traditions. While the characters, settings and concerns of such films are again frequently presented as the embodiment of an ideal version of Britishness, they are in fact quite self-consciously southern English, White and for the most part upper-class. Yet the culturally specific aristocratic past that such films delight in is so often seen as a universally applicable version of the British national heritage. Each set of traditions, as embodied by these two quite distinct sets of films, struggles for ascendancy in the national cultural formation.

## Dramas of nationality

How are representations of national identity formed in a media text? In part, they are constructed in and by the text: as the narrative unfolds, as characters are pitted one against another, so a sense of identity emerges. To this extent, character is not defined in advance, but forged in the heat of the text, by the conditions of the narrative (whether it's a news story in the tabloid press, television coverage of a major international sports event, or a Hollywood feature film). But of course there is also an historical dimension to the representation of national identity – to that extent, identity is inherited from previous representations. We assume this person is English because there is a history to representations of Englishness, and we recognize what we take to be Englishness in this particular representation. Let's examine a British film in which the question of Englishness and national identity is central to the way the text unfolds.

One of the most successful British films of the 1980s was *Chariots of Fire* (1981). That seems a fairly incontrovertible statement. But what made *Chariots* a British film? Certainly, the director, producer and scriptwriter were British, as were most of the actors. But Twentieth-Century Fox, the Hollywood studio, and Allied Stars, a company run by Dodi Fayed, an Egyptian, put up most of the money for the film. To that extent, it was a multinational project. Compare some more recent 'British' film successes: *The Full Monty* was financed by one of the American studios (Fox), two other American companies (Miramax and Universal) were behind *Shakespeare in Love* (1999), and *Elizabeth* (1998) was directed by Shekhar Kapur, an Indian, with the lead part of England's Queen Elizabeth I played by Cate Blanchett, an Australian.

The distribution of films is also of course international, even for relatively low-budget British films, since the domestic market is not large enough to cover costs. So films have to be made with the international market in mind, and this inevitably has an impact on the ways in which national identities are represented in them. Identity and character can to some extent be allowed to emerge as the text unfolds and as actions lend substance to characters. But at the same time, film-makers will often resort to stereotyping as a means of readily establishing character and identity, knowing that their films will have to work in a variety of markets, with a variety of audiences.

Stereotyping is in effect a form of shorthand, a way of establishing character by adopting recognizable and well-established conventions of representation. Such representations imply a sense of history, wherein character is established through a history of representations. Markers of identity are accrued over numerous texts. The stereotype reduces, or condenses, these markers and this history to their most basic form, and at the same time attempts to naturalize this form – that is, it attempts to make the stereotypical representation seem perfectly natural. And the more widely recognizable those condensed signs of identity are, the more readily the film can be accepted at the international box-office. Except that if the stereotype has become so familiar that audiences recognize it immediately as a stereotype, then the effect becomes comic. If that is the intended effect, there is no problem. But if the effect is unintended, it is a clear sign that the stereotype needs to be renewed, so that it can once more function as a convenient and effective representational shorthand.

If they are to be accessible to a wide range of audiences, media texts almost demand that character be developed in part through stereotyping. The problem is that stereotyping tends to reproduce the idea of a core identity, a fixed and relatively

**Figure 28.3** Contesting national identity: *Chariots of Fire* (20th Century Fox/Allied Stars/Enigma (courtesy Kobal))

stable identity. Yet as we have seen identity is invariably complex, impure, hybrid and constantly changing. No wonder then that the term stereotype is often used pejoratively: a particular characterization may be criticised for being stereotypical, meaning that it lacks a realistic dimension, it fails to match up to the reality of identity.

The theme of *Chariots of Fire* is in many ways precisely the question of national identity, of whether we can accept stereotypical representations at face value, and of whether change is possible (Figure 28.3). The narrative is organized around the stories of three great runners of the 1920s, one a Scotsman (Liddell), another an Englishman who has strong attachments to his Lithuanian Jewish family background (Abrahams), and the third a charismatic young English aristocrat (Lindsay). All must run for Great Britain in the Olympic Games. Already then, even in this pared-down version of the narrative, the question of national identity is brought to the fore. What is it to be British? What is the relationship between Scottishness, Jewishness, Englishness and Britishness? The film draws attention to the hybrid nature of national identity, and shows how it is constantly intertwined with other identities and allegiances, and particularly, in this case, ethnicity, religion, class and gender.

The key institutions in the film – especially the British Olympic team and the Cambridge college where much of the film is set – are run by the English aristocracy and upper classes. By contrast, Scottishness – and especially Liddell's overt religiosity and non-conformist principles – seems marginal. So equally does Abrahams' Jewishness and his decision to take on a professional trainer, flying in the face of the English upper-class tradition of amateurism. The impetus of the narrative sees this core/

periphery relationship modified, as the upper classes literally stand aside in order to allow Liddell and Abrahams to run in the Olympics. This is the ascendancy of the meritocracy, the new middle class; it is the emergence of a modern national identity that rejects tradition and succeeds through individual enterprise.

As a drama of national identity, then, the film investigates nationality in part by negotiating this tension between tradition and modernity, by exploring character in relation to the internal history of the nation. It pits sub-national identities against one another, forging a new vision of a modern, hybrid, even multi-cultural Britishness in the heat of the drama.

At the same time, Britishness is defined over against other nationalities: the British are different from the French, their hosts for the Olympic Games, and the Americans, their major competitors. These differences are carefully stressed in the unfolding of the narrative. In these terms, national identity seems more coherent, more stable than the internal tensions between different sub-national identities would suggest. The sense of national identity as complex, unstable and in flux is displaced by a sense of solidity and superiority by comparison with other national identities.

Yet one is always aware that this is a costume drama, and that identity is always therefore assumed. Identity is quite clearly a role, literally a masquerade – and it is important to bear in mind this sense of identity as performance, and as the product of particular historical circumstances, when faced with the apparent naturalness of so many images of the nation and nationality.

Another more recent period costume film that might be read as a drama of national identity is *Elizabeth* (Figure 28.4). In this film, England's future is bound up

**Figure 28.4** A drama of national identity: *Elizabeth* (Polygram (courtesy Kobal))

in its relations with other nation-states, and especially France, Spain, Scotland and the Vatican. These political relationships are represented in terms of religious affiliations and conflicts, on the one hand, and the marital status and inclinations of Queen Elizabeth I, on the other. What the film makes clear is that identity can never be reduced solely to national affiliation – in this case, gender identity, religious fervour and self-interest are equally important. It also makes clear the extent to which the shape of a nation can change across history.

## National identity and global culture

Both *Chariots of Fire* and *Elizabeth* were huge successes at the box-office. *Chariots* became the standard bearer for a rejuvenated British film production industry in the mid-1980s, *Elizabeth* was indicative of quality British film-making at the end of the 1990s. The success of both films was not simply that they won audiences in the home market, but that they were hits internationally – and most important of all, they were hits in the American market. The international circulation of 'national' media texts is a vital aspect of our contemporary global culture. Many would argue that the need for texts to succeed in many different markets brings with it an inevitable dilution of the national. At the level of production, the national must be reduced to internationally recognizable stereotypes if it is to have any currency. At the level of reception, so-called 'national' markets will often be saturated with texts produced or at the very least financed from outside the nation's borders.

Once again, British cinema provides an ideal example. Since the 1910s, the British box-office has been dominated by American films. The taste of British film audiences has thus to a large extent been organized around the pleasures of Hollywood cinema. While there have always been popular British films, and while some audiences have always preferred British films to American films, it remains the case that a large proportion of British audiences have over the years gained a great deal of pleasure from American films (Higson 1995).

For some cultural commentators, this has been a worrying sign of both the emergence of a 'mass' culture, and the dilution of the indigenous national culture. The problem is usually formulated in terms of the threat of Americanization, the fear that all things British will be replaced by all things American (Strinati 1992). What such arguments fail to recognize is, first, that the so-called indigenous national culture is always already a hybrid complex of cultural strands imported from many different sources; and, second, that audiences will often embrace apparently 'alien' media texts because they enable those audiences to enlarge their otherwise limited cultural repertoire.

American films may well appeal to disenfranchised working-class audiences in a still heavily class-bound British society because they offer an image of America as an open, mobile society (Nowell-Smith 1985). Central both to America's own image of itself, and to the way it presents itself to others, is the idea of the American dream – that even those from the most humble origins can make it big in the enterprise culture that is America. The narrative structure of the mainstream American film is organized around precisely this dream that individuals can always fulfil their wishes.

The beginning of the Hollywood film will very often introduce an individual who has a goal to achieve. The happy ending shows that goal being achieved. Combine this narrative structure with the *mise-en-scène*[1] of the American dream and lavish production values and it is no wonder that such films appeal to audiences world-wide.

## The future: the local and the global

Many would argue that there is little future for national identity. Traditionalists will always seek to preserve the most conservative version of the nation and nationality, but the nation itself will continue to be threatened by the globalization of culture, politics and the economy. The development of new technologies which enable the generation of media texts that need no passport to cross national boundaries, and which do so constantly and effortlessly, means that those boundaries will become increasingly blurred. There is likely to be no buffer zone between the global and the local. But of course the global – and before it, the national – can only ever be a hybrid amalgam of local identities and cultures.

The international concentration of ownership and control of the media industries, and the development of technologies that enable texts to be disseminated internationally with the greatest of ease, suggests that images of the nation and national identity will be confined to the realm of nostalgia. And of course there are already many texts which seem to treat nationality in just such terms – notably the cycle of 'British' film costume dramas, or heritage films, that appeared in the two decades following the success of *Chariots of Fire*, from *A Room with a View* (1986) to *The Wings of the Dove* (Higson 1993).

For Britain, the other key developments that will undoubtedly affect the representation of nationality in the future will be the consolidation of the European Union, on the one hand, and devolution, on the other. There are already numerous pan-European media initiatives, and it seems likely that they will continue to develop. Yet there are also an increasing number of strong local or regional initiatives. Whether we like it or not, such developments are bound to have an impact on how media texts deal with the national – and on whether the national any more seems a meaningful concept.

## Questions

1   What is the role of the media in promoting a sense of national identity?

2   Most of the examples in this chapter have been taken from British films. To what extent do you think the arguments presented above are applicable to texts from other media and/or from other nations?

3   Choose any media text. How is national identity and/or the nation represented in that text?

# Note

1   Everything that appears in the film frame, including setting, costume, lighting, actors and action.

# References

Anderson, B. (1983) *Imagined Communities: Reflections on the Origin and Spread of Nationalism*, London: Verso.

Barr, C. (1998) *Ealing Studios*, revised edn, Moffat, Dumfriesshire: Cameron and Hollis.

Corrigan, T. (1992) *A Cinema Without Walls: Movies and Culture After Vietnam*, London: Routledge.

Higson, A. (1989) 'The idea of national cinema', *Screen*, 30(4): 36–46.

Higson, A. (1993) 'Re-presenting the national past: nostalgia and pastiche in the heritage film', in L. Friedman (ed.) *British Cinema and Thatcherism*, London: UCL Press, pp. 109–29.

Higson, A. (1995) *Waving the Flag: Constructing a National Cinema in Britain*, Oxford: Clarendon Press.

Higson, A. (2000) 'The instability of the national', in J. Ashby and A. Higson (eds) *British Cinema, Past and Present*, London: Routledge.

Home Office (1977) *Report of the Committee on the Future of Broadcasting* (Annan Report), Cmnd 6753, London: HMSO.

Hurd, G. (ed.) (1984) *National Fictions: World War Two in British Film and Television*, London: BFI Publishing.

Nowell-Smith, G. (1985) 'But do we need it?', in M. Auty and N. Roddick (eds) *British Cinema Now*, London: BFI Publishing, pp. 147–58.

Strinati, D. (1992) 'The taste of America: Americanization and popular culture in Britain', in D. Strinati and S. Wagg (eds) *Come on Down? Popular Media Culture in Post-War Britain*, London: Routledge.

# Further reading

Anderson, B. (1983) *Imagined Communities: Reflections on the Origin and Spread of Nationalism*, London: Verso. A highly influential account of how the modern nation-state has emerged around the world. Anderson argues that it is through the national media and the education system that the inhabitants of a nation come to see themselves as belonging to a national community.

Barr, C. (1998) *Ealing Studios*, revised edn, Moffat, Dumfriesshire: Cameron and Hollis. A now classic and very influential examination of the British films made at Ealing Studios in the 1930s, 1940s and 1950s. How these films depict the nation is one of the themes running through the book.

Bhabha, H. K. (ed.) (1990) *Nation and Narration*, London: Routledge. A collection of articles by different writers who examine how literature from around the world evokes a sense of nationness through story-telling. Some of the essays are quite demanding in terms of the theories of representation they draw on, but they are very rewarding for what they say about nationhood and identity.

Cohen, R. (1994) *Frontiers of Identity: The British and the Others*, London: Longman. Drawing on historical scholarship and social theory, Cohen shows how the British as a people are constantly defined and redefined through their interactions with 'others'. He focuses in particular on the recent history of post-imperial adjustment, relative economic decline and European integration.

Cook, P. (1996) *Fashioning the Nation: Costume and Identity in British Cinema*, London: BFI Publishing. A short but challenging exploration of debates about British cinema as a national cinema that pays particular attention to the role costume plays in constructing a sense of identity in films.

Corner, J. and Harvey, S. (eds) (1991) *Enterprise and Heritage: Crosscurrents of National Culture*, London: Routledge. An excellent collection of articles by different authors looking at changes in British culture during the Thatcher years of the 1980s. The key theme is how the heritage industry was mobilized as a part of the enterprise culture to form new images of national past and present.

Gilroy, P. (1987) *There Ain't No Black in the Union Jack*, London: Hutchinson. Gilroy is one of Britain's leading Black cultural theorists and this is his influential account of race relations in Britain in the 1980s and of how British national culture marginalizes and often demonizes Black identities and interests.

Hall, S. (1992) 'The question of cultural identity', in S. Hall, D. Held, and T. McGrew (eds) *Modernity and its Futures*, Cambridge: Polity. An excellent and extended survey of some of the most important recent debates about the concept of cultural identity (including national identity), by one of the most important cultural theorists working in Britain in the latter part of the twentieth century.

Higson, A. (1995) *Waving the Flag: Constructing a National Cinema in Britain*, Oxford: Clarendon Press. Many of the issues that Higson explores in the current chapter are dealt with in much greater depth in this historical account of how cinema in Britain can be differentiated from American cinema, and the images of the nation its films articulate.

Hjort, M. and MacKenzie, S. (eds) (2000) *Cinema and Nation*, London: Routledge. A major new collection of writing about the idea of national cinema, and about how different national cinemas around the world operate and the images of the nation, national identity and national culture they present.

Hurd, G. (ed.) (1984) *National Fictions: World War Two in British Film and Television*, London: BFI Publishing. A short but rich collection of papers examining the role the Second World War has played in popular memory and in the development of British cinema and television, including representations of the nation in wartime and post-war films.

Morley, D. and Robins, K. (1995) *Spaces of Identity: Global Media, Electronic Landscapes and Cultural Boundaries*, London: Routledge. Two of Britain's most illuminating cultural commentators explore the ways in which changes in technology and the media have forced us to rethink the meaning of and relations between the local, the national and the global, and the collective cultural identities that emerge out of these changing spaces.

Schlesinger, P. (1991) *Media, State and Nation: Political Violence and Collective Identities*, London: Sage. A leading media sociologist looks at some of the key themes of this chapter, focusing in particular on the complexity of political communication and the part it plays in the way in which states construct their enemies, both internal and external.

*Screen* 30(4) (1989). A special issue of one the leading Film Studies journals, with several articles exploring the role of the media in producing images of the nation and national identity. Includes an essay by Andrew Higson in which he explores in more depth some of the issues raised in this chapter.

Street, S. (1997) *British National Cinema*, London: Routledge. One of a series of books from Routledge looking at different national cinemas. Street offers a very useful and accessible survey of the historical development of British cinema, focusing on its diverse cultural and industrial forms.

# Chapter 29

# Sport

SPORT AS REAL LIFE: MEDIA SPORT AND CULTURE

## NEIL BLAIN AND RAYMOND BOYLE

This chapter deals with coverage of sport by television and the press. It notes that sport has been playing a growing role in many societies, and that increasingly we consume sport as a media product. It then focuses on two themes. First, it looks at the general relationship between sport and the mass media, illustrating how sport on television, radio and the press is a major aspect of media activity, since competition for audiences relies heavily on sport. It then looks particularly at how media sports coverage is often a way in which ideas about culture and society – ideas which may in themselves have nothing to do with sport – are produced by the broadcasting and print media. The chapter especially considers how ideologies of national identity are produced, but considers other ideologies such as those of gender. These two sections are preceded by a note on the way in which television screens sport.

## Introduction

Academic study of sport *as an activity in itself* has become increasingly important because of the major and growing role sport plays around the world in most cultures and societies. But in recent years, as sport has become in the main a product which we consume through its greatly expanded presence in the mass media, there has been a rapid expansion of work on sport as a media form, and as a form which communicates to us about *culture as a whole.* This presents us, therefore, with other very important reasons for studying it academically.

This chapter deals with television broadcasting and the press but sport is very significant in the field of radio competition, where in Britain independent local radio stations have been involved in an increasingly fierce war with the BBC over sports audiences: and it is also a minor but recurrent theme in the cinema.

As we shall see, much British sports coverage is not about sport. It is often about Britishness – or Englishness or Scottishness – or regional identity, or being metropolitan or rural; or about class; or gender; or race and ethnicity, among other themes. We do not attempt to cover all these themes here but rather to selectively give some impression of the extent to which talking about sport is often in truth a way of talking about culture in general.

## A note on the forms of sports mediation

Media sport has produced formal conventions: just as TV drama has traditionally used three camera positions to cover a two-person conversation, soccer coverage has its recurrent formal conventions – albeit that they change over time, and vary nationally – with regard to matters such as camera position, shot distance, or ratios of shots of pitch action in relation to off-the-ball shots. The screening of a football match or a golf tournament is televisually very complex. Numerous formal elements are permutated in both visual and linguistic domains and in matters pertaining to commentators, for example their sheer visibility, their acts of selection and summary, as well as their status as minor stars.

There are different press conventions with regard to mode of address, and qualities of 'literariness', between different sports, and between different countries. European sports writing has long seemed to address a reader very different from its British equivalent, the contrast greatest between European reporting and the UK tabloids. Not even the UK broadsheets would claim to hear in the chants of German fans, like Italy's *Gazzetta dello Sport* did at Italia '90, 'the hereditary imprint of the roar which a thousand years ago brought fear to the hearts of Drusus and the legions when for the first time they ventured through forests without name' (25 June 1990). 'Jubilant Jerry fans yesterday blasted a Euro 96 warning to England as their heroes marched into the Semi Finals' (24 June 1996), from the English *Daily Star* a few years later, puts the matter as differently as possible.

During the 1998 World Cup, France's *L'Equipe* joked

> Welcome to the world of football! A world where the pedestrian is king, where the riot police break out into smiles, where the most beautiful avenue in the world does the Mexican wave and where car drivers toot their horns, all for good reasons (4 July 1998).

This is a level of irony (precisely about standard media accounts of the World Cup) made all the more significant when it is borne in mind that the French publication is a specialist sports paper.

Many formal characteristics are themselves of ideological significance: for example, there have been trends in the last decade towards the inclusion of female presenters, especially on sports magazine programmes, yet only in certain fields such as tennis are female commentators or expert summarizers often encountered during matches. The maleness of TV sport is still very striking in the UK media, despite a tendency towards the end of the 1990s for TV channels to use more female presenters as anchors for sports programmes.

Television is constantly innovating in the realm of sport form. Among many developments over the last decade or so, the Barcelona Olympics saw new underwater and overhead camera positions adding to the vocabulary of track, field and pool coverage while cricket has seen technological developments enabling microphones and cameras to be placed in the stumps (including Channel 4's snickometer), and several sports have seen developments in pitch-side eye-level camera work. During the Euro 2000 soccer finals many matches were covered by 17 cameras, thereby multiplying viewpoints, and sound has become more intimate, with much conversation on the field relayed in detail. Interviews, and passages of 'expert analysis', are much more flexibly cut into spaces in the flow of sporting competition, the editing rhythms of television and radio sports events becoming more adventurous and complex. Since the 1998 World Cup pioneered super slo-mo, first extensively used for field events at the 2000 Sydney Olympics, the televising of US baseball games has developed a yet more sophisticated slow motion, ultra-slo-mo, already five times slower than super-slo-mo, capable of giving new levels of detail, for example, of bat hitting ball (Kellner 2000). In the UK, during 1999, BSkyB began introducing interactive services, enabling viewer choice; for example, the choice to follow the progress of a particular sports participant through individual player-cams.

Sometimes the development of televisual sports forms such as those of darts and snooker have effectively inititiated and produced these sports as mass spectator commodities. Further forms, which might be described as para-sports, are hybrids of sports broadcasting and showbusiness, ranging from TV wrestling to programmes such as ITV's *Gladiators* and the adapted import from French television, *Fort Boyard*. Television-orientated 'sports' such as synchronized swimming often have difficulty in establishing themselves as 'real' sports and satellite television has brought to the screens other quasi-sporting spectacles from truck derbies to log-rolling.

## The sport–media relationship

Sport on television, radio and the press is a particularly significant component of media activity: competition for audiences relies heavily on sport.

Since the nineteenth century, coverage of sports has been used by newspapers both to publicize events and to attract readers (Mason 1988: 46–59; Holt 1990: 306–26). While in the circulation battles among the popular press sport has always mattered, it has also become more important in the last decade among the broadsheet press as traditionally working-class sports such as football have begun to attract an increasingly large middle-class audience.

Broadcasters in Britain have also viewed sport as a core component in their programme portfolios (Whannel 1992: 45–82, Boyle and Haynes 2000: 67–88). For television, sport was once among the cheapest forms of programming, though some sports, especially football, have now become expensive; in 1999 the average cost of BBC sport per hour was £90,000, with news and drama, by way of comparison, at £54,000 and £531,000 respectively (BBC 2000). While at certain times (such as Cup Finals, football World Cups) soccer can attract large audiences, it has also delivered substantial audiences outside peak-times, such as Channel 4's Sunday afternoon Italian football, with viewers whom advertisers are keen to reach.

For the public service BBC, sport justifies the institution's claim to be reflecting the cultural life of the country. Thus while audiences are important so too is the range of domestic sports covered, and the national access given to international sporting events (such as the Olympics) in which there is a British interest. But by 2000, one of the question marks over the future of the BBC was produced precisely by its inability to hold on to key sports such as cricket and Formula One motor-racing. When, in June 2000 BBC Television failed to retain the rights to show highlights of English

Premiership football, such was the impact this was perceived to have on the organization that press stories of crisis – 'Is the game up for the BBC?' (*The Sunday Herald* 18 June 2000) – were common. BBC trademark sports presenters like Des Lynam, Murray Walker and Richie Benaud weakened the BBC badly by leaving in the later 1990s.

The traditional patterns of sports coverage in Britain are changing, driven in part by wider technological and policy shifts in the broadcasting environment (Boyle and Haynes 2000: 206–24; Rowe 1999: 145–66).

Sport is a major site of economic contestation between terrestrial broadcasters and satellite and cable television. The introduction of increased competition from satellite and cable delivery systems pushed up the price of broadcast rights to sporting events. Satellite companies such as BSkyB regard the securing of exclusive sports rights as vital in their attempt both to increase sales of dishes and, more importantly, to increase their subscriber base among viewers. New entrants to the broadcasting market in the UK, such as the American-owned cable and communication company NTL, clearly view securing sports content (football in particular) as vital.

The escalation in the costs of rights to English football, the key content driver within the UK since 1992, clearly indicates the extent to which sports 'product' has become central in the strategic development of media companies. In 1992 BSkyB secured the exclusive live television rights for FA English Premiership football in the UK. The total deal was worth £305 million over five years and included the BBC having the sole broadcasting rights to television highlights. Other premium sporting events such as rugby league/superleague, Ryder Cup golf and overseas English Test Match cricket have all found themselves available live only on BSkyB. This means that below 20% of the television audience in the UK is able to watch these events as they happen.

In 1997, BSkyB was willing to pay £670 million for these football rights until 2001. In the process the company became one of the most profitable television stations in the world and realized that this profit was based on having live football as its exclusive premium product. The most recent rights packages (for 2001–4) have been sold for £1.4 billion, with BSkyB willing to pay £1.1 billion for the rights to show 66 matches a season, NTL/BSkyB will encrypt 40 pay-per-view games per season, with ITV showing a highlights package costing £183 million. In addition, deals will be made to secure Web-based football rights, a source of increasing revenues for the major clubs (Boyle 2000).

It is in recognition of the fast-changing new media environment, with the development of WAP-based mobile phones and the growing influence of the Internet as a key distribution network for football material, that the English FA Premier League have sold the rights for only three years (five used to be the norm). As powerful content providers they do not wish to lock themselves into deals which may exclude potential new media streams of income. Meanwhile the logic of economic interdependence between sport and television in particular saw media producers start to invest significantly in the part-ownership of a variety of British football clubs during 1999 and 2000, with BSkyB, among other media companies, buying into clubs which most celebratedly included Manchester United (Blain and O'Donnell 2000: 1–22).

However, while it is true to say that increased competition is changing the relationship between sport and television in Britain, it should also be noted that television has been instrumental in influencing sport for a number of years. But there is an acceleration in the pace of change (Boyle and Haynes 2000: iv–vii; Marqusee 2000: 38–47). We need to understand something about media sport to understand the political economy of broadcasting and the press as a whole.

Television's influence on sport goes beyond simply broadcasting events and creating individual sporting stars and teams, it has also helped to shape what we actually understand to be the nature, structure and organization of modern sport. Snooker is an obvious example of a game which for most people is a TV spectator experience; its importance and the money it attracts are a product of its televisual nature and of its stars over the years, like Stephen Hendry. But television transforms sport more actively still. The introduction of one-day cricket (including the Cricket World Cup played under floodlights) was instigated by television. In 1994, football World Cup matches were played in the searing noon heat of Orlando in the USA not for the benefit of players or fans, but for the armchair television spectator in Europe. English FA Premiership matches are frequently moved from their traditional Saturday afternoon slot to suit the needs of satellite television. Boxing world title fights take place in the middle of the night in Britain to accommodate television audiences coast-to-coast in America, with the result that a Mike Tyson outdoor fight at Hampden Park in Glasgow in June 2000 took place close to midnight (though it did last only 38 seconds!). Television has also introduced shorter snooker matches, the tie-break in tennis and the advertising-friendly breaks in American football.

In addition there has emerged a triangular relationship between sport, television and sponsorship which now financially underpins most professional sport (Whannel 1992; Rowe 1999; Boyle and Haynes 2000). The levels of sponsorship attracted by various sports are determined in part by the amount of television exposure a sport can secure, therefore sports are willing to introduce rule changes. It becomes clear that any investigation into contemporary sporting culture in Britain inevitably leads to an examination of the increasingly complex relationships which exist between various sports, the media in general and television in particular.

## Representation and media sport

The term 'representation' needs some special attention in the context of sport. How, and what, media sports coverage represents can be investigated only by moving well beyond the world of sport. In certain areas of culture, such as the domain of local – both national and regional – identity, sport has a very particular kind of force; but in general many expressions of identity are permitted in the world of sport which might be inhibited elsewhere. Norbert Elias notes that 'sport continues to constitute an area of social activity in which overt emotional engagement remains publicly acceptable' (Elias and Dunning 1993: 354) and he further observes that 'a level of national sentiment' can be found in the sports section of a newspaper which is hard to imagine elsewhere. Anthony Smith points out that 'other types of collective identity – class, gender, race, religion – may overlap or combine with national identity but they rarely succeed in undermining its hold' (Smith 1991: 143). The widespread English media deployment, in the year 2000, of the sentimental term '30 years of hurt' (first used in 1996) to describe the period between England football victories over Germany in 1966 and Euro 2000 is indicative of some oddities not just in the relationship between the countries, but in England's sense of its own identity (Blain and O'Donnell 1998: 37–56). Roy Hattersley comments of the phrase that 'the emotional exaggeration is ridiculous' ('Catastrophe at Charleroi', *The Guardian* 20 June 2000): but it is also informative.

When the *Mirror* newspaper ran its infamous 'ACHTUNG! SURRENDER' headline on the England–Germany Euro 96 clash (24 June 1996), this not only 'represented' the English and Germans as soccer combatants in an endless replay of the Second World War, which continued into accounts of England–Germany matches in 2000, but also in a different fashion represented certain very important aspects of English society, culture, and media culture. There is hardly any sense in which the media merely use sport as a metaphor. The English media in particular, and most of all in the context of international football, often consign sport itself to a subordinate role, taking over the sports field to talk about national identity and other themes instead.

In a metaphor, something is suggested as the equivalent of something else. For example, German footballers are often described, using a military metaphor, as soldiers: 'The German blitzkrieg trampled through Croatia and now their storm-troopers aim to blast Terry Venables' men out of the tournament' (*Daily Star* 24 June 1996).

But strictly speaking, sport in Britain seems to be made to carry a different sort of relationship to other forms of cultural life, to belong to that class of signs (which the field of semiotics calls *indexical*) where something gets represented by something else with which it really is connected in everyday life. The importance of sport in this respect seems to vary from culture to culture (Blain and O'Donnell 1998: 37–56; O'Donnell and Blain 1999: 211–25) and in Britain it appears to be very important.

A German football performance is felt to be truly an aspect of a wider German identity which has to do with organization, energy, commitment and aggression. Likewise, the failure at editorial and journalistic level to take women's soccer, cricket, or rugby seriously stems from a masculine belief that women cannot be competitive at a range of male activities. Sport operates through the media within culture as a way of discussing characteristics of which it is assumed to present direct evidence. In the gender field this seems to be true of lots of countries other than the UK. In the field of national identity it seems that UK journalists and readers alike place much importance on sporting performance at international level.

Media sport is a field of production with which all manner of cultural, political and psychological matters – which don't in themselves have anything to do with sport – tend to become associated. So sport, especially when consumed from the media, becomes deeply incorporated into people's sense of who they are and what other people are like.

The way in which sport is written about or televised thereby becomes a source – and possibly a unique source – of information about our beliefs, opinions and attitudes as cultures. Important examples include the attitudes men have towards women and sometimes vice versa; the attitudes one ethnic group or nationality or race has towards another; the opinions or beliefs held by Europeans about Americans or the manner in which regions of a country see each other (how Milanese see Romans, or

Londoners see Mancunians); the values we attach to questions of our own physical nature, including the characteristics of age (amazement at the technical aplomb of 17-year-old swimmer Ian Thorpe at the 2000 Sydney Olympics, or exasperation at the continued presence in the German national side of the 'old man' Lothar Matthaus, in Euro 2000); and in general, the characteristics we find admirable or distasteful in other people in a period of shifting values.

The mediation of sport provides these very powerful insights into other aspects of our values just because these values are often expressed quite accidentally or innocently, as a half-conscious or unconscious by-product of our interest in the activity of sport itself. But this isn't always so; sometimes what seems to be an article on a sporting theme – a newspaper piece, say, on Dutch or English fans, or African footballers – is either consciously or unconsciously a way of expressing views on another nationality or race, and only in form a piece about the world of sport. This means that media sport is very important not only *economically* but also *politically* and *ideologically*: 'ideology' used here in both its senses, sometimes just neutrally as a 'view of the world', but often more negatively, as a 'distortion' of actual social or cultural life. There is a lot of such distortion in sports reporting, often apparently acceptable there where it wouldn't be editorially possible elsewhere in a newspaper or in a broadcast.

And, since being a TV or newspaper journalist or editor is a position of privilege, we should bear in mind that the ideologies the mainstream media produce or reproduce when giving us accounts of sports-related matters will tend to be those of socially dominant groups. We are more likely to find out what men think about women than the other way round; more likely in Italy or France to find out what whites think about blacks than vice versa; more likely on British TV networks to find out the English view of the next World Cup than the Welsh or Scottish expectations. Conversely, the accounts which we *don't* hear tell us a lot about the groups denied a voice on TV and radio or the press.

Many examples of sport being associated with the national dimension, to pursue that one example, are evidenced in the media each week. This dimension of representation in media sport has features which are curiously static, though there is, alongside that, an element of change, as will be seen. Germanness always raises particular problems for the British media. In the early 1990s a tabloid approach to handling German identity was already well-established, the famous all-German Wimbledon final of 1991, between Boris Becker and Michael Stich, having produced from one edition of the *Star* alone such gems as 'All mein says Hun-known hero'; 'Hun-believable'; 'Stich it up your Junker'; and 'Michael's the new power Kraut' – despite these players appearing as individuals, not national representatives.

There were gathering signs of disquiet in the UK at this degree of media chauvinism and xenophobia by the mid-1990s. Euro 96 sponsors Vauxhall Motors, for example, withdrew advertising from the *Star* and the *Mirror* in protest over headlines like the latter's 'Herr we go: Krauts gun for Tel' (24 June 1996). Nonetheless, during Euro 2000, the *Daily Mirror* only after fan violence in Belgium pulled a Tony Parsons column which argued that the 'Huns' had it coming to them, and which reminded readers of 'boys in their teens who died at Anzio'. The column did appear briefly on the web site.

Beside this, usually in the broadsheets, is a more reflective language. In a fiercely critical piece on English culture during Euro 2000 Hugo Young argues that the England fan violence in Belgium says much about aspects of the English national character and culture ('Banning England would be doing everyone a favour', *Guardian* 20 June 2000) while Peter Preston argues that if the English team defines English national identity, the country is in trouble:

> Football is the instant definer of national identity; but what's the definition? Football, with its cash and cynicism and melee of glib loyalties and paper allegiances, is US . . . what does that say about us? ('Football's coming home, whatever that may be', *The Guardian* 19 June 2000).

At the beginning of the twenty-first century the tabloid language previously identified begins to co-exist in a curious way with another quite different way of talking. During the 1990s British soccer filled with overseas players to the point that, in some matches, sides like Chelsea, Arsenal and Rangers barely fielded any British players. Initial media reactions could be hostile – 'OVER-RATED OVER-PAID OVER HERE' complains one *Daily Record* headline (11 January 1999). But the massive overseas presence in British football now leads to new kinds of representations of 'foreignness'.

An article in the *Sun* recounts how Coventry's Moroccan star Moustapha Hadji can speak five languages but cannot understand team boss Gordon Strachan's Scottish accent ('No comprendo Strachanese', 16 September 2000). Interestingly, the same day's Scottish edition of the paper runs a story about how Scotland Under-21 defender Lee Wilkie is learning 'the best chat-up lines' from Italian and Spanish stars at Dundee, and is quoted as saying 'They are learning a few English words but maybe it would be better if the Scots boys learned Italian'. This story simultaneously underlines masculinist ideologies of sport, and also to an extent confirms stereotypes of 'Latin' character. But at the same time, like many media stories at the turn of the century, it shows a shift of sorts in being able to welcome the internationalization of the British game and discuss it with a sort of good-humoured bewilderment.

What seems to happen is that journalists will switch between available ways of talking about other nationalities to suit the context. There is great technical admiration in Britain among journalists, presenters and summarizers for Brazilian footballers like Rivaldo, and they are discussed with great respect, yet the media easily switch back into a different vein. Discussing the forthcoming tussle between Wales and Brazil, even the mid-market *Daily Mail* (23 May 2000) unfeelingly head-lines the preparations 'Hughes plots to squeeze all life out of the Samba stars', a characterization of the Brazilians constant over many years. This switch has occurred the moment a conflict occurs in the national dimension. And in a piece further examined below, on motor racing drivers breaking down in tears, the explanation easily slips back to available, stale accounts of national or supra-national traits: 'with Fisichella and Barrichello having Latin blood in their veins, it's only natural they should reach for their hankies' (the *Sun* 16 September 2000). This approach holds good for British regional prejudices too. 'Mangle me wurzels, there's trouble brewing in East Anglia', begins a story about Premiership returnees Ipswich Town, in the same edition.

This is not to claim that the peculiar tendency to read sport as the essence of national character is absent in the qualities: The *Sunday Herald* with a very high Scottish ABC1 readership begins a report from Euro 2000:

> Renewed hostilities between England and Germany kicked off last night at the precise moment 19.45 – that the last one ended. While the last war between the two colonial powers wreaked havoc throughout Europe and the world, this weekend it was a football match which got underway at 19.45 last night between the old rivals which brought chaos to the Belgium capital and the small city of Charleroi in southern Belgium. ('English supporters sent home in orgy of violence', 18 June 2000).

Gender representation in media sport coverage still displays deeply conservative tendencies. The tabloid's tone of the 1990s is suggested by a *Daily Star* front page during Euro 96 on half of which appears, posing provocatively and skimpily dressed, mid-decade supermodel Claudia Schiffer. 'Curvy Claudia Schiffer is one German striker we don't mind being great up front. Her wunder-bra's giving lots of support. Here's hoping that's the breast that they can do.' The right-hand side of the page has the headline printed over a photograph of Terry Venables dressed, Kitchener-style, as a military recruiting officer, over the subheading 'Jerry Venables: The England boss will be down and Kraut if the Germans have their way on Wednesday' (24 June 1996). Placing Germans as both sex and hate objects on the front of a newspaper displays a reduction in the most down-market tabloids to two of the chief determinants of sales in the UK tabloid market, sex and national chauvinism. This bizarre ideological cocktail of jingoism, male chauvinism and wartime nostalgia has little to do with sport itself – indeed the quantity of technical coverage applied to the games is limited, very much so by European comparisons.

In the era of Victoria and David Beckham, a period of intense interest in the personal lives of sports stars, the same newspaper can be found carrying a photograph of Paul Gascoigne's ex-wife Sheryl in 'a sexy low-cut frock', under the headline 'Look who's flashing it, Gazza' (16 September 2000), while the same edition carries a piece referring to 'tennis cutie' Anna Kournikova – the British tabloids call her 'Cornikova' – whose large earnings, much larger than many more successful tennis players, are based on media interest in her appearance and personal life. The next day's *Sunday People* carries a particularly detailed account of sexual activity between the chairman of a large English football club and a prostitute; and the tendency to turn women into objects of consumption in the masculine domains of sport is emphasized by the placing of adverts for sex phonelines, and other sex services and products, amidst the sports pages of some tabloids. The physical appearance of sportswomen like Kournikova likewise often determines the level of coverage they receive in the broadsheets and on television. Female sports presenters on television require in the main to be glamorous, like ITV's Gaby Logan, whatever other expert qualities they may bring to the job – which is in any case usually to ask male experts what they think about sport. The question of how women are represented by the sports media requires much more attention than we can give it here, but it has become an expanding field of study for academics in a number of its dimensions (see Hargreaves 1994: 174–208; Duncan and Messner 1998; Kane and Lenskyj 1998).

Media accounts of sporting masculinity may be changing, however. Sportsmen weeping before the camera have become a feature of media coverage, since the mythic moment of origination when English soccer player Paul Gascoigne burst into tears during the 1990 World Cup. During the 1990s, when in culture and society at large there were evident changes in British public emotional behaviour, most dramatically seen at the funeral of Princess Diana in 1997, men crying in sport also became evidence of some shifts in the understanding of masculinity. 'I started to bubble as Hearts opened bubbly', begins one *Sun* story on a player's reaction to hearing that the Edinburgh side had obtained a UEFA Cup place (23 May 2000).

'Tear We Go', says the *Sun*, in another of the awful wordplays which have become a trademark of British tabloid journalism, in a piece on racing driver Michael Schumacher's breakdown on camera after the Italian Grand Prix in September 2000. 'Super-tough Schuey went all gooey', records the article, further subcaptioning a photograph of Schumacher 'Who's Sobby Now'. A picture of his Ferrari team-mate is captioned 'Boo-Hoobens Barrichello' (his forename is Rubens) and the article recounts how both drivers – like 1999 World Champion Mika Hakkinen – have caused some surprise by weeping after races. Yet the comments from racing industry sources elicited for the piece are sympathetic, pointing out the huge strain under which F1 drivers live. This, among many other signals, represents at least two changes, a general opening of British culture to emotion (and sentimentalism); and alterations to traditional definitions of male culture.

## Conclusion

Sports coverage in the tabloids (and sometimes in the media more generally) serves cultural and specifically ideological functions often not in any important way related to the phenomenon of sport itself. Frequently a particular set of ideologies, part-produced or reproduced by the sports pages, may be associated with political attitudes of owners and editors, not least with a conservative approach to Britain's still stratified and unequal society, and a guarded or hostile stance towards Europe.

The increasingly global nature of the media may dilute the national dimension of media sports culture, but evidence suggests that local cultures are very resilient, and alternative means of delivery such as satellite and cable tend to import roughly the same ideological patterns as terrestrial broadcasting. The Web theoretically presents stronger possibilities of radicalizing ideological positions among its audiences but there is some evidence of the still fledgling Web sports pages borrowing the ideological garb of the older media, not least where they are directly developed by broadcasters or newspapers.

As we have noted, those ways of seeing the world which even the conservative sports media reproduce are not entirely immune from change. However, it won't be rapid in Britain. While over in France *L'Equipe* (13 June 2000) may lyrically imagine the French Euro 2000 side, in a botanical metaphor, as a flowering of natural talent – 'Such is the seductive power of this team in the last few days of spring, that you can hardly imagine their explosive attack will fail to last the summer' – the English press relentlessly invokes the *nation*, and not the multi-ethnic nation of early twenty-first century Europe either, as the core of its understanding of the competition.

After a report that defender Tony Adams was preparing for the Portugal game during Euro 2000 by reading Shakespeare's *Henry V*, the *Mirror* thunders:

> The game's afoot: Follow your spirit; and, upon this charge, Cry, 'God for Kevin, England and Saint George!' (12 June 2000).

Judged by a sense of European contemporariness, there is still scope for enlightenment on the British sports pages.

## Questions

1  Why is sport so important to broadcasters in the UK?

2  Analyse a set of six or so broadsheet and tabloid stories about a media sports event like a European soccer competition, or the Olympics. Discuss the accounts of key areas of identities produced therein, like gender, ethnicity and nationality.

3  What are the special characteristics of the version of national identity given by the British sports media?

## References

BBC *Annual Report and Accounts 1999/2000 Summary*, London: BBC.

Blain, N. and O'Donnell, H. (1998) 'Living without the *Sun*: European sports journalism and its readers during Euro '96', in M. Roche (ed.) *Sport, Popular Culture and Identity*, Aachen: Meyer and Meyer.

Blain, N. and O'Donnell, H. (2000) 'Current trends in media sport, and the politics of local identities: a "postmodern" debate?', *Culture, Sport, Society* 3(2).

Boyle, R. (2000) 'Sports club, multi-media company or media corporation?' paper presented at Clubs or Public Corporations: Management and Social Representations of Sport in Modern Society, Institut d'estudis Catalans, Barcelona, 13 April.

Boyle, R. and Haynes, R. (2000) *Power Play: Sport, the Media and Popular Culture*, London: Longman.

Duncan, M. C. and Messner, M. A. (1998) 'The media image of sport and gender', in L. A. Wenner (ed.) *MediaSport*, London: Routledge.

Elias, N. and Dunning, E. (1993) *Quest for Excitement: Sport and Leisure in the Civilizing Process*, Oxford: Blackwell.

Hargreaves, J. (1994) *Sporting Females*, London: Routledge.

Holt, R. (1990) *Sport and the British*, Oxford: Oxford University Press.

Kane, M. J. and Lenskyj, H. J. (1998) 'Media treatment of female athletes: issues of gender and sexualities', in L. A. Wenner (ed.) *MediaSport*, London: Routledge.

Kellner, M. (2000) 'A race that never ends', *Guardian* 9 September.

Marqusee, M. (2000) 'This sporting lie', *Index on Censorship* 29(4).

Mason, T. (1988) *Sport in Britain*, London: Faber and Faber.

O'Donnell, H. and Blain, N. (1999) 'Performing the Carmagnole: negotiating French national identity during France 98', *Journal of European Area Studies* 7(2): November.

Rowe, D. (1999) *Sport, Culture and the Media*, Buckingham: Open University Press.

Smith, A. (1991) *National Identity*, London: Penguin.

Whannel, G. (1992) *Fields in Vision: Television Sport and Cultural Transformation*, London: Routledge.

## Further reading

Blain, N., Boyle, R. and O'Donnell, H. (1993) *Sport and National Identity in the European Media*, Leicester: Leicester University Press. Still one of the few media studies accounts of mediated versions of sporting and political identities which draws a truly European comparison with examples from print media around the Continent.

Boyle, R. and Haynes, R. (2000) *Power Play: Sport, the Media and Popular Culture*, London: Longman. Provides a good overview of the key political economy and cultural representation issues surrounding the media and sport relationship including new research. Also has material on sport and new media.

Cashmore, E. Ellis (2000) *Making Sense of Sport*, 3rd edn, London: Routledge. Looks at sport in its widest context, thus includes chapters on sports violence and gambling.

Gratton, C. and Taylor, P. (2000) *Economics of Sport and Recreation*, London: E&FN Spon. A more advanced look at the economics of the sports industry. Again goes beyond the relationship with the media and examines the economics of the sports industry.

Horne, J., Tomlinson, A. and Whannel, G. (1999) *Understanding Sport: An Introduction to the Sociological and Cultural Analysis of Sport*, London: E&FN Spon. A good introduction from a broad sociological perspective on sport and society. Includes chapters on media sport and sport and identity.

Rowe, D. (1999) *Sport, Culture and the Media*, Buckingham: Open University Press. A good overview of the sports–media relationship. Includes material on sports journalism and sports photography.

## Chapter 30

# News production

NEWS VALUES

**JERRY PALMER**

'News values' are the criteria that journalists use when deciding what to report and what not to report. Various attempts have been made to account for this process in a systematic manner, and they are summarized here. Analysis of different categories of news, and different types of media, shows that any systematic analysis of news that proposes that the news process is universal in its structure is oversimplified: different types of reporting are found in different media categories. The study concludes with brief consideration of the relationship between news values and the organization of news rooms, and some ethical considerations.

## Introduction

What is 'news'? Many answers have been given to this question. Some of the best-known ones take the form of traditional aphorisms:

'Dog bites man' is not news, 'man bites dog' is (John Bogart, editor of the *New York Sun*, quoted in Mott 1950: 376).

[News is] anything that makes the reader say 'Gee whiz'. (quoted in Mott 1950: 126).

News is what somebody wants to suppress; all the rest is advertising (attributed to Lord Northcliffe in MacShane 1979: 46).

Each of these sayings tries to distinguish between the type of event that is likely to feature in news reporting and the type of event that will not. According to this approach, 'news' is a feature of events, some aspect or dimension of an event that distinguishes it from others. However, it is clear that in order to serve as the basis of distinction between events, this feature of them must be recognized as such by those who produce the reports of the events – since it is they who will make the judgement in question. Indeed, it is the ability to make this judgement – often called 'news sense' by journalists – which is the basis of professional ability in news media. 'News' is thus that set of events judged 'newsworthy', and is probably best seen not as a feature of events but as a set of criteria used by professionals in their judgements about events, criteria which enable them to make a selection of events for the purposes of reporting. Of course, it is also the case that the public who buy news media must agree with the judgements in question: if they don't, then sooner or later they will switch to another newspaper or TV channel. The criteria are to that extent publicly shared ones.

## The criteria of newsworthiness

Textbooks for use in journalist training provide definitions of the features of events that make them potentially suitable for news reporting; the most famous is Macdougall's 'timeliness, proximity, prominence, consequence and human interest' (quoted in Romano 1986: 59). However, such general principles are so general that without detailed discussion of examples they tell us relatively little. The earliest attempt to provide a more systematic definition is Galtung and Ruge (1970). They distinguish eleven features, or dimensions, of events which make them likely to be reported in news media:

1 *frequency*: the event must be complete within the publication cycle of the news organization reporting it
2 *threshold*: the event must pass a certain size threshold to qualify for sufficient importance to be newsworthy
3 *clarity*: it must be relatively clear what has actually happened
4 *cultural proximity*: it must be meaningful to the audience of the news organization in question
5 *consonance*: the event must be in accordance with the framework of understanding which typifies the culture of the potential audience
6 *unexpectedness*: within the framework of meaningfulness under cultural proximity and consonance, the event must be unexpected or rare
7 *continuity*: if an event has already been in the news, there is a good chance it will stay there
8 *composition*: coverage of events is partially dictated by the internal structure of newsgathering organizations
9 *actions of the elite*: events involving elite people or organizations are more likely to be covered than those of unimportant people
10 *personification*: events that can be seen in terms of individual people rather than abstractions
11 *negativity*: bad events are more newsworthy than good ones.

These features of events, singly or in combination, increase the chance of an event being considered newsworthy. Inevitably most reported events are characterized by more than one of these features; particular combinations of them define the type of story in question, or the 'angle' of the event that is responsible for its newsworthiness.

## An example of the application of these criteria

The usefulness of these analyses of news values can be shown by considering one news story which was prominent in English news media in the days after Tuesday, 27 June 1995. The English actor Hugh Grant, who had acquired rapid fame during the preceding 12 months due to his starring role in the internationally successful film *Four Weddings and a Funeral* (1993), was accused by the police in Los Angeles of 'lewd conduct' with a prostitute; charges were brought and the police identification photograph was made available to the news media. Grant made no attempt to deny the charge.

First, the event was reported immediately after it occurred; the report was 'timely' in that sense, although it probably would have been 'timely' even if the information had been made public some time after the event, since the public availability of the information would itself still have had news value. However, this does not exhaust the question of timeliness. First, as Galtung and Ruge (1970) argue, it is important that the event in question should be complete within the cycle of publication of the news channel; they use the example of the construction of a dam: what is reported is the beginning of the project (funding agreement, for instance) and its completion (the opening ceremony, for instance), since the gradual construction on a day-by-day basis does not usually provide events that are significant. Thus 'construction' comes to mean – in news terms – inception and completion. Another example would be the reporting of a protracted event such as a war: what is reported on a day-to-day basis is what has happened during the last 24 hours, or what has happened since the last report in the channel in question. If the latter is the case, some element of explanation of what has occurred in the time lapse is necessary and this raises the further question of the time-frame that surrounds the news cycle and is implied in reports. As Schudson (1986) shows, stories often contain multiple time-frames: in his example, a report of President Reagan meeting Chinese President Li Xiannian, the time-frames are (1) Reagan's biography – he had just recovered from a cancer operation, (2) the negotiations about Chinese–American trade, (3) Li's biography – he was one of the last survivors of the Long March, (4) the anniversary of the Korean War, in other words the long and troubled history of Chinese–American relations (Schudson 1986: 84). This multiple time-frame is necessary to supply a framework of significance for the story. Clearly, Hugh Grant's arrest does not have a time-frame which is similar to this in any detail, because of the nature of the event.

The next value to consider is 'prominence', which we can equate in this instance with Galtung and Ruge's categories of 'threshold' and 'elite': it is Grant's fame that is reponsible for the newsworthiness of the event. More exactly, it is Grant's fame in England and the USA that is responsible. Well-known in journalism is 'McLurg's law' which establishes a ratio between the size of an event and its distance from (or relevance to) the news audience (Schlesinger 1987: 117): for example, a small motorway crash in England would certainly attract local news attention if someone was killed or badly injured, and quite possibly national news too; a motorway crash in France or Germany would need to be much bigger, or involve Britons, before it would be reported in English media; if the event occurred in India or China it would require a very large number of deaths to make UK news (all such thresholds would be lowered by the relative dearth of hard news on Sundays and during the 'silly season' in August). Gans' (1980) survey of those whose actions were reported in US news media shows that roughly 75–80% of them were 'knowns', as he calls them, and the rest 'unknowns'; the majority of the knowns were in fact a group of roughly 50 people, all 'high Federal officials' (1980: 12); this analysis is certainly affected by his sample of news media, all of which had national circulations in the USA, as opposed to regional, but the general principle is not in doubt. All the media in question were also non-tabloid, which would also have an effect in this respect (see below).

In discussing 'prominence' we have already opened up the topic of 'proximity', which Galtung and Ruge call both 'proximity' and 'consonance'. In the case of Grant's arrest, prominence and proximity are effectively the same: it is his fame that is responsible for both. 'Consonance' in this instance is unproblematic since the event is perfectly comprehensible in terms of the cultural norms of our society: prostitution in relation to male sexuality, the bizarre lifestyles of the rich and famous. A category of event which poses greater problems for the cultural norms of our society, and which therefore makes the theme of 'consonance' more visible is the religious miracle. In September 1995, all UK newspapers reported a miracle in which stone statues in Hindu temples appeared to drink milk. This constituted a problem for objective, factual news reporting since miraculous events are only partially consonant with the norms of modern Western culture, and as a result UK newspapers were divided over whether to report this as a miracle or as a sham; the London *Evening Standard* (27 September 1995) presented a summary of press reporting and commented that the nature of the event posed problems for normal news procedures. Other mysterious events such as UFO sightings pose the same problem for news media.

In the case of Grant's arrest, we can consider the questions of 'proximity' and 'consonance' also in relationship to 'consequence' and Galtung and Ruge's category of 'continuity'. Grant's arrest had consequence in relationship to his future as a star and especially the launch of his latest film: it was debated whether the scandal might fit well or badly with the public persona involved in the launch (*The Guardian* G2 29 June 1995: 2–3; *Evening Standard* 29 June 1995: 13). Even more attention was paid to the potential consequences for his much-publicized relationship with Elizabeth Hurley, who was just about to be launched as the new 'face' of Estée Lauder products. As a result, 'follow-up' stories in the UK media focused on her (since Grant managed to hide for some days) and her reaction to the news: for example, photographs of her were interpreted through captions drawing attention to the emotional significance of her expression. Here we can see a fundamental news value principle in operation: the notion of 'consequence' operates both in the sense that an event may be considered newsworthy because of its likely consequences, and may remain newsworthy over time because of the way in which news attention can focus upon the unravelling of these consequences – Galtung and Ruge's 'continuity'. In the case of Grant's arrest, even the prostitute's version of events was newsworthy: she was paid $100,000 for her story by the *News of the World* (*The Guardian* G2 3 July 1995: 13).

The event was also unexpected. Inevitably the 'unexpectedness' of events conflicts with their 'consonance', in the sense that consonance indicates comprehensibility whereas unexpectedness points in the opposite direction; it is the balance between the two that is crucial, as was noted many years ago by an American commentator: '... [the journalists's] commodity is not the normal; it is the standardised exceptional' (Bent 1927, quoted in Sigal 1973: 66). This event was unexpected not of course in the sense that it is unexpected that men should consort with prostitutes, but in a much more emotionally charged sense: Grant and Hurley had become prominent public symbols of glamour, and it seemed incomprehensible that someone with that status should so dramatically be revealed to be involved in something sordid. (Although this was said in commentaries at the time, statements to this effect do not appear in news reports, which tend to avoid overt interpretation of this type.

As a result, if you looked for this 'information' in news reports it would not be there even though – arguably – this was why so much attention was paid to the event. On the implications of this 'invisibility', see Palmer 2000.)

In this wider framework, it entered a long-term debate about the nature of relationships in general; as *The Guardian* columnist Suzanne Moore put it, famous stable heterosexual relationships have become a rare breed (*The Guardian* G2 29 June 1995: 5). Even if we do not necessarily accept this interpretation, it seems likely from vox pop interviews (e.g. BBC1, *Nine O'Clock News*, 28 June 1995) and other journalists' interpretations, that the event caused questioning about the place of male sexual desire in a modern society where traditional forms of repression could not be invoked as an explanation. Clearly the event was also negative, highly personalized, and associated with elite people – here the importance of the event and the elite nature of Grant and Hurley's status are largely the same thing. Also, the 'personification' involved gave a personal identity to something that is usually publicly debated in the abstract. We could also invoke the example of the death of Leah Betts from Ecstasy poisoning in November 1995 as an example of this process: although she was not the first person to die under such circumstances (in fact she was approximately the fiftieth), the fact that she took the drug at a party at her parents' home, and that she apparently had no previous links with a drug-use subculture led to substantial news interest (during the following 5 months, some 800 press reports mentioned her name); no doubt her fate had 'personified' a debate about drug use, and many parents' fears about their children's' behaviour, which had previously lacked an individual 'face' (Palmer 2000, Chapter 1).

By 'composition', Galtung and Ruge mean that news organizations balance coverage of different areas of activity in the world according to the subdivision of news organizations into sections. This claim is substantiated by Sigal's (1973) analysis of one year of the front pages of the *New York Times* and the *Washington Post*: he shows that 'whatever the variation in world events and news flow, . . . the front page [of these papers] had a tendency to contain an equal number of stories from the national, foreign and metropolitan desks' in the newsroom (1973: 30–31). This balance is not the result of an average over time (which would not be surprising) but is achieved on a daily basis. Tuchman (1978: 33) observed the same process in a US regional daily. The explanation offered by all three studies is the bureaucratic nature of news organizations and the importance of giving different groups of journalists the amount of access they expect to news space. The Grant story happened to coincide with the election of the leader of the Conservative Party caused by the prime minister's sudden and dramatic decision to resign his position as leader and seek re-election; while it is likely that the Grant story would have been newsworthy under any circumstances, its nature made it a welcome relief on the pages of newspapers and broadcast bulletins dominated by the minutiae of political debate and produced predominantly by specialist political staff (according to *The Observer* on 2 July 1995, by the time Grant's story broke, radio stations had started to receive phone calls from listeners complaining about the amount of coverage given to the Tory leadership campaign). Whether the balance found by Sigal would obtain in tabloid or broadcast news is unclear; certainly major news stories have the effect of 'unbalancing' the front pages.

## Another approach to the criteria of newsworthiness

Gans (1980: 145–80) defines newsworthiness in terms of the 'suitability' of events, of which there are three basic forms: 'substantive', 'product' and 'competition'. Substantive suitability consists of elements of story content, essentially its importance or interest; Gans' argument here is little different from Galtung and Ruge. 'Product' suitability is based in the relationship between the story and the format of the medium or channel reporting it. It may be, for example, the size of a story in relation to the audience's presumed interest in it; or it may be the availability of some particular element in the composition of the story. For example, in the case of both Hugh Grant's arrest and the death of Leah Betts, photographs of the central characters were made available to the media close to the moment the story broke, in a way which gave them a certain rarity value. In Leah Betts' case, the photograph was taken in the intensive care unit and showed her on life-support equipment; such a photograph is extremely rare, because families rarely give permission for them. In Hugh Grant's case, the police identity photograph was made available to the media by the local police – a routine occurrence – and an enterprising agency photographer, realizing its potential, rephotographed it and made it available on the Internet very promptly; the rapid availability of a photograph, which was the exact opposite of the kind of 'glamour' pose in which film stars are usually seen, was clearly part of the profile of the story (BBC2, *Decisive Moments*, 28 December 1995). In general, all other things being equal, television is more likely to give news attention to an event where film is available than one where it is not; this has led organizations that seek publicity via the news to ensure the availability of relevant, fresh video footage at times that fit with TV channels' output schedule. Competition suitability refers to the desire not to miss something that rival channels have got, and – if possible – to 'scoop' them with an 'exclusive'.

## Categories of news

All the above are features of events which make them potentially liable to attract reportorial attention and to be selected for inclusion in news reports. However, journalists also distinguish between different categories of news: the most commonly used categories are 'hard' news, 'soft' news, 'spot' news, 'diary' news, 'breaking' news and investigative journalism.

The distinction between 'hard' and 'soft' news involves various dimensions of events. Primarily, it is a question of the importance of the event: an event which is judged important as well as interesting is more likely to be considered hard news than one which is only interesting. For example, the personal relationships of figures in the entertainment world may be mentioned in a context defined by some other feature of their lives (e.g. a court appearance), but might find more difficulty in appearing in news media without such an event (but see the distinction between tabloid and broadsheet media below). In May 1996 an earlier scientific report about the presence of traces of chemicals in babies' bottled milk which might have an effect on human fertility was widely reported in the media. Although such a report might have been considered of interest at any stage of recent history, the context of the massive 'scare' about BSE in beef – which became a major phenomenon in March 1996 – ensured that this report became 'hard' news despite the fact that it had been in the public domain for some time.

'Soft' news, on the other hand, consists of information which is considered to be relatively unimportant, or whose availability is not very directly related to the passage of time. For example, on 29 June 1996 it was reported that scientists at the Centre for Nuclear Research (CERN) in Geneva were going to do a particular experiment the following day; this was linked to the fact that it was possible because of the completion of a very expensive piece of equipment. Neither the completion of the equipment, nor perhaps the experiment, were in themselves hard news: the combination of the two, plus a striking photograph, turned a piece of information that was not very date-specific and as a result 'soft' into something with a harder edge.

Here there is an important reservation to be made: another fundamental distinction in journalism is between tabloid and broadsheet formats, and these two formats have traditionally been associated with differences in news values: the type of event which might figure in tabloid formats might not pass the threshold criteria of broadsheet media. Again the example of Hugh Grant's arrest is a good example: this event in fact did figure in both types of media, because his arrest made it hard news, but had the event consisted of somebody less authoritative than the police asserting that Grant had been guilty of the behaviour he was in fact charged with, it is possible that the allegations might have been reported in tabloid media but not in broadsheet ones. The actress Gillian Taylforth sued the *Sun* over a report in which the newspaper claimed that she had been questioned by the police over an incident of lewd conduct with her lover. The original report in the *Sun* appeared some time after the incident in question, and was little mentioned by broadsheet media until the court action: soft news subsequently became hard news because of changed circumstances.

Popularly, the differences in news values are held to be considerable, as the tabloids are accused of sensationalization and triviality, implicitly suggesting that broadsheet journalism is characterized by the opposite of these qualities. For example, the commentator Roy Greenslade, writing in the *Observer* (14 July 1996) accused tabloid news values of leading to a self-evidently inadequate coverage of the 'stand-off' between Ulster Loyalist marchers and the Royal Ulster Constabulary at Drumcree in the previous week. However, another recent journalistic commentary suggested that in the last ten years the differences between the tabloids and the broadsheets had been considerably eroded: both in design of their style of layout and in terms of the choice of stories to cover the broadsheets had become more similar to the tabloids (Matthew Engel, *The Guardian*, 3 October 1996). For instance, the coverage of an event such as Hugh Grant's US arrest would probably have received little coverage in the broadsheets before the recent past.

There are no wide-ranging systematic studies of these differences. We can address the question by considering what the potential differences are; they fall into the following categories, which are effectively different dimensions of comparison:

1 the choice of stories covered, i.e. the decision whether or not to give any space at all to a particular event
2 the treatment given to the story.

Both of these dimensions of comparison need further development:

1a Story choice can be seen primarily in terms of the importance, interest and meaning of the event in question relative to all the other events that are potential candidates for inclusion – this is the purpose of traditional studies of news values, summarised above; but it should also be seen in terms of
1b the time in the life cycle of the event at which editorial choice is to be made; this involves a calculation about whether treatment by other media makes coverage necessary or unnecessary, and – crucially – decisions about whether to continue coverage of the event after the first day in a potential news event life-cycle; analysis of this variety can only be done on a longitudinal basis, following one or more stories through at least some part of their life-cycle.

Treatment can be analysed in both quantitative and qualitative terms:

2a the amount of coverage devoted to the event
2b its place in the paper (which is an indication of the importance attributed to the event)
2c the choice of themes within the event which are seen as constituting its meaning.

The quantitative comparisons 2a and 2b need some refinement. The absolute amount of coverage devoted to a story in a newspaper is not a good indication of the importance attached to it since newspapers have very different amounts of space available for news reports (the 'newshole', to use US newsroom jargon), and therefore analysis ought to be based on some device that makes allowance for this. The qualitative comparison between themes (2c) can be quantified by measuring the amount of space devoted to each theme as a percentage of report.

Analysis of a small and chronologically random sample (Palmer 2000, Chapter 2) revealed the following similarities and differences between the tabloid and the broadsheet press:

• There is substantial agreement between the two sectors about what constitutes the main story or stories on any given day. This does not imply that all papers always choose the same story as their lead story every day, but that more often than not there is majority agreement about the events to which substantial attention is to be given by the national press; exceptions are likely to come from scoops, from the fact of previous coverage producing a new agenda, and from the search for title identity. The latter probably derives mainly from commercial rivalry, where sector-specific rivalries dictate tactics rather than differentiation from other-format papers.

- Where stories are covered by a substantial proportion of the press – but neither universally nor with the degree of emphasis given to major events – story *choice* is not very likely to correlate with the tabloid/broadsheet distinction. Where this distinction is concerned, variations in story *choice* are anyway less important than variations in story *treatment*; this is as likely to be a product of title identity or of idiosyncratic news judgement as it is of format.
- A large percentage of stories to which not much attention is given are reported in only a small minority of the press, and it is difficult to discern any consistent pattern in their distribution.
- Where there are clear differences in story choice between the two press sectors they are predicated primarily on two features:
  (a) The tabloid press carries substantially less foreign stories than the broadsheet. With the exception of major political stories, the criterion of choice for tabloid inclusion of such stories is either human interest (e.g. disasters) or UK involvement in some form; availability of photographs is also important here;
  (b) The distinction between human interest stories and policy community stories; although both sectors carry both types of story, there is a clear difference of emphasis in this respect.
- Where the same stories are covered across both sectors, broadsheets extend coverage (beyond the tabloid limits) by including more material which refers to background information or policy context or a wider range of reactions to events.

This analysis probably over-emphasiszs the similarities and under-estimates the differences between the two sectors, in various ways and for methodological reasons. Firstly, in order to simplify the contours of the comparison, the mid-markets have been placed in the same category as the red-top tabloids; however, although the format of both is tabloid in the literal sense, this similarity hides a mass of differences; the mid-markets have a larger newshole (and in the case of the *Daily Mail* the difference is considerable, to the extent that in my snapshot analysis it covers more events than *The Independent*).

Second, the analysis is based upon general news pages, and many of the most obvious differences between tabloids and broadsheets are to be found elsewhere – in sports coverage, in features and in things like competitions and promotions; by the same token, this analysis omits pin-ups. In particular, the red-tops' constant attention to show-biz stories is omitted from the comparison because it is subsumed under variations in story choice. Also, the random sample which underpins this analysis does not include any days on which either of the red-top tabloids was campaigning on any issue, and overt campaigning is one of the striking differences between the two sectors.

Third, in an attempt to make valid comparisons about the treatment of topics, the analysis is disproportionately based on stories that were in fact shared across sectors. But equally interesting would be an analysis which looked at story choice based upon a selection of events that allowed the type of treatment which was typical of the paper's 'general approach' or identity, which is not separable from its sector position. For example, on 30 October 1996 the entire national press with the exception of the *Sun* put on the front page the story of the disagreement between the then Education Secretary Gillian Shepherd and the Prime Minister about corporal punishment in schools. The *Sun* led on a story about a postman who had been sacked for looking through a woman's letter box and seeing her in the nude, and relegated the 'caning' story to the inside pages. There were two possible reasons for this: the *Sun* had in fact broken the story about policy differences *à propos* corporal punishment in a brief exclusive report the previous day and perhaps felt it did not want to give maximum prominence to a second day's attention; but no doubt it is mainly a question of the type of treatment the two events lend themselves to.

'Spot' news is defined by the circumstances under which it becomes available. Much news is the result of routinized interactions between newsgathering organizations and the various sites of likely interesting or important events in our society: police stations, law courts, Parliament, political parties, large commercial enterprises, medical services, entertainment organizations, etc. (Tuchman 1978); such organizations conventionally notify news media of their upcoming activities through press releases, prearranged press conferences, etc. Such events are listed in the 'news diary' kept by media. However, other newsworthy events occur either at less predictable sites, or on less predictable occasions: accidents may happen anywhere (despite statistical patterns of regularity), scandals may be revealed by unpredictable mechanisms. 'Spot' news is the name for events that occur on unpredicted occasions, as opposed to 'diary' news.

The term 'breaking' news appears to be used in two different senses. It may be used to refer to an event which is so incomplete that its profile is hard to summarize in an authoritative and reliable manner, but whose importance or interest is sufficiently great for a tentative report to be included in a bulletin nonetheless; it is more typical of broadcast than print media (due to the different role of the passage of time in the two media) and its typical form is 'According to reports coming in while we have been on air...'. The distinctive feature of breaking news in this sense is the relatively low degree of detail of the information, deriving from its timing in relationship to the cycle of publication. It may also be used to distinguish it from investigative journalism: in the latter, the availability of information is due entirely to journalistic endeavour, whereas in breaking news the availability derives from some other source (in this sense 'breaking news' and 'spot news' overlap); this has implications for the organization of newsroom activity, for investigative journalism in general involves an exceptional effort on the part of the news organisation – journalists must be taken off routine reporting,[1] and deployed in a different way, which has cost implications for the organization; the extent to which this is possible depends ultimately on the size of the editorial budget in question.

The reliability of information about events is another feature of decisions about their inclusion (or exclusion) in news reports, and thus part of news values. Reliability derives largely from the journalistic evaluation of the sources from which information is obtained; information is reliable when it comes from a reliable source, or can be checked in some way or other (see Miller, Chapter 6 in this volume).

## Objectivity

Reliability, considered as a journalistic criterion, is inseparable from a certain conception of what type of information news should consist of. As has often been pointed out, modern journalism differs from earlier forms by its rejection of overt partisanship in news reporting and its focus upon events rather than upon overtly evaluative interpretations of events by participants in them (Schudson 1978: 4–6, 13–25; Schlesinger 1987: 15–18; Hallin 1986: 7). Central to the new form was the establishment of the 'objective' method of reporting 'hard' news: such reports were supposed to answer five questions: what, who, when, where and how? if possible supplemented by an answer to the question 'why'? (Manoff and Schudson 1986: 2–10; Sigal 1973: 66–9). Objectivity, in this analysis, consists of reporting verified facts without comment or interpretation, although most journalists recognise that the choice of which stories to cover cannot be entirely objective as it must involve elements of interpretation (Gans 1980: 182–3); as Leapman says 'The selection of news is as much a political act as commenting on it' (1992: 254). There is clear evidence of journalists choosing what to cover or not to cover on personal evaluative grounds (Goldenberg 1975: 96). Verification means conformity to specified criteria: in the BBC, until roughly 1970, it meant being on two independent agency reports (Schlesinger 1987: 90); US journalists talk about 'triangulation' as the ideal basis of reliability, in other words confirmation from two independent sources (Tuchman 1978: 85). In the UK the journalistic rule of thumb for 'routine' reporting (as opposed to 'investigative') is whether the source is competent as a public authority on the subject in question (Murphy 1991: 12); Sigal (1986: 19) and Fishman (1980) come to a similar conclusion for US print journalism. To take again the case of Hugh Grant in Los Angeles: the fact that an official representative of the police force said that the charge has been brought was sufficient proof that it had; of course, the fact of prosecution does not in itself prove guilt, and under other circumstances the person prosecuted might deny the charge (as obviously, in the case of O. J. Simpson's murder trial in 1994–5). But the objective method of reporting, in conjunction with news values, distinguishes between what actually happened, and what somebody newsworthy and authoritative claimed happened. The fact that a claim is made, and appears in the news, does not in itself imply that the claim is true – indeed, one recent academic commentator argues that news media rarely distinguish between 'accuracy' (correct reporting of what somebody claimed happened) and 'truth' (what actually did happen) (Willis 1991: 7–13). This distinction is particularly clear in political reporting, where many claims are reported simply because of the identity of the claimant. These features of journalism have led many writers to argue that objectivity in journalism has little to do with 'fact' in the scientific sense, but is instead the product of a professional routine (Gans 1980: 183; Tuchman 1978; Schudson 1991: 151). This is a key component in the professionalism of journalists, the special skill that distinguishes their work from other forms of information processing (Schlesinger 1987: 109). It has been debated whether such 'objectivity' is capable of achieving the level of independence and reliability of information that is traditionally claimed for it (Curran 1991: 98–100; Hallin 1986: 206–7; Lichtenberg 1991).

## News values and the organization of news media

The preceding discussion of news values has concentrated primarily on the nature of the events – external to the media which report them – which are likely candidates for inclusion in news media reports. However, on various occasions the discussion has strayed across the boundary between the events themselves, and features of the organizations reporting them, for example, in the role of video in determining TV news interest in a story. This is because, ultimately, 'newsworthiness' is never exclusively a feature of events, but is always related to the nature of organizations as well. These analyses refer in different ways to the distinction just drawn. Most of the 'news values' outlined in Galtung and Ruge (1970) refer to features of events, with the exception of 'frequency' and 'composition'; Gans' criteria refer partly to features of events ('substantive suitability'), but also to features of organizations ('product' and 'competition' suitability).

An obvious example is the amount of news space available – known in American journalists' jargon as the 'newshole'. Different newspapers print different amounts of pages, and on different sizes of paper.[2] Television and radio news bulletins are of different lengths. At the moment when decisions are taken about what to include and what to exclude, the amount of space available is a crucial variable. The amount is ultimately determined by economic considerations, with (in most countries, including the UK) an addition of legal obligations on broadcasting organizations to provide news and current affairs as a public service.

Less obviously, what gets selected as news is determined in part by the internal structure of news organizations. First, we should recognize that news media are indeed complex organizations in their own right, in which different people play different roles determined by the nature of the organization. Although the partially unpredictable nature of external events means that journalistic work can never be routinized to the same extent as factories or – for example – insurance offices, nonetheless, much of the production routine of news and some aspects of reporting are indeed subject to bureaucratic organization (Sigal 1973: 4; Gans 1980: 78–81, 109; Schlesinger 1987: 48; Tunstall 1971: 24–42). Publication occurs at pre-scheduled intervals which are largely independent of what happens in the outside world. Production is geared to this schedule, and reporting is similarly subject to the 'deadline'. The production routine is responsible for the elements of the definition of news which derive from the passage of time. 'Up to date' means 'since last publication': the slogan 'yesterday's news is not news' derives its meaning from the fact that the fundamental news update is daily. (More exactly, newspapers publish on this schedule. Broadcast channels update at whatever frequency they feel appropriate. In national broadcast channels, the major updates are daily in the sense that content shifts more fundamentally overnight than at any other time. However, the increasingly widespread 'rolling news' format pioneered by CNN is not subject to the same temporal logic, especially if broadcast worldwide. Internet sites are of course subject to updating at any relevant time.)

Newsrooms are also subject to an internal division of labour. The most basic element of this is the vertical division of responsibility which gives power to make decisions about story content to editors, decisions which are reflected both in the assignment of reporters to seek information about specified topics and in the instructions given to production staff (especially subeditors) about the manner in which stories are to be treated; reporters may be subject specialists (usually called 'correspondents' in the UK) or assigned to the general staff of the newsroom (Tunstall 1971: 15, 28–36). In general, the nature of working practices in news organizations and the results this has upon news representations of the world have been little studied, and most systematic data gathering on the subject is now old (Negrine 1993: 2–4); reporters have been more studied than editors and subeditors (Schudson 1991: 149). Previous analyses of the organizational aspect of journalism are divided about the importance of the division of labour for the understanding of news values. On the one hand, Gans (1980: 100) argues that the division of labour is unimportant: '. . . who makes the final story decisions has little impact on what decisions are reached, for all abide by the considerations that govern news judgment'. In a similar vein, Tuchman (1978: 67) says that the basis of journalism as a trade is that everyone can do everyone else's job (see also Negrine 1993: 5–13). On the other hand, specialist reporters are both more likely to espouse the values implicit in the activities of those whose activities they report than are general reporters, and are likely to develop a background knowledge of the area in question which enables them to contextualise events, ask probing questions of sources, etc. (Schlesinger and Tumber 1994: 150; Sigal 1973: 14–15, 19–21, 40–1, 47, 50–1; Gans 1980: 89–93, 101–5; Goldenberg 1975: 66–7, 79, 104; Gandy 1982: 104–7; Ericson *et al.* 1989: 104–13).

## News values and cultural contexts

So far this discussion of news values has been conducted entirely in media-centric terms. To go beyond this perspective we need to do two things: first, to consider the role of sources (see Miller, Chapter 6 in this volume), about which nothing more will be said here. Second, we need to consider the relationship between what is said about events, and the social and cultural contexts in which it is said; such analyses are sometimes called 'representationalist'.

Galtung and Ruge (1970) point out (under 'cultural proximity' and 'consonance') that news must indeed make sense within the context in question, but this says nothing about the extent to which there is a functional relationship between the news portrayal of events and the social context in question. Gans (1980: 36–69) addresses this question more directly than Galtung and Ruge (1970) when he shows that American news constantly affirms certain fundamental American cultural values; in other words, the way in which news presents us with an understanding of the events in question is predicated upon the basic cultural categories current in the society in which the reporting is done. However, this begs the question of the extent to which, as a result, news accounts of events reproduce the categories in which the world is understood in a society, and thus contribute towards the maintenance of a status quo by implying that the terms of a culture are always right and adequate.

This has been the subject of considerable debate over the last two decades. Most influentially, Hall *et al.* (1978) proposed that the news portrayal of events is always subject to a process of 'primary definition' by that section of society which exercises most political and economic influence (the ruling class, in the traditional sense of this term); they demonstrate this thesis through a detailed analysis of the way in which a 'crime wave' was reported in UK media, which shows that the way in which it was reported acted to reinforce a conception of the world in which state repression of any activity likely to lead to opposition would seem justified.

Countervailing analysis suggests that control over the media is much more fragmentary and subject to negotiation than Hall *et al.* (1978) admit. In a series of analyses of particular sequences of events and their news reporting a group of authors who are broadly pluralist in their political orientation indicate that the power to define the meanings of events is always negotiated between members of various ruling elites and media personnel. The result of these negotiations cannot usually be predicted from the constellation of groups or individuals involved, and therefore definitional power must be seen as the result of these negotiations, not something than precedes it and is the result of occupying the position of a 'primary definer' (Schlesinger 1989, 1990; Miller 1993a,b; Murphy 1991; Deppa *et al.* 1993; Schlesinger and Tumber 1994).

It should be stressed that this way of understanding news is not necessarily incompatible with the way outlined in the first five sections of this chapter. As Hartley (1982: 83) puts it: news values foreground 'conflict, violence, rivalry, disagreement', but these things are only comprehensible as such in terms of a background consensus on what constitutes the normality in terms of which they are defined as disruptive. Or as Chibnall (1977: 14) says, news and news values are both the product of a professional skill and a way of building consensus in a society.

## Questions

1   Take any news story and analyse what are the news values that are responsible for its appearance in the medium or channel in question.

2   Compare the coverage of a small set of stories in broadsheet, tabloid and broadcast formats: what are the differences? What are the similarities? What can you learn about the news values of each medium or channel?

3   Take a small set of news stories and analyse the extent to which the reporting conforms to the journalistic criteria of objective reporting.

## Notes

1   Unless there is a specialist group of reporters who are permanently 'off diary', in other words whose time is not pre-allocated to predictable, routinely occurring events listed in the news diary.

2   UK newspapers are usually divided into the categories of 'tabloids', 'mid-markets' and 'broadsheets' according to the composition of their readerships and the paper format

they use. The *average* daily size of the news space available in the mid-1990s in each category was approximately as follows: tabloids 2000 column centimetres, mid-markets 2500 column centimetres, broadsheets 3500 column centimetres (Collins 1999).

# References

Chibnall, S. (1977) *Law and Order News*, London: Tavistock.

Cockerell, M., Hennessy, P. and Walker, D. (1984) *Sources Close to the Prime Minister*, London: Macmillan.

Collins, J. (1999) *Food Scares and the Media*, unpublished PhD thesis, London Guildhall University.

Curran, J. (1991) 'Mass media and democracy: a re-Appraisal', in J. Curran and M. Gurevitch (eds) *Mass Media and Society*, London: Arnold, pp. 135–64.

Deppa, J. *et al.* (1993) *The Media and Disasters: Pan Am 103*, London: Fulton.

Ericson, R. V., Baranek, P. M. and Chan, J. (1989) *Negotiating Control: a Study of News Sources*, Milton Keynes: Open University Press.

Fishman, M. (1980) *The Manufacture of News*, Austin, TX: University of Texas Press.

Galtung, J. and Ruge, M. (1970) 'The structure of foreign news', in J. Tunstall (ed.) *Media Sociology*, London: Constable.

Gandy, O. (1982) *Beyond Agenda Setting*, Norwood, NJ: Ablex.

Gans, H. J. (1980) *Deciding What's News*, London: Constable.

Goldenberg, E. (1975) *Making the Papers. The Access of Resource-Poor Groups to the Metropolitan Press*, Lexington, MA: D. C. Heath.

Hall, S. *et al.* (1978) *Policing the Crisis*, London: Macmillan.

Hallin, D. (1986) *The Uncensored War: the Media and Vietnam*, Oxford: Oxford University Press.

Hartley, J. (1982) *Reading Television*, London: Methuen.

Leapman, M. (1992) *Treacherous Estate*, London: Hodder and Stoughton.

Lichtenberg, J. (1991) 'In defence of objectivity', in J. Curran and M. Gurevitch (eds), *Mass Media and Society*, London: Arnold, pp. 216–31.

MacShane, D. (1979) *Using the Media*, London: Pluto Press.

Manoff, R. K. and Schudson, M. (eds) (1986) *Reading the News*, New York: Pantheon Books.

Miller, D. (1993a) 'Official sources and "primary definition": the case of Northern Ireland', *Media, Culture and Society* 15: 385–406.

Miller, D. (1993b) 'The Northern Ireland Information Office and the media: aims, strategy and tactics', in Glasgow University Media Group, *Getting the Message*, London: Routledge.

Mott, F. (1950) *American Journalism*, New York: Macmillan.

Murphy, D. (1991) *The Stalker Affair*, London: Constable.

Negrine, R. (1993) 'The organisation of British journalism and specialist correspondents: a study of newspaper reporting', Leicester University Centre for Mass Communications Research, Discussion Papers in Mass Communications MC93/1, Leicester: Leicester University.

Palmer, J. (2000) *Spinning into Control. News Values and Source Strategies*, London: Leicester University Press/Continuum Books.

Robertson, G. and Nicol, A. (1984) *Media Law*, London: Sage.

Romano, C. (1986) 'The grisly truth about bare facts', in R. Manoff and M. Schudson (eds) *Reading the News*, New York: Pantheon Books.

Schlesinger, P. (1987) *Putting Reality Together*, 2nd edn, London: Methuen.

Schlesinger, P. (1989) 'From production to propaganda', *Media, Culture and Society* 11: 283–306.

Schlesinger, P. (1990) 'Rethinking the sociology of journalism: source strategies and the limits of media-centrism', in M. Ferguson (ed.) *Public Communication: The New Imperatives*, London: Sage.

Schlesinger, P. and Tumber, H. (1994) *Reporting Crime*, Oxford: Clarendon Press.

Schudson, M. (1978) *Discovering the News*, New York: Basic Books.

Schudson, M. (1986) 'Deadlines, datelines and history', in R. Manoff and M. Schudson (eds) *Reading the News*, New York: Pantheon Books.

Schudson, M. (1991) 'The sociology of news production revisited', in J. Curran and M. Gurevitch (eds) *Mass Media and Society*, London: Arnold,

Sigal, L. V. (1973) *Reporters and Officials*, Lexington, MA: D. C. Heath.

Sigal, L. V. (1986) 'Sources make the news', in R. Manoff and M. Schudson (eds) *Reading the News*, New York: Pantheon Books.

Tuchman, G. (1978) *Making News*, New York: Free Press.

Tunstall, J. (1971) *Journalists at Work*, London: Constable.

Weaver, P. H. (1994) *News and the Culture of Lying*, New York: Free Press.

Willis, J. (1991) *The Shadow World: Life between the News Media and Reality*, New York: Praeger.

# Further reading

Cockerell, M., Hennessy, P. and Walker, D. (1984) *Sources Close to the Prime Minister*, London: Macmillan. Analyses the basic institutional structure of source–journalist interactions in the UK political communication system, with many examples.

Curran, J. (1990) 'The new revisionism in mass communications research', *European Journal of Communication* 5: 135–64. Critical assessment of approaches to the analysis of news and current affairs.

Ericson, R. V. (1991) 'Mass media, crime, law and justice: an institutional approach', *British Journal of Criminology* 31: 219–49. Shows the necessity of grounding analysis of news reporting in the understanding of institutions.

Galtung, J. and Ruge, M. H. (1970) 'The structure of foreign news', in J. Tunstall (ed.) *Media Sociology*, London: Constable. The first systematic attempt to analyse how news values structure news reporting.

Gandy, O. (1982) *Beyond Agenda Setting*, Norwood, NJ: Ablex. Systematic survey of source behaviour, with extended case studies.

Gans, H. J. (1980) *Deciding What's News*, London: Constable. Extended and systematic internal study of how news organizations function.

Gieber, W. and Johnson, W. (1961) 'The city hall beat: a study of reporter and source roles', *Journalism Quarterly* 38: 289–97. A very early, but still interesting, analysis of reporters' relationships to a characteristic news source.

Goldenberg, E. (1975) *Making the Papers: The Access of Resource-Poor Groups to the Metropolitan Press*, Lexington, MA: D. C. Heath. Highly focused and well-theorized analysis of differential source access to a regional media system.

Harris, R. (1991) *Good and Faithful Servant: The Unauthorised Biography of Bernard Ingham*, London: Faber & Faber. Case study of one influential news source in the recent past of the UK political communications system.

Ingham, B. (1991) *Kill the Messenger*, London: Fontana. An alternative access to the material of the previous item; it is interesting to compare the two versions of the same events.

Keane, J. (1991) *The Media and Democracy*, Cambridge: Polity. Accessible philosophical study of the ethical framework within which news reporting and source-journalist interactions should be understood.

Manoff, R. K. and Schudson, M. (eds) (1986) *Reading the News*, New York: Pantheon. A collection of papers on various aspects of news production, including the operation of news values and source–journalist intereactions.

Morrison, D. and Tumber, H. (1988) *Journalists at War*, London: Sage. Extensive interview-based account of the UK media and the Falklands War.

Robertson, G. and Nicol, A. (1984) *Media Law*, London: Sage. A basic reference book to the legal constraints and opportunities that underpin journalism.

Seymour-Ure, C. (1989) 'Prime ministers' reactions to television', *Media, Culture and Society* 11: 307–25. Historical account of recent changes in the political communications system brought about by the increasing prominence of TV reporting in this system.

Sigal, L. V. (1973) *Reporters and Officials*, Lexington, MA: D. C. Heath. One of the earliest and most influential extended studies of the interactions between journalists and news sources. Says little about news values.

Chapter 31

# Parliamentary politics

THE MEDIA AND POLITICS

**IVOR GABER**

This chapter takes an overview of the reporting of politics in Britain. It traces the history of parliamentary reporting, describes the different types of political reporting, analyses the development of political broadcasting, describes the current situation and addresses the hotly disputed question, who, if anyone, is playing the major role in driving the political news agenda – the press, the broadcaster or the politicians themselves?

## Introduction

Millbank is a busy thoroughfare situated on the north bank of the River Thames at Westminster. On one side of the road stands the Palace of Westminster – the Houses of Commons and Lords – on the other, Number 4, the real centre of political power. At least that's the argument of those who claim that in Britain today the discourse of politics is now the discourse of the television studio. Number 4 Millbank houses the production offices and studios of BBC Television and Radio, ITN, Independent Radio News and Sky News and, it is argued, it is in the power of these broadcasters to determine the political agenda, and to ignore what is taking place across the road in Parliament, that has transformed the face of political communication in the UK.

## The development of parliamentary reporting

Yet just as MPs complain about the extent to which political journalists, in both the electronic and print media, have apparently seized the political news agenda and now report politics in their own terms, they have also been complaining about what they perceive to be a general decline in the actual space that newspapers devote to the coverage of parliamentary debates. There's a great irony in these calls because up until the nineteenth century MPs did everything in their power to try to prevent journalists from reporting the proceedings of Parliament.

The British Parliament first began sitting in the thirteenth century, but no formal record of its deliberations was kept. The official journal of the House of Lords dates back to 1510 and the Commons to 1547 – they recorded the Houses' decisions but not their discussions. Members risked punishment if they revealed what was actually taking place inside Parliament to anyone. This was because of fear of the monarch and/or the London mob taking exception to their deliberations. Through the next two centuries a constant battle raged between Parliament and those courageous editors and publishers who sought to report the proceedings of the Lords and Commons. This struggle climaxed in 1771 when John Wilkes, a radical journalist and MP, defied Parliament and, with the support of the London mob, began reporting its proceedings. Thus began the whole profession of parliamentary and political journalism.

In 1803 part of the Gallery of the House of Commons was set aside for the use of reporters and 81 years later the first reporters were allowed into the MPs' lobby to mingle with members and glean political intelligence. The Commons and Lords allowed the radio microphones in 1978 and in 1985 the Lords allowed the television cameras to enter. Four years later the Commons followed suit, opening up not only the deliberations of the chamber but also those of the committees.

## Political journalists

The term political journalist is a broad-brush description of those whose work involves them in writing and broadcasting about Westminster. It covers a multitude of types – in the written press six different categories of journalists involved in political reporting can be identified and in broadcasting a further four.

### *Parliamentary reporters*

The original reporters to arrive on the Westminster scene were the debate reporters – Charles Dickens was one of the first practitioners of this trade. Nowadays the vast majority of this reporting is undertaken by specialist reporters working for the official publication of the House called *Hansard*. In addition, the national newsagency, the Press Association, has a team of gallery reporters who, unlike the *Hansard* reporters, do not transcribe every word uttered in the chamber but nonetheless supply the media with a substantial and rapid reporting services. The national newspapers also used to have their own teams of gallery reporters but now only the broadsheet newspapers – specifically *The Guardian, The Independent* and particularly *The Times* and the *Daily Telegraph* – still attempt any regular parliamentary reporting at all.

In recent years Jack Straw, a leading Labour politician, has waged a campaign against the reduction in parliamentary reporting (a campaign for which he could justifiably claim some success in that the levels of parliamentary reporting in the newspapers have, in recent years, risen). As part of his campaign Straw measured the amount of press reporting of Parliament on three days in 1933, 1953, 1963, 1973, 1983 and 1992 in *The Times* and *The Guardian* (Straw 1993: 45–54). His research revealed that the space devoted to Parliament had, in *The Guardian* between 1933 and 1992, declined from an average of over 600 column inches a day to around 90;

while the decline in *The Times* had been from an average of around 900 column inches a day to around 80. Straw adduces four reasons for this decline:

- the televising of Parliament, which has led to television displacing newspapers as the most immediate source of parliamentary news
- the large Conservative majorities of the 1980s which meant that the government was always assured of winning parliamentary votes
- a generational change among broadsheet editors who came to see parliamentary debates as 'boring' and
- a consequential change in the behaviour of MPs who, seeing the trend, now use press releases and broadcast interviews as a more effective way of engaging in the national debate.

## Political correspondents

The best known political journalists are members of the so-called 'lobby' hence, lobby correspondents. Currently there are around 140 reporters holding lobby cards which entitle them to use the members' lobby of the House of Commons and there to mix with MPs; to attend off-the-record briefings which are given twice a day by the Prime Minister's Press Secretary and to receive copies of government and parliamentary publications, in advance of both the public and MPs.

The lobby, which first came into existence in the middle of the nineteenth century, has been subjected to a great deal of criticism in recent years, from both within and without. For several years in the 1980s *The Independent*, *The Guardian* and *The Scotsman* boycotted it, claiming that its influence had become pernicious, This boycott was occasioned by one particular Downing Street Press Secretary – Bernard, now Sir Bernard Ingham – who served Mrs Thatcher between 1979 and 1990 and was seen as either very good or very bad at his job, depending on one's point of view. Certainly he was ruthless in using the unattributable nature of the briefings to denigrate politicians who were out of favour with the prime minister and to boost those whose star was in the ascendant, Ingham himself has admitted that great tension exists between political reporters and the government press officers (Ingham 1994: 6–10). Eventually Mrs Thatcher was defeated, Bernard Ingham left and the boycotters returned to the fold but criticism of the lobby has continued. However, since the election of labour in May 1997 Tony Blair's Press Secretary, Alastair Campbell, has introduced changes. The Press Secretary who, until then, could only be identified as 'sources close to the Prime Minister' or, simply as 'Downing Street' can now be identified as the 'Prime Minister's Official Spokesman'; some newspapers have dispensed with this facade altogether and refer to him by name. However, the archaic rules of the lobby remain in place. Hence everything that a journalist hears or sees in the lobby is supposed to be off the record. That doesn't mean that it can't be reported but it does mean that the source of the information cannot be identified. Such a bizarre code of practice has serious implications for notions of freedom of information and, although the lobby has voted to continue its existing practices, the calls for reform (including the televising of the daily briefings) or even abolition are certain to continue (see Winstone 1996: 26–7).

## Political columnists

As the reporting of Parliament's deliberations has declined so there has been a con-comitant rise in the amount of space newspapers devote to their star-name political columnists. Many columnists are former lobby correspondents and some still retain their lobby cards. However, their work differs significantly from their colleagues in the lobby because their job is not to report the day's political news or even to break 'exclusives'. It is to talk to politicians, observe them in action and then to make their own judgements and give their own opinions, usually in line with the political bias of the papers they are writing for. Increasingly columnists such as Hugo Young on *The Guardian*, Peter Riddell on *The Times* and Donald Macintyre on *The Independent* have seen their own column inches, influence and salaries rise. It's a trend that worries many MPs who believe that it places enormous power in the hands of a very small group of people and makes them the target of enormous amounts of behind-the-scenes flattery and pressure.

## Sketchwriters

Similar to, but different from, the political columnist is the sketchwriter. Unlike the columnist, whose visits to the press gallery in the chamber, outside the weekly ritual of Prime Minister's Questions, can be rare, the sketchwriter can often be found there during long and uncontroversial debates, with perhaps only a handful of backbenchers and a minister for company. But it's at such times that the sketchwriter often finds the angle, the quirky moment which providers writers such as Simon Hoggart in *The Guardian* or Matthew Parris in *The Times* with their material. Sketchwriters have to find something witty but also trenchant to say every day and, like the columnists', it's a trade which worries MPs since the main purpose of the sketchwriter, MPs argue, is to mock their behaviour. This might be bad enough in itself but given the lack of any significant straightforward reporting of parliament, it becomes problematic in that theirs is now virtually the only perspective on the conduct of MPs now to be found in the press.

## Whitehall and Westminster correspondents

As the reporting of the deliberations of Parliament has dried up another source of news has come onstream. Known as Whitehall or Westminster Correspondents, the broadsheet newspapers have been increasing their coverage of what is cumbersomely known as the machinery of government. The first such reporter was Anthony Howard, who in the 1960s was the *Sunday Times* Whitehall Correspondent.[1] Today reporters such as David Hencke in *The Guardian* and Jill Sherman in *The Times* seek to reveal the inner workings of the civil service, exposing incompetence, corruption and plain misguided policies. Much of their work revolves around the House of Commons' Public Accounts Committee and the agency that services it, the National Audit Office. The Committee and the Audit Office exist to undertake the very same work as the journalist – the revelation of scandals and maladministration – the only difference is one of timescale. The journalist wants to break the story before its official publication, and that means even before the advance copies of the document have been delivered to members of the lobby, while the Committee and the Audit Office want to bathe in the glory of their own publicity, undistracted by premature leaks in the press. This creates an odd sort of relationship for this breed of journalists. On the one hand, they need to have good relations with members of the Public Accounts Committee and the National Audit Office for they are clearly important sources of information. However, they are also competitors because both they and the journalist want to have their versions of the story published before the other.

## Specialist correspondents

The final category of journalist who can be identified as regularly involved in political reporting is the non-political specialist. Education, defence, diplomatic correspondents, for example, all spend a significant amount of their time in and around Westminster and Whitehall covering debates, press conferences and other meetings – their reporting tends to be more forensic, they know their subjects well and it is therefore much harder for the minister, or whoever, to pull the wool over the eyes. However, paradoxically, it can also be much more difficult for them since the nature of any lobby system means that journalists require ongoing relationships with their primary sources. Any specialist correspondent seen to be 'difficult' will find his or her ability to gain access to these sources, on or off-the-record material, that much more difficult to obtain.

## Broadcast journalists

In addition to the above categories, political journalists working in radio and television can be further subdivided, although more by the form rather than the content of their work. For behind television and radio's ranks of political correspondents stand a veritable army of support staff. At a junior level there are researchers who undertake the basic research and 'phone bashing' which television and radio require.

Then there are the political writers and producers who are responsible for assembling the material – parliamentary or other actuality material, as well as interviews and reporters' 'pieces-to-camera' – which make up the news packages that are then presented by the political correspondents. Then there are the programme presenters – political specialists themselves but whose work is confined to the television and radio studios and hence needs the support of producers and researchers. And finally there are political programme editors, who are taking editorial decisions about the content of their programmes based on the advice they are receiving from their teams of political correspondents and producers.

Thus in broadcasting much of the most significant decision-taking is undertaken by broadcast journalists who have little no direct contact with the raw material – the politicians. Certainly lunches are arranged and receptions held where these behind-the-scenes broadcasters can get to know the politicians a little better but this can be no substitute for the day-to-day contact that journalists working in the lobby are able to maintain. Hence despite the great complexity of broadcast journalism, the system of restricted parliamentary access which the lobby symbolizes means that significant power still lies in the hands of the political correspondents and their unattributable sources.

# Politicians and the broadcasters

## The early days

Broadcasting itself formally began in Britain with the establishment of BBC. Initially it was the British Broadcasting Company, formed by the radio set manufacturers in 1922 to provide programmes for the 'wireless'. Under the terms of its first licence it was specifically forbidden from collecting news – the newspapers and agencies were frightened of the competition – it was allowed to broadcast 'only such news as is obtained from news agencies approved by the Postmaster General'.[2] There was just one bulletin at 7 p.m., after evening paper sales had finished. It was also specifically forbidden, by the Postmaster General, from broadcasting its own opinions on matter of public policy, nor was it allowed to broadcast on matters of political, industrial or religious controversy. However, the very first broadcasting of politics in Britain did actually take place in 1924 when leaders of the Conservative, Labour and Liberal parties were allowed to make one radio broadcast each during the election campaign of that year.

Two years later the BBC received its Royal Charter, becoming in the process the British Broadcasting Corporation. Under the terms of this first charter and its accompanying Licence the restrictions on its newsgathering were eased. One of its stated purposes was now specifically 'to collect news and information relating to current events in any part of the world and in any manner that may be thought fit and to establish and subscribe to news agencies'.

## The General Strike and the BBC

But it was in the crucible of Britain's first and only General Strike in 1926 that the BBC's relations with politicians were really forged.[3] The strike came about when the coal owners sought to cut the wages of the miners. After nine months out on strike the miners were joined by the rest of the trade union movement. This was a crucial moment for the BBC. Print workers, being highly unionized, were called out at once, but the BBC, whose staff were not organized into unions, carried on broadcasting and the BBC was to be the main source of national news throughout the nine days of the strike. Reith wrote later about this period: 'I do not say that I welcome crises, but I do welcome the opportunities which they bring' (Reith 1950: 107).

Arrangements were made for news bulletins to be broadcast at 10 a.m., 1 p.m., 4 p.m., 7 p.m. and 9.30 p.m. using agency material and official sources – at this stage the BBC had no news gathering capability of its own. The government had the power to commandeer the BBC, granted by legislation the previous year, but it and the BBC knew it would be far better if that didn't happen. (The Cabinet was divided, with Winston Churchill very strongly believing that the Corporation should be taken over for the duration of the strike.) The BBC was able to maintain a measure of independence but only with great difficulty (in this they were much assisted by the wily Prime Minister of the day, Stanley Baldwin, who preferred to 'trust the BBC').

And he was right. Lord Reith in a memo to his staff at the end of the strike wrote: '. . . . since the BBC was a national institution, and since in this crisis the

Government was acting for the people. . . . the BBC was for the Government in the crisis too'.[4] Reith admitted that the BBC 'lacked complete liberty of action' during the strike but went on to write: 'We do not believe that any other government . . . would have allowed the broadcasting authority under its control greater freedom than was enjoyed by the BBC during the crisis' (Briggs 1995: 364–6). But the BBC's less than impartial coverage of the strike had not escaped the notice of the Labour Party and TUC. They were angered by the Corporation's obvious opposition to the strike. After the strike came to an end Reith wrote 'When it was all over I wondered if it would have been better had the BBC been commandeered. My conclusion was that it would have been better for me, worse for the BBC and for the country . . .' (Reith 1950).

## The arrival of television

Television broadcasts began in the UK in 1936 but under the terms of the BBC's Charter and Licence the only news permitted was sound transmission of a recording of the main evening's radio bulletin which was broadcast at the end of the evening broadcasts over a picture of the BBC clock. In addition it transmitted two weekly film newsreels that could also be seen in cinemas around the country.

When the Second World War broke out the television transmitters were switched off – there was a fear that they could act as beacons for enemy aircraft. This was a radio war which cemented the role of the BBC as a national institution. Initially the plan was for the BBC to be placed under direct government control but it soon became apparent that the unity of purpose in the country was so great that central direction of the national broadcaster was not necessary – the BBC spoke with the same voice as the government (and incidentally the people) out of choice, not compulsion (see Calder 1969: 412–22). Although just to make sure that no dissension was voiced on the public airwaves the government introduced, and the BBC concurred with, what came to be known as the 'fourteen-day' rule; this stated that there could be no discussion on air of any matter which was due to be discussed in Parliament within the next two weeks.

Television recommenced in 1946 and the politicians were anxious to ensure that its programmes were also covered by the fourteen-day rule. One of the keenest advocates of this extension was the war-time Prime Minister Winston Churchill who declared: 'It would be shocking to have debates in this House forestalled time after time by expressions of opinions by persons who had not the status and responsibility of MPs' (quoted in Cockerell 1988: 8). The BBC offered no challenge to the extension of the rule, its basic stance towards government remained deferential and its reporting of politics remained sycophantic and unchallenging. Indeed the Corporation felt itself so regulated and fearful of disturbing the political class that, even as late as the 1955 General Election, it used the excuse of a very narrow interpretation of the Representation of the People Act to deny itself any substantial coverage of the election until the moment after the polls closed, when it began its election results programme.

## Change in the air

At the same time there was a sense of change in the air. Post-war austerity had come to an end and the spirits, both commercial and artistic, were breaking free. In the BBC this was manifest in the work of the more adventurous producers in the current affairs department, who under the inspired leadership of Grace Wyndham-Goldie, were already starting to be more abrasive and questioning in their political coverage. And it was also evidenced in the establishment of ITV, the commercial channel, and its news supplier ITN, which set out to provide as different a news service as was possible. Under its first two editors, Aiden Crawley and Geoffrey Cox, ITN sought to differentiate itself by, wherever possible, using the pictures to tell the news stories, by making personalities out of its presenters and by ending BBC habits of deference, particularly as it applied to political interviews (Crawley 1988: 304–14).

In 1956, just one year after the birth of ITN, Britain underwent its worst post-war political trauma. In the teeth of American opposition, Britain collaborated with Israel and France in invading the Egyptian-controlled Suez Canal. Far from the national unity which was the hallmark of the British media during the Second World War, the Suez Crisis sharply divided the country. In the wave of anger and controversy that swept the nation the fourteen-day rule became an irrelevancy. In the words of ITN's then editor Geoffrey Cox: 'Every interview we did at London airport, every report on public reaction, every street interview was a breach of the Fourteen Day Rule. The issues of Suez went too deeply into the lives of the public to be inhibited by such formalities' (Cox 1995: 121). A few months later the government declined to renew the fourteen-day rule when it came up for renewal in Parliament.

The combination of the advent of ITN, the Suez crisis and the Russian invasion of Hungary, also in 1956, added to the competitive transformation. The BBC was forced to take more proactive stance in terms of its reporting of politics, particularly in view of the fact that ITN interviewers did not accord politicians the same deference as had the BBC. One of ITN's most notable presenters was the later Sir Robin Day, a barrister, who began to develop a 'courtroom' style of interviewing which confronted politicians directly. In 1958, interviewing the then Prime Minister Harold Macmillan, Day caused a national outcry by asking Macmillan whether he intended to sack his Foreign Secretary who had been the subject of much criticism. In his memoirs Day has no doubts about the importance of this interview:

> The significance of my ITN interview with Macmillan is difficult to convey today. Here was the nation's leader, the most powerful and important politician of the time, coming to terms with the new medium of television. He was questioned on TV as vigorously as in Parliament. His TV performance . . . was an early recognition that television was not merely for entertainment or party propaganda, but was now a serious part of the democratic process (Day 1989: 3).

Nor did Macmillan see the interview as an ordeal or an impertinence, as some of the Conservative press of the time claimed. His biographer records; 'His first breakthrough as a "television personality" had come with a full-length interview staged by a young, brash, and virtually unknown journalist called Robin Day . . .' (Horne 1989: 149).

Despite the apparent ending of deference, television still faced enormous handicaps in the reporting of the political process at its most intense, i.e. during a General Election campaign. Indeed no real reporting took place at all since the BBC believed, and ITN initially concurred, that even if the fourteen-day rule was no more, under the legislation governing the conduct of elections the broadcasting of politicians during a campaign could be challenged as illegal. However, ITN and one of the more adventurous of the regional ITV companies – Granada – determined to challenge this interpretation of the Representation of the People Act. The ideal opportunity arose with a by-election in the North Western town of Rochdale in 1958. Not only did it fall within Granada's transmission area but one of the candidates was a former ITN newscaster. The news imperatives were strong and both companies went ahead with very straightforward election coverage – the skies did not fall in, nor did anyone mount a legal challenge.

## The politicians' response

At the same time as television was experimenting with its coverage of politics so politicians were also seeking to come to terms with the new medium. Harold Macmillan, Prime Minister between 1958 and 1963, was the first British politician who, despite his protestations to the contrary, clearly understood the importance of the medium and learned how to exploit it. He recognized that television was his single most important instrument of communication with the electorate and he knew that the style of the traditional hustings was not appropriate. 'I've never quite mastered the art of looking into the lens and treating it as one of the family' (Horne 1989) he said in a speech after his retirement thus revealing that he understood precisely how politicians should be using this new medium.

As television became ever more powerful – by the early 1960s the majority of people were claiming television as their principal news source (Blumler and McQuail 1968: 43) – it was noticeable that much of the political debate had begun to shift away from the floor of the House of Commons to the floor of the television studios. And political parties were now making televisual appeal an important factor in their choice of leader. Macmillan's Labour counterpart was Harold Wilson who won elections in 1964 and 1966 and twice in 1974. He realized that the secret of success on television was to appear as natural as possible, while in fact he and his team in fact put a great deal of thought and effort into creating such a 'natural' effect. For example, his staff noticed he had the habit of emphasizing a point with a clenched fist. This looked slightly threatening on television so they came up with the idea of Wilson holding a pipe in that hand. The pipe cured the clenched fist and, incidentally, gave him a 'man of the people look' (in private he actually smoked cigars); it also enabled him to gain precious moments for thought during television interviews as he paused to light his pipe just at the moment as a penetrating question was being posed. (Today's non-smoking environments severely restrict the use of this particular ruse.)

In subsequent campaigns Wilson adopted yet new methods to appear 'television friendly'. A make-up artist accompanied him around the UK on his election tours, a clean suit was always ready for him to change into after a day's hard campaigning and there was even a lemon and honey drink available to keep his voice in good order – although this was always dispensed from a green decanter and drunk from a green glass so that the audience would not think he was downing a glass of scotch. Wilson used to time his most pungent remarks for when he knew he was going live into a news bulletin. Live audiences could be quite startled suddenly to hear Wilson stop mid-sentence and launch into a quip against the government. Even at this early stage in the broadcasting of politics some television producers were becoming nervous about being manipulated: the BBC was reluctant cover any of Wilson's meetings live because of what they felt to be their loss of editorial control. However, ITN, which always had a more 'showbiz' approach, relished the excitement that these live sound-bites created. Sir Geoffrey Cox has described the live pictures of Harold Wilson dealing with interruptions during coverage an election speech as 'some of the most remarkable television ever seen on a news programme' (Cox 1983: 180).

## The current situation

In an important sense Macmillan and Wilson virtually bring the story up to date for it was under their leadership the two main political parties came to accept the importance of television in the electoral battles. In the forty years that divide us from them there were many further developments – not least the impact that Margaret Thatcher and her team of advisors made on the Conservative Party and the similar role played by Peter Mandelson, first as Labour's Director of Communications and then as adviser to Tony Blair. Nonetheless the pattern had been set by the 1960s – a pattern that appears to be one of ongoing conflict and strain but which in fact is more accurately characterized as 'collusive conflict' (Kellner 1993). However, it is an uneven conflict because politicians, through a range of formal and informal controls, retain ultimate power over broadcasters. So what are these controls and how do they work?

## Formal controls

The BBC operates under a charter and licence which is granted formally by Parliament, but in fact by the government of the day for a fixed term, usually ten years. Its last charter expired in 1996 and in the period prior to renewal, the BBC was perceived to be particularly sensitive to the political climate. For example, in 1995 there was a major row, which ended with the Corporation being defeated in court, over its decision to grant the Prime Minister, John Major, a full-length interview on *Panorama* – the BBC's flagship current affairs television programme – on the eve of local elections in Scotland. Nor are ITV companies immune to similar pressures; under the 1990 Broadcasting Act ITV franchises were awarded on the 'highest bidder' principle but in the past franchises were awarded on less easily quantifiable criteria – such uncertainty creates an atmosphere in which ITV companies became very sensitive to criticisms from both government and opposition. In 1990 it was widely believed that Mrs Thatcher had been determined to ensure that Thames TV did not win back its franchise because of her anger about their programme *Death on the Rock*, which examined allegations that the British army was operating a 'shoot-to-kill' policy against IRA suspects (Bolton 1990).

Nor does the granting of the charter or the awarding of the franchises end the process of government oversight. The legislation under which the broadcasters operate requires them to show 'due impartiality' on matters of political controversy, a stricture which is wide enough to permit virtually any interpretation, by the politicians, should they choose to do so. And there are other means of formal control. The level of the BBC's licence-fee is determined by a parliamentary vote. This author was recently told by a former BBC executive of a Labour Northern Ireland Secretary who expressed his displeasure at the BBC's coverage of Ulster affairs by telling him that he'd make sure that there would be no licence fee increase that year – fortunately his Home Secretary of the day didn't follows his advice.[5] In the past there have been similar battles over the size of the ITV levy. The 1990 Act ended the levy but did create a situation in which Parliament had to adjudicate between ITV and Channel 4 as to the distribution of commercial television profits.

Broadcasting legislation comes before Parliament every five years or so and such periods are always a particularly sensitive time for broadcasters. Even in periods of relative parliamentary tranquillity they still have to keep a more than wary eye on the all-party Media, Culture and Sport Committee which monitors and comments on broadcasting affairs on a regular basis. The statutory bodies that monitor programme standards and act on viewers' complaints are directly appointed by government, as are members of the BBC Board of Governors and the Independent Television Commission. In fact Mrs Thatcher used her powers of patronage in an unprecedented way by overturning the long-standing tradition which ensured that the BBC's Chairman and Deputy Chairman were appointed from different sides of the political spectrum. Under Mrs Thatcher both offices were held by appointees known to be sympathetic to the Conservatives. A similar situation arose under Labour in 2001 when concern was expressed about the appointment of a labour-supporting Chairman of the BBC Board of Governor, at a time when the Director General was also publicly identified as a labour sympathizer.

## Informal controls

Nor are these public mechanisms the end of the story. Politicians from all parties have never been slow to bring direct pressure to bear on the broadcasters. In the run-up to the 1997 General Election the Conservatives announced the rebirth of their 'media monitoring unit' – a timely reminder of the attempts by Norman Tebbit, then Chairman of the Conservative Party, almost a decade ago to increase the 'sensitivity' of the BBC to political pressure by attacking its coverage of the US bombing of Libya. Nor is such pressure solely a Conservative prerogative; Labour Prime Minister Harold Wilson sought to exercise control of the BBC by appointing Lord Hill, who had until his appointment been identified with ITV. That attempt was unsuccessful but was merely the precursor to a long-running and vitriolic feud between Wilson and the Corporation that outlived his premiership. There are many other examples of direct political pressure being applied to the broadcaster; Northern Ireland has been a particularly sensitive subject but there is also a long history of accusations of bias and inaccurate reporting which are constantly being levelled at the broadcasters by all the political parties. This is the context in which politicians' complaints about the powers of the broadcasters have to be evaluated.

## The structures of political broadcasting

Political broadcasting on British television can be seen as taking place within two main formats – first, those programmes exclusively devoted to the reporting of parliament and politics and second, the daily news and current affairs programmes.

### Parliamentary broadcasting

The televising of Parliament is undertaken by an independent production company – CCT Productions. They supply continuous coverage of the Commons and the Lords to all British and some foreign broadcasters. They are appointed and controlled by a joint committee of broadcasters and members of the Lords and Commons who form a majority of the supervising body and who entrust day-to-day supervision to a member of the parliamentary staff, the Supervisor of Broadcasting; one of whose most important jobs is ensuring that the very strict rules of coverage are observed by the broadcasters. These rules include forbidding the cameras from revealing how full, or more likely, how empty the House is; from covering any disturbance taking place in the Chamber or from framing an MP in anything more exciting than the standard medium close-up shot. Over the years CCT's coverage has nudged the guidelines along a little so that although the main rules of coverage are still followed, some latitude has been taken (and accepted by the politicians) in the selection of camera angles, which at least provides some variation in shot for the viewer and also some occasional insight into how full, or otherwise, the chamber actually is.

Committee coverage is also undertaken by CCT; this coverage is not continuous but demand-driven. CCT establishes, a week in advance, what areas the various committees will be covering and then canvasses the broadcaster to find out how much interest there is in any of those hearings. Since broadcasters have to pay for this coverage on an *ad hoc* basis this provides a good discipline for establishing where their priorities really lie (this is in contrast to coverage of the Commons and Lords, for which the broadcaster pay an annual fee).

### BBC Parliament

One of the few growth points in political coverage has been the advent of a dedicated parliamentary channel. Originally begun by a consortium of cable companies. This channel was taken over by the BBC and renamed BBC Parliament. It provides comprehensive live and recorded coverage of the chambers and committees of the House of Commons and Lords, as well as live coverage of other political events. Its audience, however, remains minuscule.

## Political programmes

Network television and radio programmes exclusively devoted to politics and parliament are mainly to be found on the BBC. On radio the Corporation broadcasts daily reports of Parliament – *Today in Parliament* and *Yesterday in Parliament*. It also broadcasts weekly political discussion programmes – *The Week in Westminster* (first broadcast in 1929) on Radio 4, *The Westminster Hour* on 5Live and *People and Politics* on the World Service. Sound broadcasting from Parliament did not begin until 1978. Today (late 2000) the BBC broadcasts weekly live coverage of Prime Minister's Question Time and other major parliamentary events on Radio 5Live.

The live broadcasting of Parliament on television did not begin until 1986 when the Lords first allowed in the cameras. When parliament is sitting the BBC broadcasts a late night television report from parliament (*Despatch Box*) and a thrice-weekly afternoon programme *Westminster Live* which consist of both live coverage of the House and interviews. It also transmits two weekly programmes devoted to politics, both on a Sunday – an interview programme based around the personality of broadcaster David Frost, *The Frost Programme*, and *On the Record* which is broadcast Sunday lunchtimes and consists of a major interview as well as reporter packages.

In comparison, between ITV, Channel 4 and Channel 5 there is only one network programme exclusively devoted to politics and parliament. *Power House* is a thrice-weekly magazine programme which mixes parliamentary coverage, with interviews and reports. However, it goes out at midday on Channel 4 and is not widely watched. The satellite channel Sky News devotes most weekday afternoons to live political coverage of the Commons and it has a weekly political interview programme on a Sunday, hosted by their well-regarded Political Editor, Adam Boulton.

## Television news and politics

Politics has played an important role on British television news but it's a role that has been in decline in recent times. Recent research indicates that between 1975 and 1999 the amount of political coverage on terrestrial television bulletins more than halved from 28% of programme content to 13% (Barnett *et al.* 2000). There are news bulletins throughout the day on three of the five terrestrial networks (the exceptions being BBC2 and Channel 4) and, of course, round-the-clock coverage on Sky News. However, the major network news programmes are on at breakfast time, lunchtime, the early evening and, the 10 o'clock flagship bulletins for BBC and ITN. However, the two programmes which probably give greatest coverage to politics occur outside of these main coverage times – Channel 4 News at 7 p.m. and *Newsnight* on BBC2 at 10.30 p.m. While Parliament is sitting the flagship bulletins will contain an average two political stories a day on the BBC and one on ITN. In a study of the BBC and ITN news which sought to identify the main sources of political news on television it was revealed that the politicians themselves were the most important single source. Reports from Parliament rarely formed stories in themselves but clips from parliamentary debates or committee hearings would go to make up part of the political correspondent's packages (see Gaber 1997).

## The dynamics of coverage

Political coverage in television bulletins is very much a joint enterprise between the bulletin producers based at their headquarters in the BBC, ITN and Sky and their political teams at Westminster. In planning and executing their daily political coverage the broadcasters and writing journalists follow well-established newsgathering routines. For most political reporters, and politicians for that matter, the day begins with BBC Radio 4's *Today* programme. *Today's* political day, like that of their television counterparts *Breakfast News* on the BBC, GMTV on ITV and Sky News, in fact begins the previous evening when in discussions between producers at the programme headquarters and their staff at Westminster plot the morning's coverage. Their reports are avidly watched and then reacted to by other broadcast journalists and reporters working for the evening newspapers. (Later in the day journalists working for the national newspapers, who obviously have later deadlines, also start picking-up on the broadcasters' political reports.) But just as the print journalists are working out how to cover stories which have been covered by radio and television, the broadcasters have themselves been reacting to newspaper reporting, either from the morning papers or the early editions of the evening papers.

Perhaps most importantly all sides will be monitoring coverage coming from the Press Association which has a large team of parliamentary and political reporters and is viewed with credibility by both journalists and politicians. Indeed just to make sure that their own output is not missed, television and radio programmes frequently alert Press Association reporters to items that they are about to, or have just, broadcast. By getting summaries of their interview material onto the Press Association wire they save other journalists the trouble of having to watch or listen to their programmes; but they also benefit from the credibility associated with the PA which makes it more likely that the item will be noticed and, even more importantly, attributed to their programme. Another vital source of 'breaking' news at Westminster is the London *Evening Standard*. Its five editions a day are avidly consumed by politicians and journalists alike and the paper plays a vital role in determining the day's political news agenda. In the fast-moving world of breaking news it is not uncommon for stories that have led the first edition to be reduced to a paragraph on an inside page in the final edition.

In addition to the media's self-regarding behaviour there are times when the politicians also get a look-in. Twice a day the Prime Minister's Press Secretary, or his deputy (there has never been a her), gives members of that quasi-secret society, the parliamentary lobby, an off-the record briefing on the day's political events. Once a week the Prime Minister and the Leader of the Opposition cross swords on the floor of the House during Prime Minister's Questions and at numerous times during the day lobby correspondents can be seen in the Members' lobby in conversation with ministers, shadow ministers, humble backbenchers and members of the parties' media teams. However, political correspondents have observed that since the inception of the Labour Government in 1997 (and presumably the tighter discipline the governing party has imposed on its backbenchers) fewer MPs now linger in the lobby to converse, and hence there are fewer journalists there as well.

The parties' media teams follow a routine very similar to that of the journalist. Their day might easily have begun the previous evening with a series of negotiations with radio and television producers about who or what was going to be provided for the morning's news programmes. They might well have been 'spinning' – in other words trying to influence the day's forthcoming coverage by talking-up a particular news item or down-playing others. The daily editorial meetings, which form such an important part of the routines of news organizations, also take place within the party's media organizations. At these meetings they try to plan the day's political initiatives and seek to anticipate any problems that might arise. This level of activity used to be reserved for election times only but has now become the norm throughout the political cycle.

## The spin doctors

Much has been written in recent years about 'spin doctors' and the culture of 'spinning'. Indeed the two terms have now passed into general conversation. However, the term 'spinning' might be new to the public discourse but the activity is as old as politics itself. Previously 'spin doctors' were called Party Press Officers and what they did was called 'briefing'. It amounts to much the same thing. Perhaps one reason why the role of the spin doctor came to such prominence in the 1990s was partly the fact that two of Labour leader Tony Blair's closest confidants were spin doctors and their influence was not confined to issues of presentation, they had major input into policy as well.

The role of the parties' (not to mention the government's) media operations is now a major factor in the political landscape and just one example will suffice. A few years ago it would have been inconceivable for political producers to feel that they had to make their 'bids' for political interviewees with, for instance, opposition frontbenchers to anyone other than the politician him- or herself; today it is almost inconceivable that such bids would not go through the relevant press officers. (The situation with ministers is somewhat different in that the activities of Whitehall press officers are not a new phenomenon.) This gives tremendous power to press officers to grant or deny access depending as to how satisfied they currently were with the coverage they were receiving from the particular outlet in question. Denial of access is a relatively minor nuisance for a newspaper but for a broadcaster it can be disastrous – a political report that does not contain the voice or picture of the central characters is, to say the least, less than satisfactory.

Control of the political news agenda is now central to both parties' campaigning strategy. Andrew Lansley, now a member of the Conservative Shadow cabinet and a former Head of Research at Conservative Central Office, has written: 'For a political party the primary objective is to control the agenda, by determining the issues of political debate . . .' (Lansley 1995). Such sentiments are echoed across the political divide. Speaking after the 1992 election Labour's former Deputy Leader Roy Hattersley said:

> The party which sets the agenda wins the election. Does anybody doubt that if the election had been fought around health, education or unemployment, the Labour Party would now be the Government? But the election was not fought around those issues, it was fought around the issue . . . of tax in particular. That agenda was set by the Conservative Party, aided and abetted by the newspapers, with the broadcasting media as accessories after the fact (Hattersley 1993).

More recently Joy Johnson, a former Director of Media, Campaigns and Elections for Labour, has written: '. . . the party that captures the news initiative will both dominate the agenda and wrong-foot their opponents'.[6]

## The power of the press

If the politicians and their media advisors are successful at establishing their own media agenda over that of the broadcasters, how do they fare in their similar battle with the press? After all, could it not be argued that in fact it's the press which in itself determines the news priorities of both the politicians and the broadcasters? Certainly this is a popular view which received powerful support after the 1992 election from Martin Linton whose research entitled 'The Sun Wot Won It' argued that the influence of tabloid newspapers was critical in understanding movements in public opinion (Linton 1995). However, while it is certainly true that on a day-to-day basis, newspapers play a major role in determining politicians' and broadcasters news priorities this is only a short-term effect. This is because newspapers in the UK, for the most part, have strong proprietorially driven political agendas, so although, for example, in the case of the 1992 election it might have been 'The Sun Wot Won It', they won it on behalf of the politicians whose bidding they were ultimately following. Therefore because of the unusually partisan nature of the vast majority of the British press, it is a largely fruitless exercise seeking to ascertain whether or not the politicians or the press control the political agenda. Despite any short-term differences of opinion, over time newspapers follow the agenda of their political allies.

## Conclusion

At different times, and in different societies, the press, television or the politicians and their allies can be seen to have been in the ascendant, in terms of the setting of the political agenda. At the start of the new millennium in Britain, its is being argued, the combination of a highly regulated broadcasting system and a highly partisan press has created a situation in which the power to set the political agenda lies in Westminster, firmly in the hands of the politicians. And given the choice –

between the press, the broadcasters and the politicians – there are those who would argue that in a democracy the politicians have as much claim, if not more, than the other two groups to be in such a position of pre-eminence. Equally in an ideal world such power should rest with the electorate.

Such an aspiration might be unrealistic in an age of mass communications but with the development of interactivity, on television, radio and the Internet, will it always remain unattainable? And that question raises the issue of how universal access to these technologies will become. For how truly democratic is a political discourse which can only be participated in by those with a required level of economic and intellectual resources? Given that the answer to that is probably not democratic at all, then the present stand-off, with politicians still holding the ring, seems to be the best compromise on offer.

## Questions

1   To what extent has the structure of political and parliamentary reporting been influenced by:
    (a)   Patterns of newspaper ownership
    (b)   The domination of broadcasting by the BBC
    (c)   The two-party system?

2   Is the fact that political news is not popular among mass media audiences a sign of the strength or weakness of our democracy?

3   To what extent are technological developments affecting how politics is viewed by the public?

## Notes

1   The then Prime Minister Harold Wilson unsuccessfully sought to scupper Howard's appointment by instructing his ministers to have no dealings with him. See Pimlott (1993: 443).
2   See Briggs (1995: 239–48) for a full discussion of the difficulties this restriction imposed on the new BBC.
3   For two contrasting views of the role of the BBC during the General Strike see Briggs (1995: Chapter 6, Section 3) and Tracey (1977: Chapter 8).
4   Quoted in Scannell and Cardiff (1991: 33) and castigated as a 'notorious syllogism'.
5   Author's private conversation with a former BBC Controller of Northern Ireland.
6   'Driving the News', internal labour Party document.

## References

Barnett, S., Seymour, E. and Gaber, I. (2000) *From Callaghan to Kosovo: Changing trends in British Television News 1975–1999*, London: University of Westminster.

Barnett, S. and Gaber, I. (2001) *The Westminster Tales: The 21st Century Crisis in Political Journalism*, London: Continuum.

Blumler, J. and McQuail, D. (1968) *Television in Politics: Its Uses and Influences*, London: Faber & Faber.

Bolton, R. (1990) *Death on the Rock and Other Stories*, London: W. H. Allen.

Briggs, A. (1995) *The History of Broadcasting, Vol. 1, The Birth of Broadcasting*, Oxford: Oxford University Press.

Calder, A. (1969) *The People's War: Britain 1939–42*, London: Panther.

Cockerell, M. (1988) *Live from Number 10*, London: Faber & Faber.

Cox, G. (1983) *See It Happen: The Making of ITN*, London: Bodley Head.

Cox, G. (1995) *Pioneering Television News*, London: John Libbey.

Crawley, A. (1988) *Leap Before You Look*, London: Collins.

Day, R. (1989) *Grand Inquisitor*, London: Pan.

Gaber, I. (1997) 'Television and political coverage', in C. Geraghty and D. Lusted (eds) *The Television Studies Handbook*, London: Edward Arnold.

Hattersley, R. (1993) Speech at The Westminster Consultation, unpublished transcript, Goldsmiths College, University of London.

Horne, A. (1989) *Macmillan, Vol. 2, 1956–86*, London: Macmillan.

Ingham, B. (1994) 'It's the message that matters', *British Journalism Review* 7(3): 6–10.

Kellner, P. (1993) Speech at The Westminster Consultation, unpublished transcript, Goldsmiths College, University of London.

Lansley, A. (1995) 'Politics and the media', unpublished lecture, London School of Economics.

Linton, M. (1995) 'The tabloids and the 1992 election', paper presented to the Elections, Public Opinion and Polling Conference, Political Studies Association, London, September.

Pimlott, B. (1993) *Harold Wilson*, London: HarperCollins.

Reith, J. (1950) *Into the Wind*, London: Hodder & Stoughton.

Scannell, P. and Cardiff, D. (1991) *A Social History of British Broadcasting, Vol. 1, 1922–1939*, Oxford: Blackwell.

Straw, J. (1993) 'Democracy on the spike', *British Journalism Review* 4(4): 45–54.

Tracey, M. (1977) *The Production of Political Television*, London: Routledge.

Winstone, R. (1996) 'Do we need political correspondents?', *Parliamentary Review* June: 26–7.

## Further reading

Barnett, S. and Gaber, I. (2001) *The Westminster Tales: the 21st Century Crisis in Political Journalism*, London: Continuum. An up-to-date account of the current situation argues that the media now play second fiddle to the parties' and the government's media machines.

Blumler, J. and Gurevitch, M. (1995) *The Crisis of Public Communication*, London: Routledge. An important work, which argues that modern methods of political campaigning are undermining the democratic process.

Cockerell, M. (1988) *Live from Number 10*, London: Faber & Faber. A lively anecdotal history of the relations between modern Prime Ministers and the media.

Crewe, I., Gosschalk, B. and Bartle, J. (eds) (1998) *Political Communications: Why Labour Won the General Election of 1997*, London: Frank Cass. A range of essays from academics and practitioners about every aspect of political communications during the 1997 election.

Crewe, I. and Gosschalk, B. (eds) (1995) *Political Communications: the General Election Campaign of 1992*, Cambridge: Cambridge University Press. Contains a particularly interesting debate as to why the opinion polls in 1992 wrongly predicted a Labour victory.

Franklin, R. (1994) *Packaging Politics*, London: Arnold. Persuasively argues that as a result of the media 'dumbing down', political coverage, and therefore democracy, has suffered.

Franklin, R. (1994) *Televising Democracies*, London: Routledge. A series of essays by academics and practitioners examining the consequences of the introduction of television cameras into Parliament.

Gould, P. (1998) *The Unfinished Revolution: how the modernisers saved the Labour Party*, London: Little, Brown. A key autobiographical text from a polling and communications advisor who has been a driving force behind the 'New Labour' project.

Ingham, B. (1991) *Kill the Messenger*, London: HarperCollins. A highly readable autobiography by Margaret Thatcher's Press Secretary, the first of the modern spin doctors.

Jones, N. (1995) *Soundbites and Spin Doctors*, London: Cassell. The first account by a practitioner (Jones is a BBC correspondent) of the day-to-day combat between spin doctors and journalists.

Jones, N. (1999) *Sultans of Spin; the media and the New Labour Government*, London: Gollancz. Jones updates his 1995 account and exposes how New Labour spin doctors have operated once in government.

Jones, N. (2001) *The Control Freaks: How New Labour Gets its Own Way*, London: Politico. Continues the story from where *Sultans of Spin* leaves off.

Kavanagh, D. (1995) *Electoral Campaigning*, Oxford: Blackwell. A good overview of all aspects of election campaigning in the UK.

McNair, B. (1999) *An Introduction Political Communication*, London: Routledge. An excellent introduction to the subject – makes a strong case that modern campaigning methods help, rather than hinder, public understanding of politics.

Norris, P. *et al.* (1999) *On Message: Communicating the campaign*, London: Sage. A collection of essays investigating how successful, or otherwise, the parties were in influencing the media's agenda in the 1997 election – not very, the book concludes.

Negrine, R. (1998) *Parliament and the Media: A study of Britain, Germany and France*, London: Pinter. Interesting comparative study of the different ways Parliament is reported in three European countries.

Rosenbaum, M. (1997) *From Soapbox to Soundbite: Party political campaigning in Britain since 1945*, London: Macmillan. The best historical account of the growth of modern political campaigning in Britain.

Scammell, M. (1995) *Designer Politics*, London: Macmillan. A comprehensive account of politics and public relations, particularly good on the use of PR by government. Argues that more PR means more democracy.

Seymour-Ure, C. (1996) *The Political Impact of the Mass Media*, London: Constable. A well-written overview of the subject by one of the most perceptive scholars in the field.

Street, J. (2001) *Mass Media, Politics and Democracy*, Basingstoke: Palgrave. A slightly sideways overview of the debates around political communications.

Tunstall, J. (1970) *The Westminster Lobby Correspondents*, London: Routledge. A classic text; the only study of political correspondents at work, important despite its longevity.

Wyndham-Goldie, G. (1977) *Facing the Nation: Television and Politics 1936–1976*, London: Bodley Head. Another classic; an insider's view (she was Head of BBC Current Affairs) at a crucial time in the development of political broadcasting in the UK.

## Political web sites

### British Government sites

www.ukstate.co.uk – covers all UK public sites

www.open.gov.uk – specifically UK government

www.number-10.gov.uk – takes you straight to the Prime Minister

www.parliament.uk – find *Hansard* online

### General politics sites

www.psa.ac.uk – site of the Political Studies Association

www.politicos.co.uk – lively site based around Politicos bookshop

www.ukpolitics.co.uk – probably the most comprehensive UK politics site

www.YouGov.com – lively site that acts as focus of political opinion and debate

www.epolitix.com – new site covering all aspects of politics

www.essex.ac.uk – very good on political resources

www.sosig.ac.uk – social science research papers on the Web

news.bbc.co.uk – then go to the UK Politics site – superb

www.guardian.co.uk – then go to the Politics site, almost as good as the BBC

**Chapter 32**

# News photography

'THE DIRECT APPEAL TO THE EYE'? PHOTOGRAPHY AND THE PRESS

**PATRICIA HOLLAND**

The visual image has become the focus of news communication. However, press photography is also part of a popular tradition of entertainment photography that dates back to the nineteenth century. Both entertainment and informational photography in the press carry ideological meanings. A photograph must be 'read' as well as viewed, and the processes by which it is produced and selected for publication must be understood. Each individual photograph has its own history. This understanding of the history of each picture is all the more important in the age of digital imaging.

## Photographs and the press: the centrality of the image

Whether we think of the moving pictures of television, the graphic style of the Internet or the striking photography on the pages of the daily and Sunday press, at the beginning of the twenty-first century the visual image is the focus of news communication. We expect to *see* for ourselves and not simply be told. Since 1904, when the *Daily Illustrated Mirror* became the first British paper to use photographs rather than engravings for news illustrations, the amount of space given over to visual, mostly photographic, material in the press has increased so that it is now the very being of many of our newspapers. The popular tabloids have become essentially picture papers, and the 'quality' broadsheets, especially the Sundays, have accommodated more and more photographic imagery by changing their shape and form with alarming frequency. They have sprouted tabloid sections, life-style supplements, separate sports sections, glossy magazines, illustrated reviews, comics and other pull-outs, each targeted at a special segment of the readership and providing an outlet for a wide range of high-quality photography. Accompanying web sites, with pictures as well as text, are accessed by increasing numbers of people, giving a new look and texture to news photography. Photography in the newspapers jostles with that in the multi-coloured magazines that crowd our news-stands – those consumer-based publications that specialize in cookery, DIY, computers, cars, soft porn, celebrity gossip and a host of other topics. We live in a visual culture and the press plays a central role in that culture.

The phrase 'news photography' usually brings to mind dramatic images. The action pictures which win the awards show us riots, wars and disasters. These are the photographs that take the viewer into the middle of a dramatic event and carry a sense of authenticity and conviction which can overwhelm the verbal account. The photographs which are recalled in the histories of news photography include Robert Capa's dying Republican soldier in Spain 1936; the terrified child running from a napalmed village taken by Nick Ut in Vietnam 1972, and the burnt Iraqi at the wheel of his jeep, photographed by Kenneth Jarecke during the Gulf War in 1991. Each of these gets close to the immediate experience of war and each has come to stand as a symbol for the war it represents. Nevertheless, heroic photo-journalism forms only a small part of press photography, and I shall be arguing that we cannot fully understand those photographs which seek to report the news if we do not see them within the context of newspaper imagery as a whole. Dramatic action pictures shock their audience and give rise to controversy and debate, but the richly visual context within which they are embedded is of equal importance.

Pictures in the contemporary press come from a wide range of photographic genres. They include fine-art photographs and portraits, advertising photography, travel pictures, celebrity photographs, pin-ups, snapshots, photomontages and impressionistic images, film and television publicity, sports photography and many other types. Each genre tends to have a separate place in the publication – pin-ups on page 3, food photography in the magazine section, stylish portraits of business executives on the business pages, and emotion-packed sports photography at the back. Just like the segments of the newspaper in which they appear, these different photographic genres serve different ends. Each has its own recognized 'rules' and conventions, which are understood by photographers, editors and reading public alike.

This means that photographers are expected to play a variety of different roles in relation to the subjects of their pictures and to their viewing audience. When operating as a photo-journalist, a photographer promises the viewer authenticity and veracity, playing the part of a dispassionate observer who is uninvolved with events as they unfold in front of the camera. Celebrity photographers, known as 'paparazzi' following their unscrupulous Italian prototype, are different. They must negotiate a relationship between themselves and their attention-seeking subjects which is sometimes cooperative and sometimes antagonistic. When celebrities put themselves on view, a photographer may act as a pure publicist, producing flattering and glamorous images. When the celebrity wishes to be private, the photographers become intrusive stalkers, tracking down their prey with unwelcome tenacity and powerful long lenses. The relationship between Princess Diana, often said to be the most photographed of all celebrities, and the pack of photographers who followed her every move was so intense and controversial that it became the focus of media discussion in its own right. When the princess died in a car crash in Paris in 1997, the first culprits were assumed to be the photographers who were chasing her speeding car. Especially after the death of Diana, there has been a great deal of debate on the degree of privacy due to someone in the public eye, whether Royalty, pop star or politician.

All newspapers, and especially the broadsheets, need pictures of politicians in their public roles. However, 'We don't want the pictures [they] want you to take', says *The Guardian* picture editor, Eamonn McCabe, dismissing the ready smile and the genial handshake (McCabe 1995). A competitive relationship has evolved between the politicians' public relations agents, the 'spin doctors' who try to show their party to its best advantage, and the news photographer, who must always be on the look-out for some special quality in the image. Sometimes they are happy to go along with the carefully arranged 'photo-opportunity' but often they are after something more penetrating. This can lead to disputes over accuracy, when the photographer's entertainment role overlaps with their informational one. Nevertheless, there are times when both subjects and audience accept that, when the photographer is acting as an accomplished entertainer, the literal truth may give way to witty presentation.

Award-winning *Daily Mirror* photographer, Kent Gavin, has written with pride about the professionalism which allows him to move between several different roles,

> I consider my camera to be a window through which the public can look at the world. Sometimes they will be entertained, sometimes they will be horrified and provoked into action of some kind . . . Always, I hope, they will be intrigued (Gavin 1978: 5).

In his account of his career as a news photographer he described the pictures of children with which he reported the war in Biafra (1967–70), 'What can possibly force home more the message that war is obscene than pictures of bewildered, broken children, trapped in a nightmare they cannot even begin to understand' (1978: 65). Playing a different role, he was proud of his pin-up photographs, 'If the photographer can talk her round, wind her up and verbally turn her on,' he wrote, 'the model is going to look like dynamite in the pictures, which is the entire object of the exercise' (1978: 99).

One of his favourite pictures was an exercise in visual humour, in which a little dog lifts his leg and pees on the off-stump just as the batsman strikes the ball during a cricket match. In his role as entertainer, Gavin had several goes at setting this one up, and finally got the picture with the aid of a thread tied to the leg of the dog who had obstinately refused to pee on cue.

The photography of the contemporary press remains balanced between these diverse poles – that of the real, often horrific, world; that of humour; and that of glamour – the glamour of show business, of Princess Diana, of well-known celebrities and especially of the female body.

A further component, which has gained increasing importance since colour first came to the magazine supplements in the 1960s, is consumer photography. This is the photography which celebrates a prosperous, Western life-style, and it includes fashion, food, gardens, travel and the house beautiful, promoting an ever-widening range of products and their pleasurable consumption. Life-style presentations can be difficult to distinguish from that other dominant visual feature, the advertisements. Amply funded, unhampered by the need to report or to represent the real world, free to indulge in emotion and fantasy, advertising has led the way in visual innovation.

Just as news has always been more than information, press photography has always been more than news, and problems arise when its different genres and uses overlap with each other. The coming of digital technology, which has made the manipulation of images easier than ever before, has brought a renewed awareness of how important – yet how slippery – the boundaries are (Wombell 1991; Lister 1995).

## Understanding press photography

To be properly understood, press photography in all its forms must be seen from several different perspectives, some historical and some which look at current practices. First, it must be seen as occupying an important place in the long history of the photographic medium itself, and second, it is a neglected aspect of the history of the twentieth-century mass-circulation press. The convergence of these two popular media has made all the more urgent a third way of looking at press photographs, which considers their ideological role. Photographs are central to the manner in which news and views are presented to the public. Even more importantly, they have built up their own visual vocabulary, a photographic language which deploys a range of concepts that help to shape the ways in which we understand the world. From this perspective, the most trivial of entertainment photographs carries messages which are as important as the most prestigious of news reporting.

## The popular tradition

Photography's roles as an art form and as a medium of record are well documented. What is less often discussed is its long history as a form of entertainment (Freund 1980). During the nineteenth century, entertaining photographic images were produced and consumed in a wide variety of forms, from the purchase of mounted prints and post-cards to those forerunners of the domestic television set, the lantern slide show and the stereoscope (Macdonald 1979). Many of the themes familiar from today's press photography were already in circulation in these earlier forms. Travel pictures have long been among the most popular of photographic genres; as have images of the famous and the infamous. Photographic cards of royalty, seductive actresses and murderers sold in their thousands. Sentimental pictures, photographs of pets and children, as well as half-clothed women and soft porn were all part of Victorian photographic fare. Popular photographs included records of public events – such as parades and sports meetings – and images of war, from the Crimean War in the 1850s to the Boer War in the 1890s. The photographs in the pages of twentieth-century newspapers have been, above all, a development of that popular tradition.

The history of photography and that of the press ran together at the turn of the twentieth century when the new technology of the day made it possible, for the first time, to reproduce photographs in print media as well as by chemical photographic processes. In John Tagg's words 'the era of the throwaway image had begun' (Tagg 1982: 56). From then on, each picture could be rapidly reproduced as millions of identical copies. The most familiar experience of a photograph would no longer be as a precious individual object but as an endlessly repeatable image on a printed page.

In 1904, the *Daily Illustrated Mirror* became the first British newspaper to use photographs, with pictures from the Russo-Japanese war of 1904–5. 'Our pictures do not merely accompany the printed news, they are a valuable help to the understanding of it,' declared the editorial on 28 January 1904 '. . . the direct appeal to the eye, wherever it is possible, will supplement the written word, which is designed in a more cumbrous fashion to penetrate the mind' (quoted in Wombell 1986: 76).

Newspapers such as the *Daily Mail* (launched in 1896) and the *Daily Express* (launched in 1900), as well as the *Mirror*, were aiming for the first time at a mass circulation among working-class readers. In their appeal to a wider public they became an outlet for popular taste as well as for news information. Scandal and gossip now rubbed shoulders with political and overseas reporting. Pages given over to advertisers, who paid for the space, helped to keep prices down (Curran and Seaton 1997). Paul Wombell has pointed out that the newspapers' 'direct appeal to the eye', paralleled the need of advertisers to 'catch the eye' of the reader in the expanding markets of the new century (1986: 76).

Manipulation, the juxtaposition of contrasting images and a light-hearted use of pictures were all part of the Victorian entertainment legacy. The *Daily Mirror* (it soon dropped '*Illustrated*' from its title) introduced the front-page photograph and used photography to make political points. A First World War front page of 1916 was headed 'A Contrast: British Humanity and Hun Brutality' and juxtaposed pictures of happy Germans held prisoners of war by the British with wounded British prisoners held by the Germans (Allen and Frost 1981: 19). The paper introduced a centre-page picture spread, which was often humorous and featured 'beautiful girls and playful animals' (Dunkin 1981: 8). In May 1910 the *Mirror* won a scoop with its centre-page spread of King Edward VII as he lay dead, which it had persuaded the court photographer to hand over for its exclusive use. But the Victorian custom of photographing the dead already seemed inappropriate in such a public medium, and the combination of a fascination with morbidity and an intrusion into the private lives of royalty brought accusations of bad taste (Allen and Frost 1981: 11).

The pattern fast became established in which many different photographic genres rub shoulders on the pages of the newspapers; in which the entertainment pictures draw in readers, the news pictures aim to shock and horrify as well as to inform, and the advertising sets out to stimulate consumer desire.

## Reading news photographs

Offered this richly varied fare, those who look at the photographs in the newspapers must of necessity become more than passive viewers. They must become 'readers' who interpret the image as well as looking at it, and they bring different forms of understanding to it. Sometimes this 'active viewing' has been seen as a disadvantage, leading to *mis*understanding. From the perspective of a newspaper editor, Harold Evans writes,

> The reader imposes on the photographer's work a matrix of memory, appetite, prejudice and sophistication, and when his [sic] emotions are strong, he can see the opposite of what was intended (Evans 1978: ii).

An alternative view is that this ability to carry multiple, complex meanings is in the very nature of the visual, even when, as with a photograph, the image represents the real world. Roland Barthes calls this the 'polysemy' of an image. He demonstrated how a photograph is always open to a wide variety of interpretations, partly determined by the content of the picture, partly by its context, but always drawing something from the assumptions brought to it by its 'readers' (Barthes 1977).

Barthes has identified some of the codes which go to construct news photographs and which can be brought into play when the decoding work done by an alert reader becomes conscious and analytical instead of merely intuitive (1977: 21). Similarly, in an influential article, Stuart Hall produced a detailed analysis of the processes by which news photographs are first encoded by those who produce them, and then decoded by their readers, emphasizing the ways in which interpretations are influenced by the context of the image (Hall 1973: 176).

A recognition of the shifting meanings which characterize visual imagery sometimes seems to suggest that news photography is intrinsically untrustworthy. And yet, once we have understood that the 'truth' cannot be contained within the edges of the frame, the work of understanding the codes, of 'reading' the image, of exploring the context and of recognizing the history of a photograph become central concerns, and a news photographer's commitment to truth becomes ever more important.

## Photo-journalism, objectivity and partiality

The documentary style that came to characterize photo-journalism was first developed not by newspapers, but by news picture magazines. 'In the 1950s photo-journalism meant something different from news photography and nobody in Fleet Street would have made the mistake of confusing the two,' wrote photographer, Grace Robertson, who was one of the very few women to work for the prestigious *Picture Post.* On an assignment for that magazine, 'you were very aware that you were expected to bring back a story, one with a beginning, middle and an end and not just a lot of photographically interesting images that you hoped would fit the text.' She recalled that the 'general press photographers' who used large-format cameras with flash attachments and were not at all concerned about drawing attention to themselves kidded her about the tiny 35 mm Leica with which she captured her candid shots (Robertson 1990: 4).

Picture magazines had first developed in Germany during the 1920s. As the decade progressed, many German journalists and photographers were forced to flee the Nazi regime, and the development of documentary photography was taken up elsewhere, notably by *Vu* in France (1928–38), and the first *Life* in the USA (1936–72). In Britain, *Picture Post* (1938–57) was edited by the exiled Stefan Lorant, who as editor of the *Munchener Illustrierte*, was already celebrated as one of the founders of photojournalism. The magazines gave priority to pictures over text and favoured a style in which unobtrusive cameras were used to observe events as they happened, paying attention to the visual detail of everyday life. *Picture Post* came to build up a documentary record of its times (Hall 1972: 71).

The observational style, in which photographers seek to 'capture' their subjects unawares at the precise moment which conveys the essence of a scene – what its most celebrated exponent, Henri Cartier-Bresson, described as 'the decisive moment' – has come to carry an aura of objective record (Cartier-Bresson 1952). The style was at the heart of the photo-agency Magnum, founded in 1947 by a group of photographers, including Cartier-Bresson and Robert Capa, who had been through the Second World War and were seeking to promote a style of photography which put people and human values at the centre.

Photo-journalism lays claims to neutrality and objectivity, which means that 'readers' of such pictures are justified in asking questions about photographic truth. Photo-journalists enter an unwritten contract with the public to report accurately what they see. If there is an indication that the photographer has interfered with the scene in front of the camera, its authenticity may be brought into question and the contract with the viewer may be broken. Was that starving baby separated from its mother so that it looked even more forlorn in the picture? Was that man waving a stick really shouting at the policeman or simply telling the photographer to get out of the way? Was there help at hand for those desperate people just beyond the edge of the frame?

These questions are important. However, partiality may operate in more subtle ways, not necessarily by showing untruths but by putting one set of meanings into circulation to the exclusion of others. During the Second World War, the photo-journalism of *Picture Post* helped to establish the imagery of that war for the British nation. It showed the rubble of the blitz, the determined faces under air-raid warden helmets, the gallant boys in their flying jackets and fragile little planes, and the plump women in wrap-around aprons and turbaned scarves who were keeping the country going. Photographic imagery was deployed to report on the activities of a people at war and at the same time to enhance the national morale (Kee 1989). That imagery would be recalled at future moments of national crisis.

In a different political climate, during the strikes, demonstrations and riots which hit the front pages of the national press in the 1970s and early 1980s, critics pointed out that the view from the safer spot behind the police lines influenced the public's impression of what was going on and allowed the grievances of the demonstrators to go unshown (*Camerawork* 1977). Some independent photographers and photographic agencies deliberately set out to produce pictures from another perspective.

Although the issue of objectivity is always up for negotiation, the need for factual reporting becomes ever clearer when there are limitations on access which are formally enforced, as at time of war. 'War is an anxious time in the press' writes John Taylor. News photographers are exposed to censorship and limitations, because of a 'fear of documentary realism' on the part of the authorities, at a time when information is itself a weapon (Taylor 1991). From the First World War to the Gulf, there have been disputes over censorship, propaganda and truth (Knightly 1975; Wombell 1986; Taylor 1992). A commitment to discover and make public those perspectives that governments want to conceal, is, for the news photographer, both urgent and dangerous. For the sceptical reader, even greater attention must be given to the history of each individual photograph.

## History of the individual photograph

For every photograph we see, there are certain questions which should be asked. These include who the photographer was, when, where and, most importantly, why the picture was taken. Paradoxically, the understanding of an image may depend on the answers to these questions rather than on anything that is visible within the frame.

Every photograph is the result of a complex of decisions taken not only by the person who pushes the button but also by a host of other individuals and institutions (Sontag 1979). The first decisions are taken long before the film is exposed, and are made by the body which commissions the work, usually a newspaper or a news agency such as Reuters or Associated Press. For Winston Churchill's funeral in 1965, the *Sunday Times* assigned 21 photographers to 25 different viewpoints to cover both the ceremonial and the personal. Every detail was planned well in advance. 'Picture editors Jack Hallam and Chris Angeloglou negotiated shooting positions from a church tower, a bank and office windows even before the death' (Evans 1978: 27).

Of course, photographers will take crucial decisions concerning both content and style while making their pictures. Their decisions inevitably draw on photographic codes which, as Roland Barthes pointed out, are laden with meaning (1977: 21). They may choose a wide panoramic shot or select a long lens for a close-up; they may go for a high angle which dwarfs their subject, or prefer a low angle which emphasizes the subject's height; they may look for dramatic shadows or choose the more sober effect of even lighting. At the same time, decisions are likely to be based on a pragmatic assessment of what it is the newspaper wants. At every level, prejudice and 'common sense' are at work and a wide range of political opinions and social expectations may well come into play, both in deciding what events to cover and which photographic techniques to use.

Anthropologist Mark Pedelty, accompanying war correspondents and photographers during the civil war in El Salvador during the early 1990s, observed the taking of a photograph that never made the pages of a newspaper. The picture showed the bones of a child, discovered among many others in a mass grave. Despite the startling nature of the content, the photographer, who was young and ambitious, decided not to send it back to his editor in the USA. His decision followed discussions with the other North American correspondents based in San Salvador. Their view, and that of the news organizations they represented, was that the atrocity he had documented was of dubious authenticity. It was an opinion with which the photographer instinctively agreed, even though he had, unlike them, seen and photographed the actual grave (Pedelty 1995: 159).

By contrast, *Picture Post* photographer Bert Hardy told Harold Evans about his highly successful photograph of an American soldier 'sharing his last drop of water with a dying peasant' during the Korean War. It was a felicitous image that fulfilled the expectations of both news editors and viewers, but which hardly reflected the state of affairs in which it was taken. 'I had the idea and asked a GI to give the old man some water for the sake of my picture. He said he would if I was quick – and if we used my water ration' (Evans 1978: i).

Once a photograph has been sent to a newspaper, often via a news agency, the decision making is taken over by the picture editor who selects from among the hundreds that arrive daily down the wire. There are many people in the decision-making chain, including those who plan the lay-out of the paper, the art editors, section editors and the overall editor of the paper. Most of these have a view – based on their experience and often claimed to be 'instinctive' – about which photographs 'work' and about news and marketing values. Decisions are taken about the placing of a picture – whether it is of front-page quality or deserves to be relegated to an inside page, how it will be cropped and how it will be juxtaposed with captions and text.

The most remarkable photographs will be taken up by several newspapers and they may continue to be used and re-used in many different contexts. A picture can take on a life of its own, well beyond the control of the original photographer. It may be cut out, montaged, recoloured or otherwise treated, gathering meanings as it continues to be circulated in what John Tagg has described as its 'currency' (Tagg 1982: 110).

One of the most reproduced photographs ever comes from the Spanish Civil War of 1936–9 and depends almost entirely on its caption. It shows a soldier falling backwards, arms flung out, a rifle falling from his right hand. The image is slightly out of focus and there is no background or other feature in the picture. Without more information it makes little sense. We do not know who the person is or where he is; we may not recognize the uniform; we cannot make out whether he has tripped or been pushed; there is nothing to indicate the circumstances of the action. The caption in *Life Magazine* (12 July 1937) read 'Robert Capa's camera catches a Spanish soldier the instant he is dropped by a bullet through the head in front of Cordoba'. The historian of war reporting, Phillip Knightly, points out that despite this uncertainty, the picture is widely regarded to be the best war photograph ever taken, and its circulation over the years has reinforced its status as the very image of the commitment of the anti-fascists in the Spanish war (Knightley 1975: 210). It has entered the pictorial vocabulary, becoming instantly recognizable so that the original caption is largely redundant.

## Consumerism and spectacle

The 1960s saw the beginnings of two pivotal changes in twentieth-century press photography. The first was the explosion into colour of the advertising media and consumer magazines. Magazine supplements to the Sunday newspapers began to provide a consumer-led context for news images that was richly visual. The *Sunday Times* launched its supplement in 1961 and the *Observer* in 1963. They provided a new outlet for photo-journalism, which was often problematically juxtaposed with ever lusher and more expensive advertising. Advertisements for cigarettes, home photography, furniture, food, cars and all the goods which supported the post-war readjustment to a consumer economy rubbed uneasily against the grimmer photo-stories, such as those by Don McCullin on Cyprus and Vietnam.

The second development was Rupert Murdoch's revamping of the *Sun* in 1969 as a downmarket tabloid unashamedly based on hedonism and fun, in which entertainment values became more important than news information. With the transformation of the *Sun* a new popular daily press was launched which made use of the visual to push at the hitherto guarded limits of respectability and seriousness.

## The sexualization of the popular press

The *Sun* was a reincarnation of a more sober working-class newspaper, the *Daily Herald*, which had been backed by trade unions and the Labour Party but had failed to attract sufficient advertising to survive (Curran and Seaton 1997). Like the *Daily Herald*, the *Sun* based itself on its class appeal. But by the 1970s the working-class pride in work and industry which had characterized the war years was transformed into a celebration of trivia and relaxation, of gossip and scandal, of celebrity watching, pictures of Royalty, sport and humour. A politics of pleasure, which reacted against moralism and the old-fashioned sense of working-class duty, underpinned the *Sun*'s approach. It revelled in its hatred of do-gooders, teachers and anyone who might order you about or tell you what to do, in a convergence of political opinion and entertainment values (Curran and Sparks 1991: 215). Above all came the invitation to bodily enjoyment and sexuality, which centred on the half-clothed image of a woman, the Page Three 'girl'.

Page Three rapidly developed its own culture. The Page Three girls, like Linda Lusardi, became personalities in their own right and the *Sun* described Page Three photographer, Beverley Goodway, as 'the most envied man in Britain'. Women readers were encouraged to pose as a Page Three girl, and their boyfriends were given advice on how to photograph them. The sexualization of newspaper imagery was launched as an gesture of defiant liberation. This is how the change was described in the *Sun*'s own version of its history,

> The *Sun* called its women's pages 'Pacesetters' and filled them with sex. They were produced by women *for* women. But they were subtitled 'The pages for women that men can't resist' acknowledging that there are plenty of topics that fascinate both men and women. Like sex (Grose 1989: 94).

The attitude gave the *Sun* licence to exploit the Page Three principle in its approach to images of women in general. Photographers were on the look-out for the naked breast, the nipple peeping out at a party, the see-through dress. When the task force returned after the Falklands War, the *Sun* celebrated with a front-page headline, 'Lovely to see you!' above a photograph of a young woman baring her breasts (Holland 1983: 100).

When the MP Clare Short mobilized a considerable body of feminist opinion behind her bill to ban Page Three on the grounds that it was degrading to women, the response was a vilification campaign against Clare Short herself (Snoddy 1992: 110). In the popular tabloids, the entertainment role of press photography has come to take precedence over news values. The visual documentation of royal marriages and marital problems; an uninhibited use of personal attack, often disguised as humour; and extensive features on sex which border on soft porn with images of near-naked men and women and a frankness about sexual behaviour have become the order of the day.

## Truth, entertainment and the visual

The division between the popular tabloids and the 'quality' press has increased in recent years (Curran and Seaton 1997), yet both in their own way continue to stage dramas around truth, reality and the visual. Across the different genres press photographs hold reportage and entertainment in tension, as each newspaper section continues to exert its influence on the others.

At the same time, the commitment to seek out and report on unwelcome truths has taken on a fresh urgency. The new technology of the turn of the twenty-first century has brought a communications revolution which is as profound as that which launched the mass-circulation press at the beginning of the twentieth. Satellite technology now means that photographs can be transmitted almost instantaneously from any part of the globe, so that we see much more and we see it more quickly. But, as we have discussed, a photograph has always been unstable as a guarantor of 'reality', and present-day digital technology means that changes can now be made to an image that are impossible to trace. In the present, electronic, age the role of the photographer has become, paradoxically, even more important, for, very often, it is only the photographer who can vouch for the reliability of an picture. Contemporary developments are making the work of 'reading' a press photograph and of understanding the cultural, political and historical influences which shaped it ever more important.

## Questions

1   On a given day, compare the photographs used in each of the daily newspapers. Note, in particular, what front-page pictures have been chosen, and how the presentation differs between the papers. In the light of the different aims and audiences of each paper, give an account of the differences.

2   Compare and contrast the photographic styles in the different sections of a given newspaper. Make reference to the concept of photographic genre and the activity of 'reading' a picture.

3   Discuss the representation of one particular group of people – examples might be: child victims of war; grieving mothers following a disaster; Black youth; anorexic young girls; businessmen; MPs from the Opposition. Use at least six photographs from recent newspapers to illustrate your discussion.

# References

Allen, R. and Frost, J. (1981) *Daily Mirror,* Cambridge: Patrick Stephens Ltd.

Barthes, R. (1977) 'The photographic message' and 'Rhetoric of the image', both in *Image, Music, Text,* London: Fontana.

*Camerawork* (1977) 'Lewisham: what are you taking pictures for?' London: Half Moon Photography Workshop.

Cartier-Bresson, H. (1952) *The Decisive Moment,* New York: Simon & Schuster.

Curran, J. and Seaton, J. (1997) *Power Without Responsibility,* 5th edn, London: Routledge.

Curran, J. and Sparks, C. (1991) 'Press and popular culture', *Media, Culture and Society,* 13: 215–37.

Dunkin, M. (ed.) (1981) *What a Picture,* London: Weidenfeld & Nicolson.

Evans, H. (1978) *Pictures on a Page: Photo-journalism, Graphics and Picture Editing,* London: Heinemann.

Freund, G. (1980) *Photography and Society,* London: Gordon Fraser.

Gavin, K (1978) *Flash Bang Wallop! The intimate experiences of Fleet Street's top press photographer,* London: Westbridge Books.

Grose, R. (1989) *The Sun-sation,* London: Angus and Robertson.

Hall, S. (1972) 'The social eye of *Picture Post',* in *Working papers in Cultural Studies 2,* Birmingham: University of Birmingham.

Hall, S. (1973) 'The determinations of news photographs', in S. Cohen and J. Young (eds) *The Manufacture of News: Deviance, Social Problems and the Mass Media,* London: Constable.

Holland, P. (1983) 'The Page Three Girl speaks to women, too', *Screen,* 34:3, May/June.

Kee, R. (1989) *The Picture Post Album,* London: Barrie and Jenkins.

Knightly, P. (1975) *The First Casualty,* London: Pan.

Lister, M. (ed.) (1995) *The Photographic Image in Digital Culture,* London: Routledge.

McCabe, E. (1995) 'Shots that hit the front page', *Guardian,* 24 April.

Macdonald, G. (1979) *Camera: A Victorian Eyewitness,* London: Batsford. Based on a Granada television series.

Pedelty, M. (1995) *War Stories: The Culture of Foreign Correspondents,* New York and London: Routledge.

Robertson, G. (1990) *Portfolio Magazine,* Spring, Edinburgh: Photography Workshop.

Sontag, S. (1979) *On Photography,* Harmondsworth: Penguin.

Snoddy, R. (1992) *The Good, the Bad and the Unacceptable: The Hard News about the British Press,* London: Faber and Faber.

Tagg, J. (1982) 'The currency of the photograph', in V. Burgin (ed.) *Thinking Photography,* London: Macmillan.

Taylor, J. (1991) *War Photography: Realism in the British Press,* London: Routledge.

Taylor, P. (1992) *War and the Media: Propaganda and Persuasion in the Gulf War,* Manchester: Manchester University Press.

Wombell, P. (1986) 'Face to face with themselves: photography and the First World War' in P. Holland, J. Spence and S. Watney (eds) *Photography Politics Two,* London: Comedia.

Wombell, P. (ed.) (1991) *Photovideo: Photography in the Age of the Computer,* London: Rivers Oram.

## Further reading

Becker, K. (1992) 'Photojournalism and the tabloid press', in P. Dahlgren and C. Sparks (eds) *Journalism and Popular Culture*, London, Sage. Traces the history of press photography especially in the USA, and analyses photographs in tabloid newspapers from several European countries.

Benthall, J. (1993) *Disasters, Relief and the Media*, London: I. B. Tauris. Looks at 'disaster reporting' in various media.

Carter, C. *et al.* (eds) (1998) *Gender News and Power*, London: Routledge. On the representation of women in various media including Holland, P. 'The politics of the smile: "soft news" and the sexualisation of the popular press' – more about Page Three and the sexualized image.

Hall, S. *et al.* (1978) *Policing the Crisis: Mugging, The State and Law and Order*, London: Macmillan. A classic study of how television and the press pick up and amplify a particular theme – in this case 'mugging' and the Black community.

Hartley, J. (1982) *Understanding News*, London: Methuen. A semiotic analysis of news media.

Holland, P. (1992) *What is a Child? Popular Images of Childhood*, London: Virago. On the way pictures of children are used in the press and other media.

Lister, M. (ed.) (1995) *The Photographic Image in Digital Culture*, London: Routledge. On the significance of digital technology for photography.

Seymour-Ure, C. (1991) *The British Press and Broadcasting Since 1945*, Institute of Contemporary British History Oxford: Blackwell. A historical account.

Tagg, J. (1988) *The Burden of Representation: Essays on Photographies and Histories*, London: Macmillan. Essay on the various uses of photography over the history of the medium.

Taylor, J. (1998) *Body Horror: Photojournalism, catastrophe and war*, Manchester: Manchester University Press. Analysis of the most dramatic of press pictures.

# Chapter 33

# Pornography and censorship

SEX AND CENSORIOUSNESS: PORNOGRAPHY AND CENSORSHIP IN BRITAIN

## LINDA RUTH WILLIAMS

This chapter discusses the fraught interconnection between pornography and its censorship since the 1970s. It covers problems both legal and aesthetic with the definition of pornography and obscenity, and discusses the leads which feminism has taken in thinking of pornography in the context of civil rights or freedom of speech issues. It also looks at how different kinds of representations of men and women, or of people engaging in non-mainstream sexual practices, have affected recent debate. It compares the impact of progressive changes in legislation and official guidelines on what can be produced and distributed, from the 1959 Obscene Publications Act through the 1994 Criminal Justice Act Amendment to the Video Recordings Act to the 2000 publication of the British Board of Film Classification Guidelines.

> *I shall not today attempt further to define the kinds of material I understand to be embraced within that shorthand description [hard-core pornography]. . . .* But I know it when I see it.
> (Justice Potter Stewart, 1964, quoted in Williams 1991: 5, 283 n. 9, my emphasis)

> *Advising a newsagent whom he had recently acquitted of video obscenity charges, a judge in Wales offered the following advice: 'Remember, if it's dubious, it's dirty!'*
> (Kermode 1995: 64)

The pornographic moving image is as old as cinema itself: as soon as moving bodies could be filmed, they were filmed engaging in sexual activity. Pornography in the form of written text or still image has flourished in cultures as diverse as Ancient Greece and nineteenth-century Japan; it predates the printing press and mass media. It is present wherever cultures produce and consume any kinds of images of human activity; it can be found at the periphery, if not at the heart, of all 'respectable' cultures. And if pornography has readily responded to the opportunities presented by technological innovation, censorship has just as quickly dogged its production and distribution. 'Censorship is probably as old as society' writes Sigrid Nielsen (1988: 19) in her account of feminism's response to censorship practices. In his survey of one hundred years of British film censorship Philip French is more specific: 'Wherever films were made or shown', he writes, 'censorship boards sprang up' (French 1995: 23). For the campaigning group Feminists Against Censorship, 'until feminism entered the debate, pornography and censoriousness were an inseparable couple' (Rodgerson and Wilson 1991: 25–6). The dynamic between the production and the prohibition of pornography is a complex one.

Definitions of pornography are, however, notoriously problematic, and cultural critics are no more capable of giving clear explications than are legislators. The differentiation between 'soft' erotica and 'harder' pornography is particularly difficult, since it generally rests on subjective judgements of personal disgust or arousal, making one person's soft another person's hard. For Susan Griffin (1982) pornography must be distinguished from erotica in order that the latter can be rescued from the debasing influence of the former: eroticism encourages soulful, holistic sexuality, pornography indulges power and violence (it 'is an expression not of human erotic feeling and desire, and not of a love of the life of the body, but of a fear of bodily knowledge, and a desire to silence eros': Griffin 1982: 1). There may be a firmer case for distinguishing 'soft' as legally obtainable material and 'hard' as that which cannot legitimately be seen in Britain, though changes in the 1990s shifted the boundary between the two, enabling some 'hardcore' images to be available if classified at R18. In his humorous survey of sex cinema Jonathan Ross (1995) differentiates 'between sex in films, and films which only exist to show sex': He also cites a letter from HM Customs and Excise, justifying their seizure of a laserdisc copy of the 1973 film *Deep Throat* Ross had shipped to Britain:

> [T]he importation of indecent or obscene material is prohibited by the Customs Consolidation Act 1876. The material you attempted to import has been examined, and the laser disc titled *Deep Throat* was found to contain scenes of troilism, buggery, masturbation, ejaculation, cunnilingus, fellatio and intercourse (Ross 1995: 18).

These may sound like an alarming litany of sins, but what makes *Deep Throat* pornographic is – according to Ross's definition – not the simple fact of the acts here listed but the nature of their representation, for pornography is not sex itself, nor its representation in a simulated form, it is the representation of actual sex. Unlike the censorship of scenes which may be depicting acts which are themselves violent and illegal (murder, assault, violence to animals or children), many of these acts from *Deep Throat* are not only legal between consenting adults, they are practised by the majority of the population. Take straightforward heterosexual sex, for instance. The act which might be characterized as perhaps the most 'mainstream' activity of all, upon which the generation of society depends, becomes a fringe pursuit once it is indulged via the mediation of representation, or with that representation used as an aid to real sex. The paradoxes surrounding attitudes to sexual representation are manifold: the act which is a ubiquitous factor of people's lives is strictly circumscribed when performed as a live sex act or represented on film or in photographs. But in its simulated form it is everywhere – mainstream cinema (as opposed to pornographic cinema) relies heavily on representations of simulated sex to spice up its narratives. As Laura Kipnis (1996) argues in her eminently sensible study of American pornography, some fantasies are more criminal than others, depending on where and how you act them out: as long as your public fantasy is entirely fictive then it can even be art. So what is the essential difference between what we do at home and what we might see on hardcore screens? Furthermore, what is the difference between what those hardcore screens represent – which is only for a few customers from a limited range of circumscribed outlets – and what mainstream cinema represents which is available to all at the local multiplex? Ross concludes: 'if the sex is the driving force of a picture, the only real selling point or theme, then it's a sex movie. And if what is shown is actually happening, if the actors and actresses are really doing it, then it's pornography' (Ross 1995: 3).

For feminist writer Andrea Dworkin (1981), however, this definition needs to be radically politicized. In *Pornography: Men Possessing Women*, Dworkin supports her feminist polemic with reference to the word's etymology:

> The word *pornography*, derived from the ancient Greek *porne* and *graphos*, means 'writing about whores' ... [it] does not mean 'writing about sex' or 'depictions of the erotic' or 'depictions of sexual acts' or 'depictions of nude bodies' or 'sexual representations' or any other such euphemism. It means the graphic description of women as vile whores (Dworkin 1981: 199–200).

For Linda Williams in *Hard Core: Power, Pleasure and the 'Frenzy of the Visible'* (1991), pornographic films typically include certain key elements or images which produce bodily response in the audience as an effect of the spectacle of bodily response and action on-screen. Williams analyses the ambiguities and difficulties at stake in showing both the male 'money shot' and the essentially *in*visible female orgasm (which porn is nevertheless desperate to represent), and warns against simplistic generalizations about the genre, which is as complex as any other in cinema. Porn is then not just an issue around the body (and how bodies are represented), it moves the body (to arousal), just as other 'low' cultural forms provoke tears (melodrama or romance) or screams (horror). Williams also quotes US Justice Potter Stewart's notoriously subjective explication which forms one of my epigraphs: refusing to define pornography, he nevertheless assured his court that he knew it when he saw it. As Mandy Merck (1992) has pointed out, Dawn Primarolo's 1989 Location of Pornographic Materials Bill 1989 first introduced the term 'pornography' into British legislative discourse. Primarolo's definition runs:

> 3 (1) Pornographic material means film and video and any printed matter which, for the purposes of sexual arousal or titilation, depicts women, or parts of women's bodies, as objects, things or commodities, or in sexually humiliating or degrading poses or being subject to violence.
> 
> 3 (2) The reference to women in sub-section (1) above includes men (quoted in Merck, 1992: 51; see also Rodgerson and Wilson 1991: 27–8).

Merck does, however, go on to quote Annette Kuhn's important point that pornography is largely defined in common-sense terms 'whose reference is not specified representations, but the effects that representations may be thought, in certain circumstances, to produce' (Kuhn 1984, quoted in Merck 1992: 51). Pornography, and the presumed effects of pornography, are thus bound together in law, censorship and the polemic of opposition.

This brief discussion of censorship and pornography in Britain is not predicated on the assumption that porn is an alien, decadent or a solely modern activity, even though I shall concentrate on its production and censorship in Britain since the early 1960s. I shall not refer to materials which in their actual production break British law protecting the participants from violence, such as child or bestial pornography which can only be produced by actually and illegally violating children or animals. Although it is true that such materials may often have been produced in countries where these acts were quite legal, their prosecution in Britain is possible under a number of laws, not primarily obscenity law which generally govern the prosecution of what we might call 'mainstream' adult material. Child pornography clearly infringes laws other than the obscenity or censorship legislation with which we are concerned here, so it is not generally included in debates about porn, which is mainly concerned with representations of consenting adults.

Although there is much to be said about material that is entirely and unproblematically illegal, the most recent debates have concentrated on 'borderline' material, and the kind of material which the vast majority of porn consumers are interested in: images that show adults engaging in legal acts which may fall on one side of the censorable or the prosecutable divide, or the other. How the law seeks to define this borderline of the unacceptable or the illegal, and how bodies such as the BBFC seek to implement that law, is my concern. Although the BBFC changed its name from The British Board of Film Censors to The British Board of Film Classification in 1985, it may demand cuts to film or video before a classification is awarded. (Currently, classifications are guided by age: U = Universal, suitable for all; PG = Parental Guidance, some scenes may be unsuitable for children; 12 = suitable only for 12 years and over; 15 = suitable only for 15 years and over; 18 = suitable only for adults; R18 = to be supplied only in licensed sex shops to adults. Definitions of what is and is not permitted within each category are laid out in the *BBFC Classification Guidelines* (BBFC: 2000; see also the BBFC website: www.bbfc.co.uk)). This means that any work the BBFC does not classify is effectively banned, though this is rare: as Tom Dewe Matthews writes, 'Classification has become the deciding factor in what a film can or cannot contain' (Dewe Matthews 1994: 258). Most films are made or cut to the measure of their anticipated classification, meaning that a kind of pre-censorship is at work. In the case of pornography, the crucial boundaries lie between 18 and R18, on the one hand, and R18 and that which exceeds it in sexual 'strength' or 'hardness', on the other. But the histories of how these categories are perceived need to be briefly sketched, and here I shall be looking at how the boundaries of what is considered 'obscene' have shifted as debate around sexual behaviour has affected what can and cannot be filmed, published or distributed in the UK.

Both Christian-moral and feminist pro-censor oppositions to pornography have shaped the debate; libertarians have responded with calls for a more lenient climate in which a wider range of sexual images can be produced. British censorship legislation is the most draconian in Europe; according to Dewe Matthews (1994), the UK has 'the most rigorous film censorship system in the Western World'. In his substantial diatribe against the secret, non-accountable practices of the BBFC, Dewe Matthews argues for greater awareness of the decisions which are made on our behalf. '[A]s a way of filtering culture', censorship, writes Dewe Matthews, 'lies at the core of English custom' (Dewe Matthews 1994: 1). British censorship legislation has radically affected and shaped the kind of pornography – written, photographed or filmed – which is available, leaving a wide range of materials which are perfectly legal in other EC countries until recently outside the bounds of the law.

## Shifting boundaries: classification and censorship

The 1959 Obscene Publications Act (OPA), which is one of the pieces of legislation currently in place under which pornography can be prosecuted, was an attempt to clarify vague definitions of what constituted obscenity which existed in earlier law. It did, however, retain the earlier formulation that obscenity is that which has a 'tendency to deprave and corrupt', thus emphasizing the problem as that of the *effect* material might have on those likely to come into contact with it. Top-shelf heterosexual male-orientated magazine pornography like the titles published by Paul Raymond (*Men Only, Escort, Club* etc.) or international titles such as *Playboy* work within this definition fairly successfully, avoiding images of real sex, illegal acts or violence. (For a discussion of how magazines have negotiated the terms of the OPA, see Kermode and Petley 1990; Williams 1994). Until recently, however, correspondingly 'soft' gay porn had been the subject of stringent scrutiny, and 'harder' images, themselves deemed 'hard' often only by virtue of the fact that they show actual sex between bodies which are male as well as female, was policed even more strictly. Laura Kipnis (1996) also interestingly discusses how some kinds of 'soft' imagery are deemed marginal or perverse by nature of their relative alienation from mainstream sexual practice. For instance, 'soft' images of naked fat women (in magazines such as *Jumbo Jezebel* or *Love's Savage Cupcake*) or fully dressed transvestite men (in magazines such as *Guys in Gowns* or *Petticoat Impostors*) are rarely categorized alongside their skinny, gender-aligned counterparts such as *Playboy, Penthouse* or even *Hustler.* Instead the tastes these magazines appeal to are classed as 'fringe' sexual preferences akin to hardcore, even though the magazine images may not represent actual sex, penetration, erections, etc. It seems that some naked bodies are more 'obscene' than others, while some fully clothed ones may be most obscene of all (Kipnis 1996: 64–92, 93–121).

The male member also poses a similar problem of sexual double standards. In cinema, while naked female bodies have been seen on screen and in printed image in widespread form since the 1960s, representations of the male body, and particularly of the male organ in a state of excitement, have been the subject of the most stringent censorship in post-war Britain. This is also true in America, as Kipnis argues: 'Why has there been such reticence about dealing with the issues raised by pornography in which the bodies depicted are bodies possessing penises?' (Kipnis 1996: 65; see also 130–31). The effect of this 'reticence' on both sides of the Atlantic has been that the 'obscenity' definition up to the 1990s functioned to outlaw the nude or excited man, thus reinforcing the predictable omnipresence of the heterosexually orientated naked woman.

In their role as classifiers of film and video, the BBFC are the main body which filters out the 'unacceptable' from our screens, implicitly defining and sanctioning the 'acceptable'. During the 1980s they took a more specific lead from the terms of the Williams Report (Home Office 1979) which 'argued that offensiveness ought to be the main principle of intervention, demanding an end in particular to the "unworkable" tendency-to-deprave-and-corrupt test of the Obscene Publications Act' (quoted in Brown 1982: 2, from her introduction to her interview with the then chief censor of the BBFC, James Ferman). The terms of the Williams Report subsequently fed into the Local Government and Cinematographic Acts 1982, which restricted the circulation of sexual materials to private cinema clubs and, as Mandy Merck has again pointed out, 'defined, for the first time in British legislation, the sex film':

> Moving pictures . . . concerned primarily with . . . (i) sexual activity; or (ii) acts of force or restraint which are associated with sexual activity; or . . . genital organs or urinary functions (Merck 1992: 52).

The BBFC actually has no strictly enshrined legal status, in effect acting as advisors to cinemas and local councils. Regional councils take BBFC classification as their guide that a film is suitable to be shown in their area, but they can also overrule it, retaining the discretion to refuse it a local certificate, or even give it one if the BBFC have themselves denied it any classification (for example, during the 'reign' of John Trevelyan in the 1960s and early 1970s; see Dewe Matthews 1994: Chapter 11). However, it was only in the mid-1970s that films themselves became prosecutable under the OPA; strictly speaking, they aren't a publication, but were brought within the terms of this law on the recommendation of Ferman (Dewe Matthews 1994: Chapter 13). Two more highly significant pieces of legislation regulating moving-image pornography were passed in 1984 and 1994, with the Video Recordings Act (VRA) and the Criminal Justice Act Amendment to the Video Recordings Act respectively. I will look at these more closely in the final section of this chapter.

We might then trace the relationship between pornography and censorship through a history of the kinds of images which have lain on either side of the censored divide. As far as the history of legitimate film pornography is concerned, we can, for instance, trace the erosion of thresholds of acceptability (beyond which we might say lies hard-core) through the gradual acceptance of certain body parts and bodily acts on-screen. Nudity was first allowed in mainstream cinema in the 1950s in pseudo-documentary films about naturism. (In 1958 John Trevelyan, the new secretary of the BBFC, deemed that 'breasts and buttocks, but not genitalia, would be accepted by the Board 'provided that the setting was recognisable as a nudist camp or nature reserve': Dewe Matthews 1994: 169). (Here I am using 'mainstream cinema' as including all films which gained a BBFC certificate and could thus be shown at public cinemas with (from 1951 to 1982) a U, A or X certificate (AA was added in 1970), or (from 1982 onwards) the current classifications.) The first mainstream screen orgasm was *heard* (but not seen) in Polanski's *Repulsion* in 1965. Pubic hair was first allowed in Lindsay Anderson's *If* (1968). Former BBFC chief censor John Trevelyan, who worked there until 1971, remembers

> giving a simplified description of our policy by saying that in a 'U' film we could allow a man and a girl to be seen going together to a bedroom door; that in an 'A' film they could be seen going into the bedroom and up to the bed; and that in an 'X' film they could be seen in or on the bed engaged in what appeared to be sexual intercourse provided that there was reasonable discretion in what was shown (Trevelyan 1973: 105).

However, it was only in the mid-1990s that erections could be seen on film in forms other than rare art-house classics such as Andy Warhol's *Flesh* (1970 – the first erection shown on British screens). Even the notorious Japanese tale of strangulation and arousal, Nagisa Oshima's *Ai No Corrida* (*In the Realm of the Senses*, 1976), only gained BBFC certification in 1991, and this was largely also because of its lingering art-house status. Such films were (eventually) tolerated because they were presumed to have a self-selecting, non-damageable middle-class audience, indicating that the 'tendency to deprave and corrupt' criterion is still in operation in respect of the way in which the BBFC classifies not on pure image content but in terms of how it perceives a film's potential audience. A lingering anxiety about those who need protection from 'obscenity' – children and the non-art-house video viewer – shapes many of the BBFC's decisions. This anxiety was enshrined in the 1984 and the 1994 Acts mentioned earlier.

These thresholds were crossed by a combination of the BBFC acknowledging that public opinion had changed and so liberalizing their categories, and film-makers, publishers or distributors making an argument for the artistic or scientific merit of their work. The 1959 OPA also allowed for a work to be defended on the grounds of artistic or scientific merit, and this was the defence which was mounted in support of D. H. Lawrence's sexually explicit novel *Lady Chatterley's Lover* during the famous 1960 trial which tested the terms of the Act. The novel was vindicated with the victory of Penguin Books, which had garnered a respectable range of expert witnesses testifying to its literary merit and justifying its use of what was then deemed obscene language (see Rolph 1961). (Lawrence, whose writing and paintings were subject to stringent censorship, confiscation and burning during his lifetime (his paintings still cannot be brought back into Britain), discusses obscenity and offers his own definition of pornography in two essays, '*A Propos of Lady Chatterley's Lover*' (1929) and 'Pornography and Obscenity' (1929). See Lawrence 1955.)

The door was thereby opened for similar defences to be mounted in other fields. From this point onwards it became increasingly difficult for written texts to be prosecuted under the terms of the Act, and with a few notable exceptions (such as Mary Whitehouse's successful prosecution of *Gay News* for publication of a poem about Christ having a homosexual fantasy) writing is now rarely subject to legislative censure (blasphemy is perhaps rather more vulnerable than pornography; Whitehouse's victory rested on this element of the poem, not solely its sexuality). As Sigrid Nielsen writes, a 'liberal publishing climate' developed after the Chatterley trial, when 'Obscenity trials . . . became rare, while destruction orders and private prosecutions for obscenity were eventually abolished' (Nielsen 1988: 23). However, this was to be challenged with an increased intolerance of sexual material which was to take its terms from feminism in the 1970s and after.

## Andrea Dworkin and pro-censorship feminism

The BBFC responded to social change and slowly liberalized their practices (though not quickly enough, argues Dewe Matthews; suggesting that the British public were way ahead of the British censors in what they would accept during this period: 'John Trevelyan seemed to take on the persona of King Canute' in the early 1960s. Dewe Matthews 1994: 153). A radical shift took place on British screens in the 1960s, leading to arguably the most 'permissive' period in censorship history during the early 1970s. This was the moment when BBFC-legitimized forms of cinematic sexual violence hit the screen, with the certification of *Straw Dogs* and *A Clockwork Orange* in 1971, neither of which could be deemed pornographic, but both of which contained difficult images of rape (of these, only *A Clockwork Orange* has been recently certificated on video). Bernardo Bertolucci's *Last Tango In Paris*, the art-house sex film which scandalized audiences in 1973, has retained its certificate and had no problem gaining a video certificate years later, although it was cut before its original cinema release and, according to Tom Dewe Matthews, was the first film with a BBFC certificate to be tried under the OPA. (In January 1974 Edward Shackelton, member of the right-wing Christian group the Festival of Light argued that 'the film was a record of obscenities practised by Marlon Brando and Maria Schneider and was not a fictional event', although the prosecution against United Artists failed when Judge Kenneth Jones threw the case out of court: Dewe Matthews 1994: 213.)

Certainly not certificated at that moment in the UK, but also central to the ethos of this permissive moment, was *Deep Throat* (1972), the first widely known hard-core film which was made famous after its New York trial (unlike *Chatterley*, *Deep Throat* was deemed devoid of artistic merit so the New World Theatre, where the film was being shown, was fined $3 million: Ross 1995, 16). However as Jonathan Ross has pointed out, the film's notoriety notwithstanding, this was the moment when porn came out of the closet of the stag club and was increasingly consumed by 'couples audiences':

> *Deep Throat* heralded the beginning of 'porno-chic', a short but telling phase in the history of cinema when it actually became hip and cool and fashionable to watch dirty movies, ideally with your partner, then talk endlessly about them at dinner parties (Ross 1995: 15–16).

But it was ironically at this same moment that a counter-movement was developing through both radical feminism and Christianity. Andrea Dworkin's important study which developed from her work in the women's movement in the 1970s, *Pornography: Men Possessing Women* (1981) had such a profound influence on active feminism that many of its campaigning energies during the 1970s and 1980s were diverted into the pro-censorship opposition to pornography. For Dworkin, pornography is defined by the way a film, image or text represents women as victims of masculinity; its 'major theme . . . as a genre is male power, its nature, its magnitude, its use, its meaning' (Dworkin 1981: 24). This is fixed on 'the annihilation of women's sexual integrity'; as a genre it is the textual proof and culmination of the 'seedy pact' men have made 'with and for male power' (Dworkin 1981, 47, 66). The book itself is largely a series of readings of sundry sexual materials strung together by an uncompromising polemic which defines men as objectifying sexual monsters and women as their objectified victims, who live frightened lives 'circumscribed by the sexual sadism of males': 'Force is intrinsic to male sexuality', she writes (Dworkin 1981, 136, 198). In her later book

*Intercourse* (1987) she argues that the act of penetration itself embodies this aggressive sadism, with the penis as a mutilating weapon which injects into the female body a 'polluting' substance (in her analysis of *Hustler* magazine Kipnis discusses the effects of this representation of sperm as a pollutant on wider ideas of pornography as 'dirty', and as castigated by a poetics which opposes the 'cleanliness' mainstream culture to the 'filth' of the sexual: Kipnis 1996: 140–41). The 'hit-and-run sexuality' (Dworkin 1981: 134) of the man is both aggressively controlling and out of control, finding the perfect trigger for release and vehicle for satisfaction in the pornographic representation of women. Written around the same time and emerging from the same feminist moment, Susan Griffin's *Pornography and Silence* (1982) deploys a similar argumentative armoury, although her conclusions are rather more mystical. For Griffin, 'Not women, but feelings, are the object of sadistic fantasy', and pornography's prime sin is the separation of 'culture from nature. It would desacralize matter' (Griffin 1982: 55, 49). As prone to sweeping generalizations as Dworkin, Griffin argues that,

> One can look at the whole history of civilization as a struggle between the force of eros in our lives and the mind's attempt to forget eros. We have believed pornography to be an expression of eros. But we find that after all, pornography exists to silence eros (Griffin 1982: 255).

Dworkin has no truck with Griffin's attempt to rescue the 'high' cultural term 'erotica' from its debased sister 'pornography', arguing that sexuality in its publicly expressed form is dominated and dictated by male power, so any sexual materials will be infected by masculinity's contaminating influence. Thus the Marquis de Sade is placed alongside Larry Flint, gay male pornography alongside girlie magazines, literary texts alongside pictures, *Emmanuelle* alongside *Snuff*.

Dworkin's *Pornography* had enormous currency when it appeared in Britain in the early 1980s. Essentially, however, the text is a forceful crystallization of a number of ideas already in circulation, concerning the politics of the pleasurable image, the male gaze, the psychosexuality of sadism and masochism. An argument posited by many feminists of Dworkin's generation saw pleasure and its representations as key signs or symptoms of wider sexual politics. Laura Mulvey's agenda-setting *Screen* article of 1975, 'Visual pleasure and narrative cinema', argued that Classical Hollywood film had 'coded the erotic into the language of the dominant patriarchal order'; its pleasures were guided and guarded by male desire targeted on the fetishized female object of the gaze. Mulvey's cinematic women were intrinsically imbued with what she called '*to-be-looked-at-ness*': 'Woman displayed as sexual object is the *leitmotif* of erotic spectacle: from pin-ups to strip-tease, from Ziegfeld to Busby Berkeley, she holds the look, and plays to and signifies male desire'. Thus the pornographic bleeds into the everyday in the way in which women's bodies are represented in accordance with the pattern of male fantasy; for Mulvey women's 'to-be-looked-at-ness' holds true whether they are posing for *Playboy* or starring in mainstream cinema. This basic argument was also posited in 1972 by John Berger in the book that accompanied his BBC series which challenged traditional readings of the history of art, *Ways of Seeing*. Here Berger read a number of images of women through an similar theory of the power of the gaze:

> To be born a woman has been to be born, within an allotted and confined space, into the keeping of men. . . . *men act* and *women appear*. Men look at women. Women watch themselves being looked at. This determines not only most relations between men and women but also the relation of women to themselves. The surveyor of woman in herself is male: the surveyed female. Thus she turns herself into an object – and most particularly an object of vision: a sight (Berger 1972: 46–7).

It is clear then that Dworkin is drawing on a number of wider cultural readings of the sexuality of the image, even when it is not technically pornographic, in her insistence on the objectifying power of the male gaze to submit the prone female body to the model of its desire. However, two things single out her approach and influence. First, what is peculiar about Dworkin's argument is its literalness. This ranges from the notion that porn is the explicit rendering of all male desire ('Women do not believe that men believe what pornography says about women. But they do. From the worst to the best of them, they do': Dworkin 1981: 167), to the larger position that porn is not textual expression of desire but actualized performance of that desire. Even given the argument that all pornography is intrinsically the expression of a sadistic (male) sexuality, Dworkin's critics – and most subsequent writing on pornography, it has to be said – have insisted that it must still be read as artefact, as cultural object, as the *representation* of a set of acts rather than those acts themselves. But for Dworkin porn is not representation, it *is* act; it does not just depict violence against women, it *is* violence against women. Or, in Robin Morgan's (in)famous phrase, 'pornography is the theory, rape is the practice'.

Second, *Pornography* set the agenda for a whole programme of action as Dworkin took its conclusions into a campaigning political arena, using it as springboard into a lengthy career of anti-porn, pro-censorship work. 'We will know that we are free when the pornography no longer exists' she writes in the book's conclusion (Dworkin 1981: 224), and she went about trying to achieve this by drafting, with feminist attorney Catherine MacKinnon, an ordinance which gave women the power to take legal action on the grounds that they had been damaged by pornography (the effects argument in another guise). Backed by right-wing non-feminists who had a quite different stake in the issue, the ordinance was initially passed by the City Council in Minneapolis, Minnesota in 1984, only to be vetoed by the Mayor, then taken up in Indiana by the Indianapolis City Council. After bitter campaigning by feminists on both sides of the censorship/libertarian divide, with the Dworkin/MacKinnon group primarily pitted against the Feminist Anti-Censorship Taskforce (FACT), the ordinance was finally overruled as unconstitutional by the Supreme Court in 1986 (this is cogently outlined in Rodgerson and Wilson 1991: Introduction). Nevertheless, Dworkin and MacKinnon were not slow to elicit the support of anyone who would help promote this legislation, even if it meant hitching their wagon to Moral Majority right-wing groups who had traditionally had little sympathy for feminist causes. As Lynne Segal correctly points out,

> Anti-pornography campaigning was the single feminist issue which the Right had no wish to attack; on the contrary, they welcomed and supported it, since censorship of sexual explicitness had always been central to their moral agenda (Segal 1994: 62).

In the UK, two groups sprang up during the 1980s, in part taking their cue from these American developments. I said earlier that in Britain soft-porn magazines such as those published by the Paul Raymond stable now operate relatively free from the risk of prosecution, but they were the target for at least one feminist group, objecting to both the location of soft porn and its invasion into, for instance, the daily tabloids. The Campaign Against Pornography developed out of Claire Short's 'Page Three Bill', which opposed the ubiquity of female flesh across the spectrum from the mass-circulation *Sun* to the top shelf of the newsagents. Another prominent British group, the Campaign Against Pornography and Censorship (CPC), attempted to reverse the terms of debate: in the words of its coordinator Catherine Itzin, the CPC's role was to militate against a pornography which 'actually censors women's rights and freedoms' (quoted by Mead-King 1990: 38). Emulating Dworkin and MacKinnon's argument that the core issue isn't censorship but civil liberties, Itzin's group specifically claimed that theirs was not strictly a call for censorship in itself, but rather a lesser censorship pitted against the greater 'censorship' of the sex industry which in effect restricts women's behaviour. Against these tricksy linguistic arguments Feminists Against Censorship stressed, on the one hand, that 'Films and publications which glorify non-sexual violence probably do far more damage than "Page Three" and *Hustler*' (Rodgerson and Wilson 1991: 75), and, more positively, they urged that we do not

> close down on sex and narrow the boundaries of the permissible but . . . expand the possibilities of women's sexual pleasure. After all, part of feminism had been a flowering of books, magazines and films on feminist erotic themes, encouraging women to be sexually expressive, not repressive (Rodgerson and Wilson 1991: 12).

It is this final point which I wish to expand upon in the last section of this chapter.

## New pornographies and new positions: video, safe sex and voices from the sex industry

What might one find today in pornographic magazines or films which pushes against or beyond legal definitions of the 'acceptable'? The law has perhaps served to inspire publishers or film-makers to test its terms to the limit, encouraging inventive or risky image-making which pushes at the OPA's vague definitions to see how far they can go. Still images in magazines have always been able to represent far more than their filmic counterparts, particularly regarding images of genitals. For instance, what magazine *Playbirds Continental* delightfully refer to as 'held wide open close-ups' can be found in more and less explicit forms in even 'soft' top-shelf magazines, yet the all-pervasive presence of female nudity in Western culture notwithstanding, the female genitals have until recently remained fairly shrouded on-screen. Sharon Stone's famous leg-crossing scene in Paul Verhoeven's *Basic Instinct* (1992) was considered a pioneering mainstream moment. But slightly riskier images might be found in the stock of any local video store, such as when a masturbating woman's labia are briefly visible in the American soft-porn erotic thriller *Night Rhythms* (Gregory Hippolyte, 1992) or in the porno-gothic 'nuns on heat' feast *Sacred Flesh* (2000) directed by thorn in the side of the British image-police, Nigel Wingrove. None of these images come close to what can be shown in still magazine form, however. In 1994 a leaked BBFC report about *Satin and Lace – an Erotic History of Lingerie* (1992) gave a sense of what Tom Dewe Matthews calls 'the stringent exactness' of BBFC procedure with a definition of the absurd rule regarding female genital exposure: 'The examiners said that this type of exploitation came under the so-called ILOOLI rule which declares that 'inner labia is out but outer labia can be in' (Dewe Matthews 1994: 279).

I mentioned earlier the Video Recordings Act 1984 and the Criminal Justice Act Amendment to the Video Recordings Act 1994. The first was passed after a landslide Conservative Party victory and in response to a virulent tabloid newspaper campaign against so-called 'video nasties'. The rise of video in the late 1970s and early 1980s was so rapid (and so apparently unexpected) that distribution of unclassified and uncensored material briefly proliferated unchecked. While film was covered by a number of laws and regulated by the BBFC, and 'obscene' magazines could be prosecuted under an OPA designed primarily with the published text in mind, video was another matter – no law set out specific terms for its regulation. The VRA gave the BBFC a power in respect of videos which they already held over cinema, so that under it all video materials had to be BBFC classified prior to release with 'special regard to the likelihood of video works . . . being viewed in the home' (quoted in Kermode 1995: 64). The figure of the child as vulnerable viewer seeing video materials from which she should rightly be protected has thus underpinned the BBFC's more draconian recent decisions. Since video's audience cannot be regulated as strictly as cinema's, its censorship has tended to be harsher than films' (lengthy debates over withheld video certificates for *Reservoir Dogs*, *Natural Born Killers*, *The Exorcist* and *Crash* highlighted this during the 1990s, prior to the eventual certification of each).

The Criminal Justice Act Amendment to the Video Recordings Act 1994 built upon the terms of the VRA, requiring the BBFC to pay specific attention to the possibility that children might come into contact with videos not meant for them. Coming in the wake of the James Bulger trial and tabloid tales of the role that horror film *Child's Play 3* had in that crime, the 1994 legislation concretized a pervasive fear about children as viewers of difficult material. However, the debate has largely focused on horror films, and it might be argued that the treatment of sexual material on video, which has also had to be judged under the terms of the VRA, has been rather different. Although the child viewer, ostensibly eminently 'effectable' and, for the tabloid headline writer, vulnerable to the corruptions of celluloid, haunts our legislation and even justifies the limitation of what adults are allowed to see – Philip French (1995: 29) writes that *all* 'audiences have been treated like untrustworthy children' – the battle against the powers of the VRA was until recently waged on this issue of violence rather than sex. Educational sex videos promoting consensual safe sex have, for example, been allowed to push forward the boundaries of visibility in the 1990s, against the grain of the trend set by the 'video nasties' scare and the passing of both of these pieces of legislation.

In fact, if anything, sexual material on video has been able to become even more explicit, and the market has grown rapidly. Jonathan Ross (1995: 19) writes that 'In 1990 it was estimated that in the United States the sale and rental of hard-core films accounts for one-third of the video market'. Three forces have worked to open up access to a wider range of sexual materials in the late 1980s and early 1990s. First, the growth of AIDS suggested a need to distribute explicit materials advocating safe sex practices. Second, increasingly vocal and self-motivated women from the sex industry began to develop different images, reinforced by new voices from feminism and new female audiences demanding a wider range of non-sexist pornography tailored to women's desire. Third, there was a general recognition that 'public opinion' has shifted, making adult audiences more tolerant of explicit material. The first condition has had a very clear impact on what can and cannot be seen on-screen at present. I cited above different possibilities for representing the female body across the still/moving image divide. In none of the mainstream cases cited above (*Basic Instinct, Night Rhythms* and *Sacred Flesh*) did film come near to what magazines routinely represent, nor even what can now be represented on-screen of the *male* body. Three videos released in 1993 pushed forward what can be shown within the context of a broadly 'educational' rubric: *Well Sexy Woman: a lesbian guide to sexual health, Getting it Right: safer sex for young gay men* (both produced by Pride Video in association with The Terence Higgins Trust), and *Seriously Sexy: safer sex for young people* (Paradox Films in association with The Terence Higgins Trust). All were given 18 Certificates (albeit with some cuts). They showed erections aplenty in tandem with incessant safe sex messages, which apparently worked on the understanding that arousal offered a good medium for the absorption of advice. This is again where the terms of the OPA come into play: the messages are 'educational' (urging that one should use a condom), the images instructional (showing *how* to use a condom). This is permitted under the BBFC's 18 certificate guidelines, which state, 'Where sex material genuinely seeks to inform and educate in matters such as human sexuality, safe sex and health, exceptions to the normal constraints on explicit images may be made in the public interest' (BBFC 2000: 17). Ironically this meant in practice that the need for condom-instruction ensured the foregrounding of the male body, though a similar situation did not prevail in relation to female condom use. For instance there is a moment in *Seriously Sexy* when a female condom is alluded to: the woman on-screen holds one up and then apparently inserts it, while the camera stays resolutely fixed on her body above the waist. There are many shots of how to put a male condom on an erect penis, so why no visual help with the female version? Similarly, in *Well Sexy Woman*, there are debates about safe oral sex and even a scene within which two women seem to be practising it, but apart from a fairly nebulous image of apparent oral contact, there are no explicit demonstrations of the use of dental dams, presumably because of this continued taboo about the graphic depiction of the female genitals.

In conclusion, I should like to consider the second and third challenges to the old model of the pornographic together. If feminist debate around pornography and censorship has been at best difficult, this new turn towards interest in the sex industry itself focuses a number of issues. The 1990s brought a shift in some women's attitudes towards the representations of pornography, with key voices calling for the gap between analysis of images and the working world of production and consumption to be bridged. Dworkin's highly public support only for prostitute groups which highlight the horrors of sex work, such as WHISPER (Women Hurt in Systems of Prostitution Engaged in Revolt), meant that there was no space within her agenda to view the sex industry at all positively, or even to appropriate its powers and position for women. We can approach this new debate by looking at two texts published around the same time as the new wave of safe sex videos, *Dirty Looks: Women, Pornography, Power* (Church Gibson and Gibson 1993) and the Winter 1993 edition of *Social Text* (which includes a special section edited by Anne McClintock on the sex trade). Both books do something 1970s and 1980s discussions didn't, looking more at what sex workers offer their clients (on film or in body), and what the clients want from the sex industry and its images. Their writers are often keen to mark the radical difference between their own positions and those of Dworkin, MacKinnon or Itzen, adding to the burgeoning corpus of challenges to the marriage of cultural feminism with right-wing pro-censors which I discussed above. Here the pleasures as well as the dangers of pornography and sex work are emphasized, looking towards, at the most extreme point represented in either collection, a women-orientated not male dominated 'pornotopia' (Koch 1993: 42).

These writings radically depart from the positions of anti-pornography campaigners. Yet it is ironically here, through a new tone on sexual practice and sexual purchase, that the personal and the political are really being read together again, as escort workers discuss their autonomy, cross-dressers articulate their femininity as clients in S/M scenarios, sociologists debate the difficulties of participant observation in the sex trade, and alternative female pornographers describe the new ways in which sex videos by and for women are being devised and made. One of the most prominent figures in this movement, ex-porn actress Candida Royalle, grasped a moment of opportunity in identifying the new niche of legitimized female desire. Royalle, the prototype 'couples' pornographer and president of Femme Production and Distribution Inc., tailors her products to (her perception of) female desire, casting herself as the capitalist feminist identifying her market while also stressing the risks of her work. As she writes in 'Porn in the U.S.A.', she is both a woman who 'dare[s] to break with a cultural taboo' and the capitalist who 'recognized and created the market' (Royalle 1993: 24, 32). She also claims that 'Now that [porn] is being taken into the bedroom where women – the wives, madonnas, and sisters – can see it, it's very threatening to the Right' (Royalle 1993: 29). As *Skin Two* photographer Grace Lau writes in her own 'Confessions of a complete scopophiliac' in *Dirty Looks*, 'During the 1980s, female desire became a lucrative business' (Lau 1993: 205).

The excessive figure of pornographic performance artiste Annie Sprinkle also looms large in many recent discussions. Her spectacular transformations, from hooker to porn actress to film-maker to live performer blurring the boundary between sexually arousing and avant-garde spectacle, challenge the traditional distinction between the 'high' concerns of live art and the 'low' concerns of porn. By highlighting the elements of performance, artifice and pastiche, Sprinkle problematizes models of 'natural' or 'authentic' sexual response while also evidently enjoying herself. In the process, she offers herself and her audiences, in Chris Straayer's words, 'a virtual identity orgy' (Straayer 1993: 163).

Perhaps Sprinkle is important because her work exposes a wider problem about our need to explain and categorize pornography and its effects, and our ultimate failure to do so. If legal response to controversial materials shies away from trying to define the obscene and instead focuses on 'effects', recent debate has suggested that the way in which we are moved by such images is itself highly complex. New work has celebrated the possibility of enjoying and identifying across sexual divides, picking up on a long history of gay pleasure in heterosexual images (American lesbian sex campaigner Susie Bright in particular has discussed lesbian use of male-orientated images of women in the absence of specifically tailored lesbian materials, and the male gay readership of the 1990s explosion of heterosexual women's porn such as magazines *For Women* or *Playgirl* was part of the late burgeoning twentieth-century magazine market – see Braithwaite, Chapter 8 in this volume). Two years after its publication Linda Williams (1993) revised the position upon which *Hard Core* was based – that heterosexual porn is for heterosexuals, and access to the porn of another sexuality is difficult. In 'Second Thoughts on *Hard Core*: American Obscenity Law and the Scapegoating of Deviance' she writes,

> Speaking from what I now recognise to be a false sense of fixed sexual identity . . . I was unable to see then that what I was learning from the book was actually how easy it was to identify with diverse subject positions and to desire diverse objects, indeed how polymorphously perverse the genre of pornography could be (Williams 1993: 56).

The debate is then muddied by the suggestion that there can be no single response to porn of any kind: however crude its images, what they do to us is complex. And just as our responses are fluid, so are the objects upon which we choose to fix pornographically. In an important essay dating from 1982, Susan Barrowclough opened up the possibility that hard-core porn, which offers images of men as well as women, might be giving the male viewer visual pleasures other than those obvious hetero-sexual ones which he would most readily admit to:

> Contrary to the assumption that the male uses pornography to confirm and celebrate his gender's sexual activity and dominance, is the possibility of his pleasure in identifying with a 'feminine' passivity or subordination. . . . It may be that his gaze falls, not on the female genitals (which he may be accustomed to seeing elsewhere) but on the male, and that the chief part of his pleasure, which he may disown subsequently, is homoerotic rather than heterosexual. This ambiguity pornography permits (Barrowclough 1982: 36).

There is, then, no single dominant image which is intrinsically pornographic or offers its consumer one line of straightforward pleasure. Simple as this sounds, 'Context really does matter' (Segal 1993: 15):

> *It is never possible, whatever the image to isolate it, to fix its meaning and predict some inevitable pattern of response, independently from assessing its wider representational context and the particular recreational, educational or social context in which it is being received* (Segal 1993: 15, original italics).

Sexual representations, nudity, the obscene: these remain political issues. Contem-porary attitudes to sexual material may be shifting again towards a more open sense that such representations should be welcomed as long as they can appeal to a wider sexual spectrum, including women and gays, and acts represented are always con-sensual. But this new pornography must practise in an awareness that the sexual is never apolitical, the bedroom, and its representations, is the arena of power as well as pleasure.

It is difficult to conclude by reflecting anything other than a sense of flux. The BBFC shifted its boundaries more rapidly in the period around the turn of the twenty-first century than at any other time, with the possible exception of the early 1970s. It is significant that although earlier in the 1990s apparent erections were briefly glimpsed in mainstream non-porn art-house films such as *The Adjuster* (1991, dir. Atom Egoyan) or *Les Amants Du Pont Neuf* (1991, dir. Léos Carax), by the late 1990s they could be seen penetrating vaginas in *The Idiots* (1999, dir. Von Trier) and even ejaculating in *Romance* (1999, dir. Catherine Breillat), both of which were passed uncut for the cinema at 18 because these scenes were deemed serious, sensitively handled or necessary to the narrative. The paradox of sexually explicit images being available on art-house screens but remaining problematic in porn films has thus continued to dog debates.

In 1998 Petley and Kermode noted that the BBFC were aware of 'a recent British Social Attitudes Survey [which] discovered that the public is not as concerned as some have supposed about representations of "straightforward, mutually pleasurable sex, however explicit it might be"' (Petley and Kermode: 1998, 16). This shift in public attitudes has been accompanied by a shift in viewing practices. Cinema has given way to video and home viewing as the theatre of porn, the primary space of its exhibition and consumption. This underpinned a number of anxieties which surfaced in a flurry of debates between the BBFC, the Home Office and other law-enforcement bodies, and the media from 1997 onwards. By the mid-1990s the BBFC, responding to those perceived shifts in public opinion which Petley and Kermode mention as well as an awareness of the increased availability of black-market porn materials, approved for classification at R18 more explicit videos containing, for instance, shots of penetration (but in a purely sexual rather than an artily 'serious' context). After the election of the Labour Party to power in May 1997, the Home Office (in conjunction with HM Customs and Excise and the police) expressed concern about whether some of these materials might be considered obscene by the courts. Over the next two years, during which time Ferman was replaced at the BBFC by Robin Duval as Director and Andreas Whittam Smith as President, the limits of potential obscenity were tested by videos such as *Makin' Whoopie* (which was deemed not obscene by the Video Appeals Committee), and a new set of classification guidelines were officially published in September 2000. These guidelines (which, at the time of writing, are still considered controversial by the Home Office) permit hard-core images in video materials to be sold at sex shops under the R18 certificate:

> The following content . . . may be permitted
> - aroused genitalia
> - masturbation
> - oral–genital contact including kissing, licking and sucking
> - penetration by finger, penis, tongue, vibrator or dildo
> - non-harmful fetish material
> - group sexual activity
> - ejaculation and semen
>
> . . . These guidelines make no distinction between heterosexual and homosexual activity (BBFC 2000: 19).

Under these terms, and a decade after Ross's *Deep Throat* laserdisc was seized by British Customs, the film was certified uncut at R18 by the BBFC on 8 September 2000, an act profoundly resonant of the dramatic changes which have characterized responses to porn since the 1970s. The first decade of the twenty-first century promises to see even greater developments in forms of representation, contexts for consumption and exhibition, and legislative response, particularly in light of the European Convention of Human Rights' guarantee of 'freedom of expression' which entered UK law in October 2000. The traditional analogue moving image itself, as well as the even more arcane still photograph reproduced by the printing press, look likely to become less of a focus of moral, media and legal anxiety than the new proliferating technologies of the Internet, virtual reality, satellite and cable broadcasting. These are the future territories of pornography, and its censure.

## Questions

1  Debate the usefulness of the 'tendency to deprave and corrupt' criterion of the Obscene Publications Act 1959 in assessing sexual materials.

2  Discuss the differing positions taken by women writers and campaigners, as well as female performers and producers of pornography, including examples from feminist and non-feminists, pro- and anti-censorship lobbies. Is it possible to be anti-pornography and anti-censorship at the same time?

3  How has the move from viewing sexual material in cinemas to viewing it in the home shifted the debates around pornography?

## References

Barrowclough, S. (1982) 'Not a love story', *Screen* 23(5).

BBFC (2000) *BBFC Classification Guidelines*, London: BBFC.

Berger, J. (1972) *Ways of Seeing*, Harmondsworth: Penguin.

Brown, B. (1982) 'A curious arrangement', *Screen* 23(5).

Chester, G. and Dickey, J. (eds) (1988) *Feminism and Censorship: The Current Debate*, Bridport: Prism.

Church Gibson, P. and Gibson, R. (eds) (1993) *Dirty Looks: Women, Pornography, Power*, London: British Film Institute.

Dewe Matthews, T. (1994) *Censored*, London: Chatto & Windus.

Dworkin, A. (1981) *Pornography: Men Possessing Women*, London: The Women's Press.

Dworkin, A. (1987) *Intercourse*, London: Secker & Warburg.

French, P. (1995) 'No end in sight', *Index on Censorship* 6.

Griffin, S. (1982) *Pornography and Silence: Culture's Revenge Against Nature*, London: The Women's Press.

Home Office (1979) *Report of the Committee on Obscenity and Film Censorship* (Williams Report), London: HMSO.

Kermode, M. (1995) 'Horror: on the edge of taste', *Index on Censorship* 6.

Kermode, M. and Petley, J. (1990) 'Members of the press', *Time Out* 1026 (April)

Kipnis, L. (1996): *Bound and Gagged Pornography and the Politics of Fantasy in America*, New York: Grove Press.

Koch, G. (1993) 'The body's shadow realm', in P. Church Gibson and R. Gibson (eds) *Dirty Looks: Women, Pornography, Power*, London: British Film Institute.

Kuhn, A. (1984) 'Public versus private: The case of indecency and obscentiy', *Leisure Studies* 3.

Lau, G. (1993) 'Confessions of a complete scopophiliac', in P. Church Gibson and R. Gibson (eds) *Dirty Looks: Women, Pornography, Power*, London: British Film Institute.

Lawrence, D. H. (1955) *Sex, Literature and Censorship: Essays*, London: Heinemann.

McClintock, A. (ed.) (1993) *Social Text* 37 (winter): special edition on the sex industry.

Mead-King, M. (1990) 'Should pornography come off the top shelf?' *Guardian* 15 February.

Merck, M. (1992) 'From Minneapolis to Westminster', in L. Segal and M. McIntosh (eds) *Sex Exposed: Sexuality and the Pornography Debate*, London: Virago.

Mulvey, L. (1975) 'Visual pleasure and narrative cinema', *Screen* 6.

Nielsen, S. (1988),'Books for bad women: a feminist looks at censorship', in G. Chester and J. Dickey (eds) *Feminism and Censorship: The Current Debate*, Bridport: Prism.

Petley, J. and Kermode, M. (1998) 'The censor and the state', *Sight and Sound* 8(5): May, 14–18.

Rodgerson, G. and Wilson, E. (1991) *Pornography and Censorship: The Case Against Censorship*, London: Lawrence & Wishart.

Rolph, C. H. (1961) *The Trial of Lady Chatterley: Regina v. Penguin Books Limited*, Harmondsworth: Penguin.

Ross, J. (1995): *The Incredibly Strange Film Book*, London: Simon & Schuster.

Royalle, C. (1993) 'Porn in the U.S.A.', *Social Text* 37.

Segal, L. (1993) 'Does pornography cause violence? The search for evidence', in P. Church Gibson and R. Gibson (eds) *Dirty Looks: Women, Pornography, Power*, London: British Film Institute.

Segal, L. (1994) *Straight Sex: The Politics of Pleasure*, London: Virago.

Segal, L. and McIntosh, M. (eds) (1992) *Sex Exposed: Sexuality and the Pornography Debate*, London: Virago.

Straayer, C. (1993) 'The seduction of boundaries: feminist fluidity in Annie Sprinkle's art/education/sex', in P. Church Gibson and R. Gibson (eds) *Dirty Looks: Women, Pornography, Power*, London: British Film Institute.

Trevelyan, J. (1973) *What the Censor Saw*, London: Michael Joseph.

Williams, L. (1991) *Hard Core: Power, Pleasure, and the 'Frenzy of the Visible'*, London: HarperCollins.

Williams, L. (1993) 'Second thoughts on *Hard Core*: American obscenity and the scapegoating of deviance', in P. Church Gibson and R. Gibson (eds) *Dirty Looks: Women, Pornography, Power*, London: British Film Institute.

Williams, L. R. (1994) 'The pornographic subject: feminism and censorship in the 1990s', in S. Ledger, J. McDonagh and J. Spencer (eds) *Political Gender: Texts and Contexts*, London: Harvester Wheatsheaf.

# Further reading

Gail, C. and Dickey, J. (eds) (1988): *Feminism and Censorship: The Current Debate*, Bridport: Prism. A wide-ranging set of essays which sum up key areas of the debate around pornography's censorship, and particularly feminists' responses to it, from both sides of the pro- and anti-censorship divide. Also reproduces useful primary documents such as the Policy Statement of the Campaign Against Pornography and Censorship and extracts from the Minneapolis Ordinance.

Church Gibson, P. and Gibson, R. (eds) (1993) *Dirty Looks: Women, Pornography, Power*, London: British Film Institute. Useful collection of essays addressing changes in attitudes to porn in the 1990s and containing discussion of sex work and pornographic consumption.

Dewe Matthews, T. (1994) *Censored*, London: Chatto & Windus. The definitive history of British film censorship.

Dworkin, A. (1981) *Pornography: Men Possessing Women*, London: The Women's Press. Polemical starting-point for many feminist debates, arguing that porn is a form of active violence by men against women.

Kipnis, L. (1996): *Bound and Gagged Pornography and the Politics of Fantasy in America*, New York: Grove Press. Discusses a range of differently censured forms of American pornography in the context of an argument which sees porn as a form of public fantasy.

O'Toole, L. (1998) *Pornocopia: Porn, sex, technology and desire*, London: Serpent's Tail. Provides a history of mass-market pornography since the 1960s, reading it as a genre with its own conventions and hallmarks. It contains some fascinating interview material with people working in the industry as well as with porn users.

Williams, L. (1991) *Hard Core: Power, Pleasure, and the 'Frenzy of the Visible'*, London: HarperCollins. Pathbreaking analysis which reads hard-core film as a deeply unstable genre which challenges and redefines ideas about bodily pleasure and the limits of cinematic visibility.

# Index

*A New Future for Communications*,
    Government White Paper 2000 219,
    226
administrative research 5, 196, 245–58
    Audit Bureau of Communication (ABC)
      44, 98
    Broadcasters' Audience Research Board
      (BARB) 44, 247, 250
    'Establishment Survey' 247
    Joint Industry Committee for Newspaper
      Advertising Research (JICNAR)
      44
    Joint Industry Committee for Television
      Advertising Research (JICTAR)
      247
    National Readership Survey (NRS) 108,
      245, 253–4
    newspapers/magazines readership 253
    'people meters' 246–7
    radio 251
    Radio Joint Audience Research (RAJAR)
      251
advertising 11, 39–56, 74, 107–8, 222,
    245–6
    above the line 45, 53
    agencies 43–4, 48
    audiences *see* demographics
    below the line 45, 49, 53
    brands 42, 43, 50–1, 74
    clutter 48, 207, 255
    in crisis 51–2
    wastage 12, 105, 203
age 369–82, 421
    teenagers 371–5, 378
    youth 369–82
Amendment to the Criminal Justice Act
    1994 482, 488

Annan Report (Report of the Annan
    Committee on the Future of
    Broadcasting 1977) 141, 406
audiences 5, 13, 105–17, 195–7, 203–4,
    245–58, 272–303; *see also* administrative
    research, advertising, cinema,
    demographics, 'effects', market
    research, music, radio, sport and
    television
'auteur' 19, 148–9, 161

Barthes, R. 18–19, 299–300, 469, 471
BBC 96, 106, 109, 116, 121, 123, 124, 126,
    129, 136, 137–44, 169, 172, 183–5, 195,
    198, 200, 205, 206–8, 209, 221–2, 225,
    226, 234, 237, 238, 240, 245–6, 363,
    415, 449–51, 453–8
    BBC 2 206, 238, 444, 456
    *see also* Radio 1, Radio 2, Radio 3, Radio
    4 and Radio 5
Berlusconi, S. 241
Birt, J. 183–4, 207, 222, 363
Black, C. 96
Blair, T. 72–3, 94, 96–7, 346–7, 379, 416,
    453, 458
books *see* publishing
British Telecom (BT) 142, 201, 213
Broadcasting Act 1990 121, 138, 209, 221,
    224, 366, 453
Broadcasting Act 1996 96, 97, 122, 238, 366
Broadcasting Standards Committee 143,
    221

Cable Act 1984 221
cinema 13, 148–63, 401–14
    advertising 156, 256
    audiences 156, 256

cinema (*continued*)
  Bollywood 156
  British Board of Film Classification
    (BBFC) 225, 262, 480–95; *see also*
    cinema: censorship
  censorship 260, 477–95
  Cinema Advertising Association (CAA)
    256
  co-productions 152–4
  Eastern Europe 160
  EURIMAGES 154–6, 159
  Film Council 225
  Films Act 1985 224–5
  France 148, 150–3, 156, 160
  funding 150–1
  Germany 150, 156, 159
  Hollywood 13, 156, 158, 406, 412
  IMAX 149
  Ireland 148, 150–3
  Italy 156, 158–9
  MEDIA (Measures to Encourage the
    Development of the Audiovisual
    Industry) 154, 155, 159
  Netherlands 158–9
  promotion 154–6
  Spain 160
  UK 148, 150–3, 156, 160
class 340–56
comics 11, 14–22
  copyright 20, 21
  graphic novels 21
  in the UK 14, 19–21
convergence 48, 51
cultural studies 297–8, 343

Davies Committee Report 1999 225
demographics 44, 203
  lifestyle 48, 49, 113
Department of Culture, Media and Sport
  (DCMS) 225
deregulation 12, 32, 33, 235–41, 366;
  *see also* models of media institutions
  and policy
digital video disk (DVD) 250
disability 78, 383–400
Disabled People's Movement 385
discourse 309–11
Dyke, G. 184, 207

economics 195–7, 198–216
'effects' 195–7, 259–71, 272–303
  Payne Fund studies 260

Frankfurt School 4–5, 273

gender 326–39, 423
General Agreement on Tariffs and Trade
  (GATT) 149, 227
globalization 49, 59, 67–8, 166–7, 217, 221,
  227

Human Rights Act 1998 95,

identities 309–11; *see also* age, class,
  demographics, disability, gender,
  nationality, 'race' and ethnicity and
  sexuality
ideology 307–11, 343–4, 421
information management *see* public
  relations
International Monetary Fund (IMF) 73
Internet *see* new information and
  communication technologies

journalism 12, 46, 70–88, 89–103, 181, 187

Lazarsfeld, P. 5, 196
Leavis, F. R. 4–5
lobby system 75, 76, 79, 444–6, 457

magazines *see* publishing
Major, J. 96–7
market research *see* administrative research
  and demographics
'mass culture' 4–5, 6
McLuhan, M. 24, 188
media audiences *see* audiences; *see also*
  administrative research, advertising,
  cinema, 'effects', music, radio, sport
  and television
media policy *see* policy
media studies 4–7, 80, 294–303, 343
mobile phones 45, 123
models of media institutions 231–44; *see also*
  policy and public service broadcasting
  'duopoly' model of broadcasting *see also*
    television: 'cosy duopoly'
  'integration' model of broadcasting
    233–4
  'private sector monopoly' model of
    broadcasting 234–5
moral panics 259
Murdoch, R. 81, 94–5, 96–7, 181, 195, 198,
  210–11, 221, 222, 223, 241
music 12, 13, 164–79
  audiences 173
  CDs 13, 165
  charts 13, 172–3
  club scene 13, 164, 165, 169
  concerts and tours 13, 169–70

music (*continued*)
copyright 173–4, 226
festivals 170
on the Internet 13, 164, 167, 175, 226
MP3 *see* music: on the Internet
MTV 164, 170, 171, 204
music press 13, 164, 165, 171–2, 173
music video 13, 165, 171
Napster *see* music: on the Internet
radio 13, 165, 170–3
sampling 174–5
Sony 166, 167
synergy 167
*Top of the Pops* 164, 171
Universal Music Group 167
Warner EMI 167

nationality 59, 65, 401–14, 420
new information and communication
technologies (NICTs) 13, 180–91
CD-ROMS 24, 34–5, 149, 157
e-mail 226
fax 188
Internet 35, 43, 45, 48, 50, 51, 52, 57–8,
64–5, 67–8, 121, 123, 135–6, 139,
180–91, 198, 200, 206, 212, 213–14,
218, 224, 225–6, 303, 464
World Wide Web 58, 188, 189, 213, 303
news 11–12, 57–69, 70–88, 184, 185–8,
427–43, 444–63, 464–76
Cable Network News (CNN) 58, 185, 187,
188, 438
Fox TV 81
Harlech Television (HTV) 81
Independent Radio News (IRN) 444
Independent Television News (ITN) 58,
81, 206, 444, 451–2, 453, 456–7
news agencies 57–69
news values ('newsworthiness') 65, 427–43
newspapers 12, 13, 30, 46, 79, 89–103,
181–2, 198, 202–3, 210–12, 224, 225,
239, 464–76
news photography 464–76
radio news 438
Newson, E. 266–7

Parliamentary politics 444–63
Peacock Report 1986 123, 221, 223
People First 390
policy 13, 195–7, 217–30; *see also* BBC and
public service broadcasting
pornography 13, 331–3, 477–95
child 226, 480
cyberporn 180–1, 189–90
hard-core 477, 481

Location of Pornographic Materials Bill
479
Obscene Publications Act 481–95
'soft'/erotica 473, 481, 485
'positive' and 'negative' images 359–60
Press Complaints Commission 96, 225
promotions *see* public relations
public relations 45, 49–50, 70–88, 458–9;
*see also* advertising: below the line and
above the line
public service broadcasting 195–7, 205–6,
218–19, 227; *see also* BBC and policy
publishing 11, 23–38
Amazon.com 24, 28, 32
Barnes and Noble 28
Bauer 106, 107, 116
books 11, 23–38, 198, 200
British Rate and Data (BRAD) 106
COMAG 109
copyright 30–2
East Midlands Allied Press (EMAP) 47,
106, 109, 129
FNAC 28, 29
Gruhner and Jahr (G&J) 106
International Publishing Corporation
(IPC) 47, 105, 109, 110, 116
magazines 12, 15, 27, 30, 104–20, 195,
212
News International 47; *see also* Murdoch,
R.
newspapers *see* news: newspapers
Net Book Agreement (NBA) 28
subscription 111–12
Trade-Related Aspects of Intellectual
Property (TRIPS) 24
Value Added Tax (VAT) 30, 95–6
Verlagsgruppe Bertelsmann 26, 28, 33–4,
106
World Intellectual Property Organization
23, 31

'race' and ethnicity 329, 357–68
radio 12–13, 104, 121–34, 198, 209–10;
*see also* administrative research: radio;
music: radio; and news: Independent
Radio News
advertising 122, 199–205
Atlantic 252 128, 209
audiences 121–34, 251–3
Capital 129
Choice FM 128
Classic FM 122, 128, 203, 209
Commercial Radio Companies Association
(CRCA) 251
Jazz FM 128, 209

radio (*continued*)
   LBC 209
   local 127–9
   News Direct 128
   Radio 1/One FM 121, 127, 128
   Radio 2 121, 127
   Radio 3 121, 127
   Radio 4 121, 123, 127, 130–2, 209, 457
   Radio 5 121, 127–8, 185
   Radio Authority 209
   Radio Caroline 127
   Radio London 127
   Radio Luxembourg 125, 126
   Talk Radio UK *see* TalkSPORT
   TalkSPORT 122, 128, 209
   transistors 126
   Virgin 122, 128, 203, 209
Reith, J. 124–5, 127, 130, 209, 449–50
representation 307–493
Rowland, T. 97

semiotics (semiology) 299, 420; *see also*
   Barthes, R.
sexuality 313–25, 331
spin doctors *see* public relations
sport 208, 415–26
   boxing 419
   cricket 417–18; women's 420
   football 185, 416–18, 420, 421–4;
      women's 420
   motor racing 424
   rugby 420; women's 420
   snooker 419
   tennis 421

television 12–13, 45, 51, 79, 135–47, 183–5,
   198
   audiences 145; *see also* administrative
      research, demographics, 'effects' and
      market research
   British Broadcasting Corporation (BBC)
      *see* main entry
   BSkyB (Sky/BSB) 48, 135, 138, 142, 181,
      184–5, 198, 208, 213, 221, 223, 238,
      240, 417, 418, 444, 456–7
   Canal Plus (France) 150, 157
   Carlton 136
   Channel Four 136, 138, 195, 198, 205,
      207, 221–4, 234, 238, 363–6, 405–6,
      416, 456
   Channel Five 139, 195, 205, 207, 234,
      238, 366, 456
   'cosy duopoly' 221, 234
   digital/cable/satellite 135, 138, 141–2,
      157, 184, 187–8, 207, 250, 366
   Discovery Channel 238
   Granada 136, 139, 452
   ITV (Independent Television, also
      Channel Four, Channel Five, ITV 1,
      ITV 2 and ITV Sport) 136, 137–44,
      195, 198, 200, 203, 205, 206–8, 221–2,
      223–4, 234, 237, 238, 246, 364, 406,
      451–2, 453–8
   ITC (Independent Television
      Commission) 200, 206, 224, 234, 238,
      454
   licence fee 195, 200, 204–5, 206, 208,
      222, 225, 226, 245–6, 449
   London Weekend Television (LWT)
      364
   NRK (Norway) 240
   ONdigital 48, 50; *see also* ITV
   pay-per-view (PPV) 200, 208
   SVT (Sweden) 240
   Thames TV 454
Thatcher, M. (and 'Thatcherism') 76, 96,
   98, 181, 183, 221–2, 345–6, 378, 446,
   453, 454
TiVo 184, 208

'value chain' 136–9
video 185, 225, 250, 265
Video Recordings Act 1984 221, 266, 482,
   488
'Video Violence and the Protection of
   Children' *see* Newson, E.
violence 197, 259–69, 300–3, 484
   'turn-off' 301–3
   'turn-on' 301–3
   *see also* 'effects'

World Bank 73
World Trade Organization (WTO) 24, 73,
   143, 218–19